The Black
to Eastern

Blackwell Companions to Religion

The Blackwell *Companions to Religion* series presents a collection of the most recent scholarship and knowledge about world religions. Each volume draws together newly commissioned essays by distinguished authors in the field, and is presented in a style which is accessible to undergraduate students, as well as scholars and the interested general reader. These volumes approach the subject in a creative and forward-thinking style, providing a forum in which leading scholars in the field can make their views and research available to a wider audience.

Published

The Blackwell Companion to Judaism
Edited by Jacob Neusner and Alan J. Avery-Peck

The Blackwell Companion to Sociology of Religion
Edited by Richard K. Fenn

The Blackwell Companion to the Hebrew Bible
Edited by Leo G. Perdue

The Blackwell Companion to Postmodern Theology
Edited by Graham Ward

The Blackwell Companion to Hinduism
Edited by Gavin Flood

The Blackwell Companion to Political Theology
Edited by Peter Scott and William T. Cavanaugh

The Blackwell Companion to Protestantism
Edited by Alister E. McGrath and Darren C. Marks

The Blackwell Companion to Modern Theology
Edited by Gareth Jones

The Blackwell Companion to Christian Ethics
Edited by Stanley Hauerwas and Samuel Wells

The Blackwell Companion to Religious Ethics
Edited by William Schweiker

The Blackwell Companion to Christian Spirituality
Edited by Arthur Holder

The Blackwell Companion to the Study of Religion
Edited by Robert A. Segal

The Blackwell Companion to the Qur'ān
Edited by Andrew Rippin

The Blackwell Companion to Contemporary Islamic Thought
Edited by Ibrahim M. Abu-Rabi'

The Blackwell Companion to the Bible and Culture
Edited by John F. A. Sawyer

The Blackwell Companion to Catholicism
Edited by James J. Buckley, Frederick Christian Bauerschmidt, and Trent Pomplun

The Blackwell Companion to Eastern Christianity
Edited by Ken Parry

The Blackwell Companion to the Theologians
Edited by Ian S. Markham

The Blackwell Companion to the Bible in English Literature
Edited by Rebecca Lemon, Emma Mason, John Roberts, and Christopher Rowland

The Blackwell Companion to Nineteenth-Century Theology
Edited by David Fergusson

The Blackwell Companion to the New Testament
Edited by David E. Aune

The Blackwell Companion to Religion in America
Edited by Philip Goff

Forthcoming

The Blackwell Companion to Jesus
Edited by Delbert Burkett

The Blackwell Companion to African Religions
Edited by Elias Bongmba

The Blackwell Companion to Christian Mysticism
Edited by Julia A. Lamm

The Blackwell Companion to Pastoral Theology
Edited by Bonnie Miller McLemore

The Blackwell Companion to Religion and Violence
Edited by Andrew Murphy

The Blackwell Companion to Chinese Religions
Edited by Randall Nadeau

The Blackwell Companion to Buddhism
Edited by Mario Poceski

The Blackwell Companion to Eastern Christianity

Edited by

Ken Parry

⊗WILEY-BLACKWELL

A John Wiley & Sons, Ltd., Publication

Library of Congress Cataloging-in-Publication Data

The Blackwell companion to Eastern Christianity / edited by Ken Parry.
p. cm.–(Blackwell companions to religion)
Includes bibliographical references and index.
ISBN 978-0-631-23423-4 (hardcover : alk. paper) ISBN 978-1-4443-3361-9
1. Eastern churches. I. Parry, Kenneth, 1945–
BX106.23.B53 2007
281′.5–dc22
2006038841

A catalogue record for this book is available from the British Library.

Set in 10 on 12.5 pt Photina by Toppan Best-set Premedia Limited
Printed in Singapore

1   2010

In Memoriam

My mother
Joan Parry (1920–2005)
an inspiration to all who knew her

and

David Melling (1943–2004)
philosopher, liturgist, and
generous friend

Contents

Illustrations

Map

Notes on Contributors

David Appleyard is Professor of the Languages of the Horn of Africa at the School of Oriental and African Studies, University of London. His research interests focus on the Semitic and Cushitic languages of Ethiopia and Eritrea. He has published extensively and among his recent articles is 'Definite markers in modern Ethiopian Semitic languages', in G. Khan (ed.) *Semitic Studies in Honour of Edward Ullendorff* (2005).

Dimitri Brady teaches in the Department of Adult Education for the City of Manchester. He has contributed a number of articles to K. Parry et al. (eds) *The Blackwell Dictionary of Eastern Christianity* (1999), and he researches and publishes on the hagiographical traditions of the Eastern Orthodox Churches.

Ivan Zhelev Dimitrov is Professor of Theology at the University of Sofia in Bulgaria. Since 1976 he has been a representative of the Bulgarian Orthodox Church at pan-Orthodox conferences and preparatory commissions. He specializes in New Testament Studies and has published articles in German as well as Bulgarian; among the more recent is 'Moderne Bibelübersetzungen in den Laendern des "Neuen Europa"', in K. Nikolakopoulos et al. (eds) *Orthodoxe Theologie zwischen Ost und West: Festschrift für Prof. Theodor Nikolaou* (2002).

Thomas FitzGerald is Professor of Church History and Historical Theology at Holy Cross Greek Orthodox School of Theology in Brookline, Massachusetts, and a proto-presbyter of the Ecumenical Patriarchate of Constantinople. He is the author of *The Orthodox Church* (1995) and *The Ecumenical Movement: An Introductory History* (2004).

Peter Galadza holds the Kule Family Chair in Liturgy at the Sheptytsky Institute of Eastern Christian Studies, Saint Paul University, Ottawa. He is the author of *The Theology and Liturgical Work of Andrei Sheptytsky (1865–1944)* (2004), and editor-in-chief of *The Divine Liturgy: An Anthology for Worship* (2004). From 1994 to 2004 he served as editor of *Logos: A Journal of Eastern Christian Studies*.

Alexander Grishin is Professor of Art History at the Australian National University, Canberra. He has published numerous books on art history including *A Pilgrim's Account of Cyprus: Bars'kyj's travels in Cyprus* (1996), and among his recent articles is 'Bars'kyj and the Orthodox community', in M. Angold (ed.) *The Cambridge History of Christianity*, vol. 5, *Eastern Christianity* (2006).

Hannah Hunt received her doctorate from the University of Leeds and is presently lecturing at Trinity and All Saints College, Leeds. Among her recent publications are *Joy-Bearing Grief: Tears of Contrition in the Early Syrian and Byzantine Fathers* (2004), and contributions to J. A. McGuckin (ed.) *The Westminster Handbook to Origen* (2004).

Lucy-Anne Hunt is Professor and Head of the School of History of Art and Design at Manchester Metropolitan University. She is the author of *Byzantium, Eastern Christendom and Islam: Art at the Crossroads of the Medieval Mediterranean*, 2 vols (1998 and 2000) and *The Mingana and Related Collections: A Survey of Illustrated Arabic, Greek, Eastern Christian, Persian and Turkish Manuscripts in the Selly Oak Colleges, Birmingham* (1997) and numerous articles on cross-cultural interaction in the art and culture of the medieval Eastern Mediterranean.

Vrasidas Karalis is Associate Professor of Modern Greek at the University of Sydney. He has published extensively in Byzantine and Modern Greek Studies. He has translated Michael Psellos, Doukas and Leo the Deacon into modern Greek, and he is currently working on Paul's Epistle to the Romans. He is the editor of the journal *Modern Greek Studies* (Australia and New Zealand) and the president of the Society for Literature and Aesthetics (Australia).

Basil Lourié (Father Gregory) is rector of the St Petersburg parish of Holy Martyr Elizabeth, and chief editor of *Scrinium*, a journal of church history, patristics and hagiographical studies. He is also on the editorial board of *Xristianskij Vostok* (*Christian Orient*), and his research focuses on the Christian East and Christian origins. He has recently published in Russian *A History of Byzantine Philosophy* (2006).

Peter McMylor is Senior Lecturer in Sociology at the University of Manchester. He is the author of *Alasdair MacIntyre: Critic of Modernity* (1994). His current research interests are the relationship of social theory to religion, the sociology of morality and ethics and its significance for social criticism and the sociology of intellectuals.

Heleen Murre-van den Berg is Associate Professor for the History of World Christianity at Leiden University, the Netherlands. She specializes in Middle Eastern Christianities, and has a special interest in the history of the Assyrian Church of the East. Recent publications include 'Nineteenth-century Protestant missions and Middle Eastern women: an overview', in I. M. Okkenhaug and I. Flaskerud (eds) *Gender, Religion and Change in the Middle East: Two Hundred Years of History* (2005).

Vrej Nerses Nersessian is a priest of the Armenian Apostolic Orthodox Church and Curator in charge of the books and manuscripts of the Christian Middle East at the British Library, London. Among his many publications are *Armenian Illuminated Gospel Books* (1987), *Treasures from the Ark: 1700 Years of Armenian Christian Art* (2001), and *The Bible in the Armenian Tradition* (2001).

Jeremias Norman is Emeritus Professor at the University of Washington in Seattle. He taught Chinese language and linguists at the University of Washington and at Princeton University. His book *Chinese* (1988) is widely used in university courses on Chinese linguists, and he has published not only on the Chinese language but on the languages of the Altaic group. He has long had an interest in the history of the Orthodox Church in China.

Mircea Pacurariu is Emeritus Professor of Theology at Sibiu, Romania, and Romania's foremost scholar and teacher of church history and historical theology. He is the author of many books, and an English translation of his *A History of Romanian Christianity* is to be published shortly.

Ken Parry is Senior Research Fellow in the Department of Ancient History at Macquarie University, Sydney. He specializes in early Christianity, Byzantine cultural and intellectual history, and the history of Eastern Christianity in Asia, especially China and India. Among recent publications that he has edited and contributed to are *The Blackwell Dictionary of Eastern Christianity* (1999); *From Palmyra to Zayton: Epigraphy and Iconography* (2005), and *Art, Architecture and Religion along the Silk Roads* (2008).

Radmila Radić is Senior Research Fellow at the Institute of Contemporary History of Serbia, Belgrade. She is the author, among other books, of *Verom protiv vere. Država i verske zajednice u Srbiji 1945–1953* (With Faith against Faith: The State and Religious Communities in Serbia 1945–1953) (1995), and *Država i verske zajednice 1945–1970* (The State and Religious Communities 1945–1970) (2002).

Stephen H. Rapp, Jr. is Associate Professor of History at Georgia State University, Atlanta, where he specializes in medieval Eurasian history, with an emphasis on the Caucasus region, the Byzantine and Iranian Commonwealths, Eastern Christendom, and Inner Asia. He is the founding director of the World History and Cultures programme at Georgia State University. He is the author of *Studies in Medieval Georgian Historiography: Early Texts and Eurasian Contexts* (2003).

Bryan D. Spinks is Professor of Liturgical Studies at Yale Institute of Sacred Music and Yale Divinity School. A priest of the Church of England, he served on the Church of England Liturgical Commission from 1986 until 2000. His areas of research include East Syrian and Maronite liturgy, as well as Reformation and post-Reformation worship. Among his most recent publications are *Early and Medieval Rituals and Theologies of Baptism: From the New Testament to the Council of Trent* (2006) and *Reformation and Modern Rituals and Theologies of Baptism: From Luther to Contemporary Practices* (2006).

Eva Synek is Assistant Professor at the Institute for Legal Philosophy, Law on Religion and Culture at the University of Vienna. Her main research interests are in Eastern Christianity, law and religion in Central and Eastern Europe, and legal gender studies. Among her recent publications are "Wer aber nicht völlig rein ist an Seele und Leib ...', *Reinheitstabus in Orthodoxen Kirchrecht* (2006), and R. Potz and E. Synek (in collaboration with S. Troianos) *Orthodoxes Kirchenrecht. Eine Einführung* (2007).

David Thomas is Reader in Christianity and Islam in the Department of Theology and Religion at the University of Birmingham, where he edits the journal *Islam and Christian–Muslim Relations*. He has recently edited and contributed to *Christians at the Heart of Islamic Rule, Church Life and Scholarship in 'Abbasid Iraq* (2003), and edited and translated with R. Ebied, *Muslim–Christian Polemic during the Crusades, the Letter from the People of Cyprus and Ibn Abi Talib al-Dimashqi's Reply* (2005).

Janet A. Timbie is Adjunct Associate Professor in the Department of Semitic and Egyptian Languages and Literature, Catholic University of America, Washington DC. Her main area of research is Coptic monastic literature of the fourth and fifth centuries, especially Antony and the origins of Coptic monasticism, and Shenoute and the development of Coptic-based monastic thought. Her recent publications include 'The state of research on the career of Shenoute in 2004', in *Coptica* 4 (2005).

Maria Vorozhishcheva is a researcher and scholar connected with the Department of Sociology at the University of Manchester. She has contributed a number of articles to K. Parry et al. (eds) *The Blackwell Dictionary of Eastern Christianity* (1999), and her research explores the continuing significance for modernity of classical philosophy and Christian thought.

Graham Woolfenden (Father Gregory) is a parish priest in the Ukrainian Orthodox Church of the USA (Ecumenical Patriarchate of Constantinople). Formerly a Lecturer at Ripon College, Cuddesdon, Oxford he is a visiting Lecturer at the St Sofia Orthodox Seminary in New Jersey. His recently published books are *Daily Prayer in Christian Spain* (2000) and *Daily Liturgical Prayer* (2004), and he has published articles in *St Vladimir's Theological Quarterly* and *Studia Liturgica*.

Youhanna Nessim Youssef received his doctorate from Montpellier University in France, and is currently Senior Research Associate, Centre for Early Christian Studies at the Australian Catholic University, and Senior Honorary Fellow at the University of Melbourne. He has published many articles in the field of Coptic Studies and, a book, *The Arabic Life of Severus of Antioch Attributed to Athanasius of Antioch* (2004).

Preface

The Blackwell Companion to Eastern Christianity provides readers with an opportunity to gain an overview of the different traditions that make up the vast but somewhat neglected field of Eastern Christian Studies. The chapters in this volume offer a wide range of material relating to the histories, theologies, and cultural expressions of Christian communities still largely unknown to those outside them. It offers a chance to compare and contrast the variety of traditions that constitute what are commonly known as the Eastern Orthodox and Oriental Orthodox Churches. Perhaps for the first time it is possible to trace within the covers of a single book the various strands that make up the rich tapestry of Eastern Christianity. For it is only by seeing these strands in their historical context that we can begin to comprehend and appreciate what unites the eastern churches as well as what divides them. It is my hope that this *Companion* will contribute to a new and fuller understanding of the Christian East.

The physical wall between East and West may have been demolished, but the psychological wall between them is still firmly in place, and some on both sides of it are more than keen to see that it remains that way. The old views of a despotic and corrupt East versus a pragmatic and progressive West die hard. The ghost of the eighteenth-century historian Edward Gibbon, who characterized Byzantium as a debased form of classical culture and who saw only decline where once there had been glory, still haunts the western mind. Unfortunately ignorance of the religious history of Eastern Europe and the Middle East has been only too apparent in western reactions to recent events. Samuel Huntington's 'Clash of Civilizations' perpetuates an outmoded and inaccurate perception of European history that values divisiveness and difference above compatibility and interdependence, and sees only black and white where grey predominates. There is an alternative model that needs to be pressed into service and it is one in which eastern Christians play a prominent role.

The West has only just begun to appreciate the spiritual and cultural treasures of the Christian East, and the initiatives that I have been involved with, such as *The Blackwell Dictionary of Eastern Christianity* (1999) and this *Companion*, are intended to promote informed discussion and better understanding. There is much we can learn from the East which is applicable to our own situation, but which requires openness

and careful consideration. The advancement of inter-communal dialogue and cooperation has never been more urgent than in today's climate of ethnic and religious strife.
It is no longer tenable, intentionally or otherwise, for western Christians to remain
ignorant of their coreligionists in the East, any more than it is tenable for eastern Christians to ignore the contribution of the Christian West. Eastern Christianity at its worst
can exhibit nationalism, tribalism, defensiveness, and misogyny, but at its best it can
be liturgically uplifting, theologically creative, artistically beautiful, and spiritually
inspiring.

Many Eastern Orthodox Christians are still emerging from under the shadow of
Communism, a shadow which eclipsed them shortly after the end of the Ottoman
period. At the same time many Oriental Orthodox Christians are leaving their traditional homelands in the Middle East to join diaspora communities in the West, because
of the deteriorating situation for non-Muslim minorities. For followers of both traditions
the twenty-first century is offering new opportunities while at the same time posing
new dilemmas. Both under Communism and under Islam eastern Christians have lived
constrained lives, and the roles they will play in already existing and evolving democra-
cies have yet to be determined. They have experienced different histories and faced different problems from the majority of their western counterparts, and this needs to be
taken into account when assessing their contribution and current situation. On the
other hand, many eastern Christians have yet to face issues that Christians in the West
have had to face, such as religious pluralism and greater lay participation, but these
will undoubtedly impact upon them sooner or later. For more background on the
history of Eastern Christianity the reader is referred to the introduction to *The Blackwell
Dictionary of Eastern Christianity* (1999).

This *Companion* not only offers chapters covering the history, theology and politics
of the Christian East, but also has chapters devoted to liturgy, hagiography, iconography and architecture. These topics reinforce the proposition that Eastern Christianity
deserves to be treated as a phenomenon its own right, and that its contribution needs
to be seen in the wider context of world Christian culture and civilization. Liturgical
experience has always been at the heart of eastern Christian life and this area is well
represented here. Equally, eastern Christians have expressed their faith through distinctive iconographic and architectural forms and these are also illustrated and discussed. The chapters on hagiography demonstrate the love and affection felt by eastern
Christians for their saints and heroes. Hagiography offers a fascinating insight into the
eastern Christian mind where familiarity with the saints of the Church, through liturgy
and iconography, instils a feeling of devotion and respect for the wider community.

The contents of each chapter in this *Companion* are the responsibility of their authors,
and although I may not agree with everything they write, as the editor I respect their
right to say it. Sadly two contributors died before they could finish their contributions:
Father Michael Prokurat and David Melling. Father Michael was well known in North
America for his scholarly achievements and for his contribution to Orthodox understanding, and David Melling was equally renowned for his work in promoting Eastern
Christian Studies and inter-religious dialogue in the UK. David Melling was an editor
and contributor to *The Blackwell Dictionary of Eastern Christianity*, and was instrumental
along with myself in conceiving the idea of this *Companion*. I hope one day that it will

be possible for me to realize the third part of the trilogy we planned, a *Reader in Eastern Christianity*.

It remains for me to express my thanks to the editorial staff at Blackwell Publishing for their patience and professionalism in producing this volume, especially Rebecca Harkin, publisher, Karen Wilson, editorial controller, and Mary Dortch, project manager and copy editor.

Last but not least I should like to acknowledge the rights of the Ngunnawal people on whose land our house in Canberra stands. As an Australian citizen I believe that Australia will never find its true identity in the modern world until reconciliation with the Aboriginal inhabitants of this continent has been achieved.

Ken Parry
Feast of St John of Damascus
Canberra, December 2006

CHAPTER 1

Arab Christianity

David Thomas

The history of Christianity among the Arabs is long and distinctive, stretching from within a few centuries from the time of Christ to the present, and developing its own character and forms of thought. For much of its history it has been bound up with Islam and, as far as can be seen, has employed Arabic as its main language of worship and teaching. This has meant it has remained separate from other parts of the Church for long periods, and that its writings have been largely unknown to most Christians outside.

The term 'Arab Christianity' is not easy to define with precision. It can be taken in broad terms as a definition of Christians who worship and teach their faith in Arabic, though this can include Syrian and Coptic Christians who have adopted Arabic as their everyday language. Here it will be taken in relatively general terms to designate Christians who lived in the Arabian peninsula and along the eastern frontiers of the Roman world, and later the Christians who have lived in the Arab heartlands and have continued to the present to confess their faith under Islamic rule.

The Earliest Traces of Arab Christianity

In his Letter to the Galatians, St Paul mentions that after his conversion experience he 'did not consult immediately with flesh and blood, nor did I go up to Jerusalem to those who were apostles before me, but went away to Arabia and returned again to Damascus' (1: 16–17). It is attractive, and not entirely implausible, to imagine that he went to friendly fellow believers in the hinterland east of Damascus, or even went there to preach before any of his great missionary journeys. But this brief mention cannot support such inferences; the spread of the faith to Arabia cannot safely be documented at this early stage, and not with any assurance until the third century. According to Eusebius of Caesarea, there was a bishop of Bostra on the north–south trade route east of the Jordan in the middle of this century, and also synods convened in his see and further south in Arabia Petraea at about the same time (*Ecclesiastical History* 6: 20, 37). Eusebius also suggests that the Emperor Philip the Arab (r. 244–59) was a Christian, most explicitly when he describes how the emperor wished to take part in the Easter vigil in Antioch in 244 but was barred until he had confessed his sins (*Ecclesiastical History* 6: 34). Some scholars accept the reliability of the historian's evidence, but others discount it as a rumour that is countered by other attestations to Philip's pagan beliefs (it is maybe an esteem-building retrojection analogous to later stories preserved by Christians under Islamic rule of the conversion of caliphs such as the ʿAbbasid al-Maʾmūn (r. 813–33) and the Fāṭimid al-Muʿizz (r. 969–75).

These references to Arabian bishops in the third century are complemented by mention of their successors in the fourth century attending major church councils. One of the later versions of the lists of the Council of Nicaea in 325 includes among other bishops from Arabia a certain Pamphilus of the Tayenoi, possibly the bishop of the empire's Arab confederates whom authors referred to by this generic form of the name of the Ṭayy tribe. Fifty years later, one of the bishops who attended the Synod of Antioch in 363 was Theotinus of the Arabs. And in the latter decades of the century Moses, who was an ethnic Arab, worked as bishop among the Arab confederates in Syria and was instrumental in reconciling them with the empire after they had revolted.

These references to third- and fourth-century bishops are brief, and some are equivocal. But they nevertheless point to what is anyway the likely fact that there was a Christian presence among the Arabs on the fringes of the Roman Empire this early, and that it included some degree of ecclesiastical organization. The actual tribes among whom these bishops would have been active are not named in the sources, but it is not unlikely that one of these would have been the Tanūkhids, whose territory lay between the Euphrates and the major Christian See of Antioch. They and other such tribal confederations as the Ghassānids, Lakhmids and Salīḥids occupied the territory between the Roman and Sassanian Empires to the north of the Arabian peninsula proper. They acted as important buffers between the two states, and their allegiance was keenly courted through the long centuries of warfare in which the respective imperial frontiers were repeatedly pushed east and west. Throughout the fourth century, and after it, these tribes were converted to Christianity, with the Lakhmids following the teaching of the Church of the East, and the Ghassānids adopting Miaphysitism. The Lakhmids, with their centre at Ḥīra near the southern Euphrates, were influenced by Christianity as early as the mid-fourth century, though since their allegiance was to the Persians their ruling house never followed the majority of the people into allegiance to the Church of the East. Ironically, under their pagan rule Ḥīra became a town of churches and monasteries, and the home of well-known Christian poets.

The Ghassānids had their main centre at Jābiya in the Byzantine province of Arabia, and then a later establishment at the important nomad shrine of St Sergius (martyred under Diocletian) further north near the Euphrates at Sergiopolis (Ruṣāfa), where their ruler al-Mundhir built an impressive audience hall in the later sixth century. They were staunch followers of Miaphysite teachings. Their leader Ḥārith Ibn Jabala was instrumental in having Jacob Baradeus and Theodore consecrated bishops over his territory in 542, with the consequence that Miaphysitism took firm hold in this part of the empire, and the Syrian Miaphysites became known as Jacobites.

This tribe had migrated to this area in the early fourth century and started as clients of the Salīhids, who had converted to Christianity during the reign of the Emperor Valens (r. 364–78) under the influence of monks and priests who had lived among them. One of their leaders was remembered in later times as the founder of the Monastery of Dayr Dāwūd, which still continues in northern Syria. They remained allies of the Byzantines throughout the fourth and fifth centuries, but they were gradually displaced by the Ghassānids, who were recognized in their stead as leaders of the Arabian tribes by the Emperor Justinian. They disappeared from history after the advent of Islam.

The different denominational allegiances of these tribes reflect the doctrinal disagreements that racked the Roman Empire in the fourth century and afterwards. The Christological controversies that the major councils of the fifth century failed to resolve split Christians irrevocably into the three divisions of Chalcedonians, Diophysites and Miaphysites, and imperial efforts to quell rivalries and hostilities between them had the effect of driving them further apart, both in terms of the doctrinal positions they held and, in the case of the Diophysites, the areas they inhabited. When the School of Edessa was closed in 489 it was reopened in Nisibis in the Persian Empire, and influenced the hierarchy of that area to adhere to the Antiochene Diophysite Christology, with local Christians following their leaders in the form of faith they held.

In the Arabian peninsula itself Christian presence at this time is attested in the early centuries by the existence of communities of believers and bishoprics along the eastern and southern coasts. The names of bishops belonging to the Church of the East and also references to monasteries are recorded along the Arabian Gulf from as early as the fourth and as late as the thirteenth centuries, and along the coast of Hadramawt and Yemen until the ninth century. Christian missionaries were active in parts of the interior from an early date, and the town of Najrān in the northern Yemen was particularly known for its Miaphysite population. In 520 a number of Christians there were killed by the Jewish king Dhū Nuwās, an event that, according to Muslim tradition, is recalled in the Qur'an, 85: 4–8. News of this prompted the Byzantine emperor to encourage the Miaphysite Ethiopians to invade, and from 525 until 570, when the Persians captured this area, there was Christian rule and a Miaphysite hierarchy. A ruler from this period who is well known in Islamic tradition is Abraha, who made himself king in about 530. He built a cathedral at Ṣan'a, supposedly as an alternative religious centre to the then pagan Ka'ba at Mecca, and sent an expedition against this town in revenge for the assassination of a Hijāzī ally. It failed, and its overthrow has always been linked with the reference in Chapter 105 of the Qur'an to the divine intervention against the 'owners of the elephant' that caused flocks of birds to rain pebbles on them. The birth of Muhammad is usually linked with 'the year of the elephant'.

Further north in the Hijāz the presence of Christianity in these centuries is difficult to plot with accuracy. The tribes of 'Udhrā, Judhām, Bahrā' and some of the Banu Kalb north of Madīna were converted sometime before the coming of Islam, and it has been suggested that several monasteries were established in their territories. If this could be established beyond doubt, it might prove extremely significant for explaining the knowledge of Christianity possessed by Muhammad and his Muslim followers, but nothing can be ascertained beyond inference.

The Qur'an, which is almost universally dated to the early seventh century (between 610 and 632 if the accepted Muslim chronology is taken as a guide), and the earliest strata of Islamic history yield significant if isolated details about Arab Christianity in the Ḥijāz and further north at this time. The Qur'an itself comments throughout on stories that have obvious biblical antecedents, though the relationship between the forms in the two scriptures is rarely direct, and differences of detail are the subject of vigorous debate. And there is certainly one instance of a relationship between two brief accounts in the Qur'an (3: 49 and 5: 110) of Jesus creating birds from clay, breathing into them and causing them to fly, and the same incident recorded in the *Infancy Gospel of Thomas*. In addition, it shows awareness of the key doctrines of the Trinity and divinity of Christ, though in forms that permit criticisms of them as distortions of monotheistic beliefs, the Trinity by suggesting that God is one of three (4: 171, 5: 73, 5: 116), and the divinity of Christ by suggesting that Jesus is a second God (e.g., 9: 30–1). And it furthermore refers to features of institutional Christianity, such as priests and monks (5: 82–3), monasticism (57: 27) and churches, 'with men in them celebrating his glory night and morning, men who are not distracted by commerce or profit from remembering God, keeping up the prayer, and paying the prescribed alms, fearing a day when hearts and minds will turn over' (24: 36–7), as well as corrupt practices among the clergy (9: 34) and maybe internal church divisions (13: 36). All this is suggestive of a rich Christian context in which the Qur'an originated and to which it reacts by applying its criterion of strict transcendent monotheism.

The channels by which Muḥammad may have come to know about Christian beliefs are equally difficult to detect. The Muslim tradition itself preserves some details, such as that his first wife's cousin, Waraqa Ibn Nawfal, was a Christian and thus able to interpret his first experience of prophethood in terms that conformed to biblical precedents, that he knew a Christian named Jabr who kept a market stall in Mecca, and most redolently that he met and was recognized by a Christian monk while on a caravan journey as a boy (Ibn Isḥāq 1955: 79–81, 83, 95–7). This incident was amplified in both Christian and Muslim versions in later centuries, the Muslim portraying the monk, who is usually named Baḥīrā (cf. the Syriac title *bḥīrā*, 'reverend') or Sarjis/Sergius, as performing a similar role to his relative Waraqa in recognizing Muḥammad as prophet in fulfilment of earlier expectations, and the Christian portraying him as a heretic who taught Muḥammad the distorted forms of Christianity that appear in the Qur'an. In connection with this, it is maybe significant that the Muslim tradition links Muḥammad's relationship with the Christian Jabr to an accusation levelled against the Prophet in the Qur'an: 'And we [God] know well that they say: Only a man teaches him [Muḥammad]. The speech of him at whom they falsely hint is outlandish, and this is clear Arabic speech' (16: 103). Clearly, some of Muḥammad's opponents thought that he was taught versions of biblical stories by a human teacher rather than God, as Muslim doctrine holds. And here, as well as in the Baḥīrā story, there may lurk the remnant of a link between the accounts in the Qur'an of events paralleled in the Bible and Arab Christian sources from which they derived.

These scant items do little more than stir speculation about the nature of the information that may lie behind the Qur'an (of course, the question does not arise in Islam because the Qur'an in almost universally accepted as the speech of God himself and therefore free from literary dependence). And they raise the question about the form in which Christian teachings may have circulated among Arabs in the sixth and early seventh centuries, and particularly whether the Bible or any substantial parts of it had been translated into Arabic by this time and could be heard and understood by an Arab audience.

If Christianity had spread among the Arabs from the fourth century and there were bishoprics established, with churches and cathedrals, then it is not unreasonable to imagine that there would have been a liturgy in Arabic and also an Arabic Bible to meet the spiritual needs of believers. Some scholars contend that the circumstantial evidence is strong enough to indicate that there probably were a liturgy and translation of the Bible in Arabic by this time, but this evidence is never sufficient to expel all doubts. There is nothing, as far as can presently be concluded with certainty, that provides evidence for Arabic translations until well into the Muslim era; according to an uncorroborated report by Michael the Syrian (Chabot 1899–1924, II: 431–2) the first Arabic translation of the Gospels was made in the seventh century. And so it must be inferred that Christians followed liturgy in the languages in which it had been received, Greek or Syriac, and depended on oral forms of biblical stories (the occurrence in the Qur'an of many Syriac loan words, including the form *'Īsā al-Masīḥ* from *Īshō' Mshīḥā* for Jesus Christ, would seem to suggest that there was little, if any, native religious vocabulary among Christians at this time). This is one of the most perplexing problems relating to Arab Christianity in this period, together with the immediate background from which the Qur'an emerged.

The evidence for Christianity among the Arabs suggests, therefore, that while the faith was evident among leading tribes and along major coastal trading routes, where senior clergy were established and active, it may not in the three centuries following the peace of the Church have evolved into a church or churches that enjoyed institutional and intellectual independence from the main centres within the Byzantine world. The evidence forbids any firm conclusions, though maybe it points to Christianity more in a missionary than natively established form. The one exception will be the Church of the East, which by the end of the fifth century had asserted its independence of Constantinople and set up its own patriarchate, and had begun to engage in vigorous missionary work to the east into Asia and south into Arabia. These are signs that it possessed a definite sense of identity as a church in its own right.

The Muslim tradition that the *Ka'ba* in Mecca, at this time a pagan shrine, housed a representation of the Virgin and Child among its more than three hundred images of Arabian divinities is maybe indicative of the precarious nature of Christianity in this and possibly other parts of the Arab world in the early seventh century as it competed among the multiple forms of religion in circulation.

Arab Christianity under Islam

As what can be thought in many ways to be a response to the religious and social milieu in which it came into being, the Qur'an contains numerous comments on Christians and their beliefs. It addresses them directly as *Naṣārā*, a term that is usually understood as a reference to the followers of 'the Nazarite', and is also accepted as referring to them indirectly in the term *Ahl al-kitāb*, 'People of the Book', which refers to communities in pre-Islamic times that had been given a revealed scripture by God and so shared a lineage with bearers of the Qur'an.

In some verses Christians are ranked at almost the same level as Muslims, and assured that they are accorded salvation (2: 62, 3: 55), and in one often-quoted verse they are placed next to Muslims themselves:

> And you will find the most vehement of mankind in hostility to those who believe are the Jews and the idolaters. And you will find the nearest of them in affection to those who believe are those who say: 'We are Christians'. That is because there are among them priests and monks, and because they are not proud. (5: 82)

This verse appears to link the sense of communion between the two communities of believers with the quality of humility demonstrated by Christians, presumably a palpable characteristic that Muḥammad and others witnessed for themselves.

Other verses balance such comments of approval with criticism and hostility, remarking that Christians show exclusivity in their attitudes (2: 111, 2: 120, 5: 18, etc.) and are pointedly inimical towards Muslims (3: 65, 4: 153, 5: 59, all addressed to the People of the Book). Furthermore, they mislead people into false beliefs (2: 109, 3: 69), and teach wrong things (4: 171, 5: 77), and have abandoned God's promise and ended in internal strife:

> And with those who say, 'Lo, we are Christians', we made a covenant, but they forgot a part of what they were admonished about. Therefore we have stirred up enmity and hatred among them till the Day of Resurrection, when God will inform them of their handiwork. (5: 14)

Elsewhere, the Qur'an gives content to this complaint by detailing Christians' inflated claims about Jesus, that he was God and Son of God (4: 171, 9: 30, etc.), and that the godhead is therefore plural:

> O People of the Book! Commit no excesses in your religion: nor say of God aught but the truth. Jesus Christ the son of Mary was a Messenger of God, and his word which he bestowed on Mary, and a spirit from him: so believe in God and his messengers. Say not 'Three', desist. For God is one God: glory be to him. (4: 171)

And it also suggests that the scriptures given to the People of the Book have not been handed down intact. It accuses them of concealing what is contained in their scripture (2: 140, 3: 71, 5: 15, 6: 91), of mispronouncing it in order to distort its meaning (3: 78), and of corrupting it by changing 'the words from their times and places' (4: 46, 5: 41). There is no amplification of what is intended here, and some scholars see these comments as referring only to isolated individuals among the Jewish tribes of Madīna scurrilously setting out to trick Muḥammad. But in the later Islamic tradition these verses were used as the basis for increasingly elaborate critiques of the integrity of the Bible.

It can be seen from these references that a lively debate is conducted in the Qur'an between the beliefs that were being enunciated by Muḥammad and the analogous though identifiably different beliefs of Christians and Jews. And there is evident competition for the true account of what is commonly accepted as a history of God's communication with created humanity. Thus, Abraham is severed from his intimate ties with the Jews and Christians, and identified as a Muslim:

> Abraham was not a Jew or a Christian, but he was an upright man (ḥanīf) who had surrendered (muslim), and he was not of the idolaters. (3: 67)

And above all Jesus is portrayed as a prophet from God, and no more than human.

The Qur'an goes into considerable detail about who Jesus was and what he did, in its characteristically allusive style seeming to assume prior knowledge of what it refers to. It is as though it is drawing upon an ample stock of information and addressing a particularly problematic point. It describes the annunciation of his birth to Mary in two places and at some length (3: 42–7, 19:16–35), though emphatically stating that the miracle of his virgin birth in no way implies divinity for him but is entirely due to the power of God:

> It does not befit God that he should betake to himself a son. Glory be to him! When he decrees a thing, he says to it only: 'Be', and it is. (19: 35, cf. 3: 47)

It calls him a word and spirit from God (4: 171 quoted above, 3: 45), a sign and a mercy from God (19: 21), it details his miracles of healing and resuscitation (3: 49, 5: 110), and it says that he was supported by what it calls the Holy Spirit (2: 87, 2: 253). Thus he was an elect messenger of God to a particular community, bringing them the Gospel (Injīl) from God (3: 48, 5: 46), and calling disciples to help him (3: 52). But it also insists that he was no more than human, created like Adam (3: 59), eating human food (5: 75), and a servant of God (19: 30). And it also details (61: 6) that he foretold the coming of a messenger after him, 'whose name is the Praised One' (aḥmad, derived from the same trilateral root ḥ-m-d as Muḥammad), denied being divine (5: 116–17) and, most devastatingly, was not crucified but was instead raised up to God out of the clutches of the Jews (4: 157–8). In such remarks can be detected a revision of Christian claims about Jesus to bring them into line with the dominant qur'anic discourse about the transcendence of God, his distinctiveness from all other beings, who are his creatures, and his communicating with humankind through messengers who bring his revealed utterances and are protected from harm (though not oppression and persecution) by God himself. In the context of such a discourse, Jesus emerges as a signally superior human messenger, but definitely not divine despite all the unique features that attach to him. Strangely enough, his curious respite from crucifixion in accordance with God's frustration of the Jews' scheming to kill his messenger is paralleled elsewhere by references that suggest he does die (3: 55, 5: 117), though these have been given an eschatological colour in the Islamic exegetical tradition.

All these teachings provided warrants for the Muslims' attitude towards Christians as they brought the client populations under their rule and sought ways to treat them socially and to comprehend the intellectual and religious differences that separated them from themselves. They were also guided by statements about Christians attributed to the Prophet, his *Ḥadīth*, which exerted almost as much force in practical terms as the Qur'an itself. Among the many thousands of statements that were accepted as incontrovertibly attributable to him appear such strictures as: Jews and Christians should be excluded from Arabia; followers of the cross will go to hell; on his return at the end of the world Jesus will smash the cross to pieces.

A further detail that gave Muslims a precedent for their treatment of Christians is recorded in the earliest biography of Muḥammad, which was written just over a century after his death. This recounts how a deputation of Christians from Najrān in southern Arabia came to visit him in Madīna in his latter years when he was becoming increasingly successful as a leader among the Arabs. They discussed matters of faith, and the invitation to come to a common agreement was revealed from God (Qur'an, 3: 64). When they departed, they agreed to pay tribute to the Muslims, and they were later regarded as having accepted the formal protection of the Prophet. This, together with the important injunction in the late passage Qur'an 9: 29 to fight against those People of the Book who do not do or believe what Islam teaches 'until they pay the tribute readily, being brought low', provide a basis for treatment of Christians and others in the emerging Islamic state.

Raiding parties from Madīna were sent north into the margins of Byzantine territory even in the latter years of Muḥammad's life. Under his immediate successors, the Rightly-Guided Caliphs who ruled in Madīna between 632 when he died and 661, these raids turned into invading armies that captured Egypt and North Africa, much of the Middle East, and the majority of Persia. By 715, when the Umayyads, the first dynasty of Islam, was ruling from Damascus, the empire extended from Spain in the west to the Indian Ocean, and from Central Asia in the north to the fringes of the Sahara. It took in all the former Byzantine provinces south of the Taurus Mountains and some of Anatolia beyond, and vast populations of Christians who inhabited the lands within the former imperial boundaries, as well as those who had settled in the western parts of the former Sassanian Empire along the rivers Tigris and Euphrates. Churches, monasteries with their schools, towns and cities all came under Muslim rule.

By and large, it appears that life for these new subjects did not change a great deal at first. There certainly were killings, but nothing that amounts to premeditated massacring or a policy to eradicate anyone who stood up to the new masters. In the case of many cities, in fact, the Muslim warriors refrained from pillage and kept themselves apart in their own encampments outside. Later Islamic history often typifies the takeover of particular cities in terms of a surrender agreement between the Christian inhabitants and the Muslim leaders, with suitable concessions included, and then relative freedom to continue as before. There may be considerable truth in the accounts that suggest greater leniency and restraint than was common for invading armies at the time, but Muslim historians' relations of these early times betray clear tensions over different religious sensitivities and practices: the second caliph, 'Umar Ibn al Khaṭṭāb (r. 634–44) found it necessary to place under his protection crosses on public buildings and gave personal guarantees that they would not be violated, while his generals in Syria and along the southern Euphrates stipulated that crosses might only be carried in public procession on one day a year, and then outside Muslim areas of towns. 'Abd al-Malik (r. 685–705) and other Umayyad caliphs later had crosses on public display destroyed, and replaced the image of the cross on coins with a simple pillar (the founder of the dynasty Mu'āwiya (r. 661–80) first attempted this but found people did not accept the coins). This ubiquitous Christian symbol understandably irked people whose scripture denied the historicity of the crucifixion, and the necessity for caliphs to take steps to preserve images or to remove them shows how important it was to favour one or other part of the population.

That the Umayyads considered Christianity an abiding problem and even a threat is evidenced by the fact that when the caliph 'Abd al-Malik built the Dome of the Rock in Jerusalem to commemorate the miraculous Night Journey of the Prophet from Mecca to Jerusalem and from there through the heavens, he had Qur'an verses that emphasize the oneness of God and deny Christian beliefs inscribed on prominent exterior and interior features. It was as though he was triumphantly admonishing his stubborn subjects.

By the early eighth century, Greek- and Arabic-speaking Christians and other communities who were recognized as People of the Book were in principle governed by a set of regulations that Muslims attributed to the second caliph 'Umar, and knew as the *Pact of 'Umar*. Whether they go back to him in any detailed form, and exactly what their form was in this early period, cannot be known for sure. But they certainly included the *jizya*, the poll-tax that is referred to in Qur'an 9: 29, the *kharaj*, a tax on land, and restrictions on church buildings and personal dress. Their governing principle was that the state would offer client communities protection, and they in return would observe the regulations and in addition would not bear arms. Thus they became *Ahl al-dhimma*, 'People of Protection', or simply *Dhimmis*.

It is known that the caliph 'Umar II (r. 717–20), who is remembered for his piety, reinforced these *dhimmī* measures, but for the most part little is heard about unrest between faiths in Umayyad times. The career of the Chalcedonian Greek-speaking theologian John of Damascus (c.660–c.750) is indicative, though maybe not typical, of how Christians fared at this time. The son and grandson of senior state officials in Damascus – his grandfather had handed over the keys of the city to the Muslims after the Byzantine governor had fled – he worked for many years in the caliphal chancery, all the time remaining a Christian and employing Greek for writing. Sometime in the early years of the eighth century he retired from public life and became a monk in the monastery of Mar Sabas east of Jerusalem, and there proceeded to set down the first substantial reflections on Islam that are known from a Christian author. They appear as Chapter 100 in his *On Heresies*, which forms part of his major compendium *The Fount of Wisdom*. What is striking about this reflection is that it reveals some knowledge of the teachings about Jesus in the Qur'an, but also a measure of mistakenness about other teachings in the scripture, and that it refers to Muḥammad in derogatory terms as a man fired with self-interest who learnt the contents of the Qur'an from a heretical monk, and passed it off as his own. Clearly, in John's eyes the Qur'an contained nothing to inspire or attract and could be dismissed as a sub-Christian forgery; Arabic was not a language to learn; and Islam, the faith founded by a merchant living on the desert margin, contained nothing to detain a cultured Christian who lived within the intellectual ambit of Byzantium, at least in his mind if no longer in reality.

There is more than a hint of superiority in what John writes in this chapter, disdain for a faith that seems a parasitical form of Christianity, and confidence that arguments raised by its followers against the earlier beliefs can be soundly beaten down. But it has been argued that *The Fount of Wisdom* in general can be witnessed as a definite adjustment to the new reality. For in another part of this work, *On Christian Doctrine*, John provides a sustained statement of his own Chalcedonian beliefs, which can be read as an attempt to specify the distinctiveness of this form of Christianity and to distinguish it from others, explicitly from the competing forms of Christian belief that had suddenly acquired an equal status with the 'emperor's' form, which was known as just that, 'Melkite' (from *malik*, 'king'), and implicitly from Islam. The stream of works from authors of the various denominations against the beliefs of others can be seen as part of the same process, to express what is true of a particular Christian tradition in order to establish identity, guard against apostasy, and maybe inform Muslim rulers of the difference between them and others in order to gain better treatment. This is not expressed openly, but it fully explains the great number of statements of faith written within the denominations and the polemics written against them. The advent of Islam may have helped to establish firm doctrinal differences for the first time.

Christians in this early period were not slow to realize that the presence of Arabs in their midst was not like earlier incursions of raids or expeditions but something more permanent, which demanded an explanation. And they understandably turned to the Bible. Many were fully cognizant of the fact that Muslims were continuators of the teachings of Abraham, and the historian Sebeos, writing in about 660, recognized Muḥammad as a learned man who knew the law of Moses. But Muslims were definitely a threat to the Church, and others saw them as forerunners of the last days and invoked biblical predictions such as Daniel's vision of the four beasts (Daniel 7: 2–8) to interpret the events they had set off.

Given the success of the Arab Muslims in capturing such an expanse of territory so rapidly, and the added fact that non-Muslims were faced with new taxes under the new polity, it is understandable that there should be conversions from Christianity to Islam in these first generations of Islamic rule. An eloquent testimony to what was happening in the early eighth century and the practical consequences is given in the caliph 'Umar II's demand that his governors should not prevent Christians from converting. Clearly, the provincial rulers took a pragmatic view that envisaged the loss of tax income if conversions proceeded, while the pious caliph saw only the spiritual gains if they went ahead.

It is impossible to say on what scale conversions took place in these early years of Islam, though however they proceeded they are not necessarily a sign of a faith in decline. John of Damascus in his crisp dismissal of Islam and its claims to legitimacy maybe typifies the intellectual and cultural confidence of Greek-speaking Chalcedonian Arab Christians in Syria and around. And elsewhere the Church of the East was intently engaged in the missions it had conducted throughout Asia for many years. Missionaries had been active in Arabia before Islam, and had also directed their steps into Siberia and further east. In 635, three years after the death of Muḥammad, a group of monks, among whom a certain Alopen is named, took the books of the 'luminous religion' as far as China. These missionary activities went on for hundreds of years and the bishoprics that were founded continued to receive consecrated incumbents, a sign of a church that remained vigorous rather than collapsing in apocalyptic inactivity.

Arab Christianity in the Classical Islamic World

In 750 the Umayyad dynasty was overthrown and was replaced by the 'Abbasid dynasty. With its original power base in Khurasān in the east of Persia, this was different in character from the Umayyads, owing more to Persian influence, though asserting its claim to be more Muslim. Within a few years the caliph al-Manṣūr (r. 754–75) had built a new capital on the river Tigris at Baghdad and inaugurated a dynasty that lasted, at least in name, until the coming of the Mongols in the thirteenth century. The concentration of power maintained by caliphs in the first centuries of the new rule had a profound effect on all aspects of life within the empire: Arabic became the *lingua franca* with surprising speed, and the progress of learning in a multitude of disciplines involved followers of all faiths in an amalgam of intellectual activity from which emerged a distinctive Islamic culture. The contribution of Christians to this development and their engagement with it led to the appearance of new forms of thinking and a religious literature in Arabic for the first time, at least as far as can presently be told.

The position of Christians in early 'Abbasid society was, at least in appearance, privileged. A document written by the Muslim rationalist theologian and Arabic stylist Abū 'Uthmān al-Jāḥiẓ (d. 868) in the mid-ninth century gives an intriguing insight into the freedoms they enjoyed, and is worth quoting at length,

> They are secretaries and servants to kings, physicians to nobles, perfumers and moneychangers. We know that they ride highly bred horses, and dromedary camels, play polo . . . wear fashionable silk garments, and have attendants to serve them. They call themselves Ḥasan, Ḥusayn, 'Abbās, Faḍl and 'Alī, and employ also their forenames. There remains only for them to call themselves Muḥammad, and employ the forename Abū al-Qāsim. For this very fact they are liked by the Muslims! Moreover, many of the Christians fail to wear their belts, while others hide their girdles beneath their outer garments. Many of their nobles refrain out of sheer pride from paying tribute. They return to Muslims insult for insult and blow for blow. Why indeed should the Christians not do so and even more, when our judges, or at least the majority of them, consider the blood of a patriarch or bishop as equivalent to the blood of Ja'far, 'Alī, 'Abbās and Ḥamza? (al-Jāḥiẓ in Finkel 1927: 328–9)

This gives a vivid summary of a group moving in society with few external constraints, flouting the regulations that governed it, and regarding itself as an elite. Al-Jāḥiẓ was writing a diatribe that was intended for fellow Muslims to read, so it is possible that he exaggerated the situation and even misrepresented details. But his account can still be used, although with some caution.

The first point of information it gives is that Christians occupied senior professional positions in 'Abbasid Baghdad. Like John of Damascus a century earlier, they were secretaries in the caliphal service, and there is evidence that in such positions some swayed government policy in favour of particular monasteries. They were also financiers and, maybe surprisingly, physicians to Muslim nobles. Indeed, the Bakhtishūʿ family of the School of Jundishāpūr retained this position for years, a virtual Christian dynasty maintaining the Muslim rulers in health. The practice of fathers being succeeded by sons in the same position was commonplace among Christian professionals at this time, presumably reflecting modes of education and maybe a reluctance to allow precious learning and skills to be divulged willy-nilly. It certainly permitted Christians to retain status as purveyors of 'Greek learning' at this time, and it earned them the admiration and envy of Muslims and others.

In the eighth and ninth centuries Christians also performed for Muslim rulers and nobles the important task of translating works from Greek, sometimes via Syriac, into Arabic. This was another cause of admiration and praise, and it made available the ancient learning in philosophy, mathematics, astronomy, medicine and other disciplines to monolingual Muslims. Individuals such as the Nestorians Ḥunayn Ibn Isḥāq and his son Isḥāq Ibn Ḥunayn were courted for their abilities and offered payment in gold.

Al-Jāḥiẓ clearly recognizes the senior positions that Christians with these accomplishments enjoyed, and in doing so he clearly acknowledges the pluralist nature of urban society at this time, though the assumption underlying his remark is that Muslims dictate the overall terms and Arabic is the currency of communication.

His following remarks, however, hint at something darker. The series of points he makes about Christians pursuing aristocratic lifestyles, including sports and fashionable clothes, and adopting Muslim names show both the relative freedom they appear to have experienced in Muslim society and also a seeming desire on their part to be like the majority of their neighbours, an understandable reaction by a separate minority that felt its difference keenly. There may even be a hint of this group purposely exploiting its privileged position to show its open distaste for the regulations that in principle applied to it. Thus, they concealed the distinctive marks of dress they were required to show, and refused to pay the *jizya*, the most obvious token of their subservience to Muslim rule. Were they wanting to assimilate and obliterate marks of distinction, or were they trying to assert their identity by showing the power they possessed to ignore the age-old stipulations that established the relationship between Muslims and the *Ahl al-dhimma*? It is impossible to say, but it does seem justifiable to infer that at least in this case there were Christians who held positions close to the elite of Muslim society in the ninth century, but were sorely aware they were not fully accepted as part of that society.

The fact that al-Jāḥiẓ can refer to regulations from the *Pact of ʿUmar*, such as the undertaking by the scriptural clients not to dress like Muslims but to mark themselves out as different, not to use Muslim names, and not to retaliate when struck (in fact, these Christians either flout the regulations in systematic manner, or are portrayed as such for polemical effect), indicates that this continued to govern the place of the *Ahl al-dhimma*, as it would do so for centuries after. But his careful documenting of Christian indifference shows that it cannot have been enforced in any systematic fashion. The conclusion to which this diatribe points is that Christians moved within

'Abbasid Muslim society with some freedom and status, but rarely felt entirely part of that society.

This paradoxical relationship is typified in the experiences of one of the greatest patriarchs of the Church of the East, the Catholicos Timothy I (c.728–823), who led the church for forty years from his consecration in 780. His letters show he was involved with missionaries in regions he names as Persia, Assyria, India, China and Tibet, and in one he writes with some real feeling for the wives of men who remain in remote places for long years, offering to ask his missionary priests in these places to find them. He evidently functioned as the leader of a vast church that stretched the length of the Silk Road, with all the prestige and influence that involved.

Timothy also enjoyed some status in his own city. As Patriarch of the Church of the East he was recognized by the Muslim authorities as leader of all Christians throughout the Islamic Empire. And he was given access to the caliph's immediate presence. On one occasion in 781 he was invited by the caliph al-Mahdī to join in a debate stretching over two days on the differences between Christianity and Islam. 'Debate' is maybe not the appropriate term because even in Timothy's own Syriac account (the exchange was conducted in Arabic, and is recorded in a letter to one of his friends) it is clear that he is on the defensive against questions of a discomforting and even hostile nature from al-Mahdī that required considerable ingenuity and diplomacy to answer. Obviously, he could not say anything to insult Islam, but equally he could not betray his own Christian position. It seems that while the caliph took him seriously enough to devote time and attention to inquiring about the integrity of his beliefs, he was regarded as someone outside the circle of the court who could be subjected to the indignity of searching questions.

The difficulty of Timothy's position, and also his own skill in debate, is demonstrated by the best known of the many answers he gave on matters of Christian doctrine and attitudes towards Islam:

> Our gracious and wise king said to me: 'What do you say about Muḥammad?' And I replied to his majesty: 'Muḥammad is worthy of all praise by all reasonable people, O my sovereign. He walked in the path of the prophets and trod in the track of the lovers of God. All the prophets taught the doctrine of one God, and since Muḥammad taught the doctrine of the unity of God, he walked, therefore, in the path of the prophets.' (Timothy in Mingana 1928: 197)

Evidently the caliph was satisfied with this because he did not press Timothy but moved on to other topics, presumably concluding that the Christian accepted the belief that Muḥammad was a prophet like those before him. But a Christian could also have felt satisfied, since he would have understood the patriarch to suggest that Muḥammad was only copying what the biblical prophets had done, with nothing original of his own.

It is quite clear from al-Mahdī's insistent interrogation in this meeting that he was fully aware of the differences in belief between Muslims and Christians, many of his questions being based upon what the Qur'an teaches about this, and that he thought that Christians could not presume upon the soundness of their beliefs but had to make a case for the rationality and coherence of what they taught. His attitude only reflected what the great majority of Muslims accepted. But, still on the equivocal nature of the relationship between followers of the two faiths, this disagreement and disdain did not stop leading members of society and the general populace from visiting churches and monasteries, the continuing presence of which around and within Baghdad speaks eloquently of tolerance on the part of rulers. In a repetition, or possibly continuation, of a practice followed by the pagan Lakhmid ruling house in Ḥīra, 'Abbasid caliphs themselves would visit and sometimes spend periods in monasteries, presumably to enjoy the quiet and beauty of their gardens, to witness the spectacle of their liturgy on feast days, and even to sample the wine they produced. From the tenth century a distinct genre of *diyyarāt* (from *dayr*, 'monastery') literature sprang up among Muslim authors to document the location of monasteries and give descriptions of their character and advantages.

It is clear that Christians and Muslims were intimately connected socially and professionally in early 'Abbasid society. But they were also connected intellectually. For not only did Christian translators provide the raw information from which Muslims developed their own distinctive forms of philosophy, mathematics, medicine, astronomy and so on, but they also provided a stimulus that in significant ways led to the emergence of Muslim religious self-identity.

It has long been debated among scholars of early Islamic intellectual history whether the emergence of thinking of a theological nature (the term 'theology' only loosely approximates to the discipline called *'ilm al-kalām*, 'science of debate') is dependent upon discussions among Christians that were current at the time. Differences over the relationship between divine omnipotence and human moral responsibility in Umayyad times, and over the most apt characterization of God as possessing attributes which were formally discrete from his essence at about the same time, have been put down to the direct influence of Christian debates over free will and the Trinity. Whether or not this is true is open to question.

What seems definite is that Islamic religious thinkers in late Umayyad and early 'Abbasid times appear to have defined the character of Islam in part by contrast with Christianity and other faiths. While it is difficult to be categorical about this because the vast majority of works on religious topics from this time have not survived, it can be asserted with confidence from the evidence contained in later works that most Muslim scholars at this time wrote works against Christianity and other faiths. And it can be deduced from the relatively few polemics which survive that their purpose was not only to discredit the beliefs of the other but also to employ those beliefs to demonstrate the rational coherence of Islam. These works typically did this by identifying and refuting those doctrines that were in direct contravention to the key doctrines of Islam. Thus, in the case of Christianity they restricted themselves to the doctrines of the Trinity and Incarnation (identified as the uniting of the divine and human natures in Christ), and reduced the one to a simple tritheism (echoing the qur'anic criticism of calling God 'three' or 'the third of three') which could be shown to be internally incoherent, and the other to a mingling of the divine and human, with the irrational consequences of such a claim. The result is that such doctrines are shown to be unsustainable, with the obvious outcome that the only rational possibility is Islam.

Works of this kind, although appearing to be anti-Christian polemics, have as much claim to be apologetics for Islam itself. They use key doctrines of the other faith as examples of error in those aspects that most closely concern Islam, without much concern for the faith as a whole or for other key elements within it. This trend reaches an extreme point in the tenth century when the first extant synthetic treatises of Islamic religious thinking were composed. In these the treatments of doctrines from other faiths usually occur at various points as appendices to expositions of their Islamic equivalents, where by exhibiting their own logical disarray they point up the integrity of what Muslims are enjoined to believe as the only viable possibility. In such compendiums of Muslim doctrine, Christianity, together with other faiths, becomes nothing more than a cautionary case of what is wrong in believing, and so an example that helps Muslims to know what is correct belief.

Despite this rather rough handling in polemical and theological works, Muslims in the early 'Abbasid period evidently knew a considerable amount about Christianity and its major beliefs and practices. Many surviving texts contain extensive details of doctrines such as the Trinity and two natures of Christ, while a few know about the atonement. They also know about Christian veneration of the cross and the main outlines of eucharistic services, as well as some of the contents of Christian scripture. Some Muslims evidently went to great lengths to inform themselves, and were able to distinguish between the Christologies of the major denominations, which they called Melkites, Jacobites and Nestorians. And a few had some idea of the earlier sects, including Arians, Marcionites and Sabellians, as well as proof texts Christians employed to support their doctrines. The immediate origin of this information is usually difficult to identify, though the details preserved by many early authors point to written sources, now for the most part untraceable, rather than oral reports from converts or Christians themselves.

This information, which suggests some interest in and acquaintance with Arab Christianity, did not, however, appear to influence Muslim attitudes in favour of the legitimacy of Christianity. The general estimation was that it was rationally confused in its doctrines because these were derived from a corrupted scriptural origin. Making use of the hints given in the Qur'an about alterations to the scriptures of the People of the Book, Muslim controversialists habitually demonstrated or assumed that the Gospels and other biblical books could not be trusted, either because they were misinterpreted by their possessors or because their texts themselves were distorted. This accusation of *taḥrīf*, corruption of scripture, was a commonplace from an early date, and it generated a vivid tradition of debate, with Muslims tending to argue that the original *Injīl*, the single Gospel text that had been revealed by God to Jesus for his community, had been lost or intentionally misplaced, and had been replaced by a number of reconstructions written by followers, from which four were chosen. This history could explain why Christians held wrong beliefs and doctrines, and why they persisted in wrong practices such as eating pork and failing to circumcise their sons. Such individuals as St Paul or the emperor Constantine were periodically implicated as wilful culprits into misleading the church into these nefarious ways.

An instructive sidelight on to Muslim assumptions about the Arab character of Christianity in the 'Abbasid centuries is cast by some of the accusations of *taḥrīf*. One favourite was to connect Jesus' prediction in Qur'an 61: 6 of *Aḥmad*, 'the greatly praised one', who would come after him with the Paraclete verses in the Gospel of John, and argue that the original form here was not *Parakletos* but *Periklutos*, 'renowned', 'famous'.

There is an obvious overlap in meaning between the emendation to the term in John and the qur'anic term in Jesus' prediction, though the substitution only works in Arabic where short vowels are not usually written and the two forms would therefore be virtually identical. One Muslim argued in a similar way that the resurrected Jesus' instruction to Mary Magdalene in John 20: 17 to pass on to his disciples was not 'I go to my Father and your Father', but 'I go to my Lord and your Lord', because the forms of these two words in Arabic (Father, *ab*, and Lord, *rabb*) were close enough for the change to be due to scribal error.

It is maybe understandable that Muslims should take this kind of view because by about 800 Christians had begun to employ Arabic as their language of everyday conversation and in specifically religious contexts as well. While John of Damascus before 750 could write in Greek and be understood by a local audience in Palestine, translations of biblical and other key texts into Arabic were already being made at about this time in monasteries around Jerusalem. And by the early ninth century there were theologians writing, and more significantly thinking, in Arabic and employing arguments identical to those being found in current usage among Muslims. The most famous in these first generations of Arab Christian theologians were Theodore Abū Qurra (d. *c*.830), Melkite Bishop of Ḥarrān, Ḥabīb Ibn Khidma Abū Rā'iṭa (d. *c*.835) the Jacobite, and ʿAmmār al-Baṣrī (fl. 820) the Nestorian. The surviving works of each of these authors show that they were attempting to explain their theology to Muslims in terms and concepts which their audience would understand, and were responding to arguments levelled at their beliefs with answers expressly framed for thinkers who based their ideas on the Qur'an. It is not an exaggeration to say that for a few generations in the ninth century an original form of Christianity developed in Arabic within the context of Islamic theological discourse.

Of course, this development was a practical necessity as Christians started to be confronted with questions about their faith from the qur'anic array of teachings which Muslims had available. But besides the necessities of apologetic, it is possible that Christians who were freed from the pressures of Byzantine conformity and its overriding influence developed their own native forms of thinking in a new language and intellectual grammar which they shared with Muslim counterparts. As they thought out the implications of their faith in a new context, they produced theologies that at the same time looked back to patristic antecedents and looked around to the intellectual tools and formulations that were immediately available.

Although parts of the Bible were translated into Arabic earlier, it seems likely from the available evidence that systematic translations of whole books were not accomplished until the middle of the ninth century. If there were Arabic-speaking Christian communities from much earlier times, this seems a rather late date, and as has been mentioned above some scholars suggest on circumstantial grounds that there must have been earlier translations. But not only is there no surviving copy from an earlier time, but there is a substantial lack of corroborative references as well. So it would appear that only at this time at the end of the first ʿAbbasid century was there an obvious need for Arabic versions of the scriptures, presumably as fewer and fewer Christians were able to understand them in any other language. This was certainly the case among Coptic Christians, for whom from the tenth century onwards Arabic increasingly became the language of religious writing and of worship alongside Bohairic.

Through the centuries of the 'Abbasid period the course of Arab Christianity increasingly became involved with Islam. The pressures of Islamic culture with its multiple attractions to induce minorities to conform, the ascendancy of Islamic religious thought and philosophy offering convincing rationalizations of the workings of the world and stern arguments against cherished beliefs, and the inbuilt social disparity of Christians in wider society all combined to set the churches on the defensive. How rapidly Christians converted to Islam is impossible to say, but as time goes on the confidence and sense of superiority that can be seen in such theologians as John of Damascus and Timothy I become scarce.

This is not to say that Christians within the Islamic empire necessarily felt beleaguered. The example of Yaḥyā Ibn 'Adī in the tenth century counters any such assumption. An Iraqi Jacobite Christian, he studied under a Nestorian and also the philosopher Abū Naṣr al-Fārābī, and went on to become a leading figure in philosophy and theology in Baghdad. He wrote against Christians of other denominations, and also refuted Muslim theologians and philosophers of earlier times. And he left one of the most influential treatises on morals in the Islamic world, the *Tahdhīb al-akhlāq*, *The Refinement of Morals*. He does not appear to have felt hampered in any serious way by being a Christian, though maybe the fact that major works in his theological output are not original compositions but painstaking responses to arguments put by Muslims a century earlier, and that his book on morals has so little obvious Christian character that it has often been attributed to Muslim authors, suggests that he was more aware of the all-embracing presence of Islam and the requirement to defend and conform than of verve and vigour in his own faith.

Of course, this inference can only be supposition, though it is maybe supported somewhat later by the work of a Melkite theologian, Paul of Antioch, who was Bishop of Sidon some time before the thirteenth century, probably late in the twelfth. His Arabic *Letter to a Muslim Friend* is both original and courageous, for it claims to detect in the verses of the Qur'an both support for the major doctrines of Christianity and actual articulations of these doctrines themselves. Outwardly a polite and reasoned treatise, in its unspoken intention it carries devastating criticisms of Islam. For the implication of what it maintains is that the true meaning of the Islamic revelation in its support for Christianity can only be discerned and identified with the help of Christian scripture. In other words, the Qur'an is a partial attestation to biblical truth and it depends on it.

Paul goes further. The conceit of his letter is that he has asked European experts about Islam and why they have not accepted the faith, to which they reply that the Qur'an itself proclaims it is an Arabic scripture and intended for Arabs, and they support their contention with copious quotations. What Paul implies here is that Islam is not a universal faith come to supersede Christianity or any other faith, but a local teaching intended for the desert Arabs. And Muḥammad is a local preacher, indeed sent by God, but directed only to Arabia and nowhere else. It is as though he came to bring his people to a rudimentary form of monotheism from the polytheism of their old ways.

Although such systematic views are not articulated openly in this letter, they are the unavoidable message of what it contains. They appear to be the fruit of a meditation on Islam by an Arab Christian who cannot reject this later religious phenomenon as mere charlatanism, as does John of Damascus four or so centuries earlier, and concludes that it is indeed God-sent, but with only a specific geographical relevance. Here is to be seen a continuing liveliness in Christian thinking, and indeed an anticipation of what in later centuries would be termed an inclusivist attitude towards the plurality of religions, but also a deep preoccupation with the reality of Islam, an apologetic concern to vindicate Arab Christianity in the evident difficulties it faces, and an attempt to show how the later faith has not in fact replaced the earlier but is instead dependent upon it.

This letter clearly appealed to Arab Christians (for whom it was presumably intended as a boost to faith) because it circulated among them for maybe a century before it was edited by an unknown scholar in Cyprus at the beginning of the fourteenth century and confidently sent to two Muslim scholars with the invitation to approve its arguments and acknowledge the authenticity of Christianity. Needless to say, it failed, though one cannot help noting its vivacity and boldness in identifying a relationship between Christianity and Islam in which both are part of God's dispensation, though the later faith is no rival to the earlier.

Paul may well have written his letter against the background of the crusades, and the fourteenth-century Cypriot editor certainly did. It is perhaps a mark of the degree of assimilation reached by Arab Christians who lived along the route of the crusading armies (though the ignorance of the invaders is not to be underestimated) that they were rarely distinguished in any major way from Muslims, and suffered many of the same degradations and massacres at the crusaders' hands.

The Decline of Arab Christianity

Just like Muslim Arabs living in the Mediterranean parts of Islamic domains, Arab Christians suffered considerable disruption under crusader rule. European priestly and episcopal hierarchies were established, and monastic and preaching orders began activities within the crusader kingdoms, often dislodging the older orders of priests and bishops and introducing alien forms of spirituality and worship. But devastating as this was, it was marginal when compared with what was going on further east. Through the thirteenth century the Mongols swept westwards from Central Asia and virtually destroyed the Islamic Empire in its old form. For four hundred years since the middle of the ninth century the central rule of the caliph in Baghdad had increasingly been eroded as warlords seized power in the state and local rulers asserted autonomy. But with this new Turkic threat the structure of the community was almost swept away. In 1258 Baghdad was sacked and the last 'Abbasid caliph to rule in the city was assassinated. For some time following this, Christians enjoyed a measure of freedom under rule that was not only favourable but also tipping towards conversion to Christianity itself. In fact, for some years the Patriarch of the Church of the East took up residence in one of the caliphs' palaces, and felt free enough to lead religious processions in public, maybe the first since the city had been built. But the patriarchs gradually lost the rulers' confidence, and this short period of triumph over their former Muslim overlords gave way to humiliation and persecution, in which churches and monasteries were burnt and priests and bishops killed. The eventual outcome was that the Church of the East lost its position at the heart of public life and subsided into obscurity. Church communities ceased to exist in parts of Asia where they had previously been recorded, and the leadership withdrew from Baghdad. This decline was accelerated by the active persecution of Timūr i-Leng (r. 1396–1405) and his descendants, and the once great church, with its bishoprics stretching east, north and south, was lost to the world in its seclusion between Lake Van and Lake Urmia east of the upper Tigris.

Further west, Christians in Egypt and the Mediterranean coastlands fared almost as badly. From 1250 the Mamlūks seized power in Cairo, and presided over more intensive anti-Christian activities than before. Under the earlier Fāṭimid and Ayyūbid dynasties Christians had often been able to rise to senior positions in the state. And while there had been persecutions, most notably under the Fāṭimid caliph al-Ḥākim bi-Amr Allah (r. 996–1021) when the Church of the Holy Sepulchre was destroyed and Christians were forced to distinguish themselves in public by wearing weighty wooden crosses, individuals had served as viziers and caliphal secretaries; just as under 'Abbasid rulers in eighth- and ninth-century Baghdad, there was no sustained animosity towards Christians on the part of the populace. Under the Mamlūks, however, Christians were repeatedly removed from positions to which they had been able to rise, and the mob regularly vented its frustration at inept governments by destroying churches and monasteries.

Such direct action against Christians in the Arab world was hard to bear, but it cannot have compared in power to sap the will and kill the spirit with the persistent anti-*Dhimmī* measures that influenced all aspects of relations between Christians and Muslims, particularly in public life. These measures had informed all aspects of relations between Muslim masters and Christian, together with other, subjects since an early stage in the Islamic era, as we have seen; although they were not frequently enforced in an active sense, they provided the general framework of communal, and presumably personal, relations, removing security and rendering client populations constantly on the defensive. Thus, while capable individuals might achieve prominence, they must always fear removal or worse at a ruler's whim or the mob's insistence.

This inequality of relationship and precariousness of position helps to explain why Arab Christianity ceases to have the resilience and strength of former times. With a few exceptions, such as the Copt al-Ṣafī Ibn al-'Assāl and his brothers in thirteenth-century Egypt, who not only held public office but also wrote works on their own faith and defences against Islam, there were no leading theological minds or creative intellects that left a lasting mark. And under the pressure of taxation and social discrimination there were steady numbers of conversions to Islam. This, of course, had happened since the earliest years of the new faith, but after about 1100 there seems to have been a gathering of momentum, until by the end of the Mamlūk era in the early sixteenth century Christians represented no more than 7 per cent of the total population in the Arab heartlands.

The victory of the Ottomans over the Mamlūks in 1516 brought much of the Arab Middle Eastern world under rule from Istanbul. And there was some change in circumstances for Christians. The *jizya* tax levelled against *Dhimmīs* was reduced, and financial incentive to convert was thereby removed. In addition, there was some consolidation of populations under the *millet* system, according to which each religious community adhered to its own laws and customs, with the result that populations tended to live in greater separation from one another, even within the same town, and there was less occasion for meetings and thus much less intermarriage.

As part of the Ottoman conception of the state, followers of a particular religion were all regarded as members of a single community or *millet*, each of which was thought as having one head. So just as the Muslims throughout the empire all came under the sultan, Christians of all denominations came under the Ecumenical Patriarch of the Greek Orthodox Church, an arrangement analogous to that under 'Abbasid rule when the Patriarch of the Church of the East was recognized as overall head. This arrangement naturally reduced the prestige of the leaders of other denominations, who inevitably ceased to play prominent parts in the life of the state. This did, however, change over time as a number of *millets* were given recognition and thus greater autonomy, although always under the state laws.

The separation of populations within the Ottoman Empire may have been instrumental in producing rapid expansion of Arab Christian communities in the Fertile Crescent in the sixteenth century and again in the nineteenth century when it swelled to about 20 per cent of the total population. The reduction in conversions that took place through interfaith marriage and economic incentives explains this in part, though the proximity of Christian populations to coastal areas (the combined result of attraction to the crusader states and flight from the Mongol invasions), where they came into contact with European trade and social influence, gave them greater prosperity than many Muslim communities; it also opened them to new developments in health care, such as the single measure of isolating families during epidemics rather than congregating together as Muslims tended to do. Together with widely available education, which Christians in the eastern Mediterranean lands championed, these differential factors accelerated Christian population growth in these periods within the empire.

Growth in prosperity and population led to mass emigrations. Within the Ottoman Empire population movements of Christians had taken place for centuries, as communities moved away from areas of intolerance to the greater safety of majority Christian regions, or were attracted by areas of economic boom. Then, from the mid-nineteenth century, Lebanese Christians (together with some of the Muslim population) left for America in order to avoid overpopulation, leading an exodus that continued through most of the twentieth century. There are now important communities of Arab Christians in major cities of the United States and Canada, Europe and Australia, together with religious hierarchies descended from the ancient episcopates of pre-Islamic and early Islamic times, and functioning in surroundings and against new challenges of which the leaders of old could never have dreamed.

Growth in prosperity and connections with the wider world also exposed Arab Christians to ideas that, like their predecessors under 'Abbasid rule in ninth-century

Baghdad, they mediated to the world of Ottoman Islam. In the eighteenth century, and more widely in the nineteenth century, Christians were instrumental in introducing knowledge of European advances in science, philosophy, politics, and so on. The resulting Rebirth, *Naḥḍa*, as it was called, channelled mainly through newly founded newspapers and journals, had widespread effects on intellectual, social and religious life among both Christians and Muslims in the decades leading up to and away from the year 1900. And it was particularly influential on the growth of Arab nationalism, which clamoured for regional recognition within the Ottoman Empire. The secularist Baath Party, which in different guises rose to power in Syria and Iraq, was founded by Michel 'Aflaq, who came from a Christian background.

Nevertheless, the emigration of Christians steadily increased through the later nineteenth and the twentieth centuries. And it must be said that economic attractions cannot provide a full explanation for the exodus of substantial parts of the Arab Christian population of the late Ottoman and nation-state Middle Eastern world. Where there is tension within society, and discrimination between religions, and where increased Islamization marginalizes followers of other faiths – all factors recognizable from early Islamic times and attributable by theologians and ideologues to the Qur'an and the precedent of the Prophet and his successors – there is little incentive to stay when family members press invitations to join them overseas and the prospects at home are dim. The Christian population of the Arab world had by the beginning of the present century reached a low point never seen before, and there is no sign of reversal. While the long history of Arab Christianity continues, it does so in new environments where it must learn once again to survive in the tenacious way it has done in its original homeland for more than fifteen hundred years.

References and further reading

Atiya, A. S. (1969) *A History of Eastern Christianity*. London: Methuen.
Baumer, C. (2006) *The Church of the East: An Illustrated History of Assyrian Christianity*. London: I. B. Tauris.
Browne, L. E. (1967) *The Eclipse of Christianity in Asia: From the Time of Muhammad till the Fourteenth Century*. New York: Howard Fertig.
Chabot, J.-B. (1899–1924) *Chronique de Michel le Syrien, Patriarche Jacobite d'Antioche (1166–1199), Éditée pour la première fois et traduite en français*, 4 vols. Paris: Ernest Leroux.
Cragg, K. (1992) *The Arab Christian: a History in the Middle East*. London: Mowbray.
Ebied, R. and Thomas, D. (eds.) (2005) *Muslim-Christian Polemic during the Crusades, the Letter from the People of Cyprus and Ibn Abī Ṭālib al-Dimashqī's Response*. Leiden: Brill.
Fargues, P. (1998) The Arab Christians of the Middle East: a demographic perspective. In A. Pacini (ed.) *Christian Communities in the Arab Middle East, the Challenge of the Future*. Oxford: Clarendon Press.
Finkel, J. (trans.) (1927) A Risala of al-Jahiz. *Journal of the American Oriental Society* 47: 311–34.
Griffith, S. (2001) 'Melkites', 'Jacobites' and the Christological controversies in Arabic in third/ninth century Syria. In D. Thomas (ed.) *Syrian Christians under Islam, the First Thousand Years*. Leiden: Brill.

Griffith, S. H. (2007) *The Church in the Shadow of the Mosque: Christians and Muslims in the World of Islam*. Princeton: Princeton University Press.

Grypeou, E., Swanson, M. and Thomas, D. (eds.) (2006) *The Encounter of Eastern Christianity with Early Islam*. Leiden: Brill.

Hourani, A. (1991) *A History of the Arab Peoples*. London: Faber and Faber.

Hoyland, R. (1997) *Seeing Islam as Others Saw It: a Survey and Evaluation of Christian, Jewish and Zoroastrian Writings on Early Islam*. Princeton, NJ: Darwin Press.

Ibn Isḥāq (1955) *Sīrat sayyidnā Muḥammad rasūl Allāh*, trans. A. Guillaume: *The Life of Muhammad*. Oxford: Oxford University Press.

Lamoreaux, J. C. (2005) *Theodore Abū Qurrah*. Library of the Christian East 1. Provo, Ut.: Brigham Young University Press.

Lewis, B. (1995) *The Middle East: 2000 Years of History from the Rise of Christianity to the Present Day*. London: Weidenfeld and Nicolson.

Mingana, A. (ed. and trans.) (1928) The Apology of Timothy the Patriarch before the Caliph Mahdi. *Bulletin of the John Rylands Library* 12: 137–292.

Moffett, S. H. (1992) *A History of Christianity in Asia*, vol. 1: *Beginnings to 1500*. San Francisco: HarperSanFrancisco.

—— (2005) *A History of Christianity in Asia*, vol. 2: *1500 to 1900*. Maryknoll, NY: Orbis.

Parry, K. (2003) Byzantine and Melkite Iconophiles under Iconoclasm. In Ch. Dendrinos, J. Harris, E. Harvalla-Crook and J. Herrin (eds.) *Porphyrogenita: Essays on the History and Literature of Byzantium and the Latin East in Honour of Julian Chrysostomides*. Aldershot: Ashgate.

Reynolds, G. S. (2004) *A Muslim Theologian in the Sectarian Milieu, 'Abd al-Jabbār and the Critique of Christian Origins*. Leiden: Brill.

Sabella, B. (1998) The emigration of Christian Arabs: dimensions and causes of the problem. In A. Pacini (ed.) *Christian Communities in the Arab Middle East, the Challenge of the Future*. Oxford: Clarendon Press.

Samir, S. K. (1998) The Christian communities, active members of Arab society throughout history. In A. Pacini (ed.) *Christian Communities in the Arab Middle East, the Challenge of the Future*. Oxford: Clarendon Press.

Shahīd, I. (1984) *Byzantium and the Arabs in the Fourth Century*. Washington, DC: Dumbarton Oaks Research Library.

—— (1989) *Byzantium and the Arabs in the Fifth Century*. Washington, DC: Dumbarton Oaks Research Library.

—— (1995) *Byzantium and the Arabs in the Sixth Century*, vol. 1, part. 2: *Ecclesiastical History*. Washington, DC: Dumbarton Oaks Research Library.

Thomas, D. (2001) Paul of Antioch's *Letter to a Muslim Friend* and *The Letter from Cyprus*. In D. Thomas (ed.) *Syrian Christians under Islam, the First Thousand Years*. Leiden: Brill.

—— (2003) *Christians at the Heart of Islamic Rule, Church Life and Scholarship in 'Abbasid Iraq*. Leiden: Brill.

Trimingham, J. S. (1979) *Christianity among the Arabs in Pre-Islamic Times*. London: Longman.

CHAPTER 2
Armenian Christianity

Vrej Nerses Nersessian

History

In 2001 Armenia celebrated the 1,700 years that had passed since its conversion to Christianity. Three dates have to be fixed independently to determine the precise date of the nation's conversion. They are: the conversion of King Trdat, the freeing of St Gregory the Illuminator from prison, and the consecration of St Gregory as Catholicos of Armenia. The exact year in which the conversion of King Trdat took place is not agreed among scholars. Fr. Tournebize argued that the most probable date lay between 290 and 295. E. Dulaurier, M. Ormanian, M.-L. Chaumont and Father P. Ananian, relying largely on the evidence of the *History* of Movses Khorenatsi (*c*.390–450), have calculated it to have been in or about 302. Movses records that Trdat had begun his reign in the third year of that of the Emperor Diocletian, and that St Gregory the Illuminator had 'sat on the throne of the holy apostle Thaddeus in the seventeenth year of Trdat's reign' (1978: II, 82). Diocletian's reign began in November 284, so Trdat's year of accession would have been 286 or 287, and his seventeenth 302 or 303.

H. Manandyan placed the return of Trdat to Armenia from Rome in 298 or 299, subsequent to the peace established between Rome and Persia after Galerius' victory. Hence Trdat's seventeenth year fell in 314, which is also the date of the king's conversion. Behind this conclusion lies Manandyan's proposition that Trdat could not have adopted the Christian faith before 313. The Greek version of Agat'angeghos' *History of the Armenians* puts Trdat's reliance on Diocletian in matters of faith in these terms:

> From youthful age raised and educated by you [Diocletian] . . . hailing the gods who saved our power together with ourselves, I loathe the so-called Christians. What is more, I gave over to the bitterest death [after] tortures a certain Cappadocian [named] Gregory beloved by me . . . (1976: 37)

According to Agat'angeghos' *History*, written probably in the fifth century, in the summer or autumn of 314, a council of bishops met at Caesarea in Cappadocia and consecrated Gregory as Catholicos of Armenia; Gregory then returned to Armenia and baptized King Trdat, who declared his kingdom Christian. This is consistent with another statement in Agat'angeghos that, on his return from Caesarea, Gregory had brought with him the relics of St Athenogenes, who died around 303–5. Relying on this evidence, Fr. P. Ananian agreed with Manandyan's analysis and concluded that the year 314 was also the date of the 'official' conversion of Armenia.

The non-Armenian evidence for the conversion of Armenia is limited but important. Sozomen in his *Ecclesiastical History* states:

> The Armenians, I have understood, were the first to embrace Christianity. It is said that Tiridates, then the sovereign of that nation, became a Christian by means of a marvelous divine sign which was wrought in his own house; and that he issued commands to all the subjects, by a herald, to adopt the same religion. (1855: II, viii)

Eusebius in his own *Ecclesiastical History* states that Emperor Maximinus Daia, as the governor of the Roman province of Oriens:

> had the further trouble of the war against the Armenians, men who from ancient times had been friends and allies of the Romans; but as they were Christians and exceedingly earnest in their piety towards the Deity, this hater of God, by attempting to compel them to sacrifice to idols and demons, made them foes instead of friends, and enemies instead of allies. (1927–8: 214)

This war took place in November 311 or 312; according to Eusebius, Maximinus Daia 'was worn out along with his commanders in the Armenian war' (1927–8: 286).

According to the chronology of the *Narratio de rebus Armeniae*, compiled in *c.*700, the Council of Nicaea had been held 'in the thirty-fourth year of Trdat and the twentieth after the freeing of St Gregory'. The Council of Nicaea was held in June 325, so that the release of Gregory and the subsequent conversion of the king would have taken place in 305 or 306. Furthermore, Trdat's earlier persecution of Christians in Armenia coincided with the Great Persecution that broke out on 23 February 303, led by Emperor Diocletian (*c.*284–305). The martyrdoms of Oskeank', Suk'iaseank', Princess Sandukht, and the thirty-three Christian nuns led by Gayane and Hrip'sime, are the events leading to the conversion of Armenia. John Chrysostom in his panegyric dedicated to St Gregory, written during his exile in Armenia, in 404–7, refers to the two virgin martyrs, Gayane and Hrip'sime.

In several studies published to mark the 1,700th anniversary, the above evidence has been revisited, with the observation that previous scholars have given little attention to the presence of Christianity in Armenia Minor. Agat'angeghos, the primary historian of the conversion of Armenia, focuses only on Armenia Major and the Arshakuni kingdom. But, when he wishes to explain the success of St Gregory, makes the point that on his return to Armenia following his consecration by Leontius, Bishop of Caesarea, Gregory stopped in the city of Sebaste, and 'He found there a good number of brethren whom he persuaded to accompany him so that he might elevate them to the priesthood in his own country; and a very large number he took with him' (1976: §872). Furthermore, Eusebius mentions that Dionysius of Alexandria wrote letters on repentance to the Christians of Armenia, whose bishop was Meruzanes. In *The Acts of Eustratios and his Companions*, Auxentios, Eugenios, Mardarios, and Orestes, were Armenian Christians from the cities of Sebaste, Nicopolis, Satala, and Melitine. So it is not inconceivable that Meruzanes was the bishop of Armenia Minor. The reference by Eusebius to Armenians as 'friends and allies of the Romans' is not an allusion to the Arshakuni kingdom, but to Armenia Minor; here, according to *The Acts of Eustratios and his Companions*, a military garrison was stationed, in which the five martyrs served during the reigns of Diocletian and Maximinus Daia. The *Acts of Eustratios* add weight to the view that the references of Eusebius to Armenians should be confined to the geographical territory to the west of the Euphrates called Armenia Minor, at first an independent kingdom, which was then gradually drawn into the orbit of the Roman Empire and absorbed as a province by the end of the first century CE. To his credit M. Avgerian, in his introduction to *Complete Lives and Martyrologies of Saints*, regards the five martyrs of Sebaste as 'the glorious martyrs who are the pride of the Armenians, from the territory of Armenia Minor' (1874).

Apostolicity and Missions

In *The Epic Histories* of P'awstos Buzand (425–86), and the Armenian version of the *Acts of Addai*, Christianity was first introduced into Armenia from Edessa by Thaddeus, the apostle who converted the royal princess Sandukht. From the seventh century the name of the apostle Bartholomew is also added to the apostolicity claim in Armenian historiography. These traditions corroborate historical evidence pointing to the influx of Christians from Syria and Adiabene during the second and third centuries. P'awstos Buzand speaks of Daniel 'of Syrian race', who 'set up the great and first church of the mother-of-the-churches in all Armenia' (1989: III, xiv). Tertullian, in his *Commentary on the Acts of the Apostles* lists the Armenians among those who witnessed at Pentecost the descent of the Holy Ghost on the Apostles (Acts 2: 1).

The second, more successful, attempt to establish Christianity in Armenia is credited to St Gregory the 'Second Illuminator' in the See of Cappadocia. Agat'angeghos, who attests the conversion of Armenia to Christianity by Gregory calls it 'the renewal of the Armenian priesthood', and ascribes apostolic foundations to the fresh missionary impetus by linking the Christianization of Armenia to the martyrdom of St Thaddeus. P'awstos Buzand records that St Gregory was consecrated in Caesarea and was placed 'on the throne of the apostle Thaddeus'. This expression is repeated by Movses Khorenatsi, who says that Gregory 'sat on the throne of the holy apostle Thaddeus'. In the history of the numerous apostolic origins claimed by various churches east and west, the Armenian Catholicos and historian Yovhannes V (898–929) provides as good an explanation as any:

> The establishment of the holy Christian faith spread all over the earth, and above all among the Armenian people, thanks to Bartholomew, who is one of the twelve, and

Thaddeus who is one of the seventy, who received from Our Lord Jesus Christ responsibility for evangelizing and spreading the doctrine in our land. (Nersessian 2001b: 25)

The idea of primacy in the Armenian Church is unanimous with the Orthodox tradition in its affirmation of the Church as an organic unity. To the Encyclical of Pope Leo XIII, inviting the Armenian Church 'to unite with the Church of Rome', and by this union 'to obey the Pontiff of Rome', Bishop M. Mouradeants in his reply questions the validity of the invitation:

But perhaps you invite people from Christ to Peter or from Bartholomew to Peter? If you are inviting from Christ to Peter, it is manifest that you invite from the Lord to His servant, from the Teacher to His disciple, from the Saviour to the saved, from the service of God to the service of man. If you invite people from Bartholomew to Peter, it is evident that you are inviting from like to like, from disciple to his fellow disciple, from the Apostle to the Apostle, both of whom were taught by the same teaching, received the same Holy Spirit. (23 August 1888)

Despite the triumphal narratives that idolized the heroic age of Trdat and St Gregory, the conversion of the pagan aristocracy of Armenia was a slow process. Paganism persisted for centuries in the intellectual culture, oral literature, cultic practices and religious festivals. P'awstos Buzand is very critical of this period:

For from antiquity when they had taken on the name of Christians, it was merely as [though it were] some human religion; and they did not receive it with ardent faith, but as some human folly and under duress. They did not receive it with understanding as is fitting, with hope and faith, but only those who were to some degree acquainted with Greek or Syriac learning were able to achieve some partial inkling of it. As for those who were without skill in learning and who were the great of the people – the *nakharars* as well as the *shinakan* . . . consumed themselves with vile thoughts in perverse practices, and in ancient pagan customs. (1989: III, vi, 72)

The Armenian Church had to tread a narrow path between a number of political forces and religious ideologies: Persian Zoroastrianism, and various sects such as the Manichaeans, the Messalians and Borborites. The council held in Ashtishat in 365 set down regulations banning the pagan style of funerals, such as the rending of garments, loud wailing and unbridled mourning.

Movses Khorenatsi recalls the mission of Grigoris, one of the grandsons of St Gregory, to the tribe of the Mask'utk'. It is revealing that King Trdat sent his mission because the government of the north-western regions believed that if the king wished to rule over their lands, he should send them bishops from the line of St Gregory, because they are 'seeking them ardently'. Conversely, the Mask'utk' were convinced that 'this is a ruse on the part of the king of Armenia [Trdat] to prevent us from looting his country' (1978: I, xiv, 94–5; III, iii, 255–6). Movses Daskhurantsi, sums up Mesrop Mashtots and his companions' missionary work in these terms: 'He revived the church and strengthened the faith and spread the teaching of the Gospel . . . A perfect preacher and apostle to the barbarous mountain tribes, he taught them to write in their own languages' (1961: I, 55). According to Ghazar P'arpetsi (c.437–500) by the close of the fifth century Armenia had eighteen bishoprics, and of these, six were in Georgia and Caucasian Albania. Arshak Alpoyachian (1947) and Nicholas Adontz (1970), in their analysis of the growth of the episcopal sees in Armenia, drawing upon the lists of the bishops who attended four Armenian church councils: Artashat in 450 (I and II), Dvin in 505 and 555, and Manazkert in 726, concluded that the number of bishops increased from eighteen to twenty-four, to twenty-six, to twenty-seven, and to twenty-eight by 726.

Scripture and Tradition

Armenians call the Bible *Astuadsashuntch*, which means 'breath of God', following St Paul's definition: 'All Scripture is inspired by God' (2 Tim. 3: 16). The eminent leaders of the young Church, with the help of Greek and Syriac missionaries, had achieved great success in establishing the new faith. Through the medium of the spoken language, the Gospel was communicated from the earliest period of evangelization to the very beginning of the fifth century. But hearing the Gospel was not enough to make the impression desired upon the soul. The privilege to receive with understanding as is fitting, with hope and faith, belonged only to those who were to some degree acquainted with Greek or Syriac learning.

Sahak Part'ev (c.350–439), the Catholicos, and his companion the monk Mesrop Mashtots (c.361–439) undertook the task of inventing the Armenian alphabet and translating the scriptures into Armenian. Up to that point a group called *T'argmanitch vardapetk* (Translators) trained in Edessa, Antioch, Athens and Constantinople; they orally translated into Armenian passages of scriptures that were read in church in either Greek or Syriac.

The evidence of the primary sources – Koriwn (c.390–447), Ghazar P'arpetsi and Movses Khorenatsi – shows the translation of the Bible into classical Armenian was accomplished in two stages. The first translation was done between 407 and 412, and the second after the Council of Ephesus (431), between 433 and 436. Mesrop together with his pupils began the translation of the Bible with the Proverbs of Solomon. The first sentence written in the new Armenian script was the exhortation: 'To know wisdom and instruction, to perceive the words of understanding.' Koriwn states:

> At that time our blessed and desirable land of Armenia became truly worthy of admiration, whence, by the hand of two colleagues suddenly, in an instant, Moses, the Lawgiver, along with the order of the prophets, energetic Paul, with the entire phalanx of the apostles, along with Christ's world-sustaining gospel, became Armenian-speaking.

and:

> a land that had not known even the name of the regions where all those wonderful divine acts had been performed, soon learned all the things that were, not only those that had transpired in time, but that of the eternity which had preceded, and those that had come later, the beginning and the end and all the divine traditions. (1964: XI, 34)

The origin of the canon comprising twenty-two books (in the New Testament) in Armenia shows the influence of the Syriac Peshitta version.

The second phase entailed revising the translation done in accordance with the Greek manuscripts brought back from Constantinople. Koriwn says:

> Sahak, who had translated from the Greek language into Armenian all the liturgical books and the writings of the church fathers, once more undertook, with Eznik, the retranslation of the once hastily [*p'utanaki*] done translation using the authentic [*hastatun*] copies. (1964: III, 54)

The same information is also provided by Movses Khorenatsi.

Among noteworthy features of the Armenian version of the Bible was the inclusion of certain books that elsewhere came to be regarded as apocryphal. The Old Testament included the History of Joseph and Asenath and the Testament of the Twelve Patriarchs, and the New Testament included the Epistles of the Corinthians to Paul and a Third Epistle of Paul to the Corinthians.

F. C. Conybeare (1856–1924), the English Armenian scholar, was convinced of the high value of the Armenian translation. Speaking of the Old Testament he says:

> For beauty of diction and accuracy of rendering the Armenian cannot be surpassed. The genius of the language is such as to admit a translation of any Greek document both literal and graceful; true to the order of the Greek, and even reflecting its compound words, yet without being slavish, and without violence to its own idiom. We are seldom in doubt as to what stood in the Armenian's Greek text; therefore his version has almost the same value for us as the Greek text itself, from which he worked, would possess. The same criticism is true of the Armenian New Testament as well. (2001: 119)

The translation of the Bible left a distinct mark on the whole of Armenian culture; medieval religious poetry, miniature painting, music, and architecture are deeply coloured by its influence. In a certain sense, the development of the art of calligraphy was also linked to the Bible, as it was the most frequently copied book of the Middle Ages. The 20,000 plus manuscripts that have survived, more than any other ancient version, with the exception only of the Latin Vulgate, testify to the important place they occupied in the lives of the people. In 1934–5, on the 1,500th anniversary of the translation of the Bible into classical Armenian, the Armenian Byzantinist Nicholas Adontz summed up the influence of the Bible on Armenian culture in these words:

> The Latin Vulgate did not have the same importance to the Latin centuries as the Armenian Bible to the Armenian people. The Latin literature had been in existence for a long time when the Vulgate appeared; whereas the Armenian Bible inaugurated the beginnings of a new era in which the Armenian people learning for the first time the use of the pen came to take their place in the world of human civilization. (1938: 48)

The Armenian Church sanctified the translators, commemorating them annually on 11 October, the Feast of the Holy Translators.

Christian Literature

To meet the immediate needs of the Armenian Church, to reinforce its doctrinal and liturgical activities, translations from Greek and Syriac were a conscious plan of cultural transmission. This plan called for the translation of the entire corpus of Christian knowledge.

The writings of the following church fathers were translated into Armenian, which not only speaks eloquently of the whole intellectual and spiritual vitality of the Armenian Church, but also serves as an indicator of its orientation: Ignatius of Antioch, *c*.35–*c*.107; Aristides the Apologist, about second century; Irenaeus of Lyons, *c*.200; Hippolytus of Rome, *c*.170–*c*.236; Dionysius of Alexandria, d. *c*.264; Gregory the Wonderworker, *c*.213–*c*.270; Eusebius of Caesarea, *c*.260–*c*.340; Athanasius of Alexandria, *c*.296–389; Gregory of Nazianzus, 329–89; Gregory of Nyssa, *c*.330–*c*.395; Basil of Caesarea, *c*.330–*c*.379; Cyril of Jerusalem, *c*.315–86; John Chrysostom, *c*.347–407; Epiphanius of Salamis, *c*.315–403; Evagrius Ponticus, 346–99; Aphraates, fourth century; Ephrem the Syrian, *c*.306–73; Cyril of Alexandria, d. 444. These writings are of great importance for the study of Greek and Syriac works whose originals are now lost, but have been preserved in Armenian translation.

Among these works must be mentioned the *Chronicon*, in two parts, by Eusebius of Caesarea (d. 339), which has come down to us through a fifth-century Armenian translation of the original Greek. The critical edition of the Armenian *Chronicon*, with Latin translation and excerpts preserved in later Greek sources was published by Fr. Mkrtitch Avgerian (pseud. Aucher) in 1818. In the 420s, another work by Eusebius of Caesarea, the *Ecclesiastical History*, was translated into Armenian. This is also of scholarly value, since large sections are now missing from the Syriac version from which it was translated. These lacunae have been filled with the aid of the Armenian translation.

Another important work among the early Armenian translations is *The Demonstration of the Apostolic Teaching* by Irenaeus of Lyons (d. 203), discovered in an Armenian version in 1907 by Karapet Ter Mkrttchian and published in 1913 as *Armenische Irenaeusfragmente*; it was recognized as the most important discovery in patristics of that year. The fourth and fifth books of Irenaeus' *Adversus Haereses* survive in Armenian, and these are significant for the study of his literary legacy. Because of their value the Armenian versions of Irenaeus' works have been translated and published in German, French, Russian, and English.

A considerable part of the literary legacy of the renowned first-century Jewish philosopher and theologian Philo of Alexandria has been preserved thanks to Armenian translations. The Greek originals of eight of the fifteen Philonic treatises that survive in Armenian are lost. These include: the commentaries on the books of Genesis and Exodus, two treatises on providence, as well as the homilies, *On Animals*, *On Samson*, *On Jonas* and *On God*. The commentaries on the books of Genesis and Exodus are among the more important Armenian translations and have been translated into Latin, English and French.

In Armenian literature the work of John Chrysostom (d. 407), much of it known only from Armenian translations, is second only to the Bible in the number of manuscripts produced. Among Chrysostom's Armenian translations, the *Commentary on Isaiah* – of which only the first and eighth chapters are extant in the original Greek, the remaining fifty-six existing only in Armenian – was put into circulation through a Latin translation. The *Commentary on Job* by Hesychius of Jerusalem (d. after 450), another important Byzantine exegetical work, is preserved in Armenian manuscripts. In the 1980s the Armenian version of Hesychius of Jerusalem's treatise *On St John* was discovered. The Greek original of this work is also lost.

To this day the Greek text of the *Refutation of the Articles of the Council of Chalcedon* by Timothy Aelurus (d. 477) has not been found. This important monument of the fifth-century Christological controversy has reached us through Armenian and Syriac, the latter being a condensed version of Timothy's work, while the Armenian has pre-served the complete text in its original state. Timothy Aelurus' *Refutation* had a major impact on Armenia dogma. At the beginning of the seventh century Catholicos Komitas (615–18) composed a catena based on it called *Knik' Hawatoy* (Seal of Faith), and in the thirteenth century Vardan Aygektsi compiled another catena called *Armat Hawatoy* (Root of Faith). These anti-Chalcedonian works played an important role in the struggle for independence by the Armenian Church and in the forging of its national identity.

The significance of Armenian translation is not limited to Greek works. The greatest contribution of Armenian literature to the field of patristics, are the ancient Armenian translations of the works of Ephrem the Syrian (d. 373). Since 1836, when the four volumes of Ephrem's works in Armenian were published, a great deal of research has been done in the West. These works of Ephrem were made available to the western public in translations from the Armenian into Latin or into modern western languages. For example, the *Commentary on Tatian's Diatessaron* was translated twice into Latin and into French. Based on the 1836 Armenian edition, a Latin translation of the *Commentary on the Epistles of Paul* appeared in 1893. Latin and English translations were made of the *Commentary on the Acts* (1926). The *Hymns* have been published three times, the third time in 1966 with a Latin translation facing the Armenian. The *Elegies on Nicomedia* have two editions, the second of which is accompanied by a French translation.

Doctrine and Theology

An event of overwhelming significance took place in 451, when the Armenians waged the battle of Avarayr against Sassanian Persia. For the first time a Christian nation made a declaration of the principle of the inviolability of freedom of conscience:

> From this belief no one can move us, neither angels, nor men, nor sword, nor water, nor any tortures that can be conceived or devised . . . We will, here, below, choose no other lord in thy place [referring to the king of Persia], and in heaven, we will honour no other God than Jesus Christ, for there is no other God save Him. (Eghishe 1982: II, 41)

The Fathers of the Armenian Church accept the canons of the Councils of Nicaea (325), Constantinople (381) and Ephesus (431) as 'the basis of life and guide to the path leading to God'. The Nicene-Constantinopolitan Creed recited in the Armenian liturgy has the following anathema added to it:

> As for those who say there was a time when the Son was not or there was a time when the Holy Spirit was not or that they came into being out of nothing or who say that the Son of God or the Holy Spirit are of different substance and that they are changeable or alterable, such the catholic and apostolic holy church doth anathematize.

This statement refutes Arianism, Macedonianism, Apollinarianism and Nestorianism. Gregory the Illuminator added to the Creed his prayer:

> As for us, we glorify Him who was before all ages, adoring the Holy Trinity, and the one Godhead of the Father, the Son, and the Holy Ghost, now and ever through ages and ages. Amen.

Theology and Spirituality

According to the Armenian Church the Orthodox faith is that Our Lord Jesus is perfect in his godhead and perfect in his manhood. He is God Incarnate. Catholicos Nerses IV Klayetsi (1102–73), in his Encyclical Letter says:

> The Son is begotten of the nature of the Father, but outside time. His begetting is not in the manner of the birth of man, subject to passion and transitory . . . Rather he is begotten like light from light, fire from fire, for they do not become foreign to each other in individuation, but remain one ray and one warmth of fire and of light both in the one who is generated and in the one from whom he is generated; and there is one nature for both, although they are distinguished from each other in person. In the same way the light of the Son came forth from the light of the Father and the fire of the divinity of the Son came forth from the fire of the Father, they are not other but of one and the same nature.

The Armenian doctrine of the Virgin birth and redemption is also consistent with the above exposition. Mary is 'Godbearer' (*Astuadsadsin* = Theotokos) and not 'Christbearer' (*K'ristosadsin*), a term preferred by Nestorius. In a hymn sung during the feast of Nativity and Epiphany (6 January) the birth of Christ is described by Gregory of Narek (945–1003) thus: 'The first born, of the Mother of God, Virgin Bearer of the Lord, creator becoming a true man as originally created, not in the fallen state of mortals.' Another hymn by him includes the words: 'The uncontainable in Earth and Heaven is wrapped within swaddling clothes / From the Father inseparable he seats himself in the Holy altar.'

To refute the accusation that Armenian doctrine is 'Miaphysite' in the Eutychian sense, the *Trisagion* as recited in the Armenian liturgy has: 'Holy, God, Holy and powerful, Holy and immortal, who was crucified for us.' The crucial clause is 'who was crucified for us'. This phrase is replaced by other phrases according to the occasion: 'who did rise from the dead' (Easter), or 'who was born and manifested for us' (Nativity and

Epiphany). Step'anos Siwnetsi (d. 735), in his *Commentary on the Divine Liturgy*, says that in as much as the godhead was present in Christ incarnate it was legitimate to say that 'God was crucified for us, has risen from the dead and was born and manifested for us.'

Bishop Step'anos connects the *Trisagion* to the elevation of the Gospel. Step'anos' description of this moment in the liturgy called the 'Little Entrance' confirms that the *Trisagion* is addressed to Christ only:

> At the elevation of the Gospel, with spiritual eyes, we see the Son of God seated on a throne high and lifted up. The smell of fragrant incense refers to the teaching and glorification given to those born of the font, the children of the church. . . . Here the suffusion of the Holy Spirit who came from the Father, typified by the incense, takes us all up whence we have fallen. By this incense we come to God's likeness according to his image, and as we boldly process around the table, together with the seraphim, our confession of the immortal one who is crucified for us issues forth like fragrant incense. (Nersessian 2001b: 18)

The tenor of Armenian theology is daring in accepting that God does suffer and die on the cross.

David the Invincible (590–660) defines the cross with the predicate *Astuadsenkal* (God-receiving), since for the Armenian theologian 'the tree of life' in the Book of Revelation becomes the wood of life in the shape of the cross, for Abraham saw in the Sabek tree the Cross of Christ.

The *khatchk'ar* (stone cross) in Armenian sculpture or the glorified cross in Armenian miniatures representing the life of Christ, are among the most original symbols of religious piety. The cross as the 'sign' of God or the 'wood' of life is a symbol not of death but life. One of the chants composed by Gregory of Narek and sung on Easter Sunday invokes the powerful image of Christ as lion on the cross: 'I tell of the voice of the lion / Who roared on the four-winged cross. On the four-winged cross he roared / His voice resounding in Hades.' The lion is king over all the beasts and Christ is king over all creation.

The texts prove beyond doubt the Armenian opposition to Eutychianism, Julianism, and Severianism. The Armenian theologian Catholicos Yovhannes Odznetsi (650–728) in his treatise *Against the Phantasiasts*, refutes the erroneous belief that the humanity of the Saviour was a mere appearance like the imprint of a seal on wax. He affirms that the body of Christ is real and consubstantial with ours, and that the divine and human natures exist without confusion:

> The Word, in becoming man and being called man, remained also God; and man, in becoming God and being God, never lost his own substance . . . It is evident that it is the incomprehensible union and not the transformation of the nature which leads us to say one nature of the Word Incarnate. (Nersessian 2001b: 41)

Yovhannes Odznetsi occupies a distinguished place among Armenian *catholicoi* as the only one during whose catholicate of eleven years, 717–28, two very important local synods were called, at Dvin in 719 and at Manazkert in 726, to implement substantial reform in the Armenian Church. During his tenure the patristic *florilegium* known as *Girk' T'ght'ots* (Book of Letters) and the *Kanonagirk' Hayots* (Armenian Book of Canons) were compiled to defend the Church. In his oration, delivered at the opening of the synod, he described the battered state of the Armenian Church in the aftermath of the Arab conquests and decades of ecclesiastical tug-of-war with the Byzantine Church:

> For I see many grave aberrations multiplying, not only among the lay, but also among the monastics and church primates. We, who took to the path of truth with one language, based on one proclamation, have wandered unto many trails and paths, taking up infinite and variously spurious customs, both in conduct and in worship of God.

The Greeks were not the only purveyors of alien ideas and customs. In the background to the comments of the Catholicos were the beliefs and activities of movements found in the Armenian Church: Gnostics, Borborites, Mdsghneans, Paulicians, and principally the T'ondrakians, who were also damaging the integrity and Orthodoxy of the Christian faith in Armenia. The Paulicians rejected the Church with its hierarchy, institutions and sacraments outright. To address this situation Yovhannes Odznetsi pursued a rigorous policy of restoring the unified, indigenous liturgical practices and Orthodoxy throughout Armenia.

Finally, another element of dispute concerns the doctrine of the Holy Spirit. In the Nicene Creed recited during the Armenian liturgy the words about the Holy Spirit declare: 'We believe also in the Holy Spirit, the uncreated and the perfect; who spoke in the Law and in the Prophets and in the Gospels. Who came down upon the Jordan, preached in the apostles and dwelt in the saints.' In the Nicene-Constantinopolitan Creed, accepted by both eastern and western churches, is contained the statement that the Holy Spirit 'proceeds from the Father'. To this statement the Latin West introduced an extra phrase: 'and from the Son', known as the *filioque*, which the Greeks repudiated.

Armenian theologians remaining faithful to the biblical citations on the Holy Spirit, preferred not to exceed the simple formula of the Creed. Nerses IV Klayetsi in his Encyclical confirms: 'The Holy Spirit is called the one who proceeds from the Father and is equal in glory to the Son', a position which he repeats in his song 'Arawot Lusoy' (Morn of Light): 'proceeding from the Father, pour out in my spirit utterance for your pleasure'.

The formal position of the Armenian Church is: 'The Holy Spirit proceeds from the Father and is revealed by the Son', or 'The Holy Spirit proceeds from the Father through the Son.' Kirakos Gandzaketsi in chapter 50 of his *History of Armenia*, which is an account of the dialogue on unity between Pope Innocent IV (1243–54) and the Armenian Catholicos Kostandin I Bardzrberdtsi (1221–67), reiterates his position as being 'the Spirit proceeding from the Father and revealed by the Son'.

Vanakan vardapet (1181–1251), a leading intellectual of the Getik Monastery has a 'Doctrinal Advice', on the issue of the *filioque*, which is also preserved in Kirakos Gandzaketsi's *History of Armenia*. He holds the position: 'The Holy Spirit is from the Father and from the Son'. He explains his position thus:

Do not attempt to understand this in terms of natural things, but in terms of the cognition which is within us. Otherwise, when God is called Light and Life, what do you mean to say? Is He such a light and life as we see and live? Are you capable of understanding your own soul's name and essence? This is promised us in the world to come, when 'what eye has not seen nor ear heard, neither hath entered into the heart of man, what God has prepared for those who love Him is revealed'. (Gandzaketsi 1961: 338–44)

Although Vanakan vardapet's solution was not acceptable to Armenian theologians, it demonstrates the openness of the Armenian mind to other ideas and approaches in the interpretation of the mysteries of faith.

Monasticism

The history and foundation of Armenian monasticism is explored in the topographical, archaeological and geographical works of the Mkhitarist Fathers: Ghoukas Inchichian (1822, 1835), Nerses Sarkissian (1864), and Ghewond Alishan's topographical works on the provinces of Ayrarat, Sis, Shirak and Sisouan, published in the last decade of the nineteenth century. The number of monasteries listed in the publications of Ghewond Alishan, and more recently in the monograph by Hamazasp Oskian, is as follows: Vaspourakan 189, Siunik' 150, Artsakh 126, Karin 116, Ayrarat 52, Tourouberan-Taron 48, and Cilician Armenia 62.

Armenian literary sources employ various terms to define the numerous types of monasticism: *anapat*, *vank'*, *ukht*, *menastan*, *kronastan* and *miaynaworastan*. P'awstos Buzand, writing on the life of the hermit Gind vardapet, says 'he was [Gind] the leader of the religious monks (*abeghayis*), and teacher of the hermits (*miandzants*), and prelate of solitaries (*menaketsats*), overseer of solitary-communities (*vanerayits*), and teacher of all anchorites-dwelling-in-the-desert (*anapataworats*)' (1989: VI, xvi, 239).

Ghazar P'arpetsi, in a passage in his *History*, describes the life of Mesrop Mashtots after he had accepted the monastic habit and turned to the eremitic (*anapatakan*) life and lived in the deserts (*yanapats*). Here Ghazar draws a clear distinction between the 'monastic life' and the 'eremitic life', and gives the main disciplines of the communities under rule, with special mention of clothing. Koriwn, the biographer of Mesrop Mashtots, presents it in these terms: 'He [Mesrop] experienced many kinds of hardships, in keeping with the precepts of the gospel – solitude (*zmiaynaketsut'ean vars*), mountain dwelling, hunger, thirst and living on herbs, in dark cells, clad in sackcloth, with the floor as his bed' (1964: IV, 27).

The Rule of Basil of Caesarea, with modifications, was adopted by the Armenian Church, which is to be found in Gregory the Illuminator's *Yachakhapatum*, under sermon 23. The differences in the two rules are immediately apparent. While in the Caesarean version the monasteries were to be fully endowed, so that the monks would only be concerned with prayers, in the Armenian case the monks had to work to secure their living. The fruits of their labours were to be shared among the needy, pilgrims, travellers and farm workers. Catholicos Nerses I (373–7) who convened the council in Ashtishat in 365 extended the secular interests and objectives of the monasteries.

These are implied in the names given to monasteries operating in Siunik': Got'atun (house of mercy), Aspanjakanots (place of refuge), Otarats (for foreigners), Hiwranots (hospice) and Aghk'atanots (alms-house). The monasteries with these specific disciplines were the monasteries of Rshtunik', Narek, Derjan, Horomos, Gladzor, Andzewats, Hogeats.

To the two principal tasks of monasteries, asceticism and caring, just outlined above, a new role was introduced, which proved crucial for the survival of Armenian Christianity. The dynamic educational programme that the 'senior' and 'junior' t'argmanitch initiated in 406 developed into the unique order of the vardapet (unmarried priest); he had the powers to teach, interpret the scriptures, and to excommunicate and re-admit ex-communicants, as bishops had. The monasteries became intellectual centres, whose graduates were known by epithets such as Translator, Historian, Philosopher, Grammarian, Rhetorician, Poet, Scribe, and Illuminator.

Institutions, Governance and Canon Law

According to the Sixth Canon of the Council of Nicaea, the Exarch of Caesarea had jurisdiction over the missionary districts to the east of the Exarchate. Consequently, for about sixty years after the consecration of St Gregory as catholicos, his successors were ordained by the Exarchs of Caesarea. After 373, open canonical ties with Caesarea were severed. The Armenian Church had become sufficiently strong and mature, its clergy had increased in numbers, and its authority had been established.

Of the seven General Councils designated 'Ecumenical' in the Orthodox Church, the Armenian Church acknowledges the first three: (1) Nicaea, 325; (2) Constantinople, 381; (3) Ephesus, 431. It does not accept (4) Chalcedon, 451, and has made no formal pronouncements on the remaining three: (5) Constantinople, II, 553; (6) Constantinople, III, 681; and (7) Nicaea II, 787.

Of the regional councils, accepted by the ancient churches before the division in 451, the Armenian Church has also included in its *Book of Canons* the Acts of the Councils of Ancyra, 314; Caesarea, 314; Neocaesarea, 316; Gangra, 345; Antioch, 341; Laodicea, 365; and Sardica, 343; it also includes the canons of the *Apostolic Constitutions* and of the post-Apostolic Fathers. The Armenian Church, in company with all the ancient churches, reveres and follows the teachings of all the eminent church fathers (with the exception of Pope Leo I, d. 461) of the early classical period to the end of the fifth century. Between 354 and 1652 the Armenian Church convened twenty-two local councils, which were often attended not only by bishops, but also by princes, secular leaders and clergy of lower ranks. In the council of Shahapivan (444), the second Armenian Church council, but the first of which the legislation is extant in detail, the lay attendants, addressing the bishops, are reported to have said:

> These laws are pleasing to God and good for the building up of the Church. You order them and we shall obey and execute them. And if anyone does not hold firm the provisions of these laws, be he a bishop, or a presbyter, or a freeman, or a yeomen, he shall be punished and shall pay fines. (Hakobyan 1964: 534–5)

One of the most important aspects of the Armenian Church administration is its conciliar system, that is, the administrative, as well as doctrinal, liturgical, and canonical norms are set and approved by a council, a collective and participatory decision-making process. The Council of Bishops is the highest religious authority in the Church:

> *Clerical*: catholicos, bishop, priest, deacon
> *Lay*: National Ecclesiastical Assembly, Diocesan Assembly, parish

On each level, clergy and lay cooperation is central to the overall administration and ministry of the Church. While the Church is governed according to the standards set forth in the canons, there are complementary by-laws in most dioceses that further define the role and relationship of each functionary in the church within a given region.

There are four hierarchical sees in the Armenian Church: (1) The Catholicate of All Armenians in Ejmiadsin (Armenia), (2) The Catholicate of Cilicia (Lebanon), (3) The Patriarchate of Jerusalem, and (4) The Patriarchate of Constantinople.

Liturgy, Sacraments and Music

Liturgy

The Armenian Patarag (offering) is the most important expression of the Church's faith and identity. P'awstos Buzand in his *History* describes the liturgy as 'drink[ing] from the vivifying cup of salvation in the hope of the Resurrection, that is to say of the blood of our Lord Jesus Christ'. Armenian church fathers call the Divine Liturgy *Khorhurd Khorin* (mystery profound).

An exhaustive study of the Armenian rite, with critical texts and commentary are contained in Y. Gat'rjean's *Srbazan Pataragamatoyts Hayots*. This volume contains translations of the following liturgies: (1) the Liturgy of St Basil, in the oldest Armenian version; (2) the Liturgy of St Basil in a later version; (3) the Liturgy of the Armenians (under this latter title are: (a) the Anaphora of St Sahak, (b) of St Gregory of Nazianzus, (c) of St Cyril of Alexandria, and (d) fragments of a liturgy ascribed to St John Chrysostom; (4) Mass of the Catechumens; (5) the Liturgy of St John Chrysostom; (6) the Anaphora of St Ignatius; (7) the Liturgy of the Presanctified; (8) the Liturgy of St James; (9) the Liturgy of the Romans; and (10) the Liturgy of the Armenians from the eleventh century to the present. The availability of the above listed liturgies in Armenian contributed to the final shape of the only liturgy celebrated today in the Armenian Church.

Some features of the Armenian liturgy reflect what is called the Jerusalem rite. Between 397 and 431, the Jerusalem rite of the Liturgy of St James was adopted by the Church of Antioch, with which the Armenian Church has always been in close contact. The few changes made in the Armenian liturgy in the tenth century are almost all from the Byzantine Liturgy of St John Chrysostom. And finally, during the crusades, from the twelfth to the fourteenth century, the Latin presence in Asia Minor also left its traces on the liturgical uses in Armenia. The Armenian liturgy as it is used today took its final form sometime after the year 950 but before 1177, the date when Nerses Lambronatsi wrote his commentary on the liturgy.

From the seventh century, in the Divine Liturgy unleavened bread and unmixed wine is used, as the canons of the Council of Karin (692) indicate. In place of the doctrines of consubstantiation and transubstantiation, the word used in the Armenian liturgy for the changing of the bread and the wine into the body and blood of Christ is 'transposition' (*p'okharkel*'). This word shows that material elements as such remain the same in every respect except that they receive a new function and a new power. In the Prayer of the Epiclesis, the words used in the blessing of the bread are 'make it truly the body of our Lord', over the cup, 'make it verily the blood of our Lord', and over the bread and the wine 'make them truly the body and blood of our Lord' (repeated thrice). The communion bread is placed into the mouth of the faithful in the form of the consecrated bread dipped in the wine. The priest can celebrate only one liturgy a day, and only one liturgy can be celebrated each day on the same altar.

Those who do not partake of the sacrament receive *mas*, blessed thin unleavened bread (Greek *antidoron*) at the end of the liturgy. It is also taken by the worshippers to the members of their household who have not been able to attend the church. The person giving the *mas* says 'May this be to thee a share and a portion from the holy Sacrifice.' The person receiving replies 'God is my portion for ever.'

The principal *Commentaries on the Armenian Liturgy* are those by Khosrov Andzewatsi (*c*.900–63) (Venice, 1869; English trans. New York, 1991); Nerses Lambronatsi (1153–98) (Jerusalem, 1842; Venice, 1847; Italian trans. Venice, 1851, French trans. 2000), and Yovhannes Archishetsi (1260–1330) (Ejmiadsin, 1860).

Breviary

The Armenian Breviary called *Zhamagirk'* (Book of Hours) contains psalms, collects, prayers and hymns of the canonical hours. The present Armenian office has seven hours: *Gisherayin zham*: Nocturns/Night Hour; *Aravotean zham*: Matins/Morning Hour; *Arevagali zham*: Prime/Sunrise Hour; *Chashou zham*: Typica/Midday Hour; *Erekoyan zham*: Vespers/Evening Hour; *Khaghaghakan zham*: Peace Hour and *Hangstean zham*: Compline/Rest Hours. The number seven is a mystical number and recalls the words of the psalm, 'I shall bless thee seven times in the day'.

Today in Armenian parish worship, Vespers, once celebrated every day, is usually done only on Saturday evening; the night and morning offices with the *Iwghaberits* (Oil-bearing women's service) are celebrated together in the morning on Sundays. During Lent the Peace Hour, the Rest Hour and the Sunrise Hour is celebrated on Wednesdays and Fridays. Although the Midday Hour forms part of the liturgy, it can also be said separately, when no liturgy is being celebrated, and on exceptional occasions it takes the place of the liturgy.

The *Zhamagirk'* has had several editions (Amsterdam, 1662, 1667; Constantinople, 1701, 1772). For the study of the Book of Hours the important primary sources are Khosrov Andzewatsi's *Meknut'iwn Zhamakargut'ean* (Commentary on the Book of Hours,

Constantinople, 1840), and V. Hatsuni, *Patmut'iwn Hayots Aghot'amatuytsi* (A History of the Armenian Book of Hours, Venice, 1965). The English translation of large parts of the Armenian liturgical literature can be found in F. C. Conybeare's *Rituale Armenorum* (1905), on the administration of the sacraments and the breviary rites of the Armenian Church.

Rituals

The Armenian *Mashtots* (The Ritual Book) associated with the name of Catholicos Mashtots I Eghivardetsi (897–8) contains the principal sacraments (*Khorhurd*, 'mysteries', is the word used). The *Mashtots* has three formats: (1) *P'ok'r Mashtots* (Small Mashtots) which contains the sacraments and rites performed by the priest: baptism, confirmation, marriage, burial, blessings; (2) *Mayr Mashtots* (Mother Mashtots) contains the rites performed by bishops: ordination, awarding doctoral and pastoral staffs, consecration of churches, burial of priests; (3) *Hayr Mashtots* (Father Mashtots), is exclusively for catholical rites, consecration of bishops, the blessing of the holy myron (chrism), consecration of catholicos. Each of the divisions reflects the authority and jurisdiction of the three orders: priest, bishop, and catholicos.

Baptism, ordinarily of infants (though the text applies to adults), is administered by three immersions in the name of the Trinity. Confirmation (in Armenian *droshm* or *knunk'*, seal) using holy myron (chrism) on the forehead, eyes, ears, nostril, lips, hands, heart, back and feet symbolizes the receiving of the gifts of the Holy Spirit. Straight after confirmation Holy Communion is administered. Baptism is the only sacrament which is considered unrepeatable in the Armenian Church. The unction of the sick is not practised in the Armenian Church upon lay people, and is reserved only for the three major orders (priest, bishop, catholicos). The 'last anointment' is the service of last unction performed only on deceased clergy prior to burial, and is in memory of the anointing of the body of Christ with precious oils and incense.

Ordinals

The Ordinal contains the ordination rites for the three major orders: deacon, priest and bishop. Similarly to the minor orders of the Latin rite, the Armenian Church has the orders doorkeeper, lector, exorcist, acolyte and subdeacon. Preceding these five there are also two 'offices' of psalmist and sweeper. There are both married and celibate priests in the Armenian Church. Various titles of honour are conferred on clergy in major orders. The degrees of *vardapet* (doctor, teacher) are *Dsayragoyn vardapet* (eminent teacher) and *avag* (senior = arch).

In Armenian literature there are also references to the deaconess as 'female worshipper or virgin servant active in church and superior of a nunnery'. Direct literary references to deaconesses begin in the twelfth century. Mkhitar Gosh, in his *Book of Canons* (1184), says 'There are also women ordained deacon who are styled deaconess to preach to women and read the gospel to obviate a man entering the convent.' Step'anos Orbelian, Primate of Siunik', in his *History* (1299), mentions that 'There are some women who become deaconesses to preach in nunneries . . .' In the seventeenth century the Armenian St Catherine's nunnery in New Julfa (Iran), founded in 1623, and St Stephen's nunnery in Tiflis had the custom of ordaining deaconesses. The Galfayian sisterhood, founded in 1866 in Istanbul fundamentally for the purpose of caring for orphans, is significant in that all its members were deaconesses, and the abbess a proto-deaconess. The nunnery's first abbess was ordained a deaconess by Patriarch Mesrop Naroian in 1932. The abbess ordained by Patriarch Shnork' Galustian in 1982 was, in 1990, invited to Lebanon by the Catholicate of Cilicia to found a new sisterhood. In June 1991 the monastic veil was bestowed upon the first candidate, K'narik Gayp'akian, in the cathedral at Antelias, and she was appointed abbess to the Armenian sisterhood. Accordingly the Armenian sisterhood of the Companions of St Gayane has been created next to the 'Birds Nest' orphanage at Jibeyl (Lebanon).

Calendar

The Armenian *Tonatsoyts* (Typikon) in use in the Armenian Church today received its final shape during the Catholicate of Simeon Erevantsi, who first published it in 1775. The Armenian Church adopted the Gregorian calendar on 6 November 1923 with the exception of Tiflis (Georgian diocese), and in the Armenian Patriarchate of Jerusalem where, because of the 'status quo of the Holy Places', the Julian calendar is still followed.

The Armenian calendar differs from the calendar system of the other churches, in that it is based on the weekly cycle. This follows the earlier tradition in which the days of the week, especially Sunday (and later the fast days Wednesday and Friday) were the controlling element in Christian festive celebration. The Armenian calendar respects this primitive practice in that feasts of saints can never be celebrated on Sunday, Wednesday, or Friday. Though the saints have a date assigned for remembrance in the synaxarion, when that falls on a Sunday, Wednesday, or Friday, the commemoration must be transferred. On the other hand, some important feasts of our Lord and the Virgin are transferred to the Sunday nearest their fixed date. Consequently, about 150 days of the year are put aside for fasting and penance, during which time saints cannot be commemorated. Another 150 or so days remain for the commemoration of the saints. The feasts of the Lord are observed during the remaining days of the year. Hence, all the feast days in the Armenian calendar are moveable except for these six: (1) Theophany and Nativity, 6 January; (2) Presentation of the Lord to the Temple, 14 February; (3) Annunciation, 7 April; (4) Feast of the Birth of St Mary the Virgin, 8 September; (5) Presentation of the Holy Mother-of-God, 21 November; (6) Conception of the Virgin Mary by Anne, 9 December.

The liturgical year of the Armenian Church divides into four sections: (1) The period of Theophany (Advent); (2) The Great Period of Pascha (Easter); (3) The Period of Transfiguration (Assumption); (4) The Great Period of Extra-Pascha (Exaltation).

The Armenian Church still retains the ancient tradition of celebrating both the birth and baptism of Christ together on 6 January. F. C. Conybeare maintained that until the year 440 Armenia observed only the baptism of Christ on 6 January. The Armenian Church, he said, had no commemoration of Jesus' birth. It was Catholicos Yovhannes Mandakuni (478–90) who combined the commemoration of the birth with that of the baptism in 482.

Music

Armenian religious or sacred music is contained in the following books: Sharaknots (Hymnal), Gandzaran (Canticles), Manrusmunk' (Collections of anthems, and introits) and Tagharan (Chants).

The *sharakans* (literally, 'row of pearls') are arranged in canons proper to the several days of the church year. The word derives from the root *shar* or *shark'* denoting order or sequence, and each canon is divided into rhythmical sections intended to be chanted after or instead of certain psalms and canticles, and so correspond to the Latin antiphons. Each section is distinguished in the margin by the first letter of the psalm or canticle in connection with which it is sung: (1) Orhnut'iwn (aw) or Benediction (Exod. 15); (2) Harts (hts) or Of fathers (Dan. 3); (3) Medsatsustse (m) or Shall magnify (Luke 1); (4) Oghormea (o) or Have mercy (Psalm 60) ; (5) Ter yerknits (t) or Dominum in caelis (Psalm 148); (6) Mankunk' (mk) or Pueri (Psalm 112); (7) Chashu (chsh) or Praise (extracts from psalms); (8) Hambardzi (hb) or Levavi (Psalm 120). Each of these *sharakans* or sections of a complete canon is sung in one of the eight modes, of which four are known as tones (*dzayn*, dz) and four as *koghm* (k), i.e. *plagion*.

P'awstos Buzand, in his *History*, states that St Sahak in the fifth century was 'perfectly versed in singer's letters', by which we understand the early musical notation called *khaz* (neumes). By the middle of the sixteenth century, the *khaz* system of notation ceased to develop and gradually fell out of use. At the beginning of the nineteenth century, a new system of notation was created on the basis of the old by H. Limondjian (1768–1839). In 1873 Catholicos Geworg IV (1866–82) invited the musician Nikoghayos Tashchian from Constantinople to Ejmiadsin, to notate the sacred musical books of the Church; this he did and they were published as: Hymnal (1875), Liturgy (1874) and Breviary (1878). The Hymnal has been converted to western musical notes and published in Ejmiadsin in 1997.

Traditional Armenian music is distinctive not only in terms of its sound, but also in its structure, which differs in major ways from western forms. It is monophonic, consisting of a single melodic line without support for harmony. It is built on melody-modes, as opposed to the major and minor scales used in the West.

The Armenian liturgy has been set to music employing western compositional methods by the Italian Pietro Bianchini (1877), Makar Ekmalian (1896), Amy Apcar (1897), Komitas vardapet (1933) and Khoren Mekanidjian (1985). Of these only the Ekmalian and Komitas choral settings have achieved popularity and are used in Armenian worship. The organ was introduced into church services in the twentieth century.

Homeland and Diaspora Politics

The Armenian Church was and is distinguished by its use of the Armenian language. It came into existence in a particular country, to serve a particular people. The Armenian word *Hayastaneayts*, which means '[church of] the people living in Armenia', is similar in the way it is used to the name the 'Church of England'.

The name of the centre of the Armenian Church was never derived from a locality. It was always called Catholicate of All Armenians. On the strength of this title it had the authority to establish the see wherever the political centre of the nation happened to be. Whenever the political centre of the nation shifted the catholicate moved accordingly: it was founded in Vagharshapat (re-named Ejmiadsin, which means 'Descent of the Only Begotten Son'), transferred to Dvin (481), Aghtamar (927), Argina (947), Ani (992), Hromklay (1120) and Sis (1292). The long peregrinations ended in 1441, when the see returned to Ejmiadsin, where it has remained until the present.

Events of the nineteenth century brought significant changes to the Armenian Church, under tsarist Russian and then Ottoman rule. In 1828 eastern Armenia was incorporated into the tsarist empire. Not long after, in 1836 a decree was issued by Nicholas I called *polozhenie*, that is to say, a 'Supreme Regulation for governing the Affairs of the Armenian Church in Russia', while in western Armenia under Ottoman rule the Church operated under a code of rules called the Azgayin Sahmanadrut'iwn (National Constitution), established in 1863. The Ottoman administrative system of the *millet* paved the way for the formation and recognition of distinct religious communities, not subject to the jurisdiction of the Armenian Patriarchate of Constantinople, which was established in 1461. Accordingly, in 1843 the Armenian Catholic Uniate Church was created, with its own hierarchy and its own catholicos-patriarch established as its head in Lebanon. Soon after, another independent religious community was created to comprise all the Protestants in Turkey. In 1847, by imperial edict, the First Evangelical Armenian Church was founded in Constantinople.

The most tragic period in the history of the Armenian Church, and the cause of the contemporary dispersion of the Armenian people, was that of the great massacres in Ottoman Turkey between 1894 and 1923, perpetrated by Sultan Abdul-Hamid II and the Young Turks. Around one and a half million Armenians were massacred, among them around 4,000 clergy, a great number of them graduates of the Monastery of Armash (Nicomedia) who had become the primates or diocesan bishops in the provinces of Turkish Armenia. A whole generation of devoted and highly motivated clergy perished, thus giving the example of Christian martyrdom as the supreme expression of their faithfulness to Christ, matching the martyrdom of those who perished during the great persecutions of the early Church. The number of churches and monasteries in western Armenia in 1912 numbered 2,200, of which the majority were burned, looted or destroyed.

Two major factors played a major role in the shaping of the present situation: first, the dispersion of the Armenians of Turkish Armenia across the world; second, the founding of the Soviet Socialist Republic, which held sway 1920–91.

Under the Bolsheviks, all the properties of the Church were nationalized. The theological seminary, the printing press, the library and the Museum of Holy Ejmiadsin were seized in 1921. Although freedom of worship was guaranteed, all activities of the Church were forbidden or curtailed. The parochial schools were secularized and the Church was forbidden to interfere in education. The state created and supported a church movement which by its nature and specific aims was opposed to the official, established Church, her tradition and her authority. This new movement, lasting from 1923 to 1928, was called Azat Ekeghetsi ('Free Church'), and was organized and directed by a small group of clergymen who had left the Church. Their periodical *Azat Ekeghetsi*, supported by the Union of Atheists, had little impact. The low point came in 1938, when Catholicos Khoren I Muradbekian (1932–8) was murdered by the NKVD, and over 200 clergy were either executed or exiled. Even in those hard times of Church–state relationship, Catholicos Khoren had maintained his courage and found time to undertake positive activities such as the pan-Armenian celebration in 1935 of the 1,500th anniversary of the translation of the Bible into Armenian. The encyclical he issued on this special occasion had a widespread echo in the diaspora, where all Armenian communities held special ceremonies, conferences, and publications. This was a manifestation and renewal of the faithfulness of the Armenian people to the Word of God and so to its saving power. A second encyclical, issued on 1 August 1937, officially sanctioned the idea and the need for reform in the Armenian Church. Catholicos Khoren's murder in 1938 was a setback for the movement.

Archbishop Geworg VI Tchorek'tchian (1945–54) had been elected locum tenens and then catholicos in 1941. In 1943 he exhumed Khoren's body from the graveyard of St Hrip'sime Church, and laid it to rest in the grave of the *catholicoi* in St Gayane Church; from there it was re-buried in Holy Ejmiadsin, in 1995. His collection of funds in the diaspora in 1944 was successful enough to help form the 'David of Sasun' and 'General Baghramyan' tank divisions for the Soviet army fighting the Nazi invasion. In 1944, as catholicos, he received permission to reopen the printing press in Holy Ejmiadsin, to resume the publication of the official journal *Ejmiadsin'*, to reopen the Gevorgian Theological Seminary, and to free the 283 clergymen who had been sent into internal exile. Between 1946 and 1948 he encouraged the repatriation of more than 80,000 Armenians, mainly from the Middle East. On 19 April 1945, Geworg VI was summoned to see Stalin. He died on 9 May 1954 at the age of 85.

The National Ecclesiastical Assembly, the Supreme Spiritual Council, convened in Ejmiadsin on 17 August 1955, and elected the primate of the Armenians in Romania Vazgen I Palchyan as its head, the 130th Catholicos of All Armenians. Catholicos Vazgen's reign (1955–94) marked a considerable advance in the revival of church life in Soviet Armenia. His activities included frequent pastoral visits to Armenian communities abroad. These visits were an excellent opportunity for the catholicos to become closely and personally acquainted with the situation of the Armenian people scattered all over the world. He used these journeys to forge better relations between the homeland and the diaspora. He also secured funds for cultural activities that included the restoration of churches and monasteries that were returned to the Holy See. These visits marked also high moments of spiritual and national awakening among the dispersed children of the Armenian Church.

In 1970 the Armenian Church printed 10,000 copies of the Gospels and Acts in modern Eastern Armenian, following this in 1979 with the publication of the New Testament in Western Armenian. Large publications promoting Armenian religious art and culture were a feature of Catholicos Vazgen's reign; they were intended to increase the influence of the church within Soviet Armenia, and included *Armenian Churches* (1970); *Armenian Stone Crosses* (1973); *The Treasures of Holy Ejmiadsin* (1978); he also made possible the opening of the Mary-Alek Manoukian Museum in 1982. With the tacit support of the Soviet authorities, the first memorial to the victims of the genocide of 1915 was erected in Ejmiadsin in April 1965, marking the 50th anniversary. The consequence of this action was the opening of the way for the Armenian Soviet Government to build its Memorial to the Genocide at Dsidsernakaberd 52 years after the event. Catholicos Vazgen lived long enough to see the fall of the Soviet Union and the birth of the free Third Republic of Armenia in 1991. He died on 18 August 1994, and was succeeded by Garegin I Sargisyan (1995–9) and Garegin II Nersisyan in 1999.

Inter-Church Relations and Ecumenism

In the Kingdom of Cilician Armenia (lasting 1197–1375, and now in south-east Turkey) when the survival of the kingdom depended on good relationships with the Greeks and the Latins, the Armenian Church was drawn into uninterrupted series of negotiations between the Greek Orthodox and Roman Catholic Churches. Contacts had begun in the time of Catholicos Grigor II Vkayaser 'Martyrophile' (in office 1066–1105), and Grigor III Pahlavuni (in office 1113–66) attended the Latin Council of Antioch (1141), and later sent a delegation to meet Pope Eugene III (1145–53) in Italy. Soon after, talks with the Byzantine Church resumed under Catholicos Nerses IV Klayetsi (1166–73), and continued with Nerses Lambronatsi, Archbishop of Tarsus (1153–98), and Catholicos Grigor IV called Tghay (1173–93), which all ended without any substantial result, with the death in 1180 of the Emperor Manuel I Komnenos. The negotiations had failed because, for the Armenian ecumenists, union was ideally the fruit of the communion of faith and not of administrative submission on their part, or uniformity of practices, as indicated in the following statement: 'The cause of our running away from you is that you have been pulling down our churches, destroying our altars, smashing the signs of Christ, harassing our clergy, spreading slanders in a way that even the enemies of Christ would not do, even though we live close to them [i.e., Islam countries].'

The efforts for unity with the papacy at the time of the Armenian Cilician Kingdom came to nothing also because of the insistence of the papal claim of primacy. Mkhitar Skewratsi, the Armenian representative at the council in Acre in 1261, summed up the Armenian frustration in these words: 'Whence does the Church of Rome derive the power to pass judgment on the other Apostolic sees while she herself is not subject to their judgments? We ourselves [the Armenians] have indeed the authority to bring you [the Catholic Church] to trial, following the example of the Apostles, and you have no right to deny our competency.'

The story of the relationship of the Armenians with the Roman Catholics is long and at times ignoble. An example of extreme Catholic reprisal against the Armenians in Constantinople is the almost unbelievable story of Patriarch Avedik (1702–11), who was kidnapped during the reign of Louis XIV of France (r. 1643–1715), tortured, taken to the Bastille, brainwashed and made a Latin priest, shortly after which he died. The story is told in Dumas's novel, *The Man in the Iron Mask*.

The Armenian Church, with a presence in almost all the major cities of the world, is provided with favourable opportunities for full participation in the ecumenical movement. Representatives in the capacity of observers, consultants or guests attended ecumenical conferences such as the World Conference on Faith and Order, in Lund (1952), Lausanne (1972) and Edinburgh (1973). Armenian representatives were also present at the General Assembles of the World Council of Churches in Amsterdam (1948), Evanston (1954) and New Delhi (1961). On his return from the council in Rhodes, Archbishop Tiran Nersoyan presented the working of the WCC in a booklet *Ekeghetsineru Hamashkharayin Khorhurde* (Jerusalem, 1959). In August 1962 at the Central Committee meeting in Paris, the two catholicoi (Ejmiadsin and Antelias) became full members of the World Council of Churches.

The first major ecumenical event was the meeting of the Heads of the non-Chalcedonian Churches (Coptic, Ethiopian, and Syrian) in Addis Ababa, in a conference convened by His Majesty Haile Selassie (15–21 January 1965). For several years Armenian theologians have contributed to the debate on church unity between the Eastern Orthodox or Chalcedonian and the Oriental Orthodox or non-Chalcedonian Churches. The conclusions reached in these 'unofficial consultations' have been specific, far-reaching and constructive. The first four meeting were held at Aarhus (1964), Bristol (1967), Geneva (1970) and Addis Ababa (1971). The texts of the contributions, with a full record of the discussions, were published in *The Greek Orthodox Theological Review* X, 2 (1965) and XIII, 2 (1968). Pro Oriente has since 1971 organized five 'Unofficial Theological Consultations between theologians of the Oriental Orthodox Churches and the Roman Catholic Church' in Vienna. The first theological dialogue since Chalcedon was described as 'a positive successful and hopeful step which proved that theological discussions with friendly attitudes lead to proper and useful results'.

In May 1970 Catholicos Vazgen I had an audience with Pope Paul VI, the first meeting between a catholicos and the pope since the visit to Rome of Catholicos Step'annos V Salmastetsi (1545–67). The final seal of approval was given to the theological rapprochement in December 1996, when Catholicos Garegin I and Pope John Paul II signed a Common Declaration with the intention to remove any remnants of discord or mistrust between the Armenian and Roman Churches. While the Declaration was welcomed as an ecumenical gesture, its theological basis remains controversial. In 2001, on the 1,700th anniversary of the Armenian Church, Pope John Paul paid a visit to Ejmiadzin, returning to Holy Ejmiadsin the relics of St Gregory the Illuminator.

Contacts with the Anglican Communion have been much more regular. Catholicos Vazgen I met the Archbishop of Canterbury, Geoffrey Fisher in 1956, and Archbishop Dr Donald Coggan visited Ejmiadsin in October 1977, the first head of the Anglican

Church to make such a visit. Archbishop Dr George Carey was also among the many church leaders who attended the ceremonies in Holy Ejmiadsin marking the 1,700th anniversary of the Armenian Church.

References and further reading

Adontz, N. (1938) The Armenian Bible and its significance. In *Célébration solonelle du quinzième centenaire de la tracution armenienne de la Bible*. Paris.

—— (1970) *Armenia in the Period of Justinian: The Political Conditions Based on the Naxarar System*, trans. N. G. Garsoian. Louvain: Imprimerie Orientaliste.

Agat'angeghos (1976) *History of the Armenians*, trans. R. W. Thomson. Albany, NY: State University of New York Press.

Alpoyachian, A. (1947) Hayadavanut'yan taradsman shrjanake (The Spread of Armenian Christianity). *Ejmiadsin* 3–4: 20–30; 5–6: 20–5.

Avgerian, M. (1874) *Liakatar vark' ev vkayabanut'iwn srbots, vork' kan i hin tonatsutsi Ekeghetswoy Hayastaneayts* (The Complete Lives and Martyrologies of Saints as celebrated in the Armenian church calendar), 12 vols, 2nd edn. Venice. First published 1810–15.

Conybeare, F. C. (trans.) (1905) *Rituale Armenorum, being the Administration of the Sacraments and the Breviary Rites of the Armenian Church together with the Greek Rites of Baptism and Epiphany*. Oxford: Clarendon Press.

—— (2001) *The Armenian Church: Heritage and Identity*, compiled and with introduction by V. Nersessian. New York: St Vartan Press.

Eghishe vardapet (1982) *History of Vardan and the Armenian War*, trans. R. W. Thomson. Cambridge, Mass.: Harvard University Press.

Eusebius of Caesarea (1927–8) *The Ecclesiastical History and the Martyrs of Palestine*, trans. H. J. Lawlor and J. E. L. Oulton. London: SPCK.

Gandzaketsi, K. (1961) *Patmut'iwn Hayots* (History of Armenia), critical edn. by K. Melik'. Erevan: Ohandjanyan.

Gat'rjean, Y. (1897) *Srbazan Pataragamatoyts Hayots* (The Sacred Missals of the Armenians). Vienna.

St Grigor Narekatsi (2001) *Speaking with God from the Depths of the Heart: The Armenian Prayer Book of St Gregory of Narek*. Bilingual Classical Armenian-English, ed. and trans. T. J. Samuelian. Erevan: Vem Press.

Hakobyan, V. (1964, 1971) *Kanonagirk' Hayots* (Canons of Armenian Councils), 2 vols. Erevan.

Khosrov Andzewatsi (1991) *Commentary on the Divine Liturgy*, trans. S. Peter Cowe. New York: St Vartan Press.

Koriwn (1964) *The Life of Mashtots*, trans. B. Norehad. New York: Armenian General Benevolent Union.

Movses Daskhurantsi (1961) *The History of the Caucasian Albanians*, trans. C. J. F. Dowsett. London: Oxford University Press.

Movses Khorenatsi (1978) *History of the Armenians*, trans. R. W. Thomson. Cambridge, Mass.: Harvard University Press.

Nerses de Lambron (2000) *Explication de la Divine Liturgie*, trans. I. Kechichian. Beirut: Librairie Orientale.

St Nerses Shnorhali (1996) *General Epistle*, trans. and ed. Fr. Arakel Aljalian. New York: St Nerses Armenian Seminary.

Nersessian, V. (1987) *The Tondrakian Movement: Religious Movements in the Armenian Church from the Fourth to the Tenth Centuries.* London: Kahn and Averill.

—— (1997) *A Bibliography of Articles on Armenian Studies in Western Journals, 1869–1995.* London: Curzon Press.

—— (2001a) *The Bible in the Armenian Tradition.* London: British Library.

—— (2001b) *Treasures from the Ark: 1700 Years of Armenian Christian Art.* London: British Library.

Nersoyan, T., Archbishop (1996) *Armenian Church Historical Studies: Matters of Doctrine and Administration,* ed. with an introduction by V. Nersessian. New York: St Vartan Press.

Ormanian, M. (2000) *The Church of Armenia,* trans. G. Marcar Gregory. Montreal: Armenian Holy Apostolic Church, Canadian Diocese. First English edn 1912.

P'awstos Buzand (1989) *The Epic Histories,* trans. N. G. Garsoian. Cambridge, Mass.: Harvard University Press.

Sozomen (1855) *The Ecclesiastical History.* London: Bohn's Ecclesiastical Library.

Thomson, R. W. (1995) *A Bibliography of Classical Armenian Literature to 1500 AD.* Turnhout: Brepols.

—— (trans.) (2001) *The Teaching of Saint Gregory,* rev. edn. New York: St Nerses Armenian Seminary.

CHAPTER 3
Bulgarian Christianity

Ivan Zhelev Dimitrov

Early Christianity in the Balkans

Many historical sources testify that Bulgarian Christianity has its roots in the early Christian communities and churches in the Balkan peninsula, through their influence on the local population and their evangelizing missions among the various groups of settlers. Thus the lands which in 681 became part of the Bulgarian state saw a continuous advance of Christianity between 33 CE and the sixth century. From the fourth to the sixth century the Constantinople Patriarchate stepped up its missionary activities with considerable success. The structures of the Church were steadily evolving; the number of episcopacies, of clergy, of church buildings and monasteries grew all the time. Christianity penetrated even into the highland regions. The incursions of the Slav tribes and the Bulgars in the Balkan peninsula during the sixth and the seventh centuries and the wars between the young Bulgarian state (681) and Byzantium seriously damaged the local settlements. Many fortresses, towns, churches and monasteries were destroyed. This caused a decline in the local Christian population, upset the diocesan organization and hampered the mission of evangelization. Some historical sources, however, indicate that the Slavs and the Bulgars maintained regular contacts with Byzantium and with the indigenous population of the Balkans, and that there were many instances of peaceful settlement and even of military alliances between traditional enemies. This was also true of trade and other relations, such as the exchange of prisoners of war; of the imposition of Byzantine sovereignty over some of the settlers of the present-day Bulgarian lands; and of a process of colonization and demographic change. The influence of Byzantium pervaded the young state of the Bulgars, particularly during the period of dynastic strife amid the military and tribal aristocracy (761–77). There is evidence that between the sixth and the eighth centuries there were numerous channels through which Christianity could reach the new settlers of the Balkans. Judging by diocesan records, proceedings of church councils and archaeological finds, many towns and episcopal sees survived the arrival and settlement of the Slavs and the Bulgars south of the Danube. The conquest of the Balkans and the rise of the Bulgarian Empire was not a disaster for the indigenous population and its material and spiritual culture. The settlers and the local Romanized or semi-Romanized Thraco-Illyrian Christians influenced each other's way of life and socio-economic organization, as well as each other's culture, language and religious outlook.

During the first half of the ninth century Bulgaria annexed new lands with a considerable Christian population. Tens of thousands of Byzantine prisoners of war were captured, including several eminent clerics who introduced many Bulgarians to the Christian faith. Although Christians were persecuted by the authorities, their religion infiltrated even the ruler's court. In the course of Khan Kroum's wars against Byzantium (811–14) many eminent Byzantines were captured, among whom there was a certain Kinnamon who became a tutor at the palace; here he had an opportunity to champion his Christian faith. The spread of Christianity, and the fact that it had gained a foothold even at the palace, seemed to be a sign of a growing Byzantine influence that threatened the interests of the Bulgarian state. For this reason Khan Omurtag (r. 815–32) showed himself to be a determined opponent of the foreign faith and sanctioned the persecution of the Christians. Byzantine sources speak of the martyrdom of the Bishops Manuel of Adrianople and Leo of Nicaea, the soldiers John and Leontius, presbyter Parodus and another 337 Christians whose names are unknown. The palace tutor Kinnamon was imprisoned, and spared only thanks to the intercession of the Khan's son Enravota.

Omurtag's son Malamir (r. 832–6) was more tolerant towards the Christians, but showed no mercy to his brother Enravota, who had adopted the new faith under the influence of his tutor. The Bulgarian Church venerates him under the name of Voin as the first Bulgarian Christian martyr.

Thanks to his successful strategy Khan Presian (r. 836–52) managed to annex a considerable part of Macedonia which at that time had a dense Slav population. Thus the share of the Christian population grew even further and the khan was tolerant of the Christians probably because he was trying to attract the Byzantine Slavs to the Bulgarian state.

The Conversion to Christianity

The territorial expansion of the Bulgarian Empire during the first half of the ninth century brought it in closer contact with the Christian world not only to the south but also to the north-west. The sagacious statesman Khan Boris (r. 852–89) took stock of the situation and decided to make Christianity the official religion of the realm. He was aware that the spiritual and ethnic cohesion of his people could be cemented only if its two ethnic components (Bulgars and Slavs) professed a common faith. Initially Boris intended to receive Christianity at the hands of the western (Roman) clergy. In 862 Khan Boris and King Louis the German formed an alliance which involved the adoption of Christianity. To counter this alliance and prevent any further communion with the West, Byzantium put together an anti-Bulgarian coalition, which included Great Moravia, Croatia and Serbia. In 863 the Bulgarian troops were defeated and Khan Boris signed a peace treaty with Byzantium which included the explicit provision that Bulgarian envoys should be baptised at Constantinople and thereafter the ruler and the entire people should convert to the Christian faith. The newly baptised envoys returned to the Bulgarian capital Pliska accompanied by Byzantine missionaries. The speed of events did not give Boris enough time to prepare his associates and the Bulgarian people for this momentous decision. For this reason he and his family were not baptised in a solemn public ceremony, but in secret and in the dead of night. The godfather of the ruler was the Byzantine Emperor Michael III himself, who sponsored him in baptism by proxy. Thus Khan Boris adopted the Christian faith under the name of Michael and assumed the title of *knyaz* (prince). These events took place in the autumn of 864.

The mass conversion of the Bulgarians began in the spring of 865. In some cases it was greeted with enthusiasm, in others it was marked by violence. The reaction of the boyars, which was foreseen by Michael-Boris, was not late in coming. They believed that the policy of the ruler spelt danger for the state, publicly accused him of having given his people 'a bad law' and rose against him. Helped by his loyal associates Boris managed to stem the insurrection and executed 52 of the ringleaders together with their families.

The old pagan organization was dismantled with the imposition of Christianity. The pagan temples were destroyed or transformed into Christian churches; the heathen shrines were demolished and replaced by Christian ones. Along with the Byzantine preachers Bulgaria was flooded by a large number of impostors – Greeks, Armenians and others – all of whom began to baptise with alacrity. Arab Muslims also arrived, eager to preach Islam. Boris-Michael was, therefore, faced with the urgent task of establishing and building up an autonomous national church which could keep in check the spread of other religious beliefs in his realm. Furthermore, he realized that the institution of an autonomous Bulgarian Church with the rank of patriarchate had the additional advantage of limiting the expansion of Byzantine political influence, which was being spread by Constantinople's ecclesiastical envoys.

The aspirations of Knyaz Boris did not go down well in Byzantium. The champions of the pentarchy (the concept that there should be five patriarchates; Rome, Constantinople, Alexandria, Antioch and Jerusalem) dismissed outright the possibility of Bulgaria having an autonomous church, let alone an independent patriarchate. As a result, Bulgaria renewed her political alliance with the Germans and sought the protection of the Roman Church. In the summer of 865 a Bulgarian delegation was sent to Rome to present to Pope Nicholas I a set of 115 questions concerning the organization of church and religious life, as well as the customs and traditions of the Bulgars rooted in their distant pagan past. In the autumn of the same year a special papal embassy led by two bishops, Paul of Populonia and Formosus of Porto, brought back 'The replies of Pope Nicholas I to the questions of the Bulgars' (*Reponsa papae Nikolai Primi ad consulta Bulgarorum*). These replies are an extremely important document, revealing the most burning problems of the newly Christianized Bulgarian society. However, the Pope declined to give a definitive answer to one of the most important questions – the setting up of an independent Bulgarian Church headed by a patriarch – until his legates had returned and reported on the progress of Christianization and the existing organization of the Church.

In practice the ties with the western Church meant that the Byzantine clergy would be expelled and replaced by papal missionaries. Bishop Formosus found such great favour with Boris that he petitioned the Pope to appoint him Archbishop of Bulgaria. However, the new Pope Hadrian II refused, under the pretext that the bishop was not allowed to leave his own see in Italy. Soon after that Formosus was recalled and replaced by Bishops Dominic of Treviso and Grimoald of Polimarti. Boris then asked for deacon Marinus or for a cardinal whose 'life and wisdom' made him worthy to be appointed Archbishop of Bulgaria, but got another refusal. Instead, the Holy See sent deacon Sylvester and several other clerics to Bulgaria, but Boris refused to receive them and asked once again for Formosus. The Pope responded in no uncertain terms that it was for him and for him alone to choose and appoint the future spiritual leader of the Bulgarian Church. So after three years of fruitless negotiations with Rome, Boris turned again to Constantinople. It was evident from the start that this time Byzantium would be much more accommodating and prepared to make concessions.

Meanwhile a church council, which was being held in Constantinople during 869 and 870, was debating certain contentious issues between Rome and Byzantium. At the same time a Bulgarian embassy arrived in the city led by a senior dignitary called Peter. The Bulgarian envoys were invited along with a German delegation to the concluding session on 28 February 870. Three days after the dissolution of the council, on 4 March 870, the Emperor Basil I convened at his palace an extraordinary session attended by the legates of Pope Hadrian II, the representatives of the Eastern Patriarchs and the Bulgarian envoys. Much to the surprise of the papal legates, a debate ensued on the question of ecclesiastical jurisdiction over Bulgaria, from which it transpired that the lands of the Bulgarians were already considered as part of the diocese of the Patriarchate of Constantinople. Therefore, despite the objections of the papal legates a decision was taken that Bulgaria should be granted a separate archbishopric under the jurisdiction of Constantinople. Thus the foundations were laid of the Bulgarian Church, which was closely related to the Orthodox East. Chronologically it was the eighth in seniority in the ninth-century community of Eastern Orthodox churches.

The Archbishopric and the Patriarchate of Preslav

Initially the Bulgarian Church was an autonomous archbishopric under the jurisdiction of the Patriarch of Constantinople. Its primate, with the rank of archbishop, was elected by the Bulgarian episcopate and approved by the patriarch. According to an ancient story entitled 'The miracle of the Bulgar', after the founding of the Bulgarian archbishopric, Archbishop Joseph, accompanied by other clerics, teachers and mentors arrived in Bulgaria. The anonymous author praises Knyaz Boris, who 'built churches and monasteries, installed bishops, priests and abbots, to teach and guide the people . . .' The scant historical evidence does not allow us to determine the exact territory under the pastoral care of the Bulgarian Church during the ninth and tenth centuries.

The existence of diocesan centres at Pliska, Preslav, Morava, Ohrid, Bregalnitsa, Provat, Debelt and Belgrade at this time has been established beyond doubt. Dioceses which had been set up earlier, such as the ones at Sredets, Philippopolis, Drustur, Bdin,

Skopje, and Nis and elsewhere continued to exist. Keen to have young people trained as teachers and men of letters, Boris sent many young Bulgarians, including his son Symeon, to study in Constantinople. In 886 he welcomed to his capital Pliska the disciples of the brothers Cyril and Methodius: Clement, Nahum and Angelarius, who had been expelled from Great Moravia. With their help he embarked on a wide-ranging programme of education and scholarship, resulting in the creation of the Preslav and the Ohrid schools. The prince assigned many prominent Bulgarians to the monasteries, so that they could devote themselves to full-time scholarship. Among them were his brother Doks and his son Tudor Doksov. In 889 Boris I abdicated in favour of his son Vladimir and retired to a monastery, where he could devote his time to study and literary work. In 893, however, he could no longer put up with his son's attempts to revive paganism, deposed him by force and had him blinded. After that he took an active part in the first Council of the Church and the People, convened in Preslav (893), which introduced the Slavonic liturgy, replaced the Byzantine clergy with Bulgarians – a process facilitated by the presence of the talented disciples of Cyril and Methodius, discussed the role of the Archbishop of Bulgaria in ceremonies taking place in Constantinople and dealt with some other issues.

Whereas the military and political conflicts between Bulgaria and Byzantium during the reign of Knyaz Symeon (893–927) did not damage their spiritual relations irreparably, they contributed to the strengthening of the independence of the Bulgarian Church. Thanks to the political successes and the flourishing of cultural life, and given the close relationship between Church and state, the international prestige of the Bulgarian Church was growing apace.

After his success in the battle near the river of Acheloe on 20 August 917, Symeon proclaimed himself 'Emperor of the Bulgars and the Romans'. According to the theory prevailing at the time, the status of the Church had to be equal to that of the state. In Byzantium a close relationship existed between spiritual and temporal authorities. According to the rule sanctioned by many mediaeval documents, in 919 a Council of the Church and the People officially proclaimed the autocephaly of the Bulgarian Church and the Bulgarian archbishop received the title of Patriarch. In October 927 a peace treaty was signed between Bulgaria and Byzantium. Under its provisions King Peter I, related by marriage to the Byzantine emperor, received the right to call himself Basileus. The list of bishops compiled by the seventeenth-century French scholar Du Cange contains the following information: 'Damian in Drustur, now known as Dristra. In his time Bulgaria was recognized as autocephalous. On the orders of Romanus Lecapenus he was proclaimed Patriarch by the emperor's *synclitus* (council), and was later acknowledged by John Tzimisces.' We do not know whether the autocephaly and the patriarchal status of the Church were recognized by an official canonical act, but that was most probably the case. Such an assumption is supported by the passage of Du Cange's catalogue quoted above, where the compiler emphasizes the political dimension of the act, which in his opinion was the more important one and subsequently led to ecclesiastical recognition.

The Bulgarian autocephalous Church with the status of patriarchate was sixth in honorific rank among the ancient and most venerable patriarchates in the Orthodox East. At that time the main dioceses in northern Bulgaria were Pliska, later succeeded by Preslav, Dorostol (Drustur), which was the successor of the Marcianopolis diocese in the province of Lower Moesia, Bdin (Vidin) and Moravsk (Morava), which succeeded the bishopric of Margus. The main dioceses in southern Bulgaria were Philippopolis, Sardica (Sredets), Bregalnitsa, Ohrid and Prespa. We know the names, but not the order of accession, of nine Bulgarian patriarchs between 927 and 1018: Damian, Leontius, Demetrius, Sergius, Gregory, Germanus, Nicholas, Philip and David. They resided in the capital city of Preslav and later in Dorostor (modern Silistra).

The military events and political circumstances during the second half of the tenth century played a crucial role in the fate of the First Bulgarian Patriarchate. When the Kievan Knyaz Svyatoslav overran north-eastern Bulgaria (968–9) the patriarchal see moved to Dorostol, and after the invasion of the Byzantine Emperor John I Tzimisces (971), to Sredets (modern Sofia), which became the capital of the Western Bulgarian Empire under Tsar Samuel (997–1014). Owing to pressures of strategic necessity the capital was being moved ever deeper into the south-western Bulgarian lands and so was the patriarchal court, which at the end of the tenth century eventually established itself in Ohrid, the seat of the Bulgarian Patriarchs Philip and David. After conquering Bulgaria in 1018 the Byzantine Emperor Basil II, the 'Bulgar-slayer', preserved the independence of the Bulgarian Church under the name of the Ohrid Archbishopric, whose primate received the title of Archbishop of All Bulgaria. The dioceses under his jurisdiction, listed in special royal charters issued by Basil II in 1019, 1020 and 1025, encompass the former *theme* (a region of the Byzantine Empire) of Macedonia (excluding Thessaloniki and its south-eastern part), the districts of Morava, Timok, Nishava, Epirus (excluding its southern parts), the whole of Serbia and northern Thessaly. Later on, under the successors of Basil II, a number of changes were made to the area of jurisdiction of this diocese, which was reduced in favour of the Constantinople Patriarchate. At the same time the Ohrid Archbishopric was subjected to systematic Hellenization; this was achieved by appointing mainly Greek-speaking senior clerics and introducing the Greek language in the liturgy and in church administration.

The Turnovo Archbishopric and Patriarchate

In 1186, when the Bulgarian state regained its independence, the brothers Assen and Peter rejected the spiritual ascendancy of the Ohrid Archbishopric and the Constantinople Patriarchate and set up a new ecclesiastical centre in the capital of Turnovo, by establishing the autocephalous Archbishopric of Turnovo with Archbishop Basil as its primate. As a result of negotiations between Tsar Kaloyan (r. 1197–1207) and the Roman curia in the autumn of 1204, the right of the Bulgarian ruler to be called 'king' and to mint coins was recognized and Basil was elevated to 'Archbishop of Turnovo and *primas* of all Bulgaria and Wallachia'. According to the pope the title of *primas* was equivalent to 'patriarch'. At the beginning of November 1204, at a solemn ceremony, Kaloyan was crowned king and Basil was consecrated as primas. While recognizing the primacy of the pope, the Bulgarian Church preserved its independence. The union with Rome was a great diplomatic success for Tsar Kaloyan, as it helped Bulgaria achieve international recognition.

The official and canonical recognition of the patriarchal status of the Bulgarian Orthodox Church was finally achieved during the reign of Ivan Assen II (1218–41) at a major church council in the town of Lampsakos in the Dardanelles in Asia Minor, with the consent of the Patriarch of Constantinople (then in exile at Nicaea) Germanos II (1223–40) and the other four eastern patriarchs.

The Bulgarian cleric Joachim I was enthroned as the first Patriarch of Turnovo. The territory under the ecclesiastical authority of the patriarch changed with the changes to the borders of the Second Bulgarian Empire (1186–1396). It was largest during the reign of Ivan Assen II when it comprised 14 eparchies plus the See of Turnovo and the Archbishopric of Ohrid, namely 10 metropolitan sees (Preslav, Cherven, Lovech, Sredets, Ovech, Drustur, Vidin, Syar (Serres), Philippi and Mesembria) and four episcopacies (Branicevo, Belgrade, Nis and Velbuzhd). In the fourteenth century the scope of Turnovo's jurisdiction was sharply reduced; the western eparchies were placed under the Serbian Archbishopric (elevated to the rank of patriarchate in 1346), whereas the metropolitan Sees of Varna, Vidin and those of the southern regions were subordinated to the Patriarchate of Constantinople.

The Patriarchate of Turnovo was organized along the same lines as the First Bulgarian Patriarchate of Preslav. Its primate was the patriarch, who was also a member of the *synclitus* (council of the boyars). He occasionally assumed the role of regent and had his own administrative office. The Synod, composed of the church hierarchs (metropolitans and other members of the episcopacy) and sometimes including representatives of the secular authorities, played an important role in the governance of the patriarchate. It conducted trials of heretics, ruled on property disputes and on various matters of a spiritual and temporal nature concerning the Church. When a new patriarch was elected the Synod nominated three candidates, one of whom was approved by the monarch, this being an example of the interference of the temporal authorities in the life of the Church. The patriarchate was duty-bound to support the policies of the state and straying away from its line was severely punished. Thus during the reign of Tsar Theodor Svetoslav in 1300 Patriarch Joachim III was found guilty of high treason and was pushed to his death from a cliff on the Tsarevets Hill known as the Rock of Death. The secular authorities supported the Church in its fight against various heresies and on several occasions (in 1211, 1350 and 1360) convened special councils for this purpose. During the fourteenth century the Bulgarian Orthodox Church was under the religious and spiritual influence of the Byzantine Hesychast movement. Theodosius of Turnovo and Patriarch Euthymius were among its leading supporters.

Under the Jurisdiction of the Patriarchate of Constantinople

After the capital Turnovo fell to the Ottoman Turks on 17 July 1393 Patriarch Euthymius was driven out of Tsarevets, where the patriarchal palace was located. Later he was interned in the Bachkovo monastery, where he died in April 1404. One year after the fall of Turnovo, the Patriarchate of Constantinople, taking advantage of the difficult situation, intervened directly in the administration of the Bulgarian Patriarchate. The Patriarch of Constantinople Antony IV (1389–90, 1391–7) and his Synod issued a document, a synodal decision in which they declared their interest in the vacated patriarchal throne. In actual fact, the decision authorized the Metropolitan of Mavrowallachia (Moldavia), Jeremiah, 'to move with the help of God to the holy Church of Turnovo and to be allowed to perform everything befitting a prelate freely and without restraint.' In 1395 Jeremiah was already in Turnovo. Judging by a letter of Patriarch Matthew I (1397–1410) to the Great Voivode of Moldavia Alexander the Good (r. 1400–32) in August 1401 Jeremiah was still in charge of the Turnovo diocese. We do not know who his successor was, but during the second decade of the fifteenth century (around 1416) the Patriarchate of Turnovo was completely subordinated to Constantinople. Thus the diocese of the Bulgarian Orthodox Church was brought under the jurisdiction of the Patriarchate of Constantinople, the Archbishopric of Ohrid and the Serbian Patriarchate of Ipek. The Patriarchate of Ipek and the Archbishopric of Ohrid also lost their relative independence in 1766 and 1767. In this way all Bulgarian lands were brought under the pastoral care of the Patriarchate of Constantinople.

Under the Ottomans the Bulgarian people were represented before the Sultan by the Patriarch of Constantinople and were regarded as part of the Rum *millet* (Greek people, i.e., the Christian population of the Ottoman Empire). During the first centuries of Ottoman rule this did not matter very much to the oppressed Bulgarians. Although most of the senior clerics were Greek, the Orthodox Church was a bulwark of Christianity against Islam and the only traditionally popular organization that could offer a measure of spiritual independence. The churches and monasteries were beacons of learning which, during the centuries of foreign domination, preserved and developed the Bulgarian language, literature and culture.

Struggles and Victories of the Church and the Nation

With the growth of national aspirations during the National Revival in the eighteenth and the nineteenth centuries the need to cast off the spiritual suzerainty of Constantinople emerged as one of the principal goals of the Bulgarian national revolution. The Bulgarian clergy were helping to preserve the national consciousness, the way of life and the morale of the Bulgarian people, lending them moral support and encouraging them to fight the oppressors. The drive for church independence began in the 1820s and continued among the Bulgarians in Macedonia and the Adrianople region of Thrace even after the liberation in 1878. The process evolved in various stages, under different and very specific circumstances.

The earliest stage – from 1824 to the Crimean War (1853–6) – was a popular movement to drive away the Greek bishops, replace them by Bulgarian ones and abolish the Greek language from the liturgy. In 1824 the people of Vratsa led by *kaza-vekil* Dimitraki Hadjitoshev tried to oust Bishop Methodius and replace him with a Bulgarian prelate. However, the attempt failed and the *kaza-vekil* was sentenced to death. (A *kaza-vekil* was a person elected by the Christian community under the Ottomans to represent them before the authorities.)

Towards the end of the 1830s the largest Bulgarian eparchy, the diocese of Turnovo, joined the campaign against the Greek bishops. The Metropolitan of Turnovo had the nominal title Exarch of Bulgaria – a memory of the past glory of the Patriarchate of Turnovo – and his diocese approximately coincided with the territory of the Turnovo kingdom before it fell to the Turks at the end of the fourteenth century. It was after the events provoked by the deposition of the Greek metropolitan of Turnovo that the church question became a national issue, which involved all classes of Bulgarian society and was inspired by the ideals of the National Revival.

By the beginning of the Crimean War the movement for the independence of the national Church had spread to all larger towns and the regions around them in central and north-western Bulgaria, in northern Thrace and in parts of Macedonia. The most public-spirited Bulgarian emigrants in Romania, Serbia, Russia and elsewhere were also involved in the national movement. The Bulgarian community in Constantinople did not lag behind either. The reform decree issued by the sultan after the Crimean War known as Hatt-i-Humayun (1856) provided the Bulgarians with legal grounds for activism, which gave a further impetus to the drive for independence of the national Church. The Bulgarian Church community in Constantinople was made up of emigrants and temporary residents from all corners of the Bulgarian lands and emerged as the hub of the drive for church sovereignty.

Between 1856 and 1860 almost all Bulgarian provinces joined the movement against the Greek bishops, but the Bulgarian expatriate community in Constantinople was at the centre of a series of events which slowly but ineluctably prepared the ground for the independence of the Bulgarian Church. A key stage in that process was the Easter Sunday action of 3 April 1860 when, in the historic wooden church of St Stephan the Bulgarian, Bishop Hilarion of Makariopol, expressing the will of the people, challenged the supremacy of the Ecumenical (Greek) Patriarch of Constantinople and virtually proclaimed the independence of the Bulgarian Church. Hundreds of church communities followed suit and overthrew the spiritual domination of the Greek Patriarchate.

A Joint Popular Council of clergy and laity composed of church hierarchs and representatives of the dioceses of many Bulgarian towns met in Constantinople and voiced support for a sovereign Bulgarian Church. After much vacillation, on 27 February 1870 Sultan Abdul Asis signed a firman officially declaring the Bulgarian Church a separate autonomous exarchate under the loose suzerainty of the Ecumenical Patriarchate.

Building up the Bulgarian Exarchate

Thanks to the firman the Bulgarian Church regained the independence of which it had been deprived at the beginning of the fifteenth century. The decree of the Ottoman administration was received with hostility by the Patriarchate of Constantinople, which declared it uncanonical. In fact the firman issued by the Sultan on 27 February 1870 was based on a draft prepared in 1867 by the Patriarch of Constantinople, Gregory VI, and a document drawn up by a joint Bulgarian-Greek committee in 1869 which had also been seen and revised by the Patriarch. Besides, the provisions of the firman did not in any way infringe the historical prerogatives of the Ecumenical Patriarch, nor the holy canons approved by the ecumenical and local councils of the Church. Four of its articles (3, 4, 6 and 7) clearly and unambiguously stated that the Bulgarian Exarchate should be closely associated with and, to a certain extent, even be dependent on the Patriarchate of Constantinople. The other provisions of the firman were also in harmony with the ecclesiastical canons and in line with the practice of the other churches.

Article 10 was the only one which the patriarchate may have found really difficult to countenance. It described the pastoral jurisdiction of the Bulgarian Exarchate by specifying only parts of some dioceses, that is, only the districts where the Bulgarian population was the majority. The jurisdiction of the districts with a mixed population was to be decided by plebiscite. The truth of the matter is that by Article 10 of the firman large and wealthy Bulgarian dioceses were taken away from the Patriarchate of Constantinople, depriving it of a substantial share of its revenue and creating serious obstacles to any further Greek cultural influence on the re-emergent Bulgarian nation. For that reason the patriarchate protested vehemently to the Sublime Porte and when that did not yield results, took the unwarranted decision to declare a schism.

Despite the obstructions of the patriarchate, the active supporters of the independent Bulgarian Church in Constantinople went on to establish the ecclesiastical structure of the exarchate. The First Council of the Bulgarian Church and People met in Constantinople between 23 February and 24 July 1871. It was made up of 11 clerics and 39 lay representatives. The council held 37 regular sessions. It adopted and signed the statutes for the government of the Bulgarian Exarchate at its twenty-third session on 14 May. The statutes were then translated into Turkish and submitted to the Sublime Porte for approval. Having waited in vain for two months for permission to elect an exarch, the council broke up.

Eventually an election was held on 12 February 1872. Bishop Hilarion of Lovech, the oldest Bulgarian prelate who until shortly before that had been based at the Patriarchate in Constantinople, was elected exarch. However, at the instigation of the Sublime Porte and as a result of pressure by certain political circles he was forced to resign and a second election was held. Thus, on 16 February 1872 the Metropolitan of Vidin, Anthimus I, was elected exarch.

Annoyed by the success of the Bulgarian cause, on 29 August 1872 the Greek clergy convened a grand (Greek) church council, which on 16 September declared the Bulgarian Church and people schismatic. That did not bother the Bulgarians, who were in a hurry to establish their own ecclesiastical structure, but the schism remained a blot on the name of the Bulgarian Church. After the crushing of the April Uprising which hoped to liberate Bulgaria from Ottoman rule, Exarch Anthimus showed himself to be a fervent and valiant patriot. He made sure that the European governments learned about the atrocities of the Turks in suppressing the uprising and wrote a personal letter to the Tsar of Russia asking him to intervene by military force in order to liberate Bulgaria. That provoked the wrath of the Sublime Porte, which sought to arrange his deposition with the help of some notables from the Bulgarian community in Constantinople. On 12 April 1872 Anthimus was deposed and exiled to Angora (modern Ankara). On 24 April a council of electors consisting of three metropolitans and 13 laymen met at the building of the exarchate in the Ortakoy district of Constantinople and elected as the new exarch the young Metropolitan of Lovech,

Joseph (1840–1915), who had been elevated to the episcopate in 1872, and therefore, after the establishment of the exarchate.

The External Exarchate

In 1878, after the liberation of the main Bulgarian lands from Ottoman occupation, the pastoral jurisdiction of the Bulgarian Exarchate covered three distinct political entities: the Principality of Bulgaria under the suzerainty of the Sultan, Eastern Rumelia (an autonomous region under direct Ottoman military and political rule until 1885), and Macedonia and the Adrianople region of Thrace that remained within the borders of the Ottoman Empire. Exarch Joseph believed that the episcopal seat of the exarchate had to remain in the capital city of Constantinople, since about a million and a half Bulgarians still lived in the Ottoman Empire. In order to preserve the integrity of the Bulgarian Orthodox Church and the Bulgarian Exarchate, the Constituent National Assembly, which met in Turnovo in 1879, formulated and adopted Article 39 of the Constitution of the Principality of Bulgaria. According to this, so far as the Church was concerned, the principality was 'an integral part of the Bulgarian pastoral area' and would be governed by its supreme spiritual authority regardless of its geographical location. In that way two separate exarchal jurisdictions were created: an internal and an external one – at least from the perspective of the Bulgarian population of the principality. In principle, they were the constituent parts of an organic whole but, de facto, had different forms of government developed in different ways and with different objectives, while pursuing the same overall strategic goal: the consolidation of the Bulgarian nation. The external exarchate was funded by the Treasury of the Bulgarian Principality. Money was allocated on an annual basis for the maintenance of the exarch, the exarchal administration in Constantinople, as well as the teachers and clergy employed by the exarchate.

Exarch Joseph believed that his mission was to unite all Bulgarians within and without the borders of the principality, and particularly to gain rights for the Church in Macedonia, where between 1.2 and 1.5 million Bulgarians lived. The ideal of the Bulgarian spiritual leader and his 'sublime duty' to be a tower of strength to the Bulgarian national feeling and to unite all Bulgarian sees in the fold of the Exarchate had largely come to fruition. Before the outbreak of the Balkan wars in 1912, the exarchate had seven dioceses under its jurisdiction headed by metropolitans, as well as eight in Macedonia and one for the region of Adrianople governed by 'vicars of the Exarch', namely: Kostour, Lerin (Muglen), Voden, Salonika, Polena (Koukoush), Seres, Melnik, Drama and Adrianople. This vast pastoral area included 1,600 parish churches and chapels, 73 monasteries and 1,310 clergy, whereas in the Principality of Bulgaria there were 1,987 churches, 3,101 chapels, 104 monasteries and 1,992 clergy. Besides, the exarchate managed to open and maintain in Macedonia and the Adrianople region of Thrace 1,373 Bulgarian schools, including 13 high and 87 junior high schools with a total of 2,266 teachers and 78,854 students. Of all the teachers only 19 were not born in European Turkey. It is interesting to note that the Statutes of the Exarchate adopted in 1871, which provided the basis for the operation of the Bulgarian Church, had not been approved by the Sublime Porte. A reply – either positive or otherwise – was never received. Thanks to Joseph's constant efforts, the exarchate published its own newspaper for 22 years, 'a paper political, scientific, literary and spiritual'. The first issue of *Novini* (renamed *Vesti* in 1898) came out on 27 September 1890 and the last one on 9 October 1912. Because of its criticism of the Turkish government the paper was suspended on several occasions, but was finally replaced by another one entitled *Glas*.

The exarch built the magnificent iron church of St Stephan in Constantinople, which was solemnly consecrated on 8 September 1898. On his insistence the Adrianople school for priests was moved to Constantinople in 1891, and it gradually grew into a fully-fledged six-form seminary. In 1897 it acquired its own premises and extensive grounds in the Constantinople district of Sisli and evolved into a first-class theological academy. In the autumn of 1896 the construction of a Bulgarian hospital began, also in Sisli. It was completed and consecrated on 25 April 1902. The central administration of the exarchate occupied a large four-storey building in Ortakoy until the spring of 1907, when it moved to a magnificent house with a vast garden in Sisli. Still on the initiative of Exarch Joseph in 1912 a large plot was purchased in the district of Ferikoy and used for a dedicated Bulgarian cemetery.

The Bulgarian Church after the Liberation

Initially the Principality of Bulgaria was divided into the following dioceses: Sofia, Samokov, Kyustendil, Vratsa, Vidin, Lovech, Turnovo, Dorostol and Cherven, and Varna and Preslav. After the union of the Principality of Bulgaria and Eastern Rumelia in 1885 another two dioceses were added: Plovdiv and Sliven. The diocese of Stara Zagora was created a little later (1896) and after the First Balkan War Nevrokop also joined the other Bulgarian dioceses. According to the Statutes of the Exarchate (1871) several diocese were to be merged with others after the death of their metropolitan bishops. Thus after the death of Metropolitan Hilarion in 1884 the diocese of Kyustendil ceased to exist as a separate pastoral entity and became a part of the diocese of Sofia. Then after the death of Metropolitan Dositheus the diocese of Samokov also came under the jurisdiction of Sofia. Third in line was the diocese of Lovech, which would have followed the others after the death of Exarch Joseph. The exarch, however, had made the necessary arrangements for his diocese to survive him and it exists to this day.

In 1880 and 1881 an episcopal meeting was held in Sofia in which all metropolitans of the principality took part. It debated the rules for governing the Church in liberated Bulgaria. A draft entitled 'Exarchal Statutes adapted for the Principality' was drawn up. It was based on the exarchal statutes formulated and adopted by the First Council of the Bulgarian Church and People on 14 May 1871 in Constantinople. On 4 February 1883 the Bulgarian head of state, Knyaz Alexander Battenberg, endorsed this ecclesiastical-cum-legal document and it came into force. It was amended in 1890 and 1891. Four years later new statutes were approved, which in their turn were amended in 1897 and 1900. According to the statutes the Church in the Principality was governed by a Holy Synod made up of all metropolitans, but in practice during the first four years only four of them met regularly. It was agreed that Exarch Joseph would govern the Church in the principality by means of an exarchal vicar, who was to be elected by the metropolitan bishops of the principality and approved by the exarch. Until 1894 the Holy Synod did not meet regularly, but thereafter it assumed its regular functions and dealt with all current issues of the government of the Church.

The government of the Church, however, was fraught with difficulties. In many Macedonian dioceses and in some within the principality there were cases of diarchy, that is, one diocese having two metropolitans. In Plovdiv, Sozopol, Anhialo (Pomorie), Mesembria (Nesebur) and Varna there were Greek bishops affiliated to the Patriarchate of Constantinople (under the provisions of the firman of 27 February 1870). To have them officiating in Bulgaria was in contravention of Article 39 of the Turnovo Constitution and at times this led to serious conflicts. The Greek metropolitans remained in Bulgaria as late as 1906, when in a burst of indignation at the Greek outrages against the Bulgarians in Macedonia, the Bulgarian population rose against them, took over their churches and drove them out of the principality.

Conflicts also flared up between the Holy Synod and some government departments. The Holy Synod had to wage a long war before it managed to assume responsibility for religious education in schools and to put in place provisions for financial support of the parish clergy.

During his brief reign the Bulgarian Knyaz Alexander Battenberg did not get involved in any conflicts with the Bulgarian Orthodox Church and did not show any special attitude towards it. The relationship between Church and ruler, however, changed significantly with the arrival in the principality of Knyaz Ferdinand I of Saxe-Coburg-Gotha on 10 August 1887. He was brought up in a Catholic family and listened to the advice of his zealously Catholic mother (and later on, his no less pious Catholic wife). He came to a country about which he knew nothing and where according to the Constitution 'the dominant religion is Orthodox Christianity of the Eastern rite'. Besides this, the Prime Minister Stefan Stambolov was too obsequious in his dealings with the monarch and neglectful of the interests of the Church, with whose hierarchs he was in constant conflict. At one point relations between the government and the Holy Synod even broke down because the latter refused to mention the non-Orthodox prince in the liturgy. While they were meeting in session on 30 December 1888 the members of the Synod were escorted out of Sofia by police and sent to their respective dioceses. It was only towards the end of 1889 that Stambolov's government and Ferdinand managed to iron out their differences with the ecclesiastical authorities with the active mediation of the Metropolitan of Dorostol and Cherven, Gregory. The prime minister satisfied the demand of Exarch Joseph for the convocation of an extraordinary session of the Holy Synod in Rousé. In June 1890 the members of the Synod met in Rousé and adopted a liturgical formula that mentioned Knyaz Ferdinand in the liturgy.

In the autumn of the same year the Synod met in regular session in Sofia and on 27 October the bishops paid a visit to the prince. On the same day he returned the visit, accompanied by Stefan Stambolov. The restored relations between the Church and the secular authorities survived for just one year. In 1892 an initiative of Stambolov's again pitted them against each other. In connection with the engagement of the monarch to Maria-Louisa, the government tried to amend Article 38 of the Turnovo

Constitution by including the provision that not only the first prince of Bulgaria but also his successor should not necessarily belong to the Orthodox Church. Since the amendment of Article 38 was adopted without consulting the Holy Synod, the Church put up a fight against it. Stambolov, however, persecuted the metropolitans who opposed his policies and actions. The Metropolitan of Turnovo, Clement (Droumev), was particularly badly victimized. Because of a single sermon, delivered on 14 February 1893, he was treated as if he had committed high treason. He was most brutally exiled to the Lyaskovets Monastery and a criminal trial was cooked up against him. The district court of Turnovo (with a judge and jury specially selected for their subservience to the authorities) condemned the bishop to exile for life. Subsequently the Turnovo Court of Appeal reduced the sentence to two years. Thus the 'Russophile' Clement was convicted and exiled to the Glozhené Monastery, an outrage that stands out not only in the ecclesiastical but also in the civil history of Bulgaria.

However, the prince was quick to appraise the situation, pardoned the exiled bishop and decided that the heir apparent, Knyaz Boris III, should be brought up in the Bulgarian Orthodox Church. So on 2 February 1896, in the cathedral church of St Nedelya, Exarch Joseph personally performed the sacramental anointing of the heir to the throne in the presence of the special envoy of the Russian Emperor, Knyaz Golenishchev-Kutuzov. Besides being a sign of the improved relations between the prince and the Bulgarian clergy this act also showed that the approval of Russia had been won.

The Bulgarian Orthodox Church after the Balkan Wars

The two Balkan Wars precipitated Bulgaria's first national catastrophe. After the signing of the Treaty of Bucharest in July 1913 Bulgaria lost its exarchate in European Turkey. The dioceses of the exarchate in Ohrid, Bitolya, Veles, Debur and Skopje passed to the jurisdiction of the Serbian Orthodox Church and the Salonika diocese was taken over by the Greek Church. The metropolitans of the five Macedonian dioceses were driven out by the Serbs and Archimandrite Eulogius, who was at the head of the diocese of Salonika, died by drowning at sea in July 1913. Only the metropolitan See of Maronia in western Thrace (whose titular resided in Gumurjina) remained under the jurisdiction of the Bulgarian Exarchate. The Bulgarian Church also lost its dioceses in southern Dobroudja; they passed under the jurisdiction of the Romanian Orthodox Church. In the parts of Macedonia under Serbian and Greek sovereignty, and in Romanian southern Dobroudja, the Bulgarian schools were closed and the Bulgarian teachers and priests expelled. Thereafter, the Bulgarian population was subjected to brutal assimilation.

After the Second Balkan War very few Orthodox Christians were left under Exarch Joseph's pastoral care (only in Constantinople, Adrianople and Lozengrad). For that reason, as primate of the Bulgarian Church, he decided to move the seat of the exarchate to Sofia. He left behind an Exarchal Deputation, which was governed until its closure in 1945 by Bulgarian hierarchs (the first to be appointed was the Metropolitan of Veles, Meletius). The deputation had the duty to look after the spiritual and physical welfare of the Bulgarian Christians in the Ottoman Empire and, later on, the Republic of Turkey. The Exarchal Deputation was planned as a future operational headquarters which, given favourable circumstances, was to restore the organization of the Bulgarian Church in Macedonia and the Adrianople region of Thrace.

Exarch Joseph spent a little over a year and a half in Sofia. His health was failing, but, as always, he was working tirelessly to strengthen the positions of the Church. After his death on 20 June 1915, thirty years passed before a new exarch and primate of the Bulgarian Church was elected. At the time of the exarch's death the international political situation was extremely complicated. The First World War had been raging for nearly a year, but Bulgaria was prudently keeping its neutrality. On 6 September 1915, however, a treaty with Germany was signed and the country threw in its lot with the Central Powers. At the end of September 1915 a general mobilization was ordered and on 14 October Bulgaria declared war on its western neighbours. After the country's entry into the war the Bulgarian Exarchate began to restore its external dioceses, lost a few years earlier. When at the end of November 1915 Bulgaria took back Vardar Macedonia from Serbia, the metropolitans of the Exarchate who had been expelled in 1912 returned there. Some of them remained in their dioceses until the end of their days. Thus, for example, the Metropolitan of Debur, Cosmas, died on 11 January 1916 in Kicevo and was buried in the neighbouring Monastery of the Immaculate Holy Mother of God. The Metropolitan of Strumica, Gerasimus, died on 1 December 1918 in Strumica, where he was buried.

The Bulgarian Exarchate after the First World War

The First World War ended with a crushing defeat for Bulgaria. Consequently, at the end of September 1918 the Bulgarian Exarchate lost its Macedonian dioceses again. At the Treaty of Neuilly, signed on 27 November 1919, the Bulgarian Orthodox Church lost most of its Strumica diocese (Strumica, Radovis, Valandovo), the border districts of the Sofia diocese (Tsaribrod, Bosilegrad) and western Thrace, where the diocese of Maronia, having its episcopal seat in Gumurdjina, had existed since 1913. In European Turkey the exarchate managed to preserve its Adrianople diocese, which from 1910 until the spring of 1932 was governed by Archimandrite Nikodim Atanasov (who became Bishop of Tiveriopol after his ordination on 4 April 1920). Also on Turkish territory was the temporary diocese of Lozengrad, governed between 1922 and 1925 by the Bishop of Nisava, Hilarion. He was succeeded by the former Metropolitan of Skopje, Neophyte, who also governed the neighbouring diocese of Adrianople from 1932 until his death in 1938. Afterwards it fell to the Exarchal Deputation to look after the Bulgarian Orthodox Christians in European Turkey. After the death of the former Metropolitan of Veles, Meletius, on 14 August 1924, the following hierarchs occupied the post of exarchal deputy: the former Metropolitan of Ohrid, Boris (1924–36), the Bishop of Glavinica, Clement (1936–42) and the Bishop of Velitsa, Andrew (1942–5).

After the end of the First World War a movement for church reforms grew apace in Bulgaria. It was backed by priests and lay theologians, as well as some of the hierarchs of the Church. Realizing that the new historical conditions called for reforms, on 6 November 1919 the Holy Synod decided that the Statutes of the Exarchate were to be amended. The government of Alexander Stamboliyski was informed and it approved of the initiative. To put into practice its intentions the Holy Synod appointed a commission (chaired by the Metropolitan of Varna and Preslav, Symeon) which had to prepare a well-founded draft for the amendment of the statutes. As a minister of foreign and religious affairs, however, Stamboliyski surrounded himself with a group of theologians, led by Hristo Vurgov, Peter Chernyaev and Archimandrite Stefan Abadjiev, who did not trust the bishops and their initiatives. On 15 September 1920, without consulting the Holy Synod, Stamboliyski introduced in Parliament a bill amending the Statutes of the Exarchate. The bill became law, was confirmed by royal decree and promptly promulgated. According to Article 3 of the new Act, in the space of two months the Holy Synod was obliged to prepare and convene a council of the clergy and the laity. This approach was resented by the bishops, and in December of the same year an episcopal council drew up a 'draft amendment to the law for the convocation of a Council of the Church and the People'.

Thus a fierce conflict flared up between the Holy Synod and the government, which would not budge from its position and even asked military prosecutors to start judicial proceedings against the bishops. A coup was being prepared against the hierarchs of the Church: the members of the Holy Synod were to be arrested, deposed and replaced by a provisional governing body. After much effort and compromise the conflict was eventually defused, elections for delegates were held, and the Second Council of the Church and the People was opened on 6 February 1921 at the Church of the Seven Holy Apostles of Bulgaria in the capital city of Sofia. Tsar Boris III also attended the liturgy. The regular sessions of the council began on the following day in the Parliament building. Apart from a couple of recesses, the council was in session until 16 February 1922. It is interesting to note that the Macedonian dioceses were represented by clerics and lay delegates elected from among the refugees from Macedonia.

The draft statutes tabled for discussion were genuinely democratic. According to their provisions the Council of the Church and the People was the supreme legislative authority in the Church. After their adoption the statutes comprised 568 articles divided in four sections and were essentially a detailed and systematic exposition of Bulgarian ecclesiastical law. This was a legal system based on the supreme principle of the democratic assembly, that is, it guaranteed the participation of the clergy and the laity at all levels of government, while preserving the leading role of the episcopacy. The Statutes of the Exarchate adopted by the Council of the Church and the People were approved without any amendments by an Episcopal Council held in 1922. They were then approved by Parliament on 24 January 1923. Because of the fall of Stamboliyski's government the procedure of the statutes' approval could not be brought to conclusion and they never came into force. Despite the insistence of the members of the Synod, the new statutes were never reintroduced into Parliament. A decree, having the force of a law, made some amendments to existing statutes concerning the full and the lesser Synod, the election of exarch and some other matters.

After the liberation of Bulgaria in 1878 the role of the Church gradually became less prominent and its importance decreased. The role that the Church used to play in the sphere of culture and education was taken over by the new state institutions, which were shaping the way of thinking and the world outlook of the Bulgarians. Besides, the Bulgarian clergy proved, on the whole, to be undereducated and found it difficult to adapt to the new conditions. At the end of the Russo-Turkish War there were two schools for priests, neither of which offered a complete course of study: one at the SS Peter and Paul Monastery near Lyaskovets, and the other in Samokov. In 1903 the latter was moved to Sofia and became the precursor of the Theological Seminary. The Seminary in Constantinople was closed down after the Second Balkan War (1913) and continued to function in Plovdiv, starting with the school year 1915/16. Besides the two seminaries, schools for the basic education of priests were opened at the Rila, Bachkovo and Cherepish Monasteries, in which the practical details of the church services were taught. The theological faculty of Sofia University did not open until 1923.

According to the available statistics in 1905 there were 1,992 priests in Bulgaria, of whom only two had higher theological education and a further 309 were graduates of secondary theological schools. The majority had graduated from the general secondary schools and 607 had not gone beyond the primary or even elementary level. In 1938 the number of priests had risen to 2,486 including 114 with higher theological education, 172 with secondary and 600 with primary or incomplete secondary education. The undereducated Bulgarian priests could not really minister to the spiritual needs of their parishioners or inspire and rally them round the Church.

After the outbreak of the Second World War the Bulgarian Orthodox Church had another opportunity of regaining its lost dioceses. After parts of Macedonia and Aegean Thrace were annexed by force of arms, their administration had to be organized accordingly. In the uncertain and complex conditions in the spring of 1941 the Bulgarian Exarchate was the first to prove equal to the challenge and lead the way by establishing and building up the structure of the church administration. As early as 29 April 1941 the full Synod discussed at an extraordinary session canonical measures for the restoration of the structures of the Bulgarian Church in the newly liberated dioceses.

The Holy Synod was quick to respond to the situation and promptly restored the administration of the Church in the territories that were formerly under the pastoral jurisdiction of the exarchate. It managed to do that thanks to its experience and preparedness. However, the ill-fated outcome of the war for Bulgaria and the fresh national catastrophe that followed led to the irretrievable loss of the dioceses in Macedonia and the Adrianople region of Thrace. Moreover, the lifting of the schism which followed soon thereafter confined the jurisdiction of the exarchate within the borders of the Bulgarian state.

Election of Exarch and Abolition of the Schism

After the death of Exarch Joseph in 20 June 1915, no election for a new primate of the Bulgarian Orthodox Church was held for 30 years. This was due to the indecisiveness of the Bulgarian ruling circles. Besides, there were different opinions about who should be exarch and who should be Metropolitan of Sofia, but according to the canonical rules the two positions could not be separated and many believed that only an exarch elected by the whole Church should occupy the metropolitan chair of the capital. During the three decades when the Bulgarian Church had no primate (exarch), it was governed by the Holy Synod, presided over by a vicegerent chairman, elected for a limited term of office.

Some of the bishops took advantage of the political change after 9 September 1944 to solve some of the problems of the Church. Stephan, the Metropolitan of Sofia, was the most active among them. In several broadcasts over Radio Sofia and in a message to the Russian people he declared that Nazism was an enemy of all Slavs, but will be defeated by Russia and her allies, the USA and Britain. The new Bulgarian government – the left-wing Fatherland Front coalition – was seeking popular support and was willing to help the Church. On 16 October 1944 the Holy Synod accepted the resignation of the Metropolitan of Vidin, Neophyte, and elected as its new vicegerent chairman, the Metropolitan of Sofia, Stephan. Two days later the Holy Synod decided to ask for the government's consent to the election of an exarch. The consent was immediately granted. Meanwhile the Statutes of the Exarchate were amended so as to enable a broader participation of the clergy and the laity in the election. The amendments were approved by a decree promulgated in the State Gazette. The Synod promptly issued Circular No. 52 of 4 January 1945, which set the date for the diocesan conferences on 14 January and for the election of an exarch on 21 January. Each diocese had to elect seven delegates – three clerics and four laymen – who were to meet in Sofia and elect an exarch.

The council for the election of an exarch was held in the ancient Church of St Sophia on 21 January 1945. Ninety delegates with valid credentials chose the exarch from among three metropolitan bishops: Stephen of Sofia, Neophyte of Vidin, and Michael of Dorostol and Cherven. With the largest number of votes (84) the Metropolitan of Sofia, Stephen, was elected as the third Bulgarian exarch.

Another extremely important problem was the need to have the schism abolished, since it was a burden that the Bulgarian Orthodox Church had had to live with for 73 years. That was achieved with the unstinting support of the Russian Orthodox Church, which promised to intercede with the Ecumenical Patriarchate of Constantinople. To this end, the Deputation of the Exarchate was moved from Constantinople to Sofia and the Holy Synod decided to send to Constantinople the metropolitans Boris of Nevrokop and Sophronius of Turnovo who, along with the Bishop of Veles, Andrew, were authorized to act in every way to conduct the necessary negotiations and to sign the requisite documents.

The delegates of the Bulgarian Orthodox Church met in Constantinople with the Ecumenical Patriarch and negotiated with a commission of the patriarchate (comprising the Metropolitans Maximos of Chalkidon, Germanos of Sardis and Dorotheos of Laodikeia) the conditions for the abolition of the schism. A 'Protocol on the abolition of the anomaly which has existed for years in the body of the Holy Orthodox Church' was signed on 19 February 1945, and on 22 February a special decree was issued by the Ecumenical Patriarch which contained the following statement:

We give our blessing to the autocephalous status and government of the Holy Church in Bulgaria, which shall be called the Holy Orthodox Autocephalous Bulgarian Church, and being henceforth recognised as our spiritual sister shall govern and manage her own affairs independently and in an autocephalous manner according to her rules and sovereign rights . . .

In that way, in February 1945, the jurisdiction of the Bulgarian Orthodox Church was confined to the territory of the Bulgarian state, but its complete independence (autocephaly) was recognized and it occupied its place in the family of the local autocephalous churches which comprise the worldwide Orthodox Church.

From Exarchate to Patriarchate

After the coup of 9 September 1944 the Communists began to persecute followers of the Christian religion and its institutions under various pretexts, but with the sole purpose of banishing religion from the life of society and, if possible, completely destroying it. On the face of it, the election of the exarch, the lifting of the schism and the recognition of the completely autocephalous status of the Church appear to be positive developments; however, the subsequent evolution of the international political situation created conditions in which they could be used to harm the Church. The fact that the jurisdiction of the Church was confined to the country's territory created unlimited possibilities for the new authorities to interfere in its affairs, particularly after the signing of the peace treaty in Paris on 10 February 1947. Once the international situation of Bulgaria was settled and its government recognized, the ruling Communist Party felt free to do away with the legitimate opposition, which it went on to do in the summer and autumn of 1947. The institutions of the Church were next in line. With the adoption of a new constitution on 4 December 1947 the Church was separated from the state, but it was a high-handed and forcible separation.

In fact, the separation was not a single act, but a process which had started after 9 September 1944 and was brought to its conclusion with the adoption of the Religious Denominations Act on 24 February 1949. The Act was a blow to all religious organizations in Bulgarian, but damaged the Bulgarian Orthodox Church most of all. The subordination of the Church to the secular authorities was achieved through a process that also unfolded in several stages. The main blow, aimed at the real estate of the Church, was designed to curtail its financial independence. The imposition of state control over the Church was also associated with a number of other measures, such as pressure to reduce the number of clergy, to replace or dismiss clerics of whom the authorities disapproved and to restrict the religious activity of the more zealous priests. Of the former educational institutions – two seminaries (in Sofia and in Plovdiv), one theological college and one Theological Pastoral Institute – only the Sofia Seminary had survived by 1951. Meanwhile, the theological faculty was taken out of Sofia University and transformed into a Theological Academy funded by the Holy Synod. The purpose of all these measures was to deprive the Church of well-educated clergy. A turning point in the process of subordinating the Church to the state was the removal of Exarch Stephan. His resignation was a farce, staged during a meeting of the Holy Synod on 8 September 1948. Two days later, the decision for his removal was approved by the Politburo of the Central Committee of the Bulgarian Workers' Party (Communists). On 24 November 1948 he was exiled to the village of Banya near Karlovo, banned from travelling anywhere and from performing any religious services.

The Politburo of the ruling Communist Party decided that the Bulgarian Orthodox Church needed 'new, succinct, democratic' statutes. After prolonged arguments, on 3 January 1951 the Holy Synod was forced to accept the statutes imposed by the Government and to elect Cyril, the Metropolitan of Plovdiv, as its new vicegerent chairman. It was not coincidental that the minutes of the meeting of the Synod held on that date contain the following statement: 'The Statutes of the Bulgarian Orthodox Church should now be considered as approved and should be enforced.'

The next objective of the government and the Holy Synod was the restoration of the patriarchal status of the Church. The Third Council of the Church and the People was opened with pomp and ceremony on 8 May 1953 in Sofia. Taking part were 107 electors with valid credentials (out of a total of 111). The first day was devoted to solemn speeches, verification of credentials and the appointment of committees. On the following day, 9 May, the council adopted with small amendments the Statutes of the Church. On 10 May it continued in its capacity as an electoral college. According to Article 20 of the Statutes, on 27 April 1953 the Holy Synod had elected by majority voting three metropolitans who were considered worthy of the patriarchal throne and who had been approved by the government. The short list comprised Cyril of Plovdiv, Neophyte of Vidin and Clement of Stara Zagora. On the day of the election 104 of the 107 electors favoured the Metropolitan of Plovdiv, Cyril; the Metropolitan of Vidin, Neophyte received one vote and two ballot papers were declared invalid.

Thus, on 10 May 1953 the Bulgarian Orthodox Church was officially proclaimed a patriarchate and the Metropolitan of Plovdiv, Cyril, was elected patriarch. He may be considered a successor, though indirect, of St Euthymius of Turnovo, the last Bulgarian patriarch before the fall of the Bulgarian Empire to the Ottoman Turks. On the very day of its restoration the Bulgarian Patriarchate was recognized by the Orthodox Churches of Antioch, Georgia, Russia, Romania, Czechoslovakia and Poland, whose representatives were present at the solemn enthronement of the Bulgarian Patriarch Cyril on that day. In a letter dated 6 June 1953, Patriarch Alexy II of Moscow and All Russia announced in the received canonical form that the Russian Orthodox Church recognized the restored Bulgarian Patriarchate. The Patriarchate of Antioch and the Orthodox Church of Poland also declared that they recognized the Bulgarian Patriarchate and its primate. Their official letters to this effect were dated 10 June 1953 and 19 June 1953 respectively. There followed the Patriarchate of Alexandria at the end of 1954.

In 1955 the Serbian Orthodox Church also recognized the Bulgarian Patriarchate and established canonical relations with it. Thanks to the mediation of the Patriarchate of Antioch, the Russian Orthodox Church and other sister churches, the Ecumenical Patriarchate of Constantinople at last officially recognized the restored Bulgarian Patriarchate in a congratulatory letter No. 552 of 27 July 1961, and established canonical relations with it. In the spring of 1962 a delegation of the Bulgarian Church led by Patriarch Cyril paid a historic visit to the Ecumenical Patriarchate of Constantinople, the Eastern patriarchates of Jerusalem, Antioch and Alexandria and the Greek Orthodox Church, including a visit to Mt Athos. As a result the restored Bulgarian Patriarchate was officially recognized by the primates of the Patriarchate of Jerusalem and by the Greek Church.

Patriarch Cyril

In truth the churchmen understood all too well that in the difficult conditions prevailing after 9 September 1944 it would be very hard for the Bulgarian Orthodox Church to grow and develop. For this reason they were trying to preserve the status quo and to slow down as much as possible the destruction of the organization of the Church. They hoped that Patriarch Cyril would help attain these modest objectives. Future students of the history of the Church must judge to what an extent he managed to fulfil these expectations. In fact he had to govern the Church under the close supervision of the ruling Bulgarian Communist Party. But we must now examine the state of the Church at the end of his incumbency.

The Church had 11 dioceses headed by metropolitans. It had jurisdiction over the Orthodox Christians in Bulgaria, as well as the Orthodox Bulgarians abroad. A separate twelfth diocese was created with a seat in New York for the pastoral care of the Bulgarians in the USA, Canada and Australia. There was a Deputation of the Bulgarian Church in Constantinople. There were Bulgarian churches and priests in Hungary and Romania. A Bulgarian Representation Church was established in 1948 in Moscow. In 1967 a Bulgarian Orthodox parish was founded in Austria. The large Bulgarian monastery of St George Zographou had been established for centuries on Mount Athos.

In Bulgaria the Church had 1,785 regular priests and employed some 200 old-age pensioners in its parishes. It had 3,720 churches and chapels, and 120 monasteries. Religious education was provided by the Sofia Seminary – located at the Cherepish Monastery, about 100 km outside Sofia – and the Theological Academy in Sofia. The Church had its own publishing house, which brought out several books a year that were sold at the Synodal Bookshop in Sofia and through the metropolitan centres across the country. It also published a weekly newspaper, *Tsurkoven vestnik*, and a monthly review, *Douhovna koultoura*, which carried articles on religion, philosophy, art and science. The Theological Academy regularly published an annual collection of the works of its teaching staff. Some of the parish churches, particularly in the cities, were the centres of active Orthodox Christian fraternities. In 1959 the Holy Synod appointed a commission which began the preparation for a new translation of the Bible.

The Bulgarian Patriarchate was engaged in lively exchanges with all its sister churches. During Patriarch Cyril's tenure it received delegations and dignitaries of other local Orthodox churches, as well as eminent representatives of the Anglican, Old Catholic and Reform Churches and of the World Council of Churches. For its part, the Church was sending delegations (official representatives and guests) not only to Orthodox countries and churches, but also to almost all church forums. In 1961 the

Bulgarian Orthodox Church joined the World Council of Churches. Some of its members were among the pioneers of the ecumenical movement. During Patriarch Cyril's time in office the Church tirelessly supported the cause of ecumenism and sisterly love among all churches.

Patriarch Maxim

Patriarch Cyril died on 7 March 1971 and in accordance with his dying wish was buried at the Monastery of Bachkovo. The Metropolitan of Lovech, Maxim, was elected vicegerent chairman of the Holy Synod. On 25 June 1971 the full Synod elected three candidates for the patriarchal throne: the Metropolitans Maxim of Lovech, Paisiy of Vratsa and Sofroniy of Dorostol and Cherven. On 4 July 1971 a council for the election of a patriarch composed of 101 electors was convened in Sofia and the Metropolitan of Lovech, Maxim, was elected Patriarch. He received 98 votes, Paisiy of Vratsa received one and Sofroniy of Dorostol and Cherven did not receive any votes (two of the ballot papers were blank). Thus the incumbent primate of the Church, Patriarch Maxim, was elected on 4 July 1971. Upon his election he also assumed the duties of Metropolitan of Sofia.

Patriarch Maxim, at the head of the Church for over 30 years, had – like his predecessor, Patriarch Cyril – no choice for nearly two decades but to abide by the policies of the Communist Party and the state, that is, until November 1989. He is a member of the World Peace Council and, since 1971, vice-president of the National Peace Committee, honorary member of the Foreign Affairs Committee of the World Council of Churches and member of the working group of the Prague-based Christian Peace Conference. He was awarded the Order of the People's Republic of Bulgaria, 1st class in 1974. Despite the scathing criticism against him after 1990, the schism in the Church, and the occasional pressure by the temporal authorities, he continues to direct the Holy Synod as its chairman.

In the mid-1990s there were about 4,000 Eastern Orthodox ecclesiastical buildings in Bulgaria, including 132 at the design stage and 225 under construction. This number was made up of 3,300 parish churches, 170 monasteries, 600 chapels in 2,670 towns and villages – out of a total of 5,340 towns and villages. According to recent data the Church has 1,280 priests, 120 monks and 140 nuns. The Church maintains two five-form seminaries equivalent to secondary schools in Sofia and Plovdiv with a total of 400 pupils. Higher theological education is offered by four universities: Sofia, Veliko Turnovo, Shoumen and Plovdiv's subsidiary in Kurdjali. The total number of students is 1,200, half of whom are women. The students are being prepared for the ministry, for ecclesiastical service or to become teachers of religion. Since the mid-1990s religion has been taught at primary schools as an optional subject (the choice is left to the pupils and their parents), and since 2000, experimentally – as part of a range of elective subjects, a set number of which must be chosen in the primary school curriculum. The Church and many NGOs are lobbying to have religion made a compulsory subject.

The liturgy in the Bulgarian Orthodox Church is conducted in Church Slavonic – a Russian version of Old Bulgarian – which has for a long time been totally incomprehensible to the average churchgoer. That is why a gradual transition to modern Bulgarian is being encouraged. Nowadays the biblical texts are read only in modern Bulgarian. The Orthodox liturgy of the Church uses music of two different types: Byzantine monophonic plainchant and Russian polyphonic vocal music. Both types of music are equally well received by churchgoers. The Russian type of music is usually used on solemn occasions.

The revenue of the Orthodox Church is not made public and, therefore, we have no precise data about it. It is derived mainly from the sale of objects (candles, icons, books, etc.) and services (fees for various liturgical offices), as well as from the rent of real estate (buildings, agricultural land and forests). The parishioners do not pay any church dues or taxes. The Church is experiencing serious financial difficulties because the process of returning Church property is still incomplete. At the same time, large sums of money are being invested in the building of new churches and monasteries and the restoration of existing ones. Because of its limited funds the social and educational work of the Church is rather modest. To some extent this is due to the misconception that the Church cannot go to the help of the needy and the suffering without having first ensured adequate funding. The state makes no contribution towards the support of the Church or any of the other religious denominations. It grants limited annual aid for the upkeep of listed churches of architectural or historic importance, but that subsidy falls far short of what is required.

In order to provide pastoral care to the growing Bulgarian diaspora, during Patriarch Maxim's incumbency the Church established a diocese for Western and Central Europe headed by a metropolitan residing in Berlin. The diocese comprises 18 parishes with 15 priests. A new development in the life of the Church is that it is being joined by many former Protestant communities in the USA, which turn to the Orthodox Church in search of a deeper spirituality. This is a challenge for the Church which, like most other Orthodox Churches, does not view the rest of the world as a potential field of missionary activity.

The Rift in the Church

The date 10 November 1989 marked the beginning of far-reaching democratic changes in Bulgaria. At long last the direct interference of the Bulgarian Communist Party in the affairs of the Church came to an end, but, as if by force of habit, subsequent governments have kept alive the practice of behind-the-scenes meddling. Under the government of the Union of Democratic Forces (UDF) and Prime Minister Filip Dimitrov a frontal attack designed to tear apart the Church was launched. The executioner of the Bulgarian Church was hieromonk Hristofor Subev, a former physicist. He was a Member of Parliament and chairman of its Religious Denominations Committee.

The Religious Denominations Office at the Ministry of Foreign Affairs headed at the time by the retired lawyer Metodi Spasov was also doing his bidding. On 25 May 1992 Spasov issued Act No. 92, in which he accused Patriarch Maxim of being a Communist agent who had caused the degradation of the Church. For that reason Metodi Spasov 'dismissed' Patriarch Maxim and his loyal Synod and by the same administrative act appointed a new Holy Synod chaired by the Metropolitan of Nevrokop, Pimen. Thus the split in the Bulgarian Orthodox Church – approved, supported and managed by the authorities – began with a brutal act of government interference in the affairs of the Church. The schismatics managed to win over several metropolitans and other members of the episcopate. Working by surprise and in the dead of night, on the eve of 1 June 1992 Hristofor Subev – who several days later was consecrated as Bishop of Makariopol – took over the building of the Holy Synod and the schismatics moved in. This marked the beginning of the open warfare between the legitimate Holy Synod headed by Patriarch Maxim and the schismatics, waged mainly over real estate. Churches, bishop's residences and other buildings were taken over by schismatics with threats and violence. These unseemly and shameful acts by hierarchs and clergy repulsed the faithful who, after 10 November 1989, had flocked freely and without fear to the churches and monasteries. The outrages continued with the consecration of new metropolitans and bishops by the schismatics. As a result, in many parishes schismatic bishops were installed. During the summer of 1994, a surprise night-time manoeuvre enabled the legitimate Synod to recover its building.

At the beginning of June 1994 the schismatics convened and held a Council of the Church and the People in Sofia, attended, among others, by the then Prime Minister Filip Dimitrov and the Chief Prosecutor Ivan Tatarchev. The council adopted new Statutes of the Church and canonized the nineteenth-century cleric and revolutionary Ignatiy (Vasil Levski) as St Hierodeacon Ignatiy. Afterwards the council proceeded with the election of a patriarch and on 4 June 1996 elected – from among three candidates, two of whom belonged to the legitimate Synod and had not agreed to be nominated – the Metropolitan of Nevrokop, Pimen, as a schismatic patriarch. Thus an even greater outrage was perpetrated.

In conformity with the Statutes of the Church the legitimate Synod convened the Fourth Council of the Church and the People, which was held from 2 to 4 July 1997. The council unanimously condemned the repressive actions of the atheist Communist regime and paid homage to its victims. Then a National Orthodox Conference of the Clergy and the Laity was convened in Sofia on 22 June 1998 on the initiative of the schismatics. It was attended by some members of the canonical Holy Synod. A decision was taken to convene an extraordinary National Council of the Church and the People on 20 October 1998. Worried by that decision the hierarchs of the legitimate Synod prepared the convocation of a Pan-Orthodox Church Council, which was expected to condemn the schism in the Church. On 30 September and 1 October 1998 a Holy, Extended and Supra-Jurisdictional Pan-Orthodox Council, convened at the invitation of the Bulgarian Patriarch Maxim and presided over by the Ecumenical Patriarch of Constantinople, Bartholomew, was held in the solemn setting of the patriarchal cathedral of St Alexander Nevsky in Sofia. The council brought together patriarchs and archbishops, primates of local Orthodox churches, as well as metropolitans, bishops and clergy from all churches. The representatives of the schismatics – but not 'Patriarch' Pimen – appeared in person before the Pan-Orthodox Council to ask forgiveness for the sin of perpetrating a schism and 'building of an altar of their own'. They declared that they recognized His Holiness Maxim as Patriarch of the Bulgarian Orthodox Church, renounced the ecclesiastical ranks they had received during the schism, and appeared before the Pan-Orthodox Council as ordinary monks. Taking into consideration their repentance and desire to serve the Church, out of mercy and guided by the principle of economy (*oikonomia*), the council readmitted them into the fold of Orthodoxy. Their episcopal status was recognized and they were put at the disposal of the Holy Synod. The former 'Patriarch' Pimen renounced his claims to lead the Bulgarian Church, whereby the council lifted the anathema and the excommunication which were imposed on him and granted him the title of Former Metropolitan of Nevrokop.

However, barely one day after the dissolution of the council, the 'repentant' schismatics proved that their contriteness had been hypocritical and that they had mocked not only their flock but also all participants in the august Pan-Orthodox gathering. Their penitence was a farce, designed to save them from the condemnation of such a lofty ecclesiastical forum. The schism continued. When, after a long illness, the schismatic Patriarch Pimen died on 10 April 1999, the temporal authorities did not allow the holding of an election for a new schismatic patriarch. Instead, the young and ambitious Inokentiy was elected vicegerent chairman of the schismatic Synod and granted the non-vacant title of Metropolitan of Sofia. Thus the schism and the diarchy in the Church persisted for over ten years and continued to disrupt the life of the Orthodox Bulgarians. It is abundantly clear that the breach is very deep indeed and is maintained by forces outside the Church.

Meanwhile, in 1998, following the example of the Georgian Orthodox Church, the Bulgarian Orthodox Church left the World Council of Churches and the Conference of European Churches. The reason for leaving the ecumenical movement was criticism on the part of some Christian circles, claiming that those who engaged in ecumenical contacts with non-Orthodox partners were guilty of abandoning some of the fundamental tenets of Orthodoxy. The governors of the Church did not manage to rebuff those allegations convincingly and chose to retreat as the easiest solution. In that way the Church retired into itself, or at any rate confined itself only to exchanges with other Orthodox Churches. In spite of this, the visit of Pope John Paul II to Bulgaria, which had been planned for many years, went ahead in May 2002. Any fears that it might have a negative effect on the Orthodox majority or lead to privileges for the Roman Catholic minority of about 50,000 proved totally unfounded.

On 20 December 2002 the Bulgarian Parliament passed a new Religious Denominations Act. It follows the Constitution in pointing out the historic role of the traditional Eastern Orthodox religion in the life of the Bulgarian people (according to statistical data from the mid-1990s, 87 per cent of the population of Bulgaria claim to be Orthodox Christians), whilst firmly proclaiming the complete equality of all religious denominations under the law.

Further reading

Clark, V. (2000) *Why Angels Fall: A Portrait of Orthodox Europe from Byzantium to Kosovo*. London: Macmillan.

Crampton, R. J. (2005) *A Concise History of Bulgaria*, 2nd edn. Cambridge: Cambridge University Press.

Dimitrov, I. Zh. (2001) Bulgarski tsurkovni obshtini zad granitsa (Bulgarian church communities abroad). *Douhovna koultoura* (Spiritual Culture) 12: 13–17.

Fine, J. V. A. (1983) *The Early Medieval Balkans: A Critical Survey from the Sixth to the Late Twelfth Century*. Ann Arbor: University of Michigan Press.

—— (1987) *The Late Medieval Balkans: A Critical Survey from the Late Twelfth Century to the Ottoman Conquest*. Ann Arbor: University of Michigan Press.

Giatzidis, E. (2002) *An Introduction to Postcommunist Bulgaria*. Manchester: Manchester University Press.

Hupchik, D. P. (1993) *The Bulgarians in the Seventeenth Century: Slavic Orthodox Society and Culture under Ottoman Rule*. Jefferson, Mo.: McFarland.

—— (2002) *The Balkans: From Constantinople to Communism*. London: Palgrave.

Meyendorff, J. (1996) *The Orthodox Church: Its Past and its Role in the World Today*. Crestwood, NY: St Vladimir's Seminary Press.

Obolensky, D. (1971) *The Byzantine Commonwealth: Eastern Europe, 500–1453*. London: Weidenfeld and Nicolson.

Papadakis, A. (1994) *The Christian East and the Rise of the Papacy: The Church 1071–1453 AD*. Crestwood, NY: St Vladimir's Seminary Press.

Pavlowitch, S. K. (1999) *A History of the Balkans 1804–1945*. London: Longman.

Runciman, S. (1930) *The History of the First Bulgarian Empire*. London: G. Bell & Sons.

—— (1968) *The Great Church in Captivity*. Cambridge: Cambridge University Press.

Spinka, M. (1968) *A History of Christianity in the Balkans*. Hamden, Conn.: Archon Books.

Stavrianos, L. S. (2000) *The Balkans since 1453*. London: Hurst.

Sullivan, R. E. (1966) Khan Boris and the conversion of Bulgaria: a case study of the impact of Christianity on a barbarian society. *Studies in Medieval and Renaissance History* 3: 55–139.

Todorova, M. (1997) *Imagining the Balkans*. Oxford: Oxford University Press.

CHAPTER 4

Byzantine Christianity

Hannah Hunt

Introduction

Byzantine Christianity is articulated primarily by the practical expression of its theological and spiritual life but may also be delineated by certain geographical and chronological boundaries. Christianity was the dominant, but not the sole, religion practised in the Byzantine Empire, the precise boundaries of which fluctuated according to imperial fortunes. The empire spread originally around the entire Mediterranean Sea, with the Balkan peninsula and Asia Minor economically dominant. In 560 the empire occupied a million square kilometres, but by the mid-fourteenth century, massive losses in both east and west reduced this to a fraction of its former status.

The city of Constantinople was established by Constantine the Great in 324 and dedicated on 11 May 330, on the site of a Greek city known as Byzantium. The citizens of the Byzantine Empire based on Constantinople, the New Rome, were known as *Romaioi*: Greeks who saw themselves as the true heirs of the Roman Empire. The use of the word 'Byzantium' to designate the state was adopted retrospectively in the sixteenth century. Between the fourth and sixth centuries, the city (and empire) expanded and thrived. As in the West, a relatively 'dark age' fell between the seventh and ninth centuries, when Constantinople became inward-looking, especially during the iconoclastic controversy spanning the eighth and ninth centuries.

The city occupied a strategic position between east and west, geographically and culturally poised between Europe and Asia. Its location had both strengths and weaknesses. Through the Golden Horn and the Bosporus, it controlled access to the Black Sea. However, lack of natural defences left the area vulnerable to occupation by land forces, although Constantinople was only taken twice, once by the crusaders in 1204 and again by the Ottoman Turks in 1453. The massive walls and forts built by Emperor Theodosius II (r. 408–50) and strengthened over the centuries acted as a deterrent to many invaders. The stability of the Christian Empire was always enmeshed with the political and military decisions of its emperors. In particular, Arab conquests on the fringes of the empire led in the middle Byzantine period to a demise of urban culture, with the exception of Constantinople itself; what had been thriving cities became fiercely defended forts, protected by local armies. The geographical juxtapositions of Byzantine Christianity gave rise to its diversity and its distinctiveness to contemporary western Christianity.

The Fourth Crusade resulted in exile for the emperor and patriarch during 1204–61: the imperial court moved temporarily to Nicaea when Byzantium came under Latin rule. This event formed the irreversible culmination of a process of schism between East and West which had started several centuries earlier. In terms of existence as a discrete entity, the empire experienced various reversals in its fortunes before it fell finally to Ottoman Turks in 1453, during the reign of Constantine XI Palaeologos (1149–53). His speech to the combined forces from Genoa and Venice, among others, as they faced defeat, articulates the enduring importance of the city, as its historical and geographical status was imperilled by:

> the impious and infidel enemy . . . which threatens to capture the city of Constantine the Great, your fatherland, the place of ready refuge for all Christians, the guardian of all Greeks . . . Oh my lords, my brothers, my sons, the everlasting honour of Christians is in your hands.

Perceptions of Byzantium from other perspectives convey a colourful if romanticized image of a vibrant and exotic institution, which was known the world over. William Dalrymple, writing as a modern traveller and journalist, extols this capital of Christianity as being for a millennium the richest metropolis in Europe and the most populous city west of the great Chinese silk road terminus of Xian. He explains the extraordinary attention paid to Byzantium by other contemporary cultures, noting that:

> To the Barbarian West Byzantium was an almost a mythical beacon of higher civilisation, the repository of all that had been salvaged from the wreck of classical antiquity. In their sagas, the Vikings called it merely Micklegarth, the Great City. It had no rival. (1998: 26)

Dalrymple captures the immense diversity of the city, which, when John Moschus, a Palestinian monk, visited it in the seventh century, had a population of nearly three quarters of a million. The cross-fertilization of different ethnicities brought specific challenges to the unity and coherence of Byzantine Christianity, and also gave rise to friction between various religious traditions and state structures.

Even within Byzantine Christianity, assorted spiritual and theological strands contribute to the tapestry. Constantinople was a significant host to, and much influenced by, monasticism in its various forms. Although of Egyptian origin, and not withstanding the importance of such monasteries as that of St Catherine at Mount Sinai, home to the famous seventh-century abbot John Climacus, monasticism shaped Constantinople to a considerable extent. Monasteries abounded in the city: there were over 300 by the time of Justinian in the sixth century. The metropolis was also well-endowed with secular comforts, boasting numerous imperial and princely palaces, along with many bath houses, a phenomenon which demonstrate the cohabitation of sacred and secular which was to provide a fertile if at times fraught mix. Just as Byzantine Christianity cannot be limited to sheer geographical boundaries, neither can its spiritual elements be entirely separated from the worldly. The influence of Greek philosophy, especially that of Aristotle and later Platonism, added a further complexity to the intellectual life of Byzantine Christians, and aspects of these thought-worlds stimulate much of the theology of the Byzantine world.

Friction existed between the predominantly Greek Byzantium and its Latin partners in Rome intermittently throughout the period, along with schisms based on theological and political differences within the eastern empire itself. In the eighth and ninth centuries, the procession of the Holy Spirit as articulated in the Creed became an issue: although weathered at the time, the *filioque* issue came to the fore when Rome alone added it to the Creed in 1014. Differences of opinion about the acceptability of married priests had likewise been a source of conflict before the key schism of 1054 (especially in the debate between the Patriarch Photius and Pope Nicholas 1 in the second half of the ninth century). This flared up when Franks attempted to impose celibacy in southern Italy and Greek clergy resisted. Different practices on fasting, and the use of unleavened bread (*azymes*) in the Eucharist had started at the end of the sixth century. Again, this became grounds for serious doctrinal division in 1054 when Cardinal Humbert anathematized Patriarch Michael 1 Keroularios for his support of the use of bread made with yeast. Both sides claimed biblical authority for their stance on this, as on the issue of the full authority of the pope (*plena potestas*).

Rooted in the city of Constantinople, Byzantine Christianity demonstrates a profound liturgical emphasis (which is nourished by its monastic tradition) and simultaneously a sense of catering for the spiritual needs of real people who inhabit a very physical world. It seeks to elevate God's people to heaven (witness the commonly cited story of the traveller who on entering the Great Church of Hagia Sophia said he thought he had gone to heaven), yet acknowledges the chthonic nature of humanity. The occasionally stormy relationship between Church and state expresses some of the tensions inherent in a dialogue between this world and the next. The 'eschatological meaning of the Christian message' was, according to Meyendorff, expressed by the adoption of monastic spirituality as the norm for Christian worship. The interplay of socio-political, spiritual, intellectual and doctrinal issues in Byzantine Christianity underlies its structure and organization.

Structure and Organization

The structure and internal organization of Byzantine Christianity is complex and at times unwieldy. It combines a degree of autocephaly with an adherence to the concept of Ecumenical Councils which, in theory at least, drew on all parties within Christendom in deciding on agreed doctrine and practice within the Church. The councils were instrumental in agreeing the Christian creeds, but sometimes through the negative process of anathematizing perceived heretics rather than by a positive consensus of opinion. Their canons often trespassed on secular concerns (see further below).

The New Testament gives the prototype for faith leaders competing for status as organizers of their church, and this practice continued to dog the Church well into our era. The division of the Christian world into dioceses, geographical areas each 'overseen' by an *episcopos*, was not limited to the Byzantine period or territory. However, the issue of supremacy of one patriarchate over another characterizes Byzantine Christianity. The secular counterpart to this structure may be seen in the imperial organization which demonstrates well how power-sharing and delegation become essential as a state expands beyond the control of one individual. The term 'autocephalous' is derived from canon law, and denotes the right of each diocese to choose its own bishop. In the modern Eastern Christian churches this seems to be synonymous with ethnic boundaries, hence Armenian Orthodox or Greek Orthodox and so on. Byzantine times saw the gradual evolution of this system. Canon 6 of the Council of Nicaea (325) established three separate dioceses of Rome, Alexandria and Antioch. The Emperor Justinian I in the sixth century confirmed five major sees, with an implicit hierarchy. His decree affirmed the division made at Chalcedon (451) into Rome, Constantinople, Alexandria, Antioch and Jerusalem. By the ninth century the theory of pentarchy theoretically ensured the equality of the five patriarchates.

The rivalry between patriarchates predates Chalcedon. In Canon 3 of the Council of Constantinople I (381) the Emperor Theodosius (in addition to refining significant aspects of Christological teaching) suggested that the patriarch of Constantinople be second only to the pope in Rome. The concept of Byzantium as the 'new Rome' was spawned, and the bishop began to be known as the 'patriarch' of Constantinople. The title 'ecumenical patriarch' was first used by John the Faster (d. 595), and he was rebuked for doing so by Pope Gregory (590–604), who thought he was claiming universal authority. Some of the friction between sees stemmed from theological divides and some from insensitive incursions into neighbours' jurisdictions. The five different locations for periods of exile of the anti-Arian Athanasius (*c*.296–373) indicate how the geography of heresy transcends that of the geographical patriarchates.

Whilst the day-to-day supervision and administration of worship and matters of faith were carried out within each autocephalous district, major doctrinal decisions were discussed at gatherings of the wider Church. Ecumenical Councils sought ostensibly to consult representatives from all different areas of the Church, to establish common doctrines and practices. In summoning bishops to his first Council in 325, the Emperor Constantine echoed an existing practice in the Roman Senate. Seven of these Councils were agreed to be ecumenical; numerous others were too selective or partial to count as articulating the will of the universal Christian Church. The Ecumenical Councils are, interestingly, known not only by their date but also by the location of the discussions, which were often politically motivated. All seven Ecumenical Councils accepted by the main Latin and Greek churches took place in the East, as that is where the imperial power resided. Although usually initiated by some theological debate, the canons of these councils often include major statements of ecclesiastical and political significance. Despite the enormous significance attached to their findings, the Council of Ephesus (431) was the first general council to have extant original records of proceedings.

The Council of Nicaea I (325) was called primarily to name and shame Arianism, a significant and enduring Christological heresy concerning the natures of the Son and the Father, which flourished in Alexandria. Arianism was one of the most divisive issues in the early Byzantine Church: Palestinian bishops supported Arius (d. 336); those in Jerusalem and Antioch opposed him. Constantinople I (381) attempted to resolve details of Christological divides, focusing on the issue of the term *homoousios* (of the same or of one substance). The Bishop of Antioch presided and there were no western representatives. Apollinarius (*c*.310–*c*.390) was condemned, and, as noted above, the status of Constantinople was elevated. The Council of Ephesus (431) focused on the debate between Cyril of Alexandria (d. 444) and Nestorius (d. 452), Bishop of Constantinople (an Antiochene), to do partly with the title 'Theotokos' for Mary the Mother of God. There is no doubt that the political and ecclesiastical rivalry between the two patriarchal sees of Constantinople and Alexandria complicated the opposing theologies of the two schools of Alexandria and Antioch.

The Council of Chalcedon (451) was preceded by the aptly named 'Robber Council' of Ephesus (449), which exhibited a shameful degree of violence and extortion. The bishops again were predominantly from the east of the empire, and the rejection by Chalcedon of the teachings of Nestorius and Eutyches (*c*.378–454) alienated the Miaphysites, and engendered deep divisions within eastern Christendom. The allocation of the dioceses of Asia, Pontus and Thrace to Constantinople conferred patriarchal status upon the city. The somewhat ambiguously worded Canon 28 confirmed its honorary primacy after Rome, building on the situation begun at Ephesus. Other important canons affecting the organization of Byzantine Christianity were Canon 4, which brought monasticism (an increasingly urban phenomenon) for the first time under the jurisdiction of a local bishop, and Canons 9 and 17, which gave Constantinople the power to conduct appeals from regional metropolitans. The Council of Constantinople II (553) saw an attempt by Emperor Justinian I to appease the Miaphysites or anti-Chalcedonians, and the anathematization of Origen (*c*.185–*c*.254). This constituted an attack on the Egyptian and Palestinian parties, exacerbating the rift between monks and the imperial court, and between different geographical factions. The Council of Constantinople III (681) concerned itself with the doctrine of Monotheletism, an attempt to further appease the anti-Chalcedonians, and the anathematization of Pope Honorius I (d. 638) and four patriarchs of Constantinople who had given approval to this doctrine. The Council of Nicaea II (787) met originally in Constantinople, where its final session was also heard. It affirmed the proper veneration of icons, but this was not fully accepted as an ecumenical council in the West until 880. Pope Hadrian I (d. 795) had accepted it, but Charlemagne condemned it in 794.

This brief synopsis of those Councils accepted as ecumenical shows both the doctrinal issues with which they were concerned, and also the constant entanglement of Church and state, which is a dominant feature of how Byzantine Christianity organized itself.

Relationship between Church and Secular Authority

From the time of Emperor Nero (54–68), there was conflict between the allegiance of Christians to the one God and the allegiance demanded of them by the state: it was a major reason for systematic persecution of Christians in the first few centuries of the Common Era. Whilst Christians might see their 'abiding city' as heaven, they lived in an increasingly complex world on earth, and the tensions between these two were acted out by those with any power, be it secular or sacred. The mimicking of Roman imperial structures by the Ecumenical Councils noted above is a classic example of the conflation of secular and sacred. A state could easily see its citizens' loyalty to God as subversive of the civilization it supported. One solution was the absorption of two roles into one person, as achieved by the Emperor Constantine, whose expedient 'conversion' to Christianity enabled him to declare 'I have been established by God as the supervisor of the external affairs of the Church'.

Although seen by some as a coup for Christianity, Constantine's conversion also demonstrates the first Byzantine example of caesaropapism, defined by Alexander Kazhdan as 'the allegedly unlimited power of the Byzantine emperor over the Church, including the unilateral intervention in doctrinal questions ordinarily reserved to ecclesiastical authorities'. An element of reciprocity existed, however, between the two: the contemporary Lactantius (250–320) saw Christianity as the sole defender of Roman civilization. This dynamic between emperor and patriarch was neither simple nor quite as biased towards the subordination of the sacred to the imperial cult as might appear. There are instances of the emperor becoming extremely involved in church politics and doctrine: arguably the height of caesaropapism is expressed by the roles of Empresses Irene and Theodora in their intervention in defence of the holy icons during the eighth and ninth centuries. But there were also challenges to imperial authority from the church establishment: between the fourth and ninth centuries, no fewer than twelve emperors defended positions that were later declared to be heretical. Between 906 and 920, the Church as represented by Patriarch Nicholas Mystikos and Leo VI (r. 886–912) clashed violently over the affair of the tetragamy, the emperor's controversial fourth marriage. As often in the Byzantine context, this articulates as much political as doctrinal difference: modern scholars suggest that the issue was less to do with the imperial marriage and more to do with the fact that Leo had replaced Patriarch Nicholas with Euthymius whose decisions about ordinations were then called into question.

From the time of the first Ecumenical Councils, the emperor's duty and liability to defend orthodox teaching – whether from a deeply informed theological standpoint or through the advice of his clerics – makes him a key player in the fortunes of the Church, and must surely have involved a measure of respectful understanding of the peculiar role and character of priesthood. In the fourth and fifth centuries, this dynamic between divine and human kingship was expressed through the concept of *symphonia*, an extension of the Hebraic concept that God's chosen people were in a covenantal relationship with the Almighty. Gregory of Nyssa (*c.*330–*c.*395) explains it thus in one of his orations:

> if the Emperor followed the will of God and the people preserved faith, then God would bless the affairs of the earthly dominion with his protection and favour. A *symphonia* of earth and heaven would result, especially seen in the protection of the Christian *imperium* from its enemies.

Such a concept enabled emperors such as Constantine to attribute military success to divine approbation; mention is made below in the discussion of iconoclasm of similar instances.

Whilst emperors did sometimes dominate the 'external' matters of the Church, such as its finances, and appointment of senior clergy, they were not usually so involved with its internal affairs. There were specific roles for the emperor to play within liturgical worship, but the main challenge to the patriarch's authority was often not from the emperor but from monks, whose machinations during some of the Ecumenical Councils reflected the influence they also held over the emperor. The charismatic authority of monks, whose rapid spread is demonstrated by the number of monasteries in Constantinople, formed effectively a third power base to add to that of *imperium* and *sacerdotum*. The role of monks in defending the veneration of holy icons was merely the start of their influence on affairs of state. Rivalry within the Byzantine Church caused much squabbling about the validity of ordinations (as noted above) and about the problems of being in communion with certain clergy colleagues as a result. The ordination question came to a head in the case of Photius, Patriarch of Constantinople during 858–67 and again in 877–86. He was a controversial figure because of his prior calling as a politician and the fact that he was installed as patriarch whilst still a layman. His unstable relationships with emperors epitomize the fickleness of state favour in the Byzantine period.

Influential monks included Theodore of Studios (759–826), whose devotional advice shaped monastic thought and practices far beyond the Monastery of Studios itself; he also played a significant role in the Moechian controversy (the remarriage of Constantine VI). From the tenth century, Athanasios (*c*.920–1003) of Mount Athos provided further weight for the importance of contemplation in the life of the Byzantine Christian. The articulation of the charismatic power of the monks as effectively a third source of authority alongside that of patriarch and emperor was highlighted by Symeon the New Theologian (949–1022), whose supposed cult of his spiritual father, Eulabes, at the turn of the eleventh century, was ostensibly supported by Patriarch Nicholas Chrysoberges. He sent incense and candles to support the veneration of the elder Eulabes, a Studite monk who had died around 986; this prompted Symeon, his disciple, to compose a *kontakion* (hymn). His practice of sending incense and candles continued for sixteen years but during this period Symeon fell foul of the church court and was ultimately exiled by the Holy Synod for his part in a conflict with Stephen, one time Metropolitan of Nicomedia, on the matter of the imperative that a priest only teach from direct experience of God. A previous patriarch, Sisinnios, had supported Symeon when a number of his monks rebelled against him, so clearly the charismatic stance adopted by Symeon at times served the Church and at times was seen to threaten it. The emperor of the time, Basil II (976–1025), had an ambivalent relationship with the Church; on the one hand he invoked almighty power in the manner of Constantine at Milvian Bridge; on the other, he introduced heavy taxes against large landowners, of which the Church was a prime example. Basil's equivocal attitude towards the Church is a classic example of the complexity of this aspect of Byzantine Christianity.

One aspect of church organization which demonstrated relative independence from the imperial structures was that of canon law. Modern scholarship has sought to categorize canon law according to content or period; the actuality is that 'laws' to do with church organization and administration, ethical and judicial matters affecting both the lay and religious world, grew up in a sprawling mass of documentation. Much of it inevitably involved the secular administration of the Byzantine world, but since the beginnings of canon law were in the 85 Apostolic Canons, the theological ownership of canon law was clearly established. The apostolic canons were enlarged and amended by the canons of both ecumenical and local councils (fourth to late ninth century), some of which, as mentioned elsewhere in this study, concerned themselves with non-religious governmental matters. For example, fifth-century anathemas against Arians and other heretics were similar to subsequent decrees against Jews, Muslims and other non-Christian members of the Byzantine state. Canon laws about marriage were of particular sensitivity when invoked with regard to imperial marriages (such as that of Leo VI, and Theodore of Studios' rejection of Constantine VI's remarriage).

Under three emperors, Constantine I in the fourth century, Justinian I in the sixth century and Leo VI in the tenth century, matters of church law were not so completely autonomous. Justinian's *Codex* and *Novellae* were hugely significant in shaping and collating legal practices that affected both Church and state. Cooperation between the two was articulated by the codifying work of Patriarch John III Scholasticus (565–77), who had been a lawyer in his secular life.

The conciliar phase of canon law was followed by one in which particular patriarchs dominated the field, between the late ninth and eleventh centuries. Photius supervised the *Nomocanon in Fourteen Titles*, in which the canons were arranged according to content; this grew out of the 879–80 Council in Constantinople (sometimes called the 'Eighth Ecumenical', being the last to issue canons which were recognized by both East and West). The final phase of canon law was shaped by a number of canonists; in the twelfth century, Alexius Aristenos, John Zonaras, and Theodore Balsamon, were particularly influential. Zonaras imposed a system on existing canons according to his sense of their relative importance; his idiosyncratic approach attributed more authority to apostolic and ecumenical than to conciliar or local canons. Aristenos focused on the context of canons, and Balsamon was commissioned by patriarch and emperor to impose some coherence between imperial and ecclesiastical laws. In the fourteenth century, further commentaries on canon law were undertaken by Matthew Blastares and Constantine Harmenopolous, among others.

The Byzantine Conceptual World View

Byzantine Christianity has a distinctive conceptual framework, which it shares to a great extent with the modern Eastern Orthodox Church. It is based on the concept of tradition *(paradosis)* and rooted in study of patristics and scripture. The theological definitions given by patristic authors constantly refer, intertextually, to other fathers, even where they are not named or identified clearly. In contrast to modern anxieties about plagiarism and the protection of intellectual property, Byzantine theology consciously seeks to integrate previous insights, to affirm the ideas of others within the same tradition (leading to the strongest possible refutation of heresy) in a manner which suggests a 'golden chain' of illuminated wisdom. At the same time, it integrates and synthesizes certain Christianized aspects of the Hellenistic philosophical tradition, as well as owing something to rabbinic hermeneutical devices. In other respects, too, Byzantine Christianity is Greek rather than Latin in orientation, articulated, for example, by the adoption from the early seventh century of the Greek term *Basileus* for the emperor.

Basil the Great (*c*.330–79) expresses a typically Byzantine affirmation of the place of tradition, in this case unwritten tradition, in his work *On the Holy Spirit*:

> We do not content ourselves with what was reported in Acts and in the Epistles and in the Gospels; but, both before and after reading them, we add other doctrines, received from oral teaching, and carrying much weight in the mystery of the faith.

Although dating from the earliest centuries of the Christian era, the authority of this statement endures throughout Byzantine Christianity: this, in itself, is a testament to the very concept of *paradosis*, that knowledge and insight are passed on from one generation of the faithful to another, informed by apostolic insights and enlivened by the presence of the Holy Spirit.

Scripturally based, the Christian tradition of Byzantium relied on the accumulated wisdom of inspired living saints, whose experience illuminated the love of God and his desire for perfection for all humanity. Behind this was what Meyendorff describes as a 'theocentric anthropology', known as *theosis* (divinization or deification to give it more Latinate terms). The presupposition was that humanity was made in God's image, and strove continually to be reunited with God. Through the unique sacrifice of the god-man Christ, all humanity shares in the godhead, a total participation. Maximus the Confessor (*c*.580–662) in his *Ambigua* echoes the Hellenistic understanding of the composite parts of the human person in his description of deification:

> In the same way in which the soul and the body are united, God should become accessible for participation by the soul and, through the soul's intermediary, by the body, in order that the soul might receive an unchanging character, and the body, immortality; and finally that the whole man should become God, deified by the grace of God-become-man, becoming whole man, soul and body, by nature, and becoming whole God, soul and body, by grace.

Humanity's potential to become God (first articulated by Irenaeus in the second century) raises the key issue of the Mother of God, another distinctive aspect of the conceptual life of Byzantine Christianity. The status of Jesus' human mother was the source of angry debate in Ecumenical Councils and also featured in the iconoclast controversy. Whilst the Western Church venerates Mary as the ever-virgin mother of God, the Eastern Church focuses, through the title *Theotokos*, on how her humanity expresses that of Christ – who is also divine. The nuance of the term *Theotokos* strongly affirms Mary as the bearer of God in Christ, as far more than a human incubator of a divine seed. Gregory Nazianzus (329–90) states:

> If anyone does not confess that the Virgin Mary is Theotokos, he is found to be far from God. Whoever maintains that Christ passed through the Virgin as through a channel and was not fashioned in her in a manner at the same time human and divine . . . is likewise godless.

Cyril of Alexandria's famous *Third Letter to Nestorius* continues the theme, providing the basis for Byzantine Christianity's veneration for the Holy Mother of God. In this, he states that it was 'Because the holy virgin bore in the flesh God who was united hypostatically with the flesh, for that reason we call her Mother of God.' Nestorius, and the Antiochene School argued against the use of this term. The somewhat ambiguous use of the word 'Nestorian' as a derogatory term to describe the Assyrian Church of the East is evidence of the depth of feeling about the whole issue of the Theotokos. The West's choice of the term *Dei Genitrix* leads to a focus on Mary as a maternal figure, and by extension the Church as a nurturing female. The West knows her as the blessed virgin, and thus became increasingly concerned with the virgin status not only of Mary but of her own human mother, and of Mary's perpetual virginity; the East concentrates on Mary as the bearer of God, a woman whose willing co-operation with God's will articulates an essential understanding of the act of free will. The 'sinfulness of human procreation', often seen as innate in the West, is less emphasized in the East. While East and West differed about the immaculate conception of Mary, they are both agreed on a doctrine of her assumption into heaven, and the Dormition of the Virgin became and remains a major Byzantine Orthodox feast.

A dominant characteristic of Byzantine Christianity is that its concepts and doctrine cannot be easily separated: in the Eastern Christian world, *praxis* and *theoria* are enmeshed, just as in Christ, divinity and humanity, are intertwined and indistinguishable. According to Evagrius Ponticus (346–99) in his work *On Prayer*, there can be no theorizing, no theologizing without the practical impetus of prayer and faith: 'He who truly prays is a theologian, and a theologian is he who truly prays.' In other words, theology becomes almost an apophatic experience: it is, simultaneously, entirely experiential and yet incapable of verbal expression. What the Byzantine knows of God can only be expressed by what God is not, since humanity is not capable of comprehending the entirety of God. In both apophatic theology and the enmeshing of *theoria* and *praxis*, the common link is the enlivening force of the Holy Spirit, and the need for the Christian to be fully aware of being spirit-filled; hence the significance of the teachings of Symeon the New Theologian and Gregory Palamas (*c.*1296–1359).

Great intellects of both the philosophical and theological bent have long pondered how to use human words to express transcendent matters: can language and reason, however sophisticated, apprehend something uncreated, like God? Apophatic, or negative theology, is the term used during the Byzantine period to describe this paradoxical endeavour. The Cappadocian Fathers of the fourth century were among the first Christian thinkers to consider this. Writing against Eunomios, Gregory of Nyssa diverges from Neoplatonic concepts of the incomprehensibility of God: he sees in the soul the potential to ascend to God in a direct encounter:

having by the action of the Spirit passed through the whole of the hypercosmic city, having failed to recognize the One he desires among intelligible and incorporeal beings, and abandoning all that he finds, he recognizes the One he is seeking as the only One he does not comprehend.

Apophasis (the Greek word from which 'apophatic' derives) finds its most compelling expression in the writings of Pseudo-Dionysius (an unknown author of the late fifth or early sixth century), who explored in his *Divine Names* and *Mystical Theology* (arguably the most exciting seven pages of theology extant), and in the *Celestial* and *Ecclesiastical Hierarchies* the paradox of speaking about the ineffable. He asserts that negative here means not an absence or deprivation, but rather a surfeit: God is so far beyond human comprehension that the limited faculties of human nature cannot find adequate language to describe him. Dionysius posits that a state of religious ecstasy, such as that of Moses when receiving the Ten Commandments, or Christ when transfigured on Mount Tabor effects a direct knowledge of God which transcends human speech; as the human intellect progresses it leaves language and the senses behind as an inadequate form of expressing divine truth.

In explaining what God is Dionysius acknowledges the intellectual and sensory tools given to humanity, and the limitations they impose on comprehending the Almighty:

> God is therefore known in all things and as distinct from all things. He is known through knowledge and through unknowing. Of him there is conception, reason, understanding, touch, perception, opinion, imagination, name and many other things. On the other hand he cannot be understood, words cannot contain him, and no name can lay hold of him. He is not one of the things that are and he cannot be known in any of them. He is all things in all things and he is no thing among things. He is known to all from all things and he is known to no one from anything.

The issue of the transcendence of God fuelled the debate between Gregory Palamas and Barlaam the Calabrian (*c*.1290–1348) in the mid-fourteenth century. The debate focused on a distinction between the knowable energies of God and his unfathomable divine essence. Barlaam had been Eastern Orthodox and a monastic, but joined the Catholic Church on his return to Italy in 1342. Palamas, who was Archbishop of Thessaloniki (1347–59), defended in his *Triads* the practice of Hesychast contemplative prayer as fostering the vision of the uncreated light. Rather than asserting the transcendence of God as forming a gulf between the divine and human, this perspective affirms the redemptive role of the Incarnation and the means to bridge the gap. He saw God as unknowable in his essence but comprehensible in his uncreated energies. The debate between Barlaam and Palamas highlights the conflict between the more philosophical and rationalist aspects of Christian belief, and the more intellectually demanding and experiential understanding of faith.

The ambivalent relationship between Rome and Constantinople was a longstanding source of friction in the Byzantine Church. Doctrinally, the Byzantine Church diverges from the Latin Western Church even before the schism of 1054. The three main issues contributing to this were mentioned above as the *filioque*, the *azymes*, and the rival theories about authority within the Church, including the status (marital and otherwise) of clergy. With regard to the *filioque* controversy, it needs to be noted that although a creed had been forged by the Ecumenical Councils culminating in that of Chalcedon in 451, the status of the Holy Spirit had not been adequately addressed: the focus of theological thought had been on the person of Christ and his relationship to the Father. This situation presented a Church that believed in the charismatic authority of 'illuminated' living saints with a significant challenge. Experiential wisdom, which ratified the teachings of scripture, relied on divine inspiration for its authority. So the whole issue of the 'procession of the Holy Spirit' became a rallying ground for opposite camps, culminating in the involvement of the patriarch Photius mentioned above.

Schism could be said to characterize Byzantine Christianity. During the earliest days as a Christian state, the empire was deeply divided by heated debate about creedal issues such as the correct understanding of *homoousios/homoiousios*. For many years, scholars have divided theologians of the period into Antiochene and Alexandrian in emphasis, suggesting their greater focus on, respectively, the human and divine aspects of Christ. Close reading suggests more complexity than this, but the rival claims of Antioch and Alexandria, like those of Rome and Constantinople, demonstrate the partisan nature of much Byzantine religious thought. The iconoclast controversy is another example of polarities stubbornly defended by appeals to the authority of broadly similar sources. At the heart of many of these disagreements is the fundamental desire to explain the inexplicable: the divine and human natures of Christ, and the *perichoretic* nature of the Trinity. In other words, Byzantine Christianity is conceptually rooted in Christology; much of what holds it together, and much of what divides it, finds its source in this essential matter of faith.

The vociferousness with which opinions on these matters diverge is evident from the anathemas and excommunications which litter the history of the Councils, a practice which also speaks of the immense cultural and intellectual diversity of Byzantine Christianity. The heritage of Greek philosophy, both in terms of its intellectual content (for example, ideas about the soul and creation) and its mode of discourse is another source of friction within Byzantine thought. At one extreme the expression of philosophical ideas becomes an almost secular humanism, a type of scholasticism; the term 'theologian' is even seen as a term of abuse, suggesting as it does to some a divorce between the theoretical and the practical. When studying sources from the period, it is always worth remembering that Byzantine theologians did not seek to write in a systematic and consistent manner; modern inhibitions about intellectual ownership did not exist and ideas from the many diverse cultures which fed into Constantinople were absorbed into a rich and at times indigestible mix. But at the heart of Byzantine Christianity is the focus on Christ, his person and his work, informed and enlivened by the movement of the Holy Spirit, through prayer and fasting. It is a construct which integrates the intellectual, spiritual and emotional aspects of the human person just as Christ himself integrates the human and divine, and which acknowledges the human person as made in the divine image. Issues of ecclesial authority and details of liturgical practice may thus be seen as subservient to this focus. The language employed to explain such mysteries is complex and subtle.

Dominant Figures

It is inimical to any form of Eastern Christianity to impose modern, scholastic or sys-tematic divisions into the rich and complex entirety of its thought, but it is worth noting that among the dominant figures in Byzantine Christianity are monks, priests and bishops; and theologians (in the Evagrian sense) were noted for their preaching, poetry, pastoral care or political acumen. All of these modes of expression serve to articulate doctrine and thus the faith of the Byzantine Christian; none had a monopoly of cre-dence. because innovation within the tradition was viewed with suspicion, those who found new ways of explaining the eternal mysteries of faith inevitably come to mind, and are remembered for what they said or did that was inspired or different, even when it aroused hostility among the more conservative of their contemporaries. Omissions from this necessarily brief list must be forgiven.

The Cappadocian fathers are an obvious starting point, because of their contribution to the development of monastic communities, the lifeblood of Byzantine Christianity; their articulation of Trinitarian dogma; their integration of the mystical and philo-sophical into the spiritual life of the Byzantine Church. Basil the Great renounced the secular world into which he had been educated and grafted to the existing Egyptian monasticism the structures and rules which enabled it to evolve into coenobitic monas-ticism. In this he was much informed by his friend Gregory of Nazianzus (329–89), who in addition to being an assistant (if reluctant) bishop and author of five *Theological Orations* (fundamental for an understanding of the evolving doctrine of the Holy Spirit), wrote religious poetry of great beauty. Basil left a number of lucid and influential letters on various topics. A significant achievement was his refutation of Arianism, and his contribution to the debate on whether *homoiousios* ('of like substance') or *homoousios* ('of same/one substance') was the correct term to designate the relationship between Jesus the Son and God the Father. Basil's brother Gregory, Bishop of Nyssa (330–95) was also involved in the anti-Arian polemics of the Ecumenical Councils, and is remarkable for his integration of Neoplatonic and Platonic thought into Christian writing; he also shows the influence of Origen, a massively important exegete and thinker of the previous century. Gregory's *Catechetical Orations*, polemical writings and ascetical treatises, including the remarkable *Dialogue of the Soul*, which reveals the subtle mind of his sister Macrina, were important legacies for the Byzantine Church.

Evagrius (345–99) came from Pontos in Asia Minor, and (like the Cappadocian fathers with whom he was connected) combined practical asceticism in the desert with a Christianization of Neoplatonism. His *Chapters on Prayer* and the *Praktikos* give sound counsel to monastics but also form the basis for the evolution of categorizing deadly sins. He used the word *logismos* to describe the mental process of intent which precedes action. His writings are brief but cogent, and being seized upon as Origenistic caused Evagrius to be shrouded in the mists of supposed heresy for centuries, but his works continued to circulate under different names. Once rehabilitated, the strong link he offers between Hellenism and early Christianity proved inspirational to western as well as to eastern monastic and intellectual communities.

Romanus the Melode (d. *c*.555) enjoyed considerable though short-lived fame as Byzantium's best-known hymnographer. He served as a deacon before achieving prominence as a composer of biblically based *kontakia*: their authorship is debated, although around 60 of the 85 attributed to him are probably authentic. The 'Akathistos', which may be by Romanus, is the lone survivor in the Byzantine liturgy. Various reasons for the replacement of Romanus' works within the liturgy have been put forward; these include monastic zeal about the proportion of purely biblical material, especially as the monastic *typika* increasingly framed the liturgy, and perhaps their length, which would prove problematic in an already long liturgy. As examples of Byzantine poetry they are readable and dramatic, and the inclusion within them of non-scriptural themes render them a fascinating source of comment on some current affairs. Theologically, their stance tends to stress the divine nature of Christ.

The true identity of Pseudo-Dionysius, or Dionysius the Areopagite, is unknown, and has been deduced largely from references to his works in Greek and Syriac texts from the sixth century onwards. The influence of his writings, however, is immense, and not just in the Byzantine world: arguably his concepts of negative theology are expressed in the West through the writings of the author of the anonymous fourteenth-century *Cloud of Unknowing*. In fact, some scholars believe that he was more valued in the West, as is clear from the writings of John Scotus Eriugena in the ninth century, and by Syriac-speaking Christians than in Byzantium itself. Maximus the Confessor wrote a commentary on the writings of Pseudo-Dionysius and developed some of his ideas on hypostatic unity. Although writing at the time of the mainstream Christological debates, Pseudo-Dionysius used utterly different language and concepts to explore the nature of God. He drew on the Neoplatonists and especially Proclus (d. 485) to emphasize the unity of God within a sophisticated hierarchical cosmology. The extant *Mystical Theology, Celestial Hierarchy, Ecclesiastical Hierarchy* and *Divine Names* are mentioned above and provide a deep mine of theological and philosophical treasures.

Maximus the Confessor (580–662) more even than Pseudo-Dionysius, bridged East and West retrospectively. He also accommodated both the language of negative-apophatic and positive-cataphatic theology. His main contribution was to affirm that Christ had both a human and divine will, since he had both natures; this brought him into conflict with both the imperial and ecclesiastical Monothelites of the mid-seventh century, and led ultimately to his persecution, torture and martyrdom. In common with the Cappadocians, Maximus found authentic ways of integrating Hellenistic thought and Christian faith, and also achieved a measure of authentication for the writings of Pseudo-Dionysius. His writings include the *Mystagogy, Chapters on Love* and *Chapters on Knowledge*. They expound the concept that human beings are made in the image of God, a microcosm of their creator, and have a duty to renounce the vices outlined by Evagrius in order to achieve perfect union with Christ.

John of Damascus (d. *c*.749) was a monk of Mar Sabas, near Jerusalem, and also a priest. His three treatises in defence of the holy icons gave crucial expression to the understanding of the right veneration of icons; he was able to distinguish between different types of images and suggest appropriate ways of approaching them. *Latreia,* worship or veneration, is to be reserved for God alone, while *proskynesis*, a relative veneration, is appropriate for images of Christ, his mother and the saints. These writings may have formed the basis for the discussions at the Seventh Ecumenical Council in 787, and followed on from the Christological arguments propounded by Germanus I, Patriarch of Constantinople (715–30), who was forced by an imperial groundswell of iconoclasm to resign. Their Christological stance in relation to icons and their veneration was taken up and developed further by Theodore the Studite in the ninth century. John of Damascus' tripartite *Fount of Knowledge* is a comprehensive presentation of philosophical definitions, a classification of heresies, and a systematization of Byzantine theology. It represents the culmination of Greek patristic thought in the eighth century and proved to be extremely influential in both the Greek East and the Latin West.

Theodore the Studite (759–826) contributed to Byzantine monasticism not only through major reforms at the Studios monastery in Constantinople, which during his time as abbot grew in numbers as well as discipline and fervour, but also for his writings. He based his coenobitic rule on that of Basil the Great, and was a firm believer in the need for monks to participate in labour as well as contemplative prayer. His *Hypotyposis* not only provided his own monks with guidelines, but also inspired and invigorated monastic culture generally throughout the Byzantine world. Other writings survive in Byzantine hymnography, especially parts of the proper for Great Lent; his three *Antirrhetics* defending the holy icons and over five hundred of his letters are extant. Like Symeon the New Theologian, he was exiled on several occasions by his patriarch; his advice to his monks included being prepared to accept martyrdom. One aspect of his teaching which may have been particularly influential was his list of six sacraments: baptism, known as 'illumination', the Eucharist or synaxis, holy chrism, ordination, monastic tonsure and burial of the dead.

Symeon the New Theologian's contribution to Byzantine theology has been noted already in terms of his fierce defence of the authority of charism, and the imperative for the experiential as a measure of spiritual standing within the Church. His dates were probably 949–1022. His key writings include the contentious and elegant *Hymns of Divine Love*, the *Practical and Theological Chapters* and many strident *Catecheses* on theological and ethical matters, written for his own monks at St Mamas in Constantinople and elsewhere. Symeon focuses in his teaching on the major monastic practice of spiritual fatherhood, the expression of which caused challenges to other sources of authority within Byzantine Christianity. His rather idiosyncratic stance and emphasis on the purity of the inner being fed into the Hesychast revival of the fourteenth century steered by Gregory Palamas.

Nicholas Cabasilas (1320–90) was a lay theologian, possibly later a monk, whose main contribution to Byzantine Christianity was a long commentary on the sacraments, *The Life in Christ* (which consists partly of paraphrases of Gregory Palamas) and the *Explanation of the Divine Liturgy*. His concern with prayer is reflected in the operation of grace through the celebrant of the Eucharist; the priest is a conduit of God's power and love. Despite the theological nature of these texts, he is also renowned as a humanist, much concerned with social, ethical and political issues.

Key Movements

Miaphysitism

Miaphysitism is a term applied retrospectively to a doctrinal schism originating in the early fifth century. The doctrine alleges one nature only in Christ, and was thus in direct conflict with the Chalcedonian teaching of the dual nature of Christ. It should be noted, however, that the extreme form of this doctrine advocated by Eutyches was denounced not only by Chalcedonians but by non-Chalcedonians as well. The title Miaphysitism rather than 'Monophysitism' is now used as the more accurate term for the position held by the Syrian, Coptic and Armenian Churches. Eutyches developed the thinking of Cyril of Alexandria about the union of two natures in Christ in a confusing manner, presenting the belief that before the incarnation, Christ had two natures, but after it only one. This attempt to preserve the unity of God contributed to continuing difficulties in explaining how Jesus can be fully human and fully divine, despite the apparent consensus that the Chalcedonian definition of 451 was the final word on the matter.

Its relevance for a study of Byzantine Christianity is that it became, and has remained, one of the fault lines of the Eastern Christian world. Syria and Egypt tended to favour Miaphysite positions, for them the proper understanding of Cyril of Alexandria, and originally this owed much to the rivalry between the rural communities and the cities in these two countries. By the sixth century, this particular schism was engrained, with the Armenians, Copts and Syrians expressing independence from mainstream Byzantine Orthodox teaching. Great sensitivity is required in understanding these divergent positions, which spawned controversy long after 451.

We should also mention the 'Nestorian' Church, or more accurately the Church of the East, which declared its independence in Persia before the Council of Ephesus was convened in 431 at which Nestorius, Bishop of Constantinople, was condemned. The Syriac-speaking Christians of this Church pursued a remarkable missionary enterprise in the East, settling in China by the seventh century and establishing communities in South India by the sixth century. The term 'Nestorian', like the term 'Manichaean', was used by the Byzantines to denounce segments of the Christian tradition it wanted to believe was heretical. The Church of the East repudiates this title, which was applied to it as a term of opprobrium.

Iconoclasm

As with many aspects of Byzantine life, iconoclasm derives its impetus from political, theological and even economic impetus. Volcanic eruptions, earthquakes (such as that on the island of Thera in 726) and the substantial loss of territory to the Arabs were all used by one or other side to prove divine retribution in response to inappropriate use of icons. Emperor Leo III (r. 717–40) was particularly prone to superstitious pronouncements about the very practical dangers of what he saw as idolatry. At the heart of the issue, however, is a fundamental Eastern Christian perspective of Christ. For the modern historian of the Byzantine era, the value of icons from an artistic point of view cannot be separated from their theological significance. For Byzantine and contemporary Orthodox Christians, they disclose fundamental truths about the humanity and divinity of Christ, and the special relationship the Church has with Mary, his Holy Mother. Issues concerning the type of worship that might be appropriate (*latreia* or *proskynesis*) also increased tension within the Byzantine Church.

The significance of a religious image as part of the revelation of Christian truth was strongly at odds with the Jewish and Muslim stance, which saw anthropomorphic imagery as idolatry. Indeed, it took several hundred years for Christianity to feel comfortable with icons, and a fear of Greco-Roman pagan influences inhibited their existence. Even when Christian painting became widespread from the fourth century onwards there was strong opposition from such as Eusebius of Caesarea (*c*.260–*c*.340), and Epiphanius of Salamis (*c*.315–403), who exclaimed: 'How will one describe in painting the incomprehensible, inexpressible, unthinkable and indescribable, whom even Moses could not look upon?'

As Islam encroached upon the Byzantine Empire, cultural and political factors fed into the iconoclast controversy which was dominating imperial policy during the eighth and ninth centuries. In 692, the Quinisext Council debated the Christological foundation to the portrayal of Christ in human mode. Canon 82 affirmed the correctness of icons of the Lord, and interestingly this coincided with the institution of accepting the vicarious presence of the emperor through his portrait, a classic example of the convergence of imperial and theological thought. Emperor Justinian II (685–95, and again 705–11) reflected this conflation of authorities through his replacing the image of the emperor on his coins with an image of Christ.

Leo III campaigned actively against icons from 726; ecclesiastical supporters of his stance included several bishops in Asia Minor. He replaced the iconophile patriarch of Constantinople, Germanus I, with an iconoclastic patriarch in 730. Germanus had put forward the incarnational argument in favour of icons, extolling a 'visible theophany which exalts the humiliation of God the Word'. John of Damascus at the Monastery of Mar Sabas in Palestine, wrote around this time three works in defence of holy icons, warning that to reject the material risked the dualism of Manichaeism; that God having created humanity and the world in his image, the making and venerating of images was itself divine activity.

Leo's son, Constantine V (740–75) took the debate even further. The Iconoclastic Council of 754 (this council claimed to be an Ecumenical Council) decreed that icons could only represent either Christ's humanity (in which case they were 'Nestorian', as interpreted and understood at the time), or a confusion of divinity and humanity which would result in a form of Miaphysitism. Constantine drew on his iconoclastic stance for a systematic persecution of monks, whose leader Stephen the Younger was martyred in 764. On Constantine's death, the scales began to swing in favour of the iconophiles, with the Empress of Leo IV, Irene, proving to be a catalyst in the search for episcopal support for icons. The Second Council of Nicaea, called in 787, reinstated the veneration of icons, stating that 'the honour which is paid to the image passes on to that which the image represents and he who reveres the image reveres in it the subject represented'. The Council simultaneously made statements about the limits to imperial decrees and urged new standards of church and monastic behaviour.

The Empress Irene was deposed in 802. A second period of iconoclasm was instigated by Emperor Leo V in 813 and his policy was followed by Michael II (821–9) and Theophilos (829–42). The most notable iconophiles of this second period were Theodore the Studite, who composed three *Antirrhetics* in favour of icons and Patriarch Nicephorus (806–15) who also contributed to their defence. However, it was not until 843, under the auspices of Empress Theodora, that icons were again given their rightful place, confirmed by the so-called 'Triumph of Orthodoxy' (celebrated on the last Sunday in Lent), which continues to celebrate the essential role of icons in the spiritual life of the Byzantine Christian tradition.

Mission to the Slavs

The mission to Moravia in Central Europe by the brothers Cyril (826–69) and Methodius (*c*.815–85) in the second half of the ninth century shook the Byzantine Empire out of the introspection into which it had fallen during the period of iconoclasm. Although ultimately the mission failed in Moravia, it started a process of translation and promotion that eventually saw the nations of the Balkans incorporated into a Byzantine commonwealth. It was a diplomatic and religious triumph, which renewed the prestige of Constantinople and reinvigorated the ecumenical patriarchate. The conversion of Kievan Rus' in the tenth century was further proof that the Byzantine Church was alive and well, and able to promote itself in a new sphere of influence.

What the Slavonic-speaking peoples took on when they embraced Byzantine Christianity was a cultural package and patrimony that connected them with the ancient and early Christian Mediterranean world. The invention of the Glagolitic and Cyrillic alphabets gave the emerging Slav nations not only the opportunity to celebrate the liturgy in the vernacular but the means by which to begin a literary inheritance of their own. The dividing lines between Eastern and Western Christendom were drawn at this time and they have remained in place more or less through to the present.

Dualist sects

The Bulgarian priest Bogomil (whose name is Bulgarian for Theophilus), in the first half of the tenth century, fostered a form of dualism related to the more aggressive Paulicians, a dualistic sect which originated in Armenia in the seventh century. The Paulicians believed that the material world was the evil creation of Satan, with only the soul being created by God. The Bogomils themselves rejected manifestations of non-ascetic life such as sex, marriage and consumption of meat and wine. They denounced much Byzantine theological teaching, including the incarnation, which they replaced with a docetic understanding of Christ. Whilst renouncing sacraments, churches, icons and relics they maintained an elitism of their own, led by 'the Perfect': some of this is reminiscent of Gnostic and Manichaean beliefs and practices.

Driven out of the empire by Empress Theodora in the ninth century, some Paulicians moved into the Balkans, and their converts under Bogomil became a sizable group in Bulgaria, where civil disobedience was a worrying feature of their teaching. They were denounced around 972 by Cosmas, a Bulgarian priest whose writings on the Bogomils together with those of a certain Euthymius in the eleventh century, form a substantial part of our knowledge of the sect. The threat they posed to Byzantium peaked in the twelfth century when they found favour among Constantinopolitan nobility, led by Basil the Bogomil, who was burned at the stake by Emperor Alexius Comnenus (1081–1118) in 1117. However, remnants of Bogomilism continued in Slavic areas of the empire until the fall of Constantinople in 1453. Perhaps as a result of the crusades, the Bogomils appear to have been in contact with various dualist sects in the West, most notable the Cathars. We know that Nicetas, a leader of the Bogomils in Byzantium, travelled to southern France and imposed the doctrine of absolute dualism on the Cathar community.

Hesychasm

The basis of Hesychasm (from *hesychia*, meaning tranquillity or stillness) derives from centuries of monastic experience of contemplative ecstasy, rooted in the continual recitation of the Jesus prayer, but it became more of a formal concept in the fourteenth century. The Hesychast is typically one who has renounced the world and family ties, devoting his or her life to God with complete obedience and simplicity. Superficially, this is the mode of living of all religious; Justinian's *Novella 5.3* states that *hesychia* is the goal of the solitary. The Hesychast, however, additionally experiences a direct encounter with the living God, in a vision of the uncreated light. Traditionally this experience is associated with that of Mount Tabor in the New Testament story of the Transfiguration of Christ. Certain physical postures are suggested to maximise the ability to focus on the heart, and some of these are discussed by Gregory Palamas in his *Triads*. Other proponents of this type of religious experience include Symeon the New Theologian and Gregory of Sinai (1255–1346).

With Gregory Palamas (1296–1359), who became Archbishop of Thessaloniki (1347–59), the Hesychast issue evolved into political confrontation. Palamas' *Triads in Defence of the Holy Hesychasts* explain this Athonite spiritual practice in terms of an engagement with the knowable energies of God, which are distinguished from his unknowable essence. His apophatic approach failed to appease Barlaam the Calabrian (*c.*1290–1348), who accused Palamas of Messalianism (a heresy that maintained prayer alone was sufficient for salvation), asserting that it was impossible to divide the indivisible godhead in this manner. Other critics of Palamas' distinction between the essence and energies underlying Hesychasm included Gregory Akindynos and John Kyparissiotes. The theological position of Palamas was vindicated by two synods meeting in Constantinople; as a result Palamite thought became the basis of Hesychast spirituality in the late Byzantine period. It is only recently that scholars have begun to appreciate and understand the true significance of Palamas' teaching and its impact on the Orthodox world.

Conclusion

Greek Christianity of the Byzantine period may be characterized as restrained within certain traditional and ecclesiastical parameters. Given that the religious and political history of Byzantium was very different from that of the Latin West, it is not surprising that the Byzantine Church came to see itself as the true guardian of Christian belief and practice. This is also the case in relation to the Oriental Orthodox. It was always ambivalent about its classical Greek heritage, never completely in harmony with it (for obviously reasons) and yet never completely rejecting it. This tension is apparent in its use of philosophical vocabulary to explain theological truths, and in its condemnation of those who appeared to promote secular humanism at the expense of the Christian world view.

The utilization of the patristic method of theological discourse provided it with a dynamic source of renewal and replenishment which never succumbed to scholasticism on the one hand, or other-worldly mysticism on the other. It attempted to maintain a balance between excessive rationalism and unarticulated rapture, and on the whole it achieved this. Byzantine Christianity was able to articulate its religious faith through sound (liturgy) and sight (iconography) as well as through texts, to produce an integrated world view that sustained it over one thousand years of change and development. Christianity in Byzantium was an imperial religion, and although the relationship between Church and state was not always clear or convivial, it did at least provide a sense of destiny for the Greek people. That sense of destiny was in turn passed on to the Slav nations to the north, who continued to promote the idea that a Christian state was a realizable ideal.

References and further reading

Angold, M. (2001) *Byzantium: The Bridge from Antiquity to the Middle Ages*. London: Phoenix Press.
Brubaker, L. and Haldon, J. (2001) *Byzantium in the Iconoclast Era (ca 680–850): The Sources*. Aldershot: Ashgate.
Cameron, A. (2006) *The Byzantines*. Oxford: Blackwell.
Cholij, R. (2002) *Theodore the Stoudite: The Ordering of Holiness*. Oxford: Oxford University Press.
Cunningham, M. (2002) *Faith in the Byzantine World*. Oxford: Lion Books.
Dagron, G. (2003) *Emperor and Priest: The Imperial Office in Byzantium*. Cambridge: Cambridge University Press.
Dalrymple, W. (1998) *From the Holy Mountain*. London: Flamingo.
Geanakoplos, D. J. (1984) *Byzantium: Church Society, and Civilization Seen through Contemporary Eyes*. Chicago and London: University of Chicago Press .
Gregory, T. (2005) *A History of Byzantium*. Oxford: Blackwell.
Herrin, J. (2001) *Women in Purple: Rulers of Medieval Byzantium*. London: Phoenix Press.
Hussey, J. (1986) *The Orthodox Church in the Byzantine Empire*. Oxford: Clarendon Press.
Kazhdan, A. P. (ed.) (1991) *The Oxford Dictionary of Byzantium*, 3 vols. Oxford: Oxford University Press.

Laiou, A. E. and Maguire, H. (eds.) (1992) *Byzantium: A World Civilization*. Washington, DC: Dumbarton Oaks.

Littlewood, A. R. (ed.) (1995) *Originality in Byzantine Literature Art and Music: A Collection of Essays*. Oxford: Oxbow.

Mango, C. (1980) *Byzantium: The Empire of the New Rome*. London: Weidenfeld and Nicolson.

Mass, M. (ed.) (2005) *The Cambridge Companion to the Age of Justinian*. Cambridge: Cambridge University Press.

Meyendorff, J. (1974) *Byzantine Theology: Historical Trends and Doctrinal Themes*. New York: Fordham University Press.

—— (1989) *Byzantium and the Rise of Russia: A Study of Byzantino-Russian Relations in the Fourteenth Century*. Crestwood, NY: St Vladimir's Seminary Press.

Nicol, D. M. (1992) *The Immortal Emperor: The Life and Legend of Constantine Palaiologos, Last Emperor of the Romans*. Cambridge: Canto.

—— (1995) *The Last Centuries of Byzantium 1261–1453*. Cambridge: Cambridge University Press.

Obolensky, D. (1971) *The Byzantine Commonwealth: Eastern Europe, 500–1453*. London: Weidenfeld and Nicolson.

Parry, K. (1996) *Depicting the Word: Byzantine Iconophile Thought of the Eighth and Ninth Centuries*. Leiden: Brill.

Thomas, J. and Constantinides-Hero, A. (eds.) (2000) *Byzantine Monastic Foundation Documents: A Complete Translation of the Surviving Founders' Typica and Testaments*, 5 vols. Washington, DC: Dumbarton Oaks.

Treadgold, W. (1997) *A History of the Byzantine State and Society*. Stanford, Calif.: Stanford University Press.

Whittow, M. (1996) *The Making of Orthodox Byzantium 600–1025*. London: Macmillan.

Wilson, N. G. (1996) *Scholars of Byzantium*, rev. edn. London: Duckworth.

CHAPTER 5
Coptic Christianity

Janet A. Timbie

Introduction

Coptic Christianity immediately raises definitional questions. Is it the Church of ethnic Egyptians in Egypt and elsewhere in the world? Is it Christianity originally expressed in the Coptic language? Is it a separate denomination with respect to belief and practice? Is it simply to be equated with the Coptic Orthodox Church, whose patriarch lives in Egypt while bishops and clergy serve a worldwide diaspora?

All of these descriptions fit, yet are not separately adequate. 'Copt' and its adjective 'Coptic' developed from Greek *Aigyptos/Aigyptios* (Egypt/Egyptian). This became Arabic *Qibt*; thus, English 'Copt'. It would then be correct to say that all Egyptians are Copts – and this has been said by various people in modern times for political purposes – but common understanding defines Copt as 'Egyptian Christian'. As Arabic replaced Coptic in daily life and the majority of Egyptians became Muslim, labelling Egyptian Christians as Copts or Coptic Christians followed.

For centuries, Coptic Christianity was mainly embodied in the Coptic Orthodox Church, formed by the rejection of the Christological formula of the Council of Chalcedon (451). A minority in Egypt remained in communion with Constantinople and Rome, the centres of Chalcedonian faith, and became the Melkite Church with its own patriarch in Alexandria (now known as the Greek Orthodox (Melkite) Church of Alexandria). A small Coptic Catholic Church was founded in the eighteenth century when the Coptic Orthodox Metropolitan of Jerusalem became a Catholic. Protestant missions to Egypt began in the nineteenth century in significant numbers and, after little success converting Muslims, focused on the Coptic Orthodox. Hundreds of Protestant congregations exist in Egypt, the largest of these is the Coptic Evangelical Church. In this chapter, Coptic Christianity will refer to the characteristics of the Coptic Orthodox Church, supplemented where necessary by reference to the other groups: Melkite, Catholic and Protestant.

The Coptic Orthodox Church is centred in Egypt and organized into a patriarchate (Alexandria) and a system of bishoprics, both inside and outside Egypt. Especially since

the 1960s, Coptic emigration in reaction to Islamic fundamentalism and poor economic conditions in Egypt has created a diaspora church that is strong in the United
States, Canada and Australia. Smaller groups exist in Latin America and Africa (mainly
East and South), in Gulf Arab states, and in Europe (the European Coptic Union).
Numbers are difficult to estimate. The Egyptian census of 1986 found 3,300,000 Copts
(8 per cent of the population), but this figure is unreliable since both Muslim authorities
and Copts want to minimize Coptic presence. At the same time, the Church announced
11 million members, on the basis of baptismal registers. Some sources suggested 7 or
8 million in 1990 or 8 million in 1992. Of this number, perhaps 200,000 are Coptic
Catholics and 150,000 Coptic Evangelicals. Outside Egypt, the Coptic Orthodox Church
numbers about 1,200,000. And the Coptic Orthodox Church is the largest Christian
minority in the Near East, in any Islamic state.

Language use has evolved throughout the history of the Coptic Church. When the
first Christian missionaries came to Egypt in the first century, they contacted Greek-
speaking Jews and pagans. Only in the third century is there clear evidence of conversion to Christianity by individuals with Egyptian names, probably Coptic-speaking
(Eusebius 1993). Arabic enters with the conquest (641), yet Greek and Coptic remained
the languages of the Church for a considerable period. But by the tenth century the
majority of Christians no longer understood Coptic and Christian literature (with a few
exceptions) was written in Arabic. The liturgy was translated into Arabic, apart from
certain phrases in Coptic and Greek, two centuries later. Recently there has been an
effort to promote the study of Coptic by Coptic Orthodox Christians. Though the Church
proudly traces its roots to the first century (to Mark the evangelist) it is Coptic, not
Greek, that is the focus of instruction, which is consistent with the focus on the Egyptian
ethnicity of Copts.

History

The history of Coptic Christianity is one of stark contrasts. Events in the early period
(e.g., the emergence of monasticism, Athanasius' defence of the Nicene Creed) have
influenced the entire history of Christianity. Yet later developments have taken place
completely outside the awareness of the western Christian world, as a result of the
Chalcedonian schism (451) and the Muslim conquest of Egypt (641). The Coptic Church
experienced many important changes and these did not take place in isolation; on the
contrary, there was much communication between the Christian communities of the
Near East during the long period of Muslim domination.

Origins

The traditional account of the earliest years of Christianity in Egypt is built upon small,
but striking, hints in the New Testament. The flight of the Holy Family to Egypt (Matt.
2: 13–20) is described in later apocryphal texts designating the specific sites that shel-
tered the Holy Family. Apollos, identified as a Jew from Alexandria (Acts 18: 24),

appears as a Christian missionary in Ephesus; Paul (1 Cor. 1: 12) mentions an 'Apollos' as one who taught in Corinth. Egypt is mentioned (Acts 2: 10) in the long list of nations from which Jews and converts have come to Jerusalem and then heard Peter's preaching.

The direct evidence of Christianity in Egypt in the first and second centuries is sparse, coming only in the form of partial Greek manuscripts of biblical and patristic texts: a Bodmer papyrus fragment containing John 18: 31–3, 37–8 written c.135, several Chester Beatty papyri, c.200, containing parts of the New Testament and fragments of Irenaeus' 'Against Heresies', written in the early third century, have been found in Egypt. Coptic textual evidence is later; the Gospel of John, dated late third to early fourth century, is one of the earliest. Eusebius provides a continuous narrative in the form of lists of bishops, beginning with Mark the evangelist arriving in Egypt around 43, returning to Rome, and then coming back to Egypt as bishop until his martyrdom in the early 60s. Two points stand out in the traditional account: first, the founder is not one of the twelve, and, second, there is an indication of close communication between Rome and Alexandria, which will be a factor in the resolution of doctrinal conflicts in the third and fourth centuries.

Formative period

The third century saw the growth of Christianity in Egypt and offered evidence of Coptic-speaking Christians. This growth was sporadically checked by persecution, first due to the edict of Septimius Severus in 202. Attacks on Christians by pagans in Alexandria (249) and a new edict by Decius (250) renewed the pressure. Some Christians responded with calculated avoidance of persecutors; this is the course recommended by Clement of Alexandria, and the Bishop Dionysius sought refuge in Libya during the Decian persecution. The last wave of persecution began under Diocletian in 303–4 and had a severe impact on Egypt, including the Coptic-speaking population in the Thebaid. The year of Diocletian's accession to the throne (284) became the year one in the Coptic Church calendar and all subsequent dates are labelled AM (*anno martyrum*). Persecution abated in 305, returned under Maximin Daia in 310–12, climaxing in the execution of the patriarch, Peter of Alexandria, on 25 November 311. The Edict of Toleration soon followed in 313.

On the one hand, the trend in the early period is toward centralization around the Bishop of Alexandria. Yet other evidence points to a diversity of Christian belief and practice in the first centuries. Gnostic thought in diverse forms was promoted in Egypt by important thinkers, above all, Valentinus (c.150). The Nag Hammadi texts, translated into Coptic in the fourth century, contain a variety of statements of anti-cosmic dualism as well as more mainstream sentiments. The writings of Epiphanius of Salamis (d. 403) circulated in Egypt and also gave lurid, perhaps exaggerated, descriptions of Gnostic worship in fourth-century Egypt, on the fringes of the Christian community. The situation is similar with the Manichaeans. Their missionaries arrived in Egypt in the third century and a variety of Manichaean literature was translated into Coptic (found at Medinet Madi and Dakleh Oasis). Manichaean doctrine, with its use of a Jesus myth and stark dualism, can be understood as another challenge to the evolving mainstream. Shenoute of Atripe (d. 465) criticized specific Gnostic and Manichaean concepts, which implies that these views were alive and threatening into the fifth century.

After the end of persecution, Christianity throughout the empire moved into a period of doctrinal clarification. The leadership assumed by the Egyptian Church through its patriarch is striking. The growth of monasticism and the conversion of Coptic-speaking areas did not reduce the influence of the patriarch, but seemed to enhance it, as holders of the office skilfully maintained the loyalty of Christians throughout Egypt. The Trinitarian controversy, prompted by the teaching of Arius, a priest of Alexandria, had an empire-wide impact. Arius taught of the Son that 'there was when He was not'. Only the Father is eternal and uncreated. In this Arius may have been, in some sense, carrying on the teaching of Origen. But he also represented conservative resistance to the authority of the patriarch. Arius was condemned by an Egyptian synod in 324, but continued controversy over his ideas led Constantine to summon an Ecumenical Council at Nicaea in 325, at which time the Nicene Creed was adopted and Arius condemned. Alexander of Alexandria and his deacon Athanasius carried the day, but negative reaction to the *homoousios* clause (the Son is of one essence with the Father, true God from true God) set in immediately. Athanasius became Bishop of Alexandria in 328 and from then until his death in 373 advanced Nicene theology. Exiled five times, Athanasius maintained the loyalty of clergy, monastics and Christian populace and set a pattern of centralized authority that would endure in Egypt. Nicaea was reaffirmed at the Council of Constantinople in 381, but this council also honoured Constantinople, not Alexandria, beside Rome as a leading see.

Rivalry between Constantinople and Alexandria played a role in the next theological drama: Nestorius versus Cyril of Alexandria, climaxed by the Council of Chalcedon (451). If the Nicene Creed affirmed that the Son was true God, it remained to define the relationship between divine and human in Jesus Christ. Apollinarius (d. 380) argued that the divine Word replaced the human soul in Jesus. Nestorius, Bishop of Constantinople since 428, countered by stressing the full humanity of Jesus together with his divinity and rejecting the traditional title of Theotokos for Mary. Cyril of Alexandria, bishop since 412, led the attack on Nestorius. In several works Cyril made the case for the union of God and man in Jesus Christ and crafted the statement that has symbolized Coptic Orthodoxy to the present: one incarnate nature of the Word. Cyril seems to use 'nature' (*physis*) as nearly equivalent to 'individual reality' (*hypostasis*). The Emperor Theodosius II called the third Ecumenical Council to Ephesus in 431 to resolve the issue. Alexandria and Rome were again allies. The council was a complete triumph for Cyril: his theology was affirmed and Nestorius was exiled. But as with the Nicene Creed, there was negative reaction from some and Cyril needed to negotiate a compromise Formula of Reunion with John of Antioch in 433.

Cyril died in 444 and was succeeded by Dioscorus. Various parties continued to critique the theology of Ephesus. The monk Eutyches took one extreme: the one incarnate nature was divine, since the divine nature subsumed the human. Leo of Rome countered Eutyches in a way that apparently criticized Cyril and Ephesus, though the problem was more linguistic than real. The Tome of Leo maintained Christ was one person (*persona*) in two natures, divine and human. Dioscorus of Alexandria convened a council at Ephesus in August 449 that supported Eutyches and deposed Flavian, Bishop of Constantinople and an ally of Rome. When imperial power changed hands, a new council (Chalcedon, 451) favored Leo's position and exiled Dioscorus. Chalcedon became the 'Robber Synod' of the Coptic Church, countering the western view of Ephesus II as the *latrocinium*. This was a turning point because the Egyptian Church remained loyal to Dioscorus (and his successors), in spite of the best efforts of imperial authorities.

Period of division, 451–642

Successors of Dioscorus who remained loyal to his teachings held the allegiance of most Egyptian Christians. A Chalcedonian hierarchy was installed in Alexandria, at the head of a 'Melkite' Church with little popular base. Through the latter half of the fifth and then the sixth centuries, the position of a Chalcedonian Church in Egypt depended on the efforts made by the emperor in Constantinople. In 482, Peter Mongus, anti-Chalcedonian patriarch (477–89), accepted the compromise of the Henotikon formula, leading the Emperor Zeno to withdraw support for a Chalcedonian patriarch. By contrast, the Emperor Justinian (527–65) supported a Chalcedonian hierarchy in Alexandria and a Chalcedonian purge of monasteries throughout Egypt.

Yet there is a sense that the heart of the Egyptian Church was undisturbed by the struggle in Alexandria, remaining loyal to the teachings of Athanasius, Cyril, and the successors of Dioscorus. Important teachers and leaders came to Egypt from Syria-Palestine. Severus of Antioch, deposed by the Emperor Justin, arrived in 518 and produced theological writings that form the lasting basis of the 'one nature' doctrine. Jacob Baradaeus, a Syrian monk, was ordained bishop and proceeded to travel and ordain non-Chalcedonian clergy, insuring the continuity of the separated Church in Egypt (it was from Jacob that the term 'Jacobites' for the non-Chalcedonians was derived). Evidence points to the growth of the Church at this time: church building, donations to churches and monasteries witnessed in documentary papyri, and literature. The political struggles of empires had little effect at first.

Arabization of the Coptic Church

The Arab conquest of Egypt in 642 did not receive much comment in Christian writings of the time. Compared to accounts of persecution by Chalcedonians both before and after the Persian occupation (616–28), the Arab conquest seems a fairly innocuous event in Christian sources. As non-Muslims, the Christian population was liable to the poll tax, along with taxes on land and other obligations, so the rulers had no incentive to promote large-scale conversion. Many sources indicate that the post-conquest situation of the Church changed little for several centuries. Anti-Chalcedonian and Chalcedonian congregations continued to compete, though the former remained much larger.

From time to time, oppressive measures against Christians were enacted: discrimina-
tory laws, destruction of icons, and imprisonment of the patriarch. These measures
were sometimes inspired by Muslim ideology; in the eighth and ninth centuries they
were a response to rebellions by the Coptic Christian population. In particular, the
caliph al-Mutawakkil forbade Christian processions, regulated Christian dress, and
instituted other forms of discrimination. Such measures promoted conversion, which
lowered poll tax revenue, with the result that the tax rate was doubled in 868. Thus
conversion to Islam was the result of both economic and social measures, including
clear persecution.

Rule by the Fāṭimids, from 969 to 1171, began with more favourable conditions for
Christians, but soon was marked by the very worst period of Coptic Christian history:
the reign of al-Hakim (996–1021). From 1007 to 1012 he persecuted Christians in
numerous ways: humiliating dress, destruction of churches, confiscation of property
and forced conversion (or execution). Many did convert, only to return to Christianity
when al-Hakim moderated his position. But much damage was long-lasting; monasteries that had been attacked were now abandoned. Copts seemed to settle into minority
status and the Arabization of Christianity in Egypt accelerated. The language shift is
demonstrated by the production of Coptic-Arabic grammars and word lists. Translations of Coptic Christian texts into Arabic and original compositions in Arabic are
numerous from the tenth century. Even the formal selection of Bohairic for the liturgy,
by Patriarch Gabriel II (1132–45), signalled a step in Arabization: Coptic/Bohairic has
become a sacred language. Few original Coptic compositions were produced after this.
'The Martyrdom of John of Phanidjoit' (thirteenth century, Hyvernat 1924) and the
Triadon (fourteenth century, Nagel 1983) are examples.

The rule of the Ayyūbids in Egypt (1169–1250) coincided with the peak of the crusades, which affected all Christians in the Near East. At first Copts were suspected of
supporting the crusaders; as a result, Saladin (founder of the Ayyubid dynasty) razed
the cathedral of St Mark in Alexandria. Muslim victories, including the reconquest of
Jerusalem in 1187, reduced pressure on the Copts. As hostile attention on the Copts
eased, important restoration and redecoration took place in some churches and monasteries. Recent work on the Monastery of St Antony at the Red Sea has revealed a
complete decorative programme undertaken in 1232–3.

The Mamlūk regime held power in Egypt for a much longer period, 1251–1517, and
was in general much harsher toward the Christians. The Mamlūk rulers continued to
make use of Christians in administration, though some labelled 'Copts' in records of the
period were actually recent converts to Islam. Random attacks by the Muslim population and official destruction of churches brought the Christian community very low,
and scattered Christian rebellions led to severe reprisals. This predicament led to several
attempts to ally Coptic Christians (the anti-Chalcedonian group) with Rome. European
merchants and Franciscan and Dominican missionaries were in Alexandria in the
fourteenth and fifthteenth centuries; Coptic Christians travelled to Europe in the period.
Patriarch Cyril III Ibn Laqlaq made the first gesture toward union with Rome in 1237.
Nothing came of it, but as the Christian situation deteriorated, Patriarch John XI
reached out to Rome again by sending a delegation to the Council of Florence in 1437.
Pope Eugenius IV followed with a papal bull in 1442 proclaiming the union of Coptic

Christians with Rome, but it had no effect given the lack of effective connection between Rome and Christians in Egypt.

Contact between Rome and Coptic Christians continued, however, in the Ottoman period (1517–1798) as the Christian population declined to about 200,000 (10–12 per cent of the population). Negotiations took place at several points in the sixteenth century with the approval of more than one patriarch and pope. Finally, in 1597, delegates from Alexandria signed a declaration of submission to Rome. But this lacked the support of the mass of Coptic Christians and never took effect. Other activities, by various Christian groups, began in Egypt at this period that had more lasting significance. Franciscans and Capuchins engaged in charitable and educational works leading to the conversion to Catholicism by some of the Coptic elite. Protestant influence began with the work of the German Lutheran Peter Heyling in 1632–3. But the Ottoman system of governance strengthened the hand of the Coptic Orthodox patriarch, for the Ottoman *millet* system allowed religious communities to be under the authority of their own spiritual leaders. The patriarch controlled the management of church property and private laws governing Christians, such as marriage and inheritance.

Modern Period: Bonaparte to the Present

Egypt remained a province of the Ottoman Empire into the twentieth century, but the struggle between colonial powers in the nineteenth century influenced missionary activity and promoted the growth of national consciousness among Coptic Christians. Napoleon invaded Egypt and defeated the local rulers in 1798, yet the lasting effect of his expedition was scientific, not political, as modern Egyptology began with the experts accompanying Napoleon. The British soon defeated the French and helped the local rulers regain control and restore Egypt as an Ottoman province. This was also the beginning of several years of instability that ended when Muhammad Ali, an Albanian officer of the Ottomans, took control in Egypt. His rule (1805–49) began the modernization of Egypt and to some extent integrated Coptic Christians into national life. His many ambitious projects (land reform, industrialization, etc.) included reforms in education aided by foreign missionaries. The successor of Muhammad Ali gradually improved the legal status of the Copts: the jizya tax on Copts was abolished (1855) and they were accepted for military service, Copts were represented in the Consultative Council (1866), and legal equality with Muslims was affirmed (1913, then in the constitution of 1922).

The modernization begun by Muhammad Ali was matched by the work of Patriarch Cyril IV (1854–61), who made many efforts towards reform. He encouraged education (especially for clergy), church publications and construction. Cyril helped to promote union with the Eastern Orthodox, but these negotiations were cut short by his death, under rather mysterious circumstances, at age 45. Catholic and Protestant missionary activity also steadily increased opportunities for education among Copts, so it is not surprising that tensions developed between educated laity and tradition-minded clergy. In 1874, the Majlis Milli (community council) was formed at the instigation of powerful Coptic laymen and initially accepted by Cyril V (1874–1927) to administer church property and generally support reform. Cyril V later withdrew his approval and a power struggle between the patriarch/clergy and lay leaders continued for decades under several patriarchs. A more harmonious phase in the interaction of clergy and laity began in 1910 with the creation of Sunday schools. Habib Guirguis (1876–1951), an archdeacon, perhaps inspired by Protestant models, steadily promoted them until they became part of church life in every city and village. The Sunday schools included age-group classes, youth activities, teacher conferences, and prayer groups. Many important leaders of the present Coptic Church have emerged from the Sunday school movement, and it is a vital part of the diaspora community.

But the vitality shown in these institutions (council, Sunday schools) has been repeatedly threatened by trends in Egyptian society as a whole, especially by Muslim fundamentalism. The British protectorate (1882–1952), in which British troops were stationed in Egypt and dominated the Egyptian monarchy, stimulated nationalist resistance by Egyptians. At first, Egyptian nationalism united Muslims and Christians, as in the Wafd Party, which had some Coptic leaders and achieved partial independence from the British (agreements in 1922, then 1936–7). Copts were prominent in the government of King Fuad I (1922–36) and in society at large. Meanwhile, from the 1930s, the Muslim Brothers and other Islamist organizations emerged that sought to identify Egyptian nationalism with Islam and therefore return Copts to the inferior status required by Islamic law.

Matters reached a crisis in 1952, when a military coup led by Gamel Nasser overthrew the monarchy and eliminated British influence after the Suez conflict of 1956. The Nasser years (1953–70) included land reform and nationalization of some industries. These measures reduced the economic power of the Coptic upper class and increased emigration to Europe and America. The early years of Anwar Sadat, Nasser's successor, were somewhat better for Copts, who regained some public influence. Boutros Boutros Ghali (later UN secretary general) was an important adviser to Sadat when the Camp David agreement was signed (1978), formalizing peace between Egypt and Israel. Yet the continued economic weakness of Egypt and the condemnation of Egypt by other Arab countries combined to strengthen Muslim fundamentalism. Riots in Cairo in 1981 killed Copts and burned churches; a further outbreak of anti-Christian violence took place in 1990 in Minya and Fayyum. Sadat was assassinated in 1981 by fundamentalists; also killed in the attack was Bishop Samuel, the Coptic representative to the ecumenical movement. Sadat's successor, Hosni Mubarak, has maintained peace with harsh measures against anti-government forces.

It seems that both communities in Egypt – Muslim and Christian – have turned to religion since the 1950s to gain strength and purpose during the constant economic crisis brought on by a rapidly increasing population. A shared phenomenon – the apparition of the Virgin in 1968 in Zeitun – is one example of this increased religious fervour. On the Coptic side, while emigration to diaspora centres has increased, within Egypt the monastic movement draws greater numbers of the better educated. These difficult times have produced Coptic leaders to match national leaders such as Nasser and Sadat. Patriarch Cyril VI (1959–71) led negotiations leading to greater independence for the Church of Ethiopia (1959). He promoted monastic discipline, having come to the patriarchate from a long monastic life. Cyril reduced the powers of the

Majlis Milli, but worked fairly well with Nasser, who laid the foundation stone of the new St Mark's Cathedral in 1965. Patriarch Shenouda III (1971–) has been equally forceful, but endured more difficult times. Attacks on Christians by Islamic extremists caused Shenouda to protest to Sadat and cancel Easter celebrations in 1980. Sadat responded to more violence in 1981 by confining Shenouda to his monastery in Wadi Natrun and suppressing some Muslim groups. Shenouda returned from this internal exile in 1985, after Sadat's assassination, as Mubarak maintained an uneasy status quo. Shenouda has continued the monastic revival in Egypt, but also moved to become the visible leader of a worldwide Coptic Church, touring overseas in 1989.

Scripture and Tradition

Canonical scriptures and the tradition of the Church are the acknowledged twin foundations of the Coptic Orthodox Church. Scripture must be interpreted by the Fathers of the Church; thus, the Copts are aligned with Greek Orthodoxy and Roman Catholicism, rather than with the Reformed tradition.

Scripture

The early canon (both Old and New Testaments) in Egypt is attested both by the statements of church fathers and by early biblical manuscripts. A festal letter of Athanasius (367) denounces the 'apocryphal writings' of heretics and lists two acceptable categories of writings: canonical/divine and others, which could be read for instruction. His canonical list generally follows the same order as Codex Vaticanus, written in Alexandria in the fifth century. His instructional list includes Wisdom, Sirach, Esther, Judith, and Tobit, on the Old Testament side, and the Didache and the Shepherd of Hermas on the New Testament side.

Early church leaders in Egypt did not always distinguish the canonical from the merely instructional in their manner of citation. Shenoute of Atripe (d. 465) cites Wisdom and Didache with the same formula ('as it is written') that he uses for Isaiah and the Gospels. It is difficult to define the working canon of scripture at any particular time because complete manuscripts of either Old or New Testament are rare. By the Middle Ages, the Coptic Orthodox (with many other Eastern Churches) followed the larger Alexandrian canon of Codex Vaticanus. In the nineteenth century Patriarch Cyril V withdrew canonical status from Tobit, Judith, Greek Esther, Wisdom, Sirach, Baruch, Greek Daniel and Maccabees 1–3. Many citations from these books are still an important part of the liturgy (e.g., the song of the three young men, Greek Dan. 3: 24–90).

Translation of the Bible from Greek to Coptic was decentralized; early manuscript fragments are found in various dialects of Coptic and contain a diverse selection of texts. If Christianity spread to the Coptic-speaking population by the third century, Coptic translations would be required and, in fact, the oldest Coptic Bible manuscript (Papyrus Bodmer VI) contains a third-century text of Proverbs. Other manuscripts witness to extensive translation activity in the fourth century, but only portions of this Coptic version survive. Bohairic replaced the Sahidic dialect as the literary and official church language by the eleventh century, but the Old Testament does not survive in its entirety in Bohairic, perhaps because Arabic was already the daily language of Egyptian Christians. Arabic translations of the Bible were produced in Egypt beginning in the ninth century. The Arabic versions are translated from many sources: Hebrew, Greek, Syriac, and Coptic, even Latin at a later date. Translation proceeded steadily, but some biblical books were circulating in several Arabic translations before other books were translated. The entire canon in Arabic was produced sometime before the sixteenth century. The first Arabic printed Bibles, the ancestors of those currently used by Copts, appeared in the seventeenth century (Biblia Sacra Arabica 1671).

Tradition

The traditions of the Coptic Orthodox Church include the works of its teachers and leaders, and the collections of canons. For the period preceding the Council of Chalcedon (451) there is a shared body of tradition common to the Coptic Orthodox, other Oriental Orthodox, Latins and Greeks. After 451, non-Chalcedonian writers and local collections of canons are added to the fund of traditions.

The collected canons (authoritative decisions) of the first three Ecumenical Councils (Nicaea 325, Constantinople 381, Ephesus 431) are combined with pre-451 canons of local councils. These canons are preserved in Arabic (and partially in Greek and Coptic containing somewhat different texts). Works believed to contain apostolic traditions are also important: the Didascalia, the 127 Canons of the Apostles (based on Apostolic Church Order, Egyptian Church Order, and Apostolic Constitutions), the Thirty Canons of the Apostles and the Letter of Peter to Clement.

The pre-Chalcedonian church fathers who became important in the Coptic Church – judging by translation in Coptic, then Arabic – are the bishops of Alexandria from the formative period: Athanasius (d. 373), Theophilus (d. 412), and Cyril (d. 444). Works of Basil the Great (d. 379) and Gregory of Nyssa (d. 390) are significant, along with the writings of Cyril of Jerusalem (d. 386) and John Chrysostom (d. 407). The degree of influence can be measured in Coptic and Arabic translations produced and pseudonymous writings ascribed to a particular figure.

The post-Chalcedon tradition rests on the work of early anti-Chalcedonian leaders such as Dioscorus (d. 454), Timothy Aelurus (d. 477), and Theodosius of Alexandria (d. 567). Theological leadership of the anti-Chalcedonians passed to Antioch, and the work of Severus of Antioch (d. 538), who spent time in exile in Egypt, became influential. Tradition was also passed on in collections of canons assembled by patriarchs of Alexandria at key points in the medieval period.

Yet, in a certain sense, Coptic Christianity rests on scripture more than on tradition. The works of modern Coptic Church leaders rely on a dense fabric of scriptural citations, rather than a patristic catena, to build an argument. It has been suggested that this is evidence of the influence of Protestant missionaries in Egypt; however, it may be actually evidence of the conservatism that has been present for centuries.

Theology

The early theological tradition of the Church in Egypt – through the fourth century – is central to the developing tradition of the Church in both East and West. Figures such as Clement of Alexandria, Origen and Athanasius worked in the mainstream, even if, in Origen's case, certain radical propositions were later condemned. Into the fifth century, Cyril of Alexandria defined divine and human natures in Christ in a way that influenced the entire Church. The Council of Chalcedon was the turning point at which the theology of Coptic Christianity diverged from both Latin West and Greek Orthodox East. The Copts accept only the decrees of the first three Ecumenical Councils: Nicaea, Constantinople and Ephesus. When they recite the Creed, they interpret certain phrases in a manner consistent with Cyril's teaching and counter to Chalcedon. Rather than using the 'Monophysite' label for their tradition, Copts prefer anti- or non-Chalcedonian or Miaphysite, as in the Cyrillian formula, 'one nature (*mia physis*) of the Word incarnate'. Coptic leaders maintain that Christ is 'perfect in His divinity and perfect in His humanity' and they 'do not speak of two natures after this mysterious union of Our Lord' (statement of Shenouda III at 1989 conference of Greek Orthodox and Oriental Orthodox).

God as Trinity

The doctrine of the Trinity hammered out at Nicaea (325) and Constantinople (381), with the leadership of Alexandrian bishops, remains central and is confirmed by statements in the liturgy, apart from the recitation of the Creed. In the introductory portion of the Mass, the deacon recites, 'One Holy Father, One Holy Son, One Holy Spirit. Amen. Blessed be the Lord God unto the ages. Amen.'

Christ as one

The anaphora of St Basil includes a statement of faith preceding communion that underlines certain convictions about Christ:

> I believe, I believe, I believe. I confess until my last breath that this is the life-giving body of Your only Son, Our Lord, Our God and Saviour Jesus Christ. He took it from Our Lady and Queen, Holy Mary, Mother of God. He made it one with his divinity without mixture, without confusion, without change . . . I believe in truth that His Divinity was never separated from His humanity, even for one moment or for one blink of an eye.

The goal is to avoid both the errors of Nestorius (who separated the two natures of Christ) and of Eutyches (who subsumed the human to the divine in Christ by asserting that Christ's flesh was God-made). Since Chalcedon speaks of Christ 'in two natures' (*physis*, a term that Coptic Church leaders consistently equate with person), it is unacceptably Nestorian. However, ecumenical meetings in recent decades have enabled

Coptic leaders to find common ground with Roman Catholics and Greek Orthodox (e.g., the meeting of Pope Paul VI and Patriarch Shenouda III in 1973 and the conference of Greek/Eastern Orthodox and Oriental Orthodox in 1989).

Another assertion in the liturgy separates Copts and other non-Chalcedonians from fellow Christians. Before the gospel, the *Trisagion* is chanted, including the phrase, 'Holy God, Holy Mighty One, Holy Immortal One, who was crucified for us, have mercy on us', which was added to the liturgy by Peter the Fuller, patriarch of Antioch (d. 490). As a result, Copts and other non-Chalcedonians were accused of theopaschitism, the belief that the Trinity suffered. But Copts and others assert that the *Trisagion* is addressed to the incarnate Word, not to the Trinity.

Mary the Theotokos

The Egyptian Church, led by Cyril of Alexandria, was at the high point of its influence at the Council of Ephesus (431), defending the understanding of Mary as God-bearer rather than Christ-bearer, the term preferred by Nestorius. Cyril's position is evidence of the early development of popular devotion to Mary, which is also shown in the growth of the genre of *theotokion*, a hymn praising the Virgin Mary used in the Liturgy of Hours and the Psalmodia. The perpetual virginity of Mary and her lack of personal sin are affirmed, as well as her bodily assumption into heaven. However, the Coptic Church has not explicitly affirmed a doctrine of the Immaculate Conception. The Feast of the Dormition of Mary is celebrated on 29 January, her Assumption on 22 August. A relatively new feast on 2 April commemorates the apparition of the Virgin at Zeitun, Egypt in 1968.

Spirit 'who proceeds from the Father'

'Yea, we believe in the Holy Spirit, Lord who gives life, who proceeds from the Father.' By adhering to the original form of the Nicene Creed, the Coptic Church, along with others in the East (Chalcedonian and non-Chalcedonian), rejects the development that took place in the Latin Church. The Coptic Church does not accept the double procession of the Spirit from Father and Son (the *filioque* clause of the Latin Church). A fourteenth-century textbook of Coptic theology (Yuhanna Ibn Saba, 'Precious Pearl') explains this creedal statement: 'The Holy Spirit, life of the Father and the Son, proceeds from the Father . . . that is to say, proceeds from the Father in order to go to the Son without leaving either Father or Son.'

Angels: Michael versus Satan

The existence of angels and demons, archangels such as Michael and Satan, the prince of the powers of the air (Eph. 2: 2), is affirmed in most Christian traditions. But the meagre biblical statements have been substantially developed in the Coptic tradition.

Four archangels (Gabriel, Michael, Raphael and Suriel) are honoured and Michael receives particular attention as the angel who takes over the duties of the fallen Satan. The Book of the Investiture of St Michael survives in several Coptic versions and provides a script for the feast day of his investiture, 21 November. The twelfth of each month is another Feast of Michael.

Complementing this, the activity of the demons and Satan (or Sabataniel, Samael, Iblis) is recognized. Works such as the *Sayings of the Desert Fathers* (see Ward 1975) and the saints' lives of the Synaxarion portray the demons at work in the world to undermine the efforts of Christians. Athanasius' *Life of Antony* is the prototype and its point of view is still accepted; see the work of Matta El-Meskin on the letters of Antony for evidence (Matta El-Meskin 1993).

Last things: heaven and hell

The statements of the Nicene Creed are the core of Coptic eschatology: (1) Christ will come to judge the living and the dead; (2) we await the resurrection of the dead and the life of the age to come. But Coptic theologians have also implied that there is a preliminary judgement for each soul after death, as in Shenoute's *De iudicio* (Shenoute 1996). This preliminary judgement leads the righteous to paradise to await the resurrection and the last judgement. Until recently, a special church service took place on the fortieth day after death to mark this judgement. Prayers are still offered at the fortieth day, sixth month, and one year anniversary to assist souls whose fate is uncertain, as they wait for the last judgement. Thus, while there is no belief in purgatory, the prayers of the living demonstrate belief that some of the dead may be helped toward heaven at the final judgment.

Missions and Diaspora

Beginning in the Roman period, and continuing to the present, the Coptic Church has had a special role outside Egypt in two places: Jerusalem and Ethiopia. In modern times it has become a worldwide movement.

Jerusalem

After the conversion of Constantine, many churches were built on the holy sites in Jerusalem and its environs. Fourth-century evidence shows Egyptian Church leaders visiting Jerusalem and other Egyptians making pilgrimages to the holy sites. A small Coptic church was built near the Church of the Resurrection in the Roman-Byzantine period. An organized Coptic presence in Jerusalem is confirmed by the letter of the Arab conqueror, Caliph Umar to Patriarch Sophronius of Jerusalem that names the Christian sects represented at the Church of the Resurrection. Among them at this time in the seventh century, is the Coptic Orthodox Church, no longer in communion with Rome or Constantinople. When the crusaders took control of Jerusalem, they expelled the Copts and others from their churches. Yet some twelfth-century European accounts (John of Wurzburg, 1165, and Theodoric, 1172) mention Copts among Christian sects in Jerusalem. Other sources maintain that the Coptic presence was re-established when Saladin conquered Jerusalem in 1187. There has since been a continuous Coptic presence in Jerusalem.

Coptic Orthodox Church activity in the Holy Land was originally supervised by the Coptic Archbishop of Damietta, who spent the period between Christmas and Easter in Jerusalem. In 1236 a new diocese was created, the See of Jerusalem and All the East, and Basilios I was appointed to the position by Pope Cyril II, head of the Coptic Orthodox Church. The episcopal succession is not completely clear, but it continues as the See of Jerusalem, the Near East, and Sinai. In the twentieth century this diocese was active in many parts of the Near East.

Ethiopia

The Christianization of Ethiopia seems to have come about from several different directions. Rufinus (345–410) reports that the royal house of Axum was converted by two Syrian Christians, Frumentius and Aedesius, in the fourth century. It is likely that earlier Christian contacts had been made by Egyptians moving south and by Greeks and Syrians arriving along the sea coast. Frumentius was consecrated bishop by Athanasius of Alexandria and it became customary for the patriarch of Alexandria to consecrate an Egyptian, not an Ethiopian, as archbishop of Ethiopia. After consecration, this archbishop remained in Ethiopia at the royal court. This practice continued until the rise of Ethiopian nationalism in the twentieth century demanded an indigenous hierarchy. The first Ethiopian archbishop took office in 1951 and the Ethiopian Church became completely independent in 1959.

Diaspora

A diaspora presence for the Coptic Orthodox Church is a twentieth-century development, for there was little emigration before this point. Colonialism – occupation by French and British forces in the nineteenth and early twentieth centuries – created favourable conditions for some Copts, who travelled to Europe for study and work. But this did not lead to permanent overseas communities. The emergence of a Coptic diaspora comes with the 1952 socialist revolution led by Gamal Nasser, which affected all wealthy Egyptians. Wealthy Copts began to emigrate to Europe and the United States in the 1950s. Some simply came for study and stayed to form a community.

Another wave of emigration followed the 1967 Arab-Israeli war, mainly directed toward Canada, Australia, and the United States. After 1972 immigration was sponsored by the World Council of Churches, and other religious bodies, who assisted Copts on the ground that they suffered from religious persecution. At this stage, less-educated and less-wealthy Copts joined the diaspora. There are now several dioceses for the

Coptic Orthodox outside Egypt. From 1990, bishops were appointed to East Africa, France, Jerusalem, Nubia and Khartoum. Two US dioceses have since been formed: California and Florida/Texas. Dioceses have been established in Australia, Britain and Ireland/Scotland/NE England. Coptic parishes are established in the major cities of Canada, and in several European and Arab countries. The diaspora profile continues to change and information about it is best obtained from Coptic Church organizations. The size of diaspora communities is difficult to determine, sometimes because the census does not separate Christian from Muslim Egyptians. The Coptic Orthodox in the US were estimated at 400,000 in 1999. As this is one of the largest diaspora communities, it suggests a scale for others and points to worldwide numbers.

Monasticism and Spirituality

In the Christian world at large, the best-known feature of Egyptian Church history is the development of organized ascetic practice. Patterns of monastic practice and spirituality which were forged in Egypt have influenced the Christian world to the present. Within Coptic Christianity, monasticism experienced a revival in the twentieth century as monasteries expanded and increased their influence.

Foundational developments

The search for origins of asceticism in Egypt is stimulated by hints such as Philo's description of the Therapeutae, Jewish celibates who lead a life of prayer (in *On the Contemplative Life*). Eusebius (d. *c*.340), in *Ecclesiastical History*, interpreted this as evidence of first-century Christian ascetic activity in Egypt, implying that some Christians lived ascetically in isolation or in the cities in service to the Church.

There is some evidence from the late third century that Antony (born *c*.250) began his ascetic practice as a young man under the guidance of an experienced ascetic. He eventually gathered disciples in several locations; one survives today as the Monastery of St Antony at the Red Sea. At roughly the same time, Pachomius (d. 346) began an ascetic career in a village setting in Upper Egypt under the guidance of older ascetics. He formed his own group of ascetics, in which rules and leadership structure evolved to enable more people to practice Christian asceticism. Pachomius eventually founded several communities, for men and women, in the region around Thebes. Discipline and instruction were provided by daily meetings of groups within each monastery and annual meetings of the whole entity. Communal asceticism was also growing near Panopolis at the White Monastery. Founded in the fourth century with a rule similar to the Pachomian, it evolved independently under the rule of Shenoute of Atripe (d. 465). By the early fifth century, the White Monastery complex included houses for men and women and isolated cells for hermits. All were theoretically under close supervision of the leader who maintained control by personal visits, through representatives, and through written instruction. The writings of Shenoute – monastic instructions, sermons, letters – form one of the most important collections of original Coptic literature.

The monastic settlements of Nitria, Kellia and Scetis in the desert of Lower Egypt were another area of influence in the early period. Most of the monks in these settlements lived in isolated cells, gathering for the liturgy and for informal instruction by the elders. This sort of instruction is recorded in the *Sayings of the Desert Fathers* (Ward 1975), which were preserved in several collections in many ancient languages. Contradictory sayings are sometimes recorded (extreme versus moderate fasting, for example) but the overall perspective is one in which the disciple maintains humility while the elder guides him toward a life of prayer sustained by asceticism. These settlements also attracted ascetics from the entire empire, either as visitors (John Cassian, Rufinus, Palladius and Jerome) or as residents (Evagrius Ponticus), and their writings spread the values of the desert fathers throughout the Christian world.

Two factors challenged Egyptian monasticism before the Arab conquest. First, a series of barbarian raids on Scetis in the fifth century devastated the settlement. Second, the dispute over the doctrine of the Council of Chalcedon, which permanently separated the Church of Egypt from some of the Christian world, had immediate impact on the monasteries. Most of the ascetic communities remained loyal to Dioscorus and his anti-Chalcedonian successors, while imperial authorities tried to impose Chalcedonian orthodoxy. The Pachomian monasteries virtually disappear from the record in the fifth century, perhaps indicating that they were undermined by doctrinal disputes.

The Impact of Arab Conquest

The conquest of Egypt began a long period of change for the monastic movement. Both Chalcedonian and anti-Chalcedonian monasteries existed in the early seventh century. After the conquest, the two main groups continued to compete, now using the Muslim authorities to strike at opponents when this was feasible. As the Christians of Egypt were increasingly pressured by Muslim rulers through taxation and land confiscation, leading to conversion in many instances, the monasteries became even more important as centres of Christian culture.

The *Churches and Monasteries of Egypt* (see Evetts 1895), written in the twelfth century, provides capsule histories of the important monastic sites. The history of any single monastery or monastic complex illustrates the problems faced by the Christian community. The Monastery of St Jeremiah at Saqqara was sacked soon after the conquest; by 850, it was abandoned. The Monasteries of St Antony and St Paul at the Red Sea moved back and forth between Chalcedonian and anti-Chalcedonian control from the fifth to the ninth century. From the eleventh century, these monasteries were controlled by anti-Chalcedonians, yet, for a time, also occupied by Syrian monks from the Monastery of the Syrians in the Wadi Natrun. Wall decoration, completed around 1232–3, in the Monastery of St Antony in a fully Coptic style indicates that Coptic Orthodox monks had retaken control of the monastery. The following period (thirteenth to fourteenth centuries) also saw much manuscript production and translation. Decline followed this golden age and 'snapshots' by European travellers provide the evidence: in 1395–6 more than a hundred monks lived at the Monastery of St Antony; in 1422, fifty monks lived there. At some point in the late fifteenth century the monks were attacked by Bedouins and the monastery was abandoned, then re-settled by monks during the patriarchate of Gabriel VII (1525–68). From this point the Monastery of St Antony has been continuously inhabited and it has provided leaders for the entire Coptic Orthodox Church with a series of eight patriarchs (John XVI, 1676–1718, to Cyril IV, 1854–61) at a time when the Wadi Natrun was in decline.

Scetis (Wadi Natrun) has already been mentioned as a focal point of early ascetic practice in Egypt. After the Arab conquest and up to the modern period, the monasteries of Wadi Natrun experienced the same cycles of destruction and restoration as the Monasteries of St Antony and St Paul, but not always at the same time. By the end of the fourth century, four settlements existed at Scetis that later coalesced into the Monasteries of Baramus, Macarius (Dayr Anba Maqar), Pshoi (Dayr Anba Bishoi) and John the Short. Doctrinal disputes between the followers of Julian of Halicarnassus and Severus of Antioch divided the four communities sometime after 535. Each monastery had a rival monastery within Scetis founded by the excluded followers of Severus. By the ninth century the rival Severan house of Dayr Anba Bishoi had evolved into the Monastery of the Syrians (Dayr al-Suryan). Eventually, the Coptic Orthodox Church, associated with the party of Severus, took control of all monasteries in Wadi Natrun before the Arab conquest.

Through the medieval period, the monasteries became fortified compounds with walls surrounding facilities that were more coenobitic in style (refectories, etc.). Groups of foreign monks (Syrians, Armenians, and Ethiopians) settled in Wadi Natrun, either in their own houses or in existing monasteries. These monasteries also played a key role in the preservation of Christian literature. Old texts were re-copied and new translations and compositions were produced. Eventually, the steady decline in the Christian population produced a corresponding decline at Wadi Natrun. Al-Makrizi, writing in the fifteenth century, describes in *A Short History of the Copts*, monasteries in ruins with only a few monks in each house.

The Modern Revival

The strong revival of Coptic monasteries in the twentieth century is surprising. The leadership of Cyril VI (patriarch 1959–71) was crucial, but even before Cyril's term of office, there is evidence that greater numbers of more educated people were joining monasteries (perhaps stimulated by the Sunday school movement). Monasteries that had operated continuously (e.g., St Macarius) increased their membership; others (e.g., the White Monastery) were re-founded. Under Shenouda III (1971–), the trend has continued. Some of the best-known theological and spiritual writing in the Coptic Orthodox Church once again comes from a monk: Matta El-Meskin, a monk in Wadi Natrun, whose works have circulated widely in Arabic, and in English and French translation.

Liturgy, Sacraments and Music

Many elements of the Coptic Orthodox liturgy are similar to those of other Eastern Orthodox churches. For a complete description of the rites of the Coptic Orthodox Church, the many works of O. H. E. Burmester remain the best source. This discussion will focus on those features that are distinctive. The separation of the Coptic Orthodox Church from the mainstream of East and West after Chalcedon and the Arab conquest is a partial explanation of differences. Similarity with Syrian practice is a result of contact with other non-Chalcedonian Churches after 451 and with the Monastery of the Syrians in Wadi Natrun. Monastic practice has also influenced Coptic ritual, for example in the length of the Mass (three hours), which contains much repetition of psalms and prayers, and many scriptural readings.

The liturgical year: fasts, feasts and pilgrimages

The Egyptian calendar, developed in the pharaonic period, included 12 months of 30 days and one short month of five or six days at the end of the year. The calendar of the Coptic Church retains this form of 12 named months of 30 days and a 'short month' of five or six days. The names of the Coptic months are all of Egyptian origin and relate to the agricultural cycle.

The liturgical year unfolds with a mixture of Christian and Egyptian cultural associations. The Fast of the Nativity (25 November to 6 January), a three-day fast added to a 40-day fast, marks biblical events and a miracle of the Fāṭimid period. Within this period a special liturgy honours the Virgin Mary and poetic hymns mixing Coptic and Arabic are chanted during evening vigils. The Feast of the Nativity follows on 7 January.

The Fast of Jonah, two weeks before Lent, was introduced by Patriarch Abraham the Syrian (975–9) to foster repentance; it includes the liturgical reading of the Book of Jonah. Great Lent of eight weeks begins with the week-long Fast of Heraclius, originally associated with Heraclius' attack on the Jews in 628. At present, it is suggested that this fast compensates for the non-fasting Saturdays and Sundays of Lent. The 40-day Fast of Lent may be a total fast until sunset, 3 p.m., or noon, followed by abstinence from certain foods.

Holy Week culminates in the early morning of Easter Sunday when congregants return home to end their 55-day fast. The Holy 50 days spans Easter to Pentecost and is marked by a complete absence of fasting. The Fast of the Apostles then begins on the evening of Pentecost and continues until the Feast of the Apostles on July 12, varying between 15 and 49 days in length. This feast retains a link to the agricultural cycle, since this is the period of the rise of the Nile. Well into the Christian period, a ceremony took place on the river bank asking for a good inundation and good crop. The Fast of the Virgin begins on 7 August and ends with the Feast of the Assumption on 22 August.

Pilgrimages to sites associated with the Virgin (the flight to Egypt and others) take place in this period. The pilgrimage (*mulid*) is an important part of popular religion. A procession heads to the shrine of a martyr or other figure to celebrate his or her birth in heaven. Around 60 pilgrimages take place regularly. Some attract a small number, others draw thousands to an open-air festival. Along with the shrines of individual saints, sites associated with the flight to Egypt by the Holy Family are important. Pilgrims seek healing or other blessings along with the atmosphere of communal celebration.

The liturgy of hours

There are seven canonical hours: None, Vespers, Compline, Midnight Prayer, Morning Prayer (Latin Lauds and Prime), Terce and Sext. Monasteries include a Prayer of the Veil after Compline. All these are read, while two other offices are sung: the Evening Offering of Incense and Morning Offering of Incense. These two precede the celebration of the Eucharist and so in monasteries, where the Eucharist is a daily event, the incense offerings are integrated in the daily office: Evening after Compline, Morning after Morning Prayer. Whether the day is a fast or a non-fast day affects the order of these prayers.

Sacraments

Baptism is normally performed on infants: at 40 days for boys, 80 days for girls. It may also be performed on a special occasion or at a special shrine, as in pilgrimage to a monastery. Prayer of purification of the mother begins the rite, along with an initial anointing of the candidate outside the baptistery. The candidate (or a representative) renounces Satan and makes a profession of faith. Special prayers follow for sanctification of the water in the font. Triple immersion in the name of Father, Son and Holy Spirit follows. A prayer for de-sanctification of the water is recited and the water is carefully poured out.

Confirmation follows immediately after baptism. Thirty-six signs of the cross are made with holy oil on various body parts. The newly baptized person receives communion from the priest.

Repentance is initiated by confession of sin in front of a priest, in church or at home. A prayer of absolution follows a laying-on of hands. Acts of penance usually include fasting, prostrations and prayers. A special Rite of the Jar was performed in the past (until the nineteenth century) for readmission to communion of an apostate or one who fornicated with non-Christians.

Marriage, at present, includes two separate events: engagement and the marriage ceremony. At the engagement in the bride's home, the priest blesses the marriage contract, recites special prayers, blesses the couple, and places rings on the right hand of each party. The marriage ceremony consists of a service of betrothal with three sacramental prayers and a service of crowning.

Five holy orders are consecrated: reader, subdeacon, deacon, priest and bishop. The patriarch consecrates the bishop, who ordains all others.

Anointing of the sick, in its traditional form, used to require seven priests. One priest is now sufficient, although seven prayers remain in the rite. The sick person makes a confession of sins and is anointed with special oil, as are all others present. It can be performed on any day of the week, as needed, and there is also an annual public rite on the Friday before the Saturday of Lazarus, which precedes Palm Sunday.

At the Eucharist, those who will receive communion must have abstained from sexual relations for two or three days and fasted from midnight. The leavened, Eucharistic bread (*qorban*) is prepared in a special shape and stamped with a cross pattern. Mass is celebrated by one priest with one deacon (or more) and is chanted. Evening and morning prior to Mass must include the appropriate prayers for canonical hours, as well as the evening and morning incense offering. Rites of preparation at the beginning of the Mass include the selection of a loaf and procession of gifts around the altar. Liturgy of the word includes selections from Paul, the Catholic Epistles, Acts, lives of the saints, *Trisagion* (chanted), and the Gospel. Three Eucharistic anaphoras are in use: St. Cyril (rarely celebrated; mainly in Lent), St Gregory Nazianzus (Feasts of Nativity, Epiphany, and Easter, at night) and St Basil (most often). The anaphora of Basil used by the Copts has distinctive features. The preface is underlined by statements from the congregation: 'amen' and 'we [or I] believe.' The words of institution are also accompanied by the assertions 'we believe', etc. The priest dips his finger into the blood/wine and makes the sign of the cross over the chalice and twice over the body/bread. The loaf is divided leaving the four central, stamped squares (*despotikon*) intact, surrounded by twelve pieces representing the Apostles. Small bits of each piece (pearls) are used for communion.

Men receive communion at the entrance to the sanctuary, having removed their shoes. Women receive communion in their area of the church. The body/bread is placed directly in the mouth by the priest; the blood/wine is received from a spoon. After each element, the mouth is covered with a cloth to avoid any accidental loss. The prayer of thanksgiving and the inclination are followed by sprinkling the altar and congregation with water used in the Mass. Blessing and dismissal are followed by distribution of the eulogia, the bread prepared but not selected for the service, to the congregation.

Liturgical music

Music is a very distinctive part of Coptic worship. It was an oral tradition handed down by a succession of cantors (often blind), until E. Newlandsmith and R. Moftah collaborated to transcribe Coptic music during the decade 1926–36 (Robertson 1991). At present, music is vocal and follows a single melodic line. It is sung by men, though some responses may be sung by the congregation. Cymbals and triangle punctuate the music at certain points, and the sistrum has been used in the past. The service of the Mass, as typically sung, takes three hours, six or seven during Holy Week.

Coptic music preserves elements of pharaonic and Greco-Roman music with later influence from the synagogue and the Syrian Church. The style is one of slow repetitive chant in which vowels are prolonged in complicated patterns of notes and rhythm, with much vibrato. The priest and deacon chant their parts of the liturgy alone, while a cantor leads a choir of deacons and guides the responses of the congregation.

Hierarchy and Institutions

Patriarch and clergy

The Coptic Church has a long history of concentrating power in the hands of the patriarch of Alexandria. No other bishop or city in Egypt challenged the influence of Alexandria in the early centuries. His see has been located variously in Alexandria, Cairo and Wadi Natrun. The patriarch is elected by the Holy Synod (bishops, heads of monasteries, patriarchal council of clergy), representatives of priests and deacons, and lay people. In 1971, 622 voters chose three final candidates whose names were then written on pieces of paper. The selection of Shenouda III was made by a blindfolded young boy choosing one of the papers.

Bishops must be celibate and so are usually drawn from the monasteries. However, a widower of a single marriage can be consecrated bishop. The types of bishop are metropolitan, diocesan, monastic bishop or abbot, and general bishop (in charge of certain tasks, e.g., youth affairs, rather than a territory). A recent survey lists 78 bishops including 11 from areas other than Egypt, Africa, and the Near East. Priests must be legitimate, child of a first marriage (mother's side), baptised, married only once, have never shed blood, be in good health, and have some knowledge of Coptic as well as Arabic. The parish priest cannot marry after ordination and remains in the same parish throughout his career. Readers, subdeacons and deacons assist the priest in the liturgy. Readers and subdeacons are boys from 9 to 10 years of age. Deacons could formerly be as young as 14, but the trend now is for deacons to be 21 or older and already married.

The laity

The role of the laity has been contentious in the modern era. The Majlis Milli (Community Council) originated in 1874 as the voice of lay opposition to the church hierarchy. Since 1955, its power has been curtailed, but members continue to be important advisers to the patriarch, who is now president of the Majlis. Former members of the Majlis are part of the electoral body that chooses the patriarch, as are other lay notables. But tension between clergy and laity continues as a certain clericalization of the Coptic Orthodox Church increases. An example is the Sunday schools movement, whose direction was formerly in lay hands, but has now been taken over by the bishops.

Women in the Coptic Church

The role of women is in some ways a microcosm of the history and current situation of the Coptic Church. Women were present in the Egyptian monastic movement from the earliest period. With the Arabization of Egypt, their activities became more restricted. As in the Roman Catholic and Greek Orthodox traditions, women cannot be ordained, and ordained clergy have taken greater control of church life. Yet women in the modern era have sought to contribute more to the Church, either as laywomen, nuns, or as consecrated women.

The sayings of the so-called 'desert mothers' indicate that women lived as solitary ascetics in isolated areas of Egypt in the fourth and fifth centuries. The writings of Pachomius and Shenoute show that women's communities existed under the umbrella of these coenobitic leaders through the fifth century. After the Arab conquest, women's monasticism gradually weakened, but persisted until the twelfth century. The modern monastic revival in the Coptic Orthodox Church has touched women as well. Contemplative nuns are now present at six sites in Egypt, leading a cloistered life consciously patterned on the ideals of the Pachomians. Active nuns, belonging to the Daughters of Mary in Beni Suef, may live in the convent or close to the institutions where they work, such as orphanages, clinics, etc. A role for consecrated women appeared in the 1980s. Shenouda III proposed a three stage process: (1) consecrated woman, (2) consecration as subdeaconess and (3) consecration as deaconess. The consecrated woman does not serve in the liturgy in any way; rather, she assists the needy or provides catechetical instruction. Some may progress to monastic vows and become nuns; others may progress to become deaconesses, a status reserved for older women. The conflict between the control of women in Egyptian society as a whole and the freedom sought by these consecrated women (and other female monastics) has been carefully studied by P. van Doorn-Harder (1995). Laywomen are expected to make family life their main concern, as in contemporary Egyptian society. Yet modern Coptic women combine careers with family and also pursue seminary studies in order to lead their own groups. Laywomen have volunteered in social welfare projects and at the Sunday schools. A new development took place in 1985 when women ran for seats in the Majlis Milli and voted in the election.

References and further reading

Athanasius (1994) *Life of Antony*, ed. and trans. G. Bartelink. Sources chrétiennes 100. Paris: Éditions du Cerf.

Atiya, A. (ed.) (1991) *Coptic Encyclopedia*, 8 vols. New York: Macmillan.

Bolman, E. (ed.) (2001) *Monastic Visions*. Cairo: ARCE.

Burmester, O. H. E. (1967) *The Egyptian or Coptic Church*. Cairo: Société d'archéologie copte.

Cannuyer, C. (1996) *Les Coptes*, 2nd edn. Turnhout: Brepols.

Charles, R. (ed.) (1916), *Chronicle of John of Nikiu*. Oxford: Clarendon Press.

Davis, S. (2004) *The Early Coptic Papacy*. Cairo: American University in Cairo Press.

Doorn-Harder, P. van (1995) *Contemporary Coptic Nuns*. Columbia, SC: University of South Carolina Press.

Eusebius (1993) *Ecclesiastical History*, 4th edn., ed. and trans. G. Bardy. Sources chrétiennes 31, 41, 55, 73. Paris: Éditions du Cerf.

Evetts, B. (ed. and trans.) (1895) *Churches and Monasteries of Egypt and Some Neighbouring Countries, attributed to Abu Salih the Armenian*. Oxford: Clarendon Press.

Gabra, G. (2006) *The Treasures of Coptic Art*. Cairo: American University in Cairo Press.

Grossmann, P. (2002) *Christliche Architektur in Agypten*. Leiden: Brill.

Heijer, J. den (1989) *Mawhub ibn Mansur ibn Mufarrig et l'historiographie copto-arabe. Étude sur la composition de l'Histoire des Patriarches d'Alexandrie*. Corpus Scriptorium Christianorum Orientalium 513. Louvain: Peeters.

Hyvernat, H. (ed.) (1924) *Acta Martyrum*. Corpus Scriptorum Christianorum Orientalium 86. Louvain: Typographeo republicae.

Ibn Saba, Y. (1922) *Precious Pearl*, ed. and trans. J. Périer. Patrologia Orientalis 16. Paris: Firmin-Didot.

Kamil, M. (1968) *Coptic Egypt*. Cairo: Le Scribe égyptien.

al-Makrizi, T. (1873) *A Short History of the Copts*, trans. S. Malan. London: D. Nutt.

Matta El-Meskin (1993) *Saint Antoine ascète selon l'Evangile*. Spiritualité Orientale 57. Begrolles-en-Mauge: Abbaye de Bellefontaine.

Meinardus, O. (1999) *Two Thousand Years of Coptic Christianity*. Cairo: American University in Cairo Press.

Nagel, P. (1983) *Das Triadon*. Halle: Abt. Wissenschaftspublizistik der Martin-Luther-Universität.

Robertson, M. (1991) Music, Coptic. *Coptic Encyclopedia*. New York: Macmillan.

Rufinus (1997) *Church History*, trans. P. Amidon. New York: Oxford University Press.

Severus of Ashmunein (1910) *History of the Patriarchs of Alexandria*, ed. B. Evetts. Patrologia Orientalis 1. Paris: Firmin-Didot.

Shenoute (1996) *De iudicio*, ed. and trans. H. Behlmer. Turin: Ministero per i beni culturale.

Ward, B. (trans.) (1975) *Sayings of the Desert Fathers*. Oxford: Mowbray.

Watson, J. (2000) *Among the Copts*. Brighton: Sussex Academic Press.

CHAPTER 6

Ethiopian Christianity

David Appleyard

Introduction

The Ethiopian Orthodox Church is the largest of the Oriental Orthodox or non-Chalcedonian Orthodox churches, with perhaps around 33 million members. The majority of Ethiopian Orthodox live in Ethiopia, but there are sizeable expatriate communities in the United States and Canada, in Australia, and in parts of western Europe. The Orthodox Church in Eritrea, which is historically part of the Ethiopian Orthodox Church, and formally separated only in 1993, has around 2 million members. In recent years there have also been a number of converts in the West Indies, estimated at around 90,000.

The official name of the Ethiopian Orthodox Church is in Amharic *Yä-Ityopp-əya Ortodoksawit Täwahədo Betä Krəstiyan*, or the Ethiopian Orthodox *Täwahədo* Church, in which the term *täwahədo*, lit. 'unity' or 'oneness', professes the unity of the human and divine natures in Christ and reflects the pre-Chalcedonian formula 'One Incarnate Nature of God the Word'. The early and medieval history of the Church is intimately linked with the expansion of the Aksumite state and in particular the later Christian kingdom of Ethiopia, and as such its traditional members are of the Amhara and Tigrean ethnic groups. But in the wake of the political dominance of the Amhara in the region from the late thirteenth century many other ethnic groups were drawn into the Church as part of the intertwined processes of amharization and christianization.

The language of the liturgy of the Church, however, remained and is still Ge'ez (or Ethiopic), the language of Aksum at the time of the adoption of Christianity and the subsequent translation of the Bible and the liturgy. Within the service, however, sermons are delivered in the vernacular languages, mostly Amharic or Tigrinya, but some basic Christian educational material is beginning to appear in other languages of Ethiopia as part of the greater freedom of language use that Ethiopia has seen since the early 1990s.

History

Legend and early history

The Ethiopian Orthodox Church is one the oldest officially adopted and still flourishing national churches in the world. Like most of the other ancient churches it seeks to place its origins in apostolic times, a wish that finds ready support in the confusion of the exact meaning of the name Ethiopia where it occurs in the Greek Bible. There the term is either a general label for Africa south of Egypt, or more specifically refers to ancient Nubia, the Kûsh of the Hebrew text. Thus it is a teaching of the Church today that Christianity was brought to the country by the so-called Ethiopian eunuch, the servant of the Meroitic (i.e., Nubian) Queen Candace, whose meeting with the Apostle Philip is recounted in Acts 8: 26–40. The reported evangelization and subsequent martyrdom of the Apostle Matthew in Ethiopia in the apocryphal *Gəbrä Ḥawaryat* (Ethiopian Acts of the Apostles), a tradition substantiated by the Roman Martyrology, also seeks to place the evangelization of the country in the earliest times. It is indeed not unlikely that small Christian communities existed in the early centuries of the Christian era, especially in the Aksumite capital and in Adulis, the principal sea port on the Red Sea coast, as Aksum's power and prosperity arose from its importance as a trading centre located on the crossroads of both African and Indian Ocean routes heading up the Red Sea to the Eastern Mediterranean. To date, however, no archaeological or other evidence of such probably very small and constantly changing communities has come to light.

It is only in the fourth century that we can be sure of the presence of the Christian Church in Ethiopia, with the official adoption of Christianity as the religion of the royal court, mostly probably in 333 during the patriarchate of Athanasius of Alexandria. The story of the conversion of the country is recounted first by Rufinus of Tyre (*c.*345–410), who had the story from Aedesius, one of the protagonists. Frumentius and his brother Aedesius, both native Christians from Tyre, were shipwrecked on the Red Sea coast. The two boys were taken as slaves to the royal court, and Frumentius became tutor to the king's son and Aedesius his cup-bearer. As members of the royal household and close companions to the royal family they were in an excellent position to teach the Christian faith, and a small community soon developed. Rufinus also mentions that 'Roman merchants who were Christians' were given increasing influence under Frumentius' tutelage. Upon the succession of their erstwhile student and companion, Aedesius returned to Tyre, but Frumentius went to Alexandria to seek a bishop for the growing Ethiopian community. Athanasius made him Bishop of Ethiopia and he returned to be the first in a long line of bishops appointed by the See of Alexandria. (See Munro-Hay 1997: 59–60 for the full account.) Versions of this story are repeated by other early writers, such as Theodoret of Cyrrhus and John of Nikiu, and it is also recounted in the Ethiopian *Sənkəsar* (Synaxarium). Archaeological support for the story is to be found in a most graphic way in the change of design on Aksumite coins from the pagan sun and crescent moon symbol to the cross, and the use in royal inscriptions of dedicatory phrases to the 'Lord of Heaven and Earth', replacing the old pagan dedications to the triad of gods, Maḥrəm, Bəḥer and Mədr. The choice of the term 'Lord of Heaven and Earth', and the absence of any overt mention of Christ, is probably not without significance.

The conversion of Ethiopia at this time was essentially a 'top-down' process, and the evidence is that the majority of the ordinary population retained their traditional religious beliefs and practices. It has been suggested that there might have been a political element in the conversion; Aksum was keen to preserve cordial relations with Constantinople, and it may have seemed expedient on an international front to show support so soon after Constantine's decision to make Christianity the official religion of the empire. At the same time, the ambiguous term in the inscriptions would not be too antagonistic to the home audience, since the names of the old pagan gods Bəḥer and Mədr can be translated as 'land' and 'earth', respectively. Indeed, the former is still retained in one of the Ethiopian names of God, Ǝgziabəher, literally 'lord of the land (or world)'.

It appears, then, that at first Christianity was essentially confined to the circle of the royal court, and the scriptures remained in Greek, a language certainly familiar at the time to the educated elite. It was not until the very end of the fifth and the beginning of the sixth century that the process of translating the scriptures into Ge'ez was begun. This event is associated with the arrival in Ethiopia of a group of holy men from 'Rome', i.e., various cities in the Eastern Mediterranean, remembered in Ethiopian tradition as the 'Nine Saints' or Ṣadəqan. These missionaries probably fled to Ethiopia to escape anti-Miaphysite persecution and seem to have come from various places in the Eastern Mediterranean: Constantinople, Syria, Cilicia, Caesarea. Several of their names reflect variously Greek- and Syriac-speaking origins: Päntalewon, Liqanos, 'Afṣe, 'Alef, Ṣəḥma, Guba, Yəm'ata, Gärima or Yəsḥaq, and Zä-Mika'el 'Arägawi (Sergew Hable Sellassie 1970: 115ff.). To them, and to other missionaries who are likely to have accompanied them, are attributed not only the translation of the Bible and other important texts, such as the Rule of Pachomius and probably the *De recta fide* of Cyril of Alexandria, but also the foundation of monasteries and the spreading of Christianity to the country areas away from the capital and the court. They came to occupy a cherished position in later hagiographical tradition, which surely testifies to their success in propagating the faith amongst ordinary Ethiopians. By the middle of the sixth century Aksum had become a major Christian power, such that Kaleb and his son Gäbrä Mäsqäl, two of the successors of the king who adopted Christianity, were able to mount military campaigns into Yemen at the request of Constantinople in defense of the Christians of Najran and Ṣan'a. The events of those campaigns are recalled in the Qur'an in the story of 'Abrəha and the Year of the Elephant.

The medieval period

The history of the Ethiopian Church in the years following the waning of Aksum's political power in the later sixth century is little known. The rise of Islam, and loss of Ethiopian control of the Red Sea coast, as well as economic factors all led the Christian kingdom to move its focus progressively further south into the Ethiopian highlands.

Ethiopia's relations with the nascent power of Islam are supposed by Arab historians to have been excellent. The Ethiopian kingdom was placed in Muslim tradition in the almost unique position of being a 'land of neutrality' or *dar al-hiyad*, and was not subject to attempts at conquest or conversion. This is explained by the Muslim *hadith* or tradition that the Aksumite king offered sanctuary to Muhammad's followers when the community was being persecuted, and by another *hadith* that the Aksumite king was so moved by the Prophet's revelations that he secretly converted to Islam. Muhammad himself is said to have mourned the Ethiopian king's death. Whatever the validity of these traditions, it is certain that Ethiopia remained Christian, unimpeded throughout the early centuries of Islam's expansion, and continued to receive its bishops from the Coptic patriarchate of Alexandria.

We know little of the spread of Christianity within Ethiopia during these years, but local traditions suggest a steady settlement by Christian families and building of churches as far south as northern Shoa, to the region where Addis Ababa now stands. This movement did not go unopposed by the indigenous pagan populations, however, and one of the most intriguing stories of this period of Ethiopian history concerns the legend of Queen Gudit (or Yodit, i.e., Judith) who led pagan resistance and destroyed the cathedral at Aksum. The troubles that befell the Christian kingdom in the tenth century through the activities of a pagan queen are confirmed by the Arab historian, Ibn Hawqal, and others (Munro-Hay 1997: 134–8). It is possible, to judge from later history, that various memories of resistance to the political and religious hegemony of the expanding Christian kingdom are conflated in this legend, and whatever the factual truth of the story the spread of Christianity in early medieval Ethiopia was far from a straightforward process. Hagiographies of the early medieval period, such as that of St Täklä Haymanot (1215–1313), one of the greatest and best-known Ethiopian saints, confirm the at times strong resistance to the spread of Christianity. Täklä Haymanot was born during the Zag^{w}e dynasty, which probably came to power in the preceding century, and which is associated with a renaissance in Christian culture. Two Zag^{w}e kings were later canonized by the Ethiopian Church; the most famous of them is Lalibäla, who is accredited with the founding of the famous collection of rock-hewn churches, the location of which now bears his name. Täklä Haymanot is also linked with the change of dynasty in 1269 or 1270 to the family of Yəkuno 'Amlak, the so-called Solomonic dynasty, of Amhara origin and claiming descent from the kings of Aksum and thence King Solomon and the Queen of Sheba, called Makədda in Ethiopian tradition.

It seems that during the centuries that the Christian kingdom was isolated from the rest of the Christian world except for its fragile links with the See of Alexandria, surrounded by pagan kingdoms and expanding Muslim sultanates to the south and southeast, there developed a sense of identity with the beleaguered Israel of the Old Testament. Christian Ethiopia came to see itself more and more as the inheritor of Israel and deliberately imitated Old Testament institutions. It was in this climate that the Ethiopian version of the Solomon and Sheba legend developed and was expanded, resulting in the national epic called the *Kəbrä Nägäst*, or Glory of the Kings, which probably reached its final form in the thirteenth century and which provided a literary apology for the incoming Solomonic dynasty as well as codifying the perception of Ethiopia as Israel.

Thus part of the story of Solomon and the Queen of Sheba in the Kəbrä Nägäst is the episode in which Mənilək, or Ibn Hakim, the son of their union, returned to Israel and brought back to Ethiopia forty Levites and the Ark of the Covenant. Ethiopia thus claimed to have adopted the Jewish religion before Christianity, something that cannot be substantiated, the presence of the Betä Əsra'el (Falashas) or so-called Ethiopian Jews and the existence of judaizing features in Ethiopian Christian practice notwithstanding.

During the fourteenth and fifteenth centuries the Christian kingdom continued to grow in power and size, coming into conflict with and overcoming many of the Muslim sultanates and small states to its south and south-east. This was also a period of great expansion in the Church, with the establishment of new monastic communities which formed the powerhouses of Christian culture and learning and provided the vanguard for the evangelization of newly acquired frontier regions. St Täklä Haymanot, who founded the monastery of Däbrä Libanos in what was then the southern borderlands of the Christian kingdom, has already been mentioned. He was a disciple of 'Iyäsus Mo'a (c.1211–92), who founded the monastery of Däbrä Hayq on the eastern edge of the home region of the Amharas, and another of his pupils, Ḥirutä 'Amlak, founded the island monastery of Däga 'Əsṭifanos on Lake Ṭana, on the then western frontier of the Christian kingdom (Stoffregen-Pedersen 1990: 16–19). Another great monastic leader of this period was 'Ewosṭatewos (1273–1352), who was active in the north of the kingdom, in what is now part of Eritrea. He is, however, perhaps best known as the founder of the movement which promoted the observation of two Sabbaths, Saturday as well as Sunday, for which he and his followers were persecuted by the orthodox Alexandrian party. 'Ewosṭatewos himself fled the country, spending the last fourteen years of his life in exile and dying in Armenia. After his death, many of his followers returned and together with those who had remained in Ethiopia consolidated their monastic base in the north, with many houses for nuns as well as for monks, which was unusual in the Ethiopian Church at the time.

This was indeed a fertile period for theological development in the Ethiopian Church, including the introduction of the cult of the Virgin Mary and the veneration of icons. Both of these features were introduced at the beginning of the fifteenth century, during the latter half of the reign of Dawit (r. 1380–1412), but they are perhaps more espe-cially associated with the reign of his son, Zär'a Ya'qob (r. 1434–68). In many ways, his reign marks the culmination of the expansionist developments in the Church during the preceding century and a half. The Church had been growing at a considerable rate, and the Christian faith had been imposed on erstwhile pagan peoples in the newly conquered lands without any great depth of teaching, such that many traditional beliefs and practices still remained with only a thin Christian veneer. Resort to diviners and sorcerers was common, and belief in spirits associated with prominent trees, moun-tains and expanses of water was often 'christianized' merely by association with a Christian saint. Polygamy was also widespread. Zär'a Ya'qob set about a reform of the Church to tackle not only these 'unchristian' practices, but also to address the growing divisions within the Church, typified by the rift with the followers of 'Ewosṭatewos, as well as others such as the followers of 'Əsṭifanos (d. c.1450), who refused to observe the cult of the Virgin Mary, which Zär'a Ya'qob himself championed. A compromise was reached with the followers of 'Ewosṭatewos, who were permitted to observe the two Sabbaths as long as they did not enter into conflict with those who did not wish to do so. In reforming the church, Zär'a Ya'qob's methods were at times brutal in their fervour, executing those whose pursued unorthodox practices, including his own son, and destroying their property. He also required Christians to bear as a mark of their orthodox faith the sign of the cross on their own persons as tattoos, and as a decorative design on their clothing and possessions. He was at the same time a scholar, and to him is attributed in Ethiopian tradition the *Mäṣḥafä Bərhan* or Book of Light, a major work of theology and canon law. Whether or not Zär'a Ya'qob was the author, this work was certainly written under his influence. A further indication of his deep interest in ecclesiastical affairs is his sending Ethiopian emissaries to the Council of Ferrara-Florence in 1438–41, which aimed to reunite the universal Church.

The sixteenth and seventeenth centuries

Without doubt, the most difficult and challenging period in the history of the Ethiopian Church was the sixteenth century. The Christian kingdom itself was nearly destroyed by the Muslim invasion led by Aḥmad ibn-Ibrahim al-Ghazi, known in Ethiopian tradition as Grañ, 'the left-handed', whose predominantly Somali and Afar armies with some Yemeni and Ottoman help swept through the Ethiopian highlands from the south-east between 1525 and 1543. Grañ's troops destroyed and looted churches, massacring anyone who refused to convert to Islam. For centuries there had been wars of attrition on the Ethiopian kingdom's eastern and south-eastern frontiers between Christians and Muslims, culminating in the founding of Harar as the major Muslim powerbase and centre of Islamic culture in the Horn of Africa, but it is probable that the arrival of the Ottomans in the Red Sea gave the impetus to these Muslim communities to mount the *jihad* against Ethiopia under Ahmäd Grañ.

In response to the invasion, the then king of Ethiopia, Ləbnä Dəngəl, appealed to the Portuguese for help. Ethiopia had been establishing contacts with first the Florentines and Rome and then the Portuguese since the second half of the fifteenth century, and reciprocal embassies had passed between Lisbon and the Ethiopian court. Ethiopian interest in Europe was as much prompted by a desire for technological advances, particularly in weapons and firearms. European interest in Ethiopia was rather fired by the legends of Prester John and the discovery of a potential Christian ally beyond the Islamic world. Portuguese help did not arrive until 1541, by which time Ləbnä Dəngəl was dead and his successor, Gälawdewos, was on the throne, but within two years Ahmäd Grañ was dead and his armies defeated and dispersed.

However, with the Portuguese came the Jesuits, since the Portuguese sought to act as agents of the See of Rome. Rome wished to bring Ethiopia within its fold, but failed fully to appreciate the history, nature and spiritual independence of the Ethiopian Church. The Jesuits were dismayed in particular by what they saw as the Jewish features of Ethiopian Christian practice and belief, but were initially unable to persuade the king and church leadership to alter their convictions. Following in the tradition of Ethiopian monarchs intimately concerned with religious questions, Gälawdewos

(r. 1540–59) rejected the primacy of Rome. He was moved to write a reply to Jesuit accusations against the Ethiopian Church, the confession of faith generally known as the *Confessio Claudii*, in which he clearly stated how Ethiopian beliefs and practices all had their roots in the scriptures (Ullendorff 1987). The Jesuit challenge was a bitter experience for the Ethiopian Church, and led eventually to civil war instigated by the clumsy dealings of the Jesuit Mendez, who lacked the tact and learning of his predecessor, Pero Paez. Paez had succeeded in persuading King Susnəyos (r. 1607–32) to convert, for which he was deposed and probably murdered by his son and successor, Fasilädäs (r. 1632–67), who later oversaw the expulsion of the Jesuits from Ethiopia. The country then virtually closed its doors on the West for a century and a half. The single positive result of the Jesuit experience, however, was that it forced the Ethiopian Church to re-examine its doctrinal position and define its own theology, a process that lasted nearly until the end of the nineteenth century. Out of this process arose a major renaissance in intellectual, artistic and literary activity in the Church.

The nineteenth century

From the second quarter of the eighteenth century onwards, the political structure of the Ethiopian kingdom fractured, and actual government rested in the hands of an array of local warlords and petty kings. It was not until one of these, Kasa of Qʷara, took the throne as Tewodros II in 1855 that political unity was restored. The succession of bishops sent from the See of Alexandria had always been precarious, but after a period of thirteen years without an *abunä*, or bishop, in 1841 the Ethiopian Church received an energetic young head in Abunä Sälama, who had attended a Protestant college in Cairo. Tewodros enlisted the help of Abunä Sälama in his political ambitions in return for undertaking a reform of the Church. By this period the Ethiopian Church was once again riven with doctrinal controversy, this time concerning the nature of Christ. The official doctrine was, and still is, the Alexandrian doctrine of *Täwahədo*. However, two other doctrines had developed in Ethiopia: that of *Qəbat* or 'unction', which taught that the full union of the two natures of Christ was only achieved at the time of his baptism, and *Yä-Şägga Ləjj* 'Son of Grace' which upheld the doctrine of *Sost Lədät* 'Three Births', which taught that Christ had been 'born' three times: eternally from the Father, in the flesh from the Virgin Mary, and as the incarnation through the Holy Spirit at the time of baptism. Tewodros imposed the official *Täwahədo* doctrine promoted by Abunä Sälama and the Alexandrian Church with brutal force. Like his predecessor Zär'a Ya'qob, who also sought reform of the Church, Tewodros was a deeply devout and learned man. Initially he retained good relations with the Church, and his reforms were genuinely meant to modernize what had become a huge and rambling institution, but his means of imposing reform ultimately led to his alienation from the Church and the people, and his imprisoning of Abunä Sälama, who died in captivity in 1867.

Tewodros's reign also saw the coming to a head of conflict with Protestant missionaries, who had been active in the country since earlier in the nineteenth century. Here the conflict, though, was not so much on religious grounds as due to a perceived slight by European governments, in particular the British, and the outcome was the Abyssinian Campaign of 1867–8 and Tewodros's suicide at his mountain fortress of Mäqdäla. After Tewodros's death the doctrine of *Sost Lədät* still had wide adherence, particularly in the south, in the kingdom of Shoa. In 1878 the then emperor, Yohannəs IV (r. 1872–89) and the king of Shoa, Sahlä Maryam, who had taken the historic name of Mənilək, held a council at Boru Meda which promulgated the Alexandrian teaching of *Täwahədo* and banned the *Sost Lədät* doctrine as heretical. Mənilək subsequently became Emperor of Ethiopia in 1889, and his reign, which lasted till 1913, saw the largest expansion of the Ethiopian state since the medieval period, bringing into the state many peoples who were not of the Christian tradition. Missionary work amongst these new subjects of the empire was encouraged by Mənilək and there was a concerted effort of church building, especially in those areas which had once been Christian but had been lost during the upheavals of the sixteenth century.

The twentieth century

At the beginning of the twentieth century a new wave of independence arose in the Ethiopian Church. Ever since Frumentius had been ordained the first Bishop of Ethiopia by Athanasius in the fourth century, the head of the Church had been an Egyptian appointed by the See of Alexandria. The anomaly of this situation, supported by a spurious addition to the Canon of Nicaea, was acutely felt by Ethiopians. It was also felt that reform and modernization of the Church could not be led by a foreign prelate who was more than likely ignorant of Ethiopia's history, traditions and language. With the death in 1926 of Abunä Mattewos, the last of the four bishops who had been appointed back in 1881, Ethiopia approached the See of Alexandria with the request that the new metropolitan should have the authority to consecrate native Ethiopian bishops. After a lengthy exchange, finally in 1929 Abunä Qerəllos was appointed as metropolitan, with the authority to consecrate five Ethiopian monks as diocesan bishops. During the Italian occupation (1935–41), two of the new Ethiopian bishops, Petros and Marqos, joined the resistance and were subsequently executed by the Italians. Later Qerəllos was deported to Rome, since he refused to participate in the Italians' plan to sever completely the Ethiopian Church's links with Alexandria, and the Italians installed a puppet *abunä*. After liberation in 1941, Qerəllos returned and re-opened negotiations with Alexandria about the granting of autonomy, and about the recent excommunication of bishops. Alexandria had excommunicated Abrəham, the first puppet *abunä*, who died in 1939, and his successor Yohannəs, and their followers, many of whom were as much victims of political events as real collaborators. In 1948 the Coptic Synod agreed amongst other things that after Qerəllos's death an Ethiopian metropolitan could be appointed. Qerəllos died in 1951 and Abunä Basəlyos, Bishop of Harar, became the first native Ethiopian head of the Ethiopian Church.

Undoubtedly, the greatest challenge to the Ethiopian Church in the twentieth century followed in the wake of the 1974 revolution. Although at the outset it was not a Marxist revolution, within the year power came into the hands of Colonel Mängəstu Haylä Maryam and the Revolutionary Committee, known as the *Därg*, which espoused

Marxist ideology. In 1975 the *Därg* disestablished the Church and nationalized a large part of its extensive lands, and in 1977 Tewoflos, who had succeeded Basəlyos in 1971, was arrested, imprisoned, and later executed. To replace him the *Därg* instructed the Synod to elect a new *abunä*, and a simple hermit monk was chosen who took the name of Täklä Haymanot. But Alexandria complained that it was illegal to appoint a new patriarch while his predecessor still lived or had not abdicated or been removed by the Synod for infringement of canon law, and so refused to recognize him. This marked a complete severance of relations between the Coptic Church and the Ethiopian. Täklä Haymanot died in 1988 and was replaced by Märqorewos, the erstwhile Bishop of Gondar, whose candidature had been suggested by the government. During the Marxist regime, though freedom of religious expression was an overtly declared policy, the Ethiopian Church suffered heavily, not only from the loss of a great deal of its lands and economic base, and interference in its governance, but also at the local level by some obstruction of ordinary worshippers. When the regime fell in 1991 and was replaced by a transitional government composed of erstwhile rebel movements, Abunä Märqorewos was removed from office by the Synod. A new *abunä* was elected in 1992 in the person of Pawlos, who had spent some time in exile in the United States. Märqorewos in turn fled Ethiopia and was followed by several bishops who had opposed his removal. These now live in the United States, where they set up an independent Synod and serve a large part of the Ethiopian Orthodox community resident outside Ethiopia, especially in North America.

After the collapse of the Marxist regime, Eritrea sought independence from Ethiopia, which was granted in May 1993. That same year the Church in Eritrea petitioned Pope Shenouda III to return to the jurisdiction of the Coptic Church in Egypt, who granted the petition with the agreement of the Ethiopian Orthodox Church. In Cairo in 1994 Shenouda ordained five new bishops for the Eritrean Church, and in 1998 Abba Filəppos, Bishop of Asmara, was elected as the first patriarch of the Eritrean Orthodox Church.

Doctrine

The label 'Monophysite' is rejected by the Ethiopian Church as an inaccurate reflection of the unionist Christology that they follow (hence the title of the official doctrine as *Täwahədo*, literally 'union'), which is supported by the teaching of Cyril of Alexandria. Historically, because of its linkage with the See of Alexandria, and also the strong Syrian influence in the early Ethiopian Church, Ethiopia joined the Copts, Jacobite Syrians and the Armenians in rejecting the Council of Chalcedon in 451. Owing to its relative isolation, the Ethiopian Church did not participate in the polemics arising from Chalcedon, which, for example, so exercised the Syrian Orthodox and Armenian Churches. Instead, Ethiopian theology developed quite independently from what was happening elsewhere in the Eastern Churches, and only the presence of the *abunä* sent from Egypt acted as an occasional restraint.

Nevertheless, the Ethiopian Church did have its own theological controversies, which at times led to bitter dispute and even violence, as we have seen in the historical discussion. The question of the observance of two Sabbaths, Saturday according to Old Testament practice and Sunday according to the New Testament, is perhaps the most enduring Ethiopian theological diversion from traditional practice. The origin of two Sabbath observance is associated with the monk 'Ewosṭatewos, who came from Gär'alta in the north of Ethiopia, and it is especially in the north that the followers of 'Ewosṭatewos gained most support. The movement came to have regional significance, as tensions between north and south, Tigreans and Amharas, had and has long been a feature of Ethiopian history. Although 'Ewosṭatewos was exiled, his movement lived on as one of the major monastic houses of Ethiopia, and it still has its followers today.

Another major 'heresy' of the Ethiopian Church, which arose around the same time, was espoused by the followers of 'Ǝsṭifanos (d. c.1450), who not only followed 'Ewosṭatewos in observing two Sabbaths, but also insisted on devotion solely to the persons of the Trinity. By refusing to prostrate themselves before images of the Virgin and Child they thus came into conflict with the mainstream Church, which at that time under Zär'a Ya'qob was promoting the cult of the Virgin Mary. They also disassociated themselves from the practice whereby every Christian was to have an individual Father Confessor, another of Zär'a Ya'qob's religious reforms. For these refusals they were persecuted and after several leading followers of 'Ǝsṭifanos were executed, the movement died out.

It was perhaps the presence of the Jesuits in the later sixteenth and early seventeenth centuries, however, that provided the seed for major controversies in Christological thought in the Ethiopian Church. In the centuries following the expulsion of the Jesuits, the two movements or heresies, Qǝbat or 'Unction', and Yä-Ṣägga Lǝjj or 'Son of Grace' with its adherence to the doctrine of Sost Lǝdät, 'Three Births', came into being, as we have seen above. The former arose in the eustathian monasteries in the province of Gojjam, and held that the full union of the human and divine natures of Christ was only realized at the time of baptism in the Jordan. This laid the followers of Qǝbat open to the ancient heresy that Christ was an ordinary man 'adopted' by God with the implied denial of his divinity and virgin birth. The Orthodox Täwahǝdo Church insisted on the co-eternity of the three persons of the Trinity in that 'the Son Himself is the one who anoints, the Son Himself is the one who is anointed, and the Son Himself is the anointment' (Stoffregen-Pedersen 1990: 49–50). The heresy of Yä-Ṣägga Lǝjj or 'Son of Grace' arose in the other monastic movement, in the monastery of Täklä Haymanot at Azäzo, near Gondar, and adopted the view that Christ became the Son of God by the grace of the Holy Spirit, and thus led itself to be linked with the controversy of the 'Three Births' or Sost Lǝdät, which was described above. By contrast the official Alexandrian Christology became known as Karra or 'Knife' because it 'cut off' the third 'birth' from the Holy Spirit.

Judaic features

One of the most notable features of Ethiopian Christianity that has impressed itself on travellers, including the Jesuits, is the presence of a number of practices that may be identified as 'judaic' or 'Jewish-like'. The observance of a Saturday Sabbath has already been mentioned. Others are the circumcision of infant males on the eighth day, dietary laws especially regarding the eating of pork and the proper slaughter of animals for food, and rules of ritual cleanliness, for instance in regard to entering a church and participating in the Eucharist. The performance of the church service with ritual dance by the *däbtäras* (see 'Priesthood and Hierarchy', below) has also been likened to King David dancing before the Ark. Some of these features may be practices inherited from the early Eastern Church, especially other Semitic churches such as the Syrian. Others are certainly due to internal developments within the Ethiopian Church, which venerates the Old Testament perhaps more than other Churches. This veneration has often led to a literal application of Old Testament laws and practices, and is further reflected in the position that Ethiopia has adopted at least since the early medieval period as the successor of ancient Israel. It is externalized both through the belief that Ethiopia possesses the Ark of the Covenant, said to be housed in a chapel close by the ancient cathedral of St Mary of Zion in Aksum, and in the traditions of the epic *Kəbrä Nägäst* or 'Glory of the Kings', which traces the Ethiopian royal line back to the union of Solomon and the Queen of Sheba. Regard for the Old Testament is also seen in the use of such nomenclature as *Däqiqä Ǝsra'el*, 'Children of Israel' and *Betä Ǝsra'el*, 'House of Israel' (Ullendorff 1968: esp. 73–115).

Incidentally, this tendency of the Ethiopian Church to imitate the Old Testament probably lies behind the origin of the so-called Ethiopian Jews or *Falashas*. The Amharic term *fälaša* and its Ge'ez antecedent *fälasi*, literally 'wanderer', was used to refer to anyone outside the pale of the orthodox Christian kingdom, secular or religious, exile or wandering holy man or heretic. Similarly, the term *ayhud*, 'Jew', was also used to refer to political or religious dissenters. The Ethiopian Jews, who refer to themselves as *Betä Ǝsra'el*, can only be recognized as such from the fourteenth and fifteenth centuries onwards, and seemingly owe all their major institutions, including monasticism and their scriptures, to the activity of renegade Christian monks or *fälasi*. It has been suggested that the Ethiopian Jews are another example of an Ethiopian 'heresy', arising on the frontiers of the political and ecclesiastical state, which voluntarily judaized to the extent that it refuted the Messiah in Jesus (Kaplan 1992: 77–8).

Scriptures and Literature

Ethiopian Christian literature is often said to be essentially a literature of translation. It is true that a good part of this literature, particularly from the earlier centuries of Christianity in Ethiopia, is translated. Thus, aside from the Bible itself, which was translated in the first instance from the Greek over an extended period from the late fifth to the late seventh century, if the traditional completion date of 678 is accepted, other translations were made during the same period. For instance, the *De recta fide* (*Haymanot Rətə't* in Ge'ez) of Cyril Alexandria, together with other writings by Cyril and a number of other patristic texts collectively known as the *Qerəllos*, forms one of the primary theological source texts of the Ethiopian Church. Other Christian literature that was translated during Aksumite times includes the Rule of Pachomius, a number of hagiographical works such as the Life of St Paul of Thebes, known as the *Gädlä 'Azqir*, and from secular works, the Physiologus or *Fisalgos*.

The Ethiopian text of the Old Testament was initially translated from the Greek Septuagint, but shows signs of later revision from a Syriac source, and the New Testament was translated from the Lucianic recension of the Greek Bible, which was prevalent in the See of Antioch. Both of these are strongly indicative of the Syrian influences on the early Ethiopian Church, and seem to confirm the tradition that the Nine Saints were involved in the first translations of the Bible into Ge'ez. Additionally, the whole text of the Ethiopian Bible underwent a further revision in the thirteenth and fourteenth centuries on the basis of Coptic-Arabic versions, most prominently during the long episcopate (1348–88) of Abunä Sälama the Translator, the cognomen of Fiqṭor I. The Ethiopian Bible contains a number of books not found in the western canon, including the so-called deuterocanonical books, such as the Ascension of Isaiah and the Paralipomena of Baruch, as well as the Books of Noah, Ezra, Nehemiah, Maccabees, Moses and Tobit; in addition to these it also adds a couple of books unique to the Ethiopian canon: the Book of Enoch, the complete version of which now only exists in the Ge'ez translation, and the Book of Jubilees, also known as Deutero-Genesis or *Kufale* in Ge'ez. The Ethiopian New Testament contains 35 books, uniquely including The Shepherd of Hermas. It should also be borne in mind that, as with several other Eastern Churches, there is no definitive canonical text of the Ethiopian Bible.

The fourteenth and fifteenth centuries, particularly the reigns of 'Amdä Ṣəyon (1314–44) and Zär'a Ya'qob (1434–68), saw a resurgence of translation activity, this time from Coptic literature in Arabic: liturgical texts such as the Coptic Horologion, *Mäṣhafä Sä'atat*, the Rites for the Dead, *Mäṣhafä Gənzät*, the Lectionary for Holy Week, *Gəbrä Ḥəmamat*, the Homilies of John Chrysostom and Jacob of Sarug, and the Praise of Mary, *Wəddase Maryam*, and also a large number of hagiographies, of Coptic and other Eastern saints, martyrs and Church Fathers, and so on. From the same period indigenous hagiographies, *gädlat*, or 'struggles' in Ge'ez, also start to be written, such as those of Täklä Haymanot, 'Iyäsus Mo'a and Bäṣälotä Mika'el, to name but the most famous. The great Alexandrian Synaxarium or *Sənkəsar* was also translated by the end of 'Amdä Ṣəyon's reign and was soon greatly expanded by the addition of commemorative chapters on Ethiopian saints. Over the next century, other major texts such as the Didascalia, the Harp (or Organ) of the Virgin Mary, better known by its Ge'ez name *'Arganon*, and the Miracles of Mary, *Tä'ammərä Maryam*, were translated. The latter genre provided one of the most fertile grounds for Ethiopian literature: the original text of the Miracles of Mary contained 32 miracles, but the largest known Ethiopian collections to date comprise over 300. Collections of miracles, of Jesus Christ and other leading saints of the Ethiopian Church, such as St Michael the Archangel, are among the most popular types of religious literature even today. Another popular devotional genre, poetry or hymns known as *mälkə'* or 'likeness', particularly in praise of Jesus Christ or the Virgin Mary, also originated in this period, as did the religious poetry known as *qəne* which makes use of allusion and double meaning. Aside from hagiographies, original works of this period are such as the Book of Mysteries, *Mäṣḥafä Məṣṭir*, the Book of the Nativity, *Mäṣḥafä Lədät*, and the magical work, The Disciples, or *'Ardə't*. Often ascribed to King Zär'a Ya'qob himself, or certainly composed under his direct influence, is the apologetic work known as the Book of Light, *Mäṣḥafä Bərhan*. The great collection of apologetic and doctrinal writings of the Church Fathers known as the Faith of the Fathers, or *Haymanotä 'Abäw*, was translated from Arabic at the end of the fifteenth century. It has also been suggested that the basic liturgical works, the *Mə'raf* and the *Mäwasə't* were composed only at the very end of the thirteenth century, although they are ascribed to the sixth century St Yared, the traditional creator of Ethiopian sacred music and chant. From later literature, the anti-Islamic apologetic, the Gate of Faith or *'Anqäṣä 'Amin*, written by the Yemeni convert 'Ǝnbaqom, who became the Abbot of the great monastery of Däbrä Libanos, also deserves mention.

Lastly, an enormous body of biblical exegesis and theology of the Ethiopian Church is transmitted orally in the traditional system of *andəmta* commentary, which takes its name from the Amharic *andəm* 'and one [says]', which often introduces the Amharic paraphrase and discussion of each Ge'ez phrase from scripture analysed. Only a small part of this exegetical tradition has been written down and consequently become known to western scholars (Cowley 1988).

Priesthood and Hierarchy

The basis for the regulation of ecclesiastical affairs is the text called The Laws of the Kings, or *Fətḥa Nägäst*, a translation of the Arabic Nomocanon by the Coptic scholar al-'Assāl, and the highest body of the Church is the Holy Synod, or *Qəddus Sinodos*. The highest office in the Church is that occupied in the past by the bishop or metropolitan appointed by the See of Alexandria. The office nowadays carries the title of Patriarch. The Ge'ez term *abunä*, sometimes shortened to *abun*, literally 'our father', is commonly applied to this office, though it was also applied to any notable holy man or saint. The official title of the patriarch is 'The Blessed and Holy Abunä, the Archbishop and Patriarch of Ethiopia', *Bəṣu' wä-Qəddus 'Abunä Rə'sä Liqanä Pappasat wä-Patriyark zä-Ityoppəya*. The *abunä* was the only official empowered to ordain priests, and thus in the past there was often a crisis in the priesthood in the interregna between *abunäs* sent from Egypt. Today, there are positions for eighteen archbishops (*liqä pappasat*) and bishops (*pappas*), as well as the category of auxiliary bishop or *episqopos*. Formerly, these were limited to seven in number by the pseudo-canon of Nicaea, to prevent Ethiopia from consecrating its own *abunä*. During these centuries of Egyptian control over the office of metropolitan, the leading indigenous Ethiopian office was that of the Abbot of the Monastery of Hayq, and later of Däbrä Libanos, known by the name *Ǝčäge*, who held all monastic communities under his jurisdiction. Since 1951 the offices of *abunä* and *Ǝčäge* have been merged. Married men may be ordained as priest (*qes* in Amharic, *qäšši* in Tigrinya, and *qäsis* or *kahən* in Ge'ez) or deacon, though may not marry after ordination. Bishops and monks are required to be celibate. The priest usually dresses in white with a *šämma*, or the white toga-like garment of traditional

Ethiopian attire with a simple embroidered hem, thrown across his shoulders. He also wears a distinctive white turban. Today bishops dress differently, entirely in black, not unlike their Coptic peers. The lowest rank of ordination is that of the deacon or *diyaqon*.

A peculiarly Ethiopian office in the church hierarchy is that of the *däbtära*, an unordained officiant whose role in performing the liturgy is not unlike that of the Greek *psaltēs*. However, the *däbtära* also has the role of administrator, scribe and scholar, who may also use his skills in preparing amulets and in traditional medicine and divination, which sometimes imbues him with an ambiguous reputation, serving what have been called both the 'licit' and the 'illicit' aspects of religion (Kaufmann Shelemay 1992). The education of a *däbtära* is generally longer than that or an ordinary priest, as he is often trained not only in liturgical music and dance, but also in religious poetry, canon law and theology, as well as in Ge'ez, the language of the Church. Historically, it has been suggested that the division of roles between priest and *däbtära* reflects the division of the Israelite priesthood into priest (*kōhēn*) and Levite.

In 1970 one census of church officials showed that there were 60,972 priests, 56,687 deacons and 39,010 *däbtäras* (Sergew Hable Sellassie 1970: 61). Another set of statistics from the same year, however, speaks of 75,839 priests, 67,082 deacons and 48,269 *däbtäras* (Aymro Wondmagegnehu and Joachim Motovu 1970: 125). All churches must have at least two officiating priests and several *däbtäras*, sometimes as many as eight or ten. Larger churches will also have more than two priests, fulfilling various offices, including that of *gäbäz* (or *qesä gäbäz*), who are responsible for managing the economic affairs of the church. The clergy were traditionally maintained by a combination of tithes (in kind or nowadays in money) from the local community, individual donations and gifts, and produce from the land owned by the church.

Monasticism

Monasteries have always played an important role in the Ethiopian Church since the introduction of monasticism, traditionally associated with the Nine Saints, and the oldest monasteries in the country are held to have been founded by them. The famous monastery of Däbrä Damo, north-east of the ancient capital of Aksum, was founded by Zä-Mika'el 'Arägawi at the beginning of the sixth century. Built atop a flat-topped plateau, or *amba*, with near vertical sides, it is even today only accessible to people who are hauled up with ropes. It was, however, the thirteenth and fourteenth centuries that saw the greatest expansion in Ethiopian monasticism under the leadership of some of Ethiopia's most illustrious saints, such as 'Iyäsus Mo'a, Täklä Haymanot, 'Ewostatewos and Bäṣälotä Mika'el. 'Iyäsus Mo'a (d. c.1292), who was at first a member of the monastic community at Däbrä Damo, later founded the famous monastery of Däbrä Hayq, on an island in the middle of Lake Hayq, near the edge of the eastern escarpment. From here other monasteries were established, such as the most renowned of Ethiopia's houses, that of Däbrä Libanos founded by Täklä Haymanot, who was a pupil of 'Iyäsus Mo'a. Incidentally, the word *däbr*, which figures in the name of almost all monasteries, is used to describe both a monastery and a large church, and its original meaning of 'mountain' in Ge'ez doubtless reflects the preferred location for monasteries and churches. Larger monasteries are called *gädam*, a term which in Ge'ez also meant 'wilderness'.

Today, monastic houses in Ethiopia fall into two traditions, that of Täklä Haymanot and that of 'Ewosṭatewos. Both traditions, however, base their organization on the Rule of Pachomius. Just before the revolution of 1974, it was estimated that there were over 800 establishments for men, often linked with one for women. Many of these were very small, with a dozen and a half or fewer members, though the very largest monasteries housed several hundred monks and nuns.

As in other orthodox traditions, Ethiopian monasteries can be divided into coenobitic communities that favour communal life, and those that emphasize the idiorrhythmic or individual ascetic way of life. It is additionally not uncommon for a monk or nun, living in a coenobitic community, to decide to withdraw from communal life and move away from the monastery. Traditionally, this retreat would be into an uninhabited and remote place, but since the latter part of the twentieth century there has been a movement for individual monks or nuns to establish themselves in towns and cities, while still maintaining their monastic and religious life. Ethiopian monasticism shows a remarkable degree of flexibility in respect of how an individual elects to pursue his or her calling, or indeed when they enter or leave a monastic community. Whilst many individuals may enter a monastery while still young, and traditionally children could be dedicated to the monastic life by their parents as part of a vow, others become monks or nuns only late in life, typically after being widowed. Larger monastic communities are governed by an elected council, or *guba'e*, 'synod', which in turn elects an abbot or *mämhər*, a term which also means 'teacher'. In the past, the appointment of abbots to the largest and most prestigious monasteries needed the approval of the emperor. The process of becoming a monk falls into three stages: after a period of novitiate which may last several years, the three vows of obedience, chastity and poverty are taken in succession, and at each stage the monk is invested firstly with the belt or girdle, *qənat*, a band wound round the waist and crossing the chest to make a cross pattern, secondly with the cap, *qob*, and lastly with the scapular, *askema*, usually made of braided leather and decorated with twelve crosses.

Monasteries have always been seen as the centres of Christian learning in Ethiopia, and many of the schools of higher learning are located either in or adjacent to monasteries. These higher schools fall into three brackets: the *Zema Bet*, or school of religious music and chant, the *Qəne Bet*, or school of religious poetry, and the *Mäṣhaf Bet*, or school of religious commentary. Particular monasteries have reputations as the preferred school for different studies, Däbrä Wärq, for instance, in the former province of Gojjam being famous as one of the best centres for the study of religious poetry. Monasteries have also been the repositories of valuable manuscripts, some dating back to as early as the twelfth and thirteenth centuries, and other works of religious art, such as metal processional crosses, thuribles and royal crowns, as well as icons and wall paintings. Often circumstances do not provide the ideal conditions for the proper conservation of such objects, and today there is much concern about the damage being suffered by these works of art.

Liturgy and Sacraments

The eucharistic liturgy

The principal Ethiopian liturgy is the eucharistic Mass or *qəddase*, for the celebration of which two priests and at least three deacons are required, and which runs for several hours and is conducted mostly in Ge'ez with only the readings and nowadays certain portions of the liturgy in the vernacular. The first part of the Mass, which retains the form of the ancient Mass of the Catachumens, includes recitations from the Psalms, chanted prayers and usually four readings, from the Pauline Epistles, from the non-Pauline Epistles, from the Acts of the Apostles, and from the Gospels. The second part of the Mass centres on the anaphoras, which vary according to the liturgical calendar, and is called the *fəre qəddase*, 'fruit of the Mass', or the *'akʷätetä qʷərban*, 'the sacrifice of the Eucharist'. There are uniquely fourteen anaphoras in use in the Ethiopian Church, of which the one in most common use is the Anaphora of the Twelve Apostles. The others are that of Our Lord Jesus Christ, St John Boanerges, St Mary, the Three Hundred, St Athanasius, St Basil, St Gregory of Nyssa, St Epiphanius, St John Chrysostom, St Cyril, St Jacob of Serug, St Dioscorus and St Gregory the Thaumaturge. Communion is preceded by a long prayer of penitence and 44 repetitions of the formula 'Lord, have mercy on us, O Christ.' Communion is only infrequently taken by adult Ethiopians, as participating in the Eucharist requires an exceptional state of ritual purity. Children under the age of puberty, on the other hand, receive communion more frequently, as they are more likely not to have incurred ritual impurity. Likewise, monks and nuns are accustomed to receive communion more frequently than the laity.

The service in the Ethiopian Church takes place both inside and outside the church building, incorporating on occasions the ambulatory or covered walkway which surrounds the typical Ethiopian church. The most sacred part of the service, however, the offering of the Eucharist, is performed in the Sanctuary which lies at the centre of the church.

The divine office and horologium (hours)

Other liturgical offices, which also require the participation of *däbtäras*, are celebrated in cathedrals and major churches on special feast days of the liturgical year. There are three categories of such services: *wazema*, or solemn vespers, lasting four to five hours on the eve of feast days; *mäwäddəs*, the night office before Sunday; and *səbḥatä nägh*, which corresponds to matins and lauds in western tradition. Additional offices may also be performed during special periods, such as Lent. The hours or *sä'atat* are not restricted to monastic use, but are also performed in the larger churches, sometimes in the ambulatory whilst a different service is being conducted inside the church. There are three collections of hours still in use in the Ethiopian Church: the Hours of the Copts, which is an expanded version of that used in the Coptic Church; the Hours of the Psalter, which comprises the Psalms and the 15 Canticles of the Prophets, including the Magnificat and the Canticles of Moses; and the hours of Abba Giyorgis Säglawi, an Ethiopian scholar (d. *c*.1426). The latter are chanted daily in monasteries and the larger churches.

The sacraments

Like the other Oriental Orthodox Churches the Ethiopian Church recognizes seven sacraments: baptism, confirmation, communion, confession, matrimony, unction of the sick and holy orders. Baptism or *Ṭəmqät* normally takes the form of infant baptism, 40 days after birth for boys and 80 days for girls, until which time the mother is considered to be in a state of ritual impurity. Adult baptism may also occur for converts, usually after a period of three years as a catechumen. Baptism takes the form of three total immersions, and a baptismal name is given. Ethiopians normally keep a secular name, which is used in everyday life, separately from their baptismal name. The newly baptised also receives a coloured thread called a *matäb*, which is worn around the neck, sometimes with a small cross attached. Following immediately on baptism is the rite of confirmation, called *qəb'atä meron* or 'annointment with chrism', after which communion is celebrated. Communion or *qʷərban* is, as said above (see 'The eucharistic liturgy'), regularly taken only by children and clerics. The wine is made by a deacon from dried grapes steeped in water, which together with the bread, which is leaven, is prepared in a separate building adjacent to the church, called the *Betä Ləhem* or Bethlehem. Communion is delivered by the officiating priest and deacons from the Holy of Holies, which they alone may enter. In respect of confession or *nəssəha*, each member of the church is assigned his or her individual father confessor, called in Amharic *yä-näfs abbat* or 'soul father', who usually visits his charge at home, and who thus plays an important role in family life. Marriage in the Church or *täklil* is only one of the forms of matrimony in Ethiopian tradition. Full or sacramental matrimony, which is sealed with the taking of communion by both parties, is indissoluble and remarriage may only occur after the death of one partner. For this reason, there exists a number of types of secular marriage contract, some of which may be quite temporary, and all of which are dissoluble according to customary law. The Church consequently does not recognize these, and regards couples married in this way as excommunicate and thus excluded from taking communion, though they may attend services. Unction of the sick, called *qändil* after the book which contains the rite, the *Mäṣhafä Qändil* or 'Book of the Lamp', is in practice not often performed. In the case of death, interment normally takes place on the same or the following day, and is marked by the Office of the Dead or *Fəthat*. Memorial services with offering of the Eucharist take place on the seventh, thirtieth and fortieth days after death. These are accompanied by a commemorative feast, called *täzkar*, for all the participants. Lastly, the giving of Holy Orders, or *qəddus kəhnät*, is also recognized by the Ethiopian Church as a sacrament. No unordained person may administer the sacraments, in particular the celebration of the Eucharist, or conduct religious services. As only a bishop may ordain a priest or a deacon, there were often disruptions in the past in the availability of properly trained clergy, owing to the intermittent arrival of *abunäs* sent by Alexandria. Since 1951, however, priests have been ordained by native Ethiopian bishops.

Church Buildings

The oldest surviving churches in Ethiopia, which probably date back to Late Aksumite times, preserve the original rectangular basilica style that was introduced from the eastern Mediterranean. This same style is also found in the famous rock-cut churches of Lalibäla (see next section). Most church buildings in Ethiopia today are, however, circular or octagonal in shape, and as such are probably simply larger versions of the normal domestic architectural style of the highlands. These churches, usually built on slight elevations and surrounded by a grove of trees, traditionally have thatched roofs surmounted by an ostrich egg shell or an inverted pot and a cross. Churches also normally stand within a compound which contains other buildings, such as the treasury or store house, and the *Betä Ləhem*, where the eucharistic wine and bread are prepared. The main church building is also generally surrounded by an ambulatory under the shade of the heavily overhanging eaves.

The most distinctive feature of Ethiopian church architecture, however, is the interior. This has a tripartite structure, which in the typical round church takes the form of three concentric rings with the usually square Sanctuary, *Mäqdäs*, in the centre. Here is located the Holy of Holies, *Qəddusä* (or *Qəddəstä*) *Qəddusan*, the interior of which is shielded from public view by a curtain drawn across the doorway. Only the priests and deacons may enter the Holy of Holies. Within the Holy of Holies is housed the *tabot*, a representation of the Ark of the Covenant, the original of which Ethiopian tradition says is kept at the Cathedral of St Mary of Zion in Aksum. It is the presence of the *tabot* which consecrates an Ethiopian church. The *tabot* takes the form of a large tablet of wood carved with a cruciform design, the text of the Ten Commandments, and the dedication to the saint in whose name the church is consecrated. On feast days the *tabot* is brought out of the church, wrapped in rich brocades and carried on the heads of the priests. At other times the *tabot* sits on a stand, known as the *Mänbärä Tabot*, or 'Seat of the Tabot', within the Sanctuary. The next ring is known as the *Qəddəst*, and is where communion is offered to the laity. The outermost ring of the church is the *Qəne Mahlet*, or 'Choir', where the liturgy is performed and the congregation stand. There are normally partitions to separate male and female worshippers. Those worshippers who are not in the correct state of ritual purity to enter the church may stand outside in the ambulatory or in the grounds of the church compound to hear the service. The interior walls of the church, particularly of the Sanctuary, are usually covered with wall paintings or hung with icons.

Cave churches and rock–cut churches

During the medieval period, and probably already in Late Aksumite times, there developed the habit of building churches within large caves. Perhaps from this developed the practice first of enclosing cave openings and building a church behind, and then of actually cutting into the rock face to carve out a church, or cutting down into the bedrock to construct a subterranean church. The most famous of these monolithic churches are indubitably those of Lalibäla, though similar churches do exist all over the Central Highlands. The Lalibäla churches are believed to have been constructed in imitation of the holy places of Jerusalem as a substitute place of pilgrimage when travel to the Holy Land proved too arduous and difficult. The Lalibäla churches copy exactly the features of normal church architecture of the period, including interior columns, windows and relief decoration on the walls and vaulted ceilings.

The Church Year, Pilgrimages and Local Practice

The calendar

The Ethiopian calendar follows the primitive Alexandrine Computus, though as many month names suggest, this probably came to Ethiopia in pre-Christian times. Today the year, which begins around 11 September, is normally calculated according to the Year of Mercy, or ʿAmätä Mǝḥrät, calculation of which is seven and eight years behind the Common Era. Other systems are used, especially in ecclesiastical circles, including the Year of the Martyrs, starting from the persecutions of Diocletian in 284 CE. Each year is also consecutively assigned to one of the Evangelists. Most of the feasts of the Ethiopian Church are in accord with those of other Eastern churches, with the Feast of the Cross, Mäsqäl, and Epiphany, Ṭǝmqät, being given particular prominence. Commemorative feast days for saints are also observed with special devotion, with all the saints having their annual feasts, and the more popular saints such as the Virgin Mary and the Archangels having in addition regular monthly feast days. For instance, there are ten principal and six secondary feasts of Our Lord each year, and four regular monthly feasts: Trinity on the seventh of each month, the Feast of the Cross on the tenth, the Passion on the twenty-seventh, and the Nativity on the twenty-ninth.

Pilgrimages

Pilgrimages are very popular and a major part of life in Ethiopia, among both Christians and Muslims. Ancient monasteries and tombs of saints are regularly visited by the devout, especially on appropriate feast days. One of the two most frequently visited pilgrimage sites are the shrine of St Gäbrä Mänfäs Qǝddus, popularly known as Abbo, atop the extinct volcano, Mt Zǝqʷala, south of Addis Ababa. As with other holy sites, the presence of water here in the form of a crater lake may suggest a locus of pilgrimage that predates the introduction of Christianity. The other is the great church of St Gabriel at Qullǝbi near Harar. The Holy Land is, however, the ultimate goal of the pilgrim, and the Ethiopian Church has had foundations in Jerusalem and along the Jordan Valley since its early years.

References and further reading

Aymro Wondmagegnehu and Motovu, J. (1970) *The Ethiopian Orthodox Church*. Addis Ababa: Ethiopian Orthodox Mission.

Chaillot, C. (2002) *The Ethiopian Orthodox Tewahedo Church Tradition*. Paris: Inter-Orthodox Dialogue.

Cowley, R. (1988) *Ethiopian Biblical Interpretation: A Study in Exegetical Tradition and Hermeneutics*. Cambridge: Cambridge University Press.

Getatchew Haile, Sevir Chernetsov, Nosnitsin, D. and Chaillot, C. (2006) Ethiopian Orthodox (*Täwahedo*) Church. In S. Uhlig (ed.) *Encyclopaedia Aethiopia*, vol. 2 (pp. 414–32). Wiesbaden: Harrassowitz Verlag.

Getnet Tamene (1998) Features of the Ethiopian Orthodox Church and the clergy. *Asian and African Studies* 7(1): 87–104.

Kaplan, S. (1984) *The Monastic Holy Man and the Christianization of Early Solomonic Ethiopia*. Wiesbaden: Franz Steiner Verlag.

—— (1992) *The Beta Israel (Falasha) in Ethiopia*. New York and London: New York University Press.

Kaufhold, H. (ed.) (2007) *Kleines Lexikon des Christlichen Orients*. Wiesbaden: Harrassowitz.

Kaufman Shelemay, K. (1992) The musician and transmission of religious tradition: the multiple roles of the Ethiopian *däbtära*. *Journal of Religion in Africa* 22(3): 242–60.

Munro-Hay, S. C. (1997) *Ethiopia and Alexandria: The Metropolitan Episcopacy of Ethiopia*. Bibliotheca nubica et aethiopica. Schriftenreihe zur Kulturgeschichte des Raumes um das Rote Meer 5. Warsaw and Wiesbaden: Bibliotheca nubica et aethiopica.

Sergew Hable Sellassie (ed.) (1970) *The Church of Ethiopia: A Panorama of History and Spiritual Life*. Addis Ababa: Ethiopian Orthodox Church.

—— (1972) *Ancient and Medieval Ethiopian History till 1270*. Addis Ababa: United Printers.

Stoffregen-Pedersen, K. (1990) *Les Éthiopiens*. Fils d'Abraham IX. Brussels: Brepols.

Ullendorff, E. (1968) *Ethiopia and the Bible* (The Schweich Lectures 1967). London: Oxford University Press for the British Academy.

—— (1987) The *Confessio Fidei* of King Claudius of Ethiopia. *Journal of Semitic Studies* 32: 159–76.

CHAPTER 7
Georgian Christianity

Stephen H. Rapp, Jr.

Introduction

Caucasia, the territory bounded by the Black and Caspian Seas and taking its name from the Caucasus Mountains, has been a vibrant centre of Christianity since late antiquity. By the reign of Constantine the Great, monarchs of the eastern Georgian district of K'art'li (Greek Iberia) and Armenia had already embraced the Christian God; soon afterwards Christianity also took root in nearby Lazika/Colchis and Caucasian Albania. As Cyril Toumanoff (1963) and others have demonstrated, in many respects early Christian Caucasia constituted a single historical and socio-cultural unit. However, divergent responses to the imperial contest for Caucasia and the processes leading to the establishment of separate Armenian and K'art'velian 'national' churches ultimately led to a clear religious break, beginning in the early seventh century. Despite this ecclesiastical estrangement, Armeno–Georgian relations have endured to the present day, not least because of the shared experience of invasion and conquest by foreign imperial powers as well as the persistence of the extensive, bicultural Armeno–Georgian frontier zone. Any investigation of Christianity in Georgia must therefore take into consideration the history of neighbouring lands, especially Armenia.

The Early Period

The Georgian Orthodox Church is one of the several 'national' churches of Eastern Christianity and officially traces its foundation to the alleged evangelization of western Georgia by the apostle Andrew and his companion Simon 'the Canaanite'. But this is a late tradition. The Andrew legend began to take root in Byzantium only in the ninth century, largely in response to the special apostolic authority claimed by the papacy. Embellished stories about Andrew's travels quickly spread throughout eastern Christendom. Within a century or two they were embraced and further expanded by Georgian monks working in places such as Mount Athos and St Catherine's monastery on Mount Sinai.

Several lines of archaeological evidence, including burials, have shown beyond any doubt that a small Christian presence already existed in eastern Georgia in the third century. It is possible that some Jewish colonists in the K'art'velian cities of Urbnisi and Mc'xet'a (Mtskheta), the royal seat, were early Christian adherents. Although the Jewish presence in eastern Georgia goes back to a more ancient time, these colonies were enlarged by the exodus following the Jewish Wars in the first and second centuries. The Georgian written tradition, dating from the seventh century onwards, recalls this fact by identifying some of the earliest Christian converts in K'art'li as Jews and by advancing the spurious claim that two K'art'velian Jews witnessed the Crucifixion. Along with this Jewish influence, Christian ideas also were introduced to eastern Georgia by Manichaeans and, it would seem, Gnostics.

Early Georgian Christianity is characterized by its tremendous diversity, inclusiveness, and syncretic quality. The cosmopolitanism of pre-modern Caucasia, not just in the religious sphere, owed much to the region's status as a major Eurasian crossroads and its proximity to the fabled Silk Roads. A sustained push to create a single, tightly controlled Georgian Christianity and a concomitant obsession with identifying and rooting out heresy commenced much later, in the ninth and tenth centuries, and especially so in the eleventh to thirteenth centuries, under the Byzantine-oriented Bagratids.

It is difficult to gauge the prevalence of Christianity among the eastern Georgians before the fourth century. This uncertainty changes with the conversion of King Mirian III (variants: Mirean/Mihran; r. 284–361) and his family, from whose reign Christianity acquired the protection of the monarchy; within a century or so it became the dominant faith of the realm. The earliest written story of Mirian's conversion, an event dated by many scholars to around 337, is preserved in Rufinus' *Ecclesiastical History*, which was composed in Latin in the early fifth century. The oldest extant (written) Georgian account, *The Conversion of K'art'li*, is a product of the seventh century, while a considerably more elaborate version, *The Life of Nino*, derives from the ninth or tenth century. The interrelationship of these texts and the provenance of their traditions has inspired lively debate, though most specialists accept that the historical Mirian was converted through the intercession of the foreign, perhaps Cappadocian, holy woman Nino and that he consequently favoured the Church in K'art'li by offering royal protection, supporting its administration, and contributing to the building of churches. The chief prelate, sequentially styled bishop, archbishop, and then from the end of the fifth century catholicos (Georgian *kat'alikos*), was resident at the royal city Mc'xet'a.

Over the next two centuries a network of bishoprics was established under the watchful eye of the K'art'velian king. Eastern Georgia's landscape was predominantly non-urban and so the administrative model adopted by the Church in the Roman/Byzantine Empire was not appropriate. K'art'velian bishops tended to be headquartered at the estates of the most powerful aristocratic families (e.g., C'urtavi in the Armeno–Georgian frontier zone) and, after the sixth century, at important monasteries. Extremely little is known about the early ecclesiastical hierarchy except that the Archbishop of Mc'xet'a stood at its head. According to a later written tradition, Nino herself selected the first two leaders of the Church in K'art'li. Between the fourth and sixth centuries, from King Mirian to King P'arsman VI (r. from 561), the chief prelates were foreigners; several were Greek, while others were Armenian, Syrian and Iranian ('Iranian' in this context may denote 'Manichaean'). In fact, the initial phase of Christianization was very much a pan-Caucasian phenomenon in which non-Caucasians assumed a prominent role.

The Church in K'art'li was claimed by the Patriarchate of Antioch from an early time, although in practice Caucasia was often beyond Antioch's jurisdictional reach. Up to the Arab conquest in the seventh century, when regular communications between Caucasia and Syria were disrupted, the chief bishop of the Church in K'art'li received ordination from Antioch. There is a later, dubious tradition, probably originating in the eleventh century, that the exiled fourth-century Antiochene patriarch, Eustathius, made his way to eastern Georgia and was responsible for guiding the affairs of the local church. Similarly problematic is Elguja Xint'ibidze's assertion (1996) that some of the early Cappadocian fathers, including Basil the Great, might actually have been 'Iberians', i.e., Georgians. Although there may in fact be a genealogical connection of some kind, there is no compelling reason to believe that Basil identified himself as a Georgian or that the alleged Georgian link was in some way instrumental to the formation of his ideas.

In order to propagate the faith rapidly among Mirian's subjects, Christian leaders deliberately invented a script for the K'art'velian idiom of Georgian so that biblical and other religious texts could be translated into the local language. There is considerable controversy about the origins of the Georgian script. The c.800 *Life of the Kings*, the initial text of the corpus of medieval Georgian histories known as *K'art'lis c'xovreba* (the so-called Georgian Royal Annals or 'Georgian Chronicles'), credits the first K'art'velian monarch P'arnavaz (r. 299–234 BCE) with the invention of Georgian writing in early Hellenistic times. There is, however, no direct evidence to support this fanciful claim.

For its part, the medieval Armenian tradition gives the honour of creating scripts for Armenian, Georgian, and Caucasian Albanian to the Armenian cleric Mashtots, also known as Mesrop. However, surviving manuscripts of the *vita* of Mashtots, like those transmitting *The Life of the Kings*, postdate the schism between the Armenian and K'art'velian Churches, and it is altogether possible that both have been manipulated so as to give their respective parties precedence. In terms of chronology there can be no question, however, that all three Caucasian scripts were fashioned by a Christian impulse at about the same time, in the second half of the fourth century or early fifth century. Thus, while Mashtots might not have been involved personally with overseeing the creation of the Georgian script, there is every reason to think that a Christian pan-Caucasian effort was afoot. Armenian clerics would have played a conspicuous role in the project since their Church – established just a generation previously, after the conversion of King Trdat c.314 – was the largest and organizationally the most developed among the embryonic Caucasian churches.

Thus by the end of the fourth and certainly by the start of the fifth century, Christian clerics had equipped themselves with a Georgian script, called *asomt'avruli*. The Gospels were probably the first to be rendered into Georgian. Translated ecclesiastical literature has remained important in Georgia ever since. None of these early translations have survived intact; the oldest extant Georgian manuscripts are palimpsest fragments of translations deriving from the fifth to the eighth century. They are exclusively religious in nature and transmit texts from both the Old and New Testaments, as well as liturgical, homiletic, and even apocryphal works. It should be noted that some Byzantine sources that are otherwise lost are now preserved only in Georgian translations, including Hippolytus' *Commentary on the Song of Songs*, Metrophanes of Smyrna's *Commentary on Ecclesiastes*, Eustratius of Nicaea's *Brief Memorandum on When and Why the Romans and their Church Deviated from the Divine Eastern Church*, and *On Festivals*, the last of which was fabulously attributed to Justinian I. Works originally composed in yet other languages are also uniquely preserved in Georgian, including *The Passion of Michael of Mar Saba*, which was translated from Arabic in the ninth or tenth century.

At the end of the fifth century the first known example of original Georgian literature appeared: *The Martyrdom of Shushaniki*, composed by her confessor Iakob C'urtaveli (Jacob of C'urtavi). Like other specimens of early Georgian literature, it relates the deeds of a holy person. Original Georgian literary works are rather uncommon prior to the rise of the Bagratid dynasty in the ninth century, nevertheless hagiography appears to have been the genre of choice in the initial stage of local literature. These saintly biographies were written by Christians for the strengthening and defence of the faith of Christ, but they relate relatively few details about the condition and structure of the contemporary Church in K'art'li. However, the Georgian-language *vitae* of Shushaniki (fifth century), Evstat'i (*c.*600), and Habo (variant Abo, eighth century) are testaments to the diverse, multicultural character of early Georgian Christianity. All three of these Christian heroes were non-K'art'velians who lived and were killed in eastern Georgia: Shushaniki was an Armenian princess; Evstat'i, an Iranian and son of a Zoroastrian high priest; and Habo, an Arab. What was most important in these early hagiographies is a sense of Christian affiliation, not ethnicity.

In the case of Evstat'i and Habo, saintly biographies demonstrated that Christianity could overcome its enemies and doubters. Further, the physical location of the stories in eastern Georgia was of immense importance, for it showed that even in Caucasia, so far from the Holy Land, the Christian God could work miracles and guide local affairs. Biblical history was enlarged geographically and chronologically through such traditions. The originals of such *vitae* are lost, and the copies that we do have are typically found in collections of saints' lives of the eleventh century onwards. Although all of this material is in Georgian, the vast majority of the *vitae* celebrate holy men and women from elsewhere in the Christian world. Other materials in the collections consist of ecumenical Christian patristic, homiletic, theological, and exegetical writings, these works having been translated into Georgian, often from Greek. For example, the eleventh-century Parxali *mravalt'avi* (*polycephalon*) incorporates the Georgian *vitae* of Shushaniki and Habo as well as materials relating to Nino, but also well over a hundred items of an ecumenical nature. As a consequence of this structure, Georgian saints were made every bit as legitimate as saints recognized by the universal Church, and Georgian Christianity was made part of the larger Christian experience.

The writing of saints' lives in eastern Georgia constantly evolved to reflect changing local conditions. The most ancient Georgian hagiographies are passions and martyrdoms. Then, after the foundation of monasticism in K'art'li in the sixth century, the lives and activities of other holy men (and, rarely, women), especially monks, were composed. In the seventh century a narrative of Nino's travails was put into writing. Out of this hagiographical context was produced the first written Georgian-language historiographical texts in the early ninth century. It is worth noting that medieval Georgian histories tend to focus narrowly on kings and kingship and offer relatively few clues about the state of the local church.

Original and translated Georgian literature alike reveals the southerly orientation of early Georgian Christianity, towards Jerusalem, Syria and Armenia. The earliest written versions of Nino's biography exude the eastern Georgians' deep admiration for Jerusalem. Among other things, Nino was given a direct – but possibly fabulous – connection with that city and its patriarch, and holy sites in Mc'xet'a were named in honour of its most important Christian places. A number of scholars have shown the preservation of the Jerusalem rite in original and translated Georgian sources of the pre-Bagratid period (i.e., especially before the tenth century). Of special importance are the medieval Georgian *iadgaris*, roughly the equivalent of Byzantine *tropologia*. In the words of musicologist Peter Jeffery,

> Though the original Greek manuscripts are lost, the medieval Georgian translations permit us to know what [the early Jerusalem repertories] contained, to trace their historical development, and to document the influence Jerusalem asserted on other Eastern and Western centers of liturgical chant . . . Georgian chant is in some respects our most direct witness to the period and processes in which all medieval Christian liturgical chant was formed.

T'amila Mgaloblishvili's splendid investigation (1991) of the Klarjet'ian *mravalt'avi* has substantiated the importance of the era of King Vaxtang I Gorgasali (r. 447–522) in the translation and adaptation of liturgical and other ecclesiastical materials into Georgian.

Indeed, the reign of Vaxtang has traditionally been portrayed as a period of tremendous growth for Georgian Christianity. There can be no question of the extension of bishoprics in this era as well as the translating, writing, and copying of texts both at home and by K'art'velian monks resident abroad, especially in Levantine monasteries such as Mar Sabas. The pattern of foreign monasteries as the central sites of Georgian literary production was thus established back in the fifth century. It was also at this time that we observe the eastern Georgians being drawn into the theological disputes of the larger Church. In an attempt to secure K'art'velian support and to acknowledge local support of the empire, the Byzantine government recognized – and perhaps itself instigated – the change in status of the K'art'velian chief prelate from archbishop to catholicos, around the year 480. Fully-fledged autocephaly would not be achieved, however, until the Arab conquest or later. In the sixth century eastern Georgian bishops attended ecclesiastical councils hosted by the Armenians and together with other Caucasian religious leaders voiced their opposition to Chalcedon.

However, eastern Georgia's geopolitical situation and especially the increasing weakness of its monarchy compelled the K'art'velian secular and religious elite to seek aid from Constantinople. The growing Iranian menace forced Vaxtang to seek refuge in Byzantine-controlled eastern Anatolia on at least two occasions. Sassanid influence steadily expanded in eastern Georgia: an Iranian *marzbān* was established in the recently-(re)founded city of T'bilisi (older orthography Tp'ilisi, Russian Tiflis) in 523, and according to the careful research of Toumanoff (1963), K'art'velian kingship was completely extinguished by Iran several decades later, around the year 580. Within a decade the political vacuum was filled by a series of 'presiding princes', which lasted down to the re-establishment of local kingship by the Bagratid dynasty in 888.

The Long Sixth Century is perhaps the single most developmentally significant period of Georgian Christianity. Though the K'art'velian political situation plunged deeper and deeper into crisis, the Church in K'art'li was strengthened and remade itself into a 'national' organization. During the reign of P'arsman VI (561 to 579 at latest), the so-called Thirteen Syrian Fathers under the leadership of the Iovane Zedazadneli (John 'of Zedazadeni') entered eastern Georgia and acquired the king's permission to establish a series of monasteries. Among them were Davit' Garesjeli (David 'of Garesja'), founder of the monastic complex in the Garesja (variant Gareji) desert in the eastern region of Kaxet'i, and Shio Mghwmeli, who established a monastery at the Mghwme (Mghvime) caves just upriver from Mc'xet'a. The Thirteen Syrian Fathers attracted a considerable body of local pupils and this increased the demand for books throughout the land.

It is worth recalling that while these men are credited with the implantation of monasticism in eastern Georgia, the K'art'velians had previously been acquainted with it; a considerable number of K'art'velians, like the famous anti-Chalcedonian Peter the Iberian, had journeyed abroad, especially to Jerusalem. The Syrian monks were likely anti-Chalcedonians (modern observers have variously identified them as Miaphysites and Nestorians), although our relatively late sources do not indicate how or whether this affiliation affected their labours in eastern Georgia. However, at the time of their arrival, the Church in K'art'li remained in the non-Chalcedonian camp with the Armenians and Caucasian Albanians.

Yet the anti-Chalcedonian union among Caucasian Christians was becoming increasingly fragile. P'arsman VI's reign witnessed not only the implantation of monasticism in eastern Georgia but also the 'nativization' of the K'art'velian ecclesiastical hierarchy. A dramatic shift in self-consciousness resulted in the struggle waged by the inflexible *catholicoi* of K'art'li and Armenia. According to the later sources for the episode preserved in the Armenian *Book of Letters* (*Girk' T'ght'ots'*), at first the dispute centred on the Armenian allegation that the K'art'velian Catholicos Kwrion had not dedicated his full energies to the war against 'Nestorianism'. At the heart of the struggle were three issues. First, what was the proper relationship of Christian Caucasia with the Byzantine Empire? Second, was the diversity of Christianity as practised in the eastern Georgian domains appropriate? Finally, who, if anyone, should have the right to make decisions affecting the Christians of greater Caucasia, including the definition of what constituted Orthodoxy? In other words, who, if anyone, held ultimate ecclesiastical authority in Christian Caucasia and what was the structure of the regional church hierarchy?

The Armenians believed themselves, or at least local ecclesiastical councils held under the presidency of the Armenian catholicos, to possess that ultimate, pan-

Caucasian authority. Kwrion dissented, an action not unexpected in light of the great energy and newfound boldness displayed by K'art'velian church officials. Finally, at their Third Council of Dvin, held in 607, the Armenians condemned Kwrion and his adherents, and a schism between the two Caucasian churches was set into motion. It would be another century before this break would become permanent. Though Armenian polemical works were directed against the eastern Georgians not long after Dvin III (this occurring within the larger context of the separation of the imperial and Armenian churches studied by Nina Garsoïan, 1999), the K'art'velians would seem to have 'returned fire' only much later. The earliest known such work was penned by the eleventh-century Catholicos Arsen Sap'areli ('of Sap'ara').

Kwrion's Christological orientation has proven a bone of contention: was he a Diophysite, a Miaphysite or a Monothelite? There is some evidence suggesting the last, but what is certain is that this public dispute with the Armenians brought theology squarely into the K'art'velian foreground. And to the eastern Georgians, the theological issue was inseparable from the question of relations with Byzantium. Over the course of the sixth century, the eastern Georgian elite pinned its protection and fate more and more on Constantinople, and the Armenians had objected to this and resented its possible implications. From Constantinople's perspective, such alliances required what amounted to a declaration of faith: for the K'art'velians to receive Byzantine support and assistance, they would have to embrace the imperial form of Christianity. Kwrion seems to have put his church on that path. But in the reign of the Byzantine Emperor Heraclius (610–41), a great many K'art'velian churchmen abandoned their non-Chalcedonian position. Heraclius' very appearance in K'art'li, as he was en route to Sassanid Iran, and his promotion of Byzantine Christianity, was unprecedented in Georgian history. So great was the impact that the episode is uniquely reported in three separate medieval Georgian-language histories.

The excitement stemming from Heraclius' defeat of the Iranian army and his sacking of Seleucia-Ctesiphon was short-lived. Iran and Byzantium had been exhausted from the prolonged war, and both were susceptible to the new, well-organized opponent from the south, the Arabs. Sassanid Iran was an initial target, the Arabs managing to kill the last Sassanid king in 651. Byzantine possessions in Mesopotamia were also coveted by the Arabs. The routing of a Byzantine army at Yarmuk in August 636 opened the door to Syria; by 638 Syria and Palestine, including the patriarchates at Jerusalem and Antioch, were in Muslim hands. The invasion of Christian Caucasia commenced by 640 and five years later Arab troops had penetrated eastern Georgia. In 654–5 the city of T'bilisi surrendered and eastern Georgia was occupied. As was the case in neighbouring Armenia, a major component of the Arabs' approach was the colonization of Christian Caucasia.

In the meantime, Byzantine Egypt also succumbed to the Arabs, in September 642. Egypt is mentioned here because of the infamous Patriarch Cyrus of Alexandria. It was Cyrus, a favourite of Heraclius and a staunch advocate of Monothelitism, who surrendered Egypt. This Cyrus may have a direct connection to Georgia. Zaza Alek'sidze (1968) has advanced the provocative argument that Cyrus is none other than the Catholicos Kwrion. That Cyrus was deemed personally responsible for the dramatic loss of Egypt to the infidels, and that he and his Monothelite partners were singled out and excommunicated at the Sixth Ecumenical Council in 681, may explain why Kwrion's memory was expunged from medieval Georgian sources.

By the end of the seventh or start of the eighth century, Christianity in eastern Georgia had been radically transformed. For the first time in its history, a distinct tradition of the foundation of K'art'velian Christianity was put into writing. In its original form, the succinct *Conversion of K'art'li* was produced sometime in the seventh century, presumably within a few decades of the events of 607 (Rapp and Crego 2006). Although *The Conversion* undoubtedly preserves many older, accurate memories of how Christianity triumphed in the time of Nino and Mirian, the work as a whole must also be seen in large measure as a seventh-century declaration of autonomy: the K'art'velian Church was an independent organization and, significantly, connections to the contemporaneous conversions of Armenia and Albania have for the most part been expunged. Indeed, it was in this period that the Church in K'art'li was transformed into the ethnically focused K'art'velian Church. Though observers of the time did not explicitly note the change or apply new terminology to the local church, the K'art'velian Church was strikingly different in its organization and mission. Its hierarchy, including the office of catholicos, was now monopolized by eastern Georgians, especially K'art'velians. What is more, it had now become a 'national' church, an organization by and for the dominant K'art'velian *ethnie*. This is reflected in contemporary Georgian-language *vitae*, such as the eighth-century *Martyrdom of Habo* by Iovane Sabanis-dze. In the case of Habo, an Arab migrant to the Georgian territories, conversion to Christianity was not enough: he had to embrace the local, K'art'velian, form of Christianity which entailed, inter alia, learning the Georgian language and 'converting' to K'art'velian culture. After Habo the heroes of original hagiographies tend to be K'art'velians or other Georgians; the cosmopolitanism of early K'art'velian Christianity was thus curtailed, though by virtue of Georgia's location in a prominent Eurasian crossroads this condition never completely disappeared.

K'art'velian political authority remained feeble throughout the ninth century, and as it had in previous times the local church postured to fill the void. But the Arab conquest brought changes to the K'art'velian Church. As a result of the occupation, what may have been thousands of religious and secular elites evacuated the region. Some travelled east into the mountainous far eastern regions of Kaxet'i, while many others sought refuge in the Georgian south-west, in regions such as Tao (the Armenian Tayk'), Klarjet'i and Shavshet'i, where the Arabs had been unable to extend their dominion. Over the next two centuries a K'art'li-in-exile was created, which I call neo-K'art'li. This area was instrumental in the later re-conquest of eastern Georgia. Georgian Christianity not only survived, it flourished.

From the south-western domains, it gained unprecedented access to Byzantium and the imperial church, and by the tenth century this influx of Byzantine forms and ideas led to a reorientation of the local church away from the south and towards the Byzantine Empire. A prime example of this shift in Christian orientation is the deliberate substitution of the Jerusalemite liturgy with the Constantinopolitan. At the same time, monastic institutions thrived as never before. A number of enormous, often autonomous monastic foundations were established throughout the south western domains. The chief figure associated with this development is the monk Grigol Xandzt'eli (George 'of Xandzt'a/Khandzt'a'). Xandzt'eli's biography, composed by his pupil Giorgi Merch'ule, is not only an extensive record of the growth and development of K'art'velian monasticism, but it also supplies rare glimpses into the political and everyday life of contemporary neo-K'art'li. This *vita* also expresses the idea of a K'art'velian 'national' church in so far as it makes the Georgian language (i.e., the K'art'velian dialect) not only a legitimate sacred language but also an essential component of Georgian Christianity.

Neo-K'art'li's prosperity contributed to the rejuvenation of K'art'velian political life under the Bagratids. Ironically, the Bagratids were originally an Armenian family; there is evidence that in Vaxtang's time some of them had already entered the service of the K'art'velian monarchy. But it is in the years immediately following the crushing of a disastrous uprising by Armenian noble families against the Arabs in 772 that a branch of the family migrated to neo-K'art'li, where they permanently settled and were rapidly acculturated. In 813 the Bagratid prince Ashot I seized the presiding principate and three-quarters of a century later, in 888, his relative Adarnase II restored local kingship. Great though his achievement was, Adarnase could not have guessed that the Bagratid line of kings would monopolize political power in much of Georgia for the next thousand years, up until the Russian conquest of the nineteenth century.

The greatest and most enduring achievement of the Georgian Bagratids, who had risen to power under Byzantine tutelage, was the political unification of lands on both the eastern and western sides of the Surami mountains, beginning with the union of part of K'art'li, neo-K'art'li, and the western region of Ap'xazet'i (Russian Abkhazia); this was engineered by Bagrat III in 1008. It is worth emphasizing that, up to the start of the Bagratid era, the historical and ecclesiastical experiences of eastern and western Georgia often diverged. Western territories including Ap'xazet'i, and before it Lazika and Egrisi/Colchis, fell more under the influence (and sometimes direct control) of the Roman and then the Byzantine Empire. Consequently, western Georgian Christianity developed along different lines from that in eastern territories such as K'art'li (it should be noted that labelling the western regions as 'Georgian' in this early period is extremely misleading and projects back later realities and perceptions; L. G. Khrushkova's use of 'Eastern Black Sea' (2002) in this context is more historically accurate).

Although the beginning of the conversion of western Georgia may also be traced to the fourth century, the Christianity introduced and fostered there tended to be more in line with that sanctioned by Constantinople. Bishops sitting in the western regions took part in the first and fifth ecumenical councils. Once the Bagratids took the reins of power in Ap'xazet'i, the church of western Georgia was merged with that of the East. That having been said, however, the K'art'velian Church, especially as it existed in neo-K'art'li, often exerted influence over other regions, including western Georgia, long before the Bagratids assumed control of these places. Thus religious uniformity often preceded political unity. By the eleventh century, the Bagratids had realigned local royal imagery – both in art and in the historical texts they sponsored – from its traditional southern-facing, Iranian orientation to one more attuned to Christian Byzantium. In this development, too, we must acknowledge the influence of the eastern Georgian Church and its similar reorientation from the south (in this case, Palestine, Syria and Armenia) to the west, towards the Byzantine Commonwealth. In other words, the local church's intensive adoption and adaptation of Byzantine models from the ninth and especially tenth century preceded and stimulated a similar reorientation by the political elite in the tenth and eleventh centuries.

The Medieval Bagratid Period

With the definite expansion of the K'art'velian Church beyond lands inhabited primarily by K'art'velians in the tenth and eleventh centuries, we can begin to speak properly of the Georgian Church. The growing prestige of the Church attracted the Bagratids' constant attention. Potentially, the Georgian Church was as much a powerful ally as it was a dangerous rival. When the Catholicos Melk'isedek petitioned for tax immunity around the year 1031, King Bagrat IV (r. 1027–72) had little choice but to comply, for he relied heavily on the support of the local church in his obstacle-laden quest for political consolidation and unification. A number of royal charters acknowledging such immunities along with property rights have come down to us. As early as Bagrat's time the crown sometimes attempted to restrict the powers of and even subordinate the ecclesiastical hierarchy, but these attempts, led by the Georgian Athonite Giorgi Mt'acmideli (variant Mtatsmindeli, 'of the Holy Mountain'), failed. A reflection of the increasing power and prestige of the Georgian Church is the assumption of the title 'patriarch' (*patriark'i*) by its chief prelate at some point in the eleventh century. Who authorized this alteration of status is unknown; it may very well have been self-generated, without the endorsement or even knowledge of Byzantine officials.

King Davit' II, nicknamed Aghmashenebeli ('the [Re-]Builder', r. 1089–1125), manipulated church affairs to an unprecedented degree. During his reign the first attested all-Georgian ecclesiastical councils took place, the most famous of which occurred in 1103 at the neighbouring Ruisi and Urbnisi churches not far from the city of Gori. These assemblies mimicked the Ecumenical Councils, albeit on a smaller, Caucasian scale. At least one council examined Miaphysitism, a burning issue owing to the Georgian annexation of much of Caucasian Armenia. Indeed, it was in the second half of the eleventh century that the Georgian Catholicos Arseni Sap'areli wrote a tract censuring the anti-Chalcedonian Armenians for the schism. It was in this time, under the Bagratid regime, that the Georgian Church embarked on an unprecedented programme to define, unmask and combat heresy. At the Ruisi-Urbnisi council Davit' succeeded in appointing supporters and close associates to many of the highest ecclesiastical positions. He also created a new official, the *mcignobart'-uxucesi chqondideli*, which combined a major secular position with the bishopric of Chqondidi, one of the most important episcopal sees in western Georgia. After the patriarchate, the See of Chqondidi was now the second highest position in the Georgian Church. The king's intention was to control appointments to this office in order to manipulate church affairs as part of his larger project to expand and centralize state control. However, a headstrong *mcignobart'-uxucesi chqondideli* might also turn the institution on its head by giving the Church a clear path to interfere in secular matters. This tension is evident throughout the 'golden age' of the Bagratids that ended with the Mongol conquest.

The ninth to thirteenth century witnessed an unprecedented blossoming of ecclesiastical culture. Stone churches were constructed throughout the Georgian domains, and they were decorated with beautiful frescoes. This was also a period of intensive literary output. In 897 the oldest complete copy of the Georgian Gospels was made, the so-called Adyshi variant, named for the city in the northern region of Svanet'i in which it was discovered. In the tenth century a number of Gospels appear: Urbnisi (906), Opiza (913), K'sani (early tenth century), Jruchi (936), Mount Sinai (two variants, mid-century and 978), Parxali (973), Bert'ay (988), and Tbet'i (995). As the extensive studies by Ilia Abuladze show (1944), the ninth and tenth centuries, especially the period 840 to 960, witnessed the translation of many Armenian hagiographies and other ecclesiastical texts into Georgian and vice versa. This was an attempt of the two peoples to understand one another at a time when large numbers of Armenians were subjected to Georgian political authority.

In the twelfth century, the Georgian Royal Annals, *K'art'lis c'xovreba*, were translated and adapted into Armenian. Starting in the early eleventh century we possess several royal charters granting ecclesiastical tax immunity and the like; such documents become especially plentiful in the second half of the century. The original ecclesiastical-historical compilation known as *Mok'c'evay k'art'lisay*, with its core component *The Conversion of K'art'li* (initially composed back in the seventh century), took shape in early Bagratid times. Its oldest surviving manuscripts were copied in the tenth century, and include the famous Shatberdi Codex (named for the neo-K'art'velian monastery by the same name founded by Grigol Xandzt'eli) and the N/Sin.-50 manuscript from St Catherine's monastery on Mount Sinai. *Mok'c'evay k'art'lisay* includes *The Life of Nino*, an enlarged, reworked version of *The Conversion*, which itself was written in the ninth or early tenth century.

The role of monasteries in the production and safeguarding of such texts should not be underestimated. Shatberdi in neo-K'art'li was a particularly important literary centre. Of even greater significance in this regard were Georgian monks and monastic foundations abroad. The monastic diaspora, especially in the Holy Land and Syria, played a decisive role in medieval Georgian Christianity. In the ninth to thirteenth centuries Georgian monks were resident throughout the Eastern Christian world. Monasteries dominated by Georgians or having large Georgian constituencies were also widespread. The most famous of these were Iveron (Greek for 'of the Iberians/Georgians'; the Georgians sometimes referred to it as the *k'art'velt'a monastiri*, or 'Monastery of the Georgians') on Mount Athos, St Catherine's on Mount Sinai, the Monastery of the Holy Cross in Jerusalem (rebuilt by Proxore/Prochoros 'of Shavshet'i' in the eleventh century), the Monastery of the Black Mountain near Antioch in Syria, and Petricioni near Bachkovo in Bulgaria. A large number of original Georgian compositions, especially of a theological nature, were produced in these places, and copies were sent back to Georgia. Many translations of ecclesiastical literature were also made into Georgian, especially from Greek. The eleventh century saw the formation of distinct literary schools among Georgian monks. Some advocated a free-form translation from Greek while others, including Ep'rem Mcire (Ephrem 'the Lesser'), promoted translations that slavishly reproduced the Greek even at the risk of clouding comprehension of the translated text.

The energetic 'golden age' of the medieval Georgian monarchy of the Bagratids came to an end in the thirteenth century as a consequence of the overextension of resources on the part of the Crown, the inept rule of Giorgi IV Lasha (r. 1213–23) and the casting of Mongol hegemony over much of the Caucasian isthmus. Mongol rule had several consequences. Political power was fragmented, although a shadow of royal authority endured. At times, the Mongols recognized more than one Bagratid as king simultaneously. Bagratid power within Georgia was sometimes questioned, but the Bagratids entered the post-Mongol era with their monopoly over royal authority intact. The Georgian Church also survived the Mongol onslaught, although its special position had in some ways been contested. In Ap'xazet'i, during Mongol times, a separate, rival 'patriarchate' was established (or re-established; there is a divergence of opinion over when a patriarchate in Ap'xazet'i was first created). As early as 1224, in a response to a letter announcing the enthronement of Queen Rusudan (r. 1223–45) the previous year, Pope Honorius III had invited the Georgians to join a new crusade against the Muslims. The exchange of letters continued under the pontificate of Gregory IX, and in 1240 Rusudan begged him for assistance, as the Mongol invasion was unleashed upon her country. Though the Pope could do little more than offer encouragement to the Christians of distant Caucasia, he urged the Georgians to enter formal communion with the Catholic Church. In the first half of the thirteenth century the Georgian Church was drifting into schism with the Byzantine Church, and Rusudan seems to have attempted to counterbalance Byzantine influence with that of the papacy. This is reminiscent of an earlier period, the fourth century, when King Mirian had sought to restrict the influence of Sassanid Iran by accepting the new religion of Constantine the Great.

In the reign of Rusudan and continuing throughout the thirteenth century, Franciscan and Dominican friars established a foothold in Georgia. In 1328 Pope John XXII established a see in the city of T'bilisi and in the following year appointed the Dominican John of Florence as the first Catholic bishop in Georgia. This see existed down to the early sixteenth century. Despite these inroads, Orthodox Georgians never accepted formal reunion with the Roman Church.

From the late 1380s to about 1400 the Georgian lands were invaded by the armies of Timur (Tamerlane). Many places were devastated; churches and monasteries were singled out for plunder. Local Bagratid kings were in no position to defend the embattled Church. Starting under the Mongols, autonomous non-Bagratid 'principalities' had been established in the west and south-west, including in Samc'xe, Samegrelo (Mengrelia), and Ap'xazet'i. Though a united Georgian kingdom was reassembled by the Bagratid Alek'sandre I (r. 1412–42), political union did not extend past his death; Georgia would not again be united until the establishment of Russian control in the nineteenth century. In the thirteenth to early fifteenth century, the authority of the Georgian Church was diminished. Existing churches fell into disrepair and many were destroyed.

The state of deterioration persisted for the next two centuries. The fall of Constantinople in 1453 deprived the Bagratids and the Georgian Church of potential Byzantine aid, but the psychological impact was more important than loss of material support, which for a long time had been meagre. The re-emergence of a strong Iranian state under the Safavids and the rising fortunes of the Ottomans had dramatic consequences for Georgia. The intense rivalry of these two Islamic enterprises was often played out in the Caucasian arena, a situation not unlike the earlier imperial contests fought in the isthmus by Rome and Byzantium and Iran and Islam. The Georgian political elite attempted once more to play the great powers off one another, but ultimately their Christian affiliation was a hindrance as both the Ottomans and Safavids were Islamic (compare the situation under Mirian III with Christian Byzantium and Zoroastrian Iran).

Some Georgian princes and kings converted to Islam and the Georgian Church fell upon even harder times. After their occupation of south-western Georgia in the sixteenth century, the Ottomans actively established mosques throughout the region. There were some opportunities to repair existing church buildings, as was the case with the restoration of the Sioni cathedral in T'bilisi and Sueti-c'xoveli (modern Sveti-c'xoveli, i.e., Church of the 'Life-Giving Pillar') in Mc'xet'a by King Vaxtang VI, but this was the exception rather than the norm. This was also a renewed period of Georgian martyrs. In September 1624 the queen of Kaxet'i K'et'evan was put to death by order of Shah Abbas I (r. 1587–1629). Her martyrdom was reported to the pope by Augustinian fathers, who were then resident in Iran.

The Modern Period

The fact that Catholic monks reported K'et'evan's murder reflects the renewed influence of Catholicism in the seventeenth century. This influence was made possible largely through French relations with the Ottomans and Iranians. In 1626 Theatine missionaries first visited western Georgia. One of their number, Cristoforo Castelli, produced many detailed drawings of the region and its leaders, which remain a valuable and unique source of information. From 1661 until their expulsion by the Russians in 1845 Capuchins were established in eastern Georgia, at T'bilisi. Several Bagratid princes and kings and even Georgian patriarchs flirted with Catholicism and many more were sympathetic to it. The famous scholar Vaxushti Bagrationi, a son of Vaxtang VI and author of a famous history and geography of all Georgia, was educated by Catholics based in T'bilisi. Vaxtang's uncle and adviser, Sulxan-Saba Orbeliani, actually converted to Catholicism. Orbeliani was author of several books, including the first lexicon of the Georgian language and memoirs of his travels to western Europe, which had begun in 1713. This journey was undertaken so as to solicit aid for the embattled Vaxtang VI from Pope Clement IX and the French King Louis XIV.

The resurgence of Catholicism in Georgia had other important literary consequences. In 1629 the first Georgian printing press was set up in Rome through the collaboration of the Georgian envoy Prince-Monk Nikephoros Irbak'idze and Italian scholars. Yet again we observe the importance of the tiny Georgian diaspora in the history of Georgian literature and Christianity. The first printed books in Georgian were intended to aid Catholic missionary endeavours among the Georgians and included a 3,000-word Georgian-Italian vocabulary. The first printing press in Georgia was established by Vaxtang VI in T'bilisi in 1709 and was active until 1723. Early publications were religious, and included the Four Gospels (1709) and a book of liturgies (1710). However, the first edition of the great Georgian epic, the *Vep'xistqaosani* (*The Knight in the Panther's Skin*), by the thirteenth-century poet Shot'a Rust'aveli, appeared in 1712. The next great centre of Georgian printing was Moscow, where from 1737 books were published by members of the exiled Georgian royal family. Chief among the early Moscow publications is the first complete printed edition of the Georgian Bible, dated 1743.

That Moscow (and St Petersburg) was a centre of early Georgian printing was hardly accidental. The crushing psychological blow resulting from the destruction of Christian Byzantium by the Ottomans and the bloody conflict waged in Georgia and throughout Caucasia by the Ottomans and Iranians compelled many Georgian elites to look northwards to Orthodox Russia, for support and protection. From the late fifteenth century, several embassies were exchanged between eastern Georgia and the Russian Empire. The Orthodox Christianity shared by the Georgians and Russians was crucial in the growing dialogue. And, as Kenneth Church (2001) has cogently argued, both peoples contributed to and accepted an 'extermination thesis' whereby Christian Georgian society would be wiped out in the absence of full-scale Russian intervention.

In 1783 the Bagratid king of eastern Georgia, Erekle II (r. 1762–98), and the Russian Empress Catherine the Great (r. 1762–96) agreed to make Georgia a 'protectorate' of the empire. Among other things, the Treaty of Georgievisk guaranteed the sovereignty of the Georgian monarchy and Church. After the devastating Iranian attack upon eastern Georgia and especially T'bilisi by Agha Muhammad Khan in 1795 the Georgians were unable to mount serious opposition to further Russian encroachments, and in 1801 the empire annexed eastern Georgia, in part using the 'extermination thesis' to justify its unilateral action. The remaining Georgian lands were gathered under Russian hegemony over the course of the eighteenth century.

The implications of Russian rule for the Georgian Church were numerous. The 'patriarchate' of Ap'xazet'i had already disappeared in 1795; with the establishment of their direct control over the eastern regions of K'art'li and Kaxet'i, Russia sought to curb Georgian institutions that might challenge their authority. The Georgian Church was specially targeted and its patriarchate was abolished in 1811, when Antoni II, son of King Erekle II, was forced into exile. Disenfranchised remnants of the church hierarchy were absorbed into the Russian Holy Synod. The first exarch, Metropolitan Varlaam, belonged to the Georgian nobility. But once Varlaam's tenure ended in spring 1817, his successors, starting with Feofilakt Rusanov, were ethnic Russians whose knowledge of Georgia and its culture was extremely limited.

Georgian Christianity was now subjected to the Russification sweeping across the empire. The Russian liturgy replaced the Georgian. Episcopal sees in Georgia were reorganized so as to tighten the exarch's control. Frescoes in churches were systematically whitewashed. Over the next century, church buildings were poorly maintained and by the 1860s and 1870s corruption within the exarchate was rampant. But although under attack, Georgian ecclesiastical culture was by no means forced into extinction. For example, some religious books were published in the Georgian language. In 1882 Mixail Sabinin's *Sak'art'ūēlos samot'xe* (The Paradise of Georgia), a collection of hagiographical texts celebrating the holy men and women of Georgian Christianity, was published in St Petersburg (a Russian translation also appeared). And especially from second half of the nineteenth century, Georgian academics such as Ivane Javaxishvili (Dzhavakhishvili, Dzhavakhov) embarked on the scholarly study of Georgian Christianity; their works were published in Russian and Georgian.

In May 1905 Georgian priests and bishops convened in T'bilisi (Russian Tiflis) to discuss the critical situation and to issue a call for the restoration of autocephaly. The Russians could not tolerate this bold defiance and dispatched troops to break up the meeting. Meanwhile, charges of corruption grew louder with stories of the exarchate selling icons and other ecclesiastical treasures while at the same time the physical condition of church buildings worsened. Some twenty episcopal sees were unoccupied and well over 700 parishes were without pastors. Few Georgians attended services. In spring of 1908 the Russian exarch Nikon, who was widely regarded as a Georgian sympathizer, was assassinated. These events attracted the attention of Christians abroad, including the papacy. In 1910 the Georgian Catholic priest Michel Tamarati (T'amarashvili) published in Rome his *L'Église géorgienne des origines jusqu'a nos jours*. Though it is now outdated, this book remains the most comprehensive history of Christianity in Georgia. But it also had a decidedly political purpose. Tamarati not only painted Catholicism in Georgia in the best possible light, but he also criticized the illegal abrogation of the centuries-old autocephaly of the Georgian Church and the heavy-handed policies of the Russian Empire. Indeed, Georgian Christianity had become central to the Georgian national struggle against Russian rule.

The question of Georgian autocephaly resurfaced during the revolutions of 1917. After the March uprising, a group of Georgian clerics and bishops forced their way into the offices of the exarchate and installed Georgians to replace the exarch and his staff. All-Georgian ecclesiastical councils were held in T'bilisi in September 1917 and at the Gelat'i monastery near K'ut'aisi in western Georgia in 1921. The 1917 council elected Kwrion II (Kyrion) as the catholicos-patriarch of the all-Georgian Church, and with this act full autocephaly was reclaimed. The name of the new chief prelate was an auspicious one, for it should be recalled that the first Kwrion had presided over the K'art'velian Church during its estrangement from the Armenian Church at the start of the seventh century. Needless to say, the Russian Holy Synod vehemently opposed these actions and deemed them illicit. Until the Second World War, dialogue between the two Churches virtually disappeared.

Out of the revolutions of 1917 was born the Georgian Democratic Republic. When it was established in May 1918 its Menshevik leaders tended to see no formal place for religion in the state government. Their attitudes towards religion, and the Georgian Church in particular, ranged from indifferent to hostile. However, the local church was now free from the suppression it had experienced under Russian rule. Freedom of religion was guaranteed by the new constitution, but here the Georgian Church was not specially singled out. At the same time, many political figures advocated a legal separation of Church and state; the debate over this issue continued until 22 February 1921, when such a clause was introduced into the constitution. Chapter 1, article 31 guaranteed the 'full liberty of conscience' for each citizen: 'Everyone has the right to profess his/her own religion, to change the same, or not to have any religious belief.' However, the promulgation of this Act was mostly symbolic for it occurred as Soviet troops were advancing on eastern Georgia. Later that month, independent Georgia fell to the Bolsheviks and Soviet rule was extended over the Georgian lands.

Although the government of the USSR did not dismantle the Georgian Church or rescind its autocephaly, Soviet policies and laws greatly restricted its activities; it was as if chapter 1.31 of the pre-Soviet constitution had been maintained, but with emphasis upon the right of citizens to be atheists. The Catholicos-Patriarch Ambrosi, an outspoken critic of Soviet power, was arrested in winter 1923. He remained imprisoned until shortly before his death in spring 1927. Throughout the 1930s the Georgian Church suffered the state-sponsored persecution of religion. Soviet attitudes towards religious groups were altered with the outbreak of the Second World War. The need to unite in the face of the Nazi threat led Stalin, the ethnically-Georgian leader of the USSR and a former student of the T'bilisi Theological Academy, officially to recognize major religious organizations including the Georgian Church. One of the implications of this policy was the rapprochement of the Georgian and Russian Churches. In October 1943 the Russian Church formally recognized the autocephaly of its Georgian counterpart, twenty-six years after the Georgians had reclaimed this status. However, the lifting of certain restrictions did not lead to a significant revival of Christianity in Georgia.

After the war restrictions on religious organizations re-emerged. It was in this renewed anti-religious atmosphere, in 1962, that the Georgian Church applied for admission to the World Council of Churches (WCC), an ecumenical organization representing over three hundred churches including Anglicans, Protestants and Orthodox (but not Roman Catholics). Christians around the world were made aware of the dilapidated state of the Georgian Church. Georgian scholars continued to publish works about Georgian Christianity, although such publications tended to appear in small print runs and their circulation was limited to academic circles. To this period belong the initial volumes of Ilia Abuladze's splendid *Dzveli k'art'uli agiograp'iuli literaturis dzeglebi* (Monuments of Ancient Georgian Hagiographical Literature), a series featuring critical editions of medieval Georgian *vitae*.

Corruption infected the ruling elite of the Georgian Soviet Socialist Republic in the early 1970s. The Church was not immune to this wave of corruption, a situation reminiscent of the exarchate in the late nineteenth century. Church officials were rumoured to have sold ecclesiastical treasures and the deteriorating condition of church buildings was publicized in underground samizdat pamphlets. Among the most active samizdat writers was Zviad Gamsaxurdia (Gamsakhurdia), who campaigned against corruption in the Georgian Church and drew attention to continued attempts by the Soviets to Russify it. As never before, the Georgian Orthodox Church became a potent symbol in the resistance of the Georgians to the USSR. Along with the Georgian language, the Church was a constant reminder of Georgia's distinctiveness but also the wrongs that had been inflicted by Moscow.

The Late 1970s and After

Upon his enthronement as catholicos-patriarch of all-Georgia in late 1977, Ilia II embarked on a programme to rejuvenate the Georgian Church. Vacant ecclesiastical positions were filled, church buildings were refurbished, and some new ones constructed. Serving as a president of the WCC from 1979 to 1983, he drew global

attention once again to Georgian Christianity and strengthened his Church's commitment to the ecumenical movement. Ilia also engaged the national movement, especially in the years of Mikhail Gorbachev's reforms. In early April 1989 Georgians
protested in the streets against what they perceived as threats by the Ap'xazians (Abk-
hazians) of western Georgia. It was the catholicos-patriarch who addressed the crowd,
rallying the protesters while urging calm. The brutal suppression of the demonstrators
by Soviet troops on 9 April and its aftermath helped propel Zviad Gamsaxurdia to
power. Gamsaxurdia's Round Table–Free Georgia Bloc enjoyed enormous support in
the October 1990 elections, and independence was declared from the Soviet Union on
9 April 1991, the second anniversary of the 9 April massacre. The following month
Gamsaxurdia was elected president of the Republic of Georgia.

Though Gamsaxurdia held the reins of power only until January 1992, the consequences of his regime for the Georgian Church continued to resonate. Unlike the
Menshevik-dominated Republic of Georgia earlier in the century, Gamsaxurdia's
Georgia aligned itself closely with the Georgian Orthodox Church. The Church was
crucial to Gamsaxurdia's vision of Georgian unity. He made prominent public appearances with Patriarch Ilia, and the state government specially endorsed the proselytizing
efforts of the Georgian Church. In addition, the mantra 'Georgia for Georgians' was
often heard. Gamsaxurdia reasoned that a strong Georgia depended first and foremost
upon ethnic unity among the Georgian majority; the non-Georgian populations of the
republic were termed 'guests' and, in Gamsaxurdia's mind, should not expect equal
rights with the majority.

Gamsaxurdia made innumerable enemies. In late December 1991 a coup was
launched against the president and he was forced to flee the capital in January. Ironically, Gamsaxurdia eventually ended up in the care of the Chechen leader Dzhokhar
Dudaev, who championed an independent Chechnya. Back in Georgia, the junta invited
back the former Soviet ruler of Georgia, Eduard Shevardnadze. Although the Georgian
Church remained a favoured institution in Shevardnadze's Georgia, the large-scale
official assault against ethnic minorities was for the most part rescinded. The exact legal
relationship of the Church and state was still being debated in parliament in fall 2002.
It remains uncertain how the Rose Revolution and the inauguration of the reform-
minded Mixail Saakashvili in early 2004 will affect this situation. However, Saakashvili
and his allies have maintained good relations with the patriarchate. Indeed, just prior
to his official inauguration as president, Saakashvili took an oath administered by
Patriarch Ilia II over the tomb of King Davit' II Aghmashenebeli at the monastic complex
of Gelat'i near K'ut'aisi.

At the outset of the twenty-first century, the Georgian Church is again at a crossroads. Suppressed by the Russians and Soviets and treated with indifference by the
government of the first Republic of Georgia, it was briefly given special legal status
under Gamsaxurdia and its leaders are now struggling to carve out a privileged place
in post-Soviet Georgian society. With the flood of new freedoms has come a resurgence
of religious practice in Georgia. But a substantial number of Georgians have turned
their backs on the Georgian Orthodox Church and have joined various Protestant sects
in particular. Not since the eras of Nino and Vaxtang Gorgasali has Christianity in
Georgia been so multifarious. Missionaries from western Europe and North America

have entered the country in large numbers, and Georgian Church authorities have responded to the challenge in various ways. Some have called for a special legal status for their organization, and some have even advocated the legal banning of 'foreign' religions in Georgia (ironically, as medieval Georgian sources themselves acknowledge, Christianity itself began its existence in Georgia as an imported religion). These issues lay at the heart of the 1997 crisis. In April of that year, monks from several prominent Georgian monasteries published an open letter to Ilia II criticizing the ecumenical movement as 'heresy'. In particular, they attacked 'western Protestantism' and the ecumenical movement's endorsement of women in clerical activities, its indifference to and even support of homosexuality, and its emphasis upon the 'inclusive' language of the Bible. Archimandrite Giorgi of the Shio-Mghvime monastery and his companions insisted there could be only one church and that any compromise was tantamount to heresy. Much of this anti-ecumenical attitude was the result of Protestant missionary activities in post-Soviet Georgia.

The debate broke into the open, opposition rapidly mounted, and the Georgian Church stood on the verge of internal schism. Ilia reminded dissenters of the virtues and benefits of ecumenism, but to no avail. Just a short time later, on 20 May 1997, Ilia summoned ecclesiastical leaders and the decision was reached that the Georgian Church would immediately withdraw from the World Council of Churches and also the Council of European Churches. The patriarch was in the awkward position of having been a WCC president. It is instructive that in his communication of 20 May, Ilia did not characterize the ecumenical movement as heretical; clearly, he was compelled to this act as last resort in order to avoid full-blown schism within the Georgian Church. Anti-ecumenical sentiment remains strong in some quarters. Most dramatically, the former Orthodox priest Basil Mkalavishvili has been charged with orchestrating attacks upon non-Orthodox religious groups active in Georgia. Mobs armed with clubs and carrying crosses, icons, and banners have frequently interrupted meetings of non-Orthodox groups including Pentecostalists and Baptists. By fall 2002, there had been nearly a hundred registered acts of violence against Jehovah's Witnesses, one of the prime targets of 'Father Basil' and his thugs. Despite protests from governments in Europe and the United States, Georgian authorities have been slow to crack down on this campaign of violence and intimidation and others like it. Mkalavishvili's is an extreme and unfortunate solution to a very real problem facing the contemporary Georgian Orthodox Church: the proper place of religion, and especially Georgian Orthodoxy, in a newly independent, post-Soviet, democracy.

References and further reading

Abuladze, I. (1944) K'art'uli da somxuri literaturuli urt'iert'oba IX-X ss-shi: gamokvleva da tek'stebi (Georgian–Armenian Literary Relations, 9th–10th Centuries: Study and Texts). T'bilisi: Mec'niereba.

Alek'sidze, Z. (1968) Epistlet'a cigni (The Book of Letters). T'bilisi: Mec'niereba.

Blake, R. P. (1924) Georgian theological literature. Journal of Theological Studies (October): 50–64.

Church, K. (2001) From dynastic principality to imperial district: the incorporation of Guria into the Russian Empire to 1856. PhD dissertation, University of Michigan at Ann Arbor.

Djobadze, W. (1976) *Materials for the Study of Georgian Monasteries in the Western Environs of Antioch on the Orontes.* Corpus Scriptorum Christianorum Orientalium 327, subsidia 48. Louvain: CSCO/Peeters.

—— (1992) *Early Medieval Georgian Monasteries in Historic Tao, Klarjet'i, and Shavshet'i.* Stuttgart: Franz Steiner Verlag.

van Esbroeck, M. (1975) *Les plus anciens homéliaires géorgiens: étude descriptive et historique.* Publications de l'Institut orientaliste de Louvain 10. Louvain: Catholic University of Louvain, Institut Orientaliste.

—— (1982) Église géorgienne des origines au moyen age. *Bedi Kartlisa* 40: 186–99.

Gabashvili, T. (2001) *Pilgrimage to Mount Athos, Constantinople, and Jerusalem 1755–1759,* trans. and with commentary by M. Ebanoidze and J. Wilkinson. Richmond, UK: Curzon/Caucasus World.

Garsoïan, N. G. (1996) Iran and Caucasia. In R. G. Suny (ed.) *Transcaucasia, Nationalism, and Social Change: Essays in the History of Armenia, Azerbaijan, and Georgia,* rev. edn. Ann Arbor: University of Michigan Press.

—— (1999) *L'Église arménienne et le grand schisme d'orient.* Corpus Scriptorum Christanorum Orientalium 574, subsidia 100. Louvain: Peeters.

Garsoïan, N. G. and Martin-Hisard, B. (1996) Unité et diversité de la Caucasie médiévale (IVe–XIe s.). In *Il Caucaso: Cerniera fra Culture dal Mediterraneo alla Persia.* Settimane di Studio del Centro Italiano di Studi Sull'alto Medioevo 43a. Spoleto: Presso la Sede del Centro.

Gordeziani, R. (ed.) (2004) *K'ristianobis 20 saukune sak'art'veloshi* (20 Centuries of Christianity in Georgia). T'bilisi: Logosi.

Khrushkova, L. G. (2002) *Rannekhristianskie pamiatniki Vostochnogo Prichernomor'ia (IV–VII veka)* (The Early Christian Monuments of the Eastern Littoral of the Black Sea, 4th–7th Centuries). Moscow: Nauka.

Lang, D. M. (1955) St. Euthymius the Georgian and the Barlaam and Iosasph Romance. *Bulletin of the School of Oriental and African Studies* 17: 306–25.

—— (1957) *The Last Years of the Georgian Monarchy 1658–1832.* New York: Columbia University Press.

—— (1962) *A Modern History of Soviet Georgia.* Westport, Conn.: Greenwood Press.

—— (1976) *Lives and Legends of the Georgian Saints,* 2nd rev. edn. Crestwood, NY: St Vladimir's Seminary Press.

—— (1983) Iran, Armenia, and Georgia. In *The Cambridge History of Iran,* vol. 3.1 (pp. 505–36). Cambridge: Cambridge University Press.

Melia, E. (1971) The Georgian Orthodox Church. In R. H. Marshall, Jr. (ed.) *Aspects of Religion in the Soviet Union, 1917–1967.* Chicago: University of Chicago Press.

Mgaloblishvili, T'. (1991) *Klarjuli mravalt'avi* (The Klarjet'ian Polycephalon). T'bilisi: Mec'niereba.

Rapp, S. H., Jr. (2003) *Studies in Medieval Georgian Historiography: Early Texts and Eurasian Contexts.* Corpus Scriptorum Christianorum Orientalium 601, subsidia 113. Louvain: Peeters.

Rapp, S. H., Jr. and Crego, P. C. (2006) *The Conversion of K'art'li: The Shatberdi Variant,* Kek.Inst. S-1141. *Le Muséon* 119(1–2): 169–225.

Suny, R. G. (1994) *The Making of the Georgian Nation,* rev. edn. Bloomington: Indiana University Press.

Thomson, R. W. (1996) *Rewriting Caucasian History: The Medieval Armenian Adaptation of the Georgian Chronicles, the Original Georgian Texts and the Armenian Adaptation.* Oxford: Clarendon Press.

Toumanoff, C. (1963) *Studies in Christian Caucasian History.* Washington, DC: Georgetown University Press.

Xint'ibidze (Khintibize), E. (1996) *Georgian–Byzantine Literary Contacts.* Amsterdam: Adolf M. Hakkert.

CHAPTER 8

Greek Christianity after 1453

Vrasidas Karalis

History and its Discontents

The Fall of Constantinople in 1453 was the most traumatic event in the history of
Eastern Christendom; and yet it created possibilities for the Church that had never
existed before. The political power given to the patriarch by the Ottoman sultan was
instrumental in establishing the operational agenda for the Church for centuries to
come. The fall had in itself an element of irrevocability: Christian Constantinople would
eventually be transformed into Muslim Istanbul; and the first patriarch set up the
practices and the attitudes that were to remain dominant within the Orthodox world
until today.

Scholarios (1405–72) was both the man for the times and a man of another time.
His initial agreements with Mehmed the Conqueror secured the functional character
of the Church as an institution within the empire, relieved priests from taxation and
protected the faithful from forced conversions. Yet the very same person who showed
adaptability and prudence burned Pletho's book *On the Laws* (1454) for reasons that
cannot be clearly understood (except of course his personal vendetta against him) or
theologically justified. The strategy of both adaptability and exclusion has been
interpreted as a necessity under the circumstances. However, with the exception of a
very brief period in the early sixteenth century, the Christian community lived in
prosperity and protection under the Ottoman authority. The Ottomans usually tolerated
educational establishments and education was left in the hands of each *millet* to
administer; the Church itself was responsible for how the schools were to function and
more importantly, *whether* they would function at all.

However, as a totalitarian autocracy, the Ottoman political system demanded
obedience to the sultan and imposed sometimes unbearable taxes for funding wars of
expansion. In that respect they were not very different from the Byzantine emperors,
who saw religious dissent as sedition against their authority. Scholarios' approach to
the life of the faithful may be interpreted as survival ethics matched with social

authoritarianism. We must not forget that the patriarch and the aristocracy around him became civil servants to the sultan and they were treated as such according to the loyalty they showed. Precisely because of his autocratic rule the sultan treated all civil servants in the same ruthless way, irrespective of their religion (the slaughter of Ottoman officials adds many sad pages to the history of the empire). So Scholarios knew from the beginning the rules of the new game he was invited to participate in. At the same time, the Ottomans were something of a lesser evil, to the mind of the first patriarch; with regard to the 'Franks', the Church had already made its choice years before the fall; and now it had to abide by the consequences.

There is another important aspect in those last years of Christian Constantinople: the philosophical and theological debate between Platonists and Aristotelians. Scholarios was a staunch Aristotelian, in the tradition of Thomas Aquinas and Averroes. He never hesitated to take pride in his Scholastic philosophy. At the same time his rival Pletho (1360–1452) wrote his famous treatise *On the Differences between Plato and Aristotle*, in order to show how much more satisfactory for the modern minds of his day Platonic philosophy was. Pletho was more successful in making Cosimo Medici one of his devotees, and through his patronage Bessarion (1403–72) and his other students inaugurated a new Neoplatonic movement. Scholarios on the other hand was indeed an eminent Aristotelian who failed to convert the sultan to Christianity. Furthermore, his philosophical method was also rather contradictory: Scholarios employed Aristotelian categories and conceptual forms in order to explain or even justify mystical experience and the mystery of incarnation, and to talk about the ineffability of mystery in general through rational arguments of naturalistic empiricism – quite akin to the methods of Thomas Aquinas. And yet he rejected natural theology by creating a kind of diluted apophaticism or some sort of self-negating nominalism. Scholarios' philosophy and theology expressed the continuous conflict within the Orthodox tradition between faith and knowledge, a conflict which the magisterial *Summa* had temporarily solved for the West.

The antinomies became extremely obvious and therefore highly dangerous in such times of crisis; since the Church was under threat, presumed or real, its doctrine had to be practically confirmed and consolidated. Scholarios' Aristotelianism offered the canonical framework for a regulative epistemological paradigm which had to unify theology, ecclesiology, philosophy and mathematics. Pletho's Neoplatonic allegorizations destroyed with their subjectivism any kind of stable meaning: they couldn't function as normative paradigms; they were personal, chaotic and iconoclastic at the moment that Christianity demanded stability, fixity and uniformity.

Two centuries elapsed before the process of dis-identification commenced; in the mid-seventeenth century Theophilos Korydaleus (1574–1646) interpreted Aristotle as a natural philosopher and not as a Christian apologist. His interpretation was rejected and anathematized; the solid synthesis of doctrine, method and world view established by Scholarios remained unchallenged. In 1622, Patriarch Cyril Loukaris invited Korydaleus to reorganize the Patriarchal Academy by introducing contemporary learning and secular scholarship. The reorganization met the staunch opposition of the higher clergy and was soon quashed. Korydaleus' failure became the symbol of a tension that would resurface shortly before the Enlightenment: in the uneasy relationship between faith and knowledge within the Orthodox Church and the demand of ecclesiastical authorities to be in complete control of education.

Thus, for one hundred and fifty years, the theological tradition of the East retained a strong *antirrhetic* character, against everything coming from the West. It seems also that the Church was not informed about the radical changes that were taking place in the western world, during what is called the Renaissance. It did not even sense the events that led to the Reformation, although some initial contacts between Patriarch Dionysius II (1545–54) and Lutheran representatives date back to 1549.

Meanwhile, the sixteenth century was the great apogee of the Ottoman Empire under Suleiman the Magnificent. The sultan implemented a tolerant and judicious religious policy over his multinational empire; in 1537 he granted to Christians 'the great privilege of ours, to practise our religion freely and without any impediment' (Gedeon 1996: 381). However, the Ottoman Empire was also going through a deep transformation of its own after the conquest of Egypt (1517) by Selim I (the Grim) and the relocation to the capital of a considerable number of theologians and administrators from the stronghold of Islamic traditionalism. As a result, their presence increased tension between Sunnis and Shiites, and led to consideration of the forced Islamization of the Christian population. The same was attempted in 1537 by Selim's successor Suleiman; both requests were rejected by the administration and the Grand Mufti of Constantinople as being against the teachings of the Qur'an about the 'people of the book'.

The cultural wars of the Ottomans themselves had a long-term impact on their Christian subjects; those of a fundamentalist tendency demanded the banning of coffee, smoking, dancing and singing, while asking for the official expulsion of mathematics, astronomy and natural sciences from schools. In 1577 Sultan Murad (1574–95) built in the capital one of the most advanced observatories; however a plague that was then devastating the city was interpreted by the zealous fundamentalists as the wrath of God against those who were attempting to intrude into his secrets. The sultan succumbed to the pressure and razed the whole building to the ground, so that archaeologists are unable to locate its foundations to this day.

The Orthodox Church experienced similar cultural dilemmas within the general framework of belonging to an empire in a prolonged identity crisis. The situation was even more complex because of the constant proselytization by the Roman Catholic Church and the arrival of the first Jesuits in Constantinople (1583). Orthodox dioceses were divided between Roman Catholic Venetian rulers and the Ottoman sultanate. Whereas under the latter they enjoyed relative freedom of religious expression, this was not the case in the Venetian-ruled areas. There all Orthodox bishops and metropolitans were replaced by Latin representatives of the pope. In 1480, Patriarch Maximus III had written to the Doge of Venice asking for an end to the persecution of Orthodox clergy and for permission to collect a special levy for the patriarch. The whole of the next century was marked by attempts at proselytization by the Roman Catholics, which were intensified after the eruption of the Protestant movement. Pope Clement IX replaced all Orthodox bishops with his own people (1595), a policy that alienated local populations, who yearned for the religious tolerance enjoyed by Ottoman subjects. The Church appealed to the sultan, who put an abrupt end to the proselytizing activities of the Roman Catholics in the East (1576); after that he became *de facto* the guarantor of Orthodox faith. By the end of the same century the incorporation of the Orthodox Church into the Ottoman state was complete and unopposed from within.

Theologically, the period is also of some limited interest: the main issue discussed by contemporary theologians was a remnant of the Byzantine political legacy, that of the *filioque*. The issue had been resolved at the Council of Florence (1439) with an interesting compromise about the procession of the Holy Spirit *per filium*, during the incarnation (*opus trinitatis ad extra*) – an idea going back to Epiphanius of Cyprus in the fourth century. Anthropologically, such compromise had the meaning of validating history and sanctifying human action within time. Since Jesus was the Word incarnate in history, his very presence and actions made human history and activity legitimate and crucial within the history of salvation. Orthodox theologians insisted on the question of the addition to the Creed (which is a valid point indeed) but were unable to understand the anthropological consequences of the *filioque* and *per filium* clauses. By accepting the eternity of the kingdom and the timeless nature of being, as expressed by a triumphant Christian empire (which was Byzantium when the Creed was finalized), they could not see (and cannot to this day) that the meaning of the addition indicates *the centrality of actualized faith in history*. In the West the doctrine liberated the individual from apathy and inertia and instigated human action as the only way of making Christianity a factor for constant change. However, on the Orthodox side, most theological treatises of the fifteenth century persisted in dealing with this by then obsolete issue, by employing the rhetoric of ultimate finality: nothing could change without a decision by an Ecumenical Synod.

During the same period the Roman Catholic Church had already advanced to a neo-Scholastic elaboration of the doctrine under the influence of Thomas de Vio Cajetan (1469–1534), and moved towards a new theology which enhanced the conscious historicity of the individual (despite the rejection by the pope of individual conscience): which indicates the wide range of problems discussed in that period. At the same time the flowering of Spanish mysticism under St John of the Cross (1542–91) and St Teresa of Avila (1515–82), or even Ignatius of Loyola himself (1492?–1556), gave a completely new orientation to western theology by adding the element of personalized experience of divinity. Although this had begun earlier with Franciscan spirituality in the thirteenth century, it was something already known in the East with Symeon the New Theologian (949–1022), but largely ignored until the late eighteenth century, or at least restricted to monastic circles.

Not simply because of the Ottoman rule, but because of its entrenched defensive character, the East ignored such emerging issues even within its own confines. In the early sixteenth century Ioannikios Kartanos was imprisoned after teaching a mild form of pan-entheism, advocating that the world was not created by God but was born or emanated from within him, being therefore animate (*empsychos*). Kartanos drew a distinction between God and nature, rejected the Trinity but accepted the Incarnation. As a teacher he was persistently persecuted by the Church, together with his translation of the Bible, the first into the vernacular. In the middle of the same century a certain monk Mathaios, from Macedonia, was teaching that 'Jesus descended to the underworld in his physical body in order to bring Adam and his offspring back to life' (Stephanides

1990: 714). He was forced to repent and repudiate his 'cacodoxy' by the main exponent of Orthodox belief in the same period, Pahomios Rousanos, a stern apologist for Orthodoxy.

These debates are in themselves insignificant, especially in comparison with the raging Protestant theologies of Luther and Calvin in the West; they show, however, that there was an attempt to revisit some minor doctrinal issues in a period of radical reorientation of Christian theology and that there was a somehow unconscious attempt to 'naturalize' theology against the background of the 'visible revelation'. They represented failed and rather weak attempts to change the transcendental and spiritualistic character of the dominant traditional theology by raising the issue of a new perception of reality, as it was emerging then under the influence of natural sciences, the discoveries of the New World and the challenge that Neoplatonic language posited against traditional Orthodox articulation of the doctrine.

When the scholars of the Reformation contacted Patriarch Jeremias II their famous correspondence (1573–81) showed the completely different ways of theologizing of the Reformers and Eastern theologians; to an embarrassing degree, the Orthodox response is extremely Roman Catholic in character (with the exception of the issue of transubstantiation itself). Furthermore, from their correspondence it is clear that new issues were raised by the Reformers which asked for a better knowledge of the biblical text and the semantic nuances in the epistles of Paul. It was also obvious that the Eastern Church had not revisited the text of the New Testament, in particular after the hasty and faulty, but nevertheless liberating, early edition by Erasmus (1514). The Reformers were puzzled by some interesting repetitions in the Epistle to the Romans, especially the famous 'for those he foreknew he also predestined to be conformed to the image of his Son, in order that he might be the first-born among many brethren. And those whom he predestined he also called; and those whom he called he also justified; and those whom he justified he also glorified' (Rom. 8: 29–30).

These issues were re-entering the theological debate many centuries after early ecumenical synods decided on their validity for the Christian faith; however, now they had a completely new context of understanding and at the same time they reintroduced a factor which was rather neglected in the East: personal theology in the sense of an individuated interpretation of faith. For both Orthodoxy and Roman Catholicism there could not be a personal interpretation of doctrine. But when the biblical text became a printed page and not an aural/visual experience within a Eucharistic community, it was inevitable that new interpretations would emerge and new hermeneutical approaches would appear which would not necessarily be asking for the endorsement of the official Church.

Meletios Pegas (d. 1603) was the first theologian to understand that something new was born in the West; in his native Crete he witnessed the first persecutions of Protestants on Greek soil and developed a strong antipathy against the Church of Rome. Most of his works are against the pope, the primacy, the doctrine of purgatory and the *filioque*. The climate was indeed clouded by Pope Clement IX's decision to declare (1595) that the Orthodox Chrism was not valid, that it had to be repeated by a Roman Catholic bishop and that all Orthodox clergy had to accept the union; in Italy, Greek language was forbidden in the liturgy, and the College of St Athanasius (established in Rome in 1581) became one of the main centres of anti-Orthodox propaganda. The tension was so strong that, even on issues that the two Churches could agree on, there was no ground for common understanding left. In 1583, the new Gregorian calendar was rejected by a local synod in Constantinople, although the problem had been acknowledged since the late Byzantine period, when the humanist Nikephoros Gregoras proposed correcting the calendar in 1324. But the person who was to take on his shoulders the reaction against the aggressive post-Tridentine expansion in the East was Cyril Loukaris (1570–1638), one of the most important patriarchs of the East and one of the most controversial theologians of Orthodoxy. Many books have been written about his personality and work; for the purposes of our analysis we will mention his famous *Confession of Faith* (1629 and 1633).

Loukaris' presence acted as a catalyst for an avalanche of changes that were to shake the Orthodox Church for over a century. The scope and the perspective of his actions go beyond the ideas and practices of a marginalized and subordinate bishop. Sir Steven Runciman states that 'Cyril clearly issued his Confession in the hope of strengthening his flock against Romanising tendencies, of laying the foundation of a reformed and up-to-date Orthodox Church, and of providing a basis for negotiations with other Churches' (Runciman 1968: 276). The *Confession* was part of a general plan for reforming the Church, making priesthood active in the community, educating a generation of young clergymen and finally laying the foundations for a continuous dialogue with other Christians.

At the same time Loukaris asked Maximus Kallipolites to translate the New Testament into simpler Greek; and Theophilus Korydaleus to reorganize education by incorporating secular approaches to religious knowledge. Kallipolites' translation is one of the masterpieces of Greek literary language to this day; in the prologue Loukaris himself stated that the purpose of the publication was that the 'faithful would be able to read the Bible alone and by themselves'. Korydaleus tried also to instil the spirit of Aristotelian independence from biblical tradition; he tried to isolate the Bible from any philosophical framing that could occlude the direct and personal communication of the Word of God to the faithful.

Loukaris' *Confession* had a similar function; it was a personal document in which crucial aspects of Christian doctrinal tradition were readdressed. Justification and predestination are discussed as parts of a larger plan about sacraments, worship, traditional piety and the self-perception of the Christian. His insistence on justification by faith is humanly attributed to the inability of the individual to act under difficult circumstances ('this is what human frailty testifies', chapter XIII); this is an attempt to introduce the new anthropocentrism to the East. His concept of predestination raised the issues of being 'powerless and able to do nothing' (chapter XIV), in front of historical adversity. And as Cyril states, echoing Luther and Calvin, 'the time of grace is the present life' (chapter XVIII), stressing thus the conscious historicity and moral responsibility of the individual believer, as indeed had Symeon the New Theologian done before him. And it is a surely a great historical sadness that Cyril did not cite his Byzantine predecessors on this issue.

Loukaris' *Confession* was an attempt to historicize the Eastern Orthodox Church and make its faithful into active participants in larger historical projects. As Jaroslav Pelikan notes:

> In 1629 he published a confession of faith whose intent it was to achieve a synthesis of Eastern Orthodox dogma and mildly Calvinist theology, in which the genius of each tradition would be articulated without doing violence to the other. . . . The outcome of the controversy over his confession showed that the east in fact believed and taught much more than it confessed, but it was forced to make its teaching confessionally explicit in response to the challenge. (Pelikan 1974: 282–3).

Not one of his detractors or even his students who tried to refute his confession succeeded in writing anything substantial against him.

After the upheaval caused by Loukaris and Korydaleus, the Church went through a period of intense conservatism, expressed through local synods denouncing the *Confession* and by the persistent writing of counter-confessions. The creative re-elaboration of doctrines and practices that Loukaris instigated subsided under rigid formalism and the tendency to codification. This has to be seen within the context of growing stagnation in the Ottoman Empire. After the failure to capture Vienna in 1668, it was obvious that the empire was falling into a period of introspection and was gradually turning towards its natural environment, the East, in order to recover. The orientalization of the Church became visual with the new vestments and the clothes of priests; and oriental scales in chanting were introduced progressively during the seventeenth century. The origin of such changes was Persia, as a Persian craze hit the court and the aristocracy of Constantinople after 1638 when Sultan Murad conquered Bagdad and brought with him to Constantinople the famous Persian musician Sach-Koules.

The Synod of 1672 in Jerusalem denounced Loukaris and declared his *Confession* anti-Orthodox. However, the rise of Russia under Peter the Great (r. 1689–1725) and technological progress in the West facilitated the movement of ideas and spread them first of all among the only people who were literate and had access to books, namely the clergy and aristocracy. At the beginning of the eighteenth century, the city of Ioannina, in central Greece, and many cities of the Asia Minor coastline founded their own schools, with the sponsorship of wealthy Greeks of the diaspora. From these areas a new generation of scholars emerged who were to lay the foundation for the Greek reception of the Enlightenment.

In 1723, the Ecclesiastical Court did not simply defrock Methodios Anthrakitis and ban him from teaching because 'he rejected as insignificant the teachings of the most ancient traditions of our most revered fathers'; it also threatened with excommunication 'all those who read his writings and notebooks and those who would attempt to use them for teaching or any one would like to study them'. Methodios's notebooks were ritually burnt because he was a 'pantheist' in the tradition of the Spanish mystic Miguel Molinos, whose teachings were also proscribed by the Roman Catholic Church in 1687. One of the main accusations against Methodios was that he rejected or undervalued sacramental worship by espousing the *contemplatio passiva* and that he identified God with the universe (*theopantistes*). He was forced to denounce his ideas and after he confessed his errors was allowed to teach again.

Two decades later a young monk from Corfu, Evgenios Voulgaris (1716–1806), translated into Greek John Locke's *An Essay Concerning the Human Understanding*; a translation that introduced the premises of Enlightenment into the Eastern Church. Voulgaris knew eleven languages and during his life translated into Greek, with commentaries, works by Descartes, Leibniz, Newton, Hobbes and especially Voltaire. Not all of his translations were published; but his ideas as a teacher and an intellectual gained wide currency in the period and made him the leader of the Enlightenment movement in the Orthodox world from the 1750s. In 1753, Patriarch Cyril VI invited him to become the principal of a new school of advanced studies on the monastic independent region of Mount Athos. There Evgenios reorganized the famous Athonias School, which was based on Plato's Academy and included in its curriculum the whole scope of traditional wisdom combined with modern scientific knowledge. The school started with fewer than twenty students, but within five years over two hundred followed its courses. Evgenios was a highly educated teacher and created by himself, almost without meaning to, a cultural renaissance which was to last till the beginning of the Greek revolution.

However, monks from the Athonite monasteries spread rumours that he was teaching atheist propaganda and reacted furiously against his lectures. Evgenios was forced to leave the monastic republic and found refuge in Leipzig, Berlin and finally in Russia, where he became a close friend to Catherine II. His *Logic* (1766) introduced a kind of philosophical eclecticism into Greek thought which was to become the basis for a large number of personal philosophies around the end of the century. As a philosopher Voulgaris had judgement indeed but he was totally lacking in depth; he could not develop an argument and, even worse, he could not construct one, but he was extremely efficient in showing the deficiencies in the arguments of other thinkers. His monumental *Logic* paved the way for an encyclopaedic and expository academic philosophy which was highly uncritical, and simply systematized existing ideas. The same can be said about his great *Theologicon* (published posthumously in 1872). Despite the impressive arrangement and structure of the work, the ideas expressed are underscored by a strong defensive and dismissive tone against any kind of criticism or creative questioning.

His contribution was that he paved the way for something new that was far beyond him and his understanding. However, he was in a position to sense the new conditions of being which emerged during this period of Enlightenment. As a result, Voulgaris introduced into Greek a concept and a word which did not exist until then; he translated 'toleration' as *anexithreskeia* (1768), in order to indicate the reality of religious pluralism and acceptance of heterodoxy.

> Tolerance, [he writes] which contemporary Latins call *Tolerantiam* and which we could not inappropriately perhaps call *Anexithreskeia*, is nothing more than the lenient and meek predisposition of pious soul, which according to the zeal of understanding, uses the most innocuous and harmless approach towards those who do not espouse the same religion; towards these people and their edification it either uses admonition or friendliness. Finally,

even when they are not persuaded, it accepts them with magnanimity and without resentment, feeling sad for their loss and protecting or even impeding the destruction or the corruption of others – yet he never rages against them in a tyrannical manner or with brutality or behaves inhumanly towards them. (Voulgaris 2001: 21–2)

But the movement he unleashed was too much for him at the end; living a privileged life under the protection of the Tsarina, he renounced his own ideas and regressed into a kind of blind rejection of everything contemporary or indeed of everything non-Christian. His renunciation of modernity was the dominant pattern imposed by the patriarchate during the last sixty years before the Greek Revolution. Although the Church first brought the ideas and the knowledge of western scientific and philosophical progress into the East, the growing realization that modern ideas were necessarily anti-Christian forced the patriarchate to a position similar to that of the Roman Catholic Church: all modern knowledge was dangerous for the Christian believer and as such it should be denounced and avoided.

Furthermore, the struggle between faith and knowledge took a new form when the Ecumenical Patriarchate had to deal with the rise of the fragmenting national movements. The internal differentiation from the Christian *genos* to the Hellenic *ethnos* had started to take shape by the end of eighteenth century; and the appearance of a new generation of scholars was enough to show that the one would inevitably replace the other, or at least demonstrate the implicit antagonism between these two cultural realities, which were of common origin but from then onwards were to follow different historical trajectories.

Evgenios' short-lived liberal teaching created a number of eminent intellectuals who were to reshape the cultural landscape within the Greek language and change the ways of articulating philosophical and theological statements in the Orthodox tradition. The greatest intellectual of all was the prominent philologist and classical scholar Adamantios Koraes (1748–1833) the person who inaugurated a new articulation of the Greek *ethnos* as a distinct entity within the continuum of Christian universalism. But the new ethnos had to be defined not simply culturally, in regard to the historical past, or linguistically, as has usually been the case with Greek education. For Koraes, the self-definition and self-determination of the new *ethnos* should be the result of political and social differentiation *within* existing institutions; and such differentiation had to be supported and enhanced through the study of the canonical books of the past, the classical writers and the Bible.

Koraes' project for a new *ethnos*, the Hellenic ethnos, inevitably collided with the *genos* tradition as perceived by the Church. And he realized that a kind of mild reformation was needed in order for the nation to dissociate itself politically from the autocracy of Byzantium and the Ottoman Empire. Implicitly the main target of Koraes' project was the power of the patriarchate, something that Patriarch Gregory V felt deeply. Being a philologist, Koraes' model was another earlier moderate reformer, namely Erasmus. Koraes wanted educated Christian conscience to be shaped by a close study of canonical texts, so that it could be critical, political and democratic. Shortly before his death he published, in 1831, a close study and translation of the epistle to Titus, traditionally attributed to St Paul, together with Paul's two Epistles to Timothy.

The Greek state had been established and a marked turn to an absolutist regime was becoming obvious. Koraes thought that one of the main sources of political corruption was the abuses of the Church:

> What should I say more about the bishops, what should I say to the reader in order to realise the origin of their abuses and the necessity for their abolition? The origins were the enslavement of the people to the ecclesiastical despots and to what follows slavery, that is illiteracy, which inspired clergymen to imitate courtiers, to buy titles like them and rule despotically like them, forgetting Christ's command 'it should not be like that in you'. The necessity for their abolition is a result of the need to reject all despotic mentality, if we want to protect our freedom. But who from us the people can deny all these, when he is blessed not by spiritual fathers but by untouchable hegemons? Who can show contempt towards titles and honours when he sees his bishops decorating themselves with barbaric and tyrannical adjectives, so that in the end they become as grand as to look gross and ridiculous? (Koraes 1964: 1270–80)

Koraes' students paved the way for the new adventure of Eastern Christianity in Greece and inaugurated the process of a gradual emancipation from the Patriarchate of Constantinople. Amongst them Benjamin Lesbios (1759–1824) elaborated a completely new Christian and naturalistic system of ethical principles based on a highly sophisticated philosophical system; Konstaninos Koumas (1777–1836) critically introduced Immanuel Kant's philosophy into the Greek world and attempted the first grand narrative of modern political history (*History of Human Actions*, 12 volumes, Vienna, 1824–32). They were both constructing new conditions for understanding the past by expanding the limits of interpretive language. They both advocated simplicity in worship and the need for education of the clergy, and asked for reforms of ecclesiastical structures towards more accountability and openness to the citizens of the new state. The project looked like being commonly accepted, especially when one of the first acts of the revolution was to declare Koraes the 'great national benefactor' and 'the teacher of the nation'; but the fate of two of his students, Theoklitos Pharmakides and Theophilos Kaires, would prove that on the way to realizing this something had gone horribly wrong.

Establishing a National Church

Patriarch Gregory V's excommunication of the Greek revolutionaries (1821) was not simply an indication of his conservative and highly autocratic administration; it entailed the presumption that the slightest fragmentation in patriarchal jurisdiction would create a domino effect throughout the Balkans and would lead back to the chaos of the thirteenth and fourteenth centuries. In 1766–7 the archbishoprics of Peć and Achris were annexed, with the endorsement of the sultan, to the Patriarchate of Constantinople; by the end of that century its jurisdiction was almost the same as that in tenth-century Byzantium. The Church was in total control of education and the flow of ideas; so Koraes and his students had to publish their work outside the Ottoman Empire: 'Paris,

Trieste, Venice, Amsterdam and especially Vienna,' he wrote in one of his letters, 'are today the cultural capitals of Hellenism.'

And indeed, journals, newspapers, books, translations were published in these cities, whereas in the Hellenic Museum, the school established by Gregory in Constantinople, only the patriarch's speeches and denunciations of the Enlightenment were allowed to be printed and read. However, with the rise of nationalism and ideas of self-determination, popular opinion in various Orthodox regions (Serbia, Romania, Bulgaria, etc.) turned irrevocably against the domination of the patriarch, who was almost always of Greek origin, and was so closely allied to a non-Christian ruler. One year before the Greek revolution of 1821, Patriarch Gregory V anathematized Copernicus' books together with all books of modern natural sciences; these two anathematizations were his last acts of pastoral care before he was strangled by order of the Ottomans. But the centralized system that he defended, in collusion with the Ottomans, started crumbling when the revolution begun.

After 1821 there was no immediate communication between the patriarch and the revolutionaries. There was a serious problem about the validity of all ordinations during this period, which was to be resolved later with an amicable settlement. Yet even if we accept that the Greek revolution was predominantly a national uprising, the demography of the Greek mainland and of the islands was not purely Orthodox. When the revolutionaries gathered in Epidavros, about the end of 1821, in order to agree on the constitution of their future state, they found themselves in a puzzling situation. National identity did not really mean religious affiliation; there were many Albanians, Christian and Muslim, amongst them, Roman Catholics from the Aegean islands and philhellenic Protestants from the West. The issue of Jews was also raised during these discussions. But what came out after many deliberations was enshrined in the second chapter of the 1822 Constitution as follows: 'All native inhabitants of the Greek territory who believe in Christ are Greek and enjoy all civil rights without any restriction.' The Constitution abolished slavery, social ranks and hereditary privileges. The first article of the first chapter stated: 'The predominant religion within Greek territory is that of the Eastern Orthodox Church of Christ; however, the Greek government tolerates every other religion, whose rituals and sacred mysteries can be conducted without any obstacle' (Svolos 1972: 65–6). The conscious attempt of the revolutionaries at nation-building had to deal with the serious problem of religion; national identity remained a matter of religious belief and ecclesiastical commitment. The idea that 'all those who believe in Christ and are born in Greek territory are Greek' conveyed to the early state-builders a rather inaccurate conception of their immediate reality, which was to be maintained throughout the revolution.

Yet the problem became more obvious when many more non-Greek and non-Orthodox people arrived in Greece to assist the revolutionaries (the most prominent of all being Lord Byron, who was declared an honorary Greek citizen). In 1823, the reform assembly of the revolutionaries tried to reduce tension between rival factions; to do so, the articles of the Constitution had to be qualified. The first article, about the 'predominant religion in Greek territory', was retained, but in an attempt to dissociate Greek citizenship from any specific Christian denomination it was now prescribed that:

All native inhabitants of Greek territory who believe in Christ are Greek and enjoy all civil rights without any restriction. Similarly Greeks, and enjoying the same civil rights, are those foreigners who speak Greek and want to believe in Christ, by appearing in front of regional Greek authority so they can be enlisted as Greek citizens. (Svolos 1972: 80)

In the same chapter of the Constitution an ominous article appeared for the first time:

All Greeks have the right to express their ideas in the press, under the following conditions: 1. not to say anything against Christian religion. 2. not to transgress commonly accepted principles of morality. 3. to avoid personal vilification. (ibid.)

In the final constitution of the revolution (1827) an uneasy compromise was achieved. In the first article, on religion, it was stated: 'Every person in Greece can practise his religion freely and has the same protection for its worship. The religion of the state is that of the Eastern Orthodox Church of Christ.' Unquestionably the phantom of theocracy is looming large behind such statements. The same constitution attempted for the last time to solve the question of who is Greek by incorporating four new conditions:

Greeks are: 1. all native inhabitants of Greek territory, who believe in Christ. 2. All those under the Ottoman rule, who believe in Christ and arrived or will arrive in the Greek territory in order to fight for or live in it. 3. All those born in foreign territories of Greek father. 4. All those native persons, or non-native, and their descendants, who became citizens in other countries before the formulation of this Constitution, and arrive in Greek territory giving oath of allegiance to Greece. 5. All foreigners who become Greek citizens. (Svolos 1972: 94)

Without doubt, religious belief became a nation-building exercise during the period of state formation, especially from 1828 to 1864. Furthermore, the problem of the relations between state and Church became more complex after the arrival of the first king of Greece, Otto (1833–62). Otto was Roman Catholic but apart from that he was fully immersed in the romantic classicism that was dominating Europe. When he arrived in Greece he decided to relocate the capital city from the city of Nauplion, in the Peloponnese (a place full of memories of the immediate past and of the war of liberation), to the imaginary birthplace of all European culture, Athens. The city itself became the locus of a new state ideology in which the idealized history of Periclean glory was combined with the idea that Athens was the political centre of a new state, an idea that appeared as a result of the Enlightenment. Soon after, the University of Athens was established (1837) along the lines of the ideas set out by Koraes and his project for a moderate Enlightenment. The first problems between state and Church emerged when the state decided to control the Church and reorganize it along traditional German Protestant lines, not simply for ecclesiastical reasons but because of the Russian political intervention that was taking place through the Church.

Otto's project came into conflict with two very deeply rooted factors of Greek society: first, the long historical connection with the Patriarchate of Constantinople, and second, the role of the lower clergy in particular throughout the Ottoman period and the revolution. Negotiations between the patriarchate and the first governor of the newly established state, Conte Capodistria had already started. After the assassination of Capodistria (1831) discussions were postponed but always remained as one of the national questions that had to be resolved. In 1844 a military revolt took place against Otto's autocratic regime, which led to the formulation of the first political constitution of the emerging Greek society. The person behind the idea for a new relation between Church and state was one of Koraes' best students, Theokletos Pharmakides (1784–1860). He thought that the newly established state was a new beginning for the Greek people, who had to cut themselves away from the legacy of Byzantium as represented by the patriarchate; he warned of the danger of a theocratic system that would control the body politic of the state; he was a staunch opponent of any kind of restriction on the free expression of the individual; finally he believed that 'the autonomy and the independence of the Church are inseparable from the autonomy and the independence of the state and every attack against the Church is a direct or indirect attack against the state'. His main concern was to dissociate the new Church from Constantinople by identifying it as one of the social and civil apparatuses of the state, as was the case with the Church of England. By reducing the Church to a state apparatus, he thought that the caesaropapist elements within it would recede and that it would be transformed into a place for spiritual quest. Pharmakides was a competent scholar, having published a massive four-volume exegetical commentary on the New Testament, and being a strong advocate of the translation of the Bible into a simpler Greek language. His plans were immediately deemed to be 'protestantizing', and he himself had to face the immense hostility of the educated conservative Konstaninos Oikonomos (1780–1857).

Oikonomos was a contradictory individual whose intellectual formation followed a trajectory similar to that of Voulgaris. In the beginning he was impressed by the Enlightenment and the new ideas; however, his protection by the autocratic regime in Russia, his personal friendship with Tsar Alexander I and his strong attachment to the patriarchate made him change his mind after his return to Greece in 1834. He immediately allied himself with the so-called Russian Party and instigated a strong and continuous opposition to all plans for changes that did not have the consent of the patriarchate. In 1833, Pharmakides and the Bavarian Vice-Regent Maurer had formulated a plan which proclaimed: (1) the autocephalous Church of Greece, (2) the subordination of the Church to the state, and (3) the dissolution of all monasteries with fewer than six monks. The intention was to free the Church from the powerful influence of the Russian Church and to help the state begin to reconstruct the devastated country. Oikonomos opposed this plan by establishing secret societies (the Orthodoxophile Society among them) in order to incite public unrest and galvanize all Orthodox forces in support of the protection that Russia, as a co-Orthodox country, offered to the patriarchate. He spoke repeatedly with a rhetoric that was to become the most pervasive mode of conservative Orthodox advocates, down to contemporary theologians such as Christos Yannaras. He declared that 'we have to fight against the blasphemous novelty (*kainotomia*) of becoming independent and against the charlatans and fortune-seekers, of our race or other races, who imported alien and strange miasmas against traditional customs, as though it was an example of cultural advancement' (Oikonomos 1993: 23).

The conflict between Pharmakides and Oikonomos was theoretically resolved with the victory of Pharmakides and his political supporters in the 1844 constitutional compromise. Although it seemed that the new political arrangement, by legally protecting freedom of individual conscience and expression, favoured the autocephalous Church and confirmed the need for it to take a new direction, it became clear that Pharmakides' plan had begun to disintegrate. Pharmakides was gradually neutralized and the king started negotiations with the patriarchate; in 1850 the patriarch issued the *Tomos*, a document of mutual compromises, which ratified the new reality. Pharmakides responded with the 'Anti-Tomos', an extremely passionate and provocative document which argued that any connection with the patriarchate would mean a voluntary lack of emancipation from the past and would show the self-declared inability of the Greek Church to engage into a dialogue with the most obvious institution established by post-Enlightenment modernity, that is the nation-state. It would also mean conflict between two perceptions of legitimacy and civil rights within the nation-state. His passionate response was largely ignored and the antagonism between civil society and traditional authorities was soon to come into the open, along with some serious problems of civil disorder and legitimacy.

Theophilos Kaires (1784–1853) was one of the leaders of the Greek Revolution, a deeply educated priest and a progressive pedagogue. After the revolution he established an orphanage in his native island of Andros, where with the support of local population he started preaching his personal religion. He called it *theosebeia* (God-piety) and it was a patromonistic version of Christianity, very close to Judaism and Islam, but based on a new personal, almost mystical experience of God as perceived by individual reason. Undoubtedly, Kaires was indebted to the rationalist religion of the Theophilanthropists of the French Revolution, the philosophy of Auguste Comte about the self-deified humanity, and the ideas of Quakers and George Fox. Both the Incarnation and the Trinity were symbolic re-enactments of what happens in the human heart at the moment it realizes the mysterious nature of being and its incomprehensible finality. 'Since I was a child,' he stated in his final apology at the court that was to sentence him:

> I had many doubts about the doctrines of Christian religion and its sacraments. . . . In such a confused state in which I was, there was danger in remaining religion-less; but since I could not bear such beastly existence, I decided to conform, until I should become able to solve my questions. Because as long as I remained in that state of doubt and crisis, I looked like a man fallen into a ravine, who, while he tries with all his strength to escape, falls into an even deeper abyss, since the shaky basis on which he supports his feet collapses and disintegrates. At last, one serene and quiet night as I was looking intently at the starry majestic and resplendent sky, I thought that I read on the firmament, written with golden letters, the words 'Respect God', 'Love God'. At that moment I felt that that the tribulation that had devoured my soul until then was immediately appeased and vanished. (Paschales 2000: 185)

This is the most spiritual moment in nineteenth-century Greece, a moment of harmonious fusion of the individual with the universe. It is notable that the 1840s were a period of immense spiritual and religious unrest worldwide: in China, the Tai Ping movement based on the ecstatic vision of Hung Hiu Ch'uan created a new religion of mixed Christian and Taoist origin; in Persia, the Bab, or Gateway, founded the Baha'i faith; in India, the Brahmosamaj created a Christian-Hindu syncretism and in 1851 Ramakrishna had his first revelations. In the United States, Joseph Smith (1805–44) had his first encounters with an angel who took him to the cave where the golden plates with the history of the lost tribes of Israel were safely guarded for centuries; the Mormon faith was then born as the first authentic American religion. In Europe, traditional Christianity had already been questioned by the rise of biblical criticism and the research into the personality of the historical Jesus, while philosophically Søren Kierkegaard had laid the foundations for modern existentialism. At the same time, the social question was becoming more obvious and pressing; in 1848 Karl Marx published his *Communist Manifesto*, a declaration of a new perception of a millenarian Utopia. Furthermore, within the Eastern Orthodox countries, Russia was shaken by the rise of mystical sects in the woods of Siberia and the profound challenges of western rationalism; Dostoevsky's bleak and terrifying vision of human nature started emerging as a product of such irrevocable change in the relations between individual conscience and the divine. Charles Darwin's *Origin of Species* (1859) shattered for ever the closed and self-gratifying universe of traditional Christianity and shed new light on the perception of human history as a never-ending process between progress and regression.

The case of Kaires shows how harshly the autocephalous Church of Greece could deal with dissent and diversity. The Church falsely prosecuted Kaires for proselytization and had him imprisoned twice under terrible conditions that undermined his health. At the end of 1853 he was sentenced to seven years in prison, a punishment that quickly led to his death. Two weeks later, when he had already died and been buried, the Supreme Court revoked the decision. Meanwhile, his enemies dragged his body out of his grave and threw it into limestone to be burnt for his sins against the Church.

This was only the beginning of a series of persecutions of independent intellectuals and writers that prevented any lively theological and philosophical debate developing in nineteenth-century Greece. In 1856, the writer Andreas Laskaratos (1811–1902) published his fairly innocuous satire *The Mysteries of Cephalonia*, which simply criticized manners, customs and traditions of priests in his native island. The book was immediately banned by the Church and Laskaratos was anathematized; the Church bells tolled for days and the writer was persecuted from all sides. At that time the western prefecture of the Seven (Ionian) Islands was an English protectorate, but the decision was taken at both local and national level.

> This abomination of the desert born amongst us is worthy of contempt and unworthy of any Christian care; it is worthy of being enlisted amongst the few but most horrible minds, born from time to time, who spoke out against Christian society, like spiritual monsters, stigmatised with the eternal anathema of all Christian generations. (Laskaratos 1916: 11)

But the most obvious case against free thinking took place when a young writer called Emmanuel Roides (1836–1904) published his now famous 'medieval study' under the title *Pope Joan* (1866). The storm that was unleashed was to last for decades and formed the way that the official Orthodox Church perceived creative imagination, revision of the past and understanding of intellectual life. The book is uneven structurally but stylistically is a masterpiece. Despite the fact that it depicts the medieval mores of the Roman Catholic Church, it was quite clear that the attack was against the Church as an institution. The publication of the book was immediately followed by an official denunciation and anathematization by the Orthodox Church with the protection of the Kingdom of Greece. The Synod of the Church sent to all parishes a remarkable encyclical against the 'blasphemous and malignant book' which it said was 'harmful to the body and the soul of the faithful, who should stay away from it as from a monster and a miasmatic disease and who should throw it into fire, wherever they find it, so that they themselves won't be tempted and be guilty of the eternal fires of hell' (Roides 2001: 57). Roides responded with four very powerful letters defending freedom of conscience:

> The greatest of our gifts that we maintained after the fall, or even better we developed because of the fall, since before it was rather useless, as I think, is that special force within our soul, which we call 'Conscience' and through which we distinguish between good and evil, loving the former and despising the latter. . . . Nothing can quench the light of conscience; as a great contemporary poet says 'human kind is altogether an honest man', loving good and abhorring evil. (Roides 2001: 345)

To such theologically sound language, the Church replied with a tirade of extreme abuse that had the effect of transforming the rather dilettantish writer into an intellectual hero; and this kind of persistent reaction has established the Church ever since as the main anti-intellectual force in Greek society. Roides' witty rationalism inaugurated a fresh understanding of the recorded history of the Church, from within the critical perspective of Edward Gibbon and Voltaire, through the meticulous scrutiny of primary sources and the conscious attempt to explain through the problematic of their eras. Yet his book galvanized an incipient alliance between state and Church, which were gradually coming closer, as the generation of the revolution and that of Koraes' students were dying.

By the end of the century, and despite the changes that were taking place in the patriarchate, which was rediscovering its ecumenical character, the Church of Greece was forming the concept of *synallellia*, co-synergy, with the Greek state. The identification of national borders with ecclesiastical jurisdiction contributed greatly to this new bond of co-survival between Church and state: every questioning of the Church and its historical foundations became inimical to the state and as such it was declared illegal. This collusion culminated in the bizarre inclusion in the first (later the third) article of the Constitution of the unexpected clause that 'The Greek state forbids completely any translation of the text of the Holy Scripture, without the approval of the Great Church in Constantinople.' This article has ever since been repeated in all Greek constitutions, as if the Greek state had the copyright on the New Testament. Two translations that were attempted in the first decade of the twentieth century were condemned and banned; two students were killed in the centre of Athens defending the integrity of the Orthodox faith which they believed was endangered by the act of translating. In 1911, the Constitution simply sanctioned a close alliance between the two partners in a manner that left indelible marks on the spiritual life of the Church.

The first step towards the gradual convergence became obvious in the case of the theologian Apostolos Makrakes (1831–1905). In one of his trips by boat to Constantinople as a child he experienced a vision of the Virgin over the Aegean; she enjoined him to study the Bible and become a good Christian. He studied it indeed, learned many languages and published enormous commentaries on the Bible, which are monuments to his omnivorous polymathy and yet a conspicuous demonstration of sterile literalism. It was not simply a personal issue; the banishment of any kind of creative dialogue within the Church made it impossible for new theologians to assess new methods of looking at the Bible as they were articulated in the nineteenth century outside Greece. The Theological School in Athens functioned more as seminary for priests or preachers and less as a tertiary education institution for critical thinking and advancement of knowledge. Makrakes rejected the predominant allegorical interpretation of the Bible in the Eastern Church, but he was unable to interpret its meaning contextually and culturally; he thought of the New Testament text as the direct and unmediated word of God, which was impenetrable and inscrutable. By disregarding the humanity of its writers and their very historicity, he interpreted the texts as self-explanatory documents whose meaning could be unfolded only in acts of personal intuition.

He also based his interpretation of the human phenomenon on the tripartite division by Paul in his letter to the Corinthians (1 Cor. 15: 39–49), between the carnal (*sarkikos*), psychic (*psychikos*) and spiritual (*pneumatikos*) body. He advocated the *trisyntheton* of human beings as a gradual process of evolving from the physical body to the pneumatic, through Christian baptism, with the psychic body as the result of the historical life of the individual. His teachings were immediately rejected by the Church, which advocated the mind–body dichotomy as a result of the pervasive Platonic and Manichean influence in Christian history. So Makrakes was expelled from the Church; he then formed his own Church, on the models of Evangelical and Pentecostal traditions, and introduced public confession and communion without fasting every Sunday. In 1878 the Church issued a fierce encyclical against him and forced the government to close down his school and his church. Makrakes was taken to court twice, accused of heresy, and was sentenced to two years' imprisonment. The persecutions undermined his health and Makrakes died a lonely man, abandoned by his followers and in utter poverty.

The Vicissitudes of the Twentieth Century

As was mentioned earlier, the twentieth century began with attacks on the translation of the New Testament into modern Greek and the official, albeit incomprehensible, prescription of the Greek state to be itself in control of the integrity of the text. Even the new and all-powerful star of Greek politics, Eleftherios Venizelos (1864–1936), was unable to introduce any reforms. During the tragic decade 1912–22 Venizelos found himself victim to his indecision and procrastination. Whereas he had the mandate with his absolute majority in 1910–11 to introduce constitutional changes, he opted for minor reforms in the relations between Church and state, or between various state institutions, such as the monarchy and Parliament. And yet even such cosmetic semi-reforms incited the wrath of the ecclesiastical and court establishments. The Church had gradually consolidated a functional *modus vivendi* with the aristocracy and the King; so Venizelos, who was always perceived as an intruder, by modernizing Greek power structures was questioning the two pillars of social cohesion, monarchy and Church. At the same time, the conflict went deeper as the ambitious King Constantine was presenting himself as the future emperor in Constantinople; the clash between Venizelos and the king was a conflict between civil society and religious monarchy: between Athens and Constantinople, democracy against theocracy.

During a deep political crisis that divided Greece regarding its participation in the First World War with either the English or the Germans, the Archbishop of Athens Theokletos (1848–1930) anathematized the popularly elected Prime Minister of the country in one of the most memorable events of Greek history, on 12 December 1916. In the central square of Athens, in front of an effigy of Venizelos made with the skull of a donkey and stones, he himself read the text of anathematization, in front of thousands of frenzied supporters:

> Anathema to your family who profaned Greece with you; anathema to your father who gave you his seed; anathema to your mother who nurtured such a snake in her womb; accursed and wretched man! May you stay for ever in the darkness of our religion that you didn't respect; may no one be close to you and close your eyes when you die so that you keep your eyes open even when dead and see the country you have betrayed; anathema to your soul, anathema to the chaos you have created; anathema to your memory, anathema to all who remember you, anathema, anathema, anathema.

This incident shows beyond any reasonable doubt the main characteristic of the Greek Church: the complete and utter politicization of its structure.

One year later, Theokletos was replaced by Meletios Metaxakes (1871–1935) probably the most important and most controversial leader of the Church. Meletios, like his predecessor and all his successors, was a political appointment. The Synod simply accepted him as the Archbishop of Athens, after he had already been installed by the government. He was extremely active in inter-denominational dialogue, started official discussions with the Church of England, accepted the validity of Anglican ordinations and even discussed intercommunion with them. Like Loukaris, he saw in the Protestant Churches the natural and inevitable allies of Eastern Orthodox, especially under the very difficult position the latter found themselves in during the Greek-Turkish war of 1919–22, which ended with the Asia Minor catastrophe. Meletios was Archbishop of Athens for two short years (1918–20), and was replaced in turn by his predecessor, who was appointed by the king after his return to the throne. However, Meletios become the Patriarch of Constantinople and then the Archbishop of America, where he succeeded in unifying the various Orthodox Churches. In 1931, he led the Orthodox delegation at the Anglican conference in Lambeth, where his presence and theological acumen were deeply appreciated. He died the Patriarch of Alexandria, as probably the most individual and most misunderstood primate of the Church of Greece.

After 1922, a new era started for Greece. It was the first time that the overwhelming majority of Greeks lived in the same state; the concentration of people from various cultural and even linguistic backgrounds, who were connected with a loose common identity, had to be reinforced with common rituals and practices that would consolidate an otherwise shaky social stability. From 1922, the necessity for unifying strategies transformed the Church into one of the most powerful nation-building places within the state. The actual sacred space of the church gave a sense of belonging and of orderly time to the faithful, otherwise denied by the state apparatuses, which were totally unreliable and untrustworthy and thought by the common people to be responsible for the greatest catastrophe of Greek history.

The failure in Asia Minor made the dysfunctionality of the Greek state not simply obvious but also dangerous. Since civil society failed to evolve, the population turned to the atemporal permanence of the liturgy in order to impose cohesion and symmetry onto the chaotic political life of their society. In 1923 new negotiations between state and Church secured a commonly accepted plan of operation, which supposedly ended the domination of the state over the independence of the synodical structure. The state became the guarantor of the Church as long as the Church supported its policies; in exchange the Church would support the political establishment as long as it did not try to change the status quo between them. Since then, officially the Church actively supports all governments in power, if they do not fail to protect its interests from corrosion by giving away rights to religious minorities and other sectarian groups, or by permitting attempts to tax its immense property and assets.

In 1927, the Archbishop of Athens Chrysostomos (1868–1938) came close to declaring the Church under persecution when the first socialist minister tried to confiscate some of its land properties in order to settle the Asia Minor refugees in them. At the same time another demand surfaced which was later to become a state law: in 1947 all priests became public servants and their salary has been paid by the state in toto to this day. At the same time, with the notable exception of Chrysanthos (1938–41), the Church publicly endorsed the political ideology of the state, especially anti-Communism under General Metaxas (1936–41), even to the extent of blessing concentration camps after the Civil War (1947–49), and later of officially endorsing the 1967 dictatorship. The Church was extremely active in such constitutional aberrations and strongly supported the ensuing totalitarian regimes; its political involvement was deep and pervasive. In 1944, Archbishop Damaskinos (1890–1949), that 'scheming medieval prelate', according to Winston Churchill (Brendon 2001: 193), became Vice-Regent over a divided country; it was the apogee in the career of a metropolitan who had always dreamt of political power. Appointed irregularly when the previous Archbishop Chrysanthos (1881–1949) declined to preside over the swearing in of a government subservient to German occupation forces, Damaskinos stepped in without hesitation. But he proved to be an ambitious and brave individual, who protected the Jews of Athens and saved a large part of the population from starvation. In 1967 one of the first acts of the Colonels was to impose a new archbishop, Ieronymos (1905–89), because of his 'personal merit'. One of his first concerns was to extend the status of civil servant to all employees of the Church, something that the dictatorship was happy to oblige him with. After his fall, during an in-fight among the dictators, he claimed that he was not aware of any constitutional aberration in the country (a claim echoed by his then secretary and the archbishop, Christodoulos).

The change of guard within the ranks of the dictatorship in 1973 proclaimed the rather obscure metropolitan Seraphim (1913–98) as Archbishop of Athens and Greece. He happened to be from the same village as the head of the dictatorship. There were attempts after the restoration of the Republic (1974) to introduce constitutional changes in the relations between Church and state, but the pace was slow and extremely thorny. As Legg and Roberts note:

> the alliances between clergy and politicians, whether at the local level or higher, are personal; they are clientelist in the same manner as those of other Greeks. Consequently, the church as an institution has little political power, although individuals within its may be well connected to those holding power. The church is perceived as the guarantor of traditional society; it is as opposed to modernisers today as it was in the early nineteenth century. (Legg and Roberts 1997: 105)

As late as 2002 the Archbishop of Athens, Christodoulos, organized a political rally against a law proposed by the government that would remove a person's religion from identification cards. During the rally the Archbishop held in his hands the banner of the 1821 revolution (which had supposedly then been raised by the Bishop of Patras) and called for a popular campaign against those 'who want to divorce Orthodoxy from Greece'. Such strong political involvement makes any discussion about the separation of state and Church almost impossible to this day. Yet the demography of Greek society has changed dramatically since the collapse of Communism and the wave of legal and illegal migration it unleashed.

Until 1990, almost 97 per cent of the Greek population was Greek Orthodox; now this has gone down to 86 per cent, with a tendency to fall even further. It is now clear that not all Greeks are Orthodox and that many important people who contributed to the establishment of the social polity and popular culture were Greek but of Roman Catholic, Protestant or Jewish background, and that their faiths were important to them in their self-perception and personal identity. Furthermore it has become clear how, subtly and not so subtly, these people were excluded from official representations and never included in the official books of history and culture. The gradual opening up of the social body creates a deep cultural and political anxiety for the Church, which is afraid, not that it will lose the majority, but on the contrary that it will lose its monopoly on so-called 'Greekness', which is, according to this rhetoric, coterminous with the true and authentic Church of Christ.

Such alarmist discourse unfortunately dominates the way that the nation deals with the challenges of modernity and diversity. Since the mid-1980s a strong negative attitude has prevailed over Greek Orthodox cultural debates in the country; it expresses deep suspicion of the West and all ideas that are not 'ours', as a popular theologian has stated constantly. This previously 'liberal' and open-minded theologian Christos Yannaras, who in the beginning of his career wrote some extremely interesting books such as *The Freedom of Morality*, has moved towards conservative ideas of cultural insularism, Judeophobia and sterile anti-Americanism. By constantly revising the first edition of that book, and by publishing anti-western studies, Yannaras has developed what we could call the 'contamination model' (*The Modern Greek Identity*, 1978 and more specifically *Orthodoxy and the West*, 1983); according to him, everything that came from the West, starting with a translation of Thomas Aquinas' *Summa* in 1325, 'contaminated' the purity and the authenticity of Orthodox tradition; as a result the tradition has lost its centre and is living its final historical moments (*Finis Graeciae*, 1999). Products of such contamination, and its agents, are the Greek state itself and the educational system, which distort 'our authentic Greek self-consciousness' by disseminating the ideas of atheist Enlightenment people, of the 'lighteners', as he pejoratively, calls them.

According to him, everything that the West achieved, theologically or socially, was either wrong from a theological point of view or misleading about its appropriation of common early Christian tradition. Orthodox faithful had only to visit monasteries and attend liturgies in order to remain un-contaminated by western secularism, or to dis-infect themselves from its influence. Other theologians gaining popularity through the media along the same lines, like Fr George Metallinos, identify Orthodoxy and Greek-ness racially, by stressing that only in the Greek language has Orthodoxy expressed itself in the most complete and immediate way (see *Orthodoxy and Hellenism*, 1987 and *Traditional and Alienation*, 1986, inter alia, by Metallinos). The rhetoric of the victim and of mournful victimization, constantly blaming external factors that interfere with 'us', is the most interesting psychopathological symptom of this approach, which char-acterizes people who feel marginalized but do not want to lose their marginality.

Furthermore, the marked opulence of church ceremonies, the expensive vestments, the absence of theological language and the sheer politicization of many social issues all show that the Church is gradually losing its organic popular or populist connection with the faithful and is becoming an autonomous organization which offers stable employment and secure income only to its workers. Within the context of the Greek participation in the European Union and the deep social, political and cultural crisis it created, this explains why there is no decrease in the number of ordinations every year in the country and why there is an increase of monastics. As a publicly funded organization the Church reinvests the money it receives, in this way contributing to the solution of the problem of rising unemployment; the fact that Church institutions are tax-exempted also shows how the state uses the Church in order to secure cohesion and stability. The wealth of existing funds enables the Church to invest in the building of more churches and in philanthropic organizations, thus facilitating cash flow, especially in periods of financial difficulties. So the link between Greekness and Orthodoxy goes beyond the realm of a common adventure in history or of a common language of self-articulation. In our day, it is a mutually beneficial financial arrange-ment which contributes heavily to the gross national income and solves crucial social problems.

In 1997, the metropolitan of the northern city of Drama declined to read the last rites over a baptised Orthodox Christian because, as he stated, he 'was married in a civil ceremony which, according to the teaching of our Mother Church, is not only fornica-tion and adultery but also violation of our doctrinal teachings about the sacraments'. In 1996, Greek Muslim citizens were denied the right to rebuild a collapsed minaret next to their mosque; the permission had to be signed by the local metropolitan (who of course rejected it). The same metropolitan stated that 'the Church has its own law, its specific legal system. . . . It cannot accept the legalisation of abortion or the de-penalisation of adultery together with any other anti-Evangelical or anti-Christian legislation of the state'. A prominent professor and constitutional expert, Nikos K. Alivizatos, points out that all these problems can be attributed to Article 3 of the Constitution, which, even after three revisions, declares that 'the predominant religion in Greece *is* the religion of the Eastern Orthodox Church of Christ'. And he points out:

> considering that the use of the present indicative in legal documents implies a normative content, the verb 'is' raises from time to time particular problems: according to one interpretation Orthodoxy not simply is but 'should be' the predominant religion in Greece. As has been observed, Constitutions, every constitution in their modern form, contain regulative norms and not simply descriptive statements. (Alivizatos 2001: 302)

The Church uses this ambiguity in order to control all possible challenges against its dominance and authority. And it uses it so effectively that no government thinks of renegotiating the *modus operandi* within the new social situation. The low educational level of most hierarchs, the exclusion of lay people from any decision-making process and the predominant inability to engage in a meaningful dialogue with religious minorities presently living in the country result in a kind of re-tribalization of Greek society. This brings about a looming social tension and imminent destabilization, a situation that the Church is supposedly there to counteract. The absence of any checks and balances within the Church through lay organizations means that all existing problems are not personal issues between one bishop and another; they are deep-seated structural problems which have created a defensive mentality of introversion and insularism and which will eventually reach their own threshold of resistance. The sociologist of religion Bryan R. Wilson has noted that for some traditions 'the only escape from "secular" pluralism is the retreat into *gemeinschaftlich* sects' (1966: 160). Unlike the trajectory of the Patriarchate of Constantinople, which, under the leadership and vision of Athenagoras, gradually and under difficult circumstances, embraced ecumenical pluralism, the autocephalous Church of Greece has followed the path of becoming a regional and localized cult unable to explore and offer to others its own historical experience.

In the beginning of the twenty-first century, the autocephalous Church of Greece is becoming more trenchant and fanatical in its belief in its privileged singularity, constantly raising opaque defensive mechanisms against religious pluralism and alterity; and there are no signs on the horizon to show that the problem has been identified and measures have been taken to deal with it.

The Project of Historical Christianity

C. P. Cavafy (1863–1933), the Greek poet from Alexandria, described the Greek Orthodox approach to church and religious life as follows:

I love the church: its labara,
Its silver vessels and candleholders,
The lights, the ikons, the pulpit.

When I go there, into a church of the Greeks,
With its aroma of incense,
Its liturgical chanting and harmony,
The majestic presence of the priests,
Dazzling in their ornate vestments,
The solemn rhythm of their gestures –
My thoughts turn to the glories of our race,
To the splendour of our Byzantine heritage.

(Cavafy 1975: 34)

Such middle-class understanding of the Christian experience expresses the most inter-esting element of the Orthodox psychology: the absence of interiority and introspection. In all Orthodox literature, devotional, exegetical, dogmatic or ascetic, the individual is treated as if lacking in depth, without major conflicts and sense of tragic predicament. The Platonic element in the Orthodox tradition means that the Christian does not per-ceive this life as an existential adventure after the Fall; on the contrary, it sees it through the eyes of a pre-lapsarian and primordial goodness which is supposed to be the onto-logical and structural basis of historical life.

The rejection of Augustine's anthropology has imprisoned eastern theology within the confines of a paradigm which situates humanity in a morally perfect cosmos, in a universe of occluding goodness. The concept of *hamartia* as expressed by Paul, Augustine and Luther remained an alien, almost hostile element in eastern theology. In his seminal essay on Paul, Krister Stendhal observed the following:

> Judging at least from a superficial survey of the preaching of the Churches of the East from olden times to the present, it is striking how their homiletical tradition is either one of doxology or meditative mysticism or exhortation – but it does not deal with the plagued conscience in the way in which one came to do so in the Western Churches. (Stendhal 1963: 203)

This is precisely the element missing from the eastern tradition; that of introspective conscience. The Eastern Church did not inherit a book with the traumatic narrativiza-tion of the self such as Augustine's *Confessions* in the West. Naturally, for some western-ers coming to Orthodoxy this can be an attractive alternative to an overemphasis on individual guilt and responsibility.

Nor did it inherit a tradition distinguishing the realm of history from that of God, such as that inaugurated by Augustine's *Civitas Dei*. On the contrary, because of its privileged position in the fourth, fifth and sixth centuries, when Christian dogma was formulated, it retained a triumphalist and imperial understanding of history, with the *basileia* of the Christian emperor in time as the visible symbol of the eternal kingdom of God. Eastern theology removes a sense of time from humanity, by elaborating concepts of eternity and the beyond (*epekeina*) in exactly the same way as the imperial polity perceived itself when Constantinople was established, as the Christian capital of an eternal Christian empire.

Liturgically, the Orthodox Church has maintained the Scholastic doctrine of the liturgy *ex opere operato* (*ex ergou ergasmenou*), which has led to the ritual becoming autonomous, without any reference to the individual, the faith of the participants or the actual meaning of words. The doctrine *ex opere operato* led to the conspicuous theatricality of the liturgy and the self-dramatization of its language. The ornate polysyllabic words of a sacramental Greek language were always treated as sacred objects in themselves, thus creating an auto-suggestive mechanism that de-materialized circumstances and abstracted people from their very reality. In the Orthodox liturgy with its doxological and adulational character we can detect the birthplace of the atemporal, ahistorical and immaterial universe that has been conceptually elaborated by almost the totality of Greek theology.

As Yannaras has stated, Orthodox theology is based on the concept of 'good, very good indeed' (Gen. 1: 31). Such a theological approach hindered Orthodox believers from internalizing their own history. Belief in the essential goodness of the creation deprived individual conscience of its own responsibility for actions and choices. The absence of social conscience has consolidated the identification of Eastern Churches with the national consciousness; the inability to establish a discourse about morality, psychology and anthropology determined the absence of the Church from every important social or intellectual question.

On the contrary, every time a new movement emerged the Church simply rejected it in advance and banned it from the mental horizon of the faithful. This also means that the Eastern Church underestimated the cognitive abilities of the individual. The Church mentality has remained in the numinous area of indefinable emotions and has rejected knowledge both as a means for exploring the visible revelation and as a way of studying the scriptures. Thus, notwithstanding a very few exceptions, there can be no biblical criticism in the Greek Church because any interrogation of the text as a document of human psychology simply destabilizes the authority of the collective body of bishops to define what is right or wrong. Furthermore, most pronouncements by the Greek Orthodox Church Synods consist of propositions without arguments: underestimating the cognitive faculties of the faithful, they make no attempt to convince or present a case; they simply impose presupposed 'truths' which have never been tested by the individual's life and have never been felt as psychological realities. This represents in fact a huge move away from the example set by the Byzantine fathers.

On the contrary, most of the church statements refer to the authority of tradition, the importance of the clergy, the mysterious character of priesthood or the otherworldly meaning of the liturgy. The language employed in most cases is abstract and impersonal, with constant references to sacred texts and decisions of Ecumenical Councils. The faithful always remain in the dark about the conditions producing such statements. The Orthodox Church replaces tradition with the mentality of someone engaged in continuous warfare against the opponents of Jesus Christ, of the Church itself and of the nation. The conviction that everything 'bad' comes from outside has defined the Orthodox Church to this day. So the Church functions as the 'protector of the nation', the 'bastion of true Christianity', the 'sole defender of truth', employing an exclusivist and preferentialist language which divides the world into the two categories of us and them, into pure and impure and true and untrue. Such generalizations determine the attitude of the Greek Orthodox Church to other Christian denominations and to other religions. The rejection of historical responsibility has also led to the complete de-historicization of the institution and the absolute autonomization of the clergy into a kind of tribal priest-craft, the magus of the race; at the same time it has transformed the liturgy and its time and space into the cultus of the 'chosen people', the ultimate *topos* where the divine is materialized through ritual gestures, arcane words and in-audible whispers and prayers.

This hierarchical 'reality' creates an inability for the mind to perceive the chaotic multiplicity of experience outside its continuum and from an early age distorts the mental ability to establish logical relations between experiences and create semantic unities. This marked incapacity for discursive and problematizing thinking has been punctuated only twice: first when the Russian diaspora was forced to reformulate the tradition after the experience of exile that followed the Revolution in 1917; and second in the 1960s, when a number of young theologians from Greece studied in Germany and France and were able to see the obvious advances of both Protestant and Roman Catholic theologies, especially during and after the Second Vatican Council. It was only after an exodus of the Russian theologians that the tradition was renewed and re-articulated its message, by grafting it on contemporary questions.

However, within the safe continuum of the national church the renewal momentum has proved to be impossible, and it will remain unlikely for the near future. The mental structure of the subject who grows up within the Orthodox world view cannot over-come its imposed restrictions and transcend its innate limitations with critical thinking. Since such a subject is formed within a homogeneous and closed society, it cannot synthesize empirical data, concepts and projects; it sees a fragmented, alien and hostile world, full of unknown quantities and frightening presences. Every thing is a 'sign' and not itself; it means something beyond its existence that is indecipherable and therefore threatening. Hence it reverts to the warmth of the mother Church for safety, security and protection.

Theologically, this attitude means that the Orthodox believe that the *basileia* prom-ised by Jesus is of this world; and that the *basileia* is the privilege and the predicament of a chosen nation. Even the word 'orthodox', meaning the right and correct faith, is used in order to exclude the other, Christian or non-Christian, from the *basileia*. To this day, for example, in mixed marriages with any other Christian denomination, people have to convert to Orthodoxy and be re-baptised in order for the marriage to be valid. The ritual element in the baptism service is the most essential part of the ceremonial mentality that dominates the Greek Orthodox Church. We must also mention that within such homogeneous societies, the young individual is socialized through family, school, Church and the army (for the male population). Through these mechanisms the ceremonial mentality is constantly consolidated, and during the early identification period the individual projects feelings on objects, gestures and roles as they appear phenomenologically uncontaminated by meaning and yet full of significance. Usually the national identity is closely linked to religious rituals; almost all major national cel-ebrations in Greece coincide with major religious feasts. The nation is celebrated at the sacred space of the church; so it is invested with its sacredness and becomes itself a sacred reality.

As the President of the Greek republic Konstantinos Karamanlis stated: 'The nation and Orthodoxy have become in the Greek conscience virtually synonymous' (in Clogg 1983: 208). The young individual grows up under the constant exposure to such a ritualistic mentality, which is bound to its self-awareness by the physical growth of its body and the emergence of sexuality. The whole ceremonial mentality is thus reinforced by the tension of sexual desire, which leads to its projection on the actual service and therefore to the libidinization of the sacred space itself: to this day most Greeks (even of the anti-Church left parties) prefer a religious wedding for reasons not simply related to the grandiosity of rituals. The ritual itself safeguards sexual tension and fecundity; it represents the most efficient manner of instigating sexual desire.

The crucial importance of the Orthodox liturgy creates a microcosm of meaningful order and symbolic hierarchy that gives the certainty of legitimacy to participating faithful. This fundamental attitude rejects all changes to the existing pattern. If something changes, the whole microcosm will collapse and the individual will be thrown into a state of existential *anomie* which will de-legitimize its presence in the specific society and ethnos. So any discussion about changing the andocentric priesthood is simply forbidden by the Orthodox Church, although no real biblical reason is provided and the appeal to the decisions of ecumenical synods is repeated as the only response to the question. Women cannot be ordained in the Orthodox Church because they themselves represent 'ritual prohibitions' whose activities and sheer presence would 'threaten' the dominant classificatory system of power (they cannot approach the altar and they cannot receive communion during menstruation to this day). The moment women are considered for priesthood, the whole microcosmic harmony that the faithful experiences within the sacred space of the church will disintegrate. Any change to the ceremonial mentality will simply destabilize the hierarchy and as a consequence destroy the sacredness of the nation.

The Exodus?

We have followed the 'double language' of the Orthodox Church during the last seven centuries in an attempt to critically appreciate its position in history. The Greek Orthodox Church was early taken captive by secular authority; first by Constantine, then by Justinian and his court, by other Byzantine emperors, by the Ottoman sultan and finally by the nation-state of Greece. It has always functioned as a court institution and then as one of the many state apparatuses. Its very structure is that of the Roman and Byzantine court with the later addition of the Ottoman influence. To this day it has maintained the same ceremonial character as can be found in Constantine Porphyrogenitus' famous treatise *De ceremoniis* (with the theological underpinnings of Pseudo-Dionysius' *Celestial Hierarchy*); as long as there was a Christian authority, the *basileus*, such ceremonialism affirmed its sacred character, political purpose and cultural mission. However, during the Ottoman period, this ceremonial mentality was transformed into hierocratic ritualism and led to the further alienation of the faithful from the actual text of the liturgy: although it is called the word of the *laos* (people), there is no active participation in worship of the faithful themselves, who are mechanically called to receive Holy Communion and then pay their alms to church vicars.

By identifying itself with the state the Church has disregarded the potentially 'sinful' character of power and has withdrawn from a dialogue with society – especially with those affected by such sinful character. Throughout its history within Greece, it allied itself to any government in power even when there was a serious, and obvious, case of constitutional and legal aberration in the country. By becoming public servants in the Greek nation-state, priests simply lost the authority to become moral agents and speak on behalf of the faithful. The Church actively participated in the persecution of political opponents, of whole political parties, and has allied itself to dictatorships. This persecution is not symptomatic and is definitely not circumstantial. The absence of internal democracy has led to complete identification with autocratic and authoritarian languages and epistemic regimes; the Church has remained the prominent anti-democratic force within Greek society because it hasn't accepted the premises of the modern nation-state, which was created under the project of the Enlightenment.

The leadership, prominent theologians and popular preachers of the end of the twentieth century totally reject the Enlightenment, forgetting that the very existence of the Greek Orthodox Church, or indeed of the Greek state, is owed to it. Furthermore, they reject the premises of the Enlightenment and yet they refuse to be reunited with the mother Church of Constantinople, which now they see as an opponent and an enemy. In 2004 there was a major crisis in relations between the two Churches that almost led to a complete schism and virtual excommunication; and this sad development was thwarted only after the political intervention of the Greek state, which now acts as the moderator of the social theatrics of bishops and priests.

The lack of internal democracy has also led to the Church's inability to accept new proposals or ideas; inability to deal with modern challenges has quashed any development of doctrine under contemporary challenges. This is due mainly to the lack of biblical tradition in Greece; an impartial observer might feel that the Bible is a very unwelcome book within the Greek Orthodox tradition, which sees it simply as another liturgical book and not as the profound revelation in time and place of the divine Logos. From fear of Protestant biblicism, the Orthodox Church has surrounded the Bible with moralizing trivialities and obscure allegorizations, which mean nothing and which usually end with a political proclamation against the enemies of the Church.

The Church needs to regain its ecclesiastical character as the *ecclesia* of the people; it must therefore open up and reach out to the faithful by disavowing the secular power with which it has been invested since imperial Rome and Constantinople, and rediscover its own *koinonia* of the faithful. It must rediscover the tragic character of human history as a traumatic loss of innocence for every individual – and for such loss there is a collective responsibility. Within the sacramental community of the ecclesia the faithful regain collectively the pristine gaze of prelapsarian humanitas. But within the confines of historical realities the Church must open its own Christian tradition to culture and democracy, distancing itself from Constantinian ecclesiasticism, dogmatism and ungodly hubris.

Instead of being a *volkish church* based on blood and soil, which is unfortunately what it has become, the Church must rediscover its own ecumenical character, its apostolic and liberating mission. In history, it must also rediscover its middle ground between the global spiritual authority of Roman Catholicism, the religious democracy of Protestant Christianity and the political democracy of the Enlightenment; instead of demonizing each one of them and rejecting their contribution to the development of common humanity and the Christian heritage, it must boldly synthesize them, creating an open ecclesia in which clergy and laity experience their own vulnerability as conscious moments in history in a process of spiritual unfolding. Instead of using the Greek language as the sacrament itself, or the nation as the object of worship in itself, the ecclesia must create a 'socialized individual' within the bonds of a *communio sanctorum*.

The democratization of the Church will democratize the inner self, the thinking subject, and will liberate the faithful (clergy and laity) from the seductive privileges of state power in which the current Church is completely immersed. Strangely, while a theological storm has been raging throughout the Christian world since World War II, none of this has found any kind of expression in the theological discussions within the Greek Orthodox Church; on the contrary, every new Archbishop of Athens praises his Church for having maintained the 'authentic message' of the 'original church', and dismisses everything and everyone else outside their fold. (On some occasions, even the co-Orthodox Russians have not escaped some extremely derogatory comments, precisely for being Russian Orthodox and not Greek.) No real engagement with the problems raised by secularity and postmodernity has ever been attempted within the Church; no moral reflection, no spiritual discussion or even a reasonable intellectual debate have ever been fostered or promoted by the Church.

On the contrary, as an organization protected by the state, the Greek Orthodox Church reproduces a theological rhetoric which simply justifies its policies and actions. No self-reflective discourse is established because, according to the dominant perception, there are no mistakes to admit to. While the pope was persistently asked to apologise for the sacking of Constantinople in 1204 by the Fourth Crusade, the Greek Orthodox Church cannot contemplate making its own apology to persecuted religious minorities in the country, or recognize the gross errors of its involvement in politics (or even of the slaughtering of all foreigners in Constantinople in 1182). While bishops come and go, all structures remain the same; and their occupants ignore their historical development and the changes they underwent in history.

Since spirituality has been reduced to liturgicalism and *koinonia* to ecclesiasticism, no real theological questions can arise within the mindset of the Greek Orthodox subjectivity. Ecclesiastical language and life reproduces all aspects of public life in the image of official power, employing the rhetoric of the empire and imposing an impoverished vocabulary of communication which simply limits the ability for self-critical reasoning. It constantly uses a kind of religious Newspeak, tending to attribute all contemporary problems to the addition of the *filioque* in the Creed. The Greek Orthodox Church has established and imposed a set of mis-naming strategies, which see history as dystopia and historical experience as a constant attack against the true Church of Jesus Christ, i.e., itself, or against the only Truth, which it also enshrines. Within this mentality it defines a way of living with *dolce far niente* as its dominant motto; by raising the divisive walls that isolated the triumphant Byzantium from Europe, it repeats the same errors and exhibits the same exclusivity even as it purports to be participating in the ecumenical dialogue. The real theological issues of historicity, corporeality, logical rearticulation of the doctrine through natural sciences, and the elaboration of faith through postmodern existential fragmentation and semantic nihilism do not even appear in the mental universe of the hierarchy, or of its closely attached theologians, who see everything in black and white polarities and as constant conspiracies against Orthodoxy.

The Greek Orthodox Church is in need of a new ecclesiology; it must see its tradition within the historical experience of the faithful by discarding the practices of a state-sponsored church, and reintroduce the concept of Christian universalism. In the world of fragmented postmodernity, it must regain its organic unity of a diverse community, fostering debates, dismantling bureaucratic overcentralization and creating social possibilities for a spiritual revival. The current situation is the grossest distortion of the eastern tradition: the Greek Orthodox Church has to be seen as another political party, not as an eschatological community; it is characterized by arrogance, secularism and a marked anti-intellectual mentality which, disguised under the false pretences of defending faith and opposing secularity, impose a mentality of intolerance, sterility and fundamentalism.

In Greece Orthodoxy has evolved into orthodoxism; or more precisely, as two young theologians have remarked about the Church of Greece:

> it has become a new atypical institution: we call it 'alternative theocracy'. It is a politically correct version of theocracy, which does not question the current rules of the democratic state, and at the same time it tries to dissociate itself from the similar, utterly autocratic cases of the Western Dark Ages or of contemporary Islam. And yet it never ceases to be bedevilled by the same mentality: the mentality of the primacy of spiritual authority over that of the secular state. (Arkadas and Mpekridakis 2001: 22)

When Jesus said 'Render to Caesar the things that are Caesar's and to God the things that are God's' (Mark 12: 17), the Evangelist states that 'they were all amazed at him'; obviously after many centuries the amazement has not abated in the least.

References and further reading

Alivizatos, N. K. (2001) *The Uncertain Modernisation and the Vague Constitutional Reform* (in Greek). Athens: Polis Publications.

Arkadas, D. and Mpekridakis, D. I. (2001) *Cruel Discourse, Chapters of Toxic Theology* (in Greek). Athens: Exantas.

Becker, H. (1950) *Systematic Sociology*. New York: Wiley.

Brendon, P. (2001) *Winston Churchill: A Brief Life*. London: Pimlico.

Cavafy, C. P. (1975) *Collected Poems*, trans. E. Keely and P. Sherard, ed. G. Savidis. London: Chatto and Windus.

Clogg, R. (ed.) (1983) *Greece in the 1980s*. London: Macmillan.

Gedeon, M. I. (1996) [1890] *Patriarchal Tables, Historical and Biographical Information about the Patriarchs of Constantinople from Andrew the First–called to Joakim III, 36–1884*. Athens: Syllogos pros Diadosin Ophelimon Biblion.

Koraes, A. (1964) *Collected Works*, vol. A 2 (in Greek). Athens: Dorikos Publications.

Laskaratos, A. (1916) *Poems and Other Works* (in Greek). Athens: Fexis Publications.

Legg, K. R. and Roberts, J. M. (1997) *Modern Greece: A Civilization on the Periphery*. Boulder, Colo.: Westview Press.

Oikonomos, K. (1993) [1829] *On the Pure Pronunciation of Greek Language*. Athens: Philomythos.

Paschales, D. P. (2000) [1928] *Theophilos Kaires* (in Greek). Athens: Typothito.

Pelikan, J. (1974) *The Spirit of Eastern Christendom*, vol. 2: *The Christian Tradition, a History of the Development of Doctrine*. Chicago and London: University of Chicago Press.

Roides, E. (2001) [1866] *Pope Joan*, ed. Alkis Aggelou. Athens: Estia Publications.

Runciman, S. (1968) *The Great Church in Captivity: A Study of the Patriarchate of Constantinople from the Eve of the Turkish Conquest to the Greek War of Independence*. Cambridge: Cambridge University Press.

Stendhal, K. (1963) The Apostle Paul and the introspective conscience of the West. In *The Writings of St Paul*, ed. W. A. Weeks. Norton Critical Edition. New York and London: W. W. Norton. Repr. 1972.

Stephanides, V. (1990) [1959] *Ecclesiastical History from the Beginning to this Day*. Athens: Aster.

Svolos, A. (1972) *Greek Constitutions 1822–1952: Constitutional History of Greece* (in Greek). Athens: Stochastes Publications.

Voulgaris, E. (2001) [1768] *Proposal on Toleration* (in Greek). Athens: Stachys Publications.

Wilson, B. R. (1966) *Religion in Secular Society*. London: C. A. Watts.

CHAPTER 9
Romanian Christianity

Mircea Pacurariu

Over two thousand years ago, the present territory of Romania was inhabited by Geto-Dacians, the northern wing of the Thracian people. In the second century BCE the Geto-Dacian state reached the height of its political power, after which came a decline. The Roman Empire gradually conquered some territories in the Balkan Peninsula, and made them Roman provinces: Illyricum (59 BCE), Pannonia (9 CE), and Moesia (15 CE), which was later divided into Moesia Superior and Moesia Inferior. In 46 CE, the territory between the Danube and the Black Sea (which nowadays belongs to Romania and is known as Dobrudja) was annexed to Moesia Inferior. However, in 297, it became a separate province, Scythia Minor. In 106 CE, the Roman Emperor Trajan conquered and transformed the largest part of the Dacian state into a Roman province, Dacia.

The territories annexed by the Roman Empire underwent a process of Romanization, both of the local Thraco-Getic-Dacian population, and of the language, to the extent to which one can speak of a 'Balkan Romanity', or an 'Eastern (Oriental) Romanity'. In these territories, Christianity was introduced as early as the 'apostolic age', by St Paul and his disciples.

Dacian-Roman Christianity (First to Sixth Centuries)

In the territory between the Danube and the Black Sea (the future Scythia Minor province), the new teaching of Jesus Christ was propagated by St Andrew. This was mentioned by Hippolytus of Rome (d. 236), by Origen of Alexandria (d. 254), by the church historian Eusebius of Caesarea, and by several later Byzantine writers. Some local place names and folklore traditions attest to the statements of these writers regarding St Andrew's preaching. According to recent findings, St Philip might have preached in the same territory. This is suggested by the existence of a fourth-century Gothic calendar and by the assertions of a Benedictine monk, Walafridus Strabo, who lived in a monastery in the Alps, in the ninth century.

Undoubtedly, these apostles did not only preach the Gospel and baptize Geto-Dacians and Greeks in the Greek fortresses at the Black Sea (Tomis, Callatis, Histria), but they also ordained bishops or priests among those who had converted to Christianity. In turn, these ordained others, in order to ensure the 'uninterrupted succession' of priesthood in the territories they had evangelized. However, St Andrew and St Paul should be considered 'apostles of the Dacian-Romans', the forefathers of Romanians. Similarly, Romanian Christianity should be considered of 'apostolic origin'.

In the Dacian territories north of the Danube (a Roman province after 106), the new Christian teaching was preached by missionary priests who had arrived from the south of the Danube (where St Paul preached), as well as by certain lay missionaries (colonists, traders, slaves, all of whom had shared the Christian belief before their arrival in Dacia).

As a result of massive colonization, Dacia was inhabited by people from all over the Roman world (*ex toto orbe romano*, says Eutropius). Thus a new population was born, initially called Dacian-Roman, then Romanian. A new, neo-Latin language (Romanian) was engendered, derived from the popular Latin that was spoken in Dacia at the time.

Several arguments support the idea that many Dacian-Romans were converted to Christianity before Emperor Constantine the Great issued the famous Tolerance Edict in 313. Firstly, linguists have noted that many basic Romanian words with religious meaning have been used since the third or fourth centuries. Part of these words were taken over from the popular Latin spoken by the Dacian-Romans, and were 'Christianized' and given a new meaning, whereas others were created in this vast geographical space by Christian believers. They are completely independent of their synonyms in the other neo-Latin languages. Moreover, both in the prayer 'Our Father', and in the Niceno-Constantinopolitan Symbol of Faith (325 and 381), over 90 per cent of the words are of Latin origin.

Another argument in favour of the antiquity of Romanian Christianity is represented by over one hundred early Christian archaeological items that were discovered north of the Danube. According to archaeologists, they date back to the second to fourth centuries, and their number is even higher in the former province Scythia Minor. After 271–5, when the Romans abandoned Dacia and the Roman army and administration were withdrawn to south of the Danube, certain public edifices were transformed into Christian cult sites. This occurred at Slaveni and Sucidava (in Oltenia), at Porolissum (nowadays Moigrad), probably at Morisena (nowadays Cenad, in Banat). According to some researchers, even the present-day church in Densus (near the former Roman capital Sarmizegetusa, nowadays in the Hunedoara county), which has a different architectural plan, might have initially been a funeral monument for a general in Emperor Trajan's army.

In Scythia Minor, the existence of Dacian-Roman and Romanian Christianity is attested by the large number of Christians who became martyrs, in about 300, during Diocletian's persecution (284–305). Most of them remained anonymous, but some names exist in the so-called 'martyrdom acts' (the first written documents on the Romanian territory) of the priest Epictet, his disciple, Astion of Halmyris, and later, of the soldier Emilian of Durostavna/Durostorum. We should also mention four martyrs

(Zoticos, Atalos, Kamasis and Philippos), whose relics were discovered, in 1971, in a former basilica at Niculitel, Tulcea. Many other Dacian-Romans (bishops, priests, deacons, soldiers, state officials, peasants and women) were martyred in several Roman fortresses in provinces north or south of the Danube (Pannonia Inferior, Moesia Superior, Moesia Inferior, Dacia Ripensis and Dacia Mediterranea).

The strength of Christianity in Scythia Minor after 313 is proven by an impressive number of early Christian objects (rush-lights, crosses) and by over a hundred funeral inscriptions. Moreover, 35 basilicas (of the fourth to sixth centuries) were discovered in the main fortress towns of the province (Tomis, Tropaeum Trajani, Histria, Callatis, Axiopolis and Dynogetia). The fact that bishops and priests are mentioned as martyrs in Scythia Minor strongly suggests the existence of a clerical hierarchy from a very early period. The martyrdom acts mention bishops Evangelicus, Efrem and Tit. Historical evidence points to their existence in the province metropolis, Tomis (present-day Constanta). Some high clerics were also involved in the theological controversies debated at the first four Ecumenical Councils. In the fourth century, Mark participated in the First Ecumenical Council at Nicaea (325), Betranion defended the Orthodox faith against Arianism (369), and Gerontius participated in the Second Ecumenical Council at Constantinople (381). Theotimos I was referred to, by the church historian Sozomen, as being of Scythian origin, therefore not a Dacian-Roman; in his book *De viris illustribus*, the western writer Jerome mentioned the fact that Theotimos I had written certain theological books. They have been lost, but John of Damascus cited them in the eighth century.

There is evidence of eminent Christians in subsequent centuries: fifth-century documents mention Bishop Timothy, who participated in the Third Ecumenical Council at Ephesus, in 431; John, regarded by his contemporaries as the best theologian of his time, who translated works from Greek into the Latin; Alexander and Theotimos II. Sixth-century documents refer to Bishop Paternus, who was involved in controversies caused by the so-called 'Scythian monks' in his bishopric. A massive gilded silver disc that belonged to him is housed in the Hermitage Museum in St Petersburg. Valentinianus, a reputed theologian who corresponded with Pope Vigilius (d. 555) on the issues advanced at the Fifth Ecumenical Council in Constantinople in 553 is also mentioned.

By the end of the fifth century, fourteen other bishoprics had been established in the main fortress towns in Scythia Minor, which had already become a 'metropolitan province'. The Bishop of Tomis held the office of metropolitan (*episcopus metropolitanus*). After the territorial and administrative reform made by Emperor Diocletian, the Illyricum region became a *prefectura*, encompassing a series of provinces with a predominantly Dacian-Roman population. As part of it, there were approximately forty bishoprics, fifteen of which were situated on the Danube (Pannonia Inferior, Moesia Superior, Dacia Ripensis, Dacia Mediterranea and Moesia Inferior). All of them, including the ones in Scythia Minor, were subordinated to the Bishop of Constantinople, which became a patriarchal see by a decision of the Fourth Ecumenical Council in 451. The Dacian-Roman Church was therefore connected to Rome by language and to Constantinople by faith and organization.

The first monastic settlements in Scythia Minor date back to the fourth century. The names of some reputed monks in the Christian world of the time are linked to these settlements. John Cassian (360–435), 'of Scythian origin', as his biographer Gennadius of Marseilles introduced him, was ordained deacon by John Chrysostom in Constantinople and priest in Rome. He founded two monasteries near Marseilles in the south of France. He also wrote some remarkable works in Latin, including the famous *Conferences* and *Institutes*.

Another Dacian-Roman theologian, Dionysius Exiguus (460–545), was born in Scythia Minor, but spent the largest part of his life in Rome, where he worked in the papal chancellor's office. He translated into Latin several works on theology, lives of the saints and canon law. He is especially renowned as the initiator of the current chronological system (the 'Christian era', whereby the counting of years began with the birth of Jesus Christ, albeit with an error of four or five years). Several other theologians were born in Scythia Minor: John Maxentius, the author of short theological works, and Peter the Deacon, who translated works from Greek into Latin. We cannot overlook Bishop Nicetas of Remesiana from Dacia Mediterranea, whom Bishop Paulinus of Nola in Italy presented as Dacian-Roman. He was one of the most important, widely travelled, Latin-speaking missionaries, as well as the author of dogmatic and liturgical works that have been preserved and published several times. Documents mention only one Dacian-Roman bishop, Theofilus ('of Gothia'), who participated in the Council of Nicaea (325). His name is explained by the fact that, at the time, the Goths had invaded the territory north of the Danube. In 341 he became Bishop in Constantinople, and known as Ulfilas. After he preached to the Goths for about twelve years, he had to flee to south of the Danube, and later he became an Arian. He translated the Bible into the Gothic language.

So, in Romanian territory the conversion to Christianity was not accomplished at a certain date, by the order of a political leader, as happened in neighbouring territories. After the arrival of St Paul and St Andrew, Christianization became a more definite process and lasted for several centuries, being the direct result of the contact between the native Geto-Dacian population and the Roman colonists who shared in the new faith. Romanization and Christianization were parallel processes, engendering a new people, the Romanian one, who may rightfully be called, along with the Greeks, the earliest Christian people in south-east Europe.

The Romanian Church in the Seventh to Fourteenth Centuries

This long period in the history of the Romanian people and Church is rather obscure, as the historical and archaeological sources are scarce. From the third to the end of the thirteenth century, a series of migrating peoples, of Germanic, Slavic and Asian descent, heading for western Europe, invaded this territory: Goths, Vandals, Gepids, Huns, Avars, Slavs, Hungarians, Pechenegs, Cumans and Mongols. Even when they were warrior minorities, they dominated, if temporarily, parts of Romanian geographic and ethnic space, and hindered the process of state consolidation.

As the process of Christianization had been accomplished, the Romanians assimilated part of these peoples, and even converted some of them to Christianity. Only the

Slavs left their imprint on the Romanian language and managed, for a while, to impose 'Old Church Slavonic' on the Romanian Orthodox religion. Larger numbers of Slavs settled south of the Danube. A reverse phenomenon occurred here: an important part of the Romanized population was assimilated by the Slavs, whereas another part was displaced to the south, and split into ethnic groups, which still exist in Macedonia, Albania and Greece.

South of the Danube, in present-day Bulgaria, the brothers Cyril and Methodius, the 'Apostles to the Slavs', introduced the 'Slavic-Byzantine rite', namely the liturgy and the other services officiated in the Old Slavonic spoken around Thessaloniki. In the tenth century, isolated from both Constantinople and Rome, surrounded only by Slavic peoples, the Romanians were obliged to adopt the Slavic-Byzantine rite to the detriment of the Latin one.

Gradually, after the great Avar-Slavic invasion, the political and clerical organization of the Romanians improved, even if, after 602, the bishopric sees in Scythia Minor and in the territories south of the Danube disappeared. Therefore, in the seventh to fourteenth centuries, profound social, political, ethnic and cultural changes occurred. The first Romanian political forms of organization appeared, and were to develop into the future medieval Romanian states: Transylvania, Vallachia and Moldavia. It was now that Romanians were first mentioned in history, under the Germanic name 'Vallachians', which was taken over by the Slavs and denoted a Latin speaker. Archaeological research has revealed the continuity of Romanian Christianity in this period. All over Romanian territory, archaeologists have discovered bronze crosses, clay pots with cross inscriptions, cult objects and church bells.

There is evidence of a superior hierarchy in former Scythia Minor. Two inscriptions dating to the tenth or eleventh centuries mention the Metropolitans of Tomis, Anicetus and Basil. In the fourteenth century, a Vallachian bishopric also existed in present-day Bulgarian and Serbian territories.

In the territories within the Carpathian Mountains (Transylvania, Banat, Crisana and Maramures), political units – principalities and voivodates – developed in the tenth or eleventh centuries. The voivodates of Menumorut in Crisana, Gelu in Transylvania and Glad in Banat are mentioned in the Magyar chronicle *Gesta Hungarorum*. The same document mentions another one in southern Transylvania, with a seat in Balgrad (nowadays Alba-Iulia). It is believed that each of these political rulers had a religious ruler in his fortress.

The medieval Magyar kingdom, which was consolidated in the first half of the eleventh century, began the gradual annexation of Transylvania, which was to continue until the thirteenth century. The Romanian political units were replaced with new political and administrative units, the 'royal counties'. A similar thing occurred in the Church, as Orthodox bishoprics were replaced with Catholic ones, in Biharea, Morisena, Cenad and Alba-Iulia. The strong Romanian resistance caused the kings of Hungary to bring representatives of the Papal Inquisition to Transylvania, in order to convert the Orthodox believers to the western rite. Their attempts were nevertheless unsuccessful.

In the twelfth and thirteenth centuries, a significant number of Magyars settled in Transylvania, and their number increased as many Romanian nobles were converted to Catholicism. The Magyar kings brought two other Catholic ethnic groups here: the Szeklars (whose origins are disputed) and the Saxon colonists from Flanders, the Rhineland and Saxony.

Romanian Orthodox clerics existed in the territories outside the Carpathian Mountains. A letter of Pope Gregory IX in 1234 mentioned the activity of the 'pseudo-bishops of the Greek rite', who could only be Romanians. In 1247, a diploma issued by King Bela IV of Hungary mentioned the existence of political units outside the Carpathian Mountains; the text also mentioned 'archbishops and bishops', undoubtedly Romanians. Medieval documents, particularly Russian ones, also mention a Romanian pre-state territorial organization in the future medieval state of Moldavia.

The Romanian Church in the Fourteenth to Eighteenth Centuries

Vallachia and Moldavia

In the fourteenth century, the territories in the south and east of the Carpathians united. Apart from Transylvania, two other states, Vallachia and Moldavia, appeared. Transylvania remained independent of Hungary until 1541, and for centuries these three states were at war with the expanding Ottoman Empire, attempting to preserve their ethnic uniqueness and their Orthodox faith.

In the second half of the fourteenth century, the Ottomans conquered several Greek-Byzantine states in the vicinity of the Romanian ones. The Byzantine Empire was finally taken by the Turks in 1453, and Constantinople became Istanbul. The conquests were eventually followed by large-scale conversions to Islam. At the end of the fifteenth century, only the Romanian states had maintained their independence and their own political, economic and administrative structures. But from this period the Romanian states were forced to recognize Turkish Ottoman control and pay a yearly tax (haraciu), although this demand met strong armed resistance under rulers such as Mircea the Old, Vlad the Impaler, Stephen the Great, Peter Rares and later, Michael the Brave. No conversion to Islam was enforced in the Romanian countries. The Ottomans effectively ruled over Dobrudja (1417–1878), the northern part of the territory between Prut and Nistru, Buceag (1538–1812), and some smaller territories near the Danube, such as Braila.

Under such political circumstances, the Church in Vallachia and Moldavia evolved somewhat differently from the Church in Transylvania. When Vallachia and Moldavia became feudal states, the two churches were also united. The hierarchs in each local court were replaced with a metropolitan. According to the ecclesiastical canon, which stipulated that church organization should adapt to political organization, ecclesiastical union naturally followed the political one. Moreover, in feudal times, in both Vallachia and Moldavia, the relation between state and Church was close, similar to that existing in the Byzantine Empire until 1453. More specifically, the bishop's residence was near the ruler's residence, and the voievods (princes) considered themselves the protectors of the Orthodox Church in their country. The voivods built churches, granted them lands and exempted them from certain taxes. In turn, the bishops enthroned rulers in metropolitan cathedrals, and became their private counsellors. Apart from spiritual activity, bishops were entrusted with education, book editing, social assistance, and, at times, even with external political missions. Sometimes they took over the *voievod*'s functions, if he died or was deposed.

It is also worth mentioning that the Orthodox Churches were, to a certain degree, independent of the Ecumenical Patriarch in Constantinople, especially after 1453, even if, officially, their autonomy was recognized only in 1885. This relative autonomy derived from the fact that the metropolitans were all Romanians. They were elected in the country by an electoral body made up of abbots, magnates (*boyars*), and they were appointed in office by the ruler. They maintained contact with the other Orthodox Churches, especially with those in the countries under Ottoman rule, they used the national language in church services, they canonized saints, instituted religious celebrations, introduced local elements in ecclesiastical painting, architecture and music, without asking for permission from the Ecumenical Patriarch.

In 1359, the Ecumenical Patriarchate in Constantinople officially acknowledged the existence of the Metropolitan See of Vallachia in Curtea-de-Arges (Targoviste after 1517, and Bucharest after 1668). A second see (Severin) existed east of the River Olt from 1370 to 1401. In the early 1500s (probably 1503), two bishoprics were founded in Ramnicu-Valcea and in Buzau, and in 1793 another one was founded in Curtea-de-Arges.

The Metropolitan See of Moldavia was not attested in documents until 1386, even if it might have existed before. The Ecumenical Patriarch only acknowledged it in July 1401 (after years of negotiations), when a Greek hierarch had been unsuccessfully imposed.

By the mid-fourteenth century, two bishoprics were established in Moldavia, in Radauti and in Roman. In 1598, another see was established in Husi. In the Romanian territories occupied by the Ottomans, two eparchies directly subordinated to the Ecumenical Patriarch and ruled by Greek hierarchs were founded: the metropolitan seat of Proilavia (Braila) and the seat of Dristva (nowadays Silistra in Bulgaria). They functioned until 1828 and 1878, respectively.

Several bishops in Vallachia were important figures in the history of the Church in this period. Maxim Brancovici, of Serbian origin, founded the Krušedol Monastery in Serbia; Macarie founded the first printing-house in Vallachia; Eftimie was an envoy abroad on several occasions; Luke of Cyprus was an esteemed copyist and miniaturist as well as an envoy. Bishops Teophilos and Stephen founded several printing-houses and authorized the printing of Romanian and Slavonic prayer books. Varlaam and Teodosie also supported printing, such as the first Romanian version of the Bible in 1688. Antim Ivireanul, born in Georgia, was one of the most outstanding Romanian scholars. A former monk and printer, he guided the editing of over 60 books in Romanian, Slavonic, Greek, Arabic and Georgian. He was the genuine creator of the liturgical Romanian language, which has been used, with slight alterations imposed by the very process of linguistic change, until nowadays. Other important cultural and editorial figures were Daniil, Neofit the Cretan, Grigorie II and Dositei Filitti.

Similar important bishops functioned in Moldavia: Teoctist I and Gheorghe, during the reign of Stephen the Great, Teoctist II, Teofan I, Grigorie Rosca, who all adhered to the spiritual and cultural life in their country. Gheorghe Movila and two of his brothers (future rulers) founded the Sucevita Monastery, Anastasie Crimca founded the Drago-mirna Monastery and a hospital in Suceava. He also edited theological and judicial books. Varlaam was another outstanding scholar who edited several theological and judicial books, and published a homiliary based on Greek and Slavonic sources. Dosoftei, who was canonized in 2005, was considered the first Romanian poet (*The Psalms in Verse*) and prose writer (*The Saints' Lives and Deaths*). He translated foreign theatrical plays and had printed the first prayer books in Moldavia.

In the eighteenth century, Iacob Putneanul fought for his believers' rights in Moldavia. Gavriil Callimachi (previously Metropolitan of Thessaloniki) and Iacob Stamati also patronized printing and education.

Monastic life: monasteries and hermitages

An impressive number of monasteries were built in Moldavia and Vallachia after the metropolitan sees of these countries were acknowledged. Some of them were built by the rulers (*voivods*), in the ancient Byzantine tradition of church building; others were built by landowners (*boyars*) or monks. Parish churches in towns and villages were built by the religious communities, or even by rulers, landowners, merchants and guild members.

The most renowned monasteries were built by Prince Matei Basarab, in the first half of the fifteenth century; by Prince Constantin Brancoveanu (1688–1714), who was canonized in 1992; by members of the Cantacuzino and Vacarescu families, in the seventeenth and eighteenth century respectively. In Moldavia, outstanding monasteries were built by Prince Alexander the Good in the first half of the fifteenth century, and by Stephen the Great, who was canonized in 1992. Other church and monastery founders in the sixteenth and seventeenth centuries were Princes Petru Rares and Alexandru Lapusneanu, the members of the Movilesti family, Metropolitan Anastasie Crimca and Prince Vasile Lupu. The second half of the eighteenth century witnessed a spiritual renaissance in the monasteries in Moldavia (Neamt and Secu). The initiator was Abbot Paisius Velichkovsky (1722–94) (canonized by the Russian, Ukrainian and Romanian Churches), who influenced monastic life in Russia, Georgia and the Ukraine and much of the Orthodox world.

The architecture of these monasteries was Byzantine, specific to the Orthodox East. Certain Gothic influences, particularly in Moldavia, engendered a particular architectural style in the fifteenth century. New elements appeared later in Vallachian architecture, such as the open church porch. After the death of Prince Constantin Brancoveanu this style was named after him. Native artisans usually painted the interior of the churches. A particular example is offered, in Moldavia, by the exterior painting of several monastic churches built in the sixteenth century. Probota, Humor, Moldovita, Voronet, Rasca and Sucevita have been the subject of extensive specialized studies. Extremely valuable pieces of wood carving and stone sculpture, as well as silverware, embroidery, manuscripts and miniature art, have been preserved in museums and libraries in Romania and abroad, and complete the Romanian cultural and historic patrimony.

These monasteries were the centre of intense cultural and artistic life. In the fifteenth century, 'schools of copyists' existed at Neamt and Putna, under the guidance of Gavriil Uric and Teodor Marisescu. At the beginning of the sixteenth century, the Dragomirna 'school' was patronized by Metropolitan Anastasie Crimca. The first Romanian chronicles were written in these monasteries: the Dyptich of Bistrita (fifteenth century), the Chronicle of Putna (sixteenth century), the Chronicles of the Bishops Macarie of Roman and Eftimie of Radauti (sixteenth century), the Universal Chronicle by Mihail Moxa, a monk in Vallachia, in the seventeenth century.

The monasteries and bishoprics housed the first Romanian printing-houses: Dealu, Targoviste, Plumbuita, Govora, Campulung, Iasi, Bucharest, Buzau, Snagov, Ramnic, Neamt. The first printers were from the clergy: the monk Macarie, the deacon Coresi, and in Brasov, the monk Mitrofan, future Bishop of Husi and Buzau, and Antim Ivireanul, future Metropolitan. The same monasteries housed Romanian and Slavonic schools, as well as consecrated churches, and they prepared clerks for chancellor offices or as manuscript copyists. The first schools for middle and higher education were opened here as well: the College at the Three Hierarchs Monastery in Iasi, and St Sava's Academy in Bucharest. New schools appeared in the eighteenth century in most bishopric centres, and near monasteries in urban areas: Coltea, Old St George, Antim, Princess Balasa in Bucharest, St Dumitru and Obedeanu in Craiova, Barnovschi, St Vineri and St Nicholas in Iasi. The schools at Putna, Obedeanu and Antim had special sections for the education of the clergy. In 1803, a seminary was founded at the Socola-Iasi monastery.

Many monasteries played a social or humanitarian role. Ever since the fifteenth century, ill and elderly monks as well as lay believers, had been taken care of in Putna (fifteenth century), Arges, Bistrita, Cozia (sixteenth century), Dragomirna, Sadova, Hurezi (seventeenth century), Coltea and Antim in Bucharest (eighteenth century) and in many others.

During this long period, the Orthodox Romanian Church supported the Orthodox Churches in countries that were under Ottoman rule, by printing books in Greek, Arabic and Georgian, and especially by offering material assistance to churches and schools, and social assistance settlements in the Balkans and the Near East. Several Greek printing-houses functioned in Vallachia and Moldavia with the direct support of the Romanian rulers.

Antim Ivireanul printed the first two Greek-Arabic books for the Arab Orthodox believers in Antioch; later, Prince Constantin Brancoveanu offered the printing press to Patriarch Athanasius Dabas, who kept it at Aleppo in Syria. More books in the Arabic language were printed in Iasi and Bucharest in the eighteenth century. One of Antim Ivireanu's apprentices, Mihail Stefan, was sent to Tbilisi, where he printed books in the Georgian language.

The first book in Bulgarian was printed at Ramnicu-Valcea in 1806, the first version of the Gospels was published in Bulgarian in Bucharest, under the guidance of the Metropolitan of Vallachia, and the first book teaching Bulgarian was published in Brasov, in 1824. Macarie, Filip the Moldavian, Deacon Coresi and other printers of the seventeenth century printed many books in the Slavonic language, and sent them south of the Danube, to the countries which were deficient in printing-houses.

Young Greeks studied in the Greek Academies in Iasi and Bucharest, with grants awarded by the Romanian princes, who also sponsored, especially in the eighteenth century, dozens of Greek schools in Constantinople, Athos, Ioaninia, Seres, Trebezond, Smyrna and the isles of Alexandria.

From the second half of the fourteenth century, documents of the time mention the contribution of the two Romanian states, as well as of the Romanian Orthodox Church, to the development of Mount Athos monasteries: Zographou, Dionysiou, Dochiariou, Hilandar, Pantocrator, Vatopedi, Iviron. New churches and chapels were also built here with Romanian help. The Romanians also donated money, manuscripts, books, icons, robes and liturgical vessels, many of which still exist in libraries and museums in Greece.

In the sixteenth century, when the first official donations to the monasteries on Mount Athos began, Romanian princes also gave estates, forests, vineyards, fish-pools, mills, shops and paid custom duty. The same benefits went to the monastery of St Catherine at Mount Sinai (founded by Emperor Justinian), to the monasteries at Meteora in Greece, and to some monasteries in Ioaninia, the islands of Cyprus, Patmos, Rhodos, Paros, Halki, and to the Patriarchates of Constantinople, Alexandria, Antioch and Jerusalem. This custom continued until the properties of the monasteries were secular-ized in 1863, during the reign of Alexandru Ioan Cuza. The donations helped Greek Orthodoxy survive under Ottoman rule; at the same time, they promoted Greek culture and cultivated the Greek national spirit, which ultimately led to the Greek War of Independence in 1821–8.

The Romanian countries also helped some ecclesiastical settlements in Serbia (the monasteries of Krušedol, Lopusnia, Dećani, Sopočani, Hopovo, Lipovina), and in Bul-garia (Rila, Kremikovski, built by Prince Radu the Great of Vallachia, and the churches in Svistov and Vidin, built by Prince Matei Basarab). Similar clerical settlements were built in the Ukraine, such as the Moldavian church in Lvov, built by Prince Alexandru Lapusneanu. In the first half of the seventeenth century, the cultural and clerical life of the Orthodox people in the Ukraine, who were under Polish occupation, was domi-nated by the personality of the Romanian Peter Moghila, the Metropolitan of Kiev (1633–46). The son of a Romanian Prince, he founded a new school which used Latin for instruction in Kiev, guided the activity of schools in the Ukraine and printing-houses in Kiev, Lutk, Ostrog, and wrote his famous *Orthodox Confession*, which was acknow-ledged by a pan-Orthodox Synod summoned in Iasi in 1642.

By safeguarding the national churches of the countries that were under foreign occupation, the Romanian Church supported their struggle to preserve the Orthodox spirit and their national culture.

Transylvania

Many churches provide evidence of the existence of hierarchs, priests and believers in the Principality of Transylvania by the mid-fourteenth century. Mention should be made of the earlier churches in Densus, and those in Strei, Streisangeorgiu (which has an inscription dated 1313, mentioning a painter and a priest), Santamaria Orlea, Rau de Mori, Ostrov, Sanpetru, Pesteana, Gurasada, Lesnic, Ribita, Criscior (all in Hune-doara county), and the Prislop, Ramet and Peri Monasteries. There is documentary evidence of a large number of monasteries in Banat and Western Romania.

It would have been only natural for such monasteries to have their own hierarchs. But Transylvania was under the rule of the Catholic Magyar kingdom. Under these circumstances the 'apostolic' kings of Hungary (particularly Louis the Great and Sigmund of Luxembourg in the fourteenth and fifteenth centuries) took repressive measures against the Orthodox priests and believers in Transylvania. Their hierarchs never had a permanent residence near the princes of Transylvania, who were appointed by the kings of Hungary, and were forced to live in monasteries or villages. Throughout this period, the Orthodox faith was only acknowledged as 'tolerated religion'.

Three Protestant confessions appeared in Transylvania by mid-sixteenth century: Lutheranism (to which all Saxons adhered), Calvinism and Unitarianism (which were embraced by some Magyars and Szeklers). The Orthodox Church was confronted with rather unsuccessful proselytizing from the Calvinist Magyars, and a tiny percentage of the nobility went over to this confession. Despite this unfortunate situation, the docu-ments of the time, even the Magyar ones, constantly mentioned Romanian hierarchs: Archbishop Ghelasie of Ramet in 1376 (who was sanctified), others in 1391, 1456, 1479, four metropolitans in Feleac village near Cluj (from 1488 to approximately 1550), as well as others in Geoagiu and Lancram, near Alba-Iulia.

It was only in 1572 that the state authorities allowed Romanian metropolitans to live in Alba-Iulia, which had become the capital city of the Principality of Transylvania. It became their official residence until the first part of the eighteenth century. The most representative defenders of the Orthodox faith were Ioan of Prislop (1585–1605), Teoctist (1605–22), Ghenadie (1627–40), Ilie Iorest (1640–3), who was removed by the Calvinists and canonized later, Simion Stefan (1643–56), the first editor of the Romanian version of the New Testament in Alba-Iulia in 1648 and Sava Brancovici (1656–80), who was also canonized. Several other hierarchs were active in Vad, near Cluj, where Moldavian princes established a bishopric in the sixteenth and seventeenth centuries. Others lived in Maramures and in Timisoara-Banat (e.g., Metropolitan Joseph the Saint, 1643–53), in Caransebes, in Ineu-Lipova, and later in Arad.

There were close connections between the Church in Transylvania and those in Vallachia and Moldavia. The Metropolitan of Vallachia was appointed representative of the Patriarch of Constantinople in Transylvania and had the right to ordain hier-archs. Moldavian and Vallachian princes founded many churches in Transylvania: Michael the Brave, for instance, built the cathedral and the metropolitan residence in Alba-Iulia, and Constantin Brancoveanu built the churches in Ocna-Sibiu and Fagaras, as well as the Sambata Monastery near Fagaras. Throughout the Middle Ages, there was a constant exchange of hierarchs, monks, priests, iconographers, manuscript copyists, and printers. This exchange maintained a sense of national unity in the three principalities.

In 1688, the Principality of Transylvania was annexed by the Hapsburg Empire; Banat was also annexed in 1718, and this situation remained unchanged until 1918. With direct support from the authorities in Vienna and by direct action from Magyar Jesuits, a small number of priests were pressured into accepting union with the Church of Rome, by acknowledging the four 'Florentine' points (following the model of the union of the Ukraine in Brest, 1596). In 1701, Metropolitan Atanasie Anghel of Alba-Iulia was re-ordained in Vienna, but only as bishop, subordinated to the Roman Catholic Archbishop of Esztergom in Hungary. The metropolitan seat of Alba-Iulia was thus abolished and the seat of the new bishopric united with Rome was set in Fagaras (1723) and then in Blaj (1737), where it has remained. In 1853 the pope elevated it to the status of a metropolitan, with three suffrage dioceses in Oradea, Gherla and Lugoj, which still exist.

Priests, monks and believers protested against the confessional schism of the Transylvanian Romanians, and some of them subsequently died in prisons in Vienna, and later became neo-martyrs of the Orthodox Church. In 1761–2 all Orthodox Romanian monasteries and hermitages were destroyed by direct order from the Austrian General Nicholaus Adolf von Bukow. The Orthodox Church remained without a leader for more than sixty years, and candidates to priesthood were ordained in bishopric centres in Vallachia, usually at Ramnic. It was only in 1761, as a result of memoranda and peasant uprisings that the Court in Vienna consented to the Orthodox Church having its own bishopric centre in Sibiu. To begin with it had four Serbian hierarchs, but in 1810 the national hierarchy was restored.

Despite these difficulties, the Orthodox Church in Transylvania had an essential role in the advancement of Romanian culture, as well as in the strengthening of the sense of Romanian national unity. According to some historians, the first manuscripts in Romanian might have been written in southern Transylvania. In the second half of the sixteenth century, Deacon Coresi printed over twenty-five books in Romanian and Slavonic, in Brasov. The first Romanian version of the New Testament was printed in Alba-Iulia in 1648.

A considerable number of priests, especially from St Nicholas Church in Brasov, and monks copied historical and liturgical books. In the second half of the eighteenth century, three scholars belonging to the Church united with Rome – Samuil Micu, Gheorghe Sincai and Petru Maior – wrote theological, historical and linguistic books, most of which have been preserved in manuscript form.

Elementary schools for the children in the neighbouring villages functioned within the precincts of churches and monasteries. The first schools for the systematic education of clergy were founded in Blaj in 1754, and in Sibiu in 1786.

The Romanian Orthodox Church in the Modern Period, 1821–1918

The 1821 revolution led by Tudor Vladimirescu in Vallachia led to the overthrow of the Phanariot regime in the principalities of Vallachia and Moldavia. The revolution set in motion the modernization of the Romanian political, economic and social structures. In 1859 Vallachia and Moldavia were united under Alexandru Ioan Cuza (1859–66). The name Romania was officially adopted in 1862. The country became a constitutional monarchy in 1866, under Prince (King from 1881) Charles I of Hohenzollern-Sigmaringen.

On 9 May 1877 Romania proclaimed itself independent of the Ottoman Empire. The Berlin Congress (1878) internationally acknowledged the Romania's state independence and the annexation of Dobrudja. In exchange, Bukovina, which had been annexed by the Hapsburg Empire in 1775, remained as it was. After the Treaty of 16 May 1812 between Tzarist Russia and the Ottoman Empire, Russia annexed Bessarabia. Transylvania, Banat Maramures and Crisana remained part of the Austrian Hapsburg Empire. The dualistic state of Austria-Hungary was created in 1867, and the administration of those three territories was taken over by Hungary, which intensified Romanians' struggle for independence. After World War I Romania retrieved its three regions, as a result of the National Assembly in Alba-Iulia in 1918. The Peace Treaty of Versailles (1919–20) sanctioned these national resolutions.

A series of changes in religious life occurred after the first union of Vallachia and Moldavia in 1859. During the reign of Alexandru Ioan Cuza, a series of clerical laws that were absolutely necessary to the process of modernization were adopted. Monasteries' possessions were secularized in December 1863. On 3 December 1864, the independence of the Orthodox Church and the establishment of its General Synod were proclaimed, which caused a conflict with the Ecumenical Patriarch. On 11 January 1865, the Metropolitan of Vallachia was awarded the title of Primate Metropolitan. In 1872, the Organic Law was passed, whereby the Holy Synod of the Orthodox Church was constituted, comprising all the hierarchs in office: the Primate Metropolitan as president, the Metropolitan of Moldavia, the Bishops of Ramnic, Buzau, Arges, Roman, Husi and the Lower Danube (Galati), and eight 'lieutenant' hierarchs, one for every bishopric seat.

Metropolitan Veniamin Costachi of Moldavia (1803–8 and 1812–42) founded the seminary in Socola-Iasi, an elementary school and a high school near the 'Three Hierarchs' Monastery in Iasi. He also founded an engineering school, an academy, a school of crafts, as well as several 'county' schools in other towns in Moldavia. He edited approximately 130 books, some of which were his own translations from patristic literature. Grigorie Dascalul, the Metropolitan of Vallachia (1832–4), who was canonized in 2005, was also an outstanding translator from patristic literature. The Primate Metropolitan Nifon (1850–75) founded and sponsored a seminary in Bucharest; Calinic Miclescu founded the Faculty of Theology and the printing-house for church books in Bucharest (1875–86). In Moldavia, when Calinic Miclescu was metropolitan (1863–75), he and Iosif Naniescu (1875–1902) were the founders of the impressive metropolitan cathedral in Iasi. Bishops Chesarie (1825–46), Filotei (1850–9) and Dionisie Romano (1850–73) of Buzau supervised education and printing. Bishop Calinic the Saint (1850–68) of Ramnic was one of the most outstanding representatives of Romanian Orthodox spirituality, and Melchisedec Stefanescu of the Lower Danube (1864–79) and of Roman (1879–92) was the author of many studies on the history of the Church and a full member of the Romanian Academy.

The bishopric seat of Bukovina became a metropolitan seat in 1873, with Silvestru Moraru Andrievici (1880–95) as its most significant leader. After the annexation of Bessarabia by the Russian Empire in 1812, an archbishopric seat was created in Chisinau. It was subservient to the Synod of the Orthodox Church in St Petersburg, and it was forbidden to have any connections with Moldavia or Vallachia. Only its first leader, Gavriil Banulescu-Bodoni (1813–21) was Romanian; until 1918, the hierarchs were

Russian; unfamiliar with the Romanian language or with the hopes of the Romanian believers, they had a duty to incorporate Bessarabia spiritually into the Russian Empire.

In Transylvania, the Orthodox Church was ruled by the most outstanding hierarch in Romanian history, Andrei Saguna. He was vicar in 1846, bishop in 1848 and metropolitan from 1864 to 1873. In 1864 he restored the former metropolitan seat in Transylvania, which he moved to Sibiu; he also established two bishopric centres in Arad and Caransebes. He reorganized the metropolitan seat by the Organic Statute of 1868, the principles of which lie at the foundation of subsequent church law. He transformed the old Theological School in Sibiu into an Institute with a three-year theological and a four-year pedagogical section. He founded an eight-grade school in Brasov, which functioned under the guidance of the Church until 1948 and which still bears his name. He supervised the activity of the over 800 confessional elementary schools in his bishopric (over 2,700 such schools functioned in Transylvania at the time). He also founded a printing-house in Sibiu, which still functions, publishing among historical and religious books, and *Telegraful Roman*, a newspaper that has been published uninterruptedly since 1853. The Metropolitans Miron Romanul (1874–98) and Ioan Metianu (1899–1916) continued his cultural and spiritual efforts.

Theological culture benefited from new translations from patristic and post-patristic literature, especially in the first half of the nineteenth century: textbooks for theological seminaries, translations from modern Russian literature, especially in Moldavia, from where people went to study at the Pastoral Academy in Kiev. In Transylvania emphasis was laid on historical research. The first foreign-language periodicals were translated into Romanian in that period: the national-political papers *Telegraful Roman* (1853) in Sibiu, and *Biserica Ortodoxa Romana* (1874) in Bucharest are still running. Others were short–lived: *Biserica si Scoala* in Arad (1877–1948), *Foaia Diocezana* in Caransebes (1886–1948), *Candela* in Cernauti (1882–1946), *Revista Teologica* in Sibiu (1907–16 and 1921–47), published as *Mitropolia Ardealului* since 1956. In Transylvania and Banat, many priests edited newspapers with a national, political, pedagogical, literary and economic profile.

The first modern theological seminaries were founded near each bishopric centre in Moldavia and Vallachia: Socola-Iasi (1803), Bucharest, Buzau, Arges (1836), Ramnic (1837), Husi (1852), Roman (1858), Ismail-Galati (1864). A short-lived Theological Faculty was founded as part of the University of Iasi (1860–4), and another one was founded in Cernauti (1875–1948) to replace an institute that had existed since 1827. The Faculty in Bucharest (1881–1948) continued its activity as the University Theological Institute.

Each bishopric seat in Transylvania had its own Pedagogical-Theological Institute: Sibiu (1850), Arad (1822) and Caransebes (1865). The Orthodox Church in Transylvania guided the entire Romanian education system, namely several high schools (in Blaj, Beius, Brasov, Brad), pedagogical, vocational and girls' schools, as well as over 2,700 elementary schools (these were schools open to all children and subsidized by special funds donated by the believers).

Ecclesiastical art declined. Churches and monasteries were still built in the Moldavian/Brancoveanu style that had been established in previous centuries. Some neo-classical and neo-Gothic churches were built in towns, for example the metropolitan cathedral in Iasi and Amza Church in Bucharest. Some of the former princely establishments were recreated, but their initial shape was distorted. In Transylvania the same architectural style was predominant, in hall-churches, whereas in Banat and Crisana the Baroque style was dominant. The Byzantine style prevailed in the building of the cathedral in Sibiu in 1902–6.

The painting in monasteries followed the earlier Greek-Byzantine fresco style, but neo-Renaissance tempera paintings also abounded (the church of Agapia Monastery, the Metropolitan Cathedral of Iasi). Psalm music, with a strong tradition in Moldavia and Vallachia, was also strongly represented in Transylvania.

Monastic life declined after the monasteries were secularized in 1863, and after a law was passed during the reign of Alexandru Ioan Cuza, whereby restrictions were imposed on the number of monks in each monastery. Few new monasteries were built: at Cocos, Saon, Celic-Dere in Dobrudja, Chitcani, near Tighina-Bessarabia, but at the same time new churches were built in former monasteries: at Frasinei, Horaita and Cheia.

The clergy and the hierarchs took part in social and national vindication movements: in the 1848 revolution in Vallachia, Banat and Transylvania, in the movements prior to the Union of the Provinces (1857–9), in the 1892 'Memorandum' movement in Transylvania, and as a result of their involvement, many were imprisoned. During the Russian-Turkish-Romanian war for independence in 1877, and during World War I, military priests, as well as hospital monks and nuns accompanied the army on the battlefield. From 1916 to 1918, hundreds of priests from Transylvania and Banat were deported to Hungary or imprisoned because they had fought for the union with Romania.

Inter-Orthodox links, which had been so complex in the fourteenth to eighteenth centuries, regressed after monastic properties were secularized and links were made with Greek clerical institutions. Many young Romanians studied Greek theology in Athens and in Kiev, and became outstanding translators from Greek and Russian theological literature. In the second half of the nineteenth century, many Romanians from Transylvania and Banat studied at Roman Catholic and Protestant Universities in western Europe, especially in Austria and Germany.

In the same period, the first Romanian Orthodox communities appeared in Paris, Baden-Baden, Vienna and Budapest. Some Romanian monks built churches on Mount Athos (Prodromu and Lacu hermitages) and in the Holy Land (on Mount Tabor).

As a result of massive emigration from Transylvania and Banat at the beginning of the twentieth century, the first Romanian parishes emerged in the USA and in Canada.

The Romanian Orthodox Church since 1918

1918–1944

In 1918, the union of Bessarabia, Bukovina, Transylvania and Banat with Romania led to the creation of the unitary national Romanian state, initially ruled by King Ferdinand I (1914–27). The entire confessional organization underwent significant changes, as in the former provinces there were people of religious confessions who had not been acknowledged in former Romania (the General Cult Law was passed in 1928). The 1930 census found that 72.6 per cent of the population were Romanian-Orthodox, 7.9 per cent Greek Catholic, 3.9 per cent Roman Catholic (Hungarians, Szeklers, Poles, some Romanians), 6.8 per cent Lutheran-Evangelist (Saxons), and 2 per cent Reformed (Calvin Magyars). The Jews represented 4.2 per cent at that time, while the Presbyterians, the Magyar Unitarians, the Armenian-Gregorians and the Muslim Turks and Tatars in Dobrudja made up below 2.6 per cent of the population.

In 1919, all Orthodox hierarchs became members of the Holy Synod in Bucharest. In December 1919, the Bishop of Caransebes, Miron Cristea, was elected Primate Metropolitan. Shortly afterwards the process of church union was initiated. It continued until 6 May 1925, when the Law and Organization Statute of the Orthodox Romanian Church was passed, based on the principles of Andrei Saguna's Organic Statute in Transylvania. On 4 February 1925, the Holy Synod decided to found the Romanian Orthodox Patriarchate, and to institute the primate metropolitan as patriarch. After the law was passed, Miron Cristea became the first Patriarch of Romania, on 1 November 1925. Nicodim Munteanu, the former Metropolitan of Moldavia and author of theological works and translations from Russian, from the Old and the New Testament, succeeded him from 1939 to 1948.

New bishopric centres were founded in Oradea, Cluj, Hotin (Balti), Ismail, Constanta (Tomis), Sighet (Maramures) and Timisoara. On the eve of World War II, the patriarchate had the following structure: the metropolitan seats of Vallachia (with bishopric centres in Bucharest, Ramnic, Buzau, Arges, Tomis), of Moldavia and Suceava (with centres in Iasi, Roman, Husi, Galati), of Ardeal (with centres in Sibiu, Arad, Caransebes, Oradea, Cluj, later in Timisoara), of Bukovina (with centres in Cernauti, Hotin-Balti, later Maramures-Sighet), and of Bessarabia (with centres in Chisinau and Ismail). An army bishopric centre was also established in Alba-Iulia, as well as a Missionary Centre for the Orthodox Romanians in the USA and Canada, with its headquarters in Jackson, Michigan.

Out of the representative hierarchs of this period, Metropolitan Nicolae Balan of Transylvania (1920–55) fought for national union and for the unitary organization of the Church. He was one of the pioneers of Romanian ecumenism, a leading editor of publications in Sibiu, which he made into an important theological centre. Metropolitan Irineu Mihalcescu of Moldavia (1939–47) taught at the Faculty of Theology in Bucharest for thirty-five years and was considered the best theologian in the inter-war period. Bishops Roman Ciorogariu of Oradea, Nicolae Ivan of Cluj, Iacov Antonovici of Husi and Grigorie Comsa of Arad were honorary members of the Romanian Academy.

Theological education developed in the Faculties of Bucharest, Cernauti and Chisinau (since 1926), in the Theological Academies in Transylvania and Banat (Sibiu, Arad, Caransebes, Cluj and Oradea), as well as in the seminaries that existed in every old bishopric centre. Some outstanding professors should be mentioned: in Bucharest: Ioan Irineu Mihalcescu, Teodor M. Popescu, Niculae Popescu, Nichifor Crainic, Serban Ionescu, Haralambie Roventa, Petre Vintilescu, Vasile Ispir; in Cernauti: Vasile Tarnavschi, Vasile Gheorghiu, Nicolae Cotos, Vasile Loichita, Valerian Sesan; in Chisinau:

Grigorie Pisculescu (pen-name Gala Galaction) and Vasile Radu (both of whom re-translated the Bible), Iuliu Scriban, Ioan Savin, Valeriu and Cicerone Iordachescu, Toma Bulat, Constantin Tomescu; in Sibiu: Nicolae Colan, Dumitru Staniloae; in Cluj: Liviu Munteanu; and in Arad: Ilarion Felea. Some priests were also historians (some of them were elected Members of the Romanian Academy), others were writers or folklorists. Many were missionaries, social workers, military priests or teachers of religion in middle schools.

New periodicals were published between the wars: *Biserica Ortodoxa Romana* and *Studii Teologice* in Bucharest, *Candela* in Cernauti, *Luminatorul* and *Misionarul* in Chisinau, *Revista Teologica* in Sibiu. Ecclesiastical art, particularly architecture and painting, flourished as churches were constructed especially in Transylvanian towns. The Vallachian and Moldavian styles prevailed, based on the traditional Byzantine one. New monasteries in Transylvania revived monastic life in this province.

The Orthodox Church resumed its former links with other Christian Churches. Delegates from Romania participated in the pan-Orthodox conferences in Constantinople (1923), Mount Athos (1930), the first Conference of the Professors of Theology in the Balkans (Sinaia, 1924) and the first Congress of the Theology Professors in Athens (1936). It also took part in the incipient ecumenical movement. Professors and hierarchs participated in several conferences of the three main inter-war branches: 'Practical Christianity' held in Stockholm (1925) and Berne (1926), 'Faith and Organization' in Lausanne (1927) and 'World Alliance for the Union of Peoples through the Church' in Prague (1928) and Norway (1938), with subsequent regional conferences held in Romania (1924, 1933, 1936). The links with the Anglican Church were consolidated soon after the Anglican orders had been acknowledged by the Holy Synod, and subsequent to Patriarch Miron's visit to Britain in 1936.

1944–1989

On 23 August 1944 Romania severed the links with Germany and joined the Allied Forces until the end of the war. By the truce with the Soviet Union, Romania lost Bessarabia and Northern Bukovina (which was also certified by the Paris Peace Treaty in 1947). Owing to influence from Moscow and the presence of Soviet troops on its territory, Romania was to be turned into a 'popular republic' (in 1947), which was later to become 'socialist'. Dramatic changes occurred in the political, social and economic structure of the country, especially after 1965, when Nicolae Ceausescu became the leader of the Communist Party and the state leader from 1967 until 1989. The Church was totally marginalized; it became a barely tolerated institution, permanently supervised and controlled by the state authorities, particularly the secret police, the 'Securitate'. The Church was forced to adapt to these changes in order to avoid the unfortunate situation experienced by the Russian Church after the 1917 Communist Revolution, and lest it should be abolished, as had happened to churches in China and in Albania. As early as 1948, the study of religion was forbidden in schools, services were banned in hospitals and prisons, bishopric centres were abolished, and several hierarchs were pensioned off by the state. The Faculty of Theology in Suceava (which

had taken refuge here from Chisinau) was abolished, as were four theological academies in Transylvania and Banat and all seminaries (they subsequently re-opened,
gradually, as middle schools). Newspapers and periodicals were suppressed and whatever books were still published were censored in Bucharest. Links with Orthodox communities abroad were also forbidden.

From 1945 clergymen were arrested sporadically, a practice that intensified in
1948, and from 1959 to 1964, after which all political prisoners in Romania were
released. According to recent statistics, over 1,700 (out of 9,000) Orthodox priests
and monks were arrested in that period, along with Roman Catholic, Greek Catholic
priests, Protestant and neo-Protestant ministers. A former Metropolitan of Bukovina,
Visarion Puiu, was condemned to death in his absence, three priests were executed
for having participated in the armed resistance in the Fagaras Mountains, while
many others were condemned to hard labour and died in prisons. Some priests in
Bessarabia and Bukovina were arrested by the Soviets and deported to Siberia.
Important professors of theology were arrested: in Bucharest: Nichifor Crainic, Teodor
Popescu, Dumitru Staniloae; in Chisinau: Ioan Savin, Constantin Tomescu; in Arad:
Ilarion Felea; and in Cluj: Liviu Munteanu. The last two died in prison, along with
hundreds of other priests, monks, nuns and students. The few survivors were released
only after twenty years.

Dozens of monasteries and hermitages were closed down in 1959, and the monks
and nuns excluded from the monastic orders and forced to work in industrial plants.
Massive church demolishing began in Bucharest in the 1960s. Some of the churches
were historical and cultural monuments, but the protests from the patriarchate were
ignored.

Despite these hardships, a number of tactful and visionary leaders of the Church,
among whom Patriarch Justinian Marina (1948–1977) was a providential figure,
made it possible for the Church to keep functioning, albeit within rigid confines. Earlier
on 4 August 1948, the new Law for the Organization of the Cults had been passed,
whereby fourteen cults were acknowledged: Orthodox, Roman Catholic, Armenian-
Gregorian, Old Rite Christian, Reformed (Calvinist), Lutheran-Evangelical, Synodo-
Presbyterian, Jewish, Muslim, Baptist, Adventist, Pentecostal and Evangelical-Christian.
In 1948, the Holy Synod voted for the new Romanian Orthodox Church Statute, which
had to be adapted to the new situation in the country.

The number of bishopric seats was dramatically reduced, while those in Chisinau
and Cernauti were subordinated to the Patriarchate of Moscow and had Russian hierarchs. A new bishopric seat was created in the United States as a result of Romanian
state interference in diaspora affairs, the one created in 1934 having broken the links
with Romania. A Romanian Missionary Bishopric centre was created for Central Europe
in Paris in 1972, but few western states acknowledged it. On the other hand, new
parishes were founded abroad for Romanian refugees, with priests appointed by the
Romanian church officials.

Some other hierarchs deserve mention, although their biographies cannot be given
here: Patriarch Iustin Moisescu (1977–86) and Patriarch Teoctist Arapasu, honorary
member of the Romanian Academy and previously Metropolitan of Oltenia and
Moldavia. Important metropolitans have been: Firmilian Marin of Oltenia (1947–72),

Nicolae Colan (1957–67) and Nicolae Mladin (1967–81) of Ardeal, Antonie Plamadeala of Ardeal (1982–2005), Nestor Vornicescu of Oltenia (1978–2000), Vasile Lazarescu (1947–61) and Nicolae Corneanu (since 1962) of Banat, Bishops Iosif Gafton of Ramnic and Arges (1944–84) and Vasile Coman of Oradea (1971–92). The professors who taught at the two theology institutes that had not been abolished were noteworthy for their ecumenical activity: in Bucharest: Dumitru Staniloae, Ioan Coman, Liviu Stan, Nicolae Chitescu, Ene Braniste, Alexandru Ciurea, Petru Rezus, Ioan Ramureanu; and in Sibiu: Nicolae Neaga, Grigorie Marcu, Nicolae Mladin, Milan Sesan, Dumitru Belu, Isidor Todoran, Teodor Bodogae. They published in the few periodicals that were allowed to continue after 1948. Few theological works proper were published because of the restrictions imposed by the press censor. Papers on church art and history, as well as textbooks were published, nevertheless. The patriarchate was allowed to reprint service books and three editions of the Bible. A positive development was the fact that many churches were repainted and about five hundred new ones were built throughout the country. As a result of Patriarch Justinian's efforts, the first Romanian martyrs were canonized in 1955.

The links with other churches (especially those involved in the ecumenical movement) were gradually re-established, which was convenient for the Communist regime, since it created a positive image for it. At first, these links involved only churches in socialist countries, but they were subsequently extended to the patriarchates in Istanbul, Alexandria, Jerusalem and in Antioch. The Romanian representatives made an important contribution at the pan-Orthodox Conferences in Rhodes and Chambesy in Switzerland. Links with Oriental Orthodox Churches were also established: the Armenian one in Ecimiadzin (in the former Soviet Union), the Coptic one in Egypt, the Ethiopian, and the Syrian Orthodox churches in South India. The links with the Roman Catholic Churches of Austria, Germany and Belgium and with Anglican and Protestant Churches, were consolidated by summits and by student and faculty exchange programmes.

In 1961, when the Romanian Church was able to resume its involvement in the World Council of Churches, it sent its delegates to the general meetings in New Delhi (1961), Uppsala (1968), Nairobi (1975) and Vancouver (1983). Many hierarchs and theologians were active in various boards of the Ecumenical Council, and Patriarchs Justinian and Justin visited its headquarters in Geneva. In turn, many leaders of this organization visited the Romanian hierarchs. Many Romanian theologians are active as part of the European Church Conference in Geneva, as well as in committees for dialogue with the Roman Catholic and Lutheran Churches, and with representatives of the Islamic and Judaic religions.

The Romanian Orthodox Church since 1989

After the Communist regime was abolished in 1989, profound changes and renewals occurred within the Church as well. The 1992 census established the confessional ratio in Romania: 86.6 per ent Orthodox, 5 per cent Roman-Catholic, 3.5 percent Reformed, 1 per cent Greek Catholic, and under 4 per cent other cults. From 1990, some of the abolished bishopric centres were re-established, so that, at present, the Orthodox Church has the following structure: the Metropolitan seat of Vallachia and Dobrudja, with bishopric centres in Bucharest, Constanta (Tomis), Targoviste, Buzau, Galati (the Lower Danube), Slobozia, Alexandria; the seat of Moldavia and Bukovina, with centres in Iasi, Suceava-Radauti, Roman and Husi; the seat of Transylvania, with the centres of Sibiu, Feleac and Cluj, Vad, Alba-Iulia, Oradea, Maramures (Baia-Mare) and Covasna-Harghita; the seat of Oltenia, with centres in Craiova and Ramnic, and the seat of Banat, with centres in Timisoara, Arad and Caransebes. Two new metropolitan seats created for the Romanians in Gyula (Hungary) and Varset (Yugoslavia) are subordinated to the seat of Banat. Most of these centres are run by new hierarchs, educated in Romania and abroad: Daniel Ciobotea in Iasi, Teofan Savu in Craiova, Bartolomeu Anania in Cluj, Nifon Mihaita in Targoviste, Casian Craciun in Galati.

In Chisinau, the Metropolitan seat of Bessarabia, in Chisinau, subordinated to the Holy Synod of Bucharest, functions parallel to a Metropolitan seat of the Republic of Moldova, subordinated to the Holy Synod of the Russian Orthodox Church in Moscow. A metropolitan seat was created for the Romanian diaspora in Germany, and was run by Archbishop Serafim Joanta in Nuremberg. Another one exists in Paris, run by Archbishop Iosif Pop. The two archbishopric centres in America still function, one collaborating with the patriarchate, the other under foreign jurisdiction. The number of Orthodox Romanians abroad has increased, owing to massive emigration since the late 1980s.

About fourteen new theology faculties, in Iasi, Cluj, Craiova, Timisoara, among other places, and seminaries were opened after 1990, somewhat exceeding the real needs of the Church. Editorial activity developed as theological studies, textbooks and translations from western literature were published. Archbishop Bartolomeu Anania of Cluj, an esteemed poet, playwright and theologian, published his translation of the Bible. As well as the previously existing periodicals, every bishopric centre has its own newsletter.

New monasteries appeared (Recea-Mures, Ciolpani-Bacau, Barsana and Sapanta in Maramures), and the ones that had been closed down by the Communist regime were reopened. In the early twenty-first century there were 14,373 churches and 12,000 parish priests, 359 monasteries or nunneries and 174 hermitages, with 2,810 monks and 4,795 nuns. At present the patriarchate runs 23 bishopric centres, 148 arch-priest districts, 10,412 parishes and 2,251 subsidiaries. The missionary organizations resumed their activity and the study of religion was introduced in elementary and middle schools, with graduates of theology as teachers.

Social assistance is a constant concern of the Church; every theology faculty has a social assistance section, training personnel qualified for this kind of work. The Church has established its own social work establishments in Bucharest, Iasi and Suceava; many bishopric centres pay social workers out of their own budget.

Several more Romanian saints were canonized in 1992; in the same year, the Dacian-Roman saint cult was generally adopted in Romania. Religious feeling increased and became manifest in pilgrimages (St Paraschiva on 14 October in Iasi and St Dimitrie-Basarabov on 27 October in Bucharest) attended by approximately a million people. New Romanian saints were created during 2005.

The Romanian Church has intensified its links with other churches, especially with those in the Orthodox world. Its activity as part of the World Church Board of the European Church Conference and of other inter-Christian organizations continues. Relations with the representatives of the Jewish and Muslim traditions are maintained. The relations with the Roman Catholic Church culminated in Pope John Paul II's visit to Romania in May 1999, the first visit paid by the Pontiff to a largely Orthodox country.

Further reading

Balan, I. (1996) *Romanian Patericon: Containing the Lives and Sayings of the Saints and Monastic Fathers who Labored in the Land of Romania from the Fourth to the Twentieth Centuries.* Platina, Calif.: St Herman of Alaska Brotherhood.

Caravia, P. et al. (1999) *The Imprisoned Church: Romania 1944–1989.* Bucharest: National Institute for the Study of Totalitarianism.

Dumitrascu, N. (2002) *The Mission of the Romanian Orthodox Church and its Challenges.* Cluj-Napoca: Napoca Star.

Hitchens, K. (1977) *Orthodoxy and Nationality: Andreiu Eaguna and the Rumanians of Transylvania, 1846–1873.* Cambridge, Mass.: Harvard University Press.

Obolensky, D. (1971) *The Byzantine Commonwealth: Eastern Europe, 500–1453.* London: Weidenfeld and Nicolson.

Ogden, A. (2002) *Revelations of Byzantium: The Monasteries and Painted Churches of Northern Moldavia.* Portland, Ore.: Center for Romanian Studies.

Pacurariu, M. (1991) *Pagini de Istorie Bisericeasca Romaneasca* (Pages from Romanian Church History). Cluj-Napoca: Renasterea.

—— (1991–4) *Istoria Bisericii Ortodoxe Romane* (History of the Romanian Orthodox Church), 3 vols. Bucharest: The Biblical and Mission Institute of the Romanian Orthodox Church.

—— (1994) *Geschichte der Rumanischen Orthodoxen Kirche.* Erlangen.

—— (2002) *Dictionarul Teologilor Romani* (Dictionary of Romanian Theologians). Bucharest: Encyclopaedic Publishing House.

Rus, R. (2003) *Dictionar Enciclopedic de Literatura Crestina din Primul Mileniu* (Encyclopaedic Dictionary of Christian Literature of the First Millennium). Bucharest: Lidia.

Simionovici, E. (2001) *The Sacred Monastery of Voronet: A Hearth of Romanian History and Orthodox Spirituality.* Sibiu: Thausib.

Staniloae, D. (1980) *Theology and the Church.* Crestwood, NY: St Vladimir's Seminary Press.

—— (1994) *The Experience of God.* Brookline, Mass.: Holy Cross Orthodox Press.

—— (2002) *Orthodox Spirituality: A Practical Guide for the Faithful and a Definitive Manual for the Scholar.* South Canaan, Pa.: St Tikhon's Seminary Press.

Stebbing, N. (2003) *Bearers of the Spirit: Spiritual Fatherhood in Romanian Orthodoxy.* Kalamazoo, Mich.: Cistercian Publications.

Theodorescu, R. (1994) *Bucovina: Moldavian Mural Painting in the Fifteenth and Sixteenth Centuries.* Bucharest: Romanian National Commission for UNESCO.

Turcescu, L. (2002) *Dumitru Staniloae: Tradition and Modernity in Theology.* Portland, Ore.: Center for Romanian Studies.

CHAPTER 10

Russian Christianity

Basil Lourié

Christianity in Kievan Rus: Ninth to Early Fourteenth Centuries

The legend about the visit of the Apostle Andrew to the hills of the future city of Kiev was unknown in Russia before the eleventh century. Russia, however, shared with all the South Slav Christians the cult of St Clement of Rome as the favourite saint; it was a cult that spread out from Cherson on the Black Sea, the place where he was said to have been exiled under the Emperor Trajan (r. 98–117) and where his relics were deposed. Cherson became a centre of Christianity under the Patriarchate of Constantinople, whose tradition of Byzantine Christianity was influential throughout the Caucasus and Black Sea region.

According to the Byzantine sources, there was only one Baptism of Rus, which took place in the 860s under the Patriarch Photius of Constantinople, and the Prince of Kiev, Askold (between 860 and 867, most probably in 860–1). However, the Russian ruling elite after Askold remained pagan till the second and more important Baptism of Rus in 988, which nevertheless passed unnoticed by the Byzantines.

This baptism, in 988, of the Grand Prince Vladimir and the people under his rule was preceded by that of his grandmother Olga, most probably in Constantinople, in 957. Both Vladimir and Olga were glorified in the Russian Church as 'equal to the apostles', figures parallel to Constantine the Great and his mother Helena. Vladimir brought from Cherson a bishop (or, at least, a de facto leader of the Church) for Kiev, Anastasius the Chersonite. More importantly, he took from Cherson some of the relics of St Clement and put them into the main Church of Kiev, which he had himself founded, the so-called Desyatinnaya Church of the Theotokos (consecrated in 996; *desyatinnaya* means 'receiving the tithe'). So, as a new Christian capital, Kiev became both a New Constantinople and a New Cherson. On the one hand, its Cathedral, the Desyatinnaya Church, was consecrated on 12 May, the nearest Sunday to the feast of the Consecration of Constantinople (11 May), and the dedication of it to the Theotokos was also in imitation of Constantinople, the City of the Mother of God. On the other hand, as a place of repose for the relics of St Clement, Kiev became a New Cherson.

This ideology of a 'New Cherson' did not disappear until the twelfth century, although under the son of Vladimir, Yaroslav the Wise in the 1030s, Kiev became a 'New Constantinople' first and a 'New Cherson' only secondly. This new 'spiritual localization' of Kiev was officially proclaimed in 1046 by the Metropolitan of Kiev, Hilarion, in his famous *Sermon on Law and Grace*, which is in fact a typical Byzantine-styled homily on the consecration of a new cathedral. This sermon was delivered on the last (seventh) Sunday of the Paschal period, in the near proximity of (or exactly on) the feast of the Consecration of Constantinople, during the consecration of the new cathedral at Kiev, that of St Sophia. The relics of St Clement were translated here from the Desyatinnaya Church, and this new cathedral of St Sophia was dedicated to the Theotokos, despite the fact that the Kievan St Sophia was modelled after the Great Church of Constantinople. Even if Hilarion insisted in his sermon on the Chersonite roots of Russian Christianity (placing the baptism of Vladimir in Cherson), this change of cathedral made the cult of St Clement secondary (and it was indeed overshadowed by the Constantinopolitan cult of St Andrew), with no prospect of it regaining its importance.

Being separated from the Latins by the schism of 1054, the Kievan Metropolitanate was less consistent in the policy of alienation than its Mother Church in Constantinople. After the Mongol invasion of 1237, the Russian princes had to choose: either the Pope of Rome or the Mongols (called 'Tartars' in Russia). St Alexander Nevsky managed to use the force of the Mongols to protect Russia from western conquerors. During the whole of the thirteenth century the Mongols were open to Christian preaching and even allowed a church organization in their midst, and there was no oppression of the Church from their side. The situation changed drastically in the early fourteenth century when they adopted Islam as their state religion. A result of this was the Battle of Kulikovo Field (1380), which irreversibly undermined the power of the Tartars, although the final liberation of Russia did not come until 1480.

The Church of Moscow to the Middle of the Fifteenth Century

The period begins with the transference to Moscow of the See of the Metropolitan of Russia (1325), and the establishment of the famous Russian monasteries in the middle and second half of the fourteenth century, such as those of Sergius of Radonezh (1314–92) near Moscow, and Cyril Belozerskij ('of the White Lake') in the forests of the 'Northern Thebaid' near Vologda. More important, however, is that it begins with the flowering of the Russian Hesychast tradition, followed by the general establishment of monasticism and missionary work. One of the best-known missionaries of this period was St Stephen of Perm (1340–96), who invented an alphabet for the Zyrians, a Finnish people living in the region of Perm. The period from the middle of the fourteenth century to the middle of the fifteenth century was probably the closest to the ideal of 'Holy Russia'.

The Period of Self-Proclaimed Muscovite Autocephaly (1441–1589)

This is the period of the foundation of the Russian autonomous Church and the Russian monarchy, when Moscow became the 'Third Rome', after Rome proper, and Constantinople, the New Rome. It is most obviously a key period for the subsequent history of the Russian Orthodox Church.

The autocephaly of the Moscow See was established during the years 1441–8 by the following steps. The Grand Prince of Moscow Basil II refused to accept Metropolitan Isidor, appointee of the Patriarch of Constantinople, when Isidor was sent to Moscow in 1441. Instead, he wrote a letter to the patriarch explaining the need of the Russian Church to exercise the right to elect a metropolitan by the local synod of bishops. This was a formal request for autocephaly and the only official document on this issue; his letter was never answered by the patriarch. Then, with no reply from the patriarch, the Synod of Russian Bishops in 1448 consecrated as metropolitan Jonas, a Russian candidate to the Metropolitan See since 1430. These are the facts that were subsequently veiled by the following myths: that the request for autocephaly was in response to the reunion of the Eastern and Western Churches at the Council of Florence in 1439, and that Constantinople approved the autocephaly of the Moscow See, only very much later (but long before 1589).

The story of Isidor was officially represented quite differently inside and outside of Russia. Inside, he was judged unacceptable by the Synod of Russian Bishops in 1441 because of his loyalty to the reunion with Rome that had been agreed at the Council of Florence in 1439. Outside, however, as in the aforementioned letter from the Grand Prince to the Patriarch of Constantinople, the only reason to refuse him was deemed to be personal. This was perhaps to be expected, taking into account the addressee: Patriarch Metrophanes II was a supporter of the reunion. It has been suggested, however, that Basil II asked the patriarch for autocephaly as if the latter were still a lawful church authority whose Orthodoxy was impeccable. The Grand Prince may have had opinions of his own about the distribution of ecclesiastical power and may not have cared that much about the correct confession of faith. Again it has been suggested that he was happy to ignore the actual status of the patriarch, but was willing to accept the principle of patriarchal jurisdiction over the Russian Church.

Up until his death in 1461 Metropolitan Jonas considered the western eparchies as a part of his own metropolitanate. The real situation was more complicated, however. At first, Metropolitan Jonas and his autocephaly was accepted by Casimir IV, the Roman Catholic King of Poland and Lithuania. Then, in spite of this, Casimir tried to assist the Pope of Rome in establishing in Russia the Union of Florence. To this end he accepted as Metropolitan of Kiev, Gregory the Bulgarian (1458–73), a supporter of the reunion and a disciple of Isidor, who had been consecrated in Rome by the Patriarch of Constantinople in exile, Gregory Mammas, also a supporter of the reunion. Casimir succeeded in forcing all the bishops of his kingdom to submit to Gregory.

Gregory was at first consecrated Metropolitan of Kiev and Lithuania only, but very soon (before January 1459) his jurisdiction was extended to include Moscow. The

Russian Metropolitanate therefore had two heads of different faiths. Jonas was now in a position to condemn his adversaries of heresy. This condemnation turned out to be decisive, but not in a way to please Moscow. Casimir allowed Metropolitan Gregory to address the Patriarch of Constantinople with repentance for his past support of the reunion and with acknowledgement of the patriarch's jurisdiction. Gregory's letter to the patriarch is lost, but a reply from Patriarch Dionysius I to Gregory has been found, dated 14 February 1467. The patriarch in turn acknowledged Gregory as the Metropolitan of the whole Russian Church, including Moscow, and forbade anyone to have any communion with Jonas. The patriarchate does not appear to have been aware that Jonas had died in 1461. The Grand Prince of Moscow, Ivan III, responded by forbidding any contacts with both the Patriarch of Constantinople and Metropolitan Gregory. An iron curtain had slammed down separating the Muscovite Church from both Constantinople and the Kievan Metropolitanate.

From this point in 1467 the history of Russian Christianity runs in two veins. The Western Russian Church was founded on safe canonical grounds, but unfortunately there is no room here to trace the history of the specific phenomenon of Kievan Christianity from 1467 to 1686, the date of reunification of the Kievan Metropolitanate with the Patriarchate of Moscow. The organization of the Eastern Church remained with no canonical support, and separated from communion with the post-Byzantine centres of monasticism and education still existing in the Ottoman Empire. Such communion had been the key condition for the 'Hesychast renaissance' in fourteenth-century Russia. This lack of communion was to have a fatal effect on the mechanisms of the rise of the Moscow Empire as the Third Rome. The subsequent period is probably the most definitive for the destiny of the Russian Church.

Two Strategies for the Muscovite Church: the Josephites and the Non-Possessors

The last three decades of the fifteenth century were a formative period for two alternative strategies in the development of the Muscovite Church. After a period of smouldering they flared up after the Moscow Council of 1503. They were backed by two monastic movements headed by Joseph of Volokolamsk (1440–1515) and Nil of Sora (1433–1508). Naming the followers of the latter 'Nestyazhateli' ('non-possessors', or 'those who have no possessions') is an over-simplification, because the Josephites, too, had no personal possessions, although their monasteries were rich landowners. Both parties were followers of the Hesychast tradition and both were zealous for the purity of the Orthodox faith. Thus both were active in fighting against the heresy of the Judaizers that affected the Muscovite Church from the 1470s through to the early sixteenth century. And, of course, both were preoccupied with the desire to reinforce the standing of the Muscovite Church; their mutual differences lay deeper.

In sum, the Josephites were trying to build up the Church by adding to it as much secular power as possible and by ensuring the maximum autonomy for Moscow. On the other hand, the Non-Possessors invented some extraordinary measures to diminish the secular power of the Church. They tried to block any church decisions beyond the canonical competence of the local Church of Moscow, while at the same time gently but consistently acting to re-establish intellectual, ideological and, potentially, canonical dependence on the Greeks.

The war between the two parties became open after the Council of 1503, at which both Joseph and Nil, as well as their followers, were present. The main dates and events are as follows:

Moscow Council of 1503: Main differences between the two parties became apparent, although the details of this earliest stage of the polemics are not clearly known.

1510: Debates between Joseph of Volokolamsk and the closest disciple of the late Nil of Sora (d. 1508), Vassian Patrikeev (c.1470–1545), a former prince, who had been forcibly tonsured as a monk but was still influential at court. Vassian reacted to Joseph's writings against Nil and himself.

1511: Varlaam became Metropolitan of Moscow and advocated a friendly policy towards the Non-Possessors.

1518: Maxim the Greek (surnamed Trivolis, c.1470–1555) arrived in Moscow and became a close friend and teacher of Vassian Patrikeev.

1521: Metropolitan Varlaam was uncanonically deposed (and, probably, jailed) by the Grand Prince Basil III (the details of this story are not clear, but it certainly marked a turning point in Basil III's attitude towards the Josephites).

1522: Daniel, head of the Josephites after the death of Joseph of Volokolamsk (d. 1515), became Metropolitan.

1525: Second 'marriage' (canonically treated as adultery) of Grand Prince Basil III, opposed by the Non-Possessors. His former wife Solomonia Saburova, divorced for sterility and forcibly tonsured, would later become St Sophia of Suzdal.

1525: Condemnation of Maxim the Greek by Metropolitan Daniel.

1531: Condemnation of Vassian Patrikeev and (for the second time) Maxim the Greek by Metropolitan Daniel. Vassian was to die in prison after several years of captivity.

1539: Metropolitan Daniel deposed 'by his own will' for being involved in political intrigues.

1542: Macarius became Metropolitan of Moscow (until his death in 1563), and began his programme of totally restructuring the Muscovite Church, implying a kind of compromise between the two parties.

1547: Coronation of Ivan IV ('the Terrible'; 1530–84) as the Tsar of All Russia, subsequent softening of the official attitude towards the Non-Possessors.

1547 or 1548: Maxim the Greek is released and acquitted after twenty-two years in prison and excommunication. He will never be allowed, however, to return home, being forced to live in the Holy Trinity Monastery near Moscow, where he influenced its *hegumenos*, the elder Artemius.

1551: Council of Moscow called the Stoglav ('Hundred Chapters'), the name taken from its main document; the high point of Metropolitan Macarius' programme of restructuring.

1553: A Josephite, Vassian Toporkov, nephew of Joseph of Volokolamsk and an
accuser of Maxim the Greek, together with other Josephites, exert influence
upon Tsar Ivan IV and replace the circle close to Metropolitan Macarius.

1554: Condemnation, excommunication and escape by fleeing to Lithuania of
the elder Artemius. Maxim the Greek would die soon after in 1555. The Non-
Possessors now had no leader within Russia.

1564: Escape of Prince Andrew Kurbskij (1528–83) to Lithuania, to live under
the spiritual guidance of the elder Artemius. The programme of the Non-
Possessors as a whole became that of the political opposition. In the same
year Tsar Ivan IV started his policy of terror (oprichnina).

1560s–1570s: Literary polemics between Kurbskij and Ivan IV on the current
problems of the Russian Church and the status of the power of the Tsar.

1589: Establishment of the Patriarchate of Moscow in an attempt to establish
secure canonical grounds for the Muscovite Church.

The whole period can be seen as having three major stages: first, acute opposition
of the two parties (1503–47); second, compromised church structure created by
Macarius (especially in 1547–53); and third, destruction of Macarius' system inspired
by the Josephites (from 1553 to the death of Ivan IV in 1584). This was followed in the
1580s by an attempt to reinvigorate Macarius' programme.

Canon Law for the Third Rome: the Reform Programme of the Josephites

Up to the fifteenth century Russia had no canon law except the Byzantine one. This
was naturally because the Russian Church was a part of the Patriarchate of Constantinople, which was headed by metropolitans (mostly Greeks) appointed by the patriarch. As to secular law, Russia had two systems existing in different fields: the Byzantine
law, which was used only for ideological purposes, and the local customary law, which
was the actual norm of Russian justice.

This system had been broken by the non-canonical declaration of autocephaly,
and so needed to be either replaced or restored. At the Council of 1503, Joseph of
Volokolamsk proposed a programme for the independent development of Muscovite
canon law, which had been challenged by the Non-Possessors but adopted by the
Stoglav Council of 1551. In fact, Joseph proposed to extend the existing secular legislation to cover the Church as well.

The occasion for Joseph's proposal was in fact the main cause of the 1503 Council,
the right of widowed clergy to serve. Despite the canon law of the Ecumenical Church,
the Council suspended such clergy from service with no regard for the purity of their
life. Joseph justified this decision by taking many examples from ecclesiastical law,
showing that the canons relating to church discipline were subject to change. There
was, however, another question avoided by Joseph: Who had the right to change the
canons that were proclaimed or, at least, adopted by the Ecumenical Councils? Joseph's

answer was implicit but clear: it was the Muscovite Church, whose authority was now equal to that of the Ecumenical Councils.

Naturally, the theory that the state where the Muscovite Church resided was now the very Christian *oikoumene*, translated from Byzantium, was to be developed over the next years. Indeed, in 1523–4 the elder Philotheus wrote an epistle to the Grand Prince Basil III (which became known to all the ideologists of the epoch) in which he proclaimed the Muscovite state to be the Third and Last Rome, the place of the earthly sojourn of the indestructible Christian Empire. Of course, the councils of the Church of the Third Rome would have the authority of Ecumenical Councils. The next step was the coronation of Ivan IV as Tsar of All Russia in 1547 (his father Basil III was only a Grand Prince, not a Tsar) according to the coronation rite of the Byzantine emperors.

Now, having an Ecumenical Church and an emperor, the only wish that remained was an Ecumenical Council. This was the main reason for calling the Stoglav Council in 1551. This council is understandable only in the context of convening an Ecumenical Council. Metropolitan Macarius, the main ideologist of the Stoglav Council, sincerely believed that it was possible to establish a kind of Justinian *symphonia* on the basis of the Josephite autonomy of the Muscovite Church. So he repeated (chapter 62 of the Stoglav) the famous Novella VI of Justinian on the *symphonia* between the 'priesthood' and the 'kingdom'. The very desire to re-state such things, which had been part of Russian canon law since the time of the Baptism of Rus, resulted from the need to demonstrate the new authority of Moscow, where even the basic elements of the canon law of the Ecumenical Church needed to be approved for its own legitimacy. That section of the 'Hundred Chapters' which provides answers to the 'Tsar's questions' chooses to recall the Ecumenical Councils convoked by the Byzantine emperors, especially the First Ecumenical Council called by Constantine the Great. At the same time, and quite naturally, chapter 79 of the Stoglav Council quotes Joseph of Volokolamsk's 1503 defence of the primacy of the Muscovite authority over that of the Ecumenical Councils.

The Hundred Chapters consist mostly of decisions which offer no apparent contradiction of Ecumenical canon law, being those important for the everyday life of the Russian Church. The Council, however, failed at times to distinguish between dogma, church discipline and local customs. For instance, it anathematized all those who made the sign of cross otherwise than with two fingers (chapter 31). Such a dogmatization of Russian ecclesiastical and native customs became a specific feature of the epoch and of the official ideology of the circle of Metropolitan Macarius.

The Byzantine idea of a *symphonia* between Church and state was compromised by Ivan IV, who finally made the Metropolitans legitimize his bloody and adulterous public life. The Church as an organization turned out to be unable to resist because of its lack of canonicity: indeed, its autonomy in relation to the Ecumenical Church turned into being a slave of a tyrant. In the long term, the Stoglav Council became a delayed-action mine which was to blow up the entire building of the Russian Church in the seventeenth century. The Moscow Councils of 1666–7 would anathematize it as uncanonical and start the Great Schism (*Raskol*) of the Russian Church.

A Counter-Reform Programme of the Non-Possessors

At the Council of 1503 the Non-Possessors put forward an antidote to the Josephites. They considered the prime danger to be any rise in the secular power of the Church. So, in accordance with the Byzantine tradition, they were against capital punishment for heretics, although they were not of course against it for civil criminals. But their main aim was the complete dissolution of lands belonging to the monasteries. In the Orthodox Church in general monasticism was the element whose influence (or lack thereof) was always definitive for its ideology and spiritual condition. So the Non-Possessors were striking at the most vital element of the whole church organization.

Monks should eat from the labour of their hands, or from receiving alms, they argued, with abundant reference to the monastic rules and regulations. This was a brilliant idea which allowed the resolution of three problems simultaneously: to win over the Grand Prince at the expense of the Josephites, to destroy the material base of the Josephite movement, and, most importantly, to preserve the independence of the church organization from the secular powers, to the extent of making it impossible for it to be a great landowner. The Russian nineteenth-century canonist and church historian, A. Pavlov, argued that the servility of the church hierarchy since the 1520s was a direct result of the victory of the Josephites who chained the church establishment to its acres.

Both the Josephite reformation and the Non-Possessor counter-reform started from an innovation. The former was elaborating the idea of the autonomy of the Muscovite Church; the latter wanted the reform of monasticism which, although not forbidden by canon law, was not obligatory either. In fact, monasteries both in Byzantium and in Russia were allowed to possess lands and the Josephites were right in justifying their stand by citing examples from the lives of earlier Byzantine and Russian saints. In answer to this the Non-Possessors said: 'They possessed, but possessed without passion.' So the Non-Possessors positioned their reform as necessary only as it applied 'here and now', to the Muscovite Church of their time.

At first, the Non-Possessors managed to gain power at the court of the Grand Prince Basil III, and Metropolitan Varlaam (1511–21) was their protector. With the blessing of Metropolitan Varlaam, in 1517 Vassian Patrikeev prepared the first edition of the Canonical Law Code (*Kormchaya*), shortly after reworking it with the help of Maxim the Greek, the first post-Byzantine intellectual and ascetic involved in the church life of Moscow since the early fifteenth century. He arrived in Russia after the Grand Prince appealed to the Athonite monasteries to send him a person able to translate ecclesiastical texts from Greek into Slavonic. Instead of staying for a couple of years, however, he spent the rest of his life in Russia and became venerated after his death as a holy confessor and a great theologian.

Together with Vassian, Maxim became a leader of the Non-Possessors. Their collective work, the canonical code, was accepted by the Grand Prince and was almost accepted by a church council. But here the Non-Possessors and their protector Varlaam fell into disfavour. Basil III had gradually perceived what the real difference was between the two church parties: the Non-Possessors were seeking an independent Church while the Josephites were seeking a Church submissive to the state. Maxim the Greek asked questions about the origin of the Muscovite autocephaly. He was told that there was a charter which gave the patriarch's blessing for it, but nobody was able to produce the document. In 1525 he would be condemned for his refusal to acknowledge the Muscovite autocephaly.

After the unlawful 'marriage' of the Grand Prince Basil III, who took his second wife in order to produce an heir (the future Tsar Ivan IV), any links between him and the Non-Possessors were broken. The wedding ceremony had been performed by the leader of the Josephites, Metropolitan Daniel, who justified his action by reference to the alleged specific rights of the tsar. It should be noted, however, that such a view of imperial adultery had been condemned in Byzantium as a result of the second marriage of Emperor Constantine VI (r. 780–97), the so-called Moechian Controversy. From 1525 the Non-Possessors were severely persecuted and their leaders jailed on trumped-up charges. The situation partially changed in 1547, but only for a short period. The earlier centres of the Russian Hesychast movement, such as the Holy Trinity Monastery near Moscow and the St Cyril of the White Lake Monastery near Vologda, became great sources of revenue for the Church. The Josephites of the second half of the sixteenth century ceased to be Hesychasts, and the Hesychast tradition was shifted further to the north, to the monastery on the Solovki Islands in the White Sea, the main centre for about a century.

The Non-Possessors' Programme as the Political Opposition: Prince Andrew Kurbskij

Seen through the eyes of the Non-Possessors, Russia under Ivan the Terrible was in a situation worse than under the Mongols. Then, at the time of the Battle of Kulikovo Field (1380), the Hesychast leaders put forward a programme called by one modern scholar (G. M. Prokhorov) 'political Hesychasm', which forced Grand Prince Dimitrij to start a war against the Tartars. The second half of the sixteenth century saw another 'political Hesychast' initiative, which was a plan of a war against Moscow for the sake of Orthodoxy. The leader of this Hesychast political opposition was the émigré Prince Kurbskij, who had once been a general close to Ivan the Terrible. Prince Kurbskij lived in the Kingdom of Poland under the spiritual guidance of the elder Artemius, a great Hesychast figure and a theologian comparable to Maxim the Greek.

The Orthodox faith and even Russian culture was still a great force in Lithuania and Poland. Different projects for unification of all three states, not only Poland and Lithuania, but also the Muscovite state, were always on the agenda. In fact the Russian Empire included all three of them from 1795 to 1917. Therefore, a move to support the King of Poland against the Tsar of Moscow contained nothing anti-Russian in itself. Indeed Ivan IV himself was invited in 1572–5 to become King of Poland. The wars between Muscovite Russia and Poland were often similar to civil wars.

Up to his death in 1583 Prince Kurbskij acted as a general of the Polish king in his wars against Ivan IV. This would have been impossible without the blessing of Artemius and the moral support of the wide circle of Orthodox zealots. In Lithuania,

Prince Kurbskij was known as the principal protector of the Orthodox faith from both secular enemies and religious heretics. The whole tradition of West Russian Orthodox polemical literature goes back to the entourage of Kurbskij at his Lithuanian manor. In no way can Prince Kurbskij's activity be considered as something marginal with respect to 'mainstream' Orthodoxy. Kurbskij himself was continuing an international Hesychast policy already initiated in 1546–7 by the so-called *Excerpt on the Second Marriage of Basil III*, a pamphlet against both Basil III and Ivan IV. The core of this work was produced by Athonite monks and it was distributed through a very influential person and theologian, the *Protos* of Mount Athos, Gabriel, a Serb.

The main and new topic of the literary polemics between Kurbskij and Ivan IV in the 1560s–1570s (including the open letters to each other) was the nature of imperial (tsarist) power. Prince Kurbskij condemned the Josephites because they were guilty by association of the tyranny of Ivan IV. Supported by the Josephites, Ivan the Terrible, the first Russian tsar, considered himself to be a sacred person led by a kind of divine inspiration. Kurbskij wrote to him that, on the contrary, he was a human being in need of the council of other human beings who may be wiser than himself. Ivan was interested in developing a doctrine of the 'sacred king', an idea which very much affected subsequent Russian history and which has never been accepted unequivocally. Kurbskij treated the tsar in line with the Byzantine tradition where the personality of the emperor was easily separated from his elevated status. So, in Kurbskij's mind, there was no need to look for justification for the war against an impious tsar.

Kurbskij's works became widespread and very much part of the ideological quest of the seventeenth century. As for Ivan IV, he contributed decisively to the development of two extremes in Russian attitudes towards the tsar: the tsar as the 'sacred king' and the tsar as the Antichrist. When a son of Ivan IV, Feodor, inherited the Moscow throne, the Muscovite Church organization seemed unable to rise from the ruins without help from outside. Such was the collapse of the first attempt by the Church at self-sufficiency.

The Patriarchate of Moscow: Establishment, Fall, and Reconstruction (1589–1633)

Establishment of the Patriarchate of Moscow: the Third Rome without autonomy?

The period from 1585 to 1605 was a time of revival for the Muscovite Church, after its illegal autocephaly had been abolished through the act of establishing the Patriarchate of Moscow in 1589. Officially, as was said in the Charter of the Patriarch of Constantinople, Jeremias II (1572–95), given that same year in Moscow, the patriarchate was established in response to an address by the tsar to the Patriarch of Constantinople together with the three other Eastern Orthodox patriarchs. The previous anti-canonical autocephaly of Moscow was ignored as something that had no right to exist. The borders of the new patriarchate were drawn in such a way as to imply an official acknowledgement by Moscow of the Kievan Metropolitanate within the Patriarchate of Constantinople.

In addition, the Charter of Jeremias II contained a formula mentioning Moscow as the 'Third Rome'. For him this was merely a diplomatic concession: the two Constantinopolitan Councils of 1590 and 1593 did not repeat any such formula and allotted to the new patriarchate the fifth place of honour (the tsar had asked for the third), after the ancient pentarchy of Rome, Constantinople, Alexandria, Antioch and Jerusalem.

Patriarch Jeremias II, in his concessions to the Muscovite side, went so far as to perform the rite of appointment of the first Muscovite patriarch, Job, according to the local Muscovite custom of appointing chief hierarchs, where the candidates, if they were already bishops, had to receive episcopal consecration a second time. Job, already a bishop, had to be consecrated Metropolitan of Moscow immediately before his election to the patriarchate, and then consecrated patriarch by Jeremias himself. Most probably the custom of double-consecration had become difficult since 1542 under Metropolitan Macarius. Hence, Job, the first Patriarch of Moscow, became a thrice-consecrated bishop in his elevation to the patriarchate in 1589.

In his canonical letter to Patriarch Nikon in 1656, the Patriarch of Constantinople, Paisius I, was to ask if such a violation of the canons was really a custom in Russia. Indeed, it was. It existed as a strict parallel to the Russian understanding of the tsar: the superiority of the tsar over the princes was considered analogous to that of the patriarch (at first, a de facto patriarch, Metropolitan of Moscow) over the bishops. This alleged sacramental (not only administrative) superiority of the patriarch over the bishops (and even metropolitans) was the only reason to consecrate Patriarch Job with a third and not just a second consecration. Elevation to the patriarchal throne, even for a metropolitan, was viewed as a sacrament in itself.

A specific Russian understanding of the dignity of patriarch, as it had matured during the epoch of the anti-canonical Muscovite autocephaly, was to think of it as a kind of a fourth degree of priesthood. This had been the main point of the Byzantine critique of the primacy of the Pope of Rome since the fourteenth century. This implicit papism had had no room to develop during the turbulent times and under the oppressive regime of Ivan IV, but it would become one of the main aspects of Russian church history in the seventeenth century.

From 1589 the Muscovite Church had been the canonical Church of the Third Rome, with a real emperor (the tsar) and a legal patriarch. With regard to the four Patriarchs of the East, their de facto leading position was obvious: all of them received material support from Moscow, not to say moral support, for their liberation from the Ottoman Turks.

Time of Distemper (Smuta): a simultaneous catastrophe of both 'kingdom' and 'priesthood'

The relatively short period from 1604 (and especially 1605) to 1613 was one of the crucial epochs in the history of Russia. Those who lived through it called it *Smuta* ('Distemper'). This was a catastrophe for Russian society as a whole, comparable with that of 1917. The history of this period was intensively rewritten in the 1620s, and this fact affected much subsequent Russian and Soviet historiography. Until recently many contemporary sources were not published or studied properly.

Between the death of the Tsar Boris Godunov in 1605 and the election of Michael Romanov as the first tsar of the last Russian tsarist dynasty in 1613, there was no indisputable tsar in Russia. Instead there were continuous civil wars aggravated by the participation of the Polish army (mostly Catholic), together with the Kazaks (Orthodox, but citizens of Poland). Patriarch Job had been forcibly deposed in 1605 for his loyalty to Tsar Boris and was to die in 1607. The Poles had been dominating Moscow for months, supported by an influential section of Russian society and churchmen. The majority of the Russian bishops agreed to consecrate one of their number who was loyal to the Poles, Bishop Ignatius of Ryazan', as the new patriarch. In the following year (1606) Ignatius was deposed after several victories by Russian patriots. The new patriarch was Hermogen (1606–11), who received the blessing of the then sick and elderly Job. Hermogen, the figurehead of the whole Russian nation without a tsar, had agreed to accept as the tsar a son of the King of Poland, but only with the indispensable condition of his baptism into Orthodoxy. But the Poles were planning to conquer the whole Muscovite kingdom and did not want to accept any conditions, and when Hermogen failed to reach a compromise with them they murdered him. So they returned Patriarch Ignatius (1611–12), who was once again acknowledged by an absolute majority of the Russian episcopate.

Other levels of Russian society than the higher echelons turned out to be less servile and more fervent for Orthodoxy. A peasant, Minin, and a prince, Pozharskij, led a peoples' army that liberated Moscow. Ignatius was deposed definitively. The next patriarch to be appointed was Philaret Romanov, the father of the young Tsar Michael. He would be consecrated in 1619, after returning home from Polish captivity.

The victory over the pro-Polish forces has been gained under the standard of Orthodoxy, with symbolic leaders such as the confessors Job and Hermogen, but against the majority of the Russian episcopate. The latter turned out to be, in the eyes of their contemporaries, nothing less than enemies of Orthodoxy, at least, potentially. All of the bishops who survived were stained by their communion with Patriarch Ignatius, and so, together with him they were culpable in certifying a false 'orthodoxy' for the pretenders of the tsarist throne. After the *Smuta*, the Muscovite state was without a patriarch and without authoritative bishops.

The only safe way out of such a difficulty was to elect some confessing person as the next patriarch. No such candidate, however, was forthcoming. So the choice fell on a man whose authority was grounded in the secular power of the corresponding boyar party, the father of Tsar Michael.

Patriarch Philaret: second attempt at Muscovite autonomy

Patriarch Philaret Romanov (1619–33) attained the throne of the patriarch as a substitute for the throne of the tsar. By the 1590s boyar Feodor Romanov was already a potential candidate for the tsarist throne and because of this he had been forcibly tonsured as a monk by Boris Godunov. With the beginning of the Distemper Philaret immediately supported the elevation of Ignatius as patriarch, and was consecrated Metropolitan of Rostov by him, one of the highest positions in the Russian hierarchy. Subsequently he managed to stay at the top of the church administration by his readiness to serve every secular power and every patriarch, either Hermogen or Ignatius. At the same time he was a gifted secular politician whose family benefited from the civil war. This is how his son Michael became tsar (1613–45). Until the death of his father, Michael was merely a decorative figure, and even in that role, was often sidelined. In fact, Philaret resolved the problem of union between the 'kingdom' and the 'priesthood' by unifying them both in his own person. This unity was to be short-lived, however.

The 1620s and 1630s were to become a time of acute ideological struggle. In the official Russian historiography under Philaret, the history of the *Smuta* had been rewritten in such a way that it presented Patriarch Ignatius as an evil genius of the Russian Church, while those who supported Philaret had been righteous from the beginning.

The basic element of Philaret's ecclesiastical platform was to re-establish the Muscovite autocephaly, but this time on the canonical grounds of the Patriarchate of Moscow and with a more critical distrust of the Orthodoxy of the Kievan Metropolitanate. This was because of the Union of Brest of 1596, which saw the Orthodox of the Metropolitanate of Kiev join in union with the Roman Catholics; Kiev at the time was under Polish-Lithuanian rule.

Under Philaret the Moscow Council of 1620 prescribed obligatory baptism for those Catholics and Uniates who wished to be adopted into the Orthodox Church. In the rest of the Orthodox world, and also in Russia until then, adoption through chrismation had been the norm, but this was now condemned as a crime. This was an unprecedented measure which was later abrogated by the Moscow Council of 1656, but then endorsed by the Constantinopolitan Synod of 1756.

The practice became even stricter: there is evidence in some cases of rebaptism being prescribed for Orthodox Greeks. Moreover, Orthodox Greeks could only come into communion with the Russian Church through penitence. The reason for this was simple: their faith has been compromised under Ottoman Turkish rule, because it was impossible to preserve the Orthodox faith without an Orthodox emperor or tsar. Such an idea was familiar in Moscow on the eve of the development of the Third Rome theory, although it had been refuted by Maxim the Greek. Nevertheless, before Philaret nobody in Russia had come to such a canonical conclusion in their evaluation of Greek Orthodoxy.

Philaret went further. In *The Rite of Consecration of a Bishop*, first published in Moscow about 1630, the text of the bishop's oath repeated a previous one issued by the Metropolitan of Moscow, Simeon, sometime between 1505 and 1511. In this oath the candidate swears to avoid any communion with a chief hierarch consecrated either by the Catholics or by the Patriarch of Constantinople. It is worth noting, however, that Philaret himself was consecrated by the Patriarch of Jerusalem, Theophanes IV, who was acting with the blessing of Constantinople, not to mention the fact that the first Patriarch of Moscow had been consecrated personally by the Patriarch of Constantinople.

So we have to define the church programme of Philaret as a reform whose main thrust was the autonomy of the Muscovite Church. This time, however, unlike in 1441, the need for autonomy was justified by the alleged impossibility of finding a pure Orthodoxy outside the frontiers of the tsarist regime of Russia. From such a perspective, the religious value of the Orthodox 'kingdom' became exaggerated to the same extent as that of the 'priesthood', that is, the patriarchate became something like a fourth degree of priesthood. The Muscovite Church and state left by Philaret was an isolated ideological system with increasing tension between the hypertrophied 'kingdom' and 'priesthood'.

The Great Schism (*Raskol*) and the Old Believers

Russian culture in the seventeenth century and the circle of the 'Lovers of God' (Bogoljubtsy)

The tension between the 'priesthood' and the 'kingdom' was not the only tension within Muscovite Christianity in the seventeenth century. Georges Florovsky (1979) has called it 'a century of lost equilibrium'. Russian society as a whole had drastically changed during the first half of the century; people were looking for a new ideology of moral and cultural values to replace those lost in the Distemper. In the framework imposed by the church organization under Philaret Romanov, the leading ideological group became, by the 1640s, the circle of the so-called 'Lovers of God' (Bogoljubtsy); this was headed by the spiritual father of the Tsar Alexis Mikhailovich (1645–76), archpriest Stephen Vonifatievich (d. 1656) whose power in church affairs prevailed over that of the patriarch. The Bogoljubtsy were exploring ways of reconstructing the Russian cultural tradition. As is often the case, the same narrow circle of activists produced the future leaders of two antagonistic parties, Patriarch Nikon (1652–8, d. 1681) and archpriest Avvakum Petrov (1620–82).

The Bogoljubtsy were convinced that the actual customs of Russian society were of a mixed nature where every bad thing had to be classified as 'new' and every good thing as 'old', that is, 'traditional'. So, they were trying to reconstruct 'tradition' starting from their theoretical viewpoint, but with neither access to nor the wish to access the actual Orthodox tradition prior to the early seventeenth century. All of them were convinced that they already possessed the knowledge of the 'true tradition'. Their beloved method of 'cultural reconstruction' became surgical, that is, they simply amputated what they viewed as 'new'. Therefore, they pushed through to its logical end a tendency already apparent by the early 1610s; the polarization in Russian culture of the ecclesiastical and the secular. The secular was now understood as something undesirably 'new'. The zone of transition between the ecclesiastical and the secular that existed in the cultures of both Old Rus and contemporary Kievan Rus was destroyed in Muscovy, so that the new ecclesiastical and secular cultures became, instead of being different parts of one whole, opposed to each other.

At the same time, the Bogoljubtsy accepted many things from the Kievan Metropolitanate they considered to be 'old' and 'traditional', but which in fact were new. This was an inevitable consequence of the intellectual superiority of the Kievan theologians, both Hesychasts and pro-Uniates, over their Muscovite colleagues. In Moscow, the 'Kievan' books were the only Orthodox theological texts to discuss current issues, as can easily be seen from the two great compilations printed in Moscow, the *Book of Cyril* (1644) and the *Book on Faith* (1648). The Muscovite compilers were often unable to grasp the differences between the texts issued by the two main groups of Kievan theologians, not to mention their lack of understanding of contemporary Greek theology. Such theological backwardness led to an unconscious and disorderly intellectual dependence on 'Kievan' authors at the cost of the contribution made by people like Maxim the Greek, Father Artemius, Andrew Kurbskij and Ivan Fedorov.

The circle as a whole developed the idea of Russian autonomy, this time in a form resulting from a combination of the Third Rome theory with the contemporaneous Kievan philosophy of history. An anonymous eschatological treatise published as Chapter 30 of the *Book on Faith* became a manifesto of this approach. It is still unclear whether this chapter was written in Moscow or in West Russia, but in any case it was accepted as normative in Muscovy. Instead of three Romes, there were now three main periods before three apostasies: a period of about 1,000 years before the apostasy of Rome, then one of about 600 years before the apostasy of South-West Russia (through its Union with Rome), then another of about 66 years before a disastrous impending event in Moscow. There was no room for Byzantium in this scheme, which was derived from a Kievan interpretation of the Latin post-Tridentine philosophy of history.

The anonymous author goes so far as to predict the exact date of catastrophe: 1666 = 1000 + 666 (where the number of the Beast, 666, is treated as a time-span). To evaluate the responsibility of the publishers (who were the same Bogoljubtsy) it should be noted that this prophesy was issued from the official state printing house in 1648. There are other testimonies as well that show the Bogoljubtsy understood their work from an eschatological perspective, as a means to lead the whole country to penitence before the crucial date of 1666. The most interesting fact, however, is that the prophesy concerning 1666 came true: it is the date when the Great Schism of the Russian Church was decisively defined.

The first result of the Bogoljubtsy's activity was an enforcement of Philaret's autonomous conception of the Russian Church, that is, a deeper voluntary isolation from the rest of the Orthodox world. The second result was a solidification of yet another division within Russian society, the sharp polarization between the secular and the ecclesiastical cultures, potentially leading to the isolation of the Church from the rest of Russian society.

It is hardly surprising that the third and the final result of the Bogoljubtsy's common objective led to a division and collapse of their circle in the middle of the 1650s: they turned out to be unable to reach agreement on the question of what the true tradition was, that is, what was 'old' and what was 'new'. Their tendency to isolate the Church from the life of Russian society as a whole led in turn to a struggle between former associates. Both church parties were to become unrealistic and lose control of the church structures leaving them to the secular authorities. Finally, the autonomy of the Church would result in the impossibility of improving the situation from outside. All subsequent appeals to the Eastern Patriarchs would be seen as nothing but propagandist manoeuvres of the interested powers in Russia.

Start of the Great Schism (*Raskol*)

The main facts are as follows:

1654: Patriarch Nikon, empowered by the Synod of Russian Bishops in Moscow, began his revision of the Russian liturgical books and rites. Nikon's liturgical reform resulted from his philhellenism. In fact, this was but the first, unhelpful, step towards a larger reform, which was never accomplished. Nikon's philhellenism was not directed towards contemporary Greeks; though without actual knowledge of either Greek or Greek theology, Nikon was against his will depending on contemporary Greeks. In principle, however, he was struggling for what he thought was the Byzantine heritage.

1655: Council in Moscow approved the reforms, with the participation of Macarius, the Patriarch of Antioch; Macarius anathematized the Old Russian rites proclaimed to be incorrect (especially making of the sign of cross with two fingers instead of three); the Patriarch of Constantinople Paisius wrote to Nikon opposing his reforms; there was powerful opposition to Nikon within the Church and among the nobility.

1658: Nikon voluntarily left his throne owing to the deterioration in his relations with the tsar, largely because of his own pretensions to establish the 'priesthood' over the 'kingdom'; the Muscovite Church was headed by a locum tenens; Nikon lost interest in his reforms and reverted, at least, partially, to the old rites; for example, he wrote and had published liturgical books in the pre-reform style.

1662–3: Polemics between Nikon and Paisius Ligarides, a defrocked Metropolitan of Gaza, and an international adventurer, who arrived in Moscow in the guise of a true bishop of the Patriarchate of Jerusalem.

1666: Council in Moscow with participation of the Patriarchs Macarius of Antioch and Paisius of Alexandria (by this time, both of them had been suspended by the Synod of Constantinople, whose decision was then unknown in Russia); Nikon condemned and defrocked; the Council issued a book, the *Rod of Ruling* (*Zhezl Pravleniya*) written by Simeon of Polotsk (1629–80) under heavy Latin influence; Patriarch Macarius, too, was Latin-friendly, to such an extent that in 1665 he directed to Rome his Catholic confession of faith.

1667: Council in Moscow (a continuation of that of 1666) with participation of the same two Eastern Patriarchs with the purpose of regulating the whole life of the Church. The most important decisions were: approval of the *Rod of Ruling*; anathematizing of the old Russian customs and those who followed them; the Stoglav Council was proclaimed illegal (because it was uncanonical) and abrogated.

The Council of 1667 effectively created the Schism within the Russian Church. The majority of the people and the monastics and most of the lower clergy refused to follow the hierarchy, despite extremely cruel persecutions. All the bishops, on the other hand, accepted the Council, with the one exception of Paul of Kolomna, who was deposed and died under suspicious circumstances. The leaders of the dissidents (the Old Believers or Old Ritualists) were now, by the 1670s, archpriest Avvakum Petrov and deacon Theodore Ivanov.

The consequences of the Schism would be irreparable. The state church organization, with no support from the most victimized section of the faithful, was destined to submit to the secular rulers, whose interests would move further and further away from those of the Orthodox faith.

Traditionalist reaction within the state church and the 'heresy of motleys'

Simeon of Polotsk, a Russian poet of Byelorussian origin and a pro-Latin theologian, was an informal leader of the state church up to his death in 1680. His party continued to be in power up to the *coup d'état* of 1690. The subsequent anti-Latin reaction was headed by Patriarchs Joachim (1674–90) and Adrian (1690–1700). The Moscow Council of 1690 under Patriarch Joachim anathematized Simeon of Polotsk and all like-minded pro-Latin people (Simeon is reported to have confessed openly even the *filioque*). The condemned individuals were labelled 'motleys' (*pjostrye*), that is, neither Orthodox nor Catholic (despite their adherence to Latin scholasticism they never acknowledged the jurisdiction of the pope). The same Council condemned a long list of books published in Kiev throughout the seventeenth century, including the works of Peter Mogila (1596–1647), and forced the hierarchy of the Kievan Metropolitanate to agree to this condemnation.

The main pretext of the 1690 Council was the question of when exactly the Holy Gifts became transformed in the eucharistic liturgy. This had already been discussed at Florence in 1439, when Mark of Ephesus insisted that it was at the time of the epiclesis. In the Kievan Metropolitanate and then, in Moscow (at least, since the publication of the *Skrizhal'* by Nikon) the Latin view had prevailed: that it was at the time of the Words of Institution 'This is my body' and 'This is my blood.' The Council condemned the Latin view and established that of Mark of Ephesus, and the Constantinopolitan Council of 1691 approved this statement.

This patristic reorientation of Muscovite theology would have been impossible without the help of Greek theologians (writing mostly in Latin), the brothers Likhoudes: Joannicus (c.1633/5–1717) and Sophronius (c.1652/7–1730), pupils of the Metropolitan of Philadelphia (that is, of Venice) Gerasimos Vlachos. The latter was known for his edition (along with François Combefis) of the writings of Maximus the Confessor. The Likhoudes were in a close contact with the Patriarch of Jerusalem, Dositheus (1669–1707), who was then about to publish the Byzantine anti-Latin polemics and the proceedings of the Hesychast councils of the fourteenth century. Through the brothers Likhoudes, Russia directly participated during the 1690s in recovering the Hesychast heritage.

At the same time the Schism did not allow this work to be completed. The book, the *Rod of Ruling*, as well as the Councils of 1666–7, escaped the condemnation. Patriarch Joachim expressed publicly his opinion that it made no difference whether one made the sign of cross with two fingers or with three. He was obliged, nevertheless, to persecute the Old Believers. After the death of Patriarch Adrian in 1700, Tsar Peter I intensified his church reforms when the pro-Latin party, headed by the locum tenens Stephen Yavorskij (1658–1722), came to power once again. Yavorskij reopened the discussions on the Holy Gifts, taking the side of the 'motleys'; the brothers Likhoudes answered him but no changes came about in consequence.

The Reforms of Peter I and the Synodal Period of the State Church (1700–1917)

Interruption of the autocephaly (1700–21)

Tsar Peter I (1672–1725), tsar from 1682, started his church reforms in 1698 and abolished the patriarchate to make the church organization more controllable. At first Stephen Yavorskij had been appointed the locum tenens (1700); the Moscow See was without an incumbent and Peter was looking to maintain this situation. His first solution was to subordinate the Russian Church to the four Eastern Patriarchs. As early as 1701, at the consecration of the first bishop (that of Dimitri Tuptalo, Metropolitan of Rostov) after the death of the last patriarch, a promise of submission to the Eastern Patriarchs was included in the candidate's oath. Then, in the 1710s, Peter several times addressed the patriarchs officially to resolve certain ecclesiastical matters; the Eastern Patriarchs were commemorated in the liturgy before the name of the locum tenens.

Nominally, it was a renunciation of autocephaly; in reality, it was a situation where in the face of secular control there was no autonomous centre of ecclesiastical power. Only one of the patriarchs, Dositheos of Jerusalem (d. 1707), refused to have communion with Yavorskij, calling him *graikolatinophron* ('thinking as half-Greek and as half-Latin', the same sense as in the Russian nickname 'motley', meaning neither one thing nor the other).

The changes began in 1712 when Yavorskij expressed his sympathies towards the conservative opposition. By the 1710s, notwithstanding his Latin sympathies, the conservative Russian episcopate had begun to rally round him. All of them were waiting for the re-establishment of the patriarchate by Prince Alexis, the heir of Peter the Great and the hope of the opposition, but he was eventually murdered by his father in 1718. After the affair of Prince Alexis, Peter tried to construct a new system of church government, which would prevent the re-establishment of the patriarchate after his death. For this purpose he chose to use the services of a Protestant-minded person, Theophan Prokopovich (1681–1736).

Establishment of the Holy Synod (1721)

Prokopovich was the architect of a new church order which he described in his book *Dukhovnyj Reglament* ('Ecclesiastical Order', a calque of the Lutheran term *Kirchenordnung*). This book was declared part of Russian legislation in 1721. According to the analysis provided in 1916 by P. V. Verkhovskoy, Prokopovich adapted the norms of the German and Swedish Lutheran *Kirchenordnungen*, that is, he made the organization of the Church part of the state structure, at the rank of a ministry and subject to the secular rulers on the same grounds as other state ministries. At first the church ministry was called a *collegium* (the usual name of the ministries under Peter the Great), but very soon it was renamed 'Synod', a word more familiar to people.

The bishops were obliged to act not only with the consent of the tsar, but also on behalf of the tsar, performing his will. According to canon law such a situation was illegal, and as a result the *Reglament* became the first example of church legislation which completely alienated it from the Ecumenical Church. This was the main reason the official leadership of the state church became in turn divorced from the real needs and real life of the Orthodox Church.

There was still the need, however, for confirmation of the establishment of the Synod by the Eastern Patriarchs. Peter the Great and Prokopovich immediately wrote to Constantinople, in 1721, but owing to some technical difficulties they received approbation only in 1723. It has been noted that the letter from Peter and Prokopovich contained a consciously distorted Greek translation of Peter's manifesto concerning the establishment of the Synod. They presented the Synod's work as equal to that of the patriarch, which was clearly misleading. Moreover, mentioning only *en passant* some 'instruction' (that is, the *Reglament*), they said nothing about the fact that the Synod would be a state ministry. Therefore, the Eastern Patriarchs blessed a structure that never existed: a local church headed by a collective 'patriarch'.

Yavorskij insisted that the four Eastern Patriarchs should still be commemorated. This measure would help the synodal order to be considered as merely a temporary disruption before the re-establishment of the patriarchate. Prokopovich realized the significance of this and therefore obtained the abolition of the commemoration. The synodal order was finally established.

Continuation of Peter's reforms during the eighteenth century

Prokopovich continued in power until his death in 1736. He made good use of his time brutally to crush any opposition among the episcopate, while at the same time his personal rivals became, actual or potential, enemies of the synodal establishment.

The long reign of Catherine II (1762–96) was marked by additional reforms, which destroyed the last vestiges of church independence that had survived the reforms of Peter the Great, namely, in land ownership and monasticism. Her law of 1764 cancelled out the main fruit of the victory of the Josephites in the sixteenth century, that of land ownership by the Church. Two hundred years earlier, the tsars had given lands to the Church in exchange for support for their often unstable authority. Now the state was strong enough to get back what Caesar had rendered unto Caesar. However, for those remnants of church organization that had survived the Petrine reforms, this act of deprivation meant the end of the last vestige of practical independence. From this time on (up to 1917) the hierarchs of the Russian Church were state functionaries who were paid from the state budget.

The only bishop who risked protesting openly was the Metropolitan of Rostov, Arseny Matseevich, who went so far as to characterize the anti-church policy of Catherine as a continuation of that of Peter. As a result he was dismissed, deposed, de-frocked, jailed, and deprived of monastic state, finally dying in 1779 in a narrow cell. The empress considered him to be her personal enemy, but the people venerated him as a martyr.

In the same year of 1764, Catherine issued another law imposing a severe limitation on the number of monasteries and number of monks within the remaining monasteries. According to this law most of the Russian monasteries were to be transformed into parishes. It became almost impossible for an aspiring able-bodied man to be tonsured. As a result, the renaissance of Russian monasticism led by Paisius Velichkovsky (1722–94) took place in neighbouring Romania instead of Russia.

The Nineteenth Century: Major Trends

From the early nineteenth century the Church of Russia began step by step to recover from the 'paralysis' (Dostoevsky's word) caused by Peter the Great. However, the situation for Christianity in Russian society was growing increasingly worse. In the eighteenth century, the reformed Church had been unable to hold on to its flock. The consequence of this for subsequent generations was as follows.

By the late eighteenth century the Church had lost the part of its flock consisting of the aristocracy; by the first half of the nineteenth century it had lost another part, including most of the gentry; and by the middle of the nineteenth century it had lost the middle class, especially young men. By the 1860s the absolute majority of university students were atheistic or, in the best case, agnostic. Even those who were interested in the religious quest were unable to take the church establishment seriously.

Among educated people this led to a vogue for mystical teachings, and sometimes mystical sects, especially those flavoured with Protestant pietism. This was true even of great ascetic writers such as Theophan the Recluse (1815–94), a retired bishop who translated many monastic and spiritual texts from Greek into Russian. In his early works, he found favour with fashionable Protestant authors in matters relating to the theological background of Christian asceticism, such as the vision of the divine light, which was of course part of the Orthodox Hesychast tradition. Not surprisingly, these pietistic influences were much stronger among religious writers who came from a secular milieu, such as Alexei Stepanovich Khomiakov (1804–60), the creator of the philosophical and theological school known as 'Slavophilism', and those writers of fiction who were well disposed to the Church, such as Feodor Mikhailovich Dostoevsky

(1821–81), whose name takes precedence. As far as rural people and merchants were concerned the loss of authority of the state church led to the success of these sects, especially among peasants who had moved to cities to become industrial workers.

A great ascetic writer, Bishop Ignatius (Bryanchaninov, 1807–67) as well as the Orthodox thinker Constantine Leontiev (1831–91, tonsured, as monk Clement) shared the opinion that the problem of the salvation of the Russian Church and state had lost its meaning: the catastrophe of both was inevitable in a relatively short time. Therefore, according to Leontiev, the real problem was how to live after the catastrophe. Likewise, Theophan the Recluse had evaluated the time remaining to the Russian Church as no more than a couple of generations. One can see that his prediction was not far from being wrong.

An indisputable achievement of the nineteenth century was the re-emergence of monasticism and the influence of spiritual elders (*starchestvo*). The most important centres of monasticism were: the Optina monastery near Kaluga, the Valaam monastery on an island in the Ladoga Lake, and the Monastery of St Panteleimon and other smaller centres on Mount Athos. Russians had been the main driving force behind the revival of the Athonite monasticism after the decline resulting from the Greek-Turkish war of 1821–9.

Finally, by the late nineteenth century, it was more and more noticeable that there was a return to the Church and to strict Orthodoxy by a small but active group of the intelligentsia. First among their rank was Constantine Leontiev, a disciple of the Athonite Russian elder Hieronymus, and *starets* of the Optina monastery, Ambrose.

Collapse of the State Church in 1917 and its Consequences

On the eve of the revolution the organization of the Church was controlled mainly by two powers, the secular and the hierarchical. The supreme control belonged to the secular state authorities, that is, the tsar through the *Oberprokuror*. Because of the personal piety of the last Russian Tsar Nicholas II (r. 1896–1917) and his family, the state authorities were often influenced by nonconformist individuals who, unlike the members of the Synod, understood the real needs of the Orthodox Church. Thus the canonization of Seraphim of Sarov (1759–1833), one of the most beloved saints of the Russian people in recent times, was performed in 1903 with the personal participation of the tsar and, despite some obstacles, of the Synod as well.

A further example was the condemnation of Russian Athonite monks for the heresy of 'onomatolatria' (veneration of the name of Jesus as used in the Jesus Prayer) by the Synod in 1913, but they were eventually defended by the tsar and a section of the hierarchy. The Greeks took advantage of the condemnation to provoke the Russian government to execute a massive deportation of Russian monks from Mount Athos. As a result the Russian presence on the Holy Mountain was undermined and never fully recovered. The story had a positive side to it, however: it illustrated the distance separating the Hesychast tradition from the teaching of St Gregory Palamas, and the theological distance separating the members of the Synod and the episcopate from the monastics. Some secular thinkers had already noticed the importance of Gregory Palamas for the Orthodox tradition and this had stimulated further patristic studies in the field, especially among émigrés, leading to the formation of the modern interest in 'neo-patristic' Orthodox theology.

When the February Revolution of 1917 dethroned the last Russian tsar, it pulled out the core of the edifice of the church structure. The Provisional Government, after declaring itself to be secular, continued to execute the supreme management of the Church and to be manipulated by the hierarchs in the course of preparing for a local council. However, shortly after work started on preparations for the local council the radical revolutionaries overthrew the Provisional Government, in the October Revolution of 1917. This fact made the majority of the council members vote for the patriarchate, despite their previous disgust toward such a 'papist' mode of church government. The council elected a new patriarch, Tikhon (Belavin, 1917–25). He was enthroned according to the Byzantine rite, with no second consecration by a bishop as had been the case in Muscovite Russia.

In the 1920s–1930s both former state and Old Believers' churches experienced several waves of persecution, which were directed at the complete liquidation of their bishops and monastics. The number of martyrs and confessors gained by the Russian Church during the first twenty years of the Soviet regime was probably more than the total number throughout Christian history. By the late 1920s, the former state church was divided and only one section of it was deemed legal by the Soviet authorities. This part was headed by Metropolitan Sergius Stragorodskij (1867–1944), who became in 1943 the first patriarch elected under the direction of the Communist dictator Stalin. After this date, this Church became free of persecution, but at the cost of losing all autonomy (in fact as early as 1927) and becoming a tool of Soviet internal and external politics. A second part of the divided church, illegal within Russia, was the Catacomb Church, headed by the Metropolitan of Petrograd (that is, St Petersburg), Joseph (Petrovykh, 1872–1937, martyr).

The Catacomb Church ceased to be illegal in 1990 when all its undisputed bishops died, and so it restored its hierarchy with the help of the third part of the former state church, the Russian Orthodox Church Outside Russia (ROCOR). The latter had united the émigré communities that had refused to remain in communion with Patriarch Sergius. In Russia today a large part of the former Catacomb Church exists openly under the official name of the Russian Orthodox Autonomous Church. There are also other groups claiming this legacy. ROCOR has parishes both abroad and within Russia, some of them formerly belonging to the pre-1990 Catacomb Church. There are in addition two churches created by Ukrainian bishops, which exist both in the Ukraine and in the Ukrainian diaspora, and the Byelorussian Church, also existing both in Byelorussia and in the Byelorussian diaspora.

After the beginning of the twenty-first century a process of unification between ROCOR and the Moscow Patriarchate started, and gathered speed after the intervention of the President of the Russian Federation, Vladimir Putin, in 2003. This has caused schism within ROCOR and divided it into four separate groups. The major group, headed by Metropolitan Laurus (Shkurla), is involved in the negotiations with the Moscow Patriarchate, while the other three groups, strongly opposed to such negotiations, formally acknowledge the leadership of the elderly previous Metropolitan of ROCOR, Vitaly (Ustinov). Regardless of the final outcome of the negotiations for each of the groups of the former ROCOR, it is already clear that in Russia there is no trace of the high spiritual prestige that ROCOR enjoyed with Russian believers under the Soviet regime or even in the early 1990s.

In general the interest of the Russian people in the Orthodox Church, after reaching a peak in the mid-1990s, rapidly decreased once their initial curiosity had been satisfied. However, according to sociological studies, the percentage of people who declare themselves 'Orthodox' is considerably higher than that of those who say 'yes' to the question 'Do you believe in God?' (correspondingly, about 70 per cent and 50 per cent of the population).

Until the late twentieth century, and especially in the years 1993–8, the Moscow Patriarchate was struggling for both legal and unofficial recognition as a kind of a 'state religion', trying to fill the vacuum left by the defeated Communist ideology. But these efforts should now be considered as having failed, with the partial exception of Byelorussia. On the one hand, the ruling elites of the Russian Federation, not to mention the Ukraine, consider the secular character of state power to be a fundamental principle for civil peace and the internal development of the country. On the other hand, the Moscow Patriarchate, from as early as the mid-1990s, showed that its ability to influence the electorate was rather low. Therefore, 'special preferences' to the Moscow Patriarchate are found only at the regional level and only then on the basis of corruption.

Despite an obvious decline since the late 1990s of a 'ritualistic' interest in Christianity, there are signs, especially among young people, of a growing interest in the Christian faith itself, but this interest is still far from being 'digested' by the existing Orthodox Church structures. Such a phenomenon is promising, but it does not allow us to make any firm predictions regarding the future shape of Russian Christianity.

References and further reading

Bercken, W. van den (1999) *Holy Russia and Christian Europe: East and West in the Religious Ideology of Russia*. London: SCM Press.

Buruma, I. and Margalit, A. (2004) *Occidentalism: A Short History of Anti-Westernism*. London: Atlantis Books.

Chumachenko, T. A. (2002) *Church and State in Soviet Russia: Russian Orthodoxy from World War Two to the Krushchev Years*. Armonk, NY: M. E. Sharpe.

Crummey, R. O. (1987) *The Formation of Muscovy 1304–1613*. London: Longman.

Ebuss, A. (2003) *The Russian Orthodox Tradition and Modernity*. Leiden: Brill.

Ellis, J. (1986) *The Russian Orthodox Church: A Contemporary History*. London: Croom Helm.

Fedotov, G. P. (1975) *The Russian Religious Mind*, 2 vols. Belmont, Mass.: Nordland Publishing.

Fennell, J. (1983) *The Crisis of Medieval Russia 1200–1304*. Longman: London.

—— (1995) *A History of the Russian Church to 1448*. Longman: London.

Florovsky, G. (1979) *Ways of Russian Theology*, 2 vols. Belmont, Mass.: Nordland Publishing.

Franklin, S. and Shepard, J. (1996) *The Emergence of Rus 750–1200*. London: Longman.

Knox, Z. (2004) *Russian Society and the Orthodox Church*. London: Routledge.

Maloney, G. A. (1976) *A History of Orthodox Theology since 1453*. Belmont, Mass.: Nordland Publishing.

Meyendorff, J. (1989) *Byzantium and the Rise of Russia: A Study of Byzantino-Russian Relations in the Fourteenth Century*. Crestwood, NY: St Vladimir's Seminary Press.

Meyendorff, P. (1991) *Russia, Ritual, and Reform: The Liturgical Reforms of Nikon in the 17th Century*. Crestwood, NY: St Vladimir's Seminary Press.

Nichols, R. L. and Stavrou, T. G. (eds.) (1978) *Russian Orthodoxy under the Old Regime*. Minneapolis: University of Minnesota Press.

Papadakis, A. (1994) *The Christian East and the Rise of the Papacy: The Church 1071–1453 AD*. Crestwood, NY: St Vladimir's Seminary Press.

Podskalsky, G. (1982) *Christentum und theologische Literatur in der Kiever Rus' (988–1237)*. Munich: C. H. Beck'sche Verlagsbuchhandlung.

—— (1988) *Griechische Theologie in der Zeit der Türkenherrschaft (1453–1821). Die Orthodoxie im Spannungsfeld der nachreformatorischen Konfessionen des Westens*. Munich: C. H. Beck'sche Verlagsbuchhandlung.

Pospielovsky, D. (1984) *The Russian Church under the Soviet Regime 1917–1982*, 2 vols. Crestwood, NY: St Vladimir's Seminary Press.

Runciman, S. (1968) *The Great Church in Captivity*. Cambridge: Cambridge University Press.

Tachiaos, A.-E. N. (ed.) (1992) The Legacy of Saints Cyril and Methodius to Kiev and Moscow. *Proceedings of the International Congress on the Millennium of the Conversion of Rus' to Christianity*, Thessaloniki, 26–8 November 1988. Thessaloniki: Hellenic Association for Slavic Studies.

Walicki, A. (1975) *The Slavophile Controversy: A History of a Conservative Utopia in Nineteenth-Century Russian Thought*. Oxford: Oxford University Press.

CHAPTER 11
Serbian Christianity

Radmila Radić

Introduction

Approximately 11.5 million Serbs, Montenegrins and Macedonians, are Eastern Orthodox by family background. The Serbian Orthodox Church is an autocephalous, or ecclesiastically independent, member of the Eastern Orthodox communion, located primarily in Serbia, Montenegro, Bosnia and Herzegovina, Croatia, and Macedonia. About a quarter of all ethnic Serbs live outside the Republic of Serbia, mainly in Bosnia and Herzegovina and in Croatia. The distinguishing feature of Serbian national identity is the Eastern Orthodox Christian heritage, although probably less than 10 per cent of the population actually attended church during the Communist era. Unlike Romanians or Hungarians, Serbs do not have a distinct language to set them apart from their neighbours. They speak essentially the same language as Croats and Bosnians, although some pronunciations and vocabulary are distinctive. This language, linguistically termed Serbo-Croatian, is now identified as Serbian, Croatian, or Bosnian depending on the ethnicity of the speaker. It is in its written form that Serbian differs from other Serbo-Croatian languages. Reflecting Serbian religious heritage, it uses a modified version of the Cyrillic alphabet, a script originally developed by the Byzantine missionary brothers Saints Cyril and Methodius, 'Apostles to the Slavs'.

Old Church Slavonic was the first Slavic literary language and was written in two alphabets known as Glagolitic and Cyrillic (the invention of Glagolitic has been ascribed to St Cyril). Old Church Slavonic was readily adopted in other Slavic regions, where, with local modifications, it remained the religious and literary language of Orthodox Slavs throughout the Middle Ages and continued as a liturgical language into modern times.

According to the official classification of Orthodox Patriarchates of the Ecumenical Patriarchate, the Serbian Orthodox Church is ranked sixth, following the Russian and preceding the Romanian Church. The Serbian Church See is located in Belgrade, in the patriarchate building. The head of the Serbian Church holds the title of 'Archbishop of

Peć, Metropolitan of Belgrade and Karlovac, and Serbian Patriarch'. All together there are thirty-nine dioceses. The patriarch himself is the head of the Archbishopric of Belgrade and Karlovac. There are four metropolitanates: Metropolitanate of Zagreb, Ljubljana and the Whole of Italy; Metropolitanate of Montenegro and the Littoral; Metropolitanate of Mid-West America; and Metropolitanate of Dabar and Bosna.

History

Serbs form most of the population of the former Yugoslav state and are of South Slavic origin. As early as the fifth to seventh century CE, they migrated from their ancient lands in Northern Europe to the Balkan peninsula which, at the time, constituted the northern regions of the Byzantine Empire. Christianity was introduced into the Balkans during the Roman period, but the region had largely reverted to paganism by the time the Slavs arrived. Cleavages among southern Slav tribes developed over time, particularly after the establishment in the fourth century CE of the north–south 'Theodosian Line' demarcating the eastern and western segments of the Roman Empire. Organization of the Christian Church was subsequently based on this division. Missionaries from Rome converted Slavic tribes in the West to Roman Catholicism (these tribal groups becoming progenitors of the Slovenes and Croatians), while missionaries from Constantinople converted ancestors of the Serbs and Montenegrins to Eastern Orthodoxy.

According to a Byzantine writer, the emperor and historian Constantine VII (r. 913–59), Serbian tribes adopted the new faith of Christianity very slowly, so that it took them quite a while to renounce their ancient pagan customs and convictions. The same author recorded that the first occurrence of a baptism en masse among the Serbs happened during the reign of Emperor Heraclius (r. 610–41).

The Serb tribes were finally all baptised after spending more than two hundred years in their newly inhabited homeland. The Serb adoption of the Christian faith ran parallel to the process of establishing their first organized state during the first half of the ninth century. The great missionaries to the Serbs, as well as other Slav nations, were the brothers Cyril and Methodius, known as 'Equal to the Apostles' (a spiritual title given to Emperor Constantine the Great and some saints in the Orthodox Church). The baptism of the Serbs occurred during the reign of *Knez* (Prince) Mutimir (before the year 891), when the Emperor Basil I the Macedonian (r. 867–86) ruled Byzantium, and when Photius was Patriarch of Constantinople. The first dioceses in Serbian lands are mentioned in the ninth century. Before the life and times of St Sava (d. 1236), all dioceses in Serbia were under the spiritual jurisdiction of the Archbishopric of Ohrid.

The event that crucially effected baptism not only of the Serbs but also of other Slav peoples was the invention of the Slavonic script, i.e., the Glagolitic and Cyrillic alphabets, around the middle of the ninth century. The beginnings of literacy among the Slavs are closely connected with their adoption of Christianity in their own native language. The Bible was immediately translated from Greek into Slavonic, as well as all the most necessary ecclesiastical service books. The influence of the Eastern Orthodox tradition was assured over the greater part of the Balkans, and the use of the Cyrillic alphabet became one of the most visible cultural aspects separating Serbs (together with Bulgarians, Macedonians, and Montenegrins) from Croats and Slovenes.

The schism between the Greek and the Latin Churches in 1054 coincided with a surge of Christian missionary activity in northern and eastern Europe. The West imposed a Latin liturgy on the new converts and thus made Latin the only vehicle of Christian civilization and a major instrument of ecclesiastical unity. In the Balkans, however, Christianity became integrated into the indigenous cultures of the Slavic nations, and the universal Orthodox Church evolved as a fellowship of national churches rather than as a centralized body.

Serbian tribes in Zeta, i.e., Duklja (Duklya, Doclea), including the littoral, were united during the ninth century into a single Zeta-state, known earlier under its old name Duklja. By the end of the twelfth century, the Grand Župan of Raška (around present-day Novi Pazar), Stefan Nemanjić (r. c.1169–96) managed to unite most Serbian lands into a single state. He and his successors steadily expanded into neighbouring lands in modern-day Montenegro, Bosnia and Herzegovina, and central Serbia. In his foreign policy, he was closely aligned with Byzantium, although he went to war against it several times. Byzantium also exerted a strong spiritual and cultural influence on his court and his state administration. He built many churches and monasteries, among which is the famous Studenica Monastery, named 'mother of all Serbian churches'. It was in this monastery that Stefan Nemanjić had taken his monastic vows when he abdicated in 1196, and it was there that his body was laid to rest when brought back from Hilandar Monastery on Mount Athos. It is still interred there today.

Stefan Nemanjić had three sons: Vukan, Stefan and Rastko. Born around 1175, Rastko (St Sava's baptismal name) was the youngest of the three. At the age of 16, and against his parents' wishes, he had left the court accompanied by a Russian monk and entered the monastery of St Panteleimon on Mount Athos. Father and son then together founded another monastery on Mount Athos called Hilandar in 1199, which became a centre of Serbian religious and secular culture. Sava composed a church service to his father and wrote his biography. He also wrote the Typikon or monastic rule of Karyes, the Athonite capital, for use at the hermitage of St Sabbas the Sanctified. In 1206 he returned to Serbia and brought his father's relics to Studenica in 1208. He was an archimandrite (a monastic title within the Orthodox Church) at Studenica until 1217. He built the church of Žiča, where he became archbishop, and the churches of Peć and Mileševa. In 1219, he was consecrated bishop by the Patriarch Germanus of Constantinople, who was then in exile at Nicaea. Sava as metropolitan established a number of bishoprics and monasteries in the course of completing the Christianization of the half-converted Serbs.

He also built more churches with the help of his brother Stephen the 'First-Crowned', who had been crowned king by papal legates in 1217. Sava countered his brother's affinity to the Roman Catholic Church by travelling in 1219 to Nicaea, the refuge of the exiled Patriarch of Constantinople, where he received the title of autocephalous archbishop of Serbia. Upon his return to Serbia, he crowned his brother again. Sava organized his church into bishoprics headed by his former monastic colleagues and students. He then embarked on a cultural and ecclesiastical renaissance that included the establishment of schools and the beginnings of medieval Serbian literature. He managed to complete the document called *Krmčija*, which regulated legislation concerning the newly independent Serbian Church. In 1230 he went on pilgrimage to the Holy Land and built the monastery of St John at Jerusalem. He died in Turnovo and King Vladislav translated his relics to Mileševa in 1237. The Ottoman authorities burned them in 1594, but this did not prevent the spread of his cult. Sava, as an exponent of vernacular religious culture closely associated with his family's political achievements, is a unique example of Serbian identity. Although his life has sometimes been interpreted as though he deliberately separated Serbia from Rome, his feast is kept in Catholic as well as Orthodox calendars, on 14/27 January.

The Serbian Orthodox Church existed as an archbishopric from 1219 to 1346. During that period twelve consecutive archbishops occupied the throne of St Sava and each of them headed the Church during the reign of some of the kings of the Nemanjić dynasty. The archbishopric see was originally located at the Monastery of Žiča, but in 1252, owing to the impending dangers of Tatar and Kuman invasions, it was, for security reasons, moved to Peć, a monastery located at the entrance to the remote Rugova canyon. In that period, numerous famous monasteries were erected such as Sopoćani, Gračanica, and Dečani.

As the kingdom of Serbia grew in size and prestige, and Stefan Dušan, king of Serbia from 1331, assumed the imperial title of tsar from 1346 to 1355, the archbishopric of Peć was correspondingly raised to the rank of patriarchate. After Dušan's death, the internal disunity of his state and the invasion of Ottoman forces resulted in its fragmentation into several kingdoms. The Battle of the Field of Kosovo (15 June 1389), in which the remaining Serbian forces were defeated by the Ottomans, proved to be crucial to the future of the Serbian nation. Not all Serbian lands came under Ottoman rule immediately after the Turkish victory, but Serbia became a tributary state to the Ottomans. By 1459, however, Serbia was made a Turkish *pašalik* (province). The patriarchate was (unofficially) abolished, then restored in 1557, only to be abolished again in 1766. Between 1776 and 1830 Serbian lands under Ottoman rule had bishops who were Greek nationals. They were popularly called 'Phanariots' (from the Phanar district of Constantinople, the base of the Greek Ecumenical Patriarchate) and were reputed as interested in catering neither for the real needs nor the problems of the Serbian people. Since the education of the lower clergy, mainly of Serbian origin, was neglected, these clergy often lacked basic literacy.

For more than three centuries thereafter, most Serbs were dependent tenant farmers within the Ottoman feudal system. By the mid-sixteenth century, the Balkans, and especially those areas inhabited by Serbs, became a transitory region for conquering Turkish armies going west, although the Ottoman authorities wanted to appease the Orthodox by granting concessions to their Church. At the same time many Orthodox had converted to Islam, some of them under duress, and some in order to maintain previous privileges or to attain new ones. Mass migrations out of their ancestral homeland (present-day Kosovo and southern Serbia) shifted the Serb population northwards into the Šumadija region and across the Danube and Sava rivers into what is now Vojvodina and Croatia. In 1699, the Ottomans were pushed south of the Danube by

Austrian Hapsburg armies, although Serb lands to the south remained under Ottoman rule.

Under Islamic law the Ottomans did not allow new churches to be built, and allowed old ones to be restored only with great reluctance and with numerous obstructions on their part. Many churches were turned into mosques and some were torn down. People were allowed to gather in churches and monasteries only on rare occasions, and priests and monks could openly satisfy people's religious needs only by special permission. This meant that heads of families had to take on the role of domestic priest in their families. This is one reason why the celebration of the family baptismal or patron saints day, assumed great importance in the Serbian tradition.

Until re-establishment of the Serbian Church in 1920 under the auspices of the Kingdom of Yugoslavia, there existed several independent church units of the Serbian Church: the Metropolitanate of Karlovac, the Metropolitanate of Montenegro, and the Serbian Churches in Dalmatia, Bosnia and Herzegovina, South Serbia, and Macedonia.

The movement for Serbian independence began in the Šumadija region, with uprisings under the Serbian patriots Karadjordje Petrović (in 1804–13) and Miloš Obrenović (in 1815–17). After the Russia-Turkish War of 1828–9, Serbia became an internationally recognized autonomous principality under Turkish suzerainty and Russian protection. The independence of Serbia led in 1832 to the recognition of Serbian ecclesiastical autonomy. After an insurrection against the Ottomans in Bosnia and Herzegovina in 1875, Serbia and Montenegro went to war against Turkey in 1876–8 in support of the Bosnian rebels. With Russian assistance, Serbia gained more territory as well as formal independence in 1878, though Bosnia was placed under Austrian administration. In 1879, the Serbian Church was recognized by Constantinople as autocephalous under the primacy of the Metropolitan of Belgrade. This Church, however, covered only the territory of what was called 'old Serbia'. The small state of Montenegro, always independent from the Ottomans, had its own metropolitan in Cetinje. This prelate, who was also the civil and military leader of the nation, was consecrated either in Austria, or, as in the case of the famous bishop-poet Petar II Petrović Njegoš, in St Petersburg, in 1833.

In the Austro-Hungarian Empire, two autocephalous churches, with jurisdiction over Serbs, Romanians and other Slavs, were in existence during the second half of the nineteenth century. These were the Patriarchate of Sremski-Karlovci (Karlowitz), established in 1848, which governed all the Orthodox in the Kingdom of Hungary; and the Metropolitanate of Czernowitz (now Chernovtsy) in Bukovina, which, after 1873, also exercised jurisdiction over two Serbian dioceses (Zara and Kotor) in Dalmatia. The Serbian dioceses of Bosnia and Herzegovina, acquired by Austria in 1878, remained autonomous but were never completely independent from Constantinople.

In 1908, Austria-Hungary directly annexed Bosnia; the Serbs therefore sought the aid of Montenegro, Bulgaria and Greece in regaining the last Ottoman-ruled lands in the Balkans. In the ensuing Balkan Wars of 1912–13, Serbia obtained northern and central Macedonia, but Austria compelled it to yield Albanian lands that would have given Serbia access to the sea. On 28 June 1914, in the aftermath of the Balkan Wars, a Bosnian Serb, Gavrilo Princip, assassinated the Austrian Archduke Francis Ferdinand in Sarajevo. This act precipitated World War I.

Serbia fought on the side of the Allies against the Central powers in the war. Despite the initial brilliant successes of its army, Austro-Hungarian and Bulgarian forces occupied Serbia. Upon the collapse of Austria-Hungary at the end of the war in 1918, Serbia united with Montenegro and with the former South Slav subjects of the Hapsburgs, to form a new state, the Kingdom of Serbs, Croats, and Slovenes, under the Karadjordjević dynasty. After World War I, all the Serbs were united under one ecclesiastical authority. The five groups of Serbian dioceses (Montenegro, Patriarchate of Karlovci, Dalmatia, Bosnia-Herzegovina, Old Serbia) were united in 1920–2 under one Serbian patriarch, residing in Belgrade, the capital of the new Yugoslavia. The patriarch's full title was 'Archbishop of Peć, Metropolitan of Belgrade and Karlovci, and Patriarch of the Serbs'.

The new kingdom rapidly polarized between advocates of a strongly centralized state (favoured by Serbs) and others who sought a federation that reflected historical and ethnic differences. In 1929 King Alexander I attempted to solve the problems created by the ethnic parties by declaring a royal dictatorship, changing the name of the state to Yugoslavia, and creating new *banovine* (governorships) that cut across the historical territorial units.

During World War II Serbia was dismembered and occupied by Germany, Hungary, Bulgaria, and Italy. Soldiers of the royal army, calling themselves *ćetnici* (Chetniks), formed a Serbian resistance movement, but a more determined Communist resistance under the partisans, with Soviet and Anglo-American help, liberated all of Yugoslavia by 1944. The brutal religious persecution of Orthodox priests in World War II enhanced the Church's popular standing throughout Serbia.

After World War II, Communist regimes were established in the Balkan states. The Communist regime in Yugoslavia took advantage of the Serbian Church's loyal support of the Yugoslav state to gain legitimacy in the eyes of the Serbian population. However, the Church soon came into direct conflict with the Communist policy on nationalities and lost its secular role and influence. One result of this conflict was the refusal of the Serbian Church hierarchy to recognize the Macedonian Orthodox Church, which was given self-governing status by the Yugoslav state in 1967. The canonicity of this Church has not received universal Orthodox recognition. There were no attempts, however, at liquidating the churches entirely. In Yugoslavia both church and state were legally separated. With its solid record of resistance to the Germans, the Serbian Orthodox Church was able to preserve more independence from the government than its sister Churches of Bulgaria and Romania.

The Communist governments throughout Eastern Europe collapsed during the late 1980s and early 1990s, effectively dissolving state control over churches and bringing new political and religious freedoms into the region.

Albanian agitation in the 1980s for Kosovo to become a republic within the federation was met by revision of the Serbian constitution in 1990, which left Kosovo and Vojvodina with only nominal autonomy. Most Serbs living outside Serbia resisted the disintegration of Yugoslavia, fearing persecution and discrimination by the non-Serb authorities of the seceding states, and supported the creation of Serb republics in the predominantly Serb *krajina* (region) of Croatia and in Bosnia and Herzegovina. After the disintegration of socialist Yugoslavia, in 1992 Serbia and Montenegro formed the

Federal Republic of Yugoslavia, which was replaced, in 2003, by the Union of Serbia and Montenegro. In 2006, after a referendum, Montenegro proclaimed independence from the Union.

Modern Theological Figures

From the middle of eighteenth century, the Serbian Orthodox Church used Russian church literature and the Russian language as a model. Later, Russian Slavophiles had their best bastion in the Serbian Church and they helped Serbian schools and churches in Turkish Ottoman regions. Most of the Serbian theologians in the nineteenth century studied at theological faculties in Russia, and religious books from these schools were used in Serbia. Church sermons and works of famous Russian churchmen and writers were translated, but these sermons were not comprehensible to the faithful in Serbia. In the Serbia of that time there was no strong theological thinker capable of adapting Russian ideas to the Serbian milieu. There were very few independent theological works and they were without great value. They were mostly compilations of Russian and French ethical writings lacking in wider spiritual influence. Serbian theological writing at the beginning of the twentieth century was mostly composed of apologetic and polemic works. This theology offered some knowledge and information about Christ, the Gospel, the Church and Christianity, but in essence it consisted of sterile definitions, which transformed Christian faith and life into religious and ethical systems.

In the kingdom of Serbia, because of political quarrels and dynastic conflicts, there were two streams in the Church, one of them sympathetic with Russia and the other with the liberal West. With the break out of the October Revolution in 1917 every possibility for education in Russia and Serbia stopped and theologians turned to Britain and Greece.

Bishop Nikolaj Velimirović (1880–1956) is considered to be one of the most talented. He studied in Switzerland, at Oxford and in Russia. Most authors who wrote about him pointed out that with him a new era in Serbian Orthodox theology began, which was to be continued and deepened by Justin Popović (1894–1979) and others. In his early works Velimirović was prepared to entertain some kinds of reform in Orthodoxy, which his opponents explained was the result of studying in the West. Later, Velimirović would start to show signs of his struggle with European history and culture. After that came his radical denunciation of European thinking and civilization and the glorification of Serbian and Russian peasantry. The essence of Velimirović's and Popović's thinking was a critique of European humanism, civilization, and materialism. Popović was celebrated as a famous teacher of Orthodoxy, and he wrote that because European culture takes humanity as its foundation, making humanism its main architect, European man believes he can proclaim himself God. For this reason, he thought, nihilism and anarchism would be the logical outcome of western hubris.

A whole line of younger Orthodox theologians from that time held similar opinions. Leading Serbian theologians tried to revitalize the heritage of St Sava, representing him as a saint and leader of the Serbian people. Polemical postures towards Islam, Catholicism and western culture generally, which dated from times other than that of St Sava himself, were integrated into the theological concept of *svetosavlje* (the teachings of St Sava). This theology of nationalism was used first to make possible an ideological meeting-place for all Serbs who lived in different parts of the Kingdom of Yugoslavia. Further more, *svetosavlje* was used to bridge the gap which grew between the Church and Serbian intellectuals, who were alienated as a result of the influence of western philosophical and political ways of thinking. The cult of St Sava grew in schools and in public life, as also did the promotion of the glory of the old Nemanjić dynasty. This fed into the sense of injustice from centuries of enslavement under the Ottomans, the increasing decline of Serbian dominance in Kosovo, and other issues.

After World War II, the Serbian Orthodox Church had very restricted possibilities for activities until the middle of the 1980s. Using Kosovo as an unresolved problem within Serbia and Yugoslavia, the Serbian Orthodox Church offered itself as the traditional bastion of national security and the centre of national life, as evidenced by its centuries-long role as the single institution that 'never in history betrayed the Serbian people'. The ideological basis for such an assertion emerged from the synthesis of the teachings of Nikolaj Velimirović and Justin Popović, two 'enduring examples and models of modern Serbian spirituality'.

Missions and Diaspora

From the middle of the nineteenth century and during the whole of the twentieth century, many of the faithful in the Serbian Orthodox Church emigrated to America; later emigrations were to western Europe, South America, Australia and Canada. Causes of migration were varied, from economic to political, and the process of emigrating had several phases. Émigré circles first established parishes and after these bishoprics of the Serbian Orthodox Church, because they held that the Church was a basis for traditional national culture. Bishoprics in the diaspora were under the jurisdiction of the Serbian Orthodox Church, although they had some administrative freedom for conducting their internal affairs according to the laws of the country in which they existed. During the 1960s a schism occurred inside the Serbian Orthodox Church, with one section of believers under former American-Canadian bishoprics, seceding to the new breakaway church. The schism was partly healed at the beginning of the 1990s. In the period between the two World Wars, the Serbian Orthodox Church had jurisdiction over some bishoprics in Czechoslovakia and Hungary, which were taken away from it after 1945. Today the Serbian Orthodox Church has churches in North America, South America, Africa, Australia, Austria, Belgium, France, Germany, Great Britain, Hungary, Italy, New Zealand, Sweden, Switzerland and the Netherlands.

Priesthood and Hierarchy

Each Orthodox diocese is divided into lesser units, which organically belong to the same diocese or bishopric. At the head of each diocese is the bishop, first among the priests of a local Church. He chooses representatives who, with his empowerment and blessing, serve the Church either at his side or independently. They are part of the local church hierarchy and are ordained as presbyters (priests) and deacons. These degrees of church hierarchy – bishop, presbyter and deacon – form the three degrees of Holy Orders.

For purely practical reasons, each diocese or bishopric is divided into two, three or more church congregations which are administered by specifically chosen, prominent, distinguished priests, each in the capacity of a bishop's delegate. They are given some measure of jurisdiction over other priests, and they carry the title of Episcopal Dean, or proto-presbyter. Each episcopal deanery consists of several church congregations, which further consist of several parishes. The parish is the smallest unit in the local church structure, signifying the local church in a town or a village, headed by a presbyter (priest). A parish and a church congregation may coincide, but not necessarily so, since a church congregation is usually considered to have a wider connotation. All bishops form the Holy Synaxis of Bishops, and this is the highest administrative, spiritual and legislative body within the Serbian Orthodox Church.

The Holy Synaxis or assembly of bishops convenes regularly at least once a year and solves all current questions of church life. If necessary, extraordinary assemblies may be convened, as well as the regular ones. Between each regular council of the Holy Synaxis of Bishops, the executive body of the Church is the Holy Synod of Bishops. Four bishops and the patriarch, or his representative, form it, and its main role is to put into practice all decisions made by the Holy Synaxis of Bishops.

The patriarch is first only in honour; he does not have the authority of a Roman pope, and he has no power whatsoever over other bishops. All he has is his high standing, and his voice is decisive only when cases cannot be resolved by the bishops comprising the Holy Synaxis. He is considered to be first among equals.

Monasticism and Spirituality

The Orthodox Church is well known for its long-standing tradition of monasticism. The uninterrupted monastic tradition of Orthodox Christianity can be traced to the Egyptian desert communities of the fourth and fifth centuries. In medieval Serbian society monasteries and monks played an especially significant and unique role. The monasteries of Studenica, Žiča, Peć, Mileševa, Sopoćani, Dečani, Ravanica, and many others, all founded by royal patrons, outlived the state and centuries of domination by the Ottoman Turks. It is characteristic of Serbian monasteries that they have always been open to communal life. There were times when they substituted for schools and hospitals, and they became workshops for the production of icons and illuminated manuscripts. They were often used as a place of refuge from enemy raiding parties, and, last but not least, they were places of eternal rest, as they all maintained cemeteries.

Apart from the most famous monasteries founded by members of the Nemanjić dynasty, many were originally built in remote and inaccessible regions. During times of both peace and turbulence, the monasteries remained strong spiritual centres, and under Ottoman rule they were given some sort of autonomy in exchange for annual payments of taxes to the authorities. People went on pilgrimages to venerate the relics of national saints, such as those of St Simeon at Studenica, St Sava at Mileševa, St Stefan Dečanski at Dečani, Holy Knez Lazar at Ravanica, and those of saints belonging to the Branković dynasty in Krušedol. Regular church services were carefully observed in all of these monasteries. Most of the monks were at least semi-literate, doing their utmost to spread literacy among people whilst tutoring them in the faith and in spiritual life. During the Ottoman period they spoke and wrote about the glorious Serbian past and their grandest and most significant rulers and predecessors. In addition to the above-mentioned national saints, centuries of reverence have also been devoted to St Paraskeva, St Joanikije Devički, St Basil of Ostrog and others.

At the end of the nineteenth century, and during the twentieth, commitment to the monastic life fell to a low level and many monasteries were left empty. Between the two World Wars, there was an increase in women entering convents, thanks especially to Russian émigrés. Interest in monasticism never entirely faded under Communism, and in Serbia and Montenegro, when this period had come to an end, it regained some of its strength.

The Cult of Saints

Canonization in the Eastern Orthodox Church is a solemn proclamation rather than a process. Spontaneous devotion toward an individual by the faithful establishes the usual basis for sainthood. The bishop accepts the petition, examines it, and delivers it to a commission that will render a final decision.

In the Eastern Orthodox Church, relics of saints appear less frequently, although the *antimension* (the cloth upon which the Divine Liturgy is celebrated) always contains a relic, but icons of saints appear in much greater numbers. Though cultic veneration of saints as patrons, tutelary saints, helpers and healers has increased throughout the centuries, the view that the saints are supreme examples of the Christian life of sanctification is still preserved.

Lists of saints in the Serbian Orthodox Church contain today 69 persons of Serbian origin together with another 7 Sinaitic saints (monks who came to Serbia from Mount Sinai), making a total of 76 saints. From this total, 22 of them were Serb rulers, 22 were ascetic monks, 25 were archbishops and 7 were hieromartyrs. The most famous among them was Sava of Serbia (1173–1236), founder and first archbishop of the autocephalous Serbian Church.

Pilgrimages and Local Traditions

The main feast days are those of Christ, the Theotokos, and the saints. The Serbian Orthodox Church starts Christmas celebrations forty days ahead of the feast itself. The Serbian Church, like the Churches of Russia and Jerusalem, and most monasteries on Mt Athos, continues to use the Julian calendar. Celebrations begin for Christmas with the forty-day fast, while the last three Sundays of the fast are marked by events popularly called: Children's Day, Mother's Day and Father's Day. The last two days before the feast, which are popularly called Slaying Day and Yule-Log Day or Christmas Eve, are characterized by special preparatory acts before Christmas. It is customary not to sleep on that night, but to wait with vigilant anticipation for the greatest moment – Christ's birth. Yule Log Day and Christmas incorporate several customs, such as the cornel tree, Yule Log Man, the Christmas Eve cake, a strict fast supper, the Christmas cake with golden coin, the first guest of the Christmas day in the person of a young boy, and so on.

Serbian New Year's Day is celebrated on 14 January, according to the Julian calendar. This is the Feast of Circumcision of the Lord and the Feast of St Basil the Great, author of the Holy Liturgy, and the patron of monks. This feast is also popularly called 'Little' or 'Young' Christmas. Other great feasts of faith in the Serbian Orthodox Church are Theophany (19 January), Lazarus Saturday (the Willow Day), Good Friday, Easter Day or Pascha, Ascension of Our Lord or Saviour's Day, Pentecost or Descent of the Holy Spirit. During all of these celebrations certain religious services and liturgies are performed. Easter is still reckoned by the Julian calendar by most of the Eastern Orthodox Churches, which means it does not always coincide with Easter in the West.

Besides attending services at their local church or monastery, the Orthodox faithful are recommended to visit once a year a particular saintly place (especially where there are surviving relics of Serbian saints), such as the monasteries of Studenica, Ostrog, Dečani, Ravanica and Hilandar. Pilgrimage to Jerusalem allows the pilgrim to use the special title of *haji*, which derives from the Arabic word for a pilgrim.

The Serbian Orthodox Church observes single-day fasts (every Wednesday and Friday and certain other days in a year), and seasonal fasts (Great Lent, starting seven weeks before Easter and lasting until Easter Day). There are several degrees of fasting. Fasting seasons normally exclude weddings (except by a special dispensation of the bishop) and all other larger festivals.

The Serbian Orthodox faithful observe a unique holiday called the Baptismal Feast Day or Family Patron Saint Day: *Krsna slava*. On receiving Christianity through baptism, heads of Serbian families choose a saint from the Christian calendar to be the patron saint of their family. The Baptismal Feast celebration requires: a leavened wheat flour cake, boiled wheat kernels, a beeswax candle and wine. Holy water is usually used in preparing the festal cake and the priest blesses it in the host's home several days ahead of the feast itself. He executes this ceremony by using the appropriate prayer, a cross, and a small bunch of basil flowers. It is necessary to have a consecrated home icon of the saint who is being celebrated. On the very day of the Baptismal Feast, the priest cuts the festal cake, usually in the host's home. The appropriate *troparion* is sung in honour of the saint, and the priest offers prayers for abundance of grace from the Holy Spirit and God's blessing for the whole household. The head of the household provides for all those who come into his home on that day. The Baptismal Feast is transmitted from generation to generation, from fathers to sons, so that the household does not remain without the festal candle, cake and wheat. If sons move from their father's home, they may celebrate the feast in their own homes, or, alternatively, continue celebrating in their father's home while he is still living.

Aside from the Baptismal Feast, the faithful may choose another saint to celebrate as their co-patron (*Preslava*) and this saint is celebrated in the same way. This is usually done to offer thanks to a saint who is especially venerated by them for one reason or another.

Besides Baptismal Feast Days, the faithful also celebrate their local church feast, i.e., the feast day of the saint to whom their local church is dedicated. It is customary in country towns and villages to form processions after the Holy Liturgy, and to visit crop fields, stopping beside the so-called 'testament tree', and offering prayers and litanies for a fertile crop and harvest.

Among the significant saints and events celebrated by the Serbian Orthodox are: St Ignatius, 2 January; St Steven, 9 January; Synaxis of St John the Baptist, 20 January; St Sava, 27 January; St George, 6 May; St Mark, 8 May; St Vitus, 28 June; Nativity of St John the Baptist, 7 July; St Peter, 12 July; St Ellijah, 2 August; Exaltation of the Life-Giving Cross, 27 September; Venerable Cyriacus the Anchorite, 12 October; St Thomas, 19 October; Venerable Mother Paraskeva, 27 October; St Luke, 31 October; St Demetrius, 8 November; St George, 16 November; Synaxis of Archangel Michael, 21 November; St Alimpius, 9 December; St Nicholas, 19 December.

Inter-Church Relations and Ecumenism

Between the two World Wars, many Orthodox churchmen of the Ecumenical Patriarchate of Constantinople, of Greece, of the Balkans, and of the Russian emigration took part in the ecumenical movement. Several private associations of churchmen and theologians promoted understanding between Eastern Orthodoxy and the 'Anglo-Catholic' branch of Anglicanism in this period.

After World War II, however, the Orthodox Churches of the Communist-dominated countries failed to join the newly created World Council of Churches (1948): only Constantinople and Greece did so. The situation changed drastically in 1961, when the Patriarchate of Moscow applied for membership and was soon followed by other autocephalous churches. Before and after 1961, the Orthodox consistently declared that their membership did not imply any relativistic understanding of the Christian truth, but that they were ready to discuss with all Christians the best way of restoring the lost unity of Christendom, as well as problems of common Christian action and witness in the modern world. Often, and especially at the beginning of their participation, the Orthodox delegates had recourse to separate statements, which made clear to the Protestant majorities that, in the Orthodox view, Christian unity was attainable only in the full unity of the primitive apostolic faith from which the Orthodox Church had never departed. This attitude of the Orthodox could be understood only if it made sufficiently clear that the truth, which ancient Eastern Orthodoxy claims to preserve, is maintained by the Holy Spirit in the Church as a whole, and not by any individual or any group of individuals in their own right. And also that the unity of Christians, which is the goal of the ecumenical movement, does not imply cultural, intellectual or ritual uniformity but rather a mystical fellowship in the fullness of truth as expressed in eucharistic communion.

During the papacy of John XXIII, when Roman Catholicism became actively involved in ecumenism, the Orthodox after some hesitation participated in the new situation.

The spectacular meetings in the 1960s between the Ecumenical Patriarch Athenagoras and the Pope, in Jerusalem, Istanbul and Rome, the symbolic lifting of ancient anathemas, and other gestures were signs of rapprochement, although they were sometimes mistakenly interpreted as if they were ending the Great Schism itself. In the Orthodox view, full unity can be restored only in the fullness of truth witnessed by the entire Church and sanctioned in sacramental communion.

The Serbian Orthodox Church was the last Orthodox Church to take an active part in the work of the World Council of Churches in 1965. Patriarch German was elected its president in 1968. The participation of the Serbian Church in the organization and its position on ecumenism (especially the ecumenical dialogue espoused by the Roman Catholic Church) may have caused more disagreement among the bishops than any other issue in recent years.

Ecumenism as a way of transcending narrow national and confessional interests has always had strong opponents in the Serbian Church. Not infrequently, ecumenism has been condemned as a mortal danger for Orthodoxy, or its betrayal, while the Ecumenical Patriarchate has been branded a Masonic organization in the service of the 'new world order'. The strong anti-western sentiments are most clearly expressed in the writings of Nikolaj Velimirović and Justin Popović about Europe and the West. Archimandrite Justin Popović was notably a bitter critic of both ecumenism and the WCC. In both church and non-church circles these two authors are among the most abundantly quoted domestic theologians since about the 1980s. Their followers have further elaborated their teaching that both Catholicism and Protestantism are heretical, and a betrayal of Christianity, and that Catholic ecumenism is a continuation of the centuries-old drive by the Vatican to expand its jurisdiction over the Balkans at the expense of the Serbian Orthodox Church.

During the armed conflict in the former Yugoslavia representatives of different faiths issued several joint statements and made several joint appearances. The patriarch condemned the attacks on the Bajrakli mosque and the parish office of St Ante in Belgrade, and had previously sent an eirenic response to the publication of an anti-Semitic article. But on many other occasions the Serbian Orthodox Church failed to condemn religious intolerance and discrimination. The church press has published critical articles on minor religious organizations and sects, and on the Roman Catholic Church, on quite a few occasions. Their authors have been particularly touchy about aid flowing in through humanitarian organizations connected with Protestant Churches the world over. There is an underlying concern in the Serbian Orthodox Church at large that if religious communities are allowed to operate in conditions that are more liberal then the Serbian nation may become divided along religious lines too.

In 1997, a number of monastics made an appeal to the Serbian Orthodox Church, asking it to renounce its membership of the WCC. The Serbian Orthodox Church Assembly, at a regular session that year, considered the matter and decided to propose to all Orthodox Churches, and to the Ecumenical Patriarchate, to convoke a pan-Orthodox session to consult on a joint position towards the WCC. However, not all bishops were sure that ecumenism was necessarily bad. In May 1998, the Assembly again debated the whole range of issues related to the Orthodox Church's attitude to the ecumenical movement, and bishops again disagreed with each other. The Assembly adopted the conclusions of the pan-Orthodox consultation in Thessaloniki, whose participants agreed to start official talks with the WCC on the inadmissibility of the organization's present concept, structure and methodology, and the need to place it on a new footing. That year the Serbian Orthodox Church sent two representatives to the WCC Assembly in Harare. In the meantime, the decision to pull out of the organization had neither been cancelled nor put into effect and the opponents of both ecumenism and the WCC wrote that the imported heresy could only be destroyed with the sword of the Spirit.

The NATO bombing of the former Republic of Yugoslavia in 1999 increased the feeling of deep mistrust and fear, and even hatred, of the West. More frequently, however, one can hear other, albeit toned-down opinions that the West and America are not the only cause of the domestic calamity.

Encounter with Other Religions

The Great Schism between the Eastern and the Western Church (1054) was the culmination of a gradual process of estrangement between East and West that began in the early centuries of the Byzantine Empire and continued throughout the Middle Ages. Linguistic and cultural differences, as well as political events, contributed to the estrangement. Theological differences could probably have been settled if there were not two different concepts of church authority. The growth of Roman primacy, based on the concept of the apostolic origin of the Church of Rome, which claimed not only titular but also jurisdictional authority over other churches, was incompatible with traditional Orthodox ecclesiology. The Eastern Orthodox Christians considered all churches as sister churches and understood the primacy of the Roman bishop only as *primus inter pares* among his brother bishops. For the East, the highest authority in settling doctrinal disputes could not be the authority of a single Church or a single bishop, but an Ecumenical Council of all sister churches. Owing to these serious dogmatic differences the Orthodox Churches are not in communion with the Roman Catholic and Protestant communities.

The Serbian Orthodox Church sees itself as a defender of Christianity against an Islamic onslaught in Europe on the one side, and the march of Roman Catholicism against Eastern Orthodoxy on the other. In common with other Orthodox Churches, it regards itself as the standard-bearer of the nation's authentic identity, which it has practically sacralized. Parallels of its threefold role as protector of identity, guarantor of territory, and a pledge for the future are to be found in other Orthodox Churches. The Serbian Orthodox Church bases its perceived role on the following two main and perhaps contradictory premises. First, it defends the Serb nation as a natural entity, an organic body incapable of survival and development if divided or separated from its Orthodox religious roots, for there is a strong belief that he who is not Orthodox is not a Serb. Second, it carries a deep sense of insecurity acquired during the centuries of victimization (at the hands of the Ottoman Empire, the Independent State of Croatia, and Communism). In its pastoral letters and statements in recent times the Serbian Church has likened the fate of the Serb people to that of Christ. History and a belief that they live in hostile surroundings weigh down Serb priests. This sense of victimization has been the overriding factor in the Serbian Orthodox Church's response to the Yugoslav crisis.

Even before the conflict in the former Yugoslavia, the relations between the Serbian Orthodox Church and the Roman Catholic Church were burdened by many problems, including Rome's position on the persecution of Serbs in the Independent State of Croatia (NDH) during the Second World War, the question of language and alphabet in Croatia, the Kosovo problem, the Catholic Church's attitude to the Macedonian Orthodox Church, and so on. The Roman Catholic Church objected that the Serbian Orthodox Church had 'substituted the cult of St Sava as its imperialist ideology for the Gospel'. Although Patriarch Pavle and Cardinal Kuharić met several times between 1991 and 1994, and Serbian Orthodox leaders and the Croatian president exchanged letters, relations between them became increasingly tense. Several attempts to arrange a visit by Pope John Paul II to Belgrade failed. The controversy about the number of churches destroyed, the silence of the Catholic Church about the position of the Serbian Orthodox in Croatia, and its attitude towards the expulsion of Serbs and their suffering during war operations made cooperation and dialogue between the two churches difficult. Then, after 1999, things slowly began to improve.

Homeland and Diaspora Politics

The relations between the Church and the state in the East have been shaped rather differently than in the West. Unlike the Catholic Church in Western Europe, Orthodox Churches never became independent political forces. Because they were autocephalous, Orthodox Churches functioned as one of the primary agents of nation-state integration. In Byzantine spiritual and political circles, the state and the Church were two aspects of the same phenomenon. The situation evolved from the biblical principle, 'Render unto Caesar that which is Caesar's and unto God that which is God's.' The Eastern Orthodox Church acknowledges that the state is a divine institution and preaches complete subjugation to state authority, condemning every act of disobedience regardless of the religion professed by the head of state. The ideal relationship is conceived as a close tie and mutual support between Church and state. Opposed to this principle was the 'rigorous politics' promoted by monastic orders, advocating strictness on all questions. On those occasions when the state adopted an adversarial or hostile attitude towards the Church, the latter was supposed to focus inward and humbly await the moment when 'God's justice shall prevail', for the Church is one, unchanging and eternal, while states are many and ephemeral. The close tie between the Orthodox Churches and the rulers contributed to the unique development of Orthodoxy as a form of Christianity and as a cult of the nation-state. To understand better the close link between confession and ethnos, it should be noted that as early as 451, the Council of Chalcedon determined that the territorial boundaries of the church's influence should coincide with state borders.

Among the Orthodox Churches, there exist different conceptions of the nation as a domain of church influence, and of the relation between the Church and the nation.

During the medieval period, the Serbian Church had a significant, if not the principal, role in the lives of every individual and the state as a whole. The relationship between the Church and the state was natural and harmonious, and was most often compared to the human organism and the relationship between the soul and the body. This is a case where the well-known Byzantine theory of *symphonia* between the Church and the state was applied almost to its fullest extent. The Church was materially and financially completely independent. Every diocese owned land, priests were entitled to *popovski bir* (priest's choice, i.e., those goods that a priest could take for his service instead of a cash payment) and some land which they could cultivate for their needs.

Only with the Ottoman Turkish occupation of the Balkans did the Orthodox Church hierarchy in the East directly assume civil authority. The Ecumenical Patriarch of Constantinople was thus appointed by the sultan as head (*millet-bachi*) of the entire Christian population of the Ottoman Empire. The patriarch exercised these powers until the secularization of the Turkish Republic by Kemal Atatürk in 1921. By that time, however, he had lost most of his jurisdictional powers because of the establishment of autocephalous churches in Greece, Serbia, Bulgaria and Romania.

While the Serbian Orthodox Church has been autocephalous and independent throughout its history, it has nevertheless remained closely tied to the state. It has been financially dependent on the state and thus susceptible to state influence. The Church, which viewed itself as a protector of the Serbian people, operated according to this principle. It did not regard the national question as a separate political problem, but as a form and an aspect of religion; thus it acted as a national, and not solely religious, institution. During the period after the Second World War, religious communities were gradually, and increasingly, moving from social and political life towards the margins of society. The revitalization of Orthodoxy occurred in the mid-1980s, during the period of the collapse of the socialist system and the liberalization of social relations. It was especially active during the 1990s in granting substantial moral and material support to the Serbian population in territories where war was being waged. The Serbian Orthodox contacts with other churches (especially other Orthodox) constituted an important aspect of the politics of this period.

Women and Women's Expectations

Serbian Orthodoxy, as the combination of Christianity and Serbian traditional culture, accepts and supports the traditional patriarchal order, with women having a clearly defined place and role. This implies a strict role division between the genders, with the subordination of the woman to the man, and her inferiority in a physical and intellectual sense. A woman's place is secondary in every respect, and because the woman is repenting the sin of her original ancestor, she may rescue herself only through obedience and sacrifice. According to the opinion of some Serbian Orthodox theologians, her education should not provide for more than is required by her duties in the family, while her position in society should not extend beyond the limits of her traditional role in the home. Any break of these rules through so-called 'struggle for women's rights and emancipation' is interpreted by some Serbian Orthodox theologians as a disastrous foreign influence, which destroys traditional relations and order and ultimately may lead to the ruin of the entire nation. Abortion is forbidden by the Serbian Orthodox Church, and the best form of contraception it suggests is restraining oneself.

Recent Developments

Following Bolshevik practice in Russia, the new state authorities of Communist Yugoslavia, after the Second World War, separated the Church from the state and this separation also applied to education. Religious education was taken out of primary and secondary schools and most of the real estate owned by the Church was confiscated. The Theological Faculty was expelled from the University of Belgrade. The schism in parts of the Serbian Orthodox Church in the USA and Macedonia is ongoing, and there are similar problems in Montenegro (the Montenegrin Orthodox Church was officially registered in the year 2000). The wars of the 1990s on the territory of the former Yugoslav state, in Croatia, Bosnia and Herzegovina, and in Kosovo, destroyed many churches and left empty many monasteries, parishes and archbishoprics.

The present-day Serbian Orthodox Church has over 3.500 parishes, 204 monasteries, 1,900 parish priests, some 230 monks and 1,000 nuns. There are six seminaries and two theological faculties: in Belgrade and Libertyville (USA). There is a Theological Institute in Belgrade and Spiritual Academy in Srbinje in Bosnia and Herzegovina. Today seminaries provide education for over 1,000 students and there are over 1,000 students enrolled in theological faculties and spiritual academies. In 1993 the Church established its Academy for Art and Conservation in Belgrade with several departments: iconography, fresco painting, and conservation.

The official publication of the Serbian Orthodox Church is the monthly *Glasnik* (The Messenger). There is also *Pravoslavlje* (Orthodoxy), *Misionar* (Missionary), and *Svetosavsko Zvonce* (Saint Sava Bell) for children. The Theological Faculty publishes its own periodical as does the Holy Synod and some dioceses. There are also a few religious radio stations.

Further reading

Alexander, S. (1979) *Church and State in Yugoslavia since 1945*. Cambridge: Cambridge University Press.

Barford, P. M. (2002) *The Early Slavs: Culture and Society in Early Medieval Eastern Europe*. London: British Museum Press.

Círković, S. (2005) *The Serbs*. Oxford: Oxford University Press.

Clark, V. (2000) *Why Angels Fall: A Portrait of Orthodox Europe from Byzantium to Kosovo*. London: Macmillan.

Fine, J. V. A. (1987) *The Late Medieval Balkans: A Critical Survey from the Late Twelfth Century to the Ottoman Conquest*. Ann Arbor: University of Michigan Press.

Gogich, D. (1994) *The Serbian Patericon*. Forestville, Calif.: St Paisios.

Hupchick, D. P. (2002) *The Balkans: From Constantinople to Communism*. London: Palgrave.

Journal of Ecumenical Studies, Special Issue on Pluralism, Proselytism, and Nationalism in Eastern Europe (1999, winter–spring), vol. 36(1–2).

Mojzes, P. (1994) *Yugoslavian Inferno: Ethno-Religious Warfare in the Balkans*. New York: Continuum.

—— (ed.) *Religion and the War in Bosnia*. Atlanta, Ga.: Scholars Press.

Obolensky, D. (1974) *The Byzantine Commonwealth: Eastern Europe, 500–1453*. London: Sphere Books.

Parry, K. (2001) Crisis in the Balkans: the Byzantine monuments of Kosovo. *Eastern Churches Journal* 8(3): 83–90.

Pavlowitch, K. S. (1988) *The Improbable Survivor: Yugoslavia and its Problems 1918–1988*. Columbus: Ohio State University Press.

—— (2002) *Serbia: The History behind the Name*. London: C. Hurst.

Peić, S. (1994) *Medieval Serbian Culture*. London: Alpine Fine Arts.

Petrovich, M. B. (1976) *A History of Modern Serbia, 1804–1918*, 2 vols. New York and London: Harcourt Brace Jovanovich.

Radić, R. (2000) The Church and the 'Serbian question'. In N. Popov (ed.) *The Road to War in Serbia. Trauma and Catharsis*. Budapest: EU Press.

Ramet, R. (ed.) (1988) *Eastern Christianity and Politics in the Twentieth Century*. Durham, NC: Duke University Press.

Runciman, S. (1968) *The Great Church in Captivity*. Cambridge: Cambridge University Press.

—— (1971) *The Orthodox Churches and the Secular State*. Oxford: Oxford University Press.

Soulis, G. C. (1984) *The Serbs and Byzantium during the Reign of Tsar Stephen Dušan (1331–1355) and his Successors*. Washington, DC: Dumbarton Oaks.

Subotić, G. (1998) *Art of Kosovo: The Sacred Land*. New York: Monacelli Press.

Tachiaos, A.-E. N. (2001) *Cyril and Methodius of Thessalonica: The Acculturation of the Slavs*. Crestwood, NY: St Vladimir's Seminary Press.

CHAPTER 12
Syriac Christianity

Heleen Murre-van den Berg

Introduction

The Syriac churches are among the most intriguing and fascinating sections of the eastern churches. Their heritage encompasses Greek and Jewish, Roman and Persian, western and eastern elements; this multiplicity of sources forged a number of different churches, each with its distinctive features. Generally speaking, the Syriac churches are those that trace their origins to the Syriac-speaking and Syriac-writing Christian communities of the fourth to seventh centuries in the region now covered by Syria, Israel/Palestine, Lebanon, Turkey, Iraq and Iran. These are the Maronite Church, the Syrian Orthodox Church, the Syrian Catholic Church, the Assyrian Church of the East and the Chaldean Church. The members of these churches today are dispersed all over the world, but have their homelands in the Middle East and south-western India (Kerala). In India, besides archdioceses of the Syrian Orthodox Church and of the Church of the East, additional Syriac communities are found, such as the Syro-Malabar Church (Catholic, Church of the East rite), the Malankara Orthodox Church (Syrian Orthodox rite, independent), the Mar Thoma Church (the result of a nineteenth-century reformation), the Malabar Independent Syrian Church and the Catholic Syro-Malankara Church. All of these have their origins in the Indian Syrian Church, which, at least between the eighth and the sixteenth century, was subordinate to the patriarch of the Church of the East. In this chapter, I will concentrate on the Syrian Orthodox Church and the Church of the East, and in addition pay attention to those branches of these traditions that are in union with Rome, i.e., the Syrian Catholic Church and the Chaldean Church. The Indian churches and the Maronite Church will be treated in other places in this book. Figures supplied by church leaders suggest that the total number of Christians of the various Syriac traditions towards the end of the twentieth century was more than 2.5 million. Of these, a little over half belong to the Syriac churches in India. Of the remaining 1.3 million people, about 400,000 belong to each of: the Syrian Orthodox Church outside

India, the Church of the East and the Chaldean Church; 100,000 belong to the Syrian Catholic Church.

In these four churches, Classical Syriac, the language shared by all churches of the Syriac tradition, is in active use, although at different levels in the various churches. In the Syrian Orthodox Church, Classical Syriac, called Kthobonoyo (originally the term for the written 'book' language), is not only the language of liturgy and classical theological literature, but is also used for speaking and writing, especially among the clergy. Alongside the languages of the countries of the diaspora, such as English, Swedish, German, Dutch and French, which are used within the communities and to a limited extent also in the liturgy, the languages of the home countries in the Middle East play a large role in all four churches. Of these, Arabic is the most important. In the Syrian Orthodox, the Syrian Catholic and the Chaldean churches, Arabic not only functions as the language of daily communication of many of its members but is also used in the liturgy. Among the members of the Church of the East, a modern variety of Syriac, often called Sureth by the people themselves but also known as North-Eastern Neo-Aramaic, is used not only in speaking, but also for writing and publishing. The Central Neo-Aramaic language of eastern Turkey, Turoyo, spoken by many members of the Syrian Orthodox Church, has never quite managed to reach the same level of acceptance as a literary language, but to a limited extent is used in writing, especially in diaspora communities in Sweden.

One of the most sensitive issues within the Syriac churches is that of a shared ethnic identity and the nomenclature used to denote that shared identity. The twentieth century saw the birth of 'Assyrian nationalism', through which mainly lay opinion leaders in the Syriac churches (sometimes including people from the Maronite community) of the Middle East tried to stress a common, non-denominational, secular and non-Arab identity, based on the belief in a common descent from the ancient Assyrians. The development of such an ethnic identity was stimulated on the one hand by secularization and modernization in the Middle East from the late nineteenth century onwards, on the other hand by the late twentieth-century western diaspora situation, where the older religious and denominational identities from the Middle East did not fit into existing categories. Understandably, this shift in emphasis from a religious Christian identity to a secular ethnic identity was not very well received by a large part of the clergy, although the level of acceptance differed from church to church and from region to region. Within the Church of the East, this reformulation of identity was the most easily accepted, leading to the addition of 'Assyrian' to the official name of the Church. Within the Syrian Orthodox Church, acceptance in the early years of the twentieth century, especially in the communities in the United States, was relatively widespread, but this development was brought to a stop by the clergy half a century later. An alternative 'Aramean' identity was developed, in which, through lack of great Aramean empires, more space was left for the Christian aspect of such an identity. Among the Chaldeans, who in general were much more integrated into Arab Iraqi society than their counterparts of the Church of the East, either identification with secular Arab (rather than Muslim) nationalism took place (as was also the case in some circles of the Syrian Orthodox and Syrian Catholic Church in Syria), or a distinct 'Chaldean' identity was forged. In recent years, ecumenical developments in the diaspora (see below), as well as the changing political situation in Iraq following the toppling of the Baath regime in 2003, led to a compromise between the two groups by advocating a 'Chaldo-Assyrian' identity, in order to make as strong a case as possible in the new Iraq.

History

Present-day discussions on a shared identity among the members of the Syriac churches reflect a long common history in which these churches at some points (theological and sometimes political) were on opposite sides, but on many others (such as language, literature, spirituality and social position) share a common heritage. This shared heritage was never completely lost sight of, despite fierce polemical debates and opposing political interests. The Syriac churches of today all trace back their origin to the Christian communities that developed in Syria and Mesopotamia in the second and third centuries, especially to those that in this period used some variety of Aramaic rather than Greek as their primary language. One of the first Aramaic-speaking Christian centres might have been Adiabene (present-day Arbil, in Iraq), where the local ruling house had converted to Judaism around 40 CE. This Jewish city-state had regular contacts with Palestine, and it seems possible that through this route Christianity reached Adiabene as early as the first century. From here, Christianity travelled westward as well as eastward, especially towards Aramaic-speaking Edessa (present-day Urfa, in southeast Turkey) early in the second century. At about the same time, the mainly Greek-speaking Christian communities in Palestine and western Syria, especially Antioch, began to spread their faith into the Aramaic-speaking rural regions of Syria, to what is now south-eastern Turkey and northern Syria. After the conversion of the royal house of Edessa, usually dated to the early third century (King Abgar VIII, r. 179–212), the Aramaic language of Edessa, later to be called Classical Syriac, began to establish itself as the preferred language of the Christian communities of Syria and northern Mesopotamia, functioning as a lingua franca for a wide variety of Aramaic speakers. By the third century, some form of Syriac Christianity must also have spread to southern Mesopotamia (also partly Aramaic-speaking) and the Arabian peninsula. The earliest evidence of Christianity in the latter region points to the fourth and early fifth century; the western parts, with Najran as a bishopric, subsequently coming under Syrian Orthodox influence, the eastern parts, among which are Qatar and the island of Socotra, under the Church of the East. Arab Christianity of this period was dependent on the Syriac literary tradition in liturgy, scripture and doctrine.

A relatively small number of sources, dating from the second and third centuries, give the impression that early Syriac Christianity was characterized by a rather encratic form of spirituality, which emphasized the need to renounce marriage and possessions, sometimes even as a prerequisite for baptism. Such a dedicated Christian life was organized in the institution of the ' "Sons" and "Daughters" of the covenant' (bnay and bnat qyama), who, living as virgins and serving the community, did not retreat into separate religious communities. Various types of Christianity flourished in the region, including later-to-be-condemned forms such as those espoused by Marcion (d. 165) and Bardaisan (d. 222), alongside various groups in the Gnostic tradition. In the third century, Mani (216–77) established a religion built on Christian, Jewish and Gnostic elements, which was to become a significant rival to Christianity in Asia.

The third century in Persia also saw the change from Parthian to Sassanian rule, whose first ruler Ardashir (r. 226–40) chose Zoroastrianism as the official religion of the empire. Although in general Christianity was tolerated and church life continued much as before, incidental persecutions took place in the latter half of the third century, especially at times when important Zoroastrians converted to Christianity. It was probably in this period that Christians from southern Mesopotamia took refuge in the Arabian peninsula and strengthened already existing Christian communities.

In the fourth century, political and religious developments in the Roman Empire led to a greater need for Christian unity and homogeneity. The Ecumenical Councils of Nicea (325) and Constantinople (381) condemned the Christologies of Arius and Apollinarios, who both had a number of followers in the churches of Syria and Mesopotamia. In 410, when peace between the Roman and Sassanian Empires made contacts between the two parts of the church possible, the Council of Nicea was also accepted in the Church of Persia. It was the later councils of the fifth century, however, that would become decisive in the formation of the Syriac churches. At the Council of Ephesus (431), Cyril of Alexandria and his followers succeeded in having the Antiochene teachings of Nestorius on the two natures of Christ condemned. After the council, Nestorius' followers fled to Persia and found a welcome in the Persian Church, which by that time, mainly through the works of Theodore of Mopsuestia (d. 428), was already sympathetic to Antiochene theology. Theodore's works were later to be translated into Syriac, and became the standard of orthodoxy in the Church of the East in the seventh century. The Council of Chalcedon in 451, although it did not revoke the condemnation of Nestorius, accepted a Christology that in many respects was close to Theodore's and Nestorius'. This council, however, was never officially accepted in the Church of Persia. Although the Dyophysite Antiochene theology that was admitted at the Synod of Seleucia-Ctesiphon in 486 could easily have been reconciled with the line of Chalcedon, political and geographical developments in the sixth and seventh centuries reinforced the isolated position of the Church of the East.

Meanwhile, the decisions of the Council of Chalcedon in 451 had not brought the discussions on the two natures of Christ to a conclusion. Cyril of Alexandria's followers (he himself died in 444) did not accept the decisions of this council, interpreting them as a victory of 'Nestorianism' and the result of undue imperial influence on the churches of Syria. To accommodate their opposition, Emperor Zeno in 482 promulgated the Henoticon, a dogmatic formulation that allowed for greater acceptance of Miaphysite views within the Roman Empire. Despite this concession and the occasional support of members of the imperial family (Empress Theodora being one of them), the Miaphysite party found it difficult to establish a secure position. In 518, Patriarch Severus of Antioch, one of the fierce defenders of Miaphysite Christology, was removed from his see and his followers were persecuted. Although several more attempts were made to keep this party within the imperial church, the sixth century became the period in which a separate hierarchy was consecrated, mainly through the efforts of the Bishop of Edessa, Jacob Baradeus (Yaʿqub Burdʿono), after whom this church, now known as the Syrian Orthodox Church, was called the 'Jacobite' church. It was here that the majority of the Syriac-speaking Christians of Syria and western Mesopotamia found a religious home; a minority of Syriac-speaking Christians remained in the imperial church, the Melkite or Rum-Orthodox Church of the Middle East.

The Arab and Muslim victories of the seventh century, leading to the establishment of the Muslim-ruled Umayyad Empire with its centre in Damascus, allowed for further expansion of the Syrian Orthodox Church towards the East, building upon the sixth and early seventh-century establishments in the Sassanian Empire. For the first time in history, the Church of the East and the Syrian Orthodox Church found themselves under the same political power. In many respects these churches benefited from the fact that the Umayyad dynasty maintained considerable impartiality towards all Christian churches, treating the 'heretic' non-Chalcedonian church in the same way as the Chalcedonian, imperial church. One of the first losses to Christendom, however, was that of most of the churches on the Arabian peninsula, whose members seem to have been attracted to Islam from the earliest period.

Dhimmi regulations, which slowly took shape in the first centuries of Islamic rule but built upon earlier minority regulations in the Byzantium and Sassanian Empires, provided the 'people of the book' – Jews, Christians, Zoroastrians and Mandeans – with a special status. They were protected from forced conversions and military conscription and allowed a considerable amount of self-rule and religious freedom. Certain restrictions, especially in court, as well as the *jizya*, the poll tax for the *dhimmi* groups, might in some periods have induced Christian conversion to Islam, but it seems that during most of the early centuries of Islam these factors were outweighed by a relatively mild and tolerant climate; Christians were allowed to function satisfactorily within their own communities, as well as exerting considerable influence on Muslim society as a whole. Until about the tenth century the Christian communities appear to have remained more or less stable.

It was especially after the 'Abbasid caliphs took over the leadership of the Islamic Empire and the centre of the empire moved from Damascus to the new capital Baghdad (749), that the Syriac Christians entered a period of relative prosperity and considerable cultural influence. The patriarch of the Church of the East, whose see was moved from Seleucia-Ctesiphon to nearby Baghdad in 775, became the most influential non-Muslim at the court; a development that reached its peak under Timothy I (in office 780–823) who survived four 'Abbasid caliphs. He was active not only in the field of politics and religious dialogue, but also led his church into a period of expansion, while consolidating those dioceses that had resulted from earlier missions to Central Asia and China between the seventh and ninth centuries. In this period, scholars from both Syriac churches contributed considerably to the scientific and scholarly developments of the time, by translating Greek works via Syriac into Arabic and by contributing original works to the further development of physics, mathematics, medicine, grammar, philosophy and theology. The school of Ḥunain ibn Isḥāq (d. 873) is one of the famous examples of Christian–Muslim cooperation and exchange. It is in this period that the use of Arabic, in writing and in speaking, increased considerably among the members of both Syriac churches. Despite the increase of Arabic Christian texts, however, Classical Syriac survived and held its ground, as is confirmed not only by Classical Syriac texts of the ninth to thirteenth centuries, but also by the survival of both Classical Syriac and spoken Aramaic until the present time. In the early eleventh century, the Byzantines regained parts of Anatolia and Syria, which in some areas within the 'Abbasid Empire caused anti-Christian measures, but also induced the Syrian Orthodox to move their patriarchal see from Byzantine-occupied Antioch to Amid (Diyarbakir) in eastern Anatolia in 1034.

The crusades and their partial occupation of parts of western Syria hardly affected the Syrian Orthodox Church because, as one of their influential patriarchs of the time, Michael the Great (1126–99) notes in his Chronicle, the crusaders were relatively tolerant in confessional matters. The Latin presence in the Middle East prompted early attempts at unions with Rome on the part of the Syrian Orthodox, the Maronites and the Church of the East. After the battle of Manzikert (eastern Turkey) in 1071, however, the majority of the Syrian Orthodox lived under Seljuk reign, which, after the upheavals of yet another war, allowed for relatively peaceful circumstances for the Christians. It seems likely that in this period the dioceses in southern Mesopotamia and Persia, which in the ninth century were still strongholds of the Church of the East, began to weaken. By the end of the thirteenth century, they had all but disappeared, probably because most of the Christians of these regions had converted to Islam.

It was the invasion of the Mongols that changed the situation of both churches. After Baghdad was captured in 1258 by Hülagü, who himself was an adherent of the Mongol shamanist religion, Syriac Christians for the first time enjoyed a period of governmental support. This was at least partly due to the fact that in the twelfth and thirteenth centuries the Church of the East had again spread along Central Asia into northern China, converting several Mongol tribes to Christianity. The Mongol camps had churches and many of the khans, among which was Hülagü, had Christian wives. This total reversal from the earlier situation made Christians believe that a golden age had dawned. To a certain extent this was indeed the case, and authors such as Gregory Bar 'Ebroyo (Barhebreaus), a Syrian Orthodox prelate (d. 1286) and 'Awdisho' bar Brikha, Church of the East Metropolitan of Nisibis (d. 1318), who both wrote in Syriac and Arabic, made use of this period of tranquillity to revitalize Christian Syriac scholarship, which had started to slow down in the eleventh century. Mar Yawalaha, a monk probably of Ongut descent from Mongol-occupied China, became Patriarch of the Church of the East between 1281 and 1317, and symbolized the good relationships between the Mongol rulers and the Christian Church.

This 'Syriac renaissance', however, was not to last very long, for soon the Mongols realized that Islam was too powerful a force to be disregarded if they wanted to stay in power in these western regions. The first Mongol khan to become a Muslim was Ahmad Teküdür (1282–4). His successor Argun returned to the earlier policy of religious pluralism and with the help of Yawalaha's right hand man, Rabban Sauma, requested the assistance of the West against the Muslim Mamlūks via the embassy of 1287/8, but after his death in 1291 his successors returned to Islam and gradually became less sympathetic to Christianity. The fourteenth century saw many ups and downs for the Christians in Mesopotamia and Persia, as well as the end of the communities in Central Asia and China, especially after the overturn of the Mongol Yuan dynasty by the Chinese Ming dynasty in 1368. At the end of the fourteenth century, Tamerlane's destructive campaigns dealt a final blow to many of the remaining Christian centres, especially in Persia and southern Mesopotamia. Although the political events of the fourteenth century may with some justification be seen as the main factor in the reduction of the Church of the East and the Syrian Orthodox Church to small minority churches, the enormous losses of this period can only be explained by the long period of weakening that had preceded it. The communities that survived the fourteenth century were the most traditional and the most isolated, that is, Aramaic-speaking and mainly concentrated in mountainous rural areas. In all likelihood, the communities that disappeared were more urbanized, Arabic- or Persian-speaking, and perhaps assimilated to the surrounding culture to a larger extent than their more traditional counterparts.

It was from these somewhat isolated and traditional communities that, towards the end of the fifteenth century, the Church of the East and the Syrian Orthodox Church slowly began to recover from the enormous losses of the fourteenth century. Churches and monasteries began to be restored and manuscripts were copied, to such an extent that the seventeenth and eighteenth centuries became a high point in Syriac manuscript production, especially in the Church of the East. Manuscript production was stimulated not only by relatively stable political and economic conditions, but also by the need to replace the earlier manuscript losses, many of these texts being of a liturgical nature and thus needed in everyday church life.

In the early sixteenth century northern Mesopotamia had become part of the Ottoman Empire, which after the fall of Constantinople in 1453 had grown into a new Islamic world power. The same general *dhimmi* rules were in force under Ottoman rule, and by the nineteenth century the *millet* system had grown into an intricate set of regulations. In general, as in earlier periods, the *millet* system guaranteed considerable self-rule for the Christian communities, provided that the heads of the *millets* were approved of by the Ottoman Porte and that poll taxes were paid in time. The Syrian Orthodox Church and the Church of the East, whose centres in eastern Anatolia and Mesopotamia were again far away from the political power that had moved to Istanbul, were for most of the Ottoman period not granted the status of a separate millet. They were represented at the Porte by the Armenian patriarch, although the patriarchs of both Syriac churches often did ask for Ottoman approval after being elevated to office.

In this period the relationship with the Roman Catholic Church, which had occupied church leaders during the crusades and the time of the early Mongols, again became an important political factor in both churches. In the middle of the sixteenth century, a group of clergy and lay people from the Church of the East asked for papal recognition of their candidate for the patriarchate, the monk Yuhannan Sulaqa, a move which might have been stimulated by earlier contacts between the Indian Church of the East and Portuguese missionaries. This confirmation was granted by Rome in 1553, albeit on the erroneous assumption that the patriarch in office, Shim'un VII Isho'yaw bar Mama of the Abuna family (1538/9–58), had died. Towards the end of the sixteenth century, Sulaqa's successors, who had been located in Diyarbakir and Seert, moved first to Persia, later to Hakkari (Qodshanis), and subsequently refrained from seeking papal recognition. In the seventeenth and eighteenth centuries, the traditional patriarchs of the Abuna family firmly established themselves in Rabban Hormizd near Alqosh (northern Iraq), and became the most influential patriarchate of the Church of the East. Towards the end of the seventeenth century, Capuchin missionaries became the prime agents in the conversion to Catholicism of the Bishop of Diyarbakir, who became the Chaldean patriarch Yosep I in 1681. In 1830 his line united itself with the patriarchate in Alqosh under Yuhannan Hormizd (1830–8) to become the Chaldean patriarchate. In the nineteenth century, French Dominican missionaries in Mosul contributed to the further strengthening of the Catholic Chaldean Church in northern Mesopotamia. In the meantime, the successors of Sulaqa in Qodshanis had reintroduced hereditary succession and carried the traditional patriarchal name Shimʿun. In the nineteenth and twentieth centuries, this patriarchate by a curious twist of church politics became the sole representative of traditional Church of the East leadership.

In the middle of the sixteenth century the Syrian Orthodox, too, initiated contacts with Rome. The contacts between Patriarch Ignatius ʿAbd-Allah and Pope Julius seem to have led to some kind of union. Ignatius' successors Niʿma-Allah and Dawud Shah tried to continue these contacts, but the former was accused of treason by the Ottomans and converted to Islam (later fleeing to Rome and returning to Christianity); the latter, probably also under Ottoman pressure, around 1580 declined to negotiate with a papal delegation in Mesopotamia. Almost a century later, in 1656, Bishop ʿAbdul-Ġal (later Andreas) Akhijan of Mardin converted to Catholicism under influence of Capuchin missionaries in the region, as had Yosep I. Despite formal recognition by the Ottoman authorities, this union lasted only till the death of his second successor in 1721. The most successful attempt at a union took place in 1783, when Michael Jarweh, Metropolitan of Aleppo, converted to Catholicism and was confirmed by Pope Pius VI as its first patriarch. He was supported by bishops from the Mardin region. Mardin remained the patriarchal see till 1888.

In the nineteenth century, Presbyterian and Congregationalist missionaries of the American Board of Commissioners for Foreign Missions (ABCFM) became active in the Middle East. In Iran, they were particularly successful among the Church of the East, by introducing a written language based on the spoken modern Aramaic language of the Urmia region. Later missions, among which the French Lazarists and the British Anglicans were the most important, also began printing in the vernacular and contributed to the general acceptance of this modern Aramaic language as the written language of educated men and women. Even though the American missionaries succeeded in establishing small Protestant congregations in Urmia among the followers of the Church of the East and in Ṭur ʿAbdin among the Syrian Orthodox, their contributions to the field of literacy and education proved to be more influential. Their network of primary schools, complemented by a number of high schools that later developed into colleges (Urmia, Kharput), spurred other missions and the Syriac Christians themselves into action as regards the field of education. These colleges grew into breeding grounds of young intellectuals from the different Christian minorities in Persia and in Turkey, among which the Armenians were very important. It is from these centres that nationalism, which had already started to influence Armenian intellectuals in Istanbul at an earlier date, became an important force among the Syriac communities.

Towards the end of the nineteenth century, however, circumstances in the Ottoman regions were not favourable to such types of nationalism. Political and military pressure from its powerful Eastern neighbour Russia, complemented by ongoing political pressure from European states that was aimed, among other things, at negotiating more rights for the Christian minorities, made the Ottomans very suspicious of any form of nationalism that could be explained as disloyalty to the Ottoman state. In the years 1894 to 1896 the first organized massacres of the Armenian population of Eastern Anatolia took place, because Armenians were suspected of supporting Christian Russia in its aims to occupy that region. In the First World War the Syrian communities, together with the Armenians, carried the heavy burden of the generally accepted idea that the Christians were disloyal to the Ottoman state. The Church of the East communities of Hakkari fled to Persia en masse, where those who survived the arduous trip and the attacks during the journey found temporary safety in the compounds of the American and French missions. In 1918, Turkish and Kurdish pressure made all Christians flee Urmia to British-occupied Baquba near Baghdad, losing many lives on the way. In northern Iraq, the Church of the East and the Chaldean Church had lived through the war relatively unharmed, being somewhat further away from the sensitive border regions with Russia. The Syrian Orthodox in Ṭur ʿAbdin and the larger eastern Anatolian region suffered greatly; many of the inhabitants of the Christian villages and small towns were massacred and many of those who tried to flee to the Syrian provinces did not survive the hardships of the road.

The horrors of this war gave the final impetus to a migration movement that had already started on a small scale at the end of the nineteenth century. Many Christians from the Syriac churches chose to leave the Middle East and find a new home elsewhere in the world, especially in the United States. Large Church of the East communities were formed in Chicago and in California, whereas Detroit became a centre of the Chaldean Church. Syrian Orthodox communities found homes in New Jersey and New England. France became another centre for Chaldeans from Iraq, whereas many Syrian Orthodox from Syria and Palestine settled in South America. In the second half of the twentieth century, Syrian Orthodox believers from Tur ʿAbdin and northern Syria moved to north-western Europe, to Germany, Sweden and the Netherlands, in combination with the labour migration of the early seventies and also because of an unstable political situation; later it was because conditions in Ṭur ʿAbdin worsened during the war between the Turkish army and the Kurdish PKK. The Arab–Israeli wars, the Lebanese Civil War and Gulf War of 1991 induced Syriac Christians from Israel, Lebanon and Iraq to find a home elsewhere in world: in the United States, in Australia and several European countries.

The Contemporary Situation in the Middle East and the Diaspora

Despite significant migration waves, until the early twenty-first century the majority of Syriac Christians (apart from those in India) lived in the Middle East. Of the Syrian Orthodox, about two-thirds live in the Middle East and one third in Europe and the

United States. As for the Church of the East, the balance is only slightly tilted in favour of the Middle Eastern communities: about 52 per cent in the Middle East, about 10 per cent in Russia, Armenia and Georgia and 38 per cent in North America, Europe and Australia. The Syrian Catholic Church has one diocese outside the Middle East, for the United States and Canada, whereas believers are also found in Europe and Australia. About one third of the members of the Chaldean Church live outside the Middle East, mainly in the United States and France.

The country with the largest number of Syriac Christians is Iraq. Together with smaller groups of Christians (among whom are Armenians, various Protestant and Pentecostal denominations as well as a Latin-rite Catholic Church), the total number of Christians in Iraq has been estimated at about 600,000, around 2.5 per cent of the population. Of these, the Chaldeans form the majority (about 200,000), followed by the Church of the East (115,000) and the Ancient Church of the East (43,000; this is a group that split off from the Church of the East in 1968, among other things over the introduction of the western calendar). The Syrian Orthodox and Syrian Catholic churches, which are about the same size, together number almost 100,000 members. For the Chaldean Church, Iraq always has been the geographical and political centre. Like his predecessors, the popular patriarch Raphael I Bidawid, in office 1989–2003, took up residence in Baghdad, as did his successor, Mar Emmanuel II Delly. In St Peter's Chaldean Seminary in Baghdad most of the Chaldean clergy receive their basic training. It is also the Chaldean Church, together with the Syrian Catholic and to a lesser extent the Syrian Orthodox Church, that has become the most Arabized church of the country. In the Church of the East, Aramaic has been retained to a large extent, not least because a large proportion of its membership lives in the north, where Arabic has less influence. Unfortunately, the Arabization of the Chaldean Church was consciously stimulated by the secularist and Arabic nationalist Baath regime, and encouraged the Chaldean leadership to associate themselves strongly with the regime of Saddam Hussein. The Church of the East in general was less involved here, and its members more likely to become involved in oppositional organizations such as the Assyrian Democratic Movement (ADM), which stressed its Assyrian, non-Arabic identity. Especially after the Gulf War of 1991, Assyrian parties such as ADM became important in semi-independent Kurdistan, whereas the majority of the Chaldean Church had to cope with an increasingly difficult situation in Iraq under Saddam Hussein. The overthrow of Saddam Hussein in 2003 stimulated leaders of both groups to overcome the at least partly artificial boundaries that had been caused by his regime. They started to speak of the 'Chaldo-Assyrians' rather than of Chaldeans and Assyrians. The Syrian Orthodox and Syrian Catholics, although often preferring the name 'Syriacs' for their group, usually accept the name 'Assyrians' as a general epithet for the larger group of Syriac Christians. Since the mid-1980s, the situation of the Christians in Iraq has significantly deteriorated; migration continues to deplete the communities of many of their well-educated members. The situation in post-Saddam Iraq is even less stable.

In Iran, Syriac Christians form a small group of fewer than 20,000 people within an already very small Christian minority, which constitutes less than 1 per cent of the total population. One seat in parliament is reserved for the 'Assyrians', a name that unites the members of the Church of the East and the Chaldeans ('Catholic Assyrians'). Although life in general is safe and Christians are allowed a certain amount of freedom in their religious practices, the Islamic constitution of the country does not allow Christians to occupy high governmental or military positions. Restrictions in business are in place, and the juridical system favours Muslims over religious minorities. Most Syriac Christians live in Tehran, but sizeable Church of the East and Chaldean communities are still found in Urmia, which in the nineteenth century was the centre of the Church of the East in Persia. During the First World War, many Assyrians of Iran fled north to what was then Russia. Besides a considerable Assyrian community in Moscow, the now independent countries of Georgia and Armenia have sizeable Assyrian communities, many of which have retained modern Aramaic as their language of communication. Some of these Christians officially belong to the Russian Orthodox Church, but the Church of the East also has parishes in these countries.

In Turkey, the Church of the East and the Chaldean Church have all but disappeared, although many of their village churches in Hakkari still stand today, and a refugee community in Istanbul was formed in the last decades of the twentieth century. The Syrian Orthodox Church is one of the few communities to have survived not only in the major cities, but also in its homeland Tur ʿAbdin. After the cease-fire between the PKK and the Turkish government in 1999, conditions for the Christians improved, leading not so much to a re-peopling of the ancient villages as to increasing numbers of Syrian Orthodox visitors from abroad in the summer months. These visitors add to the liveliness of the region, contribute to the maintenance of churches and monasteries, and morally support the small remaining Syrian Orthodox and Syrian Catholic communities.

In 1924, in the aftermath of the First World War, the patriarchate of the Syrian Orthodox Church was transferred to Syria, first to Homs, later to Damascus (1959). The latter city has become the centre of Syrian Orthodoxy worldwide, not only because of the new initiatives of Patriarch Ignatius Zakka I ʿIwas (from Iraq, in office since 1980) such as the new seminary in Maʿarat Saydnaya, not far from Damascus, but also because Syria has the largest community of Syrian Orthodox worldwide, about 170,000 people. A considerable number of these came from Tur ʿAbdin after the First World War, mostly settling in the north-eastern diocese of Jazira (in and around the towns Hassake and Qamishli) and in Aleppo. The latter city already had a strong Syrian Orthodox community dating back to the early days of Christianity, comparable to the Syrian Orthodox communities of the dioceses of Damascus and Homs in western Syria. The Jazira region also became the new country for the Assyrians who were driven from the Hakkari mountains in south-eastern Turkey in the First World War, thereby adding Syria to the places where a considerable Church of the East community is found (about 20,000). About 26,000 Syrian Catholics live in Syria, mainly in Aleppo and Damascus. At the time of writing, Syria and Jordan also provide shelter to Iraqi Christians who fled their country in 2003 and 2004.

The last country to be mentioned as an important place for Syriac Christianity is Lebanon. Apart from the Syriac roots of the Maronite Church and to a certain extent also of the Greek Orthodox Church, all Syriac churches have sizeable communities in this country, albeit mostly due to nineteenth- and twentieth-century migrations. Despite the fact that the Syrian Catholic community in Lebanon is smaller (with about 23,000 people) than those of Syria and Iraq, the country has become an important centre for the Syrian Catholic Church. Patriarch Ignatius Moussa Daoud, in office 1998–2001, succeeding Ignatius Antoine II Hayek, became Cardinal Prefect of the Congregation for the Oriental Churches in Rome. He was followed by Patriarch Ignatius Peter VIII, who resides in Beirut (Charfeh), where there is also a seminary.

Besides immigrant communities of Syriac churches in Egypt, Kuwait, Qatar and Jordan, the Syriac communities in Jerusalem and Bethlehem deserve to be mentioned separately. Although many of the present-day Syrian Orthodox are descended from recent migrations from Turkey, the Syrian Orthodox Church has a long history in both places, going back to early Christianity. The ongoing tension in the region has been especially hard on the Bethlehem community, most of whose members have left the country. St Mark's monastery in Jerusalem attracts visitors and pilgrims from all over the world, as does the Syrian Orthodox chapel in the Church of the Holy Sepulchre. The Church of the East no longer has a church or chapel in Jerusalem.

The Church of the East is the only church whose patriarchal see is no longer in the Middle East but in the diaspora. After years of exile in Cyprus and Great Britain, Mar Shim'un XXIII Eshay (1920–75) settled in the United States, around 1961. After his assassination in San Jose in 1975 (by another Assyrian, probably for (church) political reasons), his successor Mar Dinkha IV, who was the first to be canonically elected in 1976 after centuries of hereditary succession, moved the patriarchate to Chicago; from here he endeavoured to maintain good relations with all countries where Assyrians lived. The community in the United States and Canada, about a 100,000 people in 1996, is divided between California (San Jose, Modesto, Turlock) and the Chicago region. As mentioned above, the Syrian Orthodox and the Chaldean Church also have considerable communities in North America. In South America, especially in Brazil, Syrian Orthodox communities are found, most of these dating from the early twentieth century. In Australia, communities of Syriac churches were formed in the 1960s and 1970s, and were considerably strengthened by a migration wave after 1992.

The Syrian Orthodox communities in Europe, most of which were formed in the 1970s and 1980s, for the most part consist of Syrian Orthodox from Tur 'Abdin. The Mor Ephrem monastery and the Mart Maryam cathedral in Glanerbrug in the Netherlands developed into their European centre. Close to the German border, its extensive cemetery has become a popular site for burials of Syrian Orthodox believers from both countries, while its press, the Bar Hebraeus Verlag, caters for the needs of scholars, clergy and the faithful. Two other monasteries in Germany add to the spiritual vivacity of these diaspora communities, which consist of at least 50,000 people. Apart from smaller communities in Switzerland, Austria, Belgium and England, the community in Sweden is significant, consisting of about 40,000 people concentrated mainly in the southern Södertalje region. The Assyrian Church of the East is also present in Sweden, whereas smaller communities, most of which came into being after the Gulf War of 1991, are found in Germany and the Netherlands. Chaldeans from Turkey and Iraq had already migrated to Europe before that time, especially to France and Belgium.

In all four churches, leadership is basically in the hands of the patriarchate and the patriarchal administration, whether it is located in or outside the Middle East. However, the Synod of Bishops, in which the metropolitans and bishops of the diaspora dioceses become more and more influential, has important legislative powers in all churches, for instance in the appointment of bishops and the election of a new patriarch. In addition to the hierarchy, heads of families or larger groups play a significant role in the leadership of the community as a whole. The church leaders in particular are concerned about the ongoing migration, because in the diaspora the links with the Church tend to loosen while the communities in the Middle East become weaker.

Since about the mid-1990s, the possibilities of cheap and easily available means of international communication (mainly internet, but also increased access to the telephone and to air travel), have set off important changes within the Syriac communities worldwide. The increased exchange of news and ideas between the various diaspora communities and the churches in the Middle East fuelled the debates on ethnicity and denominational belonging, inducing members of all communities to explore the meaning of 'Assyrian', 'Syrian', 'Chaldean', 'Aramean', and 'Christian'. Until the late twentieth century, converging and diverging tendencies apparently balanced each other, but more recently the converging trends seem stronger. As already stated above, this is partly to be attributed to the situation in Iraq, where the 'Chaldo-Assyrian' group strives for a strong, united, Christian party, but this development apparently ties in with changes in the diaspora where young people from all these churches find each other at gatherings and meetings advertised under an 'Assyrian-Aramaic' flag.

Theology and Doctrine, Scripture and Tradition

Converging trends may also be detected in the fields of theology and doctrine. Here church leaders search for a common Christian, common Orthodox and common Syriac identity. Like the ethnic discussions, the theological dialogues were stimulated by the diaspora situation, where circumstances forced the faithful to cooperate with other churches. As early as 1971, the Syrian Orthodox Church signed a Common Christological Declaration with the Pope, which was reiterated in 1984. The Assyrian Church of the East reached a similar agreement in 1994, a high point in a dialogue that had started in 1984. These Christological declarations, apart from their general ecumenical significance, also allowed the faithful to take part in the other churches' celebrations of the Eucharist on special occasions. In 1994 the Pro Oriente dialogue was initiated, the 'Non-Official Consultation on Dialogue within the Syriac Tradition', building upon the earlier Vienna dialogue between the Oriental Orthodox Churches and Roman Catholic theologians, but now also including the Church of the East. In a series of six meetings up until March 2003, important themes, starting with the Christological debates of the fifth and sixth centuries, followed by the history of the Antiochene exegetical tradition in general, as well as the sacraments in the Syriac churches, were discussed with theologians and clergy of the churches of the Syriac tradition, together with a number of Roman Catholic scholars. These meetings not only added considerably to the mutual understanding within the Syriac tradition, but also fuelled a renewed interest in the theological heritage of these churches both among their own theologians and scholars from outside.

On 20 July 2001, the Chaldean Catholic Church and the Assyrian Church of the East signed a far-reaching agreement on mutual cooperation, not only on the level of the patriarchates, but also on the level of local dioceses and parishes. The leading clergy of both churches expressed the hope that their churches would increasingly work together, not least in the context of Iraq in the early twenty-first century. The Syrian Orthodox Church, like many other Orthodox churches, has been a member of the World Council of Churches since 1960, and in the context of its Faith and Order meetings the relationship between the Syrian Orthodox Church and the Eastern Orthodox Churches was also reconsidered. A number of theological consultations (between the Eastern and Oriental Orthodox churches in general) in 1991 led to agreements on mutual cooperation between the Eastern Orthodox Church of Antioch and the Syrian Orthodox Church.

The Church of the East participates in the WCC, despite opposition from some of the other Oriental Orthodox churches. This opposition, mainly from Coptic circles, has been particularly painful in the context of the Middle Eastern Council of Churches, which after long negotiations and debates in 1998 yielded to Oriental Orthodox opposition and declined membership to the Assyrian Church of the East. The Syrian Orthodox, the Syrian Catholic and the Chaldean Churches are full members of the MECC.

In the churches of the Syriac tradition, as in other Orthodox churches, women are not admitted to the priesthood. So far, no strong advocacy for such admittance is found within the churches themselves. However, the Syriac traditions have a long tradition of female involvement, especially through the office of the deaconesses. Although the position of deaconess almost disappeared during the second millennium, it has been mainly the Syrian Orthodox Church that has revived this office and encourages women, especially nuns and deaconesses, to be involved in teaching and missionary outreach. Deaconesses also play a liturgical role in the baptism of adult women. Women also often form part of the boards of local parishes, both in the diaspora and the Middle East. An interesting custom in the churches of the Syriac tradition is that of girls' alongside boys' choirs, giving young girls a visible role in the Sunday liturgy.

The Syriac churches are the proud possessors of a rich body of Christian literature, which has been faithfully transmitted through the centuries. Although scholarly research and chance discoveries have added to the traditional body of texts that was cherished within the Syriac churches, in general the scholarly view of Syriac literature through the ages is largely determined by the choices made by successive generations of church scribes and readers. Pending further research into the transmission of Syriac literature in the respective Syriac traditions, the most influential authors and texts within the Syriac churches are largely the same as the important authors that feature in the scholarly histories of Syriac literature.

Although the literary heritage of these churches is divided along denominational lines, some authors and texts are cherished in both traditions. The best example of an author dear to both churches is the fourth-century St Ephrem (d. 373; called Aprem in the Church of the East). To this day his hymns count as the standard for Syriac liturgical poetry, but they have also profoundly influenced the theological concepts of both churches. In various translations, Ephrem's hymns (including hymns later ascribed to him) have also had a lasting effect on Byzantine Orthodox traditions. In the late twentieth century his prose commentaries were rediscovered by Syriac theologians. Other early texts that have strongly influenced popular Christian imagination in all Syriac traditions are the many versions of saints' lives, some of which go back to the earliest days of Syriac Christianity.

Another important element of the common heritage of all Syriac traditions is the early Syriac Bible translation, the Peshitta. In all likelihood, the Old Testament Peshitta dates from the second and early third centuries, whereas most of the New Testament translation is supposed to have originated in the fourth and early fifth centuries. Before the 'separated' Gospel version of the New Testament Peshitta, Tatian's *Diatesseron* in Syriac was in common use, whereas an older Syriac translation of the separated Gospels is also known. From the earliest centuries, the study of scripture formed a characteristic element of the theological tradition of the Syriac churches, building upon the historically oriented exegetical methods of the Antiochene tradition, but also taking in elements of the Alexandrine allegorical readings. These range from works by Theodore of Mopsuestia and Cyril of Alexandria, translated from Greek in the period of the Christological debate, to thirteenth-century compound works such as the Gannat Bussame, 'Garden of Delights', in the Church of the East, and the work of Gregory Bar 'Ebroyo in the Syrian Orthodox Church and the Church of the East. These later collections are still used in the Syriac churches, in addition to texts by some of the earlier authors such as Jacob of Edessa (d. 708) and Dionysius Bar Salibi (d. 1171) in the Syrian Orthodox Church, and Isho'dad of Merw (ninth century) in the Church of the East. Today it is mainly within the context of the liturgy that scripture reading and reflection are part of the larger Syriac spirituality. Regular reading of the Bible (through the lectionaries of the Old Testament and the Acts of the Apostles, the Apostolic Letters, and the Gospels, respectively) make up an important part of the Sunday liturgies, as does the Psalter in the weekday services. In addition, homilies and hymns introduce the faithful to the possible interpretations of the text. As in most other Christian traditions, biblical stories play an important role in children's education.

One of the most interesting and so far underestimated sources for Syriac theology is the hymns. Ephrem and Narsai (d. 502/3), later authors such as Jacob of Sarug (d. 521) of the Syrian Orthodox Church and Giwargis Warda of Arbela and Khamis bar Qardahe (both thirteenth century) of the Church of the East, have enriched Syriac theology by their large variety of hymns, many of which were included in the liturgy. In the Ottoman period, when theological reflection was at a low ebb, East Syrian authors such as 'Attaya bar Athli (sixteenth century), Sulaqa's successor patriarch 'Abdisho' of Gazarta (d. 1571), and the priests Israel of Alqosh and Yosep of Telkepe (seventeenth century) continued to write hymns, thus transmitting the classical heritage to future generations. Today, too, many theologians (including patriarchs and bishops) find hymns the most appropriate way of expressing and elucidating the mysteries of the faith.

Of the authors who continue to influence Syrian Orthodox theology, the names of Severus of Antioch (d. 538), Philoxenus of Mabbug (d. 523), Moses bar Kepha (d. 903), and Michael the Great (d. 1199) should be mentioned, alongside the already mentioned Jacob of Sarug, Jacob of Edessa, and Gregory Bar 'Ebroyo. In the Church of the East, a similar list would include the works of Bawai the Great (d. 628), Eliya of Anbar (tenth century), Yohannan bar Zo'bi (thirteenth century), and the already mentioned Isho'dad of Merw and 'Abdisho' bar Brikha of Nisibis. 'Abdisho''s extensive works summarized the East Syrian theology and canonical history of his day and have not been surpassed. The early works by Theodore of Mopsuestia have also been rediscovered by theologians of the Church of the East. Within the Chaldean Church the heritage of authors writing in Arabic has been better preserved. This applies not only to the works of the Chaldean patriarch Yosep II of Telkepe (d. 1712), perhaps the first 'modern' theologian of the Syriac churches, but also to earlier works such as those of Eliya bar Sinnaya of Nisibis (975–1094) and Abu al-Faraj ibn al-Tayyib (d. 1043). The Syrian Orthodox philosopher Yaḥyā ibn 'Adī (d. 974), remains one of the most popular Arabic Christian authors. At several places in the Middle East, the Arabic and Syriac theological heritage is given serious attention in series and journals, such as *Al-Turāth al 'Arabī al-Masīhī* in Aleppo, the *Journal of the Syriac Academy* in Baghdad, and in the work published by the Centre for Arab-Christian Documentation and Research in Beirut.

Theological education and training takes place in a number of institutions in the Middle East, for instance in the Syrian Orthodox Seminary in Ma'arat Saydnaya (Syria) and the Chaldean Patriarchal Seminary in Baghdad. In addition, universities and seminaries in Lebanon cater for students of different Syriac denominations. Many students go to the West for advanced training. Rome is one of the most popular destinations, but Syriac students can be found at most institutions that have a specialist in Syriac or Christian Arabic studies, for example, in Washington DC and Oxford as well as several universities in Germany and the Netherlands.

The Life of the Church: Liturgy, Monasticism, Church Buildings, Pilgrimage

As in all Orthodox churches, the spiritual and theological life of the Syriac churches is centred on the liturgy. Although the two main liturgical traditions, i.e., that of the Church of the East ('the Persian' or 'East-Syrian' rite) and of the Syrian Orthodox Church (the 'West-Syrian' rite) have different origins and different focuses, they both represent ancient liturgical traditions that in form and content go back to the early days of Christianity. The Eucharistic rite of the Church of the East probably contains the most ancient elements, owing to the relative isolation of this church since its origins; it probably began in the Edessa or Nisibis region. The West Syrian rite is based on an Antiochene model, with influences from the Jerusalem rite. The Catholic counterparts of both churches have generally kept to their ancient rites and have not accepted a large amount of Latinization. Over the course of time, the rites have retained their basic forms, albeit variously adapted and added on by clerical authors.

In Syriac spirituality, the church buildings play an important role. These buildings reflect the Orthodox conception of the church as a representation of the whole cosmos, of heaven and earth, heaven being symbolized by the sanctuary (*madbha*, altar), the earth by the nave (*haykla*, temple) of the church, the two parts separated from each other by the choir. The oldest and often very beautiful examples of Syriac churches today are found in Tur ʿAbdin, in Hah, in Nusaybin (Nisibis), and in the monasteries of Mor Gabriel and Dayr az-Zaʿfaran, which date from the sixth and seventh centuries. Not many church buildings of the Church of the East have survived the Mongol ravages, although many of those in northern Iraq and western Iran were probably built on earlier foundations. Most of these churches are simple one-nave structures, without any adornments. In Mosul and its surroundings some of the churches are larger and more extensively decorated; the best-preserved monastery is that of Rabban Hormizd near Alqosh.

The Syriac tradition has not allowed icons to have the same central function as in the Byzantine tradition, although in the nineteenth and twentieth centuries many icons and religious paintings found their way into Syriac churches. There are several indications that even the Church of the East, sometimes portrayed as staunchly anti-images, allowed pictures or statues in its churches in the Middle Ages. In the Syrian Orthodox Church, the equivalent of the iconostasis is a curtain that at certain moments of the Eucharistic liturgy is closed, whereas in the Church of the East the larger part of the sanctuary is often hidden behind a stone wall.

The Syriac churches have a long monastic history, during which monasteries were the prime guardians of the literary and theological tradition. A rich monastic literature was developed out of Greek, Egyptian and Mesopotamian influences, in which the boundary between the Church of the East and the Syrian Orthodox Church was easily crossed. Up till the eighth century, eastern authors were particularly productive, although little of their work survived within the Church of the East. In the thirteenth century, Muslim mystical traditions influenced authors such as Gregory Bar ʿEbroyo, whose works were appreciated in both churches and remained in circulation up till the present day.

In the seventeenth and eighteenth centuries, monasticism declined and especially in the Church of the East, scribal traditions were taken over by the priestly families of the villages of northern Mesopotamia. In the nineteenth century, the influence of Roman Catholic missions led to a revival of monasticism, this time based on western models such as the community in the monastery of Notre Dames des Semences, built in 1861 near the old Rabban Hormizd. The monasteries of the Syrian Orthodox Church in Tur ʿAbdin were never completely deserted and have become important centres of pilgrimage and learning for Syrian Orthodox believers from all over the world. In addition, Syrian Orthodox monasteries in Europe, such as the Mor Ephrem monastery in Glanerbrug, cater for the spiritual and educational needs of the diaspora.

Pilgrimage plays an important role for members of all Syriac churches. The most important of these is the pilgrimage to Jerusalem, which throughout history was undertaken by members of all churches involved. It entitles the pilgrim to the epithet of *maqdshaya* (Syriac) or *maqdasi* (Arabic), 'holy one', often indicated by a cross tattooed on arm or hand; pilgrimages to a variety of other holy sites are popular. Such pilgrimages might consist of individual travel to some of the famous monasteries or churches of the tradition, but more often takes the form of visiting specific local monasteries or churches on the feast day, the *dukhrana*, of its saint. At such gatherings Holy Liturgy is celebrated or individual prayers at the shrine are said, and are followed by a communal meal and often by traditional dancing. These *shahra-s*, as they are called, are important communal gatherings where old friends and family meet and new ties are forged through friendship and courtship.

A large number of saints are venerated in the Syriac tradition; some of the most popular are Mar Giwargis (St George), Mar Sargis and Mart Shmuni (the mother of the seven Maccabee sons). Their stories are collected in a large variety of saints' lives and extolled in well-known hymns, which still play a role in popular Christian imagination, especially in connection to pilgrimage sites. The veneration of the Virgin Mary occupies a special position in all churches. This is partly due to strong Roman Catholic influence in the nineteenth and twentieth centuries, which introduced western Marian customs to the Middle Eastern churches (for instance women wearing blue clothing in May), but also to the fact that these influences fell on the fruitful soil of a long Syriac tradition, already attested in Ephrem's poetry, of venerating Mary as the ultimate symbol of the multifaceted and intense relationship of the Church with Christ. Note that, contrary to common opinion, the Church of the East's consistent rejection of the title 'Mother of God' never prevented its theologians and believers from honouring her in the same way as the other churches of the Syriac tradition.

As in many other traditions, popular religion also comprises what is often described as 'magic'. In the Syriac churches, especially those in Mesopotamia, priests wrote miniature scrolls with protective prayers, which were then sewn into clothing or stored away in the house. A large variety of such texts have been transmitted, suggesting a sophisticated system in which certain evils, including all kinds of diseases and disabilities, required particular prayers. The basis of a particular charm is usually formed by familiar prayers such as the Lord's Prayer, in addition to which saints such as Mar Giwargis and Mar Sargis are often invoked. In many cases the curses and distinctive phrases reflect pre-Christian Mesopotamian models. The scrolls are often adorned with simple pictures. The influence of western missionaries in the nineteenth century caused these scrolls to disappear from the foreground, although rites and amulets of protection have survived in different ways until the present day.

Conclusion

One of the most striking characteristics of the Syriac churches today is a strong sense of urgency about their identity and long-term survival. Under pressure from subtle discrimination to downright hostility from radical Islamists in the Middle East and various forms of assimilation in the diaspora, both lay and clerical leaders look for ways to sustain and create a strong common identity. Such a common 'ethnic' identity is usually found in the shared Syriac tradition of language, culture, history and religion, in comparison to which earlier dogmatic, social and political differences are downplayed. Whether such a common identity, provided it successfully includes those who cherish the traditional ties of belief and community, will also be able to form an effective barrier against political and social pressure in the Middle East and assimilation in the diaspora, will primarily depend on how well the Syriac communities in Syria and Iraq are maintained and strengthened.

Further reading

Mar Aprem Mooken (2000) *The Assyrian Church of the East in the Twentieth Century.* Moran Etho 18. Kottayam: St Ephrem Ecumenical Research Institute.

Baum, W. and Winkler, D. W. (2003) *The Church of the East: A Concise History.* London and New York: Routledge Curzon.

Baumer, C. (2006) *The Church of the East: An Illustrated History of Assyrian Christianity.* London: I. B. Tauris.

Brock, S. (1996) The 'Nestorian' Church: a lamentable misnomer. *Bulletin of the John Rylands University Library of Manchester* 78(3): 23–36.

—— (1997) *A Brief Outline of Syriac Literature.* Moran Etho 9. Kottayam: St Ephrem Ecumenical Research Institute.

Brock, S. et al. (2001) *The Hidden Pearl: The Aramaic Heritage* (3 vols and video). Trans World Film, Italy.

Chaillot, C. (1998) *The Syrian Orthodox Church of Antioch and All the East: A Brief Introduction to its Life and Spirituality.* Geneva: Inter-Orthodox Dialogue.

Coakley, J. F. (1996) The Church of the East since 1914. *Bulletin of the John Rylands University Library of Manchester* 78: 179–98.

Coakley, J. F. and Parry, K. (eds.) (1996) The Church of the East: life and thought. *Bulletin of the John Rylands University Library of Manchester* 78(3).

Gillman, I. and Klimkeit, H.-J. (1999) *Christians in Asia before 1500,* Ann Arbor: University of Michigan Press.

Joseph, J., (1983) *Muslim–Christian Relations and Inter-Christian Rivalries in the Middle East: The Case of the Jacobites in an Age of Transition.* Albany: State University of New York Press.

—— (2000) *The Modern Assyrians of the Middle East: Encounters with Western Christian Missions, Archaeologists, and Colonial Powers.* Studies in Christian Mission 26. Leiden: Brill.

Kaufhold, H. (ed.) (2007) *Kleines Lexikon des Christlichen Orients.* Wiesbaden: Harrassowitz.

Le Coz, R. (1995) *Église d'Orient: Chrétiens d'Irak, d'Iran et de Turquie.* Paris: Éditions du Cerf.

Masters, B. (2001) *Christians and Jews in the Ottoman Arab World.* Cambridge: Cambridge University Press.

Pro Oriente Foundation (1994) *Syriac Dialogue. First Non-Official Consultation on Dialogue within the Syriac Tradition*, vol. 1. Vienna. See also vol. 2, 1996; vol. 3, 1998; vol. 4, 2001; vol. 5, 2003.

Sélis, Claude (1988) *Les Syriens orthodoxies et catholiques*. Fils d'Abraham Turnhout: Éditions Brepols.

CHAPTER 13

Eastern Christianity in the United States

Thomas FitzGerald

Eastern Orthodox Churches

The Alaskan Mission

Two significant events led to the establishment of Eastern Orthodox Christianity in the United States. Firstly, monastic missionaries from the Church of Russia established missions in Alaska, beginning in 1794. At that time, the Alaskan coastland and the numerous islands between North America and Siberia, discovered and explored from 1741, was part of imperial Russia. During the first century of the existence of these missions, many thousands of natives became members of the Orthodox Church. The Alaskan Mission was one of the largest and most significant missionary endeavours sanctioned by the Church of Russia during the eighteenth and nineteenth centuries.

During this period, two missionaries were especially significant. With little formal education and without priestly orders, the monk Herman (1760–1837) came to exemplify the best qualities of the early missionaries on Kodiak Island. During his forty years of missionary work, Herman instructed the natives both about Christianity and about agricultural techniques. He staunchly defended the rights of the natives in the face of exploitation and, because of this, was twice exiled by Russian merchants to Spruce Island, which became his home. Within a few decades of his death in 1837, the natives had begun to honour him as a saint. They collected stories about his service and recorded the miracles attributed to his intercession. His formal canonization took place in 1970.

Fr. John Veniaminov (1797–1879) and his family arrived on the island of Unalaska in 1824. As part of his missionary work, the young priest created an Aleut alphabet, basing it on Cyrillic characters. A dictionary and grammar soon followed. These provided the basis for a translation of the Gospel of St Matthew and portions of the liturgy. He wrote a basic catechism entitled 'Indication of the Pathway into the Kingdom'. He also taught the natives agricultural techniques, carpentry and metalworking. During ten years on Unalaska, Fr. John constructed a school, an orphanage, and a number of chapels. Moving to New Archangel (Sitka) in 1934, he continued his remarkable missionary work among the Tlingits, who were generally hostile to the Russian merchants. Fr. John also travelled to other missionary outposts. He visited Fort Rus in Northern California in 1836 and also a number of Roman Catholic missions in the region. After the death of his wife, the devoted missionary became a monk, taking the name 'Innocent'. He subsequently was elected a bishop, in 1840. With his return to New Archangel, a new period of missionary activity developed. Innocent was elected Metropolitan of Moscow in 1868 and established the Russian Orthodox Missionary Society before his death in 1879. He was canonized in 1977 and given the title 'Apostle to America'.

Imperial Russia sold Alaska to the United States in 1867. After the sale most Russians returned to their homeland or travelled south to San Francisco, where there was a sizeable Russian colony. The Church of Russia's interest in the mission declined. When a new diocese of Alaska and the Aleutian Islands was established in 1870, the see of the bishop was moved to San Francisco. Both the diocese and the see were now outside the Russian Empire and beyond the canonical jurisdiction of the Church of Russia. Few competent clergy remained in Alaska to care for the faithful, who numbered over 10,000. Moreover, the sale opened the Alaskan territory to Protestant missionaries. With little appreciation of the Orthodox Church, they proselytized among the native Orthodox and showed little regard for their culture. The Orthodox Church, however, continued to maintain a weakened presence in the Alaskan territory and the mission continued to influence the subsequent development of Orthodoxy in the United States.

Immigration and church development

The second significant factor to contribute to the foundation of the Orthodox Church in the United States was the waves of Orthodox immigrants entering the country from the late nineteenth century through the early twentieth century. Arriving from Greece, Asia Minor, Russia, the Balkans and the Middle East, these immigrants established parishes and constructed church buildings. A number of the earliest parishes began as pan-Orthodox communities containing immigrants from various ethnic backgrounds. Among these parishes were those in New Orleans (1864), San Francisco (1868) and New York City (1870). There, a notable attempt to expose Orthodox Christianity to the wider society in New York was undertaken by Fr. Nicholas Bjerring (1831–84). Between 1879 and 1881, his journal, the *Oriental Church Magazine*, published essays on Orthodox teachings and liturgical texts in English. As the number of Orthodox immigrants increased, however, these early parishes and most subsequent parishes began to serve particular ethnic groups. Orthodox parishes serving Greek, Carpatho-Russian, Arab, Romanian, Serbian, Albanian, Bulgarian, and Ukrainian immigrants developed in various parts of the country. Since many immigrants intended to return to their homeland some day, the parishes became centres in which not only the faith was preserved but also the language and customs of the old country were maintained. There was little contact between these parishes and little sense of mission beyond the needs of a particular group.

As the centre of their religious and cultural life in a new country, these parishes were usually established with very little direction from church authorities. Most parishes serving Slavic immigrants became associated with the Russian Orthodox diocese in San Francisco. These were joined initially by some parishes serving Arab, Albanian and Romanian immigrants. The Russian Orthodox diocesan see was moved to New York in 1905 under Archbishop Tikhon Bellavin (1865–1925), later Patriarch of Moscow. The move was occasioned by the rapid increase of parishes in the eastern United States. This resulted primarily from the entrance into Orthodoxy of about fifty Carpatho-Russian parishes and their clergy who had been Eastern Catholics. The basis for this movement was the refusal of local Roman Catholic bishops and priests to honour the Eastern Catholic traditions, particularly the married priesthood. This movement to Orthodoxy was led by Fr. Alexis Toth (1853–1909). Archbishop Tikhon subsequently presented a plan to the Church of Russia in 1905 which envisioned a unified Church in America under its jurisdiction.

The largest group of Orthodox immigrants in this period was the Greek. By the year 1920, there were about 300,000 Greek immigrants in the United States, organized into about 135 parishes. With few exceptions, these parishes in the early years sought to maintain some connection with dioceses of the Church of Greece or the Ecumenical Patriarchate of Constantinople. Many of these early Greek immigrants saw themselves as temporary residents in the United States and kept in close contact with families back home.

From the early decades of the century, the Patriarchate of Constantinople affirmed its responsibility for all Orthodox living in America. However, because of the acute difficulties that the patriarchate experienced throughout the nineteenth and early twentieth centuries, it was not in a position to assert its prerogatives or to exercise its ministry adequately in America. So Orthodox ecclesiastical life in the United States developed during this period with very little hierarchical supervision and not always in harmony with accepted practices. Patriarch Meletios (Metaxakis) (1871–1935) envisioned a united Orthodox Church in the United States in his enthronement address in 1922. It was in the same year that the patriarchate established the Greek Orthodox Archdiocese of North and South America as a canonical province. However, the Greek Orthodox parishes were deeply divided in the 1920s and 1930s because of differences between Royalists and Republicans in Greece. Between 1931 and 1948, Archbishop Athenagoras Spirou (1886–1972), later Patriarch of Constantinople, did much to heal these divisions and to unify the archdiocese. Faced with the specific pastoral needs of the Greek immigrants and with the divisions among them at this time, however, the Patriarchate of Constantinople and its archdiocese could do little to widen its embrace to include all Orthodox faithful in the Americas.

Further diocesan developments soon took place. After the Bolshevik revolution of 1917, the Russian Orthodox Archdiocese in the United States was thrown into chaos as a result of the political and religious turmoil in Russia. By the year 1933, there were at least four major Russian Orthodox jurisdictions in the United States. The largest was the 'Russian Orthodox Greek Catholic Church' or 'Metropolia', which had declared itself temporarily independent from the Church of Russia in 1924. Its authority was challenged by a small number of clergy and laity associated with the 'Living Church' movement which lasted from 1922 to 1943. By the year 1927, a diocese of the 'Russian Orthodox Church Abroad' was established; it served Russian immigrants with monarchist sympathies who refused to acknowledge the official leadership of the Church of Russia in the period after Patriarch Tikhon. Repudiating both these jurisdictions, the beleaguered Church of Russia, headed by Metropolitan Sergius, established an exarchate in the United States in 1933. Each of these four rival jurisdictions claimed to be the historic continuation of the Alaskan Mission and each expressed very different attitudes toward the Church of Russia and the Communist regime.

In response to the high level of immigration in the early twentieth century, and the unsupervised growth of parishes, other autocephalous Orthodox churches wanted to create dioceses in the United States to serve their faithful. Dioceses were established by the churches of Serbia in 1921, Romania in 1930, Albania in 1932, Antioch in 1936 and Bulgaria in 1938. The Ecumenical Patriarchate also established dioceses for the Ukrainians in 1937, the Carpatho-Russians in 1938 and the Albanians in 1949. Moreover, the animosities and politics of the immigrants frequently led to the creation of other dioceses which were not under the jurisdiction of any autocephalous church. With each wave of immigration, the disputes of the Old World frequently manifested themselves in the ecclesiastical life of the Orthodox in America. While claiming to be united in faith, the Orthodox were fractured into numerous diocesan jurisdictions. Most had an Old World orientation and served a particular ethnic population. While most were related to a particular Mother Church, others were not. Some followed the revised Julian calendar and others the old Julian calendar. By the year 1933, there were no less than fifteen separate diocesan jurisdictions serving particular ethnic communities and often reflecting political perspectives related to the old homeland. There were at this time about 300 Orthodox parishes in the United States, serving nearly half a million faithful.

From the perspective of Orthodox ecclesiology, the proliferation of parallel and often competing jurisdictions on the same geographical territory was a serious anomaly. The establishment of 'ethnic' and even 'political' dioceses rather than territorial dioceses may have served the short-term needs of the immigrants. However, the ecclesiastical requirements for canonical order, integrity, and the unity of the episcopacy in a given region were sacrificed. This led to an undue emphasis upon a polity of congregationalism at the parish level and encouraged an attitude of phyletism and parochialism in church life. Uncanonical priests and renegade parishes were not uncommon. These harsh facts greatly diminished the mission and message of the Orthodox Church in the United States, especially throughout the first half of the twentieth century.

Steps towards cooperation and greater unity

Confronted with the divisions both within and beyond their flocks, Archbishop Athenagoras and Archbishop Antony (Bashir) (1898–1966) of the Syrian (Antiochian) Orthodox Archdiocese recognized the need for greater jurisdictional cooperation.

Antony in particular advocated the greater use of English in liturgical services and envisioned a more united church in the United States. Together with Antony, Athenagoras made a bold proposal for a pan-Orthodox seminary in 1934 and for a pan-Orthodox journal in 1941. Divisions among the Russian jurisdictions prevented common action on these. However, the 'Federated Orthodox Greek Catholic Primary Jurisdictions in America' was established in 1943. This was a voluntary association of the primates of the six jurisdictions that were associated with one of the patriarchates. Dedicated to increasing harmony and cooperation, the federation did much in its few years of existence to achieve greater recognition of the Orthodox Church, especially by governmental agencies. However, the largest of the Russian jurisdictions, the Russian Orthodox Metropolia, was not in communion with its patriarchate, and so was not a member of the federation. Its absence was a major weakness in it, and by 1949 the federation had ceased to function.

The decades following the Second World War were an important period of transition for the Orthodox in the United States. Most importantly, the demographics were changing. There was a notable decrease in immigration of Orthodox especially after the 1920s. This meant that the composition of most parishes was rapidly changing and they were losing their immigrant character. At the same time, new parishes were being established in the suburbs beyond the traditional centre of immigrant life in the inner cities. The majority of the parishioners were born and educated in America. They were less in contact with the politics and issues of the land of their grandparents. These people were more frequently marrying beyond their ethnic communities. There was also a gradual increase of marriages between Orthodox and Roman Catholics or Protestants. In addition, people coming from other religious traditions were beginning to embrace the Orthodox Church and its teachings. This movement would increase as time went on. Many parishes were led by clergy educated at the Holy Cross Greek Orthodox School of Theology (1937) near Boston, at St Tikhon's Seminary (1938) near Scranton, Pennsylvania or at St Vladimir's Orthodox Theological School (1938) in New York.

These developments were reflected in the gradual increase of pan-Orthodox endeavours. Orthodox from various jurisdictions began to recognize that they shared not only the same faith but also the same challenges and obligations within the American society. They began to establish a number of avenues of cooperation, especially in the areas of retreat work, religious education and campus ministry. New catechetical materials in the English language were prepared. English translations of liturgical texts were made. In addition, there was growing use of English in the liturgy and other services. Bringing together clergy and laity of a number of jurisdictions, joint liturgical services began to become more common in large cities, especially on the first Sunday of Great Lent, celebrated as the Sunday of Orthodoxy. In some cities, pan-Orthodox clergy associations and councils of churches were established. These endeavours were led by clergy and laity chiefly from the three largest jurisdictions: the Greek Orthodox Archdiocese, the Syrian (Antiochian) Orthodox Archdiocese and the Russian Orthodox Metropolia. All of these were important signs that Orthodoxy in America had entered into a new phase of its development.

There were growing pains. In some jurisdictions, new tensions developed. Those who viewed the Church chiefly as the preserver of a particular ethnic identity, political perspective, or language were troubled by these developments and the tendency toward greater cooperation. Others emphasized the importance of maintaining links with the mother churches and were troubled by the possibility of a united Church in the United States. Indeed, new divisions developed as new Orthodox immigrants arrived fleeing political changes in the Balkans. Opposing the Communist government and the Church in the homeland, rival dioceses developed among the Romanians in 1951, the Bulgarians in 1947, the Ukrainians in 1950 and 1954, and the Serbs in 1963. The larger jurisdictions, however, continued on a trajectory which recognized the growing American identity of its faithful and the Church's responsibilities in the United States.

The Standing Conference

The movement towards greater cooperation and unity among the Orthodox jurisdictions found renewed expression in the establishment of the Standing Conference of Canonical Orthodox Bishops in America (SCOBA) in 1960. Under the leadership of Archbishop Iakovos (1911–2005) of the Greek Orthodox Archdiocese, SCOBA initially brought together the representatives of eleven jurisdictions. Although SCOBA remained a conference and not a formal synod, many came to view SCOBA as a first step towards greater administrative and ministerial unity. Unlike the Federation, SCOBA included the Russian Orthodox Metropolia as well as the Moscow Patriarchal Exarchate. From the beginning, the Russian Orthodox Church Outside of Russia (the Synod Abroad) refused to cooperate, citing its opposition to those who recognized the leadership of the Church of Russia. Building upon the earlier experience of the federation, SCOBA immediately began to coordinate the various national pan-Orthodox activities that had begun in the previous decades. This included programmes related to religious education and campus ministry. SCOBA supported the establishment of the Orthodox Theological Society in 1965, an important body bringing together theologians from most jurisdictions. SCOBA also took responsibility for establishing formal bilateral theological dialogues with the Episcopal Church (1962), the Roman Catholic Church (1965), the Lutheran Church (1968), and the Reformed Churches (1968). The activities of the SCOBA jurisdictions, especially their ecumenical witness, were consistently opposed by the Russian Orthodox Church Outside of Russia, centred in the United States since 1950, and by a number of other small parishes and groups which championed the 'old calendar' but which were not in communion with any autocephalous Church.

The initial achievements of SCOBA occurred at a time with the Orthodox churches at the global level were also engaged in a process of renewed conciliarity. Between 1964 and 1968, four pan-Orthodox Conferences took place and began to address issues affecting all the autocephalous Orthodox Churches. These meetings led to the establishment of a conciliar process designed to prepare for the convocation of the Great and Holy Council. Among the topics which deserved attention by the Churches was the so-called diaspora, the developing Church in America, western Europe and elsewhere. In light of these developments, the bishops of SCOBA in 1965 proposed to the autocephalous churches that it be recognized as an Episcopal Synod, having full authority to govern the life of the Church in America within the jurisdiction of the Ecumenical Patriarchate. A similar proposal was made in 1968 with the request that the American situation be placed on the agenda of the global pan-Orthodox Conferences. While no direct action was immediately taken by the autocephalous churches, the appeals of SCOBA indicated that the situation in the United States could not be long ignored.

The conciliar process both in America and at the global level was shaken in 1970 when the Patriarchate of Moscow granted autocephaly, self-governing status, to the Russian Orthodox Metropolia, then led by Metropolitan Ireney (Bekish) (1892–1978). From that time, the Metropolia has been officially known as the Orthodox Church in America (OCA). This unprecedented action regularized the formal relationship between the Metropolia and the Church of Russia, which had been lost in 1924. However, the autocephalous status of the OCA was not recognized by the Ecumenical Patriarchate and most of the other autocephalous churches. The disputed status of the OCA, led by Metropolitan Theodosius (Lazar) (b. 1933) from 1978 to 2002, immediately increased tensions among the jurisdictions in the United States. It also led to new discussions related to the presence of Orthodoxy in the United States of America and the meaning of autocephaly. While not recognizing the autocephaly of the OCA, the Ecumenical Patriarchate determined to cooperate with it in the hope of encouraging a more comprehensive resolution for America. Moreover, in 1975, the Patriarchate of Antioch unified its two diocesan jurisdictions dating from 1936 under Metropolitan Philip Salibia (b. 1931) in the newly designated Antiochian Orthodox Christian Archdiocese. He frequently joined Metropolitan Theodosius in calling for greater unity.

Throughout the early 1970s, the Ecumenical Patriarchate initiated a number of discussions on the themes of the preconciliar process. A new list of ten topics for study was agreed upon by the representatives of the autocephalous churches in 1976. This list included the topics of the diaspora and autocephaly. After dealing with a number of other topics, the theme of the diaspora was examined in meetings of the Pre-Conciliar Conference in 1990 and 1993. In light of these discussions, a historic meeting of 29 Orthodox bishops was held in 1994. This meeting produced significant statements: 'The Church in North America' and 'Unity, Mission and Evangelism'. Both of these texts emphasized the importance of Orthodox unity and witness in America. The meeting also proposed that all the bishops meet regularly to discuss issues of common concern. Another meeting was held in 2000 with about 40 bishops present. Between these meetings, in 1995, the Ecumenical Patriarchate agreed to regularize and receive a number of Ukrainian Orthodox bishops, clergy and parishes. The historic visits to the United States of Ecumenical Patriarch Demetrios in 1990 and Ecumenical Patriarch Bartholomew in 1998 both reaffirmed the responsibility of the patriarchate for America and placed emphasis upon the need for greater canonical unity.

At the beginning of the twenty-first century, the SCOBA member jurisdictions are: the Albanian Orthodox Diocese (Bishop Ilia), the American Carpatho-Russian Orthodox Diocese (Metropolitan Nicholas), the Antiochian Orthodox Christian Archdiocese (Metropolitan Philip), the Bulgarian Eastern Orthodox Church (Metropolitan Joseph), the Greek Orthodox Archdiocese (Archbishop Demetrios), the Orthodox Church in

America (Metropolitan Herman), the Romanian Orthodox Archdiocese (Metropolitan Nicolae), the Serbian Orthodox Church (Metropolitan Christopher), the Ukrainian Orthodox Church (Metropolitan Constantine).

In addition to the SCOBA jurisdictions, there are a few dioceses and groups of parishes which use the term 'Orthodox' in their title. Some of these claim to profess the historic Orthodox faith but are not in communion with any autocephalous church. With its headquarters in New York since 1950, the Russian Orthodox Church Outside of Russia is in this category. There are some parishes serving primarily Greek immigrants who are ardent supporters of the 'old calendar' and who repudiate the activities of the SCOBA jurisdictions, especially their ecumenical witness. Such groups are viewed as schismatic since they are not in communion with any autocephalous church. Finally, there are also some groups and parishes which use the term 'Orthodox' in their title but whose relationship with the historic Orthodox Church is non-existent.

SCOBA continues to be an important body serving Orthodox cooperation and unity under the leadership of Archbishop Demetrios (b. 1928), the Exarch of the Ecumenical Patriarchate and primate of the Greek Orthodox Archdiocese. The primates of the nine jurisdictions meet twice a year. With membership including clergy and laity, twelve SCOBA commissions deal with pan-Orthodox matters related to topics such as ecumenism, religious education, youth ministry, missions, and international charities. SCOBA established a formal dialogue with Roman Catholic bishops in 1981. In 2000, it began a dialogue with Oriental Orthodox Churches. On the occasion of the new millennium, the bishops issued a historic pastoral letter titled 'And the Word became flesh and dwelt among us' which spoke about the responsibilities of the Church and the Orthodox Christian in contemporary society.

The challenges which the Orthodox face in the United States are great and serious. The ongoing division of Orthodoxy into separate jurisdictions continues to weaken its mission and witness. Within most of the jurisdictions, the process of acculturation has not always been easy. In many of them there are some who continue to view the Church chiefly as the preserver of ethnic identity. As some of the jurisdictions move beyond their reliance upon ethnic loyalties, however, they are obliged to speak more clearly about the distinctive features of the Orthodox Christian faith within a religiously pluralistic society. They must express the faith in terms which are understandable and develop ministries which respond to the spiritual needs of people living in this complex society. Within this society, the Orthodox need to distinguish between Old World cultural practices and perspectives that are not essential to the faith and those affirmations that lie at the heart of the faith. In emphasizing the importance of worship, the proper role of the laity in the liturgical life of the church, as well as in the philanthropic and administrative function, needs to be strengthened. This means that a new spirit of mission must be cultivated and that the proper relationship between clergy and laity must be expressed at all levels of Church life. In addition, the role of women and their contribution to the Church needs to be better acknowledged. With its profound belief in the loving Triune God and the theocentric nature of the human person, Orthodox Christianity has much to offer American society and contemporary Christianity in America. Yet, this offering can be made only if the Orthodox take seriously their obligations to US society and to all its people.

Today, there are about 5 million Orthodox Christians in the United States gathered into over 1,500 parishes. There are about twenty monasteries, three graduate schools of theology, a college and a number of other schools and charitable institutions associated with the Church. The Orthodox in America sponsor missionaries in Africa, Albania and Asia. Likewise, the International Orthodox Christian Charities presently provide humanitarian assistance in thirteen countries. Through their writings and lectures, Orthodox theologians from the United States are influencing the Church in many other parts the world. While still affected by jurisdictional divisions, duplication of efforts, and parochialism, Orthodoxy in the United States is no longer viewed simply as a 'dispersion' composed primarily of immigrants intent upon returning to their homeland. Rather, it can only be viewed properly as an emerging local Church. The Orthodox Church is comprised primarily of Americans of a wide variety of racial, ethnic, and religious backgrounds who all treasure the faith of Orthodox Christianity.

The Oriental Orthodox Churches

The formal division between the Orthodox Churches and the Oriental Orthodox Churches dates from the fifth century. Differences in the articulation of Christology were compounded by linguistic, cultural and political factors. With the rise of Islam in the seventh century, the divide between these two families became entrenched. While some limited contacts took place in subsequent centuries, the division was not resolved.

Each of the Oriental Orthodox Churches has its own particular history and liturgical traditions. In their historical context, each has served a particular people and has expressed very little sense of mission. In the United States too, each of these Oriental Orthodox Churches has its own identity and, until the end of the twentieth century, there was little formal contact either among themselves or between them and the Eastern Orthodox. Since the 1960s, theological dialogues between the Orthodox and Oriental Orthodox have led to an affirmation that the two families share the same faith despite 1,500 years of formal division. The discussions have also led to greater contacts especially in the Middle East, North America, Western Europe and Africa. There are about 500,000 Oriental Orthodox in the United States, gathered in the following six churches.

Coptic Orthodox   The Coptic Orthodox Patriarchate of Alexandra established a diocese serving immigrants from Egypt in 1965 in conjunction with a parish in Toronto, Canada. The first parish in the United States was established in New York in 1970. With further immigration from Egypt, the single diocese was divided into six in 1995. There are about 70 parishes.

Syrian Orthodox   Syrian Orthodox immigrants from Turkey began to arrive in the United States in the late nineteenth century. The Patriarchate of Antioch began to organize parishes in the 1920s. A visiting bishop came to the United States in 1949 and this led to the establishment of an archdiocese in 1957. The patriarchate divided the archdiocese into three vicarates in 1995. These serve 23 parishes.

Armenian Apostolic Orthodox   As early as 1889 a parish was established in Worcester, Massachusetts, serving Armenian immigrants. Then in 1898, the Catholocate of Ejmiadsin created a diocese in Worcester and sent a bishop to the United States. The diocesan centre eventually moved to New York. A separate diocese serving the western United States was established in Los Angeles in 1928. The St Nerses Seminary, now near New York City, was opened in 1961 and subsequently developed a cooperative programme with St Vladimir's Orthodox Theological Seminary. Because of greater immigration from the Middle East in the 1950s, a number of parishes became associated with the Catholocate of Cilicia, located in Lebanon. Reflecting political differences, deep divisions between the two groups eventually led Cilicia to establish a prelacy in New York and another in Los Angeles. Towards the end of the twentieth century there have been efforts to heal the rift. There are about 65 parishes related to Ejmiadsin and 33 related to Cilicia.

Ethiopian Orthodox   The Church of Ethiopia received autocephaly from the Coptic Orthodox Patriarchate in 1959. In the same year, it established a parish in New York. With the growth of parishes, a diocesan jurisdiction was established and divided into three regions in 1992. There are about 29 parishes.

Eritrean Orthodox   After Eritrea gained independence from Ethiopia in 1993, the Church there was granted autocephaly by the Coptic Orthodox Patriarchate of Alexandria, with which the Church of Ethiopia concurred. Political difficulties in Eritrea in this period led to a significant emigration of Orthodox believers to the United States. By the beginning of the twenty-first century, 19 parishes had been created and a diocesan centre established in Atlanta, Georgia.

The Malankara Syrian Orthodox   Immigrants from the region of Kerala in India led the Syrian Orthodox Patriarchate of Antioch to establish an archdiocese in New York in 1993 to serve them and assist developing parishes. However, disputes in India beginning in 1975 over the relationship of the Malankara Orthodox to the Syrian Orthodox Patriarchate led to divisions there as well as in the United States. Since 1996, a process of reconciliation has been taking place. There are two diocesan jurisdictions in the United States with about 56 parishes.

The Standing Conference of Oriental Orthodox Churches

The Oriental Orthodox jurisdictions in the United States in 1973 set up the Standing Conference of Oriental Orthodox Churches (SCOOCH). This conference is designed to strengthen the bonds among the churches and to present a common witness. The conference opened up a theological dialogue with the Roman Catholic Church in 1978. A Consultation with the Standing Conference of Canonical Orthodox Bishops was established in 2000. This consultation is designed to build upon recent theological agreements and to deepen relationships between the two families of Orthodox Christianity in the United States.

Further reading

FitzGerald, T. (1995) *The Orthodox Church.* Westport, Conn.: Greenwood Press.
Mousalimas, S. A. (2004) *From Mask to Icon: Transformation in the Arctic.* Brookline M.A.: Holy Cross Orthodox Press.
Robinson, R. (1999) *The Eastern Christian Churches: A Brief Survey,* 6th edn. Rome: Edizioni Orientalia Christiana.

CHAPTER 14
Eastern Christianity in China

Jeremias Norman

The earliest evidence for Eastern Christianity in China is the famous stele dated 781, which records in Chinese characters and Syriac script the arrival and settlement of so-called 'Nestorian' (Church of the East) Christians in Xian in 635. The first contacts between Byzantine Christianity and China may have occurred as early as the Northern Wei dynasty (386–534), when merchants from the Eastern Roman Empire were apparently living in the capital of Luoyang. Byzantine coins dating from the time of Theodosius II (r. 408–50) and Justinian (r. 527–65) have been found in Chinese archaeological sites. There is, however, no evidence that Byzantine Orthodox Christianity had any lasting effect in China at this early date.

During the time of the Mongol dynasty (1204–1368), numerous Russian Orthodox believers, including apparently some clerics, were brought to the Mongol court and some of them eventually settled in Shangdu, the Mongol capital in China. These Russians certainly brought their Orthodox religion with them, but no archaeological trace of their presence in China has been found. There is, however, archaeological evidence for the presence of the Church of the East and Catholic Christians in China under the Mongols.

The first well-documented presence of Russian Orthodox believers on Chinese territory was connected to the Russian expansion into the Amur region in the mid-seventeenth century. In 1665 a fortified settlement was established at Albazin, within the borders of the Chinese Empire. Among the people taken there was the Elder Germogen, who subsequently established the monastery of the Most Merciful Saviour not far from the outpost at Albazin; in addition, a church dedicated to the Resurrection of Christ was established in Albazin itself. The Kangxi emperor, the second ruler of the Manchu Qing dynasty (1644–1911), alarmed by the incursion of Russian settlers into areas that he considered a part of his territory, in 1685 sent troops to recover the areas of Russian intrusion. Albazin was captured, and the defeated Russians were given a choice of returning to Nerchinsk in Russia or of going to Beijing and becoming Chinese subjects. Only 45 men and a few women and children accepted the offer to move to Beijing; the remaining captives, including the Elder Germogen, returned to Russia.

The Albazinians who chose to go to Beijing took along with them Fr. Maksim Leontiev, together with some church utensils and books. Among the things they carried with them was an icon of St Nicholas the Wonderworker. At the end of 1685 the Albazinians arrived in Beijing and were cordially received by the emperor. They were settled in the north-eastern quarter of the city, where they were given a pagan temple; it was quickly converted into a church where Fr. Maksim could serve. The Albazinians were enrolled in a hereditary military unit and were thereafter considered a part of the Manchu banner troops, receiving a regular salary from the Qing government. Most of the Albazinians married local Manchu or Chinese women and in two or three generations were scarcely to be distinguished from the local population. Fr. Maksim served the Albazinians until his death in 1711 or 1712. He established the Church of St Nicholas (later reconsecrated as St Sophia), establishing an Orthodox presence in China that was to continue uninterrupted down to the present day.

During the time of Fr. Maksim's tenure other Russian clergy visited Beijing. In 1695 the Metropolitan of Tobolsk sent a priest and a deacon to the Chinese capital along with an antimension, service books and liturgical vessels; in 1696 Fr. Maksim and the newly arrived clergy consecrated the new church of St Sophia, which the Albazinians continued to call St Nicholas, after the icon they had brought from Albazin in 1685.

After the death of Fr. Maksim, the Chinese emperor agreed to allow a Russian spiritual mission to come to Beijing to look after the religious needs of the Albazinians and their descendants. The first such mission was organized by St John Maximovich of Tobolsk. The new mission arrived in Beijing at the end of 1715 or the beginning of 1716. The superior of this first mission was Archimandrite Hilarion (Lezhaisky), a graduate of the Kiev Theological Academy; he was accompanied by Priest Lavrenty and a deacon, Filimon; in addition, seven students were attached to the mission. This first official mission lasted until 1728. In 1719 Peter I sent an emissary, Lev Izmailov, to Beijing to resolve problems that had arisen in Sino-Russian trade relations. Among other matters discussed was the possibility of establishing a second Orthodox church in Beijing for visiting merchants and dignitaries subject to the Russian tsar.

Peter, at the advice of Metropolitan Feodor of Tobolsk and others, decided to send someone of episcopal rank to Beijing to the head the mission. The person chosen for this office was Hieromonk Innokenty (Kulchitsky), who was duly consecrated Bishop of Pereyaslavl in March, 1721. Owing to difficulties on the Chinese side, Bishop Innokenty was unable to take up his post in Beijing. The Treaty of Kiakhta, signed in June 1728, ushered in a new era in the history of the Russian Orthodox mission in China. According to the treaty, Russia was allowed to continue its ecclesiastical activities in Beijing; along with the allotted clergy, six students were to be permitted into China to study the local languages: Chinese, Manchu and Mongolian. The second mission was headed by Archimandrite Antony (Platkovsky); he was accompanied by a priest, a hierodeacon and six students. They established their new mission at the Russian diplomatic quarters; the Albazinians continued to be served by their priest from the first mission, Fr. Lavrenty. A new church was constructed in the diplomatic quarters; it was dedicated to the Meeting of the Lord in the Temple so that the parish feast would fall as near as possible to Chinese New Years. In 1730 the old Albazinian church of St Nicholas (officially St Sophia) was destroyed in an earthquake. A new church, dedicated to the Dormition, was consecrated in 1732. The church in the diplomatic quarter was subsequently known as the Southern Church (Nanguan) while the Albazinian church in the northern part of the city was known as the Northern Church (Beiguan).

According to the Treaty of Kiakhta, the Russian government was allowed to send one spiritual mission to Beijing every ten years, each mission to be comprised of four clerics and six laymen. Among the latter there were to be language students, church assistants, a doctor and an artist. Between 1716 and 1868, thirteen spiritual missions were sent to China. The principal duty of these missions was diplomatic rather than religious. The Beijing Spiritual Mission was in effect an arm of the Russian government at a period when other European powers were unable to station regular diplomatic representation in China. Russia, by means of its Orthodox mission, was able to maintain a continuing presence in the Chinese capital. One result of this arrangement was that the more religious aims of the mission were frequently frustrated. While the pastoral care of the Albazinians descendants was never lost sight of, little was done to spread the faith among the general population.

Even taking into account the difficulties of life in Beijing at that time, it must be admitted that these missionaries from Russia accomplished very little in the religious arena. Although they apparently made a generally good impression on the Chinese authorities, on the whole, they failed to take advantage of their favourable opportunity to spread Orthodoxy among the Chinese. Part of the problem was that the role of the missionaries was carefully controlled by the Russian government, which at that time was more concerned with diplomatic affairs than with the spread of Orthodoxy. The efforts in the purely religious area paled in comparison with that of the Roman Catholic missionaries working there at the same time. There were some exceptions: during the fifth mission (1755–71) under Archimandrite Amvrosy (Yumatov), 220 Manchus and Chinese were baptized, but most of these people may have been from among the Albazinians.

In the period between the fifth mission and 1858, when the diplomatic and ecclesiastical duties of the mission were separated, one officially appointed mission followed another. During this period there were only a handful of Albazinians and native converts at the mission and little was done to attract new believers. The Holy Synod and the civil authorities, to judge from official documents, seemed generally concerned with converting the Chinese, but for various reasons – lack of language skills on the part of the missionaries, a general lack of missionary zeal, extended isolation in an alien environment, and, regrettably in many cases, moral laxity – nothing much came of the Synod's good intentions. Things improved somewhat under the tenth mission (1821–31) under Archimandrite Peter (Kaminsky); during his tenure some 100 catechumens were baptized. During the eleventh mission (1831–40) several religious works were translated into Chinese by Fr. Theophilact.

The leader of the fourteenth mission (1858–65) was Archimandrite Gury (Karpov), one of the outstanding Russian missionaries of the nineteenth century. During his tenure, two important events took place: the Treaty of Tianjin in 1858 opened China to Christian missionaries, and in 1863 the diplomatic and religious functions of the Spiritual Mission were separated. The possibility of appointing an Orthodox bishop for Beijing was once again raised, but owing to the opposition of the Russian government, nothing came of the idea. Among his many other achievements, Fr. Gury's translation work was of great significance. In addition to revising several earlier translations of religious material, he translated the New Testament into Chinese and had it printed using traditional wooden blocks. He also translated the Psalter, the Trebnik (Book of Needs), the Sluzhebnik (a book containing the priest's and deacon's parts of the liturgy and other services), an expanded catechism, a sacred history based on the two testaments, a dialogue between a neophyte and a believer, as well as several other works.

After 1862, with the transfer of the governmental duties of the mission to diplomatic and consular officials, a new era of missionary work opened up. In 1860, Fr. Isaiah (Polikin) took up residence at the Albazinian Church of the Dormition. This zealous priest drew many people to the faith. He and Fr. Gury, both of whom had an excellent knowledge of spoken Chinese, conducted religious discussions with the Albazinians and new converts, educating them in Orthodoxy and confirming their faith. In this way they were able to prepare native catechists to aid in their missionary work. It was at this time that the mission's work spread beyond Beijing proper. When it was discovered that there were several Albazinian men living in the village of Dongdingan near Beijing, and that the families of these men were unbaptized, a catechist was sent there to preach to the people. The villagers generally were well disposed to Orthodoxy; in 1861 Fr. Isaiah baptized more than 30 people there and reported that more could be baptized after receiving adequate instruction. A small school was opened in the village to further the Christianization of the local populace. In the summer of 1862, a small chapel dedicated to St Innocent of Irkutsk was consecrated in Dongdingan. Three years of missionary work in the village resulted in 200 baptisms. At this juncture, Archimandrite Gury presented a plan to the Holy Synod for spreading and strengthening Orthodoxy in China. Among other things he proposed more translations into Chinese, the preparation of native clergy and the appointment of a bishop.

The fifteenth mission (1865–78) was under the leadership of Archimandrite Pallady (Kafarov); he had served in Beijing previously under the thirteenth mission and was already proficient in Chinese. Hieromonk Isaiah from the previous mission stayed on as a member of the new mission; Fr. Isaiah experimented with using the vernacular language in services before his death in 1871. He was replaced by hieromonk Flavian (Goretsky); Fr. Flavian was charged with the translation of a commentary on the Gospels. In 1878 he took over the direction of the mission when Archimandrite Pallady had to return to Russian because of ill health. Fr. Pallady was an eminent sinologist, some of whose works can still be consulted with profit.

The sixteenth mission (1878–88) was headed by Fr. Flavian, who was made an archimandrite in 1879. In 1882 Fr. Mitrophan Chang, a former teacher and catechist at the mission, was ordained to the priesthood in Tokyo by Bishop Nicholas Kasatkin (1836–1912), later the first archbishop of the Russian Orthodox Church in Japan.

Fr. Isaiah had earlier attempted to use vernacular Chinese in conducting services, but these experiments were not entirely successful. Fr. Flavian decided that to be effective, services would have to be in literary Chinese; to do this it would be necessary to translate the service books with the help of Chinese assistants, including the newly ordained Fr. Mitrophan. Fr. Flavian revised Fr. Isaiah's texts and undertook new translations. Among the revised translations were the Horologion (Book of Hours), the Shorter *Trebnik*, the *Sluzhebnik*, the main parts of the *Kanonik*, the *Akathists* to the Saviour, the Mother of God and the Guardian Angel. New translations of the Sunday *Oktoekhos*, services for the twelve great feasts, the services of Passion Week and Easter Week were made; in addition the memorial service for the dead (*Panikhida*) was rendered into Chinese. Several works of devotion and morality were also translated.

After Fr. Mitrophan Chang returned from Japan, Chinese services were inaugurated at the mission; Chinese services continued to be served during the entire time that Fr. Flavian was director of the mission.

An article by Fr. Nikolai (Adoratsky) which appeared in *Pravoslavnoe Obozrenie* (Orthodox Review) in 1884 reported that the Orthodox mission in China had two churches in Beijing, one in the northern part of the city (Beiguan) and another in the diplomatic quarter (Nanguan). In the church dedicated to St Innocent of Irkutsk, in the village of Dongdingan not far from Beijing, occasional services were held for the local believers. In addition, services were held from time to time in Kalgan (modern Zhangjiakou) and Tianjin. In Hankou, a city where numerous Russian tea merchants lived, a small church was built for the local Russian colony. In Beijing there were two schools, one for boys and one for girls; in these schools, pupils were instructed using translated works about Orthodoxy; they were also given instruction in traditional Chinese literature. Some of the pupils were also taught to sing and read in Slavonic. Only a very small number of them ever became proficient in Russian.

Translation work had already begun in the 1830s and 1840s, but the translations of that time were not of high quality. If a mission to the Chinese were to succeed, clearly prayers and services had to be made available in the local language. The first person to undertake a major translation project had been Fr. Isaiah (Polikin), who served in Beijing from 1858 until 1871. With the aid of Chinese assistants, he had translated the entire Horologion and abbreviated versions of the Sunday services; he had also produced a Chinese version of the Septuagint Psalter in vernacular Chinese. Fr. Isaiah encountered a dilemma in his translation work. Should services and other prayers be rendered into the vernacular so that even the most uneducated believer could understand them, or should they be in the elevated literary language in which, at that time, all official and solemn rites were performed? In nineteenth-century China, the written vernacular was still considered vulgar and unsuitable for formal use.

The problem of what kind of written language to employ in missionary work also plagued Protestant and Catholic missionaries of the same period. Fr. Isaiah made translations into both the vernacular and literary languages, but he apparently preferred the former because it could be understood more easily by his flock. Later missionaries, like Archimandrites Flavian and Pallady, believed that the literary language was more appropriate and subsequent translations were mostly done in that style. A further problem was that, whether one translated using either the literary or vernacular style, there as yet existed no standard set of theological and liturgical vocabulary.

In the 1860s Fr. Isaiah compiled a Russian-Chinese dictionary of religious words and phrases; this work was later corrected and supplemented by Archimandrite Pallady. Nowadays, looking at the nineteenth-century translations, one has the impression that the missionaries were not totally successful in their choice of language. The texts are in an artificial and idiomatic kind of language that must have been difficult for even educated Chinese to understand. Nonetheless, these early attempts remained useful for later translators as they attempted to produce more idiomatic and usable versions of liturgical and theological texts. As we will see, the problem of translation was taken up again in the later history of the mission. It is important to remember that at this time all the translations were joint efforts of the Russian clergy and their Chinese co-workers. Among the latter were Fr. Mitrophan Chang, Yevmeny Yu, the teacher Osiah and another man referred to simply as Long. During the 1880s music was provided for many of the Chinese liturgical texts and a Chinese choir was formed.

As mentioned, the sixteenth mission (1878–84) was directed by Archimandrite Flavian, who had succeeded Fr. Pallady. The seventeenth mission (1884–97), headed by Archimandrite Amfilokhy (Lutovinov), passed without any notable progress in expanding the mission. Archimandrite Innokenty (Figurovsky), head of the eighteenth mission (1897–1931) was to play a highly significant role in the history of Orthodoxy in China. A graduate of the St Petersburg Theological Academy in 1892, Archimandrite Innokenty was filled with true missionary zeal. Prior to his arrival in China, he familiarized himself with the work of western missionaries in China. After visiting Mount Athos and the Holy Land, he arrived in China in 1897. His early years at the mission were taken up with learning Chinese and English and making plans for the future of the mission.

In the spring and summer of 1900 the Boxer Uprising, an anti-Christian and anti-western movement originating in Shandong province, came to Beijing. The old Beiguan and the church at Dongdingan were burned along with other mission buildings, including the mission library. At this time there were fewer than 500 native Orthodox in Beijing and its environs. Of these, 222 were martyred by the Boxers. In view of these devastating developments, there was talk in St Petersburg of closing the Chinese mission altogether. Archimandrite Innokenty, who had returned to the Russian capital on business, was able to convince the authorities that not only should the mission not be closed, it deserved to be renewed and strengthened. Increased funding was obtained and in 1902 Fr. Innokenty was raised to episcopal rank, becoming the first Orthodox bishop in China. His newly constituted mission consisted of 34 men, mostly monastics of various ranks. The Beiguan was rebuilt and a new church in honour of St Innocent of Irkutsk was established. In 1902 the Holy Synod of the Russian Orthodox Church approved local veneration for the newly martyred Chinese. A solemn celebration of their martyrdom was held at the mission in 1903. In the same year a women's convent was instituted in Beijing with five Russian nuns from Krasnoyarsk; the first Chinese nun, Pelagia Rui, was tonsured in 1905; subsequently several other Chinese women became novices. The nuns administered a girls' school and did charity work among the poor.

The period following the Boxer Uprising was in most ways the golden age of the Chinese Orthodox mission. Under Bishop Innokenty's vigorous leadership, new churches and other missionary buildings were constructed and education work was expanded. In the period before the Russian Revolution, three native Chinese priests were ordained, one of whom, Fr. Sergei Chang, was the son of the hieromartyr Mitrophan. Bishop Innokenty strongly supported the use of Chinese in church services; with native clergy and the numerous translations made in the earlier missions, it was possible to have daily services in Chinese. Bishop Innokenty himself, alone among the Russian clergy of that time, was able to serve in Chinese.

Between 1900 and 1917 numerous new missions were created in China. The initiative in many cases came from the local people themselves. An example of this was the mission in Weihuifu in Henan province. In 1905 a local Chinese official built a church and school in his town and invited Orthodox missionaries from Beijing to establish a presence there. In the same year, the invitation was accepted and a parish and boys' school were opened; shortly thereafter 34 Chinese were baptized. From this beginning, Orthodox missionary work spread to other parts of Henan province, including the important provincial capital of Kaifeng. Just before the 1917 Revolution in Russia, there were more than 500 Orthodox believers in Henan province.

There had been a Russian church in Hankou since 1884. The presence of the St Alexander Nevsky church in Hankou attracted the interest of the Chinese in surrounding areas. In 1907 a school was opened and 34 people were baptized in the city of Yuanjiakou. At a self-organized mission in Fengkou there were 62 Orthodox believers in 1916. From these places Orthodoxy spread to several other towns in Hubei province. By 1917 there were several hundred baptized Orthodox Christians in various parts of Hubei.

From Beijing, Orthodoxy was propagated to nearby regions. Mission outposts were founded in Tianjin, Yongpingfu, Tongzhou, Zhuoxian, Fangshan and Xishan, all with numerous conversions. In 1911, 60 people were baptized in Xiaoqikou in Jiangxi province near a resort area frequented by Russian tea merchants from Hankou.

After the Boxer Uprising, Bishop Innokenty (then still an archimandrite) went to Shanghai with two Chinese assistants. In 1901 a school was opened there; in 1905 the new Church of the Transfiguration was consecrated in Shanghai and in 1908, 56 people were baptized. After 1910, missionary work in neighbouring areas was launched. Among the cities where an Orthodox presence was planted were Haimen in Jiangsu province and Hangzhou, Ningbo and Taizhou in Zhejiang province. In 1911, several hundred people were baptized in these regions.

These encouraging developments were not to continue. The Revolution in Russia changed everything. Material support for the mission ceased and great numbers of refugees from the Revolution flooded into China, changing the church situation radically. However, the mission to the Chinese did not cease altogether; the publication of a new vernacular Chinese version of the Easter service by Bishop Innokenty in 1918 witnesses to this fact. Owing to the great influx of Russian refugees, many new churches were built; between 1918 and 1924, nine churches were constructed in Harbin and eleven more in other parts of Manchuria. More and more the Beijing Spiritual Mission was forced to turn its attention to meeting the pastoral needs of these new immigrants.

Because of the new political situation in Russia, the Church in China broke off relations with the Moscow Patriarchate in 1922 and established ties with the Highest Russian Church Administration Abroad (later to be known as the Russian Orthodox Church Abroad) under Metropolitan Antony (Khrapovitsky). He had moved from his see in Kiev to Serbia, becoming the leader of the great majority of Russian Orthodox outside Russia. In the same year Archimandrite Simon was appointed Bishop of Shanghai and Archbishop Melety was appointed to the see of Harbin. In 1922 there were 300,000 Russian refugees in the Harbin diocese. In 1924 the Soviet government, laying claim to all Orthodox Church property in China, took steps to seize the holdings of the Beijing Spiritual Mission. Bishop Innokenty, through obtaining the support of influential circles in the Chinese government, was able to thwart this move by declaring that the property in question did not belong to the Russian Orthodox Church but was the property of the Chinese Orthodox Church. As a result, a Chinese Orthodox Church headed by Bishop Innokenty, came into being. The newly established church created the new dioceses of Shanghai, Tianjin, Harbin and Xinjiang.

Bishop Innokenty was made Metropolitan of Beijing by the Russian Church Abroad in 1930, just before his death in 1931. He was succeeded by Bishop Simon of Shanghai who was appointed Archbishop of Beijing, but until his death in 1933 he continued to reside in Shanghai. Archimandrite Viktor was consecrated Bishop of Shanghai in 1933; shortly thereafter he was appointed to the See of Beijing where he was to remain until 1956, when he returned to Russia.

In the 1930s and 1940s the Orthodox Church in China had a rich and varied life. Many new churches were established in areas where Russian immigrants were concentrated. In 1930, for example, there were close to 50,000 Russians in the city of Shanghai. After the old church at Zhabei was destroyed by the Japanese, the Russian community of Shanghai built the imposing cathedral of the Mother of God, Surety of Sinners, which, although it has not been used as a church since the mid-1960s, is still a well-known landmark in the city of Shanghai. In 1934 a theological seminary was established in Harbin. In Beijing there was a training school for Chinese clergy. Several notable Chinese priests were graduates of this school.

The work of translation continued during the several decades following the setting up of the Chinese Orthodox Church. As related above, the older nineteenth-century liturgical texts were mostly in a variety of the Chinese literary language. In the 1930s and 1940s great strides were made in promoting a new Chinese literary language based on the northern vernacular. Moreover, Catholic and Protestant missionaries were making effective use of this new standard in carrying out their missionary work. The native Chinese clergy of this period clearly felt the need to use the vernacular in church services in those places where there was a significant number of Chinese believers. Although some of the vernacular translations of this period survive, many others undoubtedly perished during the Cultural Revolution of 1966–76.

In 1934 hieromonk John (Maximovitch) was consecrated Bishop of Shanghai by Metropolitan Anthony of the Russian Orthodox Church Abroad. He arrived in Shanghai the same year and remained there until the Communist takeover. Bishop John was raised to the rank of archbishop in 1946. He headed sees in Europe and the

United States after leaving China. He was glorified as a saint of the Church in 1994 in San Francisco.

Soviet troops invaded Manchuria in 1945. At this time, several Russian hierarchs came under the jurisdiction of the Moscow Patriarchate. In the next few years most of the Russians in this region left China, some of them going to the Soviet Union, others to North and South America and Australia. In 1946, Archbishop Viktor of Beijing, responding to the new political realities in China, also switched allegiance to the Church in the Soviet Union. A majority of the clergy in Shanghai and Tianjin opposed his action. With the establishment of the People's Republic of China in 1950, all Orthodox believers in China effectively came under the jurisdiction of the Moscow patriarchate.

In 1950, the priest Du Runde was consecrated the first native Chinese bishop in Moscow by Patriarch Alexey, with the monastic name of Simeon; one of his co-consecrators was Archbishop Viktor, his former superior in Beijing. Bishop Simeon was appointed to the See of Shanghai, where he remained until his death in 1965.

In 1955, Patriarch Alexey sent two Russian bishops to Shanghai to discuss the granting of autonomy to the Chinese Church. Both Archbishop Viktor and Bishop Simeon (Du) took part in the meeting along with several Chinese priests from Harbin, Beijing and Tianjin. Bishop Simeon opposed autonomy for the fledgling Chinese Church, the most important reason being that the Church in China still required material support from the patriarchate if it was to survive. Nonetheless, autonomous status for the Chinese Church was approved. In 1956, the Autonomous Chinese Orthodox Church was established and all financial assistance from the Church in the Soviet Union was terminated. This circumstance, in addition to the emigration of the last remnants of the Russian population in China, necessitated the closure of a number of churches.

A second Chinese priest, Yao Fuan, was raised to the episcopal rank in 1957 with the monastic name of Vassily; he was made Archbishop of Beijing and head of the newly autonomous church. Always in poor health, Bishop Vasilly died in 1962.

The Autonomous Chinese Orthodox Church lasted barely ten years. Even during this short period, the new Church was beset by many problems. In Shanghai Bishop Simeon tried to form alliances with the Protestants and Roman Catholics, but to little avail. All Orthodox churches were closed on the eve of the Cultural Revolution. At this point, the Orthodox Church, like the other Christian bodies in China, entered a period of persecution.

When the Cultural Revolution ended in 1976 little was left of the Chinese Orthodox Church that had survived for almost three centuries up until that time. Its two bishops were dead, and the clergy were scattered and demoralized; some did not survive the decade of chaos and persecution. Yet it would be a mistake to say that the Orthodox Church in China is dead. Here and there groups of Orthodox believers survive, despite being deprived of regular clergy and pastoral care. In Beijing there are still approximately 200 Orthodox Christians, some of them descendants of the Albazinians, others descendants of later converts. One elderly and infirm priest survived until 2004, but was unable to serve because there was no church building and it is illegal in China to conduct religious services outside officially approved facilities. In 1984, the Holy

Protection Church in Harbin was reopened; the rector, Fr. Gregory Zhu, held regular services until his death in 2000. At the time of writing there were fewer than 200 Orthodox Christians in the city of Harbin, and the Chinese authorities have not allowed a priest from abroad to serve at this church.

There are larger groups of Orthodox in Inner Mongolia and Xinjiang; many of these people are part Russian, and even though they have been deprived of pastoral care for almost forty years, they still maintain a strong Orthodox identity.

A new development for Chinese Orthodoxy was the establishment of a metropolitanate in Hong Kong in 1997 and the founding of a mission in Taiwan by a monk from Mt Athos.

There were always important differences between the Orthodox mission in China and those of other confessions. Originally a purely pastoral and diplomatic undertaking, in the mid-nineteenth century the Russian Spiritual Mission expanded its horizons and began to engage in a more active preaching of the Gospel to the native Chinese. Part of this effort was a large project in which the New Testament and many Orthodox service books were translated. Missionary activity first spread to the environs of Beijing, then to other provinces. The first decade and a half after the beginning of the twentieth century were a particularly fruitful period. On the eve of the Russian Revolution, the Orthodox mission in China, under the leadership of Bishop Innokenty, appeared to have a particularly hopeful future. The events of 1917 in Russia brought an end to these hopes; the large influx of Russian refugees into China changed the entire character of Orthodoxy in the country. The native Orthodox became more and more absorbed into a growing Russian immigrant church. The Chinese Orthodox survived this transformation, but they emerged in the 1950s a small and vulnerable community. Attempts by the Moscow Patriarchate to create an autonomous church could not survive the numerous political upheavals taking place in China. Looking back, we can see that the Russian mission in China was always understaffed and underfunded. For most of the mission history its religious functions were overshadowed by its political and diplomatic duties.

Since the mid-1990s interest in the Chinese mission has begun to revive in several parts of the Orthodox world. Chinese Orthodox Christians are once again able to communicate with their co-religionists abroad. Political difficulties prevent the revival of normal religious life, but the seeds for future development are present.

Further reading

Anonymous (1916) *Kratkaja Istorija Pravolslavnoj Missii v Kitae* (A Short History of the Orthodox Mission in China). Beijing: Russian Spiritual Mission in China.

Baker, K. (2006) *A History of the Orthodox Church in China, Korea and Japan.* New York: Edwin Mellen Press.

Dawson, C. (1955) *Mission to Asia.* London: Sheed and Ward. Repr. by Harper and Row, New York, 1966.

Gardner, I., Lieu, S. and Parry, K. (eds.) (2005) *From Palmyra to Zayton: Epigraphy and Iconography.* Silk Road Studies X. Turnhout: Brepols.

Kessler, A. T. (1993) *Beyond the Great Wall: The Heritage of Genghis Khan*. Los Angeles: Natural History Museum of Los Angeles County.

Parry, K. (2006) The art of the Church of the East in China. In R. Malek (ed.) *Jingjiao: The Church of the East in China and Central Asia*. Sankt Augustin: Institut Monumenta Serica.

Petrov, V. (1968) *Rossiskaja Duxovnaja Missija v Kitae* (The Russian Spiritual Mission in China). Washington, DC: Victor Kamkin.

Yue Feng (1999) *Dongzhengjiao shi* (A History of Orthodoxy). Beijing: Zhongguo Shehui Kexueyuan.

Zhang Sui (1986) *Dongzhengjiao he dongzhengjiao zai Zhongguo* (Orthodoxy and Orthodoxy in China). Xuelin Chubanshe.

CHAPTER 15
Eastern Catholic Christianity

Peter Galadza

Introduction, Statistics and Languages

Eastern Catholicism consists of some twenty churches (before Vatican II (1965), 'Rites') united by communion with the See of Rome. Most Eastern Catholic Churches have Orthodox counterparts, that is, churches not in union with the pope. Each of them has the status of a 'particular church', or, more technically, a church *sui iuris* ('of its own law'), which in some instances corresponds to Eastern Orthodoxy's 'autonomous churches'. The exact number of *sui iuris* churches is subject to debate (see below).

The shift from 'Rites' to 'Churches' is indicative of Vatican II's desire to see these communities distinguished not only by their worship, but also by indigenous theologies, spiritualities and canonical traditions. Each of them is also to incarnate in unique fashion the unity, holiness, catholicity and apostolicity of the one Church, with the Bishop of Rome serving as the touchstone of this unity and continuity. Another shift involves the term 'uniate' to describe these churches. Since the 1950s it has been considered derogatory, even though originally it simply denoted that part of an Orthodox Church that had accepted 'the *Unia*'.

As noted above, the exact number of *sui iuris* churches is subject to debate. The Russian and Belarusan Greek Catholic Churches have not had their own bishops for some time. Can they be considered 'particular churches'? There is also the question of the Ruthenian Church. While the ('Ruthenian') Byzantine Catholic Metropolia of Pittsburgh is a *sui iuris* church in its own right, its counterpart in the Carpathian region of western Ukraine has no direct canonical connection with it. Should they be counted as one or two? Finally, in view of the fact that the Albanian Byzantine Church is composed of Roman Rite Catholics, is it a 'particular church?' Most would prefer to list the Russian, Belarusan and Albanian Churches as 'communities' (without, of course, denying their full ecclesiality). Incidentally, owing to geographical, cultural and political factors, some Eastern Catholic communities have almost no contact with each other except through Vatican, or other Roman Catholic, institutions.

Table 15.1 Church membership, jurisdictions, languages

Name of Church	Members in 1995	Members in 2003	Jurisdictions both within and beyond original territory	Dominant languages of worship
1. Ukrainian Greek Catholic	5,092,980	4,366,131	15 / 15	Ukrainian; Church Slavonic for parts of the service
2. Syro-Malabar Catholic	3,154,835	3,588,172	24 / 1	Malayalam
3. Maronite Catholic	3,304,290	3,083,754	20 / 7	Arabic; Syriac
4. Melkite Greek Catholic	1,099,265	1,295,061	18 / 7	Arabic; Greek phrases
5. Romanian Greek Catholic	2,011,635	752,500	5 / 1	Romanian
6. Ruthenian Byzantine Catholic	492,537	610,688	2 / 4	Church Slavonic; English
7. Syro-Malankara Catholic	310,500	395,476	4 / 0	Malayalam
8. Armenian Catholic	296,250	369,297	10 / 7	Classical Armenian; Arabic
9. Chaldean Catholic	312,691	343,501	17 / 2	Syriac; Arabic
10. Hungarian Greek Catholic	278,750	278,000	2 / 0	Modern Hungarian
11. Slovak Greek Catholic	238,238	221,331	2 / 1	Slovak; Church Slavonic
12. Coptic Catholic	190,262	216,990	6 / 0	Coptic and Arabic
13. Ethiopian Catholic	140,710	205,999	5 / 0	Ge'ez and Amharic
14. Syrian Catholic	109,130	112,849	11 / 3	Arabic; Syriac phrases
15. Italo-Albnian	61,597	60,548	3 / 0	Greek; Italian
16. Greek Catholics in the former Yugoslavia	48,975	48,174	2 / 0	Church Slavonic; Rusyn, Croatian, Macedonian
17. Bulgarian Byzantine Catholic	20,000	15,000	1 / 0	Church Slavonic; Bulgarian
18. Greek Byzantine Catholic	2,350	2,345	2 / 0	Byzantine Greek
19. Albanian Byzantine Catholic	1,121	2,800	1 / 0	Albanian
20. Russian Byzantine Catholic	Not av'ble	Not av'ble	0 / 0	Church Slavonic
21. Belarusan Byzantine Catholic	Not av'ble	Not av'ble	0 / 0	Belarusan; Church Slavonic

Table 15.1 provides (1) membership statistics for 1995 and 2003, (2) information regarding the number of jurisdictions (usually eparchies, that is dioceses, or other administrative units) both within and beyond their original territories, and (3) languages used for worship. Where dramatic declines in membership appear, this is due to the fact that in 1995 the numbers were inflated. As regards jurisdictions, the first number designates units located within the 'home territory' (or in some cases other non-western territories), while the second number refers to jurisdictions found in the West. Incidentally, the number of hierarchs in a given church is sometimes greater than the number of jurisdictions because some of the latter have a ruling hierarch ('ordinary') as well as one or more vicar bishops. As regards languages used in worship, since Vatican II almost all of the churches have shown a greater or lesser openness to the vernaculars of the new lands in which they find themselves (as well as their homelands). It would be impossible to list all of these here. In the case of the Ruthenian Byzantine Catholic Church, however, English is listed because it constitutes the official liturgical language in that Church's American metropolia. Finally, note that in Catholic nomenclature, 'Byzantine' is synonymous with 'Greek'. There are various reasons why some churches are referred to as 'Byzantine Catholic', and others as 'Greek Catholic', even though both designate a church of the Byzantine tradition. Incidentally, some scholars prefer 'Greco-Catholic' as a way of indicating that members of these churches are not of Greek nationality.

Among the patterns that characterize the processes by which many Eastern Churches entered into union with Rome is the following: contact with western religious orders during a period of crisis and/or reform, in which union with Rome was viewed as a progressive development, although stimulated in some instances by hopes for socio-political, educational or other privileges, while in other instances bringing on persecution from civil and/or religious authorities opposed to union.

Before turning to the individual churches, an overview of western, in particular Roman, developments as they relate to Eastern Catholicism *as a whole* is necessary.

Eleventh to thirteenth centuries: During the crusades, Armenians, Assyrians and Maronites establish positive relations with Roman Catholics.

1439: The Council of Florence achieves (in most territories only short-lived) agreement on the *filioque*, purgatory, and the Roman primacy.

1550s and later: The Catholic Reformation turns its attention to the East. With the union of Florence generally moribund, Rome decides to approach each Eastern Church separately. Tridentine ecclesiology colours the approach; unity becomes a matter of *reductio in oboedientiam* – submission to Roman authority, pure and simple.

1622: Creation of the Roman Sacred Congregation *Propaganda fide*, a missionary dicastery, to which oversight of Eastern Catholics is assigned.

1729: Rome issues a decree definitively forbidding any and all forms of worship with the Orthodox.

1742: Benedict XIV's encyclical *Etsi pastoralis* declares the Roman Rite to be superior to other Catholic Rites.

1894: Leo XIII's apostolic letter *Orientalium dignitas* proclaims equality of all Rites, and forbids the enticing of Eastern Catholics to the Roman Rite; but the letter's promulgation is blocked in the Austro-Hungarian Empire, where more than three-quarters of all Eastern Catholics live.

1907: Pius X's decree *Ea semper* for Eastern Catholics in the New World, makes the Eastern Catholic bishop fully dependent on local Roman Rite authorities, denies priests the right to chrismate ('confirm') their own faithful, and insists on clerical celibacy. These restrictions will soon be overturned, except for celibacy, which will be imposed definitively in 1929.

1917: Creation of the Sacred Congregation for the Eastern Church (later changed to 'Churches'), which replaces the Eastern Section of *Propaganda fide.*

1930s: Rome embarks on the publication of generally superb liturgical books for many of the Eastern Catholic Churches.

1964: The Vatican II decree *Orientalium ecclesiarum* proclaims (again) the equality of Rites, and stresses the need for Eastern Catholics to revive their authentic traditions.

1990: Publication of the *Code of Canons of the Eastern [Catholic] Churches.*

1994: *Orientale lumen,* John Paul II's apostolic letter marking the centenary of *Orientalium dignitas,* emphasizes the East's theological and spiritual riches.

1996: The Congregation for the Eastern Churches issues the *Instruction for Applying the Liturgical Prescriptions of the Code of Canons of the Eastern Churches,* which insists that Eastern Catholic worship should be essentially identical with its Orthodox counterparts.

Henceforth, detailed information will be given for only the four largest Eastern Catholic Churches, all of which have over one million members. As it happens, these four are so different that a focus on them provides a good sense of Eastern Catholicism's diverse profile. For regularly updated information on the smaller Eastern Catholic Churches, consult www.cnewa.org\ecc.htm.

Nomenclature, Ethnicity, Geography, History

Ukrainian Greek Catholic Church

'Ukrainian Catholic' came into use in the 1950s outside of Ukraine, replacing 'Ruthenian Greek Catholic.' 'Ruthenian' derives from the Latin form of 'Rus', the name of the mediaeval territory centred at Kiev (Kyiv), capital of present-day Ukraine. In Ukraine, the Church was known simply as the 'Greek Catholic', a term applied in the 1770s by the Hapsburgs to foster parity with Roman Catholics. Prior to this, it was called 'Uniate', a name that was retained outside the Austro-Hungarian Empire. Today, the overwhelming majority of Ukrainian Catholics are of Ukrainian ethnicity, though at the time of the Union of Brest (1596), and until the liquidation of the 'Uniate' Church in the Russian Empire in the nineteenth century, an equal number was Belarusan. In Ukraine, almost 10 per cent of the population belongs to this Church, which continues to be centred in the part of western Ukraine once controlled by the Hapsburgs.

History   In 1596 the Metropolitan of Kiev (Kyiv) and most of his suffragan bishops renewed union with Rome at the Synod of Brest (in present-day Belarus). (A previous primate of the Church, Isidore, had supported the Union of Florence.) The Metropolia of Kiev was entirely within the Polish-Lithuanian Commonwealth, and as the latter's support – and size – waned, so did the union. Ukrainian Cossacks, followed by the tsarist government, consistently opposed the union in favour of Orthodoxy. By the end of the nineteenth century, the Church was restricted to the Austro-Hungarian realm, having been banned in the Russian Empire. Owing in part to the benign treatment of Greek Catholics by the Hapsburgs, who provided, for example, university education for the clergy, a sincere commitment to Catholicism developed, reaching its height in the twentieth century. When the Soviets took control of western Ukraine after World War II and declared the Church united to the Orthodox Patriarchate of Moscow (the Pseudo-Synod of Lviv, 1946), most Greek Catholics retained their commitment to Rome and re-emerged in 1989 as Communism collapsed. This forced an announcement of the Church's de-criminalization on 1 December, during a visit of Mikhail Gorbachev to Rome. During the Soviet period, the most contentious issue was the Vatican's willingness to sacrifice this Church in the interests of dialogue with Moscow. Today, this is no longer an issue. However, the Vatican refuses to recognize a Ukrainian Catholic patriarchate, a cause championed by Cardinal Josyf Slipyj (a former primate, d. 1984) after his release in 1963 from eighteen years in Siberia. This refusal is partially a remnant of the Vatican's former *Ostpolitik*, though the more important factor is the desire to avoid perceptions of 'Catholic expansionism' in the former USSR.

Syro–Malabar Church

The designation 'Syro-Malabar', created by Rome, has been used consistently only from the end of the nineteenth century. It derives from the original liturgical tradition of this Church, that is, the East Syrian; while 'Malabar' (probably of Arabic derivation) is the name that came to be applied to its original territory, the western coast of South India, properly called Kerala. Today, there is a movement to restore the Church's original name, 'Saint Thomas Christians'. In Kerala, a territory approximately 50 miles wide and 250 miles long, the overwhelming majority of Christians are Syro-Malabars. In India as a whole, where only slightly more than 1 per cent of the population is Catholic, Syro-Malabars make up approximately a third of that number.

History   A firmly entrenched tradition has the apostle Thomas founding a Church on the south-west coast of India. A group of East Syrian (Chaldean) Christians from Persia, led by a certain Thomas of Cana, are said to have arrived in Kerala in the fourth century, followed by another group of East Syrians in the ninth. This explains the provenance of the Church's liturgy, as well as the fact that until a century after the arrival of the Portuguese in 1498, the metropolitan of the Church was always appointed by the Assyrian (Chaldean) patriarch, and was inevitably a foreigner. Effective governance of the Church, however, lay in the hands of an archdeacon – always a local, who knew Syriac – along with the yogam, a representative body of clergy and laity from the entire

Church. The Portuguese takeover of the Church began slowly with the founding of a Latin-Rite seminary around 1550. By 1597, when the Assyrian-appointed metropolitan died, a new appointment was blocked and two years later the Thomas Christians were summoned to a synod at Diamper. This initiated the destruction of virtually all of their written monuments, which were believed by the Portuguese to be tainted with Nestorianism. An ethnically foreign, Roman-Rite hierarchy was imposed until 1896, when Rome allowed three Indians to exercise episcopal authority, although regular Syro-Malabar dioceses were not created until 1923. This legacy has caused the Syro-Malabars to be the most Latinized of the Eastern Churches. In 1992, John Paul II raised the Church to major archepiscopal status. Until then, Syro-Malabars had two metropolitanates without a primatial centre.

Maronite Catholic Church

The name derives from the fourth- or fifth-century Saint Maron (also 'Maro' and 'Marun'), whose followers later founded a leading monastery. A seventh- or eighth-century monk of that monastery, John-Maron, became Patriarch of Antioch during the absence of a Byzantine hierarch there. Thus, its full name is the Antiochian Syrian Maronite Church, 'Syrian' being a reference to the earlier dominance of Syriac. Maronites are the largest church in Lebanon, comprising more than a third of all Christians and almost 20 per cent of the population. Dioceses also exist in other parts of the Middle East. Unlike most Eastern Catholic Churches, they have no direct Orthodox counterpart.

History   The Maronites were originally centred at a monastery located between Antioch and Damascus, but in the eighth century persecution by Muslims and depredations from other Christians forced them into Lebanon's remote hills. Their adherence at the time to monothelitism (while rejecting miaphysitism), might help explain their distinctiveness from both Byzantines and 'Jacobites'. In the eleventh century, the crusades, which they supported, broke the Maronites' isolation. The year 1182 saw them confirm their union with Rome, and their patriarch attended the Fourth Lateran Council (1215). The Synod of Mt Lebanon (1734) was the most prominent attempt to reform – and Latinize – the Church. The early bond with Rome, the lack of an Orthodox counterpart, and western – especially French – protection from the Ottomans, particularly in the nineteenth century, have made the Maronites among the more pro-Roman (and Latinized) of the Eastern Catholics. Since 1943, the president of Lebanon must be a Maronite, a stipulation promoted by the French to ensure Maronite security in a sea of conflicting groups. But the civil war begun in 1975 has revealed their vulnerability.

Melkite Greek Catholic Church

'Melkite', occasionally rendered 'Melchite', derives from the Syriac and Arabic for 'king': this Church accepted the Council of Chalcedon (451), promoted by the Byzan-

tine emperor (king). It is the Catholic counterpart of the (Eastern) Orthodox Patriarchate of Antioch. In the USA, 'Greek' sometimes is omitted from the name. In the Middle
East, in popular parlance, Melkites are sometimes referred to simply as 'Catholics'.
(Roman Catholics are 'Latins'.) Lebanese, Syrians, Palestinians, Jordanians and a very
small number of Egyptians form the ethnic base, while in the West an increasing
number of non-Middle-Easterners – in some parishes more than a third – make up the
membership. Owing to emigration, there are now approximately as many Melkites in
the West as in the home territories. Nonetheless, it is the largest Catholic community
in Syria and Palestine, and the second largest in Lebanon.

History Individual hierarchs of the Antiochene Patriarchate re-established communion with Rome in the late sixteenth century, but from 1724 an uninterrupted line
of patriarchs has been Catholic. In 1838, once Greek Catholics had begun to migrate
from Syria and Lebanon to Palestine and Egypt (owing to toleration there), 'Alexandria
and Jerusalem' were added to the patriarch's title. In 1848, the Ottomans ceased their
persecution of Melkite Catholics, and the patriarch returned to Damascus from exile
at Holy Saviour Monastery in Lebanon. For later history, see the sections below on
theology, and missions.

Scripture and Tradition

In occasional references – in discussions or publications – approaches range from the
standard Roman Catholic stress on scripture and tradition as the conveyors of revelation, to the more Orthodox notion of scripture as part of tradition. Owing to contact
with Roman Catholicism, Eastern Catholics tend to be less apprehensive of modern
biblical criticism than some of their Orthodox counterparts. However, they have not
made significant contributions to this area.

As for authoritative versions of scripture, nothing equivalent to the Council of
Trent's endorsement of the Vulgate and its canon exists among Eastern Catholics.
The status of versions such as the Septuagint, Peshitta, Armenian, Coptic, Ge'ez, and
Slavonic – to mention only the more prominent classical ones – derives from their liturgical use and passing allusions in Vatican, or other ecclesiastical, statements. The
vernacular versions used in most of the churches have undergone little of the kind of
review that western Christians are accustomed to. Thus, at times several different
modern translations are in use without Eastern Catholic authorities ruling on their
relative merits or status.

Doctrine, Theology and Theologians

Forty years after Vatican II freed Eastern Catholics to develop a distinctive theology, no
Eastern Catholic author or work stands out as universally significant. Only in the area
of ecclesiology, where collegiality and ecumenism have been studied, are contributions
part of larger discussions (see below). Of course, Roman Catholics have advanced

theology, as Tomaš Špidlik has done, in this case 'spiritual theology', by employing eastern sources to elaborate the holistic foundation of theologizing, but this is 'Catholic eastern theology' rather than Eastern Catholic theology.

Before Vatican II, original Eastern Catholic contributions were unimaginable; whenever attempted, they evoked denunciations. It was easier for a Roman Catholic to appropriate elements of Greek patristics, for example, than for an Eastern Catholic to do so: the former's loyalties could be presumed while the latter was often suspected of 'schismophilia'.

Before *Orientalium dignitas*, and the founding of the Pontifical Oriental Institute in 1917, Eastern Catholic theology tended simply to (1) transmit Tridentine manualism and Scholasticism into the languages of these churches, (2) interpret liturgical usages, and (3) contextualize Catholic social and pastoral reflection. In this last area, the benefits of western influence were significant, leading to involvement in education and economic betterment, and the revitalization of catechesis and preaching.

After 1917, the stress came to fall on finding eastern support for Roman doctrines. Thus Greek and Syriac texts, for example, were combed for serviceable references to Roman primacy, the procession of the Holy Spirit, the Bodily Assumption, and so on.

Today, the nascent field is characterized by an appropriation and application of Orthodox theology. To the extent that Eastern Catholics are in greater contact with western Christianity, they could forge an organic and dynamic synthesis of the two. But this has yet to occur. Another aspect of contemporary Eastern Catholic theologizing is the issue of newer Catholic doctrines proclaimed before Vatican II – during the First Vatican Council, for example. Some theologians pose the question of their authentic reception. Can they be embraced unreservedly by Eastern Catholic Churches who before Vatican II were required to be passive receptors of these formulations? Nonetheless, Eastern Catholics stress that communion with Rome guarantees a universality and unity otherwise unattainable. For them, the inability of the Orthodox Churches (1) to overcome the multiplicity of rival jurisdictions not only in the 'Old World' but also in the new, (2) to convoke a pan-Orthodox council, not to mention forge cooperation in other areas, and (3) to mitigate an almost endemic identification of church and ethnos – all of these are adduced as positive reasons for continuing recognition of Rome's authority by Eastern Catholics.

Ukrainian Greek Catholic Church

At the time of, and for three decades after, the Union of Brest, several 'Uniate' churchmen relied heavily on Greek and Slavonic sources for their theology, which, although usually polemical, signalled a flowering of religious thought, dormant during the previous three centuries. As the Church's elites came to be Roman-trained and the Catholic Reformation gained ground, reliance on Eastern sources became far less frequent (a tendency evident in Orthodox institutions as well). During the Hapsburg period theologizing was Scholastic and manualist, centred as it was at state-sponsored universities. The founding of the Greek Catholic Theological Academy in 1928 by Metropolitan Andrei Sheptytsky, a theologian in his own right, signalled the Church's commitment to finding eastern sources for Catholic doctrine, and – very significantly – to theologizing in greater dialogue with the socio-cultural situation of Greek Catholics. Today, most Ukrainian Catholic theology is thoroughly engaged with Orthodox methods and sources, though the hierarchy has yet to develop a worldwide stance on the *filioque*, for example. In North America many dioceses omit the addition. The quest for a patriarchate has stimulated reflection on collegiality and the lay movement, especially as the latter has been vocal in support of the cause.

Theologians Lev Krevza (d. 1639) was a noteworthy ecclesiologist of the early period. The two centuries after his death was a theological 'dry spell', in which writing focused on history and liturgical questions. The manualist approach is best represented by the prolific Alexander Bachynsky (d. 1933), who produced textbooks for virtually every field of theology as well as a commentary edition of the Slavonic bible, which for some scriptural books included a Ukrainian translation. Josyf Slipyj (d. 1984), first rector of the Lviv Theological Academy, did systematic theology, combining Scholasticism and Greek sources. His rival, Havryil Kostelnyk (d. 1948), produced a ground-breaking work on the epiclesis (but ended his days in Orthodoxy, as the leader of a Soviet-sponsored group that sought unification with the Moscow Patriarchate). The post-Vatican II generation is represented by: Petro B. T. Bilaniuk (d. 1998) who excelled in historical theology; Myroslaw Tataryn and Sviatoslav Shevchuk, both systematicians; Andriy Chirovsky and Borys Gudziak – ecclesiology and spiritual theology; Andrii Krawchuk and Myroslav Marynovych – ethics and social thought; and Peter Galadza – liturgy. Most of the post-conciliar theology is characterized by an appropriation of Orthodox thought, but with western critical methods and the strong complementarity of Catholic thinking. While most of this work has appeared in the West, the re-emergence of theology in Ukraine will cause this to change.

Syro–Malabar Church

As most of the written legacy of the Saint Thomas Christians was branded 'Nestorian' and destroyed after the Synod of Diamper (1599), a ressourcement of the Syro-Malabar theological tradition has been extremely difficult. In addition, because the East Syrian ('Chaldean') tradition is viewed as a later imposition – much more benign, but nonetheless just as alien as the Latin – the stress is laid on developing an authentically Indian theology. Since Vatican II, several hundred theological publications have appeared. Many of them might be characterized as an appropriation of mainstream post-conciliar Roman Catholic theology.

Theologians Joseph Pathrapamkal and Antony Edanad have employed a spiritual reading of scripture to dialogue with the socio-cultural situation of India. The former has even reflected on biblical notions of righteousness as related to the Hindu notion of Dharma. Placid Podipara, Xavier Koodapuzha and A. M. Mundadan have made significant contributions to a pan-Indian ecclesiology in which dynamic interaction among all of the churches of India – with a view to curing that country's social ills – is stressed just as much as communion with Rome. Elements of a liberation theology are also evident in Mundadan's work. As might be expected, liturgical theology is the area where Syro-Malabar theology is most distinctive, grounded as it is in East Syriac texts as well as a contemporary concern for enculturation. Here, the work of Jacob Vellian is significant.

Maronite Catholic Church

Today, Maronites are reappropriating the Syriac theology of classical authors such as Aphraat, Ephrem and Isaac of Nineveh. Being Semitic, and thus less philosophical than the Greek or Latin traditions, this theology resonates well with the postmodern stress on symbols, imagery and paradox. In spite of extensive liturgical reforms, the Maronites continue to recite the *filioque*, an addition widely accepted only in 1736.

Theologians   Joseph S. Assemani (1687–1768) (not to be confused with Joseph A. Assemani, d. 1782, the prolific Maronite liturgist) laid the foundation for modern Syriac studies with his editions of historical documents, patristic works (especially Ephrem), saints' lives and canon law. After Vatican II, Seely Beggiani became prominent in the area of historical theology, culling elements of a systematic theology from the writings of the Syriac fathers, who also inspire his spiritual theology.

Melkite Greek Catholic Church

Of all Eastern Catholics, the Melkites have been the most assertive in questioning the centralizing ecclesiology of Vatican I, even in its Vatican II incarnation. Even before the former Council, Patriarch Germanos Adam (d. 1809) argued the rights of his local Church, and drew accusations of 'Gallicanism'. Patriarch Gregory Yusef II opposed *Pastor aeternus*, and when compelled to sign the document, added 'preserving all the rights and privileges of the patriarchs'.

Immediately after Vatican II, Melkites almost universally ceased pronouncing the *filioque* in the Creed, although little pneumatological reflection accompanied the shift; it was more a matter of symbolizing the theological distinctiveness endorsed by Vatican II.

In the area of ethics, Archbishop Joseph Raya, a popularizing theologian, questioned Catholicism's stance on birth control, insisting that married couples should be free to follow their consciences.

Theologians   Metropolitan Germanos Adam combined Catholic apologetics, conciliarism and an appreciation for eastern emphases such as the epiclesis. Patriarch Maximos III Mazloum (d. 1855), usually considered the greatest of the patriarchs, also wrote theology. In the twentieth century, J. Nasrallah was prolific in historical theology. Churchmen Elias Zoghby, Peter Medawar and Neophytos Edelby stand out as creative ecclesiologists, along with Orestes Kerame, who prepared many of Patriarch

Maximos IV's electrifying interventions at Vatican II. Georges Habra has published seven volumes (in French) on fundamental theology, exegesis, eschatology and ethics. They are characterized by an application of scriptural and patristic insights to existential questions. Habra is thus the only Eastern Catholic theologian who has ventured beyond a focus on particular questions and historical theology to produce a broad synthesis of more universal significance. The average Eastern Catholic has tended to rely on Roman Catholic thinkers for such syntheses.

Missions and Diaspora

Until Vatican II, Eastern Catholics desiring to work in foreign missions had to transfer to the Roman Rite. This, coupled with the legacy of the Ottoman ban on proselytizing, and similar Communist restrictions, has coloured Eastern Catholic attitudes towards sharing the faith. As for emigration, it has usually resulted from economic and/or political strife. The economic crisis in the former Eastern Bloc in the 1990s and later, and turmoil in the Middle East have greatly increased the number of Eastern Catholics in the West.

Ukrainian Greek Catholic Church

The first parish in the West was founded in Pennsylvania in 1884. The married clergy who followed their flocks to the New World were sometimes suspended by Roman Catholic bishops (triggering movements to Orthodoxy). The first bishop for the USA was assigned in 1907, and upon his death in 1916, the Vatican divided Slav Greek Catholics by creating distinct structures for those from Austrian-controlled Galicia on the one hand, and the Hungarian part of Transcarpathia (the jurisdiction now known as the Byzantine Catholic Metropolia of Pittsburgh), on the other. Other jurisdictions for the USA were created between the 1950s and 1980s in Stamford, Connecticut; Chicago; and Parma, Ohio; and in Canada, between 1910 and the 1980s, in Winnipeg, Edmonton, Toronto, Saskatoon and New Westminster, British Columbia. Since World War II jurisdictions have existed in Brazil and Argentina, Australia, Germany, France, England; and new ones have been created in Poland.

While a large influx of post-Word War II political emigrés greatly expanded membership in the West, their ethno-centrism prevented an organic indigenization that would have attracted non-Ukrainians. Nonetheless, especially in North American communities dominated by descendants of pre-World War II immigrants, English is the usual language for worship, and non-Ukrainians are found among the membership.

Syro–Malabar Church

Until the 1990s, Syro-Malabar clergy hoping to minister outside the territory of Kerala had to transfer to the Roman Rite. This was particularly ironic, as they are the original Christians of India. Today, hundreds of thousands of Syro-Malabars live in other parts of India. While eleven dioceses for the Syro-Malabars outside Kerala have been created since 1977, these are nonetheless under the direct jurisdiction of Rome rather than the Major Archbishop. Beyond these dioceses, however, large numbers of Syro-Malabars (e.g., 12,000 in the area of Chennai/Mylapore alone) do not have a single parish, even though the Church has a large surplus of vocations who could minister to them. In western countries and the Gulf region, to which Indians flock for employment, the tendency is to presume that the Syro-Malabars will assimilate to the Roman Rite. The only diocese for Syro-Malabars outside of India, the Eparchy of Saint Thomas in Chicago, was finally created in 2001, and a mission was recently established in Italy.

Maronite Catholic Church

The first parish in the Americas was founded in the early 1890s. Even without a bishop, the National Association of Maronites worked for the establishment of a seminary in Washington, which occurred in 1961. An American diocese has existed since 1971 (divided into two – Brooklyn and Los Angeles – in 1994). Others were then founded in Canada, Australia, Mexico, Argentina and Brazil. While a commitment to the Lebanese cause creates a certain insularity, their western liturgical ethos and tradition of Lebanese cosmopolitanism sometimes facilitate non-Middle-Eastern membership.

Melkite Greek Catholic Church

Emigration to the West began around 1850, and 1889 saw the arrival of the first permanent priest in the USA. Even though a bishop was not assigned to America until 1966, a seminary was founded in Methuen, Massachusetts in 1954. Since Vatican II, dioceses have existed in America, Brazil, Canada, Mexico, Australia and Venezuela. Owing to their lack of identity with a single national or ethnic group, and their willingness to use the vernaculars of their adopted homelands, in America the Melkites have had noticeable success in attracting new members. There, services were being conducted in English as early as 1951, in spite of objections from Roman Catholic authorities.

Priesthood and Hierarchy

Table 15.2 provides the following information: (1) location of the primate, and his title and (2) the proportion of married (diocesan) clergy to that of celibate diocesan clergy. Notwithstanding Vatican II's declaration of the equality of all 'Rites', Roman authorities continue to oppose the open ordination of married candidates to the priesthood outside of Eastern Catholic 'homelands.' Thus, in spite of the severe shortage of clergy in the USA, the only married priests usually permitted to serve there are immigrants from Eastern Europe or the Middle East. In Italy and France, however, married priests are not even allowed to immigrate to serve their communities.

Table 15.2 Eastern Catholic primatial sees and proportion of married priests

Name of Church	Residence and title of primate or senior hierarch	Proportion of married diocesan priests
1. Ukrainian Greek Catholic	Kiev (Kyiv), Ukraine: Major Archbishop of Kyiv and Halyč (seeking patriarchal status)	In Ukraine, about 90%; outside: about 40%
2. Syro-Malabar Catholic	Ernakulam, India: Major Archbishop of Ernakulam-Angamaly	Optional celibacy eliminated
3. Maronite Catholic	Bherké, Lebanon: Patriarch of Antioch of the Maronites	In the Middle East, about 50%; outside: none
4. Melkite Greek Catholic	Damascus, Syria: Patriarch of Antioch of the Greek Catholics	In the Middle East, less than 50%; outside: few
5. Romanian Greek Catholic	Blaj, Romania: Major Archbishop of Făgăraş and Alba Julia	In Romania, a majority; outside: few
6. Ruthenian Byzantine Catholic	Pittsburgh, Pennsylvania: Metropolitan of Pittsburgh of the Byzantines	Almost no married priests
7. Syro-Malankara Catholic	Trivandrum, Kerala State, India: Major Archbishop of Trivandrum of the Syro-Malakarese	Optional celibacy eliminated in 1930s
8. Armenian Catholic	Beirut, Lebanon: Patriarch of Cilicia	Almost no married priests
9. Chaldean Catholic	Baghdad, Iraq: Patriarch of Babylon of the Chaldeans	Very few married priests
10. Hungarian Greek Catholic	Nyíregyháza, Hungary: Bishop of Hajdúdorog	More than half
11. Slovak Greek Catholic	Prešov, Slovakia: Bishop of Prešov of Catholics of the Byzantine Rite	More than half
12. Coptic Catholic	Cairo, Egypt: Patriarch of Alexandria of the Copts	Optional celibacy eliminated in 1898
13. Ethiopian Catholic	Addis Ababa, Ethiopia: Archbishop of Addis Ababa of the Ethiopians	Almost no married priests
14. Syrian Catholic	Beirut, Lebanon: Patriarch of Antioch of the Syrians	Optional celibacy eliminated in 1888
15. Italo-Albanian	Lungro and Piana degli Albanesi: two equal sees	Very few married priests
16. Greek Catholics in the former Yugoslavia	Zagreb, Croatia: Bishop of Križevci	Approximately 75%
17. Bulgarian Byzantine Catholic	Sofia, Bulgaria: Apostolic Exarch for Catholics of the Byzantine-Slav Rite in Bulgaria	More than half
18. Greek Byzantine Catholic	Athens, Greece: Apostolic Exarch for Catholics of the Byzantine Rite in Greece	No married priests

Eastern Catholics, like their Orthodox and Roman Catholic counterparts, have the three major orders of bishop, presbyter and deacon. However, unlike the Roman Church, they have retained the minor orders as in the Orthodox Church. Where optional celibacy has not been banned or restricted by the Vatican, candidates for ordination must be married before receiving the diaconate, and all bishops must be celibate (again, as in the Orthodox Church). At the time of the Council of Florence, several eastern hierarchs were made cardinals. In 1856, the Archbishop of Lviv became the first Eastern Catholic cardinal of the post-Florentine period, and thereafter that number has steadily increased, so that at the beginning of the twenty-first century there are several of them. However, especially among the Melkites, there has been considerable debate about the advisability of having eastern hierarchs invested with the title, 'Cardinal of the Roman Church'.

As for offices or titles particular to the various churches, almost all of the Eastern Catholic Churches have retained or revived the titles used in their Orthodox counterparts: 'mitred archpriest (among the Byzantine Slavs) and 'archpriest' or 'protopresbyter' (among the Byzantines at large); 'chorbishop' and 'periodeutes' (among those of the Syriac tradition); and 'vartapet' (among the Armenians). 'Archimandrite' and 'hegoumen' are still used in religious communities in particular, though 'protoarchimandrite' was created as an equivalent of 'superior-general' for religious orders. In many instances, Eastern Catholics have also adopted the Roman Catholic titles 'monsignor' '(papal) chamberlain', and 'prelate', as well as the general western title 'canon'. All these are used with exactly the same significance as in the Roman Rite except for 'monsignor', which the Maronites use as an additional title for chorbishops.

Spirituality

To a greater or lesser extent all of the Eastern Catholic Churches have incorporated elements of Carmelite, Ignatian and Liguorian spiritualities, to mention just a few western forms. This was a natural result of the training received by their clerical elites in the West, as well as contact with Latin religious orders. When appropriated authentically and without disdain for eastern traditions, these spiritualities have borne outstanding fruit: they lead to new forms of contemplation and social action, as well as practices like retreats and spiritual exercises. However, inauthentic appropriations appeared in the attempts of some churchmen to manipulate the western forms as symbols of confessional identity or socio-political distinction. Another occasional byproduct of such westernization was the neglect of indigenous spiritual resources. Consequently, today there are more practitioners of the Jesus Prayer among western Christians – to give just one example – than among Eastern Catholics, where the rosary remains better known. Such examples could be multiplied.

The Catholic Church's pro-Orthodox ecumenism, endorsed by John Paul II, has generated interest in the spirituality of icons, works such as the *Philokalia*, and chants such as the *akathistos* hymn. The biblical, liturgical, spiritual and social justice movements, prominent in some parts of western Christianity, also resonate among educated and more committed Eastern Catholics. Just as in the case of theology, a dynamic, new synthesis of eastern and western could be forged, but this has yet to occur. It is actually those Roman Catholics engaged in a ressourcement of classical Christiantiy – whether eastern or western – who are at the forefront of such a process.

Monasticism

The 1990 *Code of Canons of the Eastern Churches* lists seven categories of the 'consecrated life': (1) Societies of Apostolic Life, (2) Secular Institutes, (3) Societies of Common Life in the Manner of the Religious, (4) Congregations, (5) Orders, (6) Hermitages and (7) Monasteries. The differences among these generally pertain to the nature of the vows taken and the relative rigour of lifestyle. The most prominent communities tend to be the 'exempt Orders', that is, religious communities not under the jurisdiction of the local hierarch, a system adapted from the West (though with some parallels – on a smaller scale – in Orthodoxy, e.g. the Stauropegial monasteries).

Ukrainian Greek Catholic Church

The Basilian (male) Order, reformed according to Jesuit models in 1617 and 1882, is the institutional continuation of the line of monasticism pre-dating the Union of Brest. The analogous Basilian Sisters remained more traditional in their organization far longer, for example, less centralized. The year 1892 saw the creation of Ukraine's first entirely active women's congregation, the Sisters Servants of Mary Immaculate. Eventually, however, the Basilian Sisters became just as active in apostolates such as teaching and patient care. In 1906 Metropolitan Andrey Sheptytsky renewed a traditional form of monasticism with the founding of the Studites, who have a female counterpart. That year also saw the formation of a Ukrainian Province of the Redemptorists. Several smaller congregations (Holy Family, Saint Joseph, Vincentians and Mother of God) also exist. In the West, the Basilians, Sister Servants of Mary Immaculate and Redemptorists are the most numerous. The total number of religious throughout the world approximates 1,000.

Syro–Malabar Church

Until Kuriakos Elias Chavara (d. 1871) helped found the Carmelites of Mary Immaculate and the Congregation of the Mother of Carmel, there were no Syro-Malabar religious communities. It is suggested that before the sixteenth century the monasticism which may have existed in Kerala was eremitical. However, today this church has an astounding 209 religious orders, with more than 30,000 female religious and 4,000 male. Forty-nine of these communities are of Syro-Malabar origin, one is Syro-Malankara, and the rest are of Latin origin (Franciscans, Ursulines, etc.) with roots either in India or abroad. It was after Vatican II that Syro-Malabar provinces of these Latin orders were created. The most prominent male community remains the Carmelites of Mary Immaculate.

Maronite Catholic Church

The three exempt orders of men are (1) the Lebanese Maronite Order, (2) the Congregation of Saint Anthony the Great (Antonines) and (3) the Mariamists, or Order of the Blessed Virgin Mary. The congregation of the Lebanese Missionaries of Kreim (Kreimists) also exists. The first three are seventeenth- and eighteenth-century configurations of earlier Maronite monasticism, while the Kreimists date from 1865. The Maronites have a larger number of female communities: in addition to counterparts of the Antonines and Lebanese Maronite Order, there are the Holy Family Sisters, Sisters of Saint Theresa, Sisters of Our Lady of the Meadow, Sisters of Saint John the Baptist of Hrash, and the Sisters of the Blessed Sacrament. All of the latter date from the nineteenth and twentieth centuries.

Melkite Greek Catholic Church

The Melkites have five religious communities of men and an equal number of female ones, though none of the latter exists in the West. The male communities, of which the first three are exempt Orders centred in Lebanon, are: (1) the Basilian Salvatoreans (from the Rule of Saint Basil and the Holy Saviour Monastery), established in 1683; (2) the stricter, and more eastern, Basilians of Saint John the Baptist of Shouer (or Saor), founded in the early 1700s; (3) the Aleppo Basilians, who separated from the Shouerites in 1829; (4) the Paulists, a congregation established in 1903; (5) the new Monastery of the Resurrection. Three female Orders correspond in name to the male ones, and the two congregations of women are the Missionaries of Our Lady of Perpetual Help, and the Sisters of Our Lady of Good Service.

Liturgy, Sacraments and Music

All the churches with 'Greek' in their name are of the Byzantine Rite, while the Armenian, Coptic, Ethiopian Churches, etc. are of those respective Rites. The Chaldean Catholic Church is of the East Syrian Rite, and the Syrian Catholic and Syro-Malankara Churches of the West Syrian.

Since Vatican II all of the Eastern Catholic Churches – to a greater or lesser extent – have embarked on a process of liturgical reform, usually consisting of a re-appropriation of eastern elements. But this process has been very fluid and unique for each of the churches. Thus it is virtually impossible to describe it in more than general terms.

Ukrainian Greek Catholic Church

Owing to the western Ukraine's position on the frontier between the East Slavic Orthodox and western Catholic civilizations, Ukrainian Catholic worship manifests an unpredictable mix of East and West: One can witness lengthy, entirely chanted, Slav-Byzantine-style services with high icon screens (whether in Ukraine or the West), and at the same time abbreviated, read, western-style services with no screen. In a city like Lviv, the Church's heartland, these differences can be observed in parishes within blocks of each other, even though the Church's *official* service books are very eastern. As for the Gregorian calendar, attempts in the past by Latin or Polish authorities to impose it have led to the retention of the Julian calendar within Ukraine. Elsewhere, however, almost two-thirds of all communities use the former. Since the eighteenth century, chorales – some of them quite beautiful – have been sung during worship. This distinguishes Ukrainian Catholic worship from most Orthodox.

Syro–Malabar Church

While East Syrian in origin, between 1599 and the 1950s the Rite was Latinized almost beyond recognition, though Syriac continued to be used until Vatican II, when the vernacular, Malayalam, was adopted. Pius XII had attempted a restoration of East Syrian usage, but after being estranged from it for so many centuries, Syro-Malabars generally rejected it. In 1998, after decades of Rome's insistence on greater orientalization ('Chaldeanization') on the one hand, and its rejection by the majority of Syro-Malabars on the other, the Major Archbishop and his Synod were given complete freedom to regulate worship. The liturgical question – along with the lack of parity for Syro-Malabars outside Kerala – has remained the most divisive issue facing the Church. The challenge, in the view of liturgists, is to enculturate worship effectively into Indian realities, and to show sensitivity to the faithful who have become essentially Roman Rite in their liturgical ethos. As regards details, Syro-Malabars continue to use unleavened bread, and priests tend to celebrate the Eucharist *versus populum,* though recently a compromise had been struck that would have had them face *versus altare* during the anaphora. An abbreviated and simpler order for the Eucharist – developed in 1968 but rejected by Rome – continues to dominate. After Vatican II, Syro-Malabars began composing hymns heavily influenced by Indian motifs.

Maronite Catholic Church

The Maronite Rite is an independent tradition related to the West Syrian on the one hand and the East Syrian on the other. Ancient Syriac usages were preserved by the monks during the Church's seclusion in the mountains. In 1606 the Maronites became the first easterners to adopt the Gregorian calendar. Structurally, the Eucharist is a variant of the Syriac Liturgy of Saint James and (unlike their Liturgy of the Hours) became heavily Latinized, a trend that was curbed in 1992 with the publication of a new liturgicon. Nonetheless, the Eucharist is said facing the people, organs are almost ubiquitous, and unleavened communion wafers – albeit intincted – continue to be used. Six anaphoras (of the Syriac tradition's several dozen) are regularly employed today. Maronites have been energetic in composing modern hymns (of varying quality), which supplement their reserved, traditional chant. Latin additions to the calendar have been the feasts of the Sacred Heart and Corpus Christi.

Melkite Greek Catholic Church

The Gregorian calendar was adopted in 1857. Because the Melkites are among the least Latinized Eastern Catholics, even in the West some parishes continue to celebrate Matins on Sunday, and unlike their Orthodox counterpart in North America, neither organs nor Italianate polyphony are used, and congregational singing is encouraged. Byzantine chant dominates, though modern hymns, borrowed from the Maronites, may be heard before and after the Liturgy or during communion. Before Vatican II, Corpus Christi was a prominent feast (introduced in 1737), for which Arabic hymnography was composed by Maximos III.

Institutions

Because ecclesiastical institutions are important as sources of information regarding their respective churches, a list of these for all of the Eastern Catholic Churches, rather than only the four largest, is provided below. They are listed according to the size of their membership.

Ukrainian Greek Catholic Church   The Ukrainian Catholic University in Lviv has one of the few university-level theology faculties in all of Ukraine, and publishes the journal *Bohoslovia*. (Other institutions doing academic work in religion reflect the limitations of the transfer of Soviet professors of 'scientific atheism' to 'religious studies', or, on the other hand, the limitations of a catechetical approach – dominant in the newly revived seminaries.) In Rome, the Church sponsors a branch of the university and a metochion at Piazza Madonna dei Monti, while the Vatican supports Saint Josaphat's Seminary and Pokrova graduate residence. In Canada, the Sheptytsky Institute of Eastern Christian Studies of Saint Paul University's Faculty of Theology (Ottawa) is the only institution in the western hemisphere that grants degrees in Eastern Christian Studies from the bachelor's to doctoral level. The institute publishes *Logos: A Journal of Eastern Christian Studies*. Seminaries exist in Ottawa, Washington, DC, and Stamford, Connecticut.

Syro–Malabar Church   Three inter-diocesan major seminaries (one of them pontifical) are operated by the Church in Kerala, along with another twelve sponsored either by dioceses or religious orders. The Paurastya Vidyapitham, or Oriental Institute of Religious Studies, located at Vadavathoor has embarked on an ambitious programme of publishing, with several hundred works appearing to date. It is also a centre for international theological conferences.

Maronite Catholic Church   Rome's Maronite College was founded in 1584, and though converted to other uses intermittently during the last two hundred years, it is again an institution for Maronites. The Lebanese Maronite Order operates the University of the Holy Spirit in Kaslik (founded in 1961), and in 1987 the Lebanese Mariamists opened the University of Notre Dame, modeled on American institutions of higher learning. A patriarchal seminary exists at Ghazir and a diocesan one near Tripoli.

Melkite Greek Catholic Church   The Church currently sponsors three major seminaries: Saint Anne's Patriarchal Seminary at Raboué, Lebanon; Holy Saviour Seminary at Beit Sahour in Israel; and Saint Basil's in Methuen, Massachusetts. Harissa, Lebanon, is the site of a prominent theological institute and publishing house operated by the Melkite Paulists. Sophia Press in Boston has published some of the best translations of Byzantine liturgical texts available. Even some Orthodox use these translations.

Armenian Catholic Church   The Mechitarist Fathers operate important institutes of research on the Island of San Lazzaro, Venice, and in Vienna. Their work is revered as much by the Armenian Orthodox as by Catholics. An Armenian seminary has existed at Bzoummar, Lebanon since 1771, and Rome's Armenian College was created by the Vatican in 1883.

Byzantine Catholic Metropolia of Pittsburgh   Saint Cyril and Methodius Seminary in Pittsburgh has recently opened its programmes to lay persons and gained accreditation through the Association of Theological Schools. It also operates a Cantor's Institute. The journal *Diakonia*, closely associated with the Church during the 1980s and 1990s, was published by Jesuits working in Eastern Christian Studies at the University of Scranton, but ceased publication after the transfer of the university's Eastern Christian collection to Slovakia.

Coptic Catholic Church   Maadi, a suburb of Cairo, is the site of Saint Leo's Patriarchal Seminary, and the Church sponsors a hospital in the town of Assiut.

Chaldean Catholic Church   In spite of difficulties, the Church has attempted to maintain Saint Peter's Patriarchal Seminary in Baghdad.

Ethiopian Catholic Church   Rome established a college for the Ethiopians inside the Vatican walls in 1919 and seminaries are maintained in Addis Ababa and Adigrat (Ethiopia), and Asmara and Keren (Eritrea).

Syrian Catholic Church   The historic monastery of Sharfeh in Lebanon is the site of a patriarchal seminary and publishing house.

Syro–Malankara Catholic Church   Since 1958 the Church has operated the Kurisumala Ashram, where Cistercian spirituality is combined with elements of Hindu asceticism and the West Syrian liturgical tradition. Hindus as well as Christians participate in its programmes. The Church has a college and major seminary in Trivandrum (and six colleges elsewhere), as well as the renowned Saint Ephrem Ecumenical Research Institute in Kottayam, which publishes *The Harp*. It also operates more than a dozen hospitals and almost 300 schools.

Ruthenian Greek Catholic Church   A seminary was founded in Uzhhorod by the Hapsburgs in the 1770s, and was revived in the early 1990s.

Romanian Greek Catholic Church   The Romanian College in Rome was created by the Vatican in 1936. After the fall of Communism, seminaries were established in the cities of Cluj, Baia Mare and Oradea, as the former seminaries in Blaj, Oradea Mare and Gherla were not returned to the Church.

Byzantine Catholics in Former Yugoslavia   Saints Cyril and Methodius Seminary in Zagreb was built in 1685 and continues to operate. Seminarians take their classes at the city's university.

Slovak Greek Catholic Church   Since 1990, a theological faculty has been part of Safarik University in Kosice. A theological faculty is also part of the newly established University of Prešov.

Hungarian Greek Catholic Church   A prominent seminary has existed in Nyiregyháza for several decades, and is at the forefront of an easternization movement.

Greek Byzantine Catholic Church   The Greek College was established in Rome in 1576, though it has always been more than a college for Greeks, serving Catholics of all the Byzantine Churches at one time or another. In Greece, the Church operates one of the most renowned hospitals in all the country, the Pammakaristos, founded in Athens in 1944.

Governance and Canon Law

After more than fifty years of preparation – interrupted by Vatican II – the *Code of Canons of the Eastern Churches* was promulgated by Pope John Paul II in 1990. The new Code only contains canons applicable to all the Eastern Catholic Churches. Each individual church is also required to develop a particular law regulating aspects of its life that differ from the other churches. Once completed, this *ius particularis* must be approved by Rome.

As regards governance, the 1990 Code places Eastern Catholic Churches into one of five different categories, depending on the status of their primate (or the lack thereof): (1) patriarchal, to which belong the Armenian, Chaldean, Coptic, Maronite, Melkite and Syrian; (2) major archepiscopal, a category created for the Ukrainian Catholic Church during Vatican II, to which the Syro-Malabar Church was added in 1992, and the Syro-Malankara and Romanian Churches in 2005; (3) metropolitan *sui iuris* ('of their own law') to which belong the American Ruthenian and Ethiopian; (4) other churches, *sui iuris*: Bulgarian, Greek, Hungarian, Italo-Albanian, Slovak, and a diocese for all of the former Yugoslavia; (5) churches with no hierarchy of their own Rite. The term *sui iuris* is added to the categories below the major archepiscopal, because metropolitanates and dioceses as such are not usually 'churches with their own law'.

Patriarchal churches elect their own primate (in synod), who only requests communion with the pope. For their home territories, these synods also elect their own bishops, from a list of candidates previously approved by Rome. In the case of major archepiscopal churches, the election of the primate must be *approved* by the pope; and for metropolitan churches the pope names the primate from a list of at least three candidates provided by the church's council of bishops. Outside the home territories, Vatican involvement is much more direct, imitating procedures used in the Roman Rite.

Note that patriarchal and major archepiscopal churches have permanent synods of five bishops, who usually meet more frequently than the full synod. Churches of these two categories gather occasionally in ecclesial council, with presbyteral, monastic, lay and institutional delegates from all of the dioceses. However, such councils enjoy only advisory roles.

There is no correlation between size and status among Eastern Catholic Churches. The Ukrainian Catholic and Syro-Malabar Churches, for example, are far larger than most of the patriarchal churches. However, these latter usually owe their status to the fact that at the time of their reunion with Rome, they had a patriarch (or catholicos).

Pilgrimages and Local Traditions

Ukrainian Greek Catholic Church   In Ukraine, the three most important sites – all of them possessing miraculous Marian icons, or copies thereof, and all located near Lviv – are Zarvanytsia, Hoshiv and Univ. In North America, female religious communities in Sloatsburg, New York; Ancaster, Ontario; and Fox Chase, Pennsylvania, all have annual pilgrimages.

Syro–Malabar Church   Many of the important pilgrimage sites are associated with Saint Thomas: his grave at Mylapore (Chennai), and the mountain where, according to tradition, he prayed – Malayatoor (near Kaladi), along with six churches founded by him. The most important of the many Marian shrines is at Velankanni (Tamil Nadu).

Maronite Catholic Church   The Marian shrine at Harissa, above the bay of Jounieh in Lebanon, is the premiere pilgrimage site (on 15 August), attracting not only Christians but Muslims as well. Saint Sharbel's monastery at Annaya is also a prominent shrine.

Melkite Greek Catholic Church   Although the Melkites do not claim any miracle-working icons, pilgrimage sites include Maloula (60 km from Damascus), associated with the Prophet Elias; the basilica of Our Lady of the Waiting at Maghdoshi; a miniature of Hagia Sophia at Harissa; and the famed Monastery of the Holy Saviour near Sidon.

Inter-Church Relations and Ecumenism

Presently, the existence of Eastern Catholic Churches – particularly in the former USSR – and continued Vatican support for them, is considered by some Orthodox, especially in Greece and Russia, to be the greatest impediment to East–West rapprochement. They are accused of having 'betrayed Orthodoxy' in part in order to benefit from privileges available to Catholics.

Ukrainian Greek Catholic Church   Officially, the Church has been very committed to ecumenism. Its primate, Myroslav Lubachivsky (d. 2000) wholeheartedly endorsed the Balamand Statement, and his successor, Lubomyr Husar, is a specialist in East–West relations. From 1992 to 1998, the Kievan Church Study Group energetically explored the possibility of 'double communion': restoring communion with the Ukrainian Catholic Church's mother church, Constantinople, without breaking communion with Rome. Though never disbanded, since 1997 the group has been moribund. Within Ukraine, believers generally divide between those committed to reunion primarily out of ethno-national motives, and those still wary of relations with a church that they have come to identify with the USSR. These two approaches are generally mirrored in the West. Consequently, almost all encounters are with those Ukrainian Orthodox Churches not within Moscow's jurisdiction. Of course, the fact that the Ukrainian Greek Catholic Church (UGCC) is viewed by many Orthodox as the greatest stumbling block to East–West rapprochement has not benefited its attempts to find dialogue partners.

Syro–Malabar Church   Most Syro-Malabars are very committed to restoring the unity of Indian Christianity, a unity that reigned until the reaction against Portuguese religious oppression in 1653 at Mattancherry (the 'Coonan Cross Oath') where Saint Thomas Christians vowed to reject Jesuit directives, and thus created the Mar Thoma Church. The 'quest for an Indian Church' as it is called, is fervently supported by most Syro-Malabars.

Maronite Catholic Church   Among the Syriac Churches of the Middle East, Maronites are frequently considered 'honest brokers' because of the lack of a direct Orthodox counterpart. Bishops Matar of Beirut and Sayyah of Palestine have been particularly active in the Middle Eastern Conference of Churches.

Melkite Greek Catholic Church   Melkites and Orthodox have come to develop extremely good relations, in part because of shared difficulties with Islam and the absence of ethno-national issues dividing them. In the Middle East, priests of the two churches occasionally con-celebrate the Eucharist, in spite of canonical prohibitions, and even in the West, the laity regularly receive at each others' altars. Baptisms and weddings are often con-celebrated. In 1975, the Melkite Synod requested permission from the Vatican to inaugurate 'double communion' (with Rome and the Orthodox), but it was denied. An official bilateral dialogue with the Orthodox Patriarchate of Antioch was inaugurated in 1995, and that same year saw the most pioneering event of contemporary East–West ecumenism in the 'Zoghby–Khodr' initiative: Bishop Zoghby signed a declaration stating: 'I believe in everything taught by the Eastern Orthodox Church, and I am in communion with the Bishop of Rome within the limits recognized by the Holy Fathers of the East during the first millennium and before the separation.' Georges Khodr, the influential Orthodox Metropolitan of Byblos and Batroun officially declared: 'I consider this profession of faith by Bishop Elias Zoghby to create the necessary and sufficient conditions to establish the unity of the Orthodox Churches with Rome.' Rome has refused to sanction this initiative.

Encounter with Other Religions

Ukrainian Greek Catholic Church   The Ukrainian Catholic University's Institute of Religion and Society has sponsored several inter-faith conferences, and Myroslav Marynovych, the Institute's director, has worked very closely with Jewish intellectuals to foster dialogue. Cardinal Husar meets regularly with Ukraine's chief rabbi and Muslim leaders. Within the Church at large, however, this is not an area of dynamic activity.

Syro–Malabar Church   Owing to the fact that many Syro-Malabars consider the Hindu spiritual tradition equivalent to the Greek philosophical tradition as a *praeparatio evangelica*, dialogue with Hinduism involves an intense and creative appropriation of the latter rather than just encounter and acquaintanceship. All of the Church's major educational institutions are involved in this dialogue.

Maronite Catholic Church   The Maronite universities are centres of inter-faith dialogue, and the recent Patriarchal Assembly included Drouze and Muslim observers (in addition to Orthodox).

Melkite Greek Catholic Church   Of all the churches in the Middle-East, the Melkites are the most involved in dialogue with Muslims. The Paulists of Harissa administer an institute for Christian–Muslim dialogue.

Cult of Saints

Ukrainian Greek Catholic Church   In addition to almost twenty saints of the Kievan Rus' period (shared with the Orthodox) Ukrainian Catholics venerate St Josaphat Kuntsevych, Archbishop of Polotsk (12 November), martyred in 1621 by opponents of the Union, and canonized in 1867. His status remains a bone of contention between Catholics and Orthodox. In 2001, John Paul II finally beatified 27 victims of Soviet and Nazi oppression as well as the first superior of the Sisters Servants of Mary Immaculate, Josaphata Hordyshevska (d. 1919). Oddly enough, the Church has no post-patristic Latin saints in its calendar, though in 1891 Roman authorities attempted to introduce 40 of them (who had little relation to the Eastern Church).

Syro–Malabar Church   In addition to the pronounced cult of Saint Thomas, shared by other Indian Christians, Syro-Malabars venerate Blessed Chavara and Blessed Alphonsa, beatified in 1986, during John Paul II's visit to Kerala. Of all the Eastern Catholic Churches, the Syro-Malabars have the greatest devotion to various Latins saints.

Maronite Catholic Church   In addition to Saint Maron (9 February) commemorated by other Eastern Churches, the saints particular to the Maronites are John-Maron (2 March); Sharbel (23 July), a nineteenth-century hermit canonized in 1977 whose body remained incorrupt for many decades; Saint Rebecca (Rafqa) (23 March), a nun who died in 1914 and was canonized in 2001, and Nematallah Hardini, a nineteenth-century monk canonized in 2004. Maronites who have been beatified include the Mass-abki brothers (10 July), three laymen – two of them with families – who were martyred in Damascus in 1860, and proclaimed blessed in 1926. At least ten Latin saints, from Thomas Aquinas to Vincent de Paul, are found in their calendar.

Melkite Greek Catholic Church   The Melkites have no unique saints. Beyond the Byzantine calendar, French influence around 1900 generated a strong devotion to Thérèse of Lisieux. Saint Rita is also popular. These two stand out as western additions. After Vatican II, Gregory Palamas was restored to their calendar. In the West, Melkites have included Russian and Ukrainian saints in some of their service books.

Images and Church Buildings

Ukrainian Greek Catholic Church   The baroque period brought a synthesis in architecture and painting – in some cases quite appealing – of western, Byzantine and folk elements. By the nineteenth century less tasteful forms came to dominate, consisting of poorer renditions of a stylized Italianate. By the early twentieth century, a style dubbed 'neo-Byzantine' emerged, which did not always succeed in blending the abstract and realist in proper proportions (a requirement of true Byzantine imagery). Sheptytsky endorsed a more authentic form of Byzantine art and architecture, but it was his successor, Slipyj, who managed to construct the magnificent cathedral of Saint Sophia in Rome in 1968. In the West, one witnesses a full array of styles, from that represented by Saint Sophia, to thoroughly modern and westernized forms. The Montreal architect Radoslav Zuk represents the latter trend.

Syro–Malabar Church   Before the sixteenth century, Syro-Malabar churches had conspicuous affinities in design and decoration with Hindu temples. After 1599, they became almost indistinguishable from Portuguese Catholic structures. Contemporary religious art sometimes reflects the ethereal stylization associated with Hindu images, and newer church architecture is attempting a similar indigenization.

Maronite Catholic Church   Early Maronite churches were very simple, owing to the community's poverty; they resembled larger homes, and were sometimes carved into the sides of cliffs. In the modern period they became almost identical to Italian or other western European churches, and included large numbers of statues, which some communities retain. Presently, modern architecture dominates, though an attempt has been made to adapt traditional elements such as central rounded domes. Maronites never had chancel barriers (though during the height of Latinization they had communion rails). However, older churches were sometimes covered with frescoes and mosaics. Maronites consider the illustrations found in the Rabbula Gospel to be the best expression of their classical iconographic heritage and there is a movement to promote such imagery.

Melkite Greek Catholic Church   The beginning of the eighteenth century saw the growth of Syro-Arabic elements in Melkite iconography, subsequently coupled with Italianate naturalism. Today, a comprehensive return to Byzantine forms is evident. As for architecture, Ottoman restrictions on the external display of Christianity had previously prevented the construction of noteworthy churches. Today, adaptations of Byzantine styles dominate.

Homeland and Diaspora Politics

Ukrainian Greek Catholic Church   As a 'Church of the people', usually devoid of state sponsorship, the UGCC became very much identified with the Ukrainian national cause, especially as centuries of devastation (and a veritable 'brain drain' to the north and west) left the clergy as the only social elite. While on the one hand this enabled the Church to stand with the people in their daily struggles, it also engendered a deleterious ethno-centrism, from which the Church is emerging only now, after Ukrainian independence (1991). In post-Soviet Ukraine, the Church consistently endorses democratic values while avoiding conspicuous political roles. Should the government become more authoritarian, this endorsement of democracy might bring the Church into conflict with the state. Outside Ukraine, western Canada is the only region where Ukrainian Catholics have played significant political roles, but naturally they do so as Ukrainian-Canadians rather than members of a religious group.

Syro-Malabar Church   Syro-Malabars were avid supporters of the awakening of Indian consciousness in the run up to independence in 1947, and they have committed themselves repeatedly to what their literature calls 'the national resurgence and renewal'. In Kerala, they are a force to be reckoned with in politics, owing to their large social service and educational network, as well as their involvement in the media.

Recently the Church – along with Muslim communities – was subjected to clandestine surveillance and information-gathering by government circles hoping to control minorities.

Maronite Catholic Church   The prominence of the Maronites in Lebanese politics derives from the community's historical evolution from a religious body into a polity. After the Lebanese civil war that began in 1975, factionalism and political disenchantment increased so much among Lebanese Christians that they began to turn again to the Maronite hierarchy for political leadership. The patriarch and bishops are especially trusted with three issues: the status of southern Lebanon, the economic crisis, and electoral reform. Since the Taif Agreement of 1989, the Maronite president's position was even weaker, thus making the hierarchy a natural focus of leadership. In the USA, Maronites have organized to influence American Middle East policy (e.g., the Syria Accountability Act).

Melkite Greek Catholic Church   In Lebanon, Melkites play a moderating role between Muslims and Maronites, and are a respected political force in Syria. In Israel, the Church fully supports the Palestinian cause without, of course, condoning violence. Most Melkites insist that Archbishop Hilarion Capucci, who was arrested and imprisoned in 1974 for transporting arms, was framed.

Women and Women's Expectations

In the homelands, in Churches such as the Ukrainian Catholic, clergy wives traditionally played prominent roles in social work and education; and during the Soviet era, owing to a greater immunity from government reprisals, older women in particular exercised leadership in the 'Uniate' underground. Today, while most of the Eastern Catholic Churches have active women's organizations, and some have seen the wives of clergy organize for retreats and workshops, nothing approaching modern Christian feminism is evident. Ironically, in spite of contact with western Christianity, Eastern Catholics, unlike some of their Orthodox counterparts, have not officially promoted the restoration of the female diaconate. Also, female altar servers are a rarity, and generally prohibited by explicit guidelines or custom. However, women are frequently cantors, lectors, parish council members and episcopal chancery officials; and during the recent Maronite and Ukrainian Catholic Patriarchal assemblies, almost half of the delegates were women.

Recent Developments and Social Involvement

Ukrainian Catholic Church   The Church has taken advantage of the resources provided by Caritas International to establish a network of social services – even in eastern Ukraine. However, only one hospital is entirely operated by the Church. Zenia Kushpeta, a Canadian, has brought the Faith and Light movement (of Jean Vanier) to Ukraine, and the indigenous Fund of St Volodymyr, concentrated in western Ukraine, provides social services. Ukrainian Catholics are pivotal in efforts such as Children of Chernobyl, though strictly speaking these are secular rather than ecclesial projects. In Canada, the Sisters Servants have operated hospitals, and many parishes indirectly sponsor seniors' homes. In Winnipeg, the Redemptorists established Welcome House, and in Toronto the Church sponsored the Saint John the Compassionate Mission to serve street people.

Syro–Malabar Church   Involvement in social welfare and education increased more than a hundredfold in the twentieth century. The Church operates 124 hospitals, 211 orphanages, 121 seniors facilities, more than 150 colleges of various kinds, over 1,000 primary schools and 248 'industrial training and production centres'. The Church's commitment to education has helped to make Kerala the leading state in India for literacy rates. Emblematic of Indian realities is the Church's sponsorship of three leprosy care centres. Bishop Jacob Manathodath, an authority on enculturation, has been prominent in protesting the deleterious effects of globalization and human rights violations, and has called upon the Church of India to become poor herself, rather than simply preaching poverty. Bishop Gratian Mundadan has also been vocal about the Indian Church's need to avoid institutional opulence.

Maronite Catholic Church   In Lebanon, the Church operates hospitals, clinics, geriatric and psychiatric services, services for the disabled, as well as paramedic training facilities.

Melkite Greek Catholic Church   Father Elias Chacour, author of *Blood Brothers* and *We Belong to the Land*, and founder of Mar Elias College in Galilee, has been nominated for the Nobel Peace Prize three times for his work in Arab–Israeli reconciliation. Father Emile Shoufani (see *Le Curéde Nazareth*), director for twenty years of Saint Joseph School in Nazareth, where Muslims, Jews and Christians study together, has also worked to bring these communities closer. In the Middle East, Melkites operate hospitals, orphanages and housing projects. In New York, two of their priests operate inner-city storefront missions for the needy.

Further reading

Arangassery, L. (1999) *A Handbook on Catholic Eastern Churches*. Changanassery, India: HIRS Publications.
Attwater, D. (1961) *The Christian Churches of the East*, vol. 1: *Churches in Communion with Rome*. Milwaukee: Bruce Publishing.
Eastern Catholic Diocesan Directors (1997) *To the Ends of the Earth: Aspects of Eastern Catholic Church History*. Pittsburgh: God with Us Publications.
Fortesque, A. (1923) *The Uniate Eastern Churches*. London: Burns, Oates and Washbourne.
Galadza, P. (1998) What is Eastern Catholic theology? Some ecclesial and programmatic dimensions. *Logos: A Journal of Eastern Christian Studies* 39: 59–70.
Koodapuzha, X. (1988) *Oriental Churches: Theological Dimensions*. Vadavathoor, India: Oriental Institute of Religious Studies.

Nedungatt, G. (ed.) (2002) *A Guide to the Eastern Code: A Commentary on the Code of Canons of the Eastern Churches.* Rome: Pontificio Istituto Orientale.

Nichols, A. (1992) *Rome and the Eastern Churches.* Collegeville, Minn.: Liturgical Press.

Pospishil, V. (1979) *Ex Occidente Lex, From the West – the Law: The Eastern Catholic Churches under the Tutelage of the Holy See of Rome.* Cartaret, NJ: Saint Mary's Religious Action Fund.

Roberson, R. (1999) *The Eastern Churches: A Brief Survey,* 6th edn. Rome: Edizioni Orientalia Christiana. (This book is regularly updated at www.cnewa.org/ecc.htm.)

Roberti, J.-C. (1992) *Les Uniates.* Paris: Éditions du Cerf.

Roccasalvo, J. L. (1992) *The Eastern Catholic Churches: An Introduction to their Worship and Spirituality.* Collegeville, Minn.: Liturgical Press.

Suttner, E. (1991) *Church Unity: Union of Uniatism?* Rome: Centre for Indian and Inter-religious Studies.

Taft, R. (1996) *The Christian East: Its Institutions and its Thought – A Critical Reflection,* Orientalia Christiana Analecta 251. Rome: Pontificio Istituto Orientale.

—— (1998) Eastern Catholic theology: Is there any such thing? Reflections of a practitioner. *Logos: A Journal of Eastern Christian Studies* 39: 13–58.

CHAPTER 16

Eastern Christian Liturgical Traditions
Eastern Orthodox

Graham Woolfenden

The Emperor Constantine founded the city of Constantinople in 324, and by 381 the bishop was regarded as second only to the bishop of Rome. After the break with Rome in 1054, he was regarded as the first among equals of the Orthodox episcopate. His cathedral, the Great Church, was dedicated in 360 and known as Hagia Sophia from around 430. The original building was replaced by that created for the Emperor Justinian in 537. It became a mosque after 1453, but was made a museum in 1934. This church was the principal place of development for what became the Byzantine liturgical tradition.

Early liturgical influences came from the Greek language traditions of the Syrian city of Antioch. For centuries the standard anaphora or eucharistic prayer for Sundays was that attributed to St Basil the Great (d. 379). John Chrysostom became bishop of Constantinople in 398, and may have brought with him from Antioch a version of the anaphora of the Apostles edited for his own use, which became in turn part of the Byzantine tradition (Taft 1992).

The liturgical rites were originally solemn but simple, making use of readings and psalms to recall Christ's acts of salvation. The daily office of the Great Church, the *akolouthia asmatiki* or 'sung' office was largely made up of psalms and other scriptural texts and made good use of the large number of clergy and singers available to this imperial foundation.

Some major changes in the liturgical tradition were introduced from the time of the monastic reformer Theodore of Studios (759–826), and were given impetus by the struggle with iconoclasm. For example, Palestinian monks had begun to elaborate the Jerusalem tradition with a rich liturgical poetry from the seventh century, most especially at the daily offices, and this became influential in Constantinople. Eventually the Palestinian monastic office (itself based on the framework of the Jerusalem cathedral office), was combined with the priestly prayers and litanies of the Constantinopolitan office to form the synthesis that is the contemporary Byzantine round of daily prayer.

At the same time, Jerusalem increasingly accepted many features of Constantinopolitan provenance, especially in the Divine Liturgy. The resulting hybrid office shows its composite origins most vividly in the last few days of Holy Week, when the passion accounts are read several times in forms that reflect the traditions of both cities.

The flowering of Greek language liturgical poetry was of such magnitude that the material was collected into several different books. The Sunday and weekday cycles were codified as the *Octoechos* (book of the eight tones) in the eighth century. The Lent and Paschal cycles of the *Triodion* (book of three odes, as in Lenten Matins) were codified from the tenth century, with the Paschal services later entitled *Pentecostarion*. From the same era, the material for fixed feasts such as Christmas was collected into the twelve-volume *Menaion* (book of the month). The unchanging parts of the offices were and are to be found in the Horologion/*Chasoslov*, the book of hours, and the priests' prayers are in the *Euchologion* (*Sluzhebnik* in Slavonic). To these would be added the Psalter and a separate priest's book for other services, known in Slavonic as a *Trebnik* or book of rites. In the tenth century another kind of book appeared, intended as a guide to all the other liturgical works, and known as the *Typikon*.

By the twelfth century, fusion of the Palestinian tradition of the monastery of Mar Sabas and the Great Church of the Holy Wisdom was complete. The hybrid usages of Constantinople had, since the ninth century, been spreading beyond Greece and Asia Minor through the work of the brothers Cyril and Methodius, and their successors based at Ohrid in Macedonia. The southern Slav peoples, the Serbs and Bulgars became Christians in this liturgical tradition, as did the Romanians, who used Slavonic in all their church services until relatively modern times, although they ordinarily speak a Romance language. The conversion of Kievan Rus', beginning in 988, ensured the enormous spread of Byzantine liturgical traditions amongst the east Slav peoples, in what became the Russian Empire, and beyond.

The Georgians had adopted Christianity in the fourth century and retained strong links with Antioch and Jerusalem. The bishops and people of the ancient sees of Antioch, Alexandria and Jerusalem who remained Chalcedonian, and the churches connected with them such as that of Georgia, eventually became heavily Byzantinized. As a result, the Greek recension of the Jerusalem Liturgy of St James is now only used in a few places once a year, and will not be discussed here.

The authoritative editions of the *Typika* and the *diataxeis* (compendia of rubrics) codified the variant readings in the ancient manuscripts. The most influential *diataxis*, that of the mid-fourteenth-century Patriarch Philotheos Kokkinos was eventually included in the early printed books. Orthodox liturgical books were first printed in Greek, in Rome and Venice from 1526 onwards, Slavonic ones appearing not long afterwards in Muscovy and in what is now Ukraine.

In what follows we will sometimes differentiate between Greek and Russian customs (which do not denote any difference in faith). Greek liturgical customs are observed by the Greek- and Arabic-speaking churches of the ancient Patriarchates of Constantinople, Alexandria, Antioch and Jerusalem; the Church of Greece and the Church of Cyprus (the latter retains a distinctive, older *Typikon*). Russian customs are found amongst the Russians, Ukrainians, Belorussians, and the Georgians (who were heavily Russianized from the eighteenth century onwards). Serbs, Bulgarians and Romanians follow broadly Russian customs with a variety of other, sometimes local, influences. The Byzantine Rite Catholics of Ukraine, the Carpathians and Romania have adopted a number of Latin usages, though efforts are being made to stamp these out. This Latinization was somewhat less marked among the Greek Rite Catholics of the Middle East.

It is a commonly observed phenomenon that liturgical centres at a distance from the place of origin are more likely to conserve older ritual traditions. This is especially true in the Byzantine liturgical tradition; the Russians have often faithfully preserved older Constantinopolitan practice. The Russian *Typikon* declares that it is that of the monastery of St Sabas (near Jerusalem), whereas the Greek '*Typikon* of the Great Church of Christ' (i.e., the See of Constantinople), was edited in the early nineteenth century to reflect changes in the practices of the Greek-speaking churches.

The Setting of the Liturgy and Other Services

Since the Middle Ages, the typical Byzantine church has been a centrally planned building with an attached sanctuary at the east end. Entrance should be through a narthex, a space large enough for some services to be held there. The central space, the nave, may be largely devoid of seating, as people normally stand.

Greek churches usually provide lecterns for the cantors, either side of the east end of the nave. A throne is often provided for the bishop by the choir on the right hand side. Russian churches have a platform, the *solea*, in front of the sanctuary, the central part of which, jutting out into the nave, is the place of preaching and receiving communion, and is called the 'ambo', a word reserved by the Greeks for a pulpit in the nave from which the Gospel is read when a deacon serves. Russian churches often have a raised platform for the bishop in the centre of the nave which may also serve as a place for the deacon to read the gospel.

The sanctuary or bema is screened by the *templon* or iconostasis, a barrier covered with icons and with three doors. The central or holy doors are used by bishops, priests or deacons during the more important services. Others use the side doors. Secondary sanctuaries are common in Russia. All sanctuaries contain a cuboid altar or holy table, placed so as to allow processions to pass easily around its east side. On the left side of the sanctuary, or in a separate chamber, is the table of preparation or *prothesis*. On the right side may be the *diaconicon*, where vestments are kept. In the apse there should be a central throne for the bishop and seats for the priests around it. These last are now often absent from Greek churches.

Outside the time of the eucharistic liturgy, nothing is placed on the altar except those things that normally remain there. These are the *antimension*, a consecrated cloth without which no celebration may take place, the Gospel book placed on top of it, a hand cross, and cloths for wiping the mouths of the communicants, and nowadays, a container for the reserved holy gifts (they were once kept on the table of preparation). Candles are often placed around rather than on the altar, and in Russian practice a seven-branch lamp stand is placed at the rear of the altar.

The Daily Round of Prayer

The order of the daily services begins with Vespers on the previous night. This is followed by Compline (or 'After Dinner'), then the Midnight Office, Matins, the First, Third,
Sixth Hours and the Divine Liturgy. Then the Ninth Hour immediately before the next
Vespers completes the cycle. The services are now usually grouped; common Russian
practice is to serve Ninth Hour, Vespers, Little Compline, Matins and the First Hour in
the evening, and then Midnight, Third and Sixth Hours and Divine Liturgy in the
morning. An early-twentieth-century book recommended a time between 4 and 5 a.m.
for the morning offices, with early Liturgy at 6 or 6.30, late Liturgy at 9 a.m. Vespers
were between 3.30 and 5 p.m. depending on the time of year, but the festal All-Night
Vigil would start at 6 p.m. Russian parishes that do not have a daily Liturgy will have
at least the 'All-Night Vigil' of Vespers, Matins and First Hour on Saturday evening and
the eves of feasts; with Liturgy following the Third and Sixth Hours in the morning.
(See also Mother Mary 1969.)

In Greek, Middle Eastern and Balkan churches, daily liturgy is rare, but it is not
uncommon for Vespers and Matins to be celebrated each evening and morning. On
Mount Athos, Midnight, Matins and the First Hour start around 3.30 a.m., followed in
turn by Hours and Liturgy (on weekdays, the Liturgy may be in a subsidiary church).
The main meal is now served if not a fasting day, and then in the evening, Ninth Hour
and Vespers precede dinner, Compline follows it.

The Evening Office of Vespers (Greek: *Hesperinos,*
Slavonic: *Vechernya*)

(NB: The psalms are numbered according to the Septuagint.)

This important office begins the daily liturgical round and comes in a number of
forms. Little Vespers is celebrated with the Ninth Hour in the afternoon before an All-
Night Vigil. If there is no vigil, the Ninth Hour immediately precedes festal Vespers. The
Vespers that comprises the first part of a Vigil is called Great Vespers, and is more or
less the same as any Sunday or festal Vespers. Vespers from Sunday to Friday evenings
inclusive is called Daily Vespers. In the Great Fast (Lent) weekday Vespers follows a
special order which may also be observed in other fasting seasons. On Wednesdays,
Fridays, and certain other days of Lent, Vespers is combined with communion from the
reserved species and called the Liturgy of the Presanctified Gifts. On the eves of Christmas, Epiphany, and the Annunciation (if it falls on a weekday), and on Holy Thursday
and Holy Saturday, Vespers is combined with the Divine Liturgy.

The standard opening blessing, 'Blessed be our God, always, now and ever and to
the ages of ages' is replaced by a more elaborate one, 'Glory to the Holy Consubstantial,
Undivided and Life-Giving Trinity . . .' when there is a Vigil. A series of opening prayers
that include the 'Our Father' precede all groups of offices, the last element 'Come let us
worship God our King' (based on Psalm 94) signals the beginning of each new hour.
The first proper element of Vespers is Psalm 103, a thanksgiving for creation, during

which the priest reads the seven lamp-lighting prayers of the Constantinopolitan cathedral rite. If the service is part of an All-Night Vigil then special refrains are sung by the choir (otherwise the psalm is read by a single reader). This Vigil singing can be very elaborate, and during it the whole church and all present are incensed. The deacon then chants the Great Litany or *synapte* with its general petitions, found at the beginning of almost all Byzantine liturgical services, 'In peace, let us pray to the Lord. Lord have mercy.'

There now follows the reading of the Psalter. The psalms are divided into twenty divisions called *kathismata*. One is recited at Vespers every day (except Sunday), and two (normally) at Matins. The *kathismata* are further divided into three *staseis* or antiphons, and it is common to sing just the first antiphon, Psalms 1–3, or select verses thereof, on Saturday nights and the eves of feasts. Ideally the Psalter is read weekly, and twice weekly in Lent, but in non-monastic churches the reading is usually omitted or abbreviated. After the *kathisma* or in some cases after each antiphon, there is a short litany beginning: 'Again and again, in peace let us pray to the Lord.' This probably replaces a prayer, and the saying of the first three of the lamp-lighting prayers at each antiphon in the Liturgy of the Presanctified is a relic of that custom. (For the old Constantinople office see Woolfenden 2004: 93–120.)

The central part of Vespers begins with the singing of the first verses of Psalm 140, 'Lord I have cried to you, hear me', and the words, 'Let my prayer come before you like incense' have given rise to a daily incensation at this point. Most of the remaining verses of Psalms 140, 141, 129 and 116 are omitted, but not the last ones, when poetic stanzas called *stikhira* are inserted between the psalm verses: ten on feasts, six on weekdays, four at Little Vespers. *Stikhira* are appointed according to the day and feast. At the *stikhira* with the doxology, 'Glory be . . .', there is an entry procession and the singing of the ancient hymn 'Hail gladdening light'. There is no entrance procession on weekdays or at Little Vespers.

After the entrance there is a form of responsorial psalm called the *prokeimenon*, e.g., the response for Sunday: 'The Lord is king, he is robed in majesty'. On the eve of feasts there is a series of three readings from the Old Testament (though on the feasts of Apostles they are from the New). On Lenten weekdays there are two readings from Genesis and Proverbs (Exodus and Job in Holy Week), each preceded by a *prokeimenon* taken from the psalms in order (see Mother Mary 1978). Between them, when Presanctified is celebrated, the congregation is blessed with a candle and the censer at the words 'The light of Christ enlightens all', possibly an ancient evening light ceremony. Similarly a repeat of the verses of Psalm 140 'Let my prayer arise' after the readings at Presanctified may also derive from the cathedral office of Constantinople.

On feasts the *prokeimenon* is followed by the litany known as the *ektene* which has a thrice repeated 'Lord have mercy', and then the ancient prayer, 'Vouchsafe, O Lord to keep us this night'. On weekdays this prayer follows the *prokeimenon* directly. The next litany, 'Let us complete our evening prayer to the Lord' asks for more personal needs such as a guardian 'angel of peace' and forgiveness of sins, and is followed by an ancient prayer of blessing and dismissal, the prayer over the people. On the eve of feasts, the procession known as the *Litiya* now takes place. *Stikhira* accompany the procession to the narthex or the back of the church, and there are lengthy intercessions with multiple

'Lord have mercy's'. The return to the sanctuary is accompanied by further *stikhira*, the *Aposticha*, a version of which are also chanted on non-festal days. The canticle 'Lord now let your servant, depart in peace' is said or sung, followed by prayers including 'Our Father', after which come the *troparia* or dismissal hymn(s) of the day.

The festal *troparia* introduce a blessing of bread, wheat, wine and oil, originally intended to sustain those present through the night watch. The first ten verses of Psalm 33 once accompanied their distribution. On weekdays the *ektene* is sung after the *troparia* and then comes the dismissal rite. Lenten Vespers concludes with the same four *troparia* each night, accompanied by prostrations, further prayers, and the penitential Prayer of St Ephrem, 'O Lord and Master of my life'.

After the solemn singing of 'Let my prayer arise', the Liturgy of the Presanctified is more like an ordinary Liturgy (see below). At Vesperal Divine Liturgies, the psalms for the day of the week are not recited and the Old Testament readings of Vespers are juxtaposed with those of the Liturgy, which then continues as normal.

Compline or 'After Dinner' has two forms. Great Compline is used on Monday to Friday in Lent and other fasting seasons, and also on Christmas, Theophany and Annunciation eves, when it forms the All-Night Vigil with Matins. The service is in three parts, the first comprising a group of six psalms (4, 6, 12, 24, 30 and 90), verses from Isaiah with the refrain 'God is with us' and other prayers that suit the end of the day, seeking divine protection for the night. The second part, largely made up of Psalms 50, 101 and the Prayer of Manasses, is a service of penance, and the third, which includes Psalms 69, 142, the 'Glory to God in the Highest', and two lengthy prayers to the Mother of God and to the Saviour, entrusts the night to God. Little Compline is an abbreviated version of this, retaining Psalms 50, 69 and 142, and often including a canon (see below). In both cases the service normally finishes with an act of mutual forgiveness and a highly simplified litany. The Midnight Office on weekdays largely comprises Psalm 118, and on Sunday, a canon in honour of the Trinity. It closes with prayers and the same litany as that used at Compline.

The Night to Morning Service of Matins (*Orthros, Utrenya*)

When Matins is not preceded by any other office, it begins with a short additional service of Psalms 19 and 20, some *troparia*, and a short litany. This so-called 'Royal Office' may be derived from the preliminary rites of the sung cathedral office (Larina 2006). The main service begins with the blessing 'Glory to the Holy . . .' (see above) and after introductory verses come the Six Psalms, 3, 37, 62, 87, 102 and 142. During the second set of three psalms the priest says twelve dawn prayers, which were also part of the chanted office. The Six Psalms are all appropriate to a vigil before dawn, and the whole first part of this service may be seen as awaiting the light of the new day. After the psalms and the *synapte*, the deacon leads the responsorial chant of verses from Psalm 117, 'The Lord is God and has appeared unto us' or on fasting weekdays, the more ancient daily chant of 'Alleluia' with verses from Isaiah 26, 'My spirit seeks thee early in the morning, O God.' In both cases *troparia* follow.

The night vigil continues with the reading of the Psalter in course. Short litanies and *troparia* called sessional hymns follow each *kathisma* (see above). At certain times of the year, *kathisma* 18 is read every evening at Vespers, and three *kathismata* at Matins, otherwise only two.

On Sundays and feasts there is now inserted a cathedral vigil, similar to that described by Egeria (Wilkinson 1999: 144–5). On feasts the *Polyeleos* is sung, Psalms 134 and 135 with 'Alleluia' responses. Slav churches and the monasteries of Mount Athos add Psalm 136, 'By the waters of Babylon' on the three pre-Lent Sundays. On ordinary Sundays Psalm 118 is to be sung, followed by a series of verses with the response 'Blessed are thou, O Lord, teach me thy statutes', the *Evlogitaria*. The psalms may be omitted or radically abbreviated, but an incensation is carried out in preparation for the Gospel.

Further chants, the *hypakoe*, the Graduals, and a *prokeimenon*, precede one of a series of eleven resurrection Gospels, read by the priest at the altar. On feasts, in Russian churches, the Matins Gospel is read in the centre of the church, and an additional chant, the 'Magnification' is inserted after *Polyeleos*. After the resurrection Gospel all sing 'We have seen the resurrection of Christ', and then Psalm 50, some verses and a prayer. It is customary at this point for the faithful to come and venerate the Gospel book. On feasts they may instead venerate the festal icon and be anointed with some of the oil blessed at the end of Vespers.

Psalm 50 marks the beginning of the morning part of the office, and is also found, without festal verses and prayers, straight after the psalmody on weekdays. This psalm leads into the major feature of the morning office, the canon.

The canon of Matins is a series of nine biblical canticles or odes, grouped in threes. The first: Exod. 15: 1–19 (the Song of the Sea), Deut. 32:1–43 and I Sam. 2: 1–10 (the Song of Hannah). The second is Hab. 3: 2–19, Isa. 26: 9–21 and Jonah 2: 2–9. The last group is made up of the two songs of the three young men in the furnace from Dan. 3 and the Lucan canticles 'Magnificat' and 'Benedictus', which together form the ninth ode. From around the eighth century it became customary to add poetic refrains of increasing length, and the biblical verses are now wholly omitted, except on the weekdays of Lent, and in the monasteries of Mount Athos and a very few other places, being effectively replaced by the poetry (ode 2 is normally left out altogether, and only a few penitential canons include a poetic version). The first of the poetic verses, the *heirmos* will often preserve a memory of the biblical canticle, e.g., the well-known 'On beholding the sea of life', recalling the canticle of Jonah and used in services for the dead. In Russian usage only the *heirmos* is sung and the *troparia* read, and in some Greek usages the *troparia* are sung. (See Mother Mary 1978 for details of the three ode canons in Lent.)

The use of more than one canon was instrumental in the disappearance of the biblical verses. Four are usually appointed for Sunday and three for weekdays. Further poetic stanzas follow the third and sixth odes, notably the *kontakion*, which is often the remnant of a much more extended poem. During the eighth ode, originally 'Benedicite', there is an incensation, which is continued during the singing of the Magnificat (only replaced on great feasts), and before the ninth poetic ode. This may have once marked a procession from the narthex to the nave in the Constantinopolitan cathedral office.

After the canon is a poetic piece called *photogogikon* or *exaposteilarion*, which once signalled sunrise, the time to praise the risen Lord in the morning psalms of praise, 148–50. On Sundays, feasts and solemn days, these psalms have *stikhira* as at Vespers. The doxology 'Glory to God in the Highest' is the conclusion to and climax of Matins; it is sung on festal days but recited on weekdays in a variant form. On Sundays and feasts Matins is concluded by the *ektene*, the litany 'Let us complete our morning prayer to the Lord' and a prayer over the people. On weekdays, 'Let us complete . . .' follows the lesser doxology, and then *Aposticha* verses as at Vespers, prayers including the 'Our Father', the *troparia* of the day, and the *ektene*.

The Hours of Prayer in the Day

The First, Third, Sixth and Ninth Hours all share a similar structure. They have three fixed psalms (5, 89 and 100 at the First, 16, 24 and 50 at the Third, 53, 54 and 90 at the Sixth and 83, 84 and 85 at the Ninth), then usually the *troparion* and *kontakion* of the day, some appropriate verses of scripture, a prayer common to all the hours and a prayer for each hour. In fasting seasons the *troparia* are the same every day and reflect the traditional themes of the hours: respectively, early morning, the sending of the Holy Spirit, the crucifixion, and the death of Christ. The Books of Hours also provides 'inter-hours' for fasting seasons outside of Lent, but they are now rarely used. In Lent the weekday hours may include the reading of a *kathisma*, and the Sixth Hour has a daily reading from Isaiah (Ezekiel in Holy Week), with *prokeimena* before and after it. On three days in the year, Christmas and Epiphany eves and Good Friday, there is a special form of the Hours, celebrated (mid-morning) as one service called Royal Hours. Each hour retains one of its usual psalms (5, 50, 90 and 85) alongside two others chosen for the day. There are poetic verses and Old Testament, Epistle and Gospel readings.

The Divine Liturgy

The eucharistic service may be conveniently divided into four parts, the *prothesis* or preparation, the service of three antiphons and prayers (called an *enarxis*), the Liturgy of the Catechumens (or of the word) and the Liturgy of the Faithful.

Preparation

The liturgical books begin with the prayers said by the priest and deacon on entering church, and at their vesting and washing of hands. Then, at the table of the preparation, the priest takes the first of a series of loaves (the modern Greek custom of using one loaf for all that follows is not envisaged by the rubrics), and, saying verses from Isaiah 53: 7–8 'He was led as a sheep to the slaughter' etc., he cuts out a square of bread called the Lamb. This is placed on the *diskos* or paten, and wine with a little water is poured into the chalice by the deacon. The priest takes a particle from the next loaf in honour of the Mother of God, placing it beside the Lamb. From the third he takes nine particles in honour of nine orders of saints and places them on the other side. From the fourth and fifth loaves he takes particles to remember by name, first the living and then the departed. (Only the Lamb is used for communion.) The preparation is concluded by the priest veiling the *diskos* and chalice, incensing the gifts and saying a prayer, which is the oldest part of this rite (being known in the ninth century). Most of this rite was medieval elaboration of a simple selection of the bread and wine from amongst the peoples' offerings, and originally took place in an outside sacristy, the *skeuophylakion*, which at Hagia Sophia was to the north east of the main church (see Taft 1975).

The enarxis

The deacon incenses the church, and the priest begins with the blessing: 'Blessed be the kingdom of the Father, the Son and the Holy Spirit . . .' The deacon says the *synapte* while the priest says a prayer. Then is sung the first antiphon (in Russian churches usually Psalm 102), and there is a small litany while the priest says another prayer. The second antiphon (Russian usage, Psalm 145) always includes the hymn 'Only-begotten Son and Word of God', and is followed by another short litany and prayer. The third antiphon is usually the Beatitudes.

This service of antiphons and prayers was originally a processional service sung on days when the Sunday or festal observance began at one church and processed to another, most especially Hagia Sophia, for the Eucharist. By the ninth or tenth centuries, when there was no procession through the city, a priest and deacon would begin the service of three antiphons, and the bishop would only enter after it. In the contemporary rite, when a bishop celebrates, he remains in the body of the church during the service of the antiphons and only enters the sanctuary at the so-called 'Little Entrance'.

The Liturgy of the Catechumens

The 'Little Entrance' was originally the entry into church. The deacon carries the Gospel book and precedes the priest around the altar and out of the north door to come before the holy doors. The procession goes to collect the bishop from the body of the church when he celebrates. Appropriate verses followed by the *troparia* and *kontakia* of the day are sung as the clergy enter the sanctuary. The singing of the *trisagion*, 'Holy God, Holy mighty, Holy Immortal have mercy on us' was probably the refrain of the original entry chant. The clergy move during this chant to their places behind the altar, the bishop going to the central throne in the apse, thus completing the entry rite.

After the greeting 'Peace be to all', there is a *prokeimenon* proper to the day, and then the Epistle is read. Incensation in preparation for the Gospel should take place during the 'Alleluia' chant that follows, but is often begun during the reading. A deacon receives the Gospel book and a blessing from the celebrant and may read in the body of the church, either in the centre (Russian usage) or from a bema to one side (Greek usage).

Anciently sermons were preached after the Gospel and this practice is again common in many places, especially in western Europe and America. Other practices include preaching at the end of the Liturgy and even during the communion of the clergy, if there are a large number of concelebrants.

The originally penitential litany known as the *ektene* has been imported into the rite at this point, and may be followed by a Litany for the Departed. A further litany follows for the catechumens, who were then dismissed (often omitted today), and there are two short Litanies of the Faithful. This was the original location of the *synapte*. The two prayers said by the priest are for the preparation of the clergy, and that God will hear the prayers of the faithful.

The Liturgy of the Faithful

This begins with the singing of the Cherubic Hymn and the Great Entrance. The bread and wine prepared in the outside *skeuophylakion* used to be brought in a solemn procession to the altar, which came to be seen as a burial procession of Christ whose resurrection would be celebrated in the anaphora. The hymn, 'Let us who mystically represent the Cherubim' may have replaced a psalm sung at this point. When a bishop celebrates nowadays he receives the gifts at the holy doors, but a celebrating priest and deacon carry the chalice and the paten in procession from the preparation table, through the north door (around the church in Greek usage) and in through the holy doors.

A further litany accompanies the priest's prayer of approach to the altar, and after that, the exchange of the kiss of peace (nowadays only between the clergy), is followed by the singing or saying of the Nicene-Constantinopolitan creed (introduced to the liturgy in the early sixth century).

The anaphora or eucharistic prayer follows the same Antiochene shape whether it is that attributed to St Basil (now used only on ten days annually), or to St John Chrysostom. The opening dialogue includes the call to lift the hearts, and the reply 'Let us give thanks to the Lord' is sung at length while the priest prays the opening thanksgiving for God's creative and redemptive work. The last words of this thanksgiving are sung aloud to introduce the hymn 'Holy, holy, holy', and the priest continues to thank God more especially for the saving work of Christ. This leads to the chanting aloud of the words of institution, with the response 'Amen'. During the second 'Amen', the priest commemorates the saving acts of Crucifixion, Resurrection, Ascension and sending the Holy Spirit, and the paten and chalice are elevated in a gesture of offering. The singers again continue while the priest invokes the Spirit upon the people and the gifts, and specifically prays for consecration of the gifts, so that the communicants may benefit from their reception. The Mother of God is commemorated by a hymn that may change for certain feasts, and the priest continues to intercede for the living and the dead, he is audible again when he prays for the bishop, and the prayer finishes with a doxology chanted aloud.

After the greeting of the people, another litany with the 'angel of peace' petitions covers the prayer of preparation for the Lord's Prayer. 'Our Father' is usually sung or said by all, and is followed by a prayer of inclination originally intended as a blessing over those who were not receiving communion, and who would now leave (Taft 2000: 166–97). After another prayer the priest breaks the Lamb into four, saying 'The Holy things for the Holy People', the ancient invitation to communion.

One of the four parts is placed in the chalice, followed by some hot water, a custom which may be a remnant of Greco-Roman symposium practice (Taft 2000: 441–502), and now seen as a symbol of the warmth of the Holy Spirit. The second part is used for the communion of the clergy, and the other two are cut into much smaller particles and placed in the chalice for the communion of the faithful. It is normal to close the doors and curtain of the altar during the communion of the clergy and then open them to bring out the chalice for the people with suitable invitation.

Communion has become much more frequent in parts of the contemporary Orthodox Church, and one will see large queues before several chalices in Russian and Ukrainian churches. In other part of the Orthodox world, only a few people, mostly children, will receive communion, except on great festivals.

As in all traditional liturgies, the remaining rites are quite short. Two brief hymns, 'We have seen the true light' and 'Let our mouths be filled with thy praise O Lord' are followed by a short litany of thanksgiving. The prayer 'Behind the ambo' said in the centre of the church by Russian priests and before the icon of the Saviour by Greeks was the ancient final prayer that followed the monition 'Let us depart in peace'. The prayer is now followed by chants that once accompanied the distribution of blessed bread, a blessing, and the dismissal prayer drawn from the offices. Nowadays blessed bread is distributed after the final prayer. The bread, known as *antidoron* (in place of the gifts), should be what was cut off the loaf when extracting the Lamb.

The Initiation Rites

There are a number of preparatory rites before baptism: eight days after the birth, the naming of the child; then, forty days after the birth, the 'churching' of the mother and child. Traditionally, the mother would then attend church again, and the child would begin to do so. The first attendance at church by the mother and child together is usually shortly followed by the baptism.

The present baptismal rite was intended for adults, and to be spread over a period of time. Most of the rite as we know it today was complete by the eighth-century Barberini codex (see Parenti and Velkovska 1995). The first prayer accompanied enrolment as a catechumen, and there then followed three exorcisms and an exorcistic prayer. Now done together, these were spread over several weeks of catechumenal instruction. Having been thoroughly prepared to turn away from the pagan world, the candidate renounces Satan, even spitting upon him, and turns to Christ, reciting the Nicene-Constantinopolitan Creed. The responses and profession of faith are made by the godparents when the candidate is an infant. The catechumenate is concluded by a prayer that the candidate may be worthy to receive the grace and power of baptism.

The catechumenal rites are carried out in the narthex or at the back of the church and the baptism rite proper starts with the candidate and sponsors going with the priest to the font in the centre of the church. (In many modern Russian churches the font is in a separate side chapel or church building.) The rite begins with 'Blessed is the kingdom . . .' and the *synapte*. The priest then blesses the water in a prayer that praises God for creation, with special reference to the life-giving powers of water. The prayer calls for the Spirit to be sent upon the waters of the font, that there may be redemption, sanctification, cleansing, incorruption, life and so on for the baptizand. The priest blesses olive oil, recalling the sprig of olive brought by the dove to Noah, as a protection against all evil. He pours some oil into the water, and anoints the candidate with the oil, preferably all over the body.

The baptism follows immediately, the candidate being immersed in water three times with the words 'The servant of God N is baptized in the name of the Father, Amen. And of the Son, Amen. And of the Holy Spirit, Amen.' Where possible, the whole body is dipped in the water, but if this is not possible many Orthodox are content to pour water over the head.

The newly baptized person is wrapped in a sheet or towel and Psalm 31, 'Blessed are they whose iniquities are forgiven' is sung. The newly baptized is anointed again, this time with the *myron* or chrism. Chrism is usually blessed periodically by the head of each autocephalous church as there is need; not usually an annual event as it is in the West. To the olive oil is added a complex mixture of sweet-smelling essences which takes several days to mix completely. The priest at baptism takes the chrism and says a prayer that blesses God who has regenerated this person by water and the Spirit, and prays that he or she may now receive the seal of the Holy Spirit, the communion in the body and blood of Christ, and life in the Orthodox Church. The baptized is then anointed on the forehead, eyes, nostrils, mouth, ears, breast, hands and feet; the priest saying each time 'The Seal of the Gift of the Holy Spirit. Amen.'

Many western theologians, and an older generation of Orthodox divines, saw this anointing with chrism as equivalent to western confirmation. The rite is, however, an integral part of the baptism and the texts indicate that baptism is itself a place of the pouring out of the Spirit. Orthodox initiation is an integrated rite of baptismal bath and the gift of the Spirit, leading to the reception of communion by all the baptized. There is nothing similar to the western medieval development of a distinct sacramental rite of confirmation reserved to the bishop.

Having been anointed with chrism, the newly baptized is dressed in a white robe, and is led around the font by the priest, the choir singing 'As many as have been baptized into Christ, have put on Christ, Alleluia'. Anciently, this would have been the point when the newly baptized were taken into church for the Liturgy, and an Epistle (Rom. 6: 3–11) and Gospel (Matt. 28: 16–20) are read at this point.

The remaining ceremonies were originally carried out a week later and include a ceremonial washing off of the oil. The white robe is removed with a prayer and the neophyte is tonsured as a sign of a life offered to God. Holy Communion is often given to the newly baptized at this point, or he or she receives it the following week. A final, later ceremony, also known as 'churching' concludes the rite. The priest conducts the neophyte around the altar, holding him, if a child, in his arms. Females are normally simply placed before the holy doors. Finally the priest gives a newly baptized child back to his or her mother (not the godparent) to be received anew as a gift from God.

Renewing the Spotless Robe: the Mystery of Confession

Many of the prayers given in the *Euchologia* for penance and confession had their origin in canonical penance and communal reconciliation. Practice nowadays varies quite widely; many Orthodox use the sacrament only rarely when conscious of a very serious sin, while others (especially Russians) confess before every reception of communion.

It is common for confessions to be heard in the open church, by the priest standing beside a lectern on which are placed the cross and a Gospel book. The penitent stands in front of the lectern and it is clear, as one exhortation says, that 'I am but a witness, bearing testimony before him of all the things which you have to say to me.' The rites often include Psalm 50, *troparia* of penance, and a prayer recalling the prophet Nathan's absolution of David's sin. If there is limited time, this last prayer alone may be used before the actual confession. After the confession and the setting of a penance if appropriate, the priest puts his stole over the head of the penitent and says the absolution prayer. The Greek prayer for the penitent's forgiveness begins 'May God who pardoned David through Nathan the prophet when he confessed his sins . . .' In Russian usage, there are two prayers, the first of which is also a prayer for forgiveness and emphasizes reconciliation in the words 'Reconcile and unite him [or her] to the Holy Church.' The second prayer, which first appeared in seventeenth-century books under western influence, contains an indicative formula, 'I . . . through the power given unto me by Him, do forgive and absolve you from all your sins . . .' After the dismissal a Russian priest will give (or may withhold) a blessing to go to communion.

The Liturgical Calendar

Pascha, Easter, the feast of the Lord's resurrection is the feast of feasts for Christians of this tradition. Lent, known as the 'Great Fast' or the 'Great Forty Days' came to include the major period of preparation and exorcism for those to be baptized (Talley 1990). The forty days finishes with Lazarus Saturday, which was a baptismal day (the liturgy includes the singing of 'As many as have been baptized into Christ'). The Great or Holy Week is seen as additional to the forty, and starts with the Entry into Jerusalem, Palm Sunday. Lent is preceded by a preparatory period of three weeks (four Sundays), with no fasting the first week, the normal Wednesday and Friday fast in the next week and no meat eaten in the third.

The weekdays of Lent proper, beginning with 'Clean Monday', the first day of the first week, are aliturgical but the Liturgy of the Presanctified is celebrated on Wednesday and Friday and certain other days. The full Liturgy of St John Chrysostom is served on Saturdays, usually for the departed, and the Liturgy of St Basil on the five Sundays. All the weekday services are characterized by frequent prostrations, especially at the prayer of St Ephrem the Syrian, 'O Lord and Master of my life'. During fasting periods it is traditional to abstain from meat, fish and dairy products.

Palm Sunday is reckoned one of the twelve Great Feasts. Palms, olive or pussy willow branches are blessed and distributed at Matins. Up to Thursday the offices are simpler than usual but have lengthy readings of scripture (Woolfenden 2002), and the Liturgy of the Presanctified is served each day. On Holy Thursday there may once have been a reconciliation of penitents. The Liturgy of St Basil is combined with Vespers and after it, a bishop, and certain abbots, may wash the feet of twelve priests. Although intended to be an evening celebration, this liturgy is now usually in the morning. In the evening the Matins of Good Friday takes place. This very lengthy service includes twelve Gospel readings, and originated in an overnight stational procession through Jerusalem (Calivas 1992). Between the readings are sung some of the most impressive examples of Byzantine poetry. One of the most famous stanzas is 'Today he who hung the earth upon the waters is hung on the tree . . . We worship thy passion O Christ, show us also thy glorious resurrection.'

On Good Friday morning at the Royal Hours, each Gospel passion is read in turn. In Greek usage Vespers follows immediately; the Russians delay it until the afternoon. The Vespers Gospel is a harmony from all four Gospels recounting the death of Christ, and the so-called winding-sheet (*epitaphios* or *plashchenitza*), a large embroidered representation of Christ lying in the tomb, is brought out and placed in the centre of the church. (A number of more recent dramatic ceremonies, such as taking the figure from the cross and wrapping it in a sheet during the Gospel at Vespers, have spread quite widely through the Orthodox world from Greece; see Calivas 1992: 68.)

Good Friday evening is the time of one of the most popular services, the Matins of Holy Saturday with the Lamentations at the tomb. These last are a series of verses interspersed through Psalm 118, and dating from about the twelfth or thirteenth century. At the end of this service there is a very moving procession with the winding-sheet, round the outside of the church, after which the readings look forward to the Resurrection.

Another vesperal Liturgy of St Basil, again now normally celebrated in the morning of Holy Saturday, is in fact the ancient Easter Vigil. It was during the fifteen Old Testament readings of this service that the main group of baptisms was to be performed. Traditionally all remained in church after the service until early Sunday morning. Nowadays the special Resurrection Matins is celebrated at midnight after a procession, and the Liturgy of St John Chrysostom follows. This service is famous for the paschal joy which suffuses it, the frequent singing of the paschal *troparion* and the exchange of the Easter greeting; 'Christ is risen!' with the reply, 'He is risen indeed!'

Throughout the paschal period there is no kneeling and the Easter *troparion* is sung at all services. Easter or Bright Week is particularly festive; there is also a feast of mid-Pentecost. Pascha itself closes with Ascension Thursday after forty days, and the Pentecost season with Trinity or Pentecost Sunday. Special prayers at Vespers on that Sunday reintroduce kneeling and the next day, Monday, is the day of the Holy Spirit (Woolfenden 1996).

Throughout the year the services of Sundays (and ordinary weekdays outside the fasting and festal seasons) are grouped into a cycle according to the eight tones of the chant. The resurrection hymns of Sunday are only omitted on Great Feasts of the Lord.

The mid-winter feasts of Christmas and Theophany on 25 December and 6 January are both feasts of the Incarnation, closely connected with one another. The Christian East adopted Theophany first, but by the end of the fourth century East and West celebrated both feasts. Christmas has a preparation of six weeks' fasting, but only the last week refers to the coming feast and there is nothing like the western Advent. Royal Hours are celebrated on Christmas and Epiphany eves and there is also a vigil Liturgy of St Basil, which has now become less important than the morning liturgy of St John Chrysostom. The Byzantine tradition concentrates all the birth narratives, including the Magi, at Christmas. Theophany is very much the feast of the Baptism of Christ, being marked by the very important ceremony of the great Blessing of Water, done outside if possible, after which homes are blessed. The period between the two feasts is free of fasting, which brings them together as one period of rejoicing.

Fasting is very much part of Byzantine liturgical life. Besides the Lenten and Nativity fasts already mentioned, there is a fasting period that starts one week after Pentecost and leads to the feast of Saints Peter and Paul (29 June). A two-week fast precedes the feast of the Dormition of the Mother of God (15 August), and apart from fast-free periods, Wednesday and Fridays are normally observed as fasting days.

The liturgical year commences on 1 September. Other major feasts that have not so far been mentioned are: the Birth of the Mother of God (8 September), the Universal Exaltation of the Holy Cross (14 September), the Entry of the Mother of God into the Temple (21 November), the Meeting of the Lord (2 February), the Annunciation (25 March), and the Transfiguration (6 August). Many of these feasts have traditional ceremonies proper to that day, for example in Greece, grapes, and in Russia, apples, are blessed on the Transfiguration. It should also be remembered that the Orthodox and Greco-Catholics of the former Soviet Union, the Serbs and many Russians and Ukrainians in the diaspora still use the Julian calendar, so that, for example, Christmas falls on 7 January in the civil calendar.

Other Pastoral Rites

The marriage service begins with the Service of Betrothal (Meyendorff 1975), in Russian churches held at the door of the church. After the opening blessing 'Blessed be our God' and the *synapte* with prayers for those who are pledging themselves to each other, the rings are blessed and exchanged. The rite finishes with a prayer of blessing and originally took place quite separately from the marriage itself. In some places, for example Cyprus, this was the case until quite recently. Nowadays the rite is celebrated on the same day as the crowning. There are no vows as such, but the rite of betrothal is considered as a binding contract before God.

The marriage itself, or crowning, begins with the couple processing together into the church to Psalm 127 (to the words 'Your wife will be like a fruitful vine within your house'). The couple stands on a cloth before a table in the centre of the church, holding candles. (In Russian usage there are questions establishing freedom to marry that date from the seventeenth century.) The opening exclamation 'Blessed is the kingdom . . .' leads to an expanded *synapte*, and a series of prayers evoking the examples of married couples in the scriptures. Crowns are then taken from the table and placed on the heads of the bride and groom. In Greek churches the crowns are light wreathes of flowers, in Russian and other churches they are metal and either adjustable so as to be used by different couples, or heavily ornate and so have to be held above the heads of the couple. An Epistle and Gospel are read (Eph. 5: 20–33 and John 2:1–11), and after further litanies, a common cup of wine is blessed and shared by the bride and groom. Finally the priest leads them around the table three times as the *troparia* are sung that start 'Rejoice, O Isaiah! A virgin is with child.' This 'dance of Isaiah' may be seen as symbolizing their journey through life together.

In former times the crowns were worn for eight days, but are now removed with prayers immediately after the procession. The service is concluded, and the newly married receive the congratulations of their family and friends.

The Orthodox Church permits the remarriage in church of divorced persons under certain circumstances. In this case the rite of second marriage, which has a more penitential rite of betrothal, may be used.

The seriously ill are anointed with olive oil blessed for that purpose in a service which ideally requires the presence of seven priests. The service begins in a way similar to Matins, with a canon that stresses the healing and reconciling uses of oil. After a prayer to sanctify the oil, there is a series of seven Epistles (the first is Jas. 5: 10–17), Gospels and prayers for healing, the Gospels and prayers being read by each priest in turn. After his prayer, each priest anoints the sick person. After the seventh prayer, all the priests hold the Gospel book open over the patient's head for a final prayer for forgiveness. In emergencies the service may be abbreviated, and is considered to have been fulfilled as long as the priest carried out at least one anointing. The anointing service is often celebrated in church in Holy Week or at other times of the year, for example, in the early weeks of Lent. Since it is intended for healing, then children, for example, may only be anointed if they are truly sick.

The liturgical books expect the priest to minister at the deathbed for the service of the parting of the soul from the body. The funeral service itself begins at the home (or the funeral home nowadays) with brief *troparia* and a litany. On arrival in church the service continues with Psalm 90 and Psalm 118 (usually abbreviated) and the *evlogitaria* verses for the departed. The shape of Matins continues to be apparent as Psalm 50 is read and followed by the canon in tone 6, 'Crossing the deep on foot as though it were dry land'. After the sixth ode is sung the well-known *kontakion*, 'Give rest, O Christ, to the soul of thy servant with the saints'. The canon is followed by further poetic verses such as 'All human things are vanity, all that remain not after death', then the Beatitudes with verses, and an Epistle (1 Thess. 4: 13–17) and a Gospel (John 5: 24–30). The priest reads the prayer 'O God of spirits and of all flesh' several times during the service. After a litany the choir sing the verses 'Come brethren, giving thanks to God let us give the last kiss to the dead' and all come to greet the departed with a kiss (the casket being left open during the service). At the end a prayer of absolution is read over the body. All go to the cemetery (the Orthodox Church does not normally permit cremation) for the very brief service of committal, at which the priest scatters earth over the remains, and pours oil and empties the censer over them as well.

A major feature of Orthodox prayer for the departed is the *panikhida* or *parastas*, *mnemosynon* in Greek. This service, again following the general pattern of Matins, and, abbreviated according to need, is celebrated at the place of death or in church immediately after death. It is also served on the third, ninth and fortieth days after death, and thereafter on the anniversary. The word *panikhida* refers to the fact that this was once a vigil extending through the night. There are further opportunities to remember the dead on certain Saturdays in the year.

The structure of Matins also characterizes the many kinds of devotional service (known, for example, in Slavonic as a *moleben*). Typically they begin with the opening prayers, a psalm (e.g., 142), the chant of the 'The Lord is God' with verses of Psalm 117 and *troparia*, Psalm 50, a vestigial poetic canon and a *prokeimenon* and appropriate Gospel reading. Then there is a litany with opportunities to pray for particular needs, and an often lengthy concluding prayer. A similar shape is found in such services as the blessing of a new home, in which the Gospel is the story of Zacchaeus from Luke 19. This service also includes a blessing of oil, and anointing and incensing of the house.

Even the contents of devotional prayer books are arranged in a way that reflects the public liturgical services, which therefore may penetrate every aspect of people's lives. Again, the year is punctuated by various blessings as was mentioned above, many of which may be used on other occasions. One of the most striking services of blessing is that of the waters at Theophany, 6 January. Appropriate verses accompany the procession to the place of blessing, which may be the sea or a river. There are then three readings from Isaiah (the last begins 'Therefore with joy you will draw water from the wells of salvation', Isa. 12: 3). The short Epistle and the Marcan Gospel of the Baptism of Christ lead to a litany and the long and beautiful prayer of blessing. The prayer is similar to that used to bless baptismal water but its supplication is for more general healing and sanctification. A cross is dipped or thrown into the water (sometimes recovered by a swimmer) and all present are sprinkled with the water and drink from it.

Ordinations may be divided into those that are given before the Liturgy begins, and the major sacramental orders given during it (for further material, see Bradshaw 1990). The first group: tonsure, reader and subdeacon, were once administered outside the church, in the *skeuophylakion*. They are now given in the centre of the church, and the tonsure is almost always given at the same time as a man is made a reader. This service and that to ordain a subdeacon have short prayers for the appropriate grace. A new reader reads an Epistle, and a new subdeacon receives a basin, ewer and towel (one of his tasks is to wash the bishop's hands).

All the major orders start with the candidate being brought ceremonially to the bishop. In the case of a deacon this takes place immediately after the anaphora: of a priest, directly after the Great Entrance, and in the case of a bishop, after the *trisagion*. (A bishop's consecration is preceded by a rite of election and profession of faith, usually the night before.) The candidate is taken around the altar three times as 'Rejoice Isaiah' is sung. The bishop then says the formula 'The Divine Grace which always heals that which is infirm . . . elevates through the laying on of hands N the most devout *subdeacon to be a deacon . . .*' The candidate for diaconate kneels on one knee as the bishop says two prayers with his hand on his head. The new deacon is then vested and acclaimed to be worthy, with the exclamation 'Axios!', and takes his place with the other deacons. A candidate for priesthood is conducted about the altar by two priests, and after the 'Divine grace' formula kneels on both knees as the bishop lays on hands and says another two prayers. He is also vested to the cries of 'Axios'. After the 'Divine grace' formula, a new bishop kneels while his consecrators (at least three bishops are needed) hold the Gospel book open over his head as the two ordination prayers are said. The new bishop is vested then to the 'Axios' acclamations, but only receives his pastoral staff at the end of the Liturgy. It should be noted that anciently the 'Axios' acclamations were part of the process of selection and preceded the ordination prayers; they were moved after them so as to avoid partisan disturbances.

Byzantine Liturgical Music

All services are normally sung, or at the very least read on a reciting note. This is to prevent too great emphasis on the idiosyncrasies of clergy and readers (Gardner 1980). There are strict rules forbidding the use of any musical instrument. (Pipe organs are, however, sometimes found in the USA and the Ionian islands).

The monophonic liturgical music of Constantinople was at first syllabic and congregational. After *c.*850 it became more elaborate and melismatic, and could only be performed by professional choirs or cantors (*ODB*). A small group of cantors singing together or solo is normal in Greek and Arab churches. The soloist will sing the elaborate chant while other singers execute a dominant drone, the *ison*. The greater part of the melodies have been systematized into the eight tones. Within each tone there are sets of model melodies that can be further elaborated, for example the melodies of the *stikhira*, the *heirmoi* of the canons, and the *troparia* and *kontakia*. Greek books provide for entire liturgies to be sung in the appropriate tone. The tones are numbered one to four and then as plagal of the first, etc., except that the seventh is called 'grave tone'.

As the Byzantine liturgical books were translated into other languages, especially Slavonic, the syllabic melodies were adapted to the different structure of the Slavonic language and somewhat simplified (the tones are numbered 1 to 8). Early adaptations in Bulgaria tried to stay closer to the original Greek melodies, but in Rus' (modern Ukraine, Russia and Belarus), the melodies developed in a new way, often influenced by western styles of chant (Gardner 2000). The basic chants remained simple enough to be sung congregationally, but were more elaborate in monasteries and cathedrals. Congregational singing of the chant has remained common to the present day in parts of Ukraine and among the Carpatho-Rusyn diaspora.

An early style of polyphonic singing developed in seventeenth-century Muscovy, and a more westernized style later characterized Kiev and St Petersburg. Harmonized music sung by choirs of men and boys eventually became normal throughout the Russian Church (women singers only became common after the Revolution). The style was set by the Imperial Chapel and the Synodal choir in Moscow. A more traditional and ecclesial style was developed under the leadership of composers such as Kastalsky, and may be seen in the works, e.g., of Rachmaninov, as compared to the freer compositional style of the church music of Tchaikovsky.

Harmonized church music, often Russian, may be heard in Greek churches, but in some places efforts are being made to restore congregational singing. In Russia it is now normal for certain pieces, such as the Creed and Lord's Prayer, to be sung by all present. However the ongoing availability of good choirs has ensured that Slav liturgical music will continue to be predominantly harmonized. The same is also true of Romania, which has both vigorous chant traditions and impressive harmony. Bulgaria has further developed the Russian romantic choral tradition.

References and further reading

Bradshaw, P. F. (1990) *Ordination Rites of the Ancient Churches of East and West.* New York: Pueblo.

Calivas, A. C. (1992) *Great Week and Pascha in the Greek Orthodox Church.* Brookline, Mass.: Holy Cross.

Gardner, J. von (1980) *Russian Church Singing,* vol 1. Crestwood, NY: St Vladimir's Seminary Press.

—— (2000) *Russian Church Singing,* vol. 2. Crestwood, NY: St Vladimir's Seminary Press.

Larina, Sister Vassa (2006) The origins and history of the Royal Office at the beginning of Matins. Paper given at the first conference of Societas Orientalium Liturgiarum, Eichstätt, Germany, July.

Mother Mary and Kallistos Ware (1969) *The Festal Menaion.* London: Faber and Faber.

—— and —— (1978) *The Lenten Triodion.* London: Faber and Faber.

Mateos, J. (1971) *La Célébration de la Parole dans la Liturgie Byzantine.* Orientalia Christiana Analecta 191. Rome: Pontificio Istituto Orientale.

Meyendorff, J. (1975) *Marriage: An Orthodox Perspective.* Crestwood, NY: St Vladimir's Seminary Press.

ODB: Oxford Dictionary of Byzantium (1991) ed. A. Kazhdan. Oxford: Oxford University Press.

Parenti, S. and Velkovska, E. (eds.) (1995) *L'Eucologio Barberini gr. 336.* Rome: Centro Liturgico Vincenziano/ Edizioni Liturgiche.

Schmemann, A. (1969) *Great Lent.* Crestwood, NY: St Vladimir's Seminary Press.

—— (1974) *Of Water and the Spirit.* Crestwood, NY: St Vladimir's Seminary Press.

Schulz, H.-J. (1986) *The Byzantine Liturgy.* New York: Pueblo.

Taft, R. F. (1975) *The Great Entrance.* Orientalia Christiana Analecta 200. Rome: Pontificium Institutum Studiorum Orientalium.

—— (1992) *The Byzantine Rite, a Short History.* Collegeville, Minn.: Liturgical Press.

—— (2000) *The Pre-Communion Rites.* Orientalia Christiana Analecta 261. Rome: Pontificio Istituto Orientale.

Talley, T. J. (1990) *The Origins of the Liturgical Year.* Collegeville, Minn.: Liturgical Press.

Uspensky, N. D. (1985) *Evening Worship in the Orthodox Church.* Crestwood, NY: St Vladimir's Seminary Press.

Wellesz, E. (1961) *A History of Byzantine Music and Hymnography.* Oxford: Oxford University Press.

Wilkinson, J. (1999) *Egeria's Travels.* Warminster: Aris and Phillips.

Woolfenden, G. (Father Gregory) (1996) The fifty days of Pascha: the Byzantine tradition. In C. Irvine (ed.) *Celebrating the Easter Mystery.* London: Mowbray.

—— (2001) *Joyful Light.* Witney: St Stephen's Press.

—— (2002) From betrayal to faith . . .. *Eastern Churches Journal* 8(1): 59–84.

—— (2004) *Daily Liturgical Prayer.* Farnborough: Ashgate.

CHAPTER 17

Eastern Christian Liturgical Traditions
Oriental Orthodox

Bryan D. Spinks

The non-Chalcedonian Churches divide into two distinct theological groupings. On the one hand are the so-called Miaphysite Churches: Syrian Orthodox and their Indian subbranches; Armenian; Coptic and Ethiopic. On the other is the so-called Diophysite Church, the Church of the East or Assyrian Church. However, in terms of liturgical traditions and their interrelationship, the alignments are rather different. The Syriac-speaking churches – Syrian Orthodox, Church of the East, and the Chalcedonian Maronite Church – once shared a common theological literature, and liturgical ordos or structures. Their traditions are shared by the ecclesiastical offshoots of the Church of the East, such as the Syro-Malabar Church and the Chaldean Church, and, from the Syrian Orthodox, such churches as the Syrian Catholic, Malankara Orthodox, Syrian Jacobite and Mar Thoma Church. The Armenian Church was influenced first by Cappadocian Greek-speaking and Syriac-speaking missionaries, then by Byzantium, and also by Rome, and these influences are reflected in its liturgical traditions. The Coptic Church has preserved some liturgical forms which seem to be indigenous, and others which show clear signs of influence from Palestine and Syria. The Ethiopic Church owed its origins – and, until the twentieth century, its patriarch – to the Coptic Church, but its liturgy shows some considerable eclectic independence in its development. In all these churches it is difficult to date the developed mature liturgical forms.

The Syriac Churches: Early Liturgical Traditions

At one time scholars were of the opinion that the Syriac liturgies were branches of a common Antiochene liturgical tradition, with two forks, East and West Syrian. The Maronite rite was seen as a variant of the West Syrian rite. However, more recent scholarship has emphasized that the East Syrian rite was centred on Edessa, not Antioch, and that the Maronite liturgical tradition seems to have blended some elements from the Edessan tradition with elements from the Antiochene tradition. (Macomber 1973).

Furthermore, there was a distinct difference of culture between Greek-speaking Antioch and the surrounding Syriac-speaking hinterland. It seems that the majority of the later adherents of the Syrian Orthodox church came from the hinterlands, and for its liturgical use that church seems to have drawn upon a possible Aramaic/Syriac version of the Jerusalem or Palestinian liturgy.

Several early documents give us some idea of the liturgical diversity of the third and fourth centuries. These include the Apocryphal Acts of Thomas, around the early third century; the Didascalia, from North Syria, early third century; the Apostolic Constitutions from the region of Antioch, c.360–80; and the Gospel of Philip. The Acts of Thomas gives accounts of a number of baptisms and celebrations of the Eucharist. It exists in Greek and Syriac, but it is thought that, although Syriac was the original language, the present Syriac recension is a later version, and that the Greek may preserve earlier readings. In two accounts in the Greek version, initiation seems to be by anointing only.

Rites of initiation

The fact that we have two recensions with differences in the liturgical descriptions suggests a diversity of practice in these communities. However, what they yield overall is an emerging pattern of initiation by anointing followed by baptism, with an emphasis on calling the Spirit to come upon and sanctify the oil. The main baptismal images used are of protection and new birth. This ritual sequence is confirmed in the Didascalia, where an anointing of the candidate's head was followed by anointing of the whole body, and then baptism in water. The theological emphasis is on messianic status and new birth. However, the Gospel of Philip, which may have originated in Edessa and reflects beliefs which would later be deemed Gnostic, seems to know the sequence to be baptism and then anointing – though again with considerable emphasis on the anointing. Even here, though, the main image is on the messianic status of the newly baptized who receive the Spirit, which is associated with the anointing.

The Apostolic Constitutions was written in Greek and reflects a Greek-speaking community in the region of Antioch. The author tends to espouse a semi-Arian Christology. He uses a number of sources, including the Didache and the Didascalia, and therefore has duplications. In the rite, which is original or peculiar to the document, we have a pre-baptismal and post-baptismal anointing. The first oil is blessed 'for the remission of sins, and the first preparation for the confession of baptism, so that the candidate, when he is anointed, may be freed from all ungodliness, and may become worthy of initiation, according to the command of the Only-Begotten' (7: 42). The water is blessed in a prayer which gives thanks for the wonderful works of God. After the baptism the candidate is anointed with *myron* (chrism), with an emphasis on cleansing.

As far as evidence for the Palestinian, or Jerusalem, usage is concerned, our first clues come in the Mystagogical Catecheses of Cyril of Jerusalem. (For a trenchant defence of Cyril's authorship, see Doval 2001.) Cyril's rite of baptism included – after instruction – a ritualized renunciation of Satan and commitment to Christ, stripping of clothes, anointing, baptism, post-baptismal anointing with chrism, which Cyril associated with the gift of the Holy Spirit, and the putting on of a white garment.

An early Syriac commentary on the liturgy (British Library Additional MS 14496) was used by subsequent East and West Syrian commentators. It exists in several recensions, some of which reflect use of a pre-baptismal anointing only, which seemed to be the East Syrian usage, and some a post-baptismal anointing, which seems to have been the West Syrian usage (Brock 1980).

Eucharistic rites

In the accounts of the Eucharist in the Acts of Thomas it appears that wine was not always used; sometimes there is reference to bread only. However, when examples of prayer over the elements is given, several take the form of an invocation of the Spirit to come upon the element(s), rather like the invocation on the oil in the baptismal accounts. On the other hand, in Apostolic Constitutions VIII, the Eucharist is outlined as having readings from the Law, Prophets, Letters and Gospels; a sermon; the dismissal, in the form of litanies and prayers, of catechumens, the possessed and penitents; a litany for church and world; the exchange of the Peace; and a eucharistic prayer over the bread and wine which gives thanks for creation and salvation history in the Old Covenant, with the singing of the sanctus; thanks for the work of Jesus Christ leading into an institution narrative; a petition for the Holy Spirit 'to show [*apophenei*] this bread body of your Christ, and this cup blood of your Christ'; and then intercessions for living and departed. The rite concluded with a thanksgiving and dismissal prayer, which was for protection.

Important also for prehistory is the anaphora or eucharistic prayer attributed to Addai and Mari. This prayer is one of three eucharistic prayers still used by the Church of the East, and is also used in the Chaldean and Syro-Malabar Churches. A version of it is also preserved (but no longer used) by the Maronites, called 'St Peter III', or 'Sharar'. What is remarkable about this eucharistic prayer, at least by later standards, is that it contains no institution narrative. It gives glory to God, contains the sanctus, gives thanks for the Incarnation, commemorates the offering on the altar, and remembers the righteous fathers. It contains a petition for the Spirit to come upon the elements of bread and wine, for benefit of the communicants:

> May he (she) come, O Lord, your Holy Spirit and rest upon this oblation of your servants, and bless and hallow it, that it may be to us, O Lord, for the pardon of debts and the forgiveness of sins, and a great hope of resurrection from the dead and a new life in the kingdom of heaven with all who have been pleasing before you.

In terms of having a calling of the Spirit upon the bread and wine, but no institution narrative, this prayer stands in a tradition at least parallel with the invocations in the Acts of Thomas. The interpretation of the evidence from Cyril of Jerusalem is somewhat contested on this matter. Cyril attests to the kiss of peace, the dialogue beginning *sursum corda*, and then thanksgiving over the bread and wine, with mention of heaven, earth, sun, moon, and stars, leading into angelic beings and the sanctus. He then mentions the calling of the Holy Spirit upon the elements, followed by intercessions for the living and then the departed. The thanksgiving is followed by the Lord's Prayer, the sancta sanctis ('holy things for holy people') and communion. There is no mention of an institution narrative forming part of the eucharistic prayer. Some scholars suggest that, as in Addai and Mari, there was no narrative at this time. Others argue that Cyril passes over it because he had already discussed it in a previous lecture.

Finally we may note that the Syrian Orthodox, Church of the East and Maronites all ascribe hymns and prayers to Ephrem, the great fourth-century Syrian theologian, to whom they gave the title, 'Harp of the Spirit'.

The East Syrian Tradition (Church of the East, Chaldean and Syro-Malabar Churches)

This Church is descended from those churches and bishops in the regions of Edessa who refused to condemn the fifth-century Bishop of Constantinople, Nestorius. Gathered under a Catholicos, the Church eventually found itself in the Sassanian Empire, and thus somewhat insulated from other Eastern churches. Its missionary endeavours reached China as well as India. Its Catholic offshoots are known as the Chaldean Church, and in India, the Syro-Malabar Church.

Whatever forms may have been used in the areas which were later to become the Church of the East, a move towards standardization was made as early as the Synod of Seleucia-Ctesiphon in 410. In Canon 13, that Synod decreed that the eucharistic liturgy should in the future be uniformly celebrated according to 'the western rite that the Bishops Isaac (Seleucia-Ctesiphon) and Marutha (Martyropolis) have taught us' (Macomber 1973: 239). A further standardization and reform of the East Syrian rites is attributed to Catholicos Iso'yahb III (650–9). According to a ninth-century source, 'before the time of Mar Iso'yahb of Adiabene the Catholicos, the orders of the services were performed in a confused manner in every place; but by means of this man the services of all the church acquired connected order' (Jones 1964: 164). According to the Catalogue of 'Abdiso, Iso'yabh 'arranged an order of the Church-Book of the cycle of the year, and Ordination-formularies for all orders, and the Office of Reconciliator' (ibid.). He is reputed to have been responsible for redacting the present baptismal rite, and for prefacing services with a common opening, and for some hymns. The Liturgical Homilies of Narsai and the Commentary on the Divine Liturgy by Gabriel Qatraya give us some information of the rites prior to Iso'yahb III. The manuscript texts which have come down to us – all post-Iso'yahb – show considerable homogeneity.

Eucharistic rites

The Holy Qurbana, or Eucharist, is contained in the Hudra and Taksa. It contains three anaphoras or eucharistic prayers: Addai and Mari, Nestorius and Theodore the Interpreter. If there were other anaphoras at one time, these have not survived. Addai and

Mari seems to be the most ancient. Those of Nestorius and Theodore may have been the work of Mar Aba the Great, who was Catholicos from 540 to 552. The anaphora of Nestorius is inspired by those of John Chrysostom and Basil; that of Theodore seems to have been inspired by Nestorius and Addai and Mari, and the liturgical homilies of Theodore of Mopsuestia. However, both show considerable cultural and linguistic inculturation, and are very far from being just translations (Spinks 1999).

Addai and Mari is the main rite used. Nestorius is used on five occasions: Epiphany, the Friday of John the Baptist, the memorial of the Greek Doctors, the Wednesday of the Rogation of the Ninevites, and Maundy Thursday; and Theodore is used from the first Sunday of the Annunciation-Nativity period until the Sunday of Hosanna. Addai and Mari has a structure peculiar to itself; Nestorius and Theodore follow what is called the East Syrian pattern, in which, after the narrative of institution and *anamnesis*, come the intercessions, and only then, as a climax before the doxology, the *epiklesis* or calling on the Spirit to come upon the bread and wine.

The structure of the eucharistic liturgy can be divided as follows:

1   Entrance
2   Liturgy of the Word from *trisagion* to dismissal of catechumens
3   Pre-anaphora: from the transfer of the elements to diptychs
4   Anaphora
5   Preparation for communion: from 'Have mercy' to sancta sanctis
6   Communion and concluding rites.

At least for understanding the commentaries, it should be remembered that the older arrangements of many East Syrian churches included a bema in the nave from which the Liturgy of the Word was celebrated. Only at the equivalent of the Great Entrance did all the clergy move from the bema into the sanctuary.

Beginning with a Trinitarian invocation, the rite commences with an eastern short version of Gloria in excelsis and Lord's Prayer, interwoven with a *qanona*, which in fact is a form of the sanctus. There follows a prayer, the *marmita*, prayer of the anthem of the sanctuary, the anthem of the sanctuary (*onita d'qanke*), the procession to the bema, veneration of the cross, the Prayer before Laku Mara, Laku Mara, and a concluding collect. The *marmita* is in fact three psalms with farcings and gloria. The *aqqapta*, which is said when there is no *marmita*, seems to have been the original entrance versicle of the bishop. The Laku Mara is a form of a *troparion*, celebrating Christ as the source of our resurrection; it is repeated together with the psalm words, 'I have [sic] washed my hands in innocency.' From the commentaries we surmise that the earliest rites began with a greeting and the Liturgy of the Word. The *onita d'qanke* and *marmita* were added by the seventh century, and, in the ninth century, the Lord's Prayer, and finally Gloria and Veneration of the Cross.

The Liturgy of the Word opens with the *trisagion*. There is a reading from the Law and Prophets (Prophets and Acts on Sundays of Eastertide). There is a *suraya* (responsorial psalm), prayer before the Epistle, Epistle reading, followed by *turgama* (commentary), the *zummara* (alleluia chant), gospel procession and reading of the Gospel, and homily. This is followed by the litany-style prayers, blessings, and dismissal of the catechumens. There is nothing particularly East Syrian about this section, though, like the West Syrian, it has retained or replicated the Torah and Neviim readings as in the synagogue.

In the pre-anaphora the manuscripts vary on the sequence, since some presuppose at least two priests, with certain ceremonies taking place in the sanctuary, and others taking place in the bema at the same time. Other manuscripts seem to attempt to rationalize the structure for one priest. We have the anthem of the mysteries; the washing of the hands; the transfer and unveiling of the mysteries, during which the *onita d-raze* is chanted; procession to the sanctuary; the Creed; diaconal proclamation; prayers of access, and the first *ghanta* and *kussape*, which are here preparatory prayers; the kiss of peace; and the diptychs. The mysteries are censed. The three eucharistic prayers used have been mentioned above. Unlike other traditions, the prayers are interrupted by *kussape* prayers by and for the priest, and the text of the eucharistic prayer is also rubrically divided into *ghanata* and *qanone*.

The communion rites are mainly concerned with an elaborate fraction, with the Lord's Prayer and sancta sanctis. The old rite of penance has, in truncated form, been placed before the peoples' communion, as a communion preparation. After communion there is a *teshbota*, a kiss of peace in the sanctuary, and blessing. The custom of blessed bread is also known. Peculiar to the East Syrian tradition is the *malka*, or holy leaven, which is required to be added to the bread baked for the communion. Made of wheat flour, salt, olive oil, and a few drops of water, it actually contains no leaven at all. However, it is regarded as a *raza* (mystery), and is mentioned frequently after the tenth century. It has attracted a legendary explanation, that it represents loaves given to the twelve Apostles at the Last Supper.

Rites of initiation

The baptismal rite as described by Narsai in his homilies retained the sequence found in many of the early Syrian documents, namely a pre-baptismal anointing followed by baptism and communion. Narsai also knows of a renunciation of the devil. In the ordo that has come down to us, which tradition ascribes to Iso'yahb III, we find no such ritualization of the devil, but we do find the use of a horn of oil, and what seems to be a post-baptismal laying on of hands.

The ordo assumes that the candidates will be infants, and seems to be the first ordo so adapted. It commences with the Trinitarian invocation, Lord's Prayer and Gloria, as in the Eucharist – a standardized opening. There follows a prayer which introduces the psalmody, then an imposition of hands, and anointing. The entry to the baptistery is accompanied by a number of chants, and a *karuzuta* or litany by the deacon. The priest prays the *suraya*, Psalm 110. Another *karazuta* follows, and a canon. An Epistle and Gospel are read, with a further prayer of imposition. Then comes a blessing of oil, the prayer genre being similar to a eucharistic prayer, with the East Syrian *sursum corda*, sanctus and an *epiklesis*. Oil from the horn is used to consecrate by co-mingling the oil for the baptism. (Supposedly the horn originally consisted of water from Christ's baptism, and water from his side, to which oil was added after Pentecost, and each Apostle took a horn with some of this mixture.) A shorter blessing of the water follows, and oil from the horn is poured into the water. The candidates are anointed and baptized. After the baptism there is a canon, and a signing and laying on of hands. No rubric suggests that oil be used at the signing, but the practice seems to be that oil from the horn is used again (Irving 1902). Crowns (linen cloths) are also placed on the candidates.

Daily offices

We know very little about the shape of daily prayer in this tradition. The services have compositions attributed to Ephrem, Jacob of Nisibis, Simeon bar Sabba'e, Maruta of Maipharkat, Narsai and Babai the Great. According to Bar Hebraeus, it was Simon bar Sabba'e who was responsible for arranging the daily office into two choirs or weeks. Weeks are classed as even or uneven, depending on whether they follow an even or uneven Sunday in the calendar. Two choirs alternate the privilege of intoning the office: the first choir on Monday, Wednesday and Friday of uneven weeks, and the second choir on Tuesday and Thursday, with the order reversed in even weeks. According to the study of Robert Taft (1986), the three-day Hours and Compline have all but disappeared, Terce and Sext surviving only in Lenten ferias, and Compline on some feasts.

Ramsa (Vespers) and Sapra (Matins) are regarded by scholars as having almost a pure cathedral shape; that is, unlike most traditions, they have resisted the wholesale incorporation of elements from the monastic office. Ramsa begins with *marmita*, the psalmody of which seems to be the remains of None; Onita of incense; Laku Mara hymn; *suraya*, and antiphon (*onita d qdam*). Then follow the fixed Cathedral psalms: 141, 142, 119: 105–12; 117; followed by *suraya*, *onita d-bata*, and intercessions in the form of *karazuta*; *trisagion* and collect; and blessing. There is also a stational procession.

Sapra has fixed morning psalms; and then the Lauds psalms: 148, 150, 117, with collect; *onita d-sapra*, Laku Mara, benedicte or miserere (festal/ferial), Gloria in excelsis; *trisagion* and Lord's Prayer; prayers and blessing. There are no readings of scripture other than at Eastertide, these being a hallmark of the monastic usage.

There are also Nocturns (Lelya) and a Vigil.

Marriage rites

The marriage service, as in all eastern rites, comprises the betrothal and the marriage. The betrothal consists of:

1   Consent. A woman (in older tradition) is sent to the bride's house, offering a ring.
2   Joining of hands by the priest, in the home.

The marriage liturgy has four parts:

1   The blessing of a cup of wine with *hnana*, dust from a saint's tomb. The bless-
    ing includes the placing of a cross and a ring in the cup, and drinking from
    the cup.
2   Blessing of the marriage clothes
3   Crowning of bride and groom
4   Blessing of the bed chamber.

The texts of the service view marriage as another Cana of Galilee. The imagery of Christ
the bridegroom is adopted and amalgamated with the imagery from the Book of Revelation, where the lamb is slain, suggesting that the dowry is a costly sacrifice and demonstration of pure love – the blood of the covenant. The ring is a type of 'the ring' which
features in salvation history – of Joseph, of Rebecca, and of the Church espoused to
Christ. It carries the salvation history of all rings in scripture. The *hnana* is regarded as
eschatological drink, appropriate for the eschatological symbolism of human marriage.
The crowning represents royal status, and the bridal chamber takes on the role of the
heavenly sanctuary.

Funeral rites

The East Syrian funeral rites share with other eastern rites the feature of having distinct
rites for clergy, men, women and children. In this tradition, in its original Middle
Eastern setting, the body was taken to the church only in the case of clergy. For lay
people the body is prepared in the home, and taken in procession to the place of burial.
The body is washed and clothed in a white garment during which several *moutwas*
(psalmody and anthem) are recited. The processional chant follows, with prayers at the
grave.

Ordination rites

The ordination rites have some elements in common with the Georgian rite, suggesting
some common origin at an early stage of development. According to East Syrian tradition, the rites were the work of the patriarchs Mar Aba the Great, Iso'yabh III, Cyprian,
Bishop of Nisibis *c*.767, and Gabriel, Metropolitan of Bassorah *c*.884.

The rites begin with the standard opening of Gloria and Lord's Prayer, followed by
prayer and psalmody. The rite provides for the ordination of readers, with benediction
and the laying of the bishop's hand on the head, followed by signing and the giving of
a stole. There is a similar rite for subdeacons. The Ordering of Deacons begins with a
series of prayers and canons (psalmody), with a prayer requesting the grace of the Holy
Spirit to perfect this ministry, with the laying on of the right hand, and a further prayer.
The formula says:

N has been set apart, consecrated and perfected to the work of the ministry of the Church, and to the Levitical and Stephanite office, in the name of the Father, and of the Son, and of the Holy Spirit. Amen.

Canons and prayers follow. The Ordering of Priests has a similar structure, with the ordination prayer reflecting the office of presbyterate. The formula links the order with the Aaronic priesthood. The Ordering of Bishops has a similar structure. There are also rites for an archdeacon, the patriarch's archdeacon, and metropolitan.

The West Syrian Tradition (Syrian Orthodox)

The West Syrian Syriac tradition is represented by the Syrian Orthodox Church, which is the descendent of those Antiochene Christians who refused to accept the Christology of Chalcedon. Their patroness was the Byzantine Empress Theodora, and their founding theologians were Severus of Antioch, Jacob Baradeus, Jacob of Serug and Philoxenus of Mabbug. Though the tradition was originally bilingual, Greek usage gave way to the vernacular Syriac, and all the liturgical rites were translated into Syriac. Since the Antiochene hinterland had in any case used Syriac, the hymns of Ephrem provided a rich resource. However, it was the Palestinian or Jerusalem usage which seems to have formed the heart of the eucharistic liturgy, St James, together with a version of the Liturgy of St John Chrysostom known as the Twelve Apostles. A collection of chants for the liturgical year, known as the Oktoekhos, was reputedly made by Severus of Antioch, and translated into Syriac by James of Edessa. In fact, translation and retranslation seems to have taken place more than once (Varghese 1998). Borrowing from Byzantine and Jerusalem usage continued long after the Christological divisions.

Eucharistic rites

A number of commentaries exist which give some idea of how the eucharistic liturgy grew; in fact, additions continued to have been made even in the nineteenth century. Significant commentaries are those of George of the Arabs, Moses bar Kepha, John of Dara, Jacob of Eddesa and Dionysius Bar Salibi.

The present rite (*qurbono*, offering) commences with prayers for the preparation of the priest and vesting, together with *prothesis*, or preparation of the elements of bread and wine. Varghese comments that what was a simple act of preparation of bread and wine has become a long ceremony which occupies at least a third of the eucharistic celebration (Varghese 1998). As the priest enters the sanctuary, the curtain is drawn closed and the entire preparation takes place behind the curtain. It consists of the First and Second Service, also called the services of Melchizedek and Aaron. The first includes an opening prayer, Psalm 51, entry into the sanctuary, kissing and going around the altars, arrangement of the bread and wine, and a service of penitence: *promion-sedro*, *qolo*, *etro* and *hutomo* (anthems, prayers of penitence, and thanksgiving). The second consists of prayer, washing of the hands, vesting, kneeling before the altar, commemorations, *promion-sedro*, censing of the paten and chalice, *hutomo*, with *qaumo* (*trisagion*, Lord's Prayer and Creed).

The Mass of the Catechumens begins with the Ma'nitho of Severus, *trisagion*, and the Old Testament lections, three being provided from the Law, Writings and Prophets. The *trisagion* is the non-Chalcedonian form, and is followed by the Epistle and Gospel. Then come a further *promion*, *sedro* and *etro* (incense). The Nicene Creed follows, with the washing of the hands, and a prayer of approach for worthiness. The celebrant ascends to the altar and offers the prayer of the peace, together with a prayer of approach and the prayer of the veil, which mentions this 'fearful and unbloody sacrifice'.

The Syrian Orthodox tradition has something in the region of eighty anaphoras which it either uses or once used. These vary considerably in date of composition, length and quality. Twelve Apostles and St James are fourth- or fifth-century in origin, though the former seems to be a sixth- or seventh-century translation. H. Fuchs attempted some broad classification, noting translations from Greek and original Syriac compositions, with dates ranging from the seventh to the fifteenth century, in the case of the anaphora of Ignatius Behnan (Fuchs 1926). One good example is the anaphora attributed to Severus of Antioch. There is no extant Greek anaphora like St James and Twelve Apostles. However, parallels do exist. Echoes of St James occur in Severus, and there are slight linguistic parallels at one point with the Greek Coptic rite of St Mark. Furthermore Severus' theology of *theoria* is also echoed in the anaphora. While it cannot be proved that Severus is the author, he certainly could have authored such a prayer in Greek (Spinks 2005). However, despite the diversity that has existed in the number of anaphoras, the structure remains that identified by scholars as Syro-Byzantine, with oratio theologica, sanctus and benedictus, oratio christologica, institution narrative, *anamnesis*, *epiklesis* and intercessions.

The Anaphora of St James is something of a classic, having a Trinitarian structure. It may be the result of an amalgamation of an older Jerusalem usage with elements from the anaphora of St Basil. It begins by proclaiming that God is worshipped by the very creation itself: sun, moon, stars, earth, sea and Jerusalem. After the sanctus and benedictus, the prayer rehearses the creation of humanity, the Fall, and the sending of Christ, leading into the words of institution. An *anamnesis* and offering leads into a lengthy *epiklesis*, telling of the work of the Holy Spirit and asking God to send forth the Spirit so that he (the grammatical gender in Syriac is she) may tabernacle in the bread and wine. Lengthy intercessions follow, and these differ somewhat in manuscripts and between the Syrian Orthodox, Indian Syrian Orthodox and Mar Thoma Churches.

After the anaphora, there is a further greeting of peace and a blessing, which form the beginning of the fraction and commixture, for which the curtain is drawn closed. The fraction has a prayer attributed to Bar Salibi, a hymn of Jacob of Sarug, and three prayers for the commixture. After the fraction and commixture, the curtain is drawn back, and the Lord's Prayer and sancta sanctis follow. After communion there is a thanksgiving and dismissal, though further dismissal rites take place in the sanctuary once more after the curtain is drawn.

Rites of initiation

The Syrian Orthodox Church developed several baptismal ordos, suggesting regional differences, and these are attributed to Severus of Antioch, Timothy of Alexandria, and for emergency use, Philoxenus of Mabbug. What is common is that this tradition follows that found in Apostolic Constitutions in having a significant post-baptismal anointing with *myron*.

Timothy of Alexandria has the same structure as Severus, and a number of prayers in common. According to Sebastian Brock, it dates from the sixth century (Brock 1972). However, the rite now in use is that of Severus, though the recensions used in the Syrian Orthodox, Malankara Church in India, and Mar Thoma Church of India, have some variations (Tovey 1998). The Syrian Orthodox recension (printed text 1974) consists of two services. The first is the service of the catechumens, and consists of opening Gloria to the Trinity, prayer of worthiness, Psalm 51, hymn 'O Lord by your baptism', *quqal'yon* (Psalm 29: 1, 3, 4), prayer and *eqbo*. This is followed by *husoyo* (absolution) and *promion*, *sedro*, *qolo* and *etro*, psalm and lections, insufflation, consignation, exorcism, *apotaxis* and *synaxis*, Creed and anointing.

The second service begins with the Gloria to the Trinity, and a prayer for mixing the water with the power and operation of the Holy Spirit. After a number of brief prayers, the candidate is anointed with the oil of anointing. This is followed by *eqbo* and *husoyo*, and then *premion*, *sedro*, hymn, and *etro*. After a series of prayers, the water is signed, *myron* is poured into the water, and the water is blessed: 'May this water be blessed and sanctified so as to become a divine regenerating laver.' The candidate is anointed with the oil of anointing, first on the forehead, and then the whole body, and is baptized. After the baptism the candidate is anointed with the *myron*, accompanied by prayer with hand-laying. The formula of anointing is, 'By the holy myron which is Christ's sweet fragrance, the seal of the true faith, and the perfection of the Holy Spirit's gifts, N is sealed.' After a series of prayers including the Lord's Prayer, the candidate is crowned with a ribbon, and then given communion. Male candidates are processed three times round the altar. There is a prayer for the removal of the crown (ribbon) after seven days.

Daily offices

The Daily Office of the Syrian Orthodox as celebrated in Jerusalem today groups the offices into two; None, Vespers and Compline at 4 p.m. in winter, and Nocturns, Matins with Terce and Sext at 6.30 a.m. Scholars note a difference between what is termed the use of Antioch and that of Tikrit. Vespers (Ramso) commences with the common liturgical opening, prayer, Psalm 51 and a variable psalm. This may indicate the influence of the monastic office. There then follows a preparatory prayer and the core of Eastern Vespers, Psalms 141, 142, 119: 105–17, and 117. Then comes *husoyo*, *promion*, *sedro*, with incensing, *qolo*, *etro*, *qolo*, *bo'utho*, *hullolo*, Gospel, *tesmesto*, final prayers including *trisagion* and Lord's Prayer, and *hutomo*. A form of Compline is usually attached to Vespers. It includes Psalm 4, *promion, sedro, qolo, bo'utho,* Psalm 91 and 121, *tesbohta,* Creed and blessing. Matins (Lilyo and Safro) includes fixed psalmody at various points, *eqbo, husoyo, bo'utho,* as well as *sedro,* Magnificat (recited twice, once in Lilyo and then again in Safro) and Gloria in excelsis. The major part of Lilyo is made up of three units called *qawme* (stations) and *'eddone* (periods). The minor Hours are made up of poetic material and prayers. They have an opening prayer, and *promion, sedro, qolo* and *bo'utho.* Their theme tends to be watchfulness and following God's will, guided by the saints and the Theotokos.

Marriage rites

The marriage rite has the usual eastern brief betrothal, with joining the right hands. Though certain services in western countries include vows, the traditional rite begins with the standard opening of Gloria to the Trinity, prayer and Psalm 51, hymn, prayer, *quqal'yon* (Psalms 45, 1, 2, 9), *eqbo, husoyo, promion, sedro,* hymn and *etro.* Then comes a lavish blessing of the rings, including the petition, 'May these rings be blessed and may they be for the fulfilment of gladness to the children of the Holy Church.' A blessing of bride and groom follows. The second service is the blessing of the crowns or garlands, which again has the stylized beginning from Gloria to *etro,* followed by lections. The priest recites:

> O Lord, who did adorn the sky with luminaries: the sun, the moon, and the stars; O God, who did crown the earth with fruits, flowers, and blossoms of all kinds; O Jesus Christ who did crown kings, priests, and prophets, O Compassionate One, who did bestow his triumph upon his worshippers in return for their heroic combat to keep the faith; Lord, who crowned King David with the crown of victory; O God, who encircled the ocean like a crown around all the earth; O Good One, who blessed the year by his grace, put your right hand, full of mercy and compassion, upon the heads upon which these crowns are placed. Grant them that they also may crown their children with righteousness, justice and mirth. May your peace and concord abide with them throughout their lives forever. Amen. (Metropolitan Samuel 1974)

Chants follow while the priest waves the crowns over their heads. Prayers are also recited over the best man and bridesmaid. An admonition, joining of hands, and removal of the crowns follow, with Lord's Prayer, Creed and Hymn of the Blessed Virgin Mary. A rubric notes the custom of drinking from a common cup of wine.

Funeral rites

As with the Church of the East, funeral rites are provided for males, females, children and clerics. The rite is known as the *tekso d'oufoyo,* or order of enshrouding. The overall structure of each is similar, and consists of three services. Here we describe the rites for females. It begins with the *trisagion,* Lord's Prayer, Gloria to the Trinity, prayer and Psalm 51. A hymn follows, in this case beginning, 'O Christ, who has promised resurrection to Adam's mortal children, we beseech you to raise and quicken your handmaid who has slept trusting you.' Then follows a *quqal'yon* (Psalm 123: 1–3), *eqbo, husoyo, promion, sedro, eqbo* and *etro*. A hymn, 'Sarah died', follows, and then a hymn, 'Sorrow not'. This first service concludes with the supplication of St James, *trisagion* and Lord's Prayer.

The second service begins with Gloria to the Trinity, prayer, *quqal'yon* (Psalm 103: 2 and 4), *eqbo, husoyo, promion, sedro, eqbo* and *etro*, two hymns, and the supplication of St Ephrem. The third service has the same structure, but after the two hymns comes the supplication of St Balai, a canticle, 'O how bitter the cup', an Epistle reading, a Gospel reading, litany and burial. The rite concludes with the *trisagion*, Lord's Prayer, Nicene Creed, *quqal'yon* of the departed, the *kaumo* of the departed, and the supplication of St Balai. A memorial for the third and fortieth days and the first anniversary are provided to follow the Divine Liturgy.

Ordination rites

The present ordination rites are attributed to Michael the Syrian, patriarch from 1166 to 1199, and rites are provided for cantor, reader, subdeacon, deacon, presbyter and bishop as well as for the institution of an archdeacon, chorepiscopos, visitor, abbot and abbess. The rite for ordination of a deacon, for example, after introductory prayers, canticles and scripture reading, has a prayer by the bishop and the admonition:

> The grace of our Lord Jesus Christ, which always supplies our deficiencies through the will of God the Father, with the power of the Holy Spirit, advances from the order of subdeacons to the rank of deacon this man standing here . . .'

The bishop prays that the candidate will be made worthy and, after touching the communion mysteries, places his hands on the candidate's head, raises and lowers them three times, and prays the ordination prayer, which makes reference to Stephen. After another prayer, the archdeacon and bishop acclaim the candidate as deacon. A prayer of thanksgiving by the bishop, prayed silently, follows. Some of the prayers have parallels in the Byzantine and Melkite rites.

The Maronite Tradition

The forebears of the Maronite Church seem to have shared liturgical roots with both the Church of the East and the Syrian Orthodox, but their acceptance of Chalcedon separated them from both. Over the course of time the Maronite rites have been transformed by successive waves of Syrian Orthodox influence, and then, after the crusades, when the Maronites established communion with Rome, Latin influences. Thus, for example, the Roman rite of penance was introduced, and the Roman marriage vow was incorporated into the Maronite marriage rite. Latin vesture for the Mass is quite common. However, from the 1940s, and then gaining momentum with encouragement from Vatican II, the Latinization has been partly reversed. More authentic Syriac texts have been established (though now in Arabic), and oriental vesture reintroduced. The Diocese of Maron in the USA pioneered English-language versions of the rites.

Eucharistic rites

The usual liturgy used is that of the Twelve Apostles, the anaphora of which is the Syriac form of the Anaphora of St John Chrysostom. Scholars speculate that the Syriac preserves an earlier version than the Greek, but, according to Sebastian Brock, the Syriac style and vocabulary date it to the sixth or seventh century. The present ordo also contains the Anaphora of St Peter, St James, and 'Anaphora of the Roman Church'. Other anaphoras were once used but have now fallen in disuse, a process which began at least as early as the authorization of the first printed missals in 1596. Amongst these is 'Sharar' or St Peter III. This anaphora is a twin of the East Syrian Addai and Mari. The Maronite version has a distinctive form of institution narrative and *anamnesis*, as well as lengthy intercessions. It has been argued that this anaphora perhaps preserves the institution narrative which somehow fell out of the East Syrian prayer. This is unlikely; it seems rather that the Maronite version has been expanded and modified to bring it into line with later expectations of what constitutes a eucharistic prayer (for a recent attempt, but one that is flawed by presuppositions of Jewish origins, see Jammo 2002). Sharar seems to have been suppressed in the missal of 1716, though an abbreviation was made for use as the liturgy of the presanctified (Hayek 1964).

The present ordo begins with prayers of preparation at the altar and preparation of the offerings, echoing the Syrian Orthodox rite, but much shorter. What was apparently the original beginning is now entitled 'Preparing the faithful' and has a doxology, a prayer, a form of the Gloria in excelsis, followed by *husoyo, promion* and *sedro*. As in the Syrian Orthodox rite, the *trisagion* introduces the readings, though in the Chalcedonian version. Provision is made for a homily, followed by the Creed and the Peace. The modern division here suggests western influence, where the Creed seems to belong to the Liturgy of the Word rather than being part of the pre-anaphoral liturgy. A sure sign of Latinization is the enlargement of the printed words of institution in the printed missal, whereas the *epiklesis* is in the same print as the rest of the anaphora. It is true that the congregation is unlikely to be aware of this, but the Maronite clergy tend to do manual acts and elevations which underscore the Latin view of the importance of the words of institution as words of consecration. A penitential prayer follows and then sancta sanctis and communion. There is a short thanksgiving and dismissal.

Rites of initiation

The baptismal rite of the Maronites is attributed to Jacob of Sarug, though there is a shorter form named after St Basil. A thorough study of the manuscript tradition was undertaken by Mouhanna, and certainly there were considerable variations in the manuscripts. The present text of the rite was published in 1942. The structure of the rite is very similar to that of the Syrian Orthodox. There is provision for a rite of admission with a prayer over the mother, and a prayer over the candidate. After a *qolo*, there is the giving of the name with the words:

N, may the seal of the holy cross, symbol of victory, be your shelter and protection until the day you receive the seal of Christ through the waters of baptism. Then, when you are granted this seal of your Lord, you will enter and join with his spiritual flock, for ever. Amen.

The preparatory rites begin with the common opening of 'Glory to the Trinity,' prayer and Psalm 51, *husoyo, promion, sedro, qolo* and *etro*. The *trisagion*, with 'baptismal propers', is sung: 'O Christ, baptized in the river Jordan, have mercy on us.' After a *mazmoro* come the readings, and provision for a homily. There follows a rite for the catechumens which includes exorcisms, renunciation of Satan, and the recitation of the Creed. In some of the manuscripts there is indication that an anointing with oil followed.

In the present rite a lengthy blessing of the font follows, with diaconal biddings to prayer, a greeting, and then an actual blessing prayer. This begins with a form of *sursum corda* with one response which is reminiscent of the Church of the East formulation. The prayer is patterned on the anaphora, and includes sanctus and benedictus, and an extremely long invocation of the Holy Spirit. The emphasis in this prayer is on the font as womb, and passing from being an earthly Adam to rebirth as a heavenly Adam. The celebrant signs the font with the cross before the blessing, and during the blessing *myron* is poured into the water in the form of a cross.

The final part of the rite begins with a greeting, and the catechumens are signed with oil. The baptism is by triple immersion and the Trinitarian formula, 'N is baptized a lamb in the flock of Christ in the name of the Father (amen) and of the Son (amen) and of the Holy Spirit, for eternal life (amen).' The baptizands are clothed in a white garment, and signed with *myron*, and there is an optional 'crowning'. A procession in the Church with *qolo* follows, and there may be a Eucharist; if there is no Eucharist the rite ends with a prayer and the removal of the 'crown'.

Daily offices

The Maronite daily office, as might be expected, has much in common with that of the Syrian Orthdox. Ramso has the common opening with introductory prayer, alleluia with refrains, and Psalm 51. A preparatory prayer is followed by the same fixed evening psalms as the Syrian Orthodox. These are followed by *soghito*, or hymn, 'The Resurrection of Christ', and then by *promion, sedro, qolo* and *etro*. For example, the *promion* for the first Sunday of the Annunciations to Zechariah, has the following:

> Praise, glory and honour to the Most High
> who sent his messenger into his sanctuary,
> to announce to the priest Zechariah the conception of the Forerunner.
> To the Good One is due glory and honour this evening,
> and all the days of our lives, now and for ever. Amen.

Incense is offered during this praise.

Mazmoro follows, and readings. This is followed by bu'otho (supplications), and hutomo with trisagion, Lord's Prayer, final prayers and dismissal. Lilyo follows the same structure as the Syrian Orthodox. Safro includes Magnificat, Psalms 63, 91, 51, nuhro (Hymn of St Ephrem) and benedicite (Tabet 1972). The form of Safro (Matins) provided by the Diocese of St Maron in the USA has a revised structure, and represents a simplification of the older rite. Thus it begins with the opening doxology and prayer with greeting, followed by a short Gloria, prayer and psalm of the day, prayer, nuhro, hymn and a prayer before the fixed morning psalms – Psalms 148–150, and 117. Then follow the Canticle of the Three Children (benedicite), promion, sedro, qolo and etro, mazmoro, readings, Gloria in excelsis and a concluding prayer.

Marriage rites

The marriage service exists in a number of older recensions, the oldest being Berke 22. One remarkable characteristic of some of the older manuscripts is that, as in the Coptic tradition, the Maronite marriage rites in some areas included a rite of anointing. The text of Renaudot given by Denzinger, coming after the ratification of the betrothal and before the exchange of rings, reads:

> When our Lord Jesus Christ found himself in the house of Simon, a sinful woman knocked at the door and approached Jesus bearing ointment. She anointed his feet and her sins were forgiven her. This sinful woman carried an ointment. She entered the house of Simon and the Lord replied to her expectancy and said to her, 'Your sins are forgiven and your bad deeds are pardoned.

This anointing seems to be used in an almost exorcistic and purificatory sense rather like oil of healing. According to Van Overstraeten, it was included because of the influence of the Canon Laws of the Coptic Ibn-el-Assal in the thirteenth century (Van Overstraeten 1974). However, the Coptic prayer is full of messianic significance, and is not exorcistic and purificatory. The manuscript Vat Syr.477, dated sixteenth or seventeenth century, has a different prayer:

> God the Father, you commanded your servant Samuel to anoint David Son of Jesse. And he was your prophet, and he kept your commandments and judged your people justly before you. And you raised by means of anointing priests, kings and prophets. Even now, Lord God, let your power and your right hand full of mercies rest upon this oil and sanctify it and grant to your servants whom we anoint with it pardon of their debts and forgiveness of sins, and laudable fellowship and loving unity. And rule over them with tranquillity all

the days of their life, through the prayers of the Mother of God, Mary and all the saints for ever. Amen. Amen.

This seems to combine messianic themes with the purificatory theme. However, the practice seems to have disappeared after the seventeenth century, whatever the original theme may have been. The present text of the rite was published in 1942, and consists of the Covenant (betrothal) and Crowning (marriage). The Covenant takes place in the home, with the exchange of consent, and the blessing and giving of rings. There is also provision for blessing of cincture, clothing and jewellery.

The Crowning is a longer rite, opening with the Gloria patri, prayer, and Psalm 128, a husoyo with promion, sedro, qolo, etro, trisagion and readings. There follows a karazuta and a homily. Then comes the actual crowning rite. After a diaconal proclamation and qolo come vows, showing distinct Latin Catholic influence. The blessing and giving of rings follows, and then the crowns are blessed, with Psalm 21: 2–5 for the bridegroom, and Psalm 45: 11–12, 14 for the bride. For the latter the celebrant prays:

> May God who crowned all the holy women and blessed Sarah, Rebecca and Rachel,
> bless you, be merciful to you, and exalt you with the crown of glory.
> Adorned with the fruits of the Spirit,
> may you flourish as a blessed vine in the midst of the Church;
> may the Lord dwell with your husband in love and abiding peace;
> (may you bring forth children pleasing to God)
> through the intercession of Mary, Mother of God, and all the saints.

The 'witnesses' – best man and maid of honour – are also crowned.

After the crowning comes the Hymn of St Ephrem, with the theme of Christ as the spouse, and then the removal of the crowns. A prayer over the bride and groom follows, and the rite ends with a concluding prayer and blessing.

Funeral rites

The burial rite is contained in the Book of Ginnazat. The earliest known text dates from 1266 and contains offices for burial of clergy and monks. In this text the rite begins in the house with psalmody, husoyo, mazmoro or qolo. There is a procession to the church for a service of psalmody, readings, office of incense, rite of farewell and procession to the grave. Clergy to be buried are anointed. After burial there is a final prayer. The custom as witnessed in 1986 was that only the parish priest and close family attend the burial. The congregation disperse with the farewell.

Ordination rites

The ordination rites are a late compilation, though clearly drawing on earlier material. Thus there are parallels not only with the Syrian Orthodox, but also the Melkite rite, the Byzantine rite for deacons, and the Apostolic Constitutions. The prayer for the ordination of priests includes the petition:

> Now also, Lord God, we pray you and beseech your many mercies, that you would look on us with the eye of your mercy and strengthen this your servant N, who bends his neck before your holy altar and before our lowliness, that he may receive from us sinners this imposition of hands of your Holy Spirit, that he may fulfil this angelic ministry and be worthy to minister your true and divine doctrine for the strength and stability of the holy Church.

The Armenian Orthodox Church

Armenian tradition traces its origins to the Apostles Thaddeus and Bartholomew, but the great missionary of Armenia was St Gregory Partev or Gregory the Illuminator (Enlightener), *c.*240–332. Perhaps as early as 301 Christianity was the prevailing religion in Armenia. Gregory was from Caesarea in Cappadocia, but it is clear that parts of Armenia were influenced by Syriac-speaking Christianity, with ties to Edessa. Thus we find a two-fold liturgical influence, followed by Byzantine influence, and then in the twelfth century, Latin influence. All these influences have left telltale marks, in varying degrees, on the liturgical rites.

Eucharistic rites

Today the Armenian Church uses a single eucharistic liturgy and eucharistic prayer, attributed to St Athanasius of Alexandria, which seems to be an amalgamation of elements from the liturgies of St James, St Basil and St John Chrysostom. However, in the ancient manuscripts the following anaphoras are found in translation:

St John Chrysostom (Byzantine)
St Basil (Byzantine)
St James (Syriac)
St Ignatius (Syriac)
The Roman canon missae (Latin)

In addition we find the following:

St Gregory the Illuminator (earlier pre-Byzantine version of St Basil)
St Gregory of Nazianzus
St Cyril of Alexandria
St Isaac the Parthian

The last three seem to have been independent compilations. An important commentary on the liturgy by Khosrov Andzewatsi gives evidence of the shape of the liturgy in the tenth century in Vaspurakan province.

The present liturgy of St Athanasius begins with prayers of vesting, which take place privately. This is followed by the purification and accession of the ministers, during which the congregation stands. The purification includes pouring water over the hands of the celebrant, and the accession has clear parallels with the preparation in the Latin rite. This is followed by the *prothesis*, which is a brief preparation and blessing of the bread (unleavened) and wine (not mixed with water). The *prothesis* takes place with the curtain drawn shut. Then comes the synaxis, beginning with the censing of the congregation as the celebrant walks in its midst. Next follows the *enarxis* which consists of blessing, the *monogenes*, introit, bidding of peace, and chanting of the three antiphons. Then comes the Little Entrance, with a non-Chalcedonian form of the *trisagion*, the Great Litany and the lections. The Creed follows together with the anathema:

> As for those who say there was a time when the Son was not or there was a time when the Holy Spirit was not or that they came into being out of nothing or who say that the Son of God or the Holy Spirit be of different substance and that they be changeable or alterable, such doth the Catholic and Apostolic Church anathematize.

There then follow prayers and a litany entitled 'The Prayers after the Lections'.

The Eucharist proper begins with the Great Entrance, the transfer of the elements from the *prothesis* table to the altar, and the Peace. The anaphora follows and, as might be expected, is Syro-Byzantine in structure. There are diptyches and then the Lord's Prayer. A prayer of inclination introduces the elevation, and while the sancta sanctis is sung, the priest prays privately. The intinction and fraction precede the communion. The prayers provided as a preparation to communion are quite extensive, and are followed by a thanksgiving, with blessing and dismissal, which includes the last Gospel (John 1: 1–14) from the Roman rite.

Rites of initiation

If the eucharistic liturgy shows clear Greek and Latin influence, the baptismal rite witnesses to the early Syrian influence, with a stress on the pneumatic imagery of John 3, and an absence of verbal exorcisms. The present rite includes prayers after the eighth day for making a catechumen, and for mother and child after forty days. The rite begins with prayers and psalms, a renunciation of Satan and a Trinitarian confession. The Creed is recited together with Psalm 118. There is a blessing of the oil, and blessing of the water, and this includes pouring the blessed oil into the water. The prayer of blessing the oil associates it with the Holy Spirit and with priests, kings and prophets (cf. The Didascalia from North Syria). Scholars speculate that there was once a pre-baptismal anointing at this point, as in the Syrian tradition, but that it was later transferred to after the rite.

The emphasis on the baptism in water concerns enlightenment, redemption and adoption and being co-heirs, rather than the image of death and resurrection; as in the Syrian rites, the font is a womb rather than a tomb. Baptism is by triple immersion.

After the baptism comes the Lord's Prayer, a prayer, and the anointing. There is also a vesting prayer, which mentions the 'garment of salvation'. The candidate is then taken to the bema (sanctuary) and the rubric directs that communion is given. A rubric also mentions the crown, or white hood, which is to be worn for eight days.

Daily offices

The daily offices seem to preserve some elements of the early Cappadocian offices, but also show Jerusalem influence (Winkler 1997 and Woolfenden 2004). There are in fact nine offices provided: Vespers, the Hour of Peace, the Hour of Rest, Night Office, Matins, Prime, Terce, Sext and None. Commentaries on the office by Yovhannes Odznetsi (c.728) and Khosrov Andzewatsi (c.950) give some idea of the forms at an earlier time. Important modern studies on reconstructing the development of the Night Office and Vespers have been made by Gabriele Winkler. The core of Vespers in the Cappadocian and Jerusalem usage is conjectured to have been lucernarium with Phos hilaron, Psalm 140 and intercessions (Taft 1986), and these of course occur in Armenian Vespers. The present structure of Vespers consists of an introduction formed by the Lord's Prayer, Psalm 55: 17–18, and Psalm 86, followed by lucernarium with a prayer for blessing light, Phos hilaron or other hymn of light, the evening proclamation ('Let my prayer rise before you as incense'), a litany, prayer and prayer of inclination. The prayer of blessing is a fine prayer:

> Blessed Lord, who dwellest on high, and praised is the glory of thy majesty; who establishedst the luminaries on high, and sentest forth light by day, and the moon and the world of mankind. Thou madest the sun to give light by day, and the moon and the stars to give light by night, and the light of the lamp. Thou art light laudable, holy and primal light. From thee doth the darkness flee. And do thou, Christ, send forth thy living light into our hearts. And let us with one accord say, blessed is the name of thy holy glory. And to thee we sing a hymn of praise and glory to Father and Son.

At one time the service may have ended with the prayer of inclination, but in the course of time it has been extended. There thus follows the *trisagion* with prayers, Psalm 121, a prayer for those in need, and dismissal psalms (91, 123, 54), to which are added the Proclamation of the Cross, Psalm 122, Psalm 100, final invocation and Lord's Prayer.

The Hour of Peace commences with part of Psalm 34 and then a 'canon' of six psalms, the psalter being divided into eight canons, with cento-like prayers drawn from scripture and prayers. The Hour of Rest uses much of Psalm 119.

The Night Office opens with, 'Lord, if you will open my lips, my mouth shall sing thy praises' recited three times, and a benediction of the Trinity. Psalms 3, 88, 103, 143 follow, then hymns and supplications, prayer, a canon of psalmody and canticle, intercessions and prayers. Matins begins with Psalm 90: 14–17 and Gloria Patri, followed by a number of canticles: Daniel 3, Magnificat, Benedictus and Nunc dimittis. It may be that these are vestiges of Vigil. In the text given by Conybeare (1905), Psalm 51 and then 148–150 follow, with anthem and Gloria in excelsis, proclamation (according to occasion), and Prayer of the Resurrection. Then come litany and collect, Angel of Peace petitions, prayer of blessing and *trisagion*. The rite continues with a devotional addition, with bidding, responsory, Gospel of healing and anthem, bidding and blessing. The remaining Hours share a similar structure, with blessing God the Holy Spirit, psalm, hymns, prayer, and proclamation (bidding) and prayer and Lord's Prayer, although None is longer, with additional material.

Marriage rites

The marriage rite is preceded by a short betrothal rite consisting of Psalm 4, scripture readings and a prayer. The prayer texts for the actual rite for marriage, or the putting on of crowns, vary in the manuscript tradition. Psalm 21 is followed by readings from Genesis, Isaiah, Ephesians, Matthew and John. A number of prayers follow, alluding to the themes of creation and the wedding at Cana in Galilee, asking that the couple be kept spotless, be fruitful, and attain the joy of the heavenly bridal chamber. The couple are crowned with the crown of comeliness. In some manuscripts the crowning prayer is much richer, and alludes to Old Testament types.

The more recent rites have included as part of betrothal the presentation and blessing of gifts (now abandoned), the blessing of robes, and joining of hands. And in the marriage rite itself, the blessing of a common cup, which seems to have been an imitation of Byzantine practice, has not survived.

Funeral rites

The burial rite consists of a service of psalmody, readings and prayers in church or in the house; the funeral procession to the place of burial; a short office; committal; sealing of the grave; and return to the house of the deceased. For lay burial the rite begins with three psalms (Gobola), a prayer concerned with creation of humanity and asking that this person be ranked with the saints of the kingdom, and the Lord's Prayer with paraphrase. This is followed by a psalm, Epistle and Gospel readings. The procession to the grave is followed by prayers, Psalm 116 and a litany with a hundredfold Kyrie. Two lengthy prayers are said to seal the grave, followed by a hymn. On returning to the home, Psalm 44 and a prayer are recited. Provision is made for an office for the second day.

Rites for burial of the clergy are more elaborate. The rite for a priest includes this prayer:

> Lord God, creator of all creatures, thou with thy mighty power didst go down into the nether hell, and unleash the power of death. And thou didst set free the spirits therein, and translate them unto thy deathless abode of rest. We pray thee, Lord, mingle the spirit of

this priest N or M with the ranks of those who love thy holy name. And do thou bless thy great congregation of us who stand before thee; and make us worthy to glorify Father and Son and holy Spirit, now and ever and to the eternity of eternities. Amen.

It includes the following on behalf of the deceased:

Hail to thee, holy church. Hail to thee, altar of holiness. Hail to you, ranks of the priesthood. I have set forth again on the road to the creator of heaven.

Ordination rites

According to Bernard Botte, the rites of ordination are influenced by the Byzantine rite, but Paul Bradshaw maintains that this may be true in terms of structure, but not text (Bradshaw 1990). The only slight parallels that Bradshaw could trace were with the Georgian rite, and that for readers and deaconesses only. Provision is made for the appointment of a reader and subdeacon with appropriate psalm and prayer. The rite for a deacon begins with Psalms 15 and 25, and then the assembly and God are addressed in prayer with the laying on of the bishop's hand. Amongst the petitions in the prayer for ordination of priests is the following:

Give him apostolic grace to expel and drive away the diseases of sufferings and all foul spirits from humanity; by laying his hands on them and calling on your all-powerful name, let him bestow in grace assistance and healing on the afflicted.

In comparison to other Eastern rites, the ordination rites are quite simple and straightforward.

The Coptic Orthodox Church

Although something about worship in Egypt may be gleaned from Clement and Origen, the first liturgical compilation of note is the Canons of Hippolytus (c.336) and the eucology attributed to Bishop Sarapion of Thmuis (c.350). The former is one redaction of the so-called apostolic tradition attributed to Hippolytus, the integrity of which has been seriously challenged in late twentieth-century scholarship. The latter is a collection of prayers, some probably by Serapion, but by no means all from the same author. It includes prayers for catechumens; for oil before and after baptism; for sanctification of the waters of baptism; prayers with laying on of hands for deacons, priests and bishops; prayers for the sick; and an anaphora with a distinct shape, showing traces of the use of the Didache, which in some parts of Egypt was regarded as canonical scripture. However, in the process which led to the emergence of a regional as opposed to a local liturgy, we find Syrian or Cappadocian influence combined with what seems to have been the indigenous usage of Alexandria. It appears that the present forms of the rites are due to the work of Patriarch Gabriel V (c.1411).

Eucharistic rites

Thus, for the eucharistic liturgy there were three rites, existing in Greek and Coptic: St Basil, St Gregory of Nazianzus and St Mark (in Coptic entitled St Cyril). In the older tradition, St Basil was the rite used for ordinary days of the year, St Gregory for seven major feasts, and St Cyril (St. Mark) was used in the month of Kiyahk and during Lent. In modern practice the liturgy of St Basil is used, and parts of the anaphora of Gregory are added-on solemnities. St Cyril is rarely used because of its length and little-known melodies.

The *prothesis*, as in all eastern liturgies, is a later addition, though its length in the Coptic rite it is more akin to the Syrian. In Arabic the title is *hamal*, lamb. It includes prayers for worthiness for the celebrant, and short formulae while the bread is arranged. The prayer said secretly over the bread and wine contains an *epiklesis*; it has been suggested that it is the remnant of an ancient eucharistic anaphora. It includes the petition:

> O lover of humanity, make your face to shine upon this bread, and upon this cup, which we have set on this your priestly table. Bless them, sanctify them, hallow them, and change them, that this bread may become indeed your holy body, and the mixture in this cup, your precious blood.

Given the relatively late date of the *prothesis*, this may be simply an instance of anticipating the later rite, which seems to be a characteristic of many later medieval developments. After the *prothesis* comes the prayer of incense and the lection, with *trisagion* between a reading from Acts and the Gospel. The lections are interspersed with formulae recited by priest and deacon. The liturgy of the faithful begins with the prayer of the veil, and litanic intercessions. This is followed by the Creed and the kiss of peace. The anaphora of St Basil is regarded as an early form of the anaphora, pre-dating the Byzantine recension, which is almost certainly an expansion by Basil himself. The problem is explaining how or why the earlier recension found in Egypt should be named after Basil. It is suggested that it was the Anaphora of Cappadocia that Basil brought with him in his extended visit to Egypt.

As with Basil, the Anaphora of Gregory is of the West Syrian pattern. This is a lengthy anaphora addressed throughout to the Son. Jose Sanchez Caro has argued that the 'I–thou' style of this anaphora has much in common with the homilies and poems of St Gregory of Nazianzus, and could have been written or expanded by him (Sanchez Caro 1983). Others have pointed out the use of 'for my sake' for the work of the Son, which again is characteristic of Gregory's style. According to Albert Gerhards, it was an anti-Arian Cappadocian prayer, expanded to become anti-Nestorian, and then 'Eygptianized' (Gerhards 1984).

The Anaphora of St Cyril (St Mark) has its own distinctive Egyptian structure. Fragments of comparable Egyptian anaphoras exist, including the so-called 'Strasbourg Papyrus' Gr.234, which is regarded as being an earlier version of St Cyril. It begins with an opening praise of God for creation, in words paralleled in Nehemiah 9, and then, with reference to 'reasonable sacrifice and this unbloody service', uses Malachai 1: 11.

The reference to sacrifice becomes a springboard for extremely lengthy intercessions before a return to the theme of praise, and the sanctus. A feature of the Egyptian tradition is that the benedictus is not used after sanctus. This seems to be partly because the Egyptian eucharistic prayers (Serapion, St Cyril, and the various fragments) use the wording of the sanctus to develop the first *epiklesis* or calling on God to send his power/Spirit to bless the elements. This leads into the institution narrative, second *epiklesis* and final doxology. The benedictus would interrupt this flow.

The anaphora is followed by the consignation, fraction and Lord's Prayer. Communion includes a 'confession' which has to do with the Theotokos and unity of the divinity and humanity in Christ. The rite ends with a thanksgiving, inclination, and lengthy prayer of dismissal.

Rites of initiation

The rite of baptism begins with prayers over the catechumens, and a prayer for oil of the catechumens, which is exorcistic in theme. Exorcisms follow, together with anointing with the oil of exorcism. The rite then replicates much of the eucharistic rite, with four lections, psalmody, intercessions, *sursum corda*, blessing of water (modelled on the eucharistic prayer) into which chrism (*myron*) is poured. The blessing of the water asks God to:

> Show forth yourself and look upon this your creature, this water; give it the grace of the Jordan, and the power and the strength of heaven; and by the descent of your Holy Spirit upon it, hallow it with the blessing of the Jordan. Amen.

The candidate is led to the font, and then immersed three times, using the active western formula. The rite provides a prayer for deconsecrating the water after the baptism. Anointing with chrism follows, with the formula:

> In the name of the Father and of the Son and of the Holy Spirit. An unction of the grace of the Holy Spirit; an unction of the pledge of the kingdom of heaven; an unction of participation in eternal and immortal life. A holy unction of Christ our God, and a seal that shall not be loosed. The perfection of the grace of the Holy Spirit, and the breastplate of the faith and the truth. You are anointed, N, with holy oil, in the name of the Father and of the Son and of the Holy Spirit. Amen.

A rubric directs anointing with thirty-six crosses. There follows a laying on of hands, clothing in a white garment, signing and breathing on the candidates, a crowning and the giving of a girdle.

Daily offices

John Cassian in the fourth century gives some gleanings of the daily services of the monks in Egypt. However, the present divine office was reformed by Patriarch Gabriel, with the result that it is heavily monastic in ethos. The present form has eight services: Morning, Terce, Sext, None, Eleventh Hour (Vespers) and Compline, together with Prayer of the Veil, and Midnight. The structure of each hardly varies. There are fixed initial prayers, twelve psalms, a Gospel reading, poetic refrains called *psali*, Kyrie eleison some 40 to 50 times, *trisagion*, Lord's Prayer, dismissal prayer of absolution, and a final prayer. Psalms 119–28 are used at Vespers, and 129–50 at Compline. Some of the *psali* have parallels in the Byzantine *troparia* and Theotokia.

In addition to these monastic offices, there are offices of Evening and Morning Incense, and it is thought that these are relics of the 'cathedral' offices. The rite for the evening begins with fixed introductory prayers, continues with the invitatory with praise of Mary and the saints, the putting on of incense, the evening incense prayer, censing the altar, intercessions for the dead and sick, *trisagion*, Lord's Prayer, 'Hail to You', preface to Creed, Creed, blessing with candles and cross, litany, prayer of the Gospel, psalm verse, Gospel, three great prayers and censing, Lord's Prayer, three prayers of absolution, veneration of the cross and Gospel, and ends with the final blessing. There is also provision for a daily choral service called Psalmodia, which has three forms. It can precede the Evening Office of Incense, or come between Midnight and Morning Prayer, or between Morning Prayer and the Morning Office of Incense. The structure consists of fixed initial prayers and Psalm 50, a fixed psalmody or canticles, *psali*, Theotokia (theological hymn of the day), Lobsh of the Theotokia (another poetic piece), a hymn of the day (Difnar) and conclusion.

Marriage rites

One of the significant things regarding the marriage rite of the Coptic Church is that, like the Maronite rite, it once contained an anointing of bride and groom, though this has fallen into disuse in the modern rite. For the rite of betrothal, the bride and family go to the church, and the bride is escorted to a special place on the women's side of the church. The groom arrives and is seated in the men's division of the church. A fairly lengthy Liturgy of the Word prefaces the betrothal rite, which consists of three betrothal prayers, two of which are followed by short congregational prayers. The prayers centre on the theme of creation and the well-being of the couple. The father of the groom presents wedding attire, which is blessed by the priest. A ring is placed on the finger of the groom, who is led to the bride; the groom removes the ring and places it on the bride's finger, and they are regarded as betrothed.

The marriage rite begins with a question of consent, and then comes a Liturgy of the Word. After the Gospel there is a special litany which includes,

> You who blessed the wedding celebrated at Cana in Galilee and by the power of your divinity changed water into real wine, bless and protect the marriage of your servants N and N, keeping them in peace, unity and love . . .

Another litany follows, then the Creed, and then three prayers: one for the couple to become one flesh, one for multiplying blessings, and a third for protection in the future. The anointing rite once followed, but now the service continues with the crowning (the 'messianic' connection may have been the reason for the anointing to be adopted, though the theme of the anointing prayers was more for protection than coronation). The crowning is followed by signing and blessing, and then the removal of the crowns.

Funeral rites

The burial office, according to Burmester (1967), begins with a prayer of thanksgiving and the *trisagion*. The office in church begins with a prayer of thanksgiving, the Gloria and the Lord's Prayer. Psalm 51 follows, and then a number of extracts from psalms, ending with Psalm 114. A prayer of incense follows, with Epistle, *trisagion* and Gospel. Prayers for peace, the patriarch and clergy, and for the faithful follow, and then the burial prayer. Then come the Lord's Prayer, a prayer to Christ for absolution and prayer for the safe journey of the departed to paradise follow. This prayer was once said over the grave, though now it is frequently said in the church. There is a further absolution and blessing.

Ordination rites

The ordination rites in their present form date from around the fourteenth century, and provide for the ordination of reader, subdeacon, deacon, presbyter, *hegoumenos* (abbot), archdeacon and bishop. There is a special form for the consecration of the patriarch. There are some echoes of the forms found in Apostolic Constitutions, and the Syrian Orthodox rites. The rite for presbyters has a rubric outlining their qualities, and candidates are vested in deacon's attire with *orarium* (stole) over the arm. Prayers and formulae require a turning to the west, to the altar and to the east. The rites include signing the candidate with three crosses on the forehead. There is also an admonition to the candidate.

The Ethiopian Orthodox *Täwahǝdo* Church

Ethiopia received Christianity from Egypt, and until the late twentieth century, the patriarch was a Copt consecrated by the Coptic patriarch. There are certainly liturgical borrowings from Egypt, for example, the ordination rites. Furthermore, it would seem that the areas of Egypt which redacted or used the canons of Hippolytus, or the Hippolytan genre (Sinados and Testament of our Lord) were influential, and became the normal liturgy of this Church. However, we also find Syrian influences, together with medieval indigenous creativity to give the liturgical texts a characteristic style. In addition, living alongside Muslims and Falashas has also influenced the imagery and concepts of the liturgical material. The result is a very distinct liturgical tradition.

Eucharistic rites

The normal eucharistic liturgy is that of the Apostles, underneath which lies the Hippolytan literature. The text of the rite begins with the preparation and vesting of the ministers, and one of these is attributed to St Basil. Vessels are also prepared. The celebrating priest prays the Lord's Prayer, and then begins the *prothesis*. The *enarxis* begins with a summons to prayer, the giving of the peace, and diaconal biddings and intercessions, after which the priest says another prayer attributed to Basil, and the Absolution of the Son (cf. Coptic funeral rite). More intercessions follow. Then come censing with prayers of incense, and intercessions for peace, the patriarch, and the congregation. Epistle readings (Pauline and Catholic), and a reading from Acts with prayers and acclamations come next. More censing, the *trisagion* and intercessions lead to the Gospel, followed by the dismissal of the catechumens.

The pre-anaphora includes the Peace, some intercessions and the Creed. The Anaphora of the Apostles is that attributed to Hippolytus, heavily interpolated and greatly expanded. After an initial brief thanksgiving come intercessions. Thanksgiving is briefly resumed and a sanctus introduced, followed by the Hippolytan institution narrative, brief *epiklesis*, petition for gathering the church and benedictus. The Lord's Prayer and various other prayers lead to the fraction, the consignation and communion. Thanksgiving after communion includes an exhortation, psalm verses, parts of the Lord's Prayer, prayer of inclination and dismissal.

In addition to this rite, E. Hammerschmidt (1961) listed eighteen other anaphoras, though it is doubtful that all were used. Some are translations, for example, St Mark/Cyril, and St James. Others are indigenous compositions, such as Epiphanius, John the Evangelist and Mary Cyriacos. The latter addresses Mary, and contains a long list of Old Testament worthies leading to the conception of Mary, a statement of Trinitarian doctrine, and then the recitation of the Creed before further praise of the Virgin, and the institution narrative. According to Getatchew Haile (1981), some of these anaphoras date from a Trinitarian controversy in the fifteenth century in which dissidents and Orthodox both authored new anaphoras reflecting the struggle.

Other rites

The baptismal rite of the Ethiopic church is similar to that of the Coptic, which is what we would expect. Likewise the ordination prayers, more obviously so because the Coptic Church supplied bishops for this Church. The office has some peculiarities of its own, and studies of these rites are still in their infancy. The liturgical book, the Me'eraf, gives the ordinary of the cathedral office, while the *deggua* has antiphons proper to the season, and the *qene* contains the poetic elements. Vespers (Wazema) has an opening prayer, proper hymn, supplication for travellers, Psalm 23 with proper antiphon and first evening *qene*. A supplication for rain is followed by Psalm 92 with antiphon and second *qene*. Supplication for the king is followed by Psalm 140, with antiphon and third *qene*. There follows Liton, which is a thanksgiving, readings from Epistles and

Acts, followed by Daniel 3: 52–6, with antiphon and final *qene*. A chant before the Gospel and Gospel follow, and three prayers for the evening. The office concludes with petitions, doxology, Creed, Lord's Prayer and dismissal.

Mawaddes, or Vigil, begins with thanksgiving, *trisagion* and *kidan* of the morning. The remainder of the service consists mainly of groups of psalms which are each followed by intercessory prayers, such as for rain and the fruits of the earth. At a festal vigil the whole psalter is recited. Morning prayer (*sebhata naghe*) has three different forms. The festal form begins with an opening prayer, and a prayer of absolution, the *ezl* (proper), Liton, a series of psalms, with supplication for the sick. There are canticles, Psalms 148–50, supplications, reading of the Gospel, and further psalmody before ending with the Creed and Lord's Prayer. The minor Hours tend to be mainly recitation of psalms.

The marriage rite is similar to the Coptic rite, but includes a ceremony of cutting a piece of the groom's hair and placing it on the head of the bride, and then vice versa. It is celebrated with the Eucharist, and the crowning takes place at the end.

The burial rite includes preparation of the body, accompanied by psalms, reading from the Gospel of John, and the 'praises of Mary'. Psalms and the 'praises of Mary' are appointed for the burial. Many of the customs of the rite are found in the Ethiopic translation of the *Testamentum Domini*. Because this Church believes that only on the Last Day will a person's fate be known, it is quite proper to pray for the departed. According to Rowell, burial practice includes the winding of a strip of parchment, inscribed with a mixture of prayers and magical formulae, around the body (Rowell 1977).

References and further reading

Bradshaw, P. F. (1990) *Ordination Rites of the Ancient Churches of East and West*. New York: Pueblo.

Brock, S (1972) Studies in the early history of the Syrian Orthodox baptismal liturgy. *Journal of Theological Studies* NS 23: 16–64.

—— (1980) Some early Syriac baptismal commentaries. *Orientalia Christiana Periodica* 46: 20–61.

Burmester, O. H. E. (1967) *The Egyptian or Coptic Church*. Cairo: Publications de la société d'archéologie copte.

Conybeare, F. C. (1905) *Rituale Armenorum*. Oxford: Clarendon Press.

Doval, A. (2001) *Cyril of Jerusalem, Mystagogue: The Authorship of the Mystatagogic Catecheses*. Washington, DC: Catholic University Press of America.

Fuchs, H. (1926) *Die Anaphora des monophysitischen Patriarchen Johannan I, Aschendorff*. Westfalen: Munster.

Gerhards, A. (1984) *Die griechische Gregoriosanaphora*. Aschendorff: Munster.

Haile, G. (1981) Religious controversies and the growth of Ethiopic literature in the fourteenth and fifteenth centuries. *Oriens Christianus*, 4th ser. 65: 102–36.

Hammerschmidt, E. (1961) *Studies in the Ethiopic Anaphoras*. Berlin: Akademie-Verlag.

Hayek, M. (1964) *Liturgie Maronite: Historie et textes eucharistiques*. Paris: Maison Mame.

Irving, F. F. (1902) *The Ceremonial Use of Oil among the East Syrians.* Oxford: Occasional Paper of the Eastern Church Association, NS 4: 3–28.

Jammo, S. (2002) The Anaphora of the Apostles Addai and Mari: a study of structure and historical background. *Orientalia Christiana Periodica* 68: 5–35.

Jones, B. H. (1964) The history of the Nestorian liturgies. *Anglican Theological Review* 46: 155–76.

Macomber, W. F. (1973) A theory on the origins of the Syrian, Maronite and Chaldean rites. *Orientalia Christiana Periodica* 39: 235–42.

Metropolitan Mar Athanasius Yeshue Samuel (1974) *The Order of Solemnization of the Sacrament of Matrimony.* Lebanon.

Metzger, M. (ed.) (1985–7) *Les Constitutions Apostoliques,* 3 vols, Sources Chretiennes. Paris: Éditions du Cerf.

Mouhanna, A (1980) *Les Rites de l'initiation dans l'église maronite.* Rome: Pontificio Istituto Orientale.

Rowell, G. (1977) *The Liturgy of the Christian Burial.* London: SPCK.

Sanchez Caro, J. M. (1983) *Eucharistia e Historia de la Salvacion.* Madrid: Biblioteca de Autores Christianos.

Spinks, B. D. (1993) *Worship: Prayers from the East.* Washington, DC: Pastoral Press.

—— (1999) *Mar Nestorius and Mar Theodore the Interpreter: The Forgotten Eucharistic Prayers of East Syria,* Alcuin/GROW Joint Liturgical Study 45. Cambridge: Grove Books.

—— (2005) The anaphora attributed to Severus of Antioch: a note on its character and theology. In J. Getcha and A. Lossky (eds.) *Thusia aineseos: Mélanges liturgiques offerts à la mémoire de l'archevêque Georges Wagner (1930–1993).* Paris: Presses Saint-Serge.

Tabet, J. (1972) *L'Office Commun Maronite.* Kaslik: Bibliothèque de l'Université Saint-Esprit.

Taft, R. F. (1986) *The Liturgy of the Hours in East and West.* Collegeville, Minn.: Liturgical Press.

Tovey, P. (1998) *Essays in West Syrian Liturgy.* Oriental Institute of Religious Studies India 199. Kottayam.

Van Overstraeten, J.-G. (1974) Le rite de l'onction des époux dans la liturgie copte du marriage. *Parole d'Orient* 5: 49–93.

Varghese, B. (1998) Early history of the preparation rites in the Syrian Orthodox Anaphora. In *Symposium Syriacum* VII. Rome: Pontificio Istituto Orientale.

Winkler, G. (1997) *Studies in Early Christian Liturgy and its Context.* Aldershot: Ashgate.

Woolfenden, G. (2004) *Daily Liturgical Prayer.* Aldershot: Ashgate.

CHAPTER 18

Eastern Christian Iconographic and Architectural Traditions
Eastern Orthodox

Alexander Grishin

Introduction

The Eastern Orthodox traditions in art and architecture may date back to earliest Christianity, but they received their initial codification only in the opening decades of the fourth century. This is particularly true of the time when Emperor Constantine the Great endorsed Christianity as an official religion of the Roman Empire and moved its capital from pagan Rome, in the West, to Byzantium, in the East, which he renamed Constantinople. The Eastern Roman Empire, or the Byzantine Empire as it became subsequently known, served as the cradle of Orthodox art and Christianity and survived for over a millennium until its capital, Constantinople, was captured by the Ottoman Turks in 1453. Although losing much of its imperial prestige and patronage, the Eastern Orthodox traditions in art and architecture continued to flourish during the period of occupation and continue to the present day.

Many of the Slav countries of Eastern Europe inherited the Eastern Orthodox traditions in art virtually at the moment of their conversion to Christianity, and Byzantine painters and architects followed Byzantine missionaries, clergy and imperial diplomats. In each of these countries, over time, local national traditions emerged and built on the foundations of Byzantine architectural and iconographic conventions, which led one scholar to describe the phenomenon as a Byzantine commonwealth (Obolensky 1971).

The Early Christian Period

The origins of the Eastern Orthodox Christian traditions of art and architecture are not clearly documented. Within the oral and later literary traditions of the Orthodox Church, earliest Christian art dates back to Christ's lifetime and to the foundation of the Roman Empire under Augustus. The Church taught that: 'the tradition of making images . . . existed even at the time of the preaching of Christianity by the Apostles' (Seventh Ecumenical Council, 787). In later literary sources there are also references to paintings made of the Virgin Mary from life by the Evangelist Luke and to miraculous images of Christ created by the Saviour himself. However the earliest surviving archaeo-logical evidence is from the second and third centuries and is characterized by an enormous diversity in the representations of Christ and the Apostles, suggesting that there was no single dominant image for their portrayal dating from a very early period, as was the case, for example, in imperial portraiture. Much of the earliest Christian art survives in the form of third-century house churches, such as that at Dura Europos on the Euphrates in Syria, and in the funerary catacombs, including those of Domitilla, S. Callisto and Priscilla in Rome, and consists of painted wall decorations, carvings, as well as small votive souvenirs.

After the Edict of Milan (313) and the legalization of the Christian faith, the basilica, both as found in Roman secular architecture and in synagogue basilicas, was widely adapted for Christian use for churches that were required to house huge congregations. As an architectural form, the basilica in its simplest plan could consist of a single longitudinal nave, but in more complex manifestations could incorporate five or more aisles separated by colonnades. The longitudinal aisles were frequently crossed by a horizontal transept and surmounted by a clerestory or a second-storey gallery level. Basilicas almost inevitably had a protruding semicircular apse at the east end and sometimes an entrance vestibule (a narthex), and a courtyard (an atrium), at the west end. Other architectural forms of the time included the centrally planned funerary martyria and baptisteries, which also became widespread and attained a degree of standardization. Emperor Constantine and his mother St Helena were in part respon-sible for a major campaign of building churches in the main cities of the empire and in the holy sites of Palestine. These included St Peter's and St Giovanni in the Lateran in Rome and large churches in Jerusalem and Bethlehem, none of which has survived in its original state.

Although some pagan structures were adapted for Christian use, for example, in Thessaloniki the mausoleum of Emperor Galerius (d. 311) was converted into a church possibly in the fourth century and is now known as Hagios Georgios, by the fourth and fifth centuries function-built large-scale Christian buildings appeared in considerable numbers throughout the Roman Empire. In figurative imagery, in the third, fourth and fifth centuries, we encounter a great stylistic and iconographic diversity, reflecting the many different visual traditions on which the early Christians drew as sources. The imperial Roman tradition undoubtedly played a role (Grabar 1968), as did other con-ventions in Roman imagery (Mathews 1993), as well as Jewish and eastern art forms. There are instances where King David may have been derived from a pagan image of Orpheus, an image of Christ may have been based on the sun god Helios and the beard-less handsome Good Shepherd may have originated in pagan bucolic pastoral imagery. In contrast to early literary sources which attest to the existence of extensive figurative imagery both in painting and free-standing sculpture, the actual survival of earliest Christian art is limited and geographically restricted. It is difficult to determine the impact of the Mosaic ban on graven images (Exod. 20: 4), or for that matter, the inter-dependence of Roman and Judaic traditions, but in its earliest manifestations as found

on painted arcosolia in catacombs and on carved sarcophagi, there are frequent symbolic, emblematic and allegorical images of salvation such as anchors, fish, peacocks
and simple figurative compositions of the Good Shepherd, Jonah and the whale and
Daniel in the lions' den.

From the fourth and fifth centuries there survive a number of extensive monumental
cycles of New and Old Testament imagery, such as the mosaics in Sta Maria Maggiore
in Rome 432–40, as well as complex interwoven pagan and Christian imagery as in
the partially preserved mosaic decorations of the mausoleum of Emperor Constantine's
daughter, Constantinia (d. 353), the church of Sta Constanza in Rome. Generally in
such monuments as the so-called mausoleum of Galla Placidia in Ravenna, 450, and
the apsidal decorations of Hosios David in Thessaloniki, c.425–50, the mosaics exhibit
a great diversity in imagery and of adopted artistic strategies. Evidence from numerous
churches, including St John Studios in Constantinople and Theotokos Acheiropoietos
in Thessaloniki, both from the mid-fifth century, suggests that the larger churches had
low stone carved sanctuary screens, an ambon (pulpit) and quite elaborately decorated
altars. Little of this early figurative carving has survived, nor has the precious metalwork or church plate which is mentioned in the literary sources.

In the fourth and fifth centuries there developed different traditions of Eastern Christian monasticism. Pilgrimage both to the Holy Land – the sites made sacred by the life
of Christ on earth – and to the tombs of Christian martyrs and to sites associated with
holy men also became increasingly popular. An early saint who gained a reputation
throughout Christendom was St Symeon the Stylite (d. 459) who spent 36 years standing on a 16-metre high pillar. This form of aerial penance did not go unnoticed and
large numbers of worshippers flocked to his pillar to hear his teachings and to witness
his miracles. A huge monastery in the form of a four-arm basilica was built around his
pillar at Qal'at Sim'an in Syria, 75 km north-east of Antioch (see plate 18.1). Pilgrims
brought back from such sacred sites, as well as from the Holy Land, small souvenirs in
the form of tokens in precious or base metals, terracotta or metal ampullae which contained sacred oils and ointments, as well as carved ivories and painted images. These
reliquary souvenirs frequently reproduced the main image from the site and hence
disseminated this iconography throughout the Christian empire.

The Sixth Century

If the earliest period in Christian art is characterized by its diversity and by the meta-
morphosis of various pagan traditions into a Christian iconography, the sixth century
may be viewed as a period of synthesis and consolidation. By the sixth century Constantinople had become the undisputed capital of the Roman Empire, while old Rome
and the western provinces were increasingly subjected to periods of disorder and constant pillage. Emperor Justinian (r. 527–65), who did much to militarily recapture the
territory of the empire and to temporarily restore its former borders, also undertook a
huge building campaign. While it is difficult to generalize, the basilica appears to have
remained the main architectural form for Christian churches throughout the empire,

so when Justinian built the fortress monastery of St Catherine at Mount Sinai, c.548–65, the main church of the monastery, the *katholikon*, was in the form of a modest masonry-built basilica.

In Constantinople, the sixth century witnessed a number of impressive experiments with domed architecture including the churches of SS Sergius and Bacchus, St Eirene and St Polyeuktos. The most spectacular church to be built in the capital in the sixth century, and arguably in the whole history of Byzantium, was the cathedral of the city dedicated to Holy Wisdom, Hagia Sophia. It was built on the site of two earlier basilica churches which had been destroyed by fires. Justinian's architects, Isidoros of Miletos and Anthemios of Tralles, between 532 and 537 erected a miraculous structure with a huge floating dome suspended between two semi-domes. The church has needed only a few minor repairs and stands to the present day, one of the most recognizable symbols of Eastern Orthodox Christianity (see plates 18.2 and 18.3). In subsequent history, many Orthodox communities throughout the empire and eastern Europe built their own versions of Hagia Sophia, but never attained the scale or the eccentric architectural boldness of the church in Constantinople.

Although Justinian's court chronicler, Prokopios, documents a vast array of buildings with splendid figurative mosaic decorations, relatively little survives in the capital. The original mosaics in Hagia Sophia itself, many of which survive (plate 18.4), in view of the building's enormous scale, appear to have been largely nonfigurative, consisting of a lacework of geometric ornament, foliage and crosses suspended against the sea of a golden mosaic background. From the sixth century, the best examples of religious mosaics survive in the provinces, particularly Ravenna, in the churches of San Vitale (plate 18.5) and San Apollinare Nuovo, at St Catherine at Mount Sinai and in some mosaic panels in the church of Hagios Demetrios in Thessaloniki. While the fragmentary and random pattern of survival cautions against sweeping generalizations, it appears that by the sixth century workshops and artists throughout the empire were producing mosaics of a very high quality and on a vast scale. The fact that virtually the same imagery is encountered in the few scattered surviving manuscripts, in the applied arts, and in what survives of monumental church decorations, suggests that a basic religious iconography was already in place, frequently modified by regional traditions.

Icons, in the form of painted panels depicting religious iconography, which have become almost synonymous with Eastern Orthodox Christianity (Cormack 1997), survive from the sixth century at the monastery of St Catherine at Mount Sinai. The survival appears to be random and a result of the remoteness of the location and the strength of its fortifications. These images of saints in encaustic (painted with wax and pigments) on wooden panels point to possible roots in funerary portraiture in late antiquity, while such literary sources as the apocryphal Acts of St John suggest that this form of Christian portraiture may go back to a very early date. Some icons, like the sixth-century Sinai Pantokrator (the image of Christ as the ruler of all) (plate 18.6), may be a copy of the image of Christ which decorated the Chalke Gate of the Great Palace in Constantinople. Other icons were in liturgical use and were placed on low chancel barriers which separated the congregation and the sanctuary or on separate icon stands – the *proskynetaria*.

It appears that some of the icons at Sinai may have been sent by Justinian as a gift to the monastery when he reinforced the walls, rebuilt the church, and re-endowed that sacred site associated with Moses and the tablets of the Law (Forsyth and Weitzmann 1973). Other imperial gifts in the sixth century included precious silks and other textiles with religious iconography, finely carved ivories and steatites, and church plate. As with the Church Ecumenical Councils, the first of which was held under Emperor Constantine at Nicaea in 325, in religious art there was a desire to establish a degree of standardization and Orthodoxy. Local saint and relic cults were tolerated and survived, as did the celebration of local sacred sites, but as in the religious calendar, in art, there emerged a dominant tradition of iconography.

Iconoclasm

The destruction of the image of Christ over the Chalke Gate of the Great Palace in Constantinople in 726 on the orders of Emperor Leo III may have marked the official beginnings of iconoclasm, but the roots of the conflict go back much earlier and may reflect the possible clash between the more iconoclastic eastern traditions where the Mosaic ban on graven images prevailed and the Hellenistic heritage. After the death of Justinian the Byzantine Empire sustained a number of serious military defeats and had lost much of its western territories, the victorious armies of Islam pressed from the East while the Slavs and the Avars attacked from the North. On several occasions the capital itself was under siege and the days of the empire must have appeared numbered. In addition, the Byzantines had endured a number of natural catastrophes and outbreaks of the plague. It was at a time of military threat to the empire and when the imperial coffers were empty, that a military emperor from the Syrian borderlands, Leo III, banned the public display of figurative religious images. The iconoclasts (literally meaning the breakers of icons), possibly as much for political reasons as theological ones, viewed icons and the cult of relics as a form of idolatry and as the possible cause for some of their military and civil misfortunes. Like their Muslim foes they forbade the depiction of figural images and destroyed some of the icons and monumental images which were on prominent view. The defenders of images, the iconodules or iconophiles, argued that an icon is not venerated as an idol and that veneration shown to an icon was conveyed 'by our spiritual eyes towards the prototype' (Seventh Ecumenical Council, 787), whether this be Christ, the Virgin or the saints. Despite the restoration of icons briefly under Empress Eirene between 787 and 814, iconoclasm lasted over a century, until 843.

The impact of iconoclasm is difficult to estimate. Certainly some religious art was destroyed, iconophile monks, clergy and artists were martyred and some illuminated manuscripts were burnt. Monumental iconoclast crosses appeared in the apses of some major churches during the iconoclast period, including Hagia Eirene in Constantinople, c.753 (plate 18.7), the Koimesis Church in Nicaea and Hagia Sophia in Thessaloniki (Brubaker and Haldon 2001). Nevertheless, it was an economically depressed period with a shrinking population in a time when more resources were devoted to military survival than to the creation of new churches and their decoration. In areas including

Cappadocia, Cyprus, Sinai and parts of the West, the iconoclast decrees from distant Constantinople appear to have been ignored and figurative art production continued, as fleeing icon painters may have found refuge in areas outside of Constantinople's control and may have played a significant role in the creation of some of the art associated with the Carolingian rulers of western Europe. The brilliant theologian, St John of Damascus (d. c.750), found refuge in the Monastery of Mar Sabas in Palestine and wrote brilliantly in defence of the icon. Some monks in Constantinople at the Studite monastery retained their iconophile sympathies, and although persecuted, seem to have produced a number of illuminated psalters, such as the Khludov Psalter, c.850, which vividly illustrated their antagonism towards the iconoclast heretics.

After a century of iconoclasm the Eastern Orthodox Church neither lost the technical skills for the production of art in many mediums, nor the knowledge of the iconographic conventions, but had formulated a theory of religious art in such detail and clarity that it has remained valid to the present day. Although the second half of the ninth century continued to be a period of political turmoil and economic insecurity and of limited art production, Byzantine post-iconoclast art was produced under a far more standardized iconographic schema. In 864, the conversion of Boris I brought the Bulgars into the Christian fold and at the same time missionary activities were under way in other Slav countries. Also in the 860s a protracted dispute between the pope in Rome, Nicholas I, and the patriarch in Constantinople, Photios, demonstrated the extent to which the Roman Church, which was now increasingly under the protection of the Franks rather than the Byzantines, had drifted away from the rest of the Christian Church. This separation culminated in the schism between the Orthodox Church and the Church of Rome in 1054.

After the triumph of Orthodoxy, huge figurative mosaics appeared in Hagia Sophia in Constantinople including the immense Theotokos and Child between archangels in the apse which was dedicated in 867 (plate 18.8). Below it an inscription proclaims: 'The images which the impostors [the iconoclasts] had cast down here the pious emperors have again set up.' In the post-iconoclast period there was a strongly expressed desire to restore religious iconography with an emphasis placed on continuing the presumed golden age which preceded the iconoclast heresy. In some of the new churches built in Constantinople after iconoclasm, like the Theotokos of the Pharos, c.842–67, and the Nea Ekklesia, consecrated in 880, neither of which survives, literary sources record the emergence of the smaller compact Byzantine church; this was to become the principal church design throughout the empire and was to continue to the present. Architecturally, the church was domed and had a symbolically inscribed cross: the cruciform shape may have been a symbolic reference to the crucifixion, while the dome an allusion to the celestial dome of heaven. In the classic cross-in-square church, the main vaults are in the shape of a Greek cross inscribed within a square, creating a nine bay core. The central dome is usually supported on columns and is flanked by four barrel vaults with the corner bays surmounted by four smaller domes. In this typical five-dome church, the liturgical west is frequently marked by an entrance narthex, while the apse protrudes from the eastern end. Although the Nea Ekklesia may have been an early example of a cross-in-square church in the capital, it is possible that earlier prototypes lie in Armenia or Asia Minor. If the basilica was the prevalent architectural form for the early Christian church, the cross-in-square church became the dominant architectural form in post-iconoclast church architecture.

Symbolically, the interior of the domed cross-in-square church was conceived as a microcosm of the Christian universe arranged within a hierarchal order. The ninth-century iconographic programmes of church decoration generally placed Christ in the dome (sometimes in the form of an Ascension as in the dome mosaic in Hagia Sophia in Thessaloniki, 885–6), the Virgin was located in the apsidal conch, while the minor vaults were occupied with various episodes or feasts selected from the life of Christ and sometimes from the life of the Virgin Mary. Frequently the lower walls of the church bore images of individual saints and the hagiographical cycles. In this ordered hierarchy, Christ appeared as the godhead in the highest point in the church like a heavenly celestial zone frequently surrounded by angels and prophets. Below this was the festive zone, a celebration of Christ's life on earth, where the great feasts of the church were revealed liturgically to the congregation, while below this on the lowest level, the one physically and spiritually closest to the congregation, were the saints (Demus 1948). While this programme of church decoration has many antecedents and certainly exhibits a considerable amount of variation, as a general observation, it appeared as a creation of the post-iconoclast period and then with considerable uniformity it was repeated throughout the empire.

Macedonian and Komnenian Dynasties

Byzantine art from the end of iconoclasm in 843 to the fall of Constantinople to the armies of the Fourth Crusade in 1204 is frequently termed Middle Byzantine. The whole period is dominated by two imperial dynasties, the Macedonian dynasty, which dominated the imperial throne between 867 and 1056, and the Komnenian dynasty, between 1081 and 1185. The cross-in-square church which entered metropolitan use in the ninth century became the norm in Byzantine architecture and in the tenth century became widespread throughout the empire. The Russian prince Vladimir of Kiev, who was baptised probably around 988–9 and who married Anna, the daughter of the Byzantine Emperor Basil II, by 996 had Byzantine architects working in his capital; they built a cross-in-square church, the Tithe Church in Kiev. In mainland Greece, near Delphi, between 946 and 955 a variant of the cross-in-square design was employed in the building of the Theotokos church at Hosios Loukas (originally dedicated to Hagia Barbara), while in Thessaloniki an impressive cross-in-square church of Panagia ton Chalkeon was built in 1028. On Mount Athos, the holy monastic peninsula founded by St Athanasios in the tenth century, about twenty monastic cross-in-square churches were eventually built, two of the earliest being the Theotokos church at the Vatopedi Monastery in 972 and the Koimesis church at the Iviron Monastery in 976.

In contrast to the metropolitan churches of earlier centuries, the cross-in-square churches constructed during the Macedonian dynasty were generally small in scale and frequently employed a decorative brickwork on their exterior, the so-called cloisonné style. If the early Christian basilicas sought huge enclosed spaces for large congregations, while the imperial churches of the sixth century made a statement concerning imperial power, wealth and grandeur, the new cross-in-square churches reflected a shrinking demography, and often had as patrons members of the military or civil aristocracy, and on many occasions were designated as monastic churches and also were designed to serve as the founder's tomb. Implicit in this patronage was the commemoration of the founder by the monastic community in perpetuity, something which was frequently written into the *typikon* or charter of the monastery. These churches created a more intimate atmosphere for worship and where the original liturgical furnishings survive, as in the rock-cut churches of Cappadocia or at Hosios Loukas, it appears that the sanctuary screens grew considerably in height, creating a physical barrier between the inner sanctuary containing the altar and the lay worshipper. These templon screens, apart from accommodating 'holy doors' which enabled the clergy to go in and out of the sanctuary, also served for the display of icons (Epstein 1981). So rather than an opaque barrier, it became like a visual parable where to the Orthodox faithful the iconography was revealed both liturgically and in the process of private prayer. After iconoclasm, icon painters strove to be non-naturalistic, usually employing gold backgrounds; they were deliberately symbolic and faithfully preserved the prescribed characteristics of the original prototype.

As a large number of these Middle Byzantine churches has survived with much of their decorations, there is room for some generalizations. Churches like the *katholikon* at Hosios Loukas with mosaics and frescoes from the 1020s, the *katholikon* at Nea Moni on Chios, with mosaics from *c.*1042–55, the frescoes and mosaics in the cathedral of St Sophia in Kiev, *c.*1043–6, the frescoes in the column churches in the Göreme Valley in Cappadocia, *c.*1060s, and the mosaics in the *katholikon* church at Daphni, on the outskirts of Athens, dating from *c.*1100 (plates 18.9 and 18.10), can all be described as churches where the decorations and architecture form a single Christian microcosm. While from monument to monument there are considerable stylistic differences and some scholars have separated them into metropolitan and provincial trends noting different classicizing or hieratic elements, stylistically the emphasis was placed on preserving the spiritual characteristics of the figures and on conveying the symbolic iconography of the scenes. Although the individual churches may reflect local cults and peculiarities, the main liturgical feasts of the Church were always celebrated. The *Dodekaorton*, the twelve principal feasts of the Church, were frequently included on the vaults or on the upper reaches of the walls. These feasts were: the Annunciation to the Virgin, the Nativity of Christ, the Presentation of Christ in the Temple, the Baptism of Christ, the Transfiguration, the Raising of Lazarus, the Entry into Jerusalem, the Crucifixion, the Anastasis, the Ascension, Pentecost and the Koimesis. Although in some churches there were more Marian feasts or other scenes from the Passion cycle, which could reflect the dedication of the church, the main feasts of the Orthodox church calendar became also the main images depicted within the church. There was more variation in the inclusion of saints, so that in a major monastic church like Hosios Loukas (plate 18.11) there was a great multitude of monastic saints included in the iconographic programme, while in Nea Moni, a church with an imperial founder, there were more warrior saints and others saints who had major cults in the capital. The church, its architecture and its decorations, formed a single symbolic and liturgical whole, a sacred space which existed outside temporal time.

If some of the monumental art during the Middle Byzantine period seemed more private and intimate than that which preceded it, this is particularly evident in some of the illuminated manuscripts, carved ivories and other religious artefacts of exquisite quality. Four manuscripts in particular, the Paris Gregory, c.879–83, and the Paris Psalter, c.950–70, both in the Bibliothèque Nationale in Paris, and the Leo Bible, c.930–40, and the Joshua Roll, mid-tenth century, both in the Biblioteca Vaticana in Rome, have been singled out by scholars as part of a so-called Macedonian Renaissance because of their use of classicizing motifs. Unlike the western traditions of art, in the context of Byzantine art this is not a particularly useful concept, as Byzantine art never lost its links with the Hellenistic heritage and unlike the West, where there was a conscious rejection of medieval spiritualism and the desire to revive classical pagan art and values, within the Eastern Orthodox tradition one may speak of a perennial classicism which found stronger expression at some periods than in others, but which was never totally abandoned.

Although in literary sources the Byzantines in the eleventh and twelfth centuries continued to refer to themselves as 'Romans', one could argue that real identity lay with the physical manifestations of Orthodoxy: the Church and its sacred iconography, particularly as expressed in its icons. Even regimes which vied with the Byzantines for political supremacy, such as the Normans in Sicily and the Venetians, imitated Byzantine conventions in their architectural forms and mosaic decorations, as part of their bid for imperial legitimacy. There exist only scant physical remains of the monumental cycles of decorations in Constantinople from this period, in contrast to the wealth of examples from Greece, Cyprus, Cappadocia, the Balkans and Russia. While every church and monastery has its own history and peculiarities, there are many features which they share. Generally the wealthier foundations, sometimes with imperial connections or popular pilgrim cults, employed the expensive mosaic tesserae for the decorations of the vaults and marble revetment to cover the lower reaches of the walls. Other churches and monasteries employed the much cheaper medium of frescoes and in some rare instances, for example St Sophia in Kiev, they combined mosaics for the more prominent parts of the church, executed probably by imported Byzantine artists, and frescoes for other sections, where there is evidence of local participation. Frescoes were generally painted in water soluble pigments directly into freshly laid sections of plaster and then completed on the dry surface of the wall with pigments mixed with a binder, with gold leaf sometimes added for the haloes and other details. Frescoes frequently covered the entire wall surface of the church, leading to more extensive iconographic programmes than with mosaics. Even in churches of relatively modest proportions, for example the three so-called column churches – Elmali Kilise, Çarikli Kilise and Karanlik Kilise – in the Göreme Valley monastic complex in Cappadocia, there are up to fifteen feast scenes and a considerable number of images of individual saints (see plate 18.12).

It was also in the frescoed churches of the eleventh and twelfth centuries that strongly expressed individual artistic talents appear in Byzantine art. Although very few Byzantine artists of this time can be identified by name, when one looks at the frescoes in St Sophia in Ohrid, c.1037–56, or St. Panteleimon at Nerezi, 1164, both in Macedonia, or at Panagia Phobiotissa in Asinou, 1105/6, or Panagia of Arakos in Lagoudera, 1192, both on Cyprus, one immediately recognizes the presence of a strong individual artistic genius. In some instances one is able tentatively to follow the progress of these artists and their related workshops as they travelled from one monument to the next, whether it be within Cappadocia or moving between the churches in Macedonia, Kastoria, Cyprus or in the Balkans (Skawran 1982; Stylianou 1985). If many of the important iconographic conventions by this time had found their resolution and relatively minor variations were tolerated by the Church and patrons, the spiritual intensity through which this iconography was communicated and the artistic strategies employed varied considerably.

In Byzantine manuscripts of the time, both in their texts and their illuminations, there appears a certain standardization as well as an unprecedented richness and variety in the large number of surviving examples (Carr 1987). It is difficult to speculate on the extent to which profusely illustrated manuscripts, such as the Menologion of Basil II, c.976–1025, in the Biblioteca Vaticana, of which only the first of two volumes survives, or the lavish eleventh-century Gospel lectionaries from the Dionysiou Monastery on Mount Athos and at the Biblioteca Vaticana, are chance survivals or characteristic of a much broader tradition. What is clear is that there was a considerable level of production of high quality illuminated manuscripts which disseminated Middle Byzantine iconographic conventions very widely. There also survives quite a large number of very high quality Byzantine icons, enamels and examples of precious metal work from this period.

What is much more speculative is the manner in which the Orthodox worshipper used religious images. From the iconophile writings of the eighth and ninth centuries, as well as from the evidence found in liturgical manuscripts and in scenes of various aspects of the liturgy found in other illuminations, especially in Gospel lectionaries and the menologia, we know that Byzantine Christians from this period frequently venerated icons on their knees, kissed icons and carried icons in procession on feast days and took them around city walls at times of crisis. The icons did symbolize the spiritual presence of the saints depicted on them and prayer and veneration shown to the icons were communicated directly to the spiritual beings depicted on them. With narrative images, such as feast scenes, they were not read simply as literary illustrations, but they were 'prayed through' in an allegorical and spiritual manner, one revealed by the liturgy, where the faithful partook of some of the mysteries of the scene (Ouspensky 1992). In an icon of the Nativity of Christ, for example, the cave in which Christ was born also related to the womb of the Virgin and the actual cave crypt in the church at Bethlehem, and allegorically prefigured the tomb of the sepulchre. The Christ Child in the swaddling clothes in the manager related both to the text of the Gospel of St Luke as revealed in the Christmas liturgy, as well as to the funerary shroud and the sepulchre in which the body of Christ was placed. In this way, every detail of the sacred iconography became like a visual parable, which was gradually revealed to the faithful. Specific icons were venerated on specific occasions and certain parts of the church were metaphysically associated with a sacred topography.

Aesthetics certainly played a role in Byzantine religious art at the time. The learned eleventh-century Byzantine historian, Michael Psellos, noted on one occasion:

> I am a most careful viewer of icons: but one icon astonished me by its indescribable beauty, paralysing my senses like a thunderbolt, and vanquishing me of my power of judgement in the matter. Its subject was the Mother of God. (Cormack 1997: 35)

Cults formed around some remarkable icons, some of which were known as *Acheiropoietos* (not made by human hands); others were thought as being created by saints, like images of the Theotokos painted by the Evangelist Luke. An icon of the Virgin and Child was brought from Constantinople to Kiev in 1131 and then moved to the principality of Vladimir, from which it acquired its name *Our Lady of Vladimir* and became the most holy image of Russia. Other icons appeared miraculously and were interpreted as heavenly signs which called on people to establish monasteries in their honour in those locations.

Palaiologue Dynasty

The friction between the Orthodox Byzantine Empire and the Roman Catholic West came to a head when the armies of the Fourth Crusade, in alliance with the Venetians, in 1204 attacked, sacked and occupied Constantinople. A primary objective was to loot the capital of the weakened Byzantine Empire and vast quantities of relics and treasures were exported to the West, with Venice as the chief beneficiary. Much was destroyed as well; antiquities and Christian monuments were melted down to retrieve the bronze and precious metals. The Byzantine aristocracy who survived the sack scattered to form independent principalities at Nicaea, at Epiros, on the west coast of Greece with a capital at Arta, and at Trebizond on the Black Sea. Together with the Bulgars, Serbs, Seljuk Turks and the Mongols, they all competed with the crusaders to seize control of the empire, until in 1261 the Byzantines from Nicaea gained control of Constantinople and Emperor Michael VIII Palaiologos came to the throne, and the city returned to Orthodox hands.

Unlike the Latin Kingdom of Jerusalem, where one can speak of a hybrid 'crusader art', apart from the destruction, there is little material evidence of the half-century of crusader occupation, although in one of the Byzantine churches converted to the Latin rite, now known as Kalendarhane Camii, there is a fragmentarily preserved St Francis cycle which must have been executed after St Francis's death in 1228 and the Byzantine recapture of the city in 1261. While in exile, the Byzantine principalities continued to commission art and art production continued, but through the accidents of survival little remains in Nicaea. The cathedral of Hagia Sophia in Trebizond, *c.*1238–63, is possibly the most significant frescoed, purely Byzantine, monument from this period. Certainly during this period, and arguably later, the main centres for art production lay outside the spheres of direct Byzantine political control; there is evidence of Byzantine artists at this time working in Russia, Bulgaria, Serbia and Georgia. This Byzantine commonwealth was multi-ethnic and multilingual, but unified more through faith, liturgy and art than through any sort of military or political alliance.

The restoration of Byzantine rule in Constantinople in 1261, like the Orthodox victory over iconoclasm, led to a period of extensive restoration and rebuilding, and like that period, this one has also been viewed by some cultural historians as one of great revival: a 'Palaiologan renaissance'. However, the Byzantine Empire from 1261 to its final collapse to the Ottoman Turks in 1453 led a very precarious existence, where the Byzantine principalities in exile did not form a single united front, but sought various alliances with traditional foes, while the Bulgars, Serbs, Seljuks and finally the Ottomans all made territorial incursions and threatened the survival of the empire. Attempts to find a unity with the western Church for reasons of political expediency were rejected by the Byzantine Church at home, the prevailing view being that it was better to die and face martyrdom than to compromise one's faith. One can argue that in this late phase of Byzantine art one can frequently note elements of nervous intro-spection and of heightened spiritualism.

In the south gallery of Hagia Sophia in Constantinople, in an area usually reserved for Church Councils and the members of the imperial family, a huge mosaic of the Deesis was created, probably shortly after 1261, where each of the figures is more than twice life-size. The Deesis, the image of Christ, flanked by the Virgin and John the Baptist, in Byzantine iconography served in an abbreviated form as an image of the Last Judgement, where before Christ the Judge, the Virgin and John the Baptist inter-cede for humankind. In this Deesis, despite its monumental scale, Christ has a most wonderful and caring expression, like a human, his head casts a shadow on his neck and he comes to help and save, rather than to judge and condemn. The mosaic is beautifully modelled in the faces and hands in very fine tesserae, and is reminiscent of the painterly qualities encountered on the sixth century Sinai icon of Christ. Stylistic parallels may also be drawn with the frescoes in Hagia Sophia in Trebizond and with some of the Serbian churches, like those in the Church of the Holy Trinity at Sopocani of the late thirteenth century. It is interesting that the church and the emperor selected this image of intercession before the Last Judgement as the principal icon to erect in the Great Church on restoration of power, when the empire faced such an uncertain future.

A considerable amount of painting and mosaics survives in Constantinople from this late period, although most of the churches in which they are found are restorations of earlier buildings, rather than new creations. It appears that frequently an exo-narthex and a funerary side chapel (*parekklesion*) were added to an existing structure to restore and re-endow a church and to give it a funerary function for the new donor. In this manner a military man and his widow restored the church of Theotokos Pam-makaristos between the 1260s and 1308, and a major imperial bureaucrat, Theodore Metochites, restored the Chora Monastery between *c*.1315 and 1321 (Underwood 1966–75; Belting et al. 1978; Mango 2000). Both contain extensive cycles of mosaics and frescoes of an amazing complexity and intricacy in the narrative aspects of the iconography and a growing theological sophistication. Although art historians have frequently described the style as one of refined elegance with a strong classicizing ten-dency, the elongated figures with their small heads and graceful gestures, with sweep-ing accentuating draperies and the marked colour and shadow contrasts, as prayer images, denote an intense spiritualism, whereby the beholder is invited to contemplate a divine spiritual mystery, rather than to simply read a familiar story. In the mosaics in the Church of the Holy Apostles in Thessaloniki, *c.*1310–14, and in the frescoes of Hagios Nikolaos Orphanos, also in Thessaloniki, *c.*1320, and the Theotokos Hodegetria (Aphendiko) in the Brontocheion Monastery at Mistras, *c.*1311–22, there are parallel stylistic developments which suggest that this was a general tendency rather than an isolated phenomenon. One could argue that the new spiritualism of Hesychasm, the ideas of St Gregory Palamas and Symeon the New Theologian, all found reflection in some paintings and icons of this period.

Whereas in discussion of earlier Byzantine art chance survivals dictated the choice of examples, in the Palaiologan period large numbers of churches, icons and manuscripts survive in mainland Greece, Athos, the Balkans, Russia, Cyprus and Crete. Although the quality may not be of a constant level amongst the 600 painted churches mainly from the fourteenth and fifteenth centuries on Crete or in the cluster of churches at Mistras, the density and concentration of surviving monuments allows us a much better basis for generalizing about Byzantine art and architecture on the eve of the military defeat of the empire by the Ottoman Turks.

Orthodox Traditions of Art outside the Boundaries of the Byzantine Empire

By the early eleventh century a Byzantine commonwealth existed which stretched from the Gulf of Finland to Crete and from the Adriatic to the Caucasus, where a community of nations in varying degrees owed allegiance to Byzantium, the Byzantine Church and its cultural traditions. In the first instance, many of the countries of the Slav North emerged as military rivals to the Byzantines and even after their conversion to Christianity some hostilities continued. Another unifying element was the Cyrillo-Methodian heritage of Old Church Slavonic into which the Greek New Testament and the liturgical offices had been translated; by the tenth and eleventh centuries also a whole mass of patristic and related literature was available in this native Slav language. It meant that Moravia, Bohemia, Croatia, Bulgaria and Russia all shared a literary heritage which provided access to Orthodox Christianity in a native language and perhaps negated the need to study Greek. By implication, this also barred access to the classical heritage, so that the literary traditions of Slav East Europe incorporated the Byzantine Greek tradition without recourse to its pagan Hellenistic foundations. The same may be argued concerning the visual arts and that by the ninth and tenth centuries the theology of the icon, the liturgical iconography and the techniques of its production were all in place and the Slav peoples inherited Byzantine iconography in a very pure form, but without recourse to the waves of Hellenism that constantly resurfaced in Byzantium.

By the thirteenth century Byzantine political domination diminished, particularly during the Latin occupation of the capital, and major concessions were made to local ecclesiastical autonomy. For example, in 1219 a Serb, St Sava, was consecrated as Archbishop of Serbia and he established an autocephalous Orthodox Church; in 1235 the Bulgarian Church was recognized as an autonomous patriarchate; and in 1250 a

Russian monk, Cyril, was consecrated as Metropolitan of Kiev. Although many of the political bonds loosened, and finally disappeared with the fall of Constantinople in 1453, and Moscow had proclaimed its position as the Third Rome and the protector of the Orthodox faithful and of the Orthodox traditions, the Byzantine religious, cultural and artistic links remained largely intact.

The relationship between the Byzantine heritage and the development of national schools in all cases is a complex phenomenon. In the first instance, in Bulgaria, Serbia and Russia, Byzantine artists appeared in the early years after the acceptance of Christianity and one could argue that the frescoes in St Sophia in Ohrid, c.1040, the mosaics in St Sophia in Kiev, c.1043–6, and the frescoes in the Bachkovo ossuary in Bulgaria, c.1083, are the works of mainly Byzantine artists. It also needs to be noted that Byzantine artists commanded enormous prestige by the local East European rulers, even in times of political dispute with Constantinople. There are numerous documented examples from the Palaiologan period of records of Byzantine artists working in the Slav lands, and on numerous occasions art in the Balkans and Russia has been attributed to Byzantine masters on stylistic grounds. Nevertheless, without violating the principles of Byzantine Orthodox iconography, distinctive local traditions did arise in the nations of East Europe, which enriched the existing cultural heritage.

The Balkans and Romania

The boundaries of the different nation states have been particularly fluid in the Balkans and it may be unwise to attempt to differentiate eastern Serbian and western Bulgarian art or to distinguish the Bulgarian, Serbian and Byzantine strands in the art of Macedonia. The frescoes in St Sophia in Ohrid, c.1040, or in the church of St Panteleimon in Nerezi of 1164 (plate 18.13), may show evidence of the participation by local artists, but ultimately bear the stamp of Byzantine artists and the theology of Byzantine patrons. However, by the late twelfth century and early thirteenth century, church architecture in the Balkans demonstrates a certain hybrid mixture of Byzantine, western Romanesque and indigenous traditions.

The Monastery of the Virgin at Studenica was founded by the Serbian Grand Župan Stefan Nemanjić in 1192. Its immaculate ashlar construction with a marbled exterior and extensive relief carvings appears very un-Byzantine and suggests that masons were invited here from the Adriatic littoral; however, the domed square core flanked by barrel vaults clearly reflects Byzantine conventions. The other peculiarity is the general oval plan, which is in contrast to the rectangular structures in Byzantine and Romanesque architecture, and which appears in Studenica and then recurs in numerous other Serbian churches including Mileševa, Sopoćani and Dečani. The frescoes in the *katholikon* of Studenica, dated by inscription to 1209, which include a vast Crucifixion (plate 18.14), remain faithful to Byzantine iconographic conventions, while the Slav inscriptions suggest the participation of local artists. Although Serbia at this time flirted with western Catholicism, Stefan Nemanjić's youngest son, Rastko, became a monk on Athos and took the name of Sava and later became the first archbishop of the independent Serbian Orthodox Church. Two years after his death in 1235, his remains were translated to the Church of the Ascension at the monastery in Mileševa, which had been founded in 1230, and which was built in the same hybrid architectural style as Studenica. The frescoes again retain the purity of Byzantine iconography and although there is an inscription that they were painted by Demetrios, George and Theodore, the ethnicity of the artists is unclear. There seems little evidence to suggest that the artists were anything other than Serbs, but possibly working in collaboration with Greek artists, and certainly working within the eastern Orthodox Byzantine tradition and in the process creating some of the most powerful and moving images of the thirteenth century.

At Sopoćani, King Stefan Uroš founded a monastery to which he translated the remains of his father, St Stefan Nemanjić, in 1266, and probably at the same time had the *katholikon*, the Church of the Holy Trinity, decorated. Again it is a case of hybrid Romanesque, Byzantine and indigenous architectural forms which created large expanses of wall surfaces that were decorated with Byzantine iconography including an immense image of the Koimesis. The inclusion of secular imagery dealing with the life of the donors (Sopoćani was designed as the mausoleum for the royal house) does have Byzantine precedence, but as it was created at a time when few works survive in the Byzantine capital it is difficult to point to precise parallels. The tendency amongst some western art historians to categorize this art stylistically as metropolitan, provincial, monastic or courtly (Rice 1968) is not particularly useful, as unlike western European developments in art where such stylistic morphology can lead to the designation of different schools of art, Orthodox religious iconography was in many ways a conservative tradition which had been liturgically prescribed, and the emergence of a Serbian national school occurred within these conventions.

There has also been a tendency to view the art of the Balkans of the thirteenth century as a surrogate for artistic developments in the inner provinces of the empire from which very little monumental art survives. The argument of centre and periphery within the Byzantine context is difficult to maintain as the extant art from the Balkans in the thirteenth century was primarily a religious art serving a liturgical function, while its secular associations in the form of donor portraits also adhered to well-established conventions. It can be argued that the same workshop responsible for the mosaics in Hosios Loukas in Greece later travelled to Kiev to work on the mosaics in St Sophia, while other artists worked in Thrace, Macedonia and Greece, or travelled to Cappadocia and Cyprus. A Byzantine artist trained in Constantinople later worked in Novgorod and Moscow and it becomes highly problematic to attempt to establish an ethnicity for the artist who decorated the chapel of the Holy Trinity at the Serbian Hilandar monastery of Mount Athos in a style similar to that of Sopoćani. It is possible to speak of an Orthodox artistic tradition in the thirteenth and fourteenth centuries which thrived on its multi-ethnicity and multi-nationality, but which was essentially a single and united tradition with numerous regional variations.

Outside Sofia in Bulgaria there still exists a wonderful church dedicated to SS Nicholas and Panteleimon at Boyana, with frescoes dated 1259 executed in a Byzantine style and with a taste for realism in detail. Earlier, during the first Bulgarian kingdom (681–1061), together with the three-aisle basilicas there appeared centrally planned domed triconch churches like St Panteleimon in Ohrid, c.893. During the

Plate 18.1 Church of St Symeon the Stylite, Qal'at Sim'an, Syria, c.476–90. Exterior view from the north-east (Photo: Sasha Grishin)

Plate 18.2 Hagia Sophia, Constantinople, 532–7. Exterior view from the south (Photo: Sasha Grishin)

Plate 18.3 Hagia Sophia, Constantinople, 532–7. Interior view facing apse (Photo: Sasha Grishin)

Plate 18.4 Deesis, mosaic, c.1261. Hagia Sophia, Constantinople, south gallery (Photo: Sasha Grishin)

Plate 18.5 Emperor Justinian, chancel mosaic, San Vitale, Ravenna, c.546–7. Detail of larger panel of Emperor Justinian with Bishop Maximian, clergy, courtiers and soldiers (Photo: Sasha Grishin)

Plate 18.6 Christ Pantocrator, encaustic icon, sixth century. Monastery of St Catherine, Mount Sinai (Photo: Sasha Grishin)

Plate 18.7 Apsidal cross, mosaic. Hagia Eirene, Constantinople, c.753 (Photo: Sasha Grishin)

Plate 18.8 Theotokos and Child, apsidal mosaic, 967. Hagia Sophia, Constantinople
(Photo: Sasha Grishin)

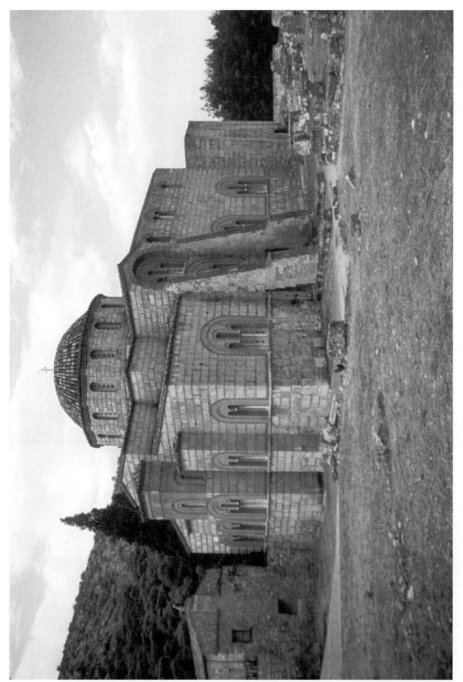

Plate 18.9 Monastery of Daphni, *katholikon*, near Athens, Greece, c.1100. Exterior view from north-east (Photo: Sasha Grishin)

Plate 18.10   Pantocrator, dome mosaic. Daphni *katholikon*, *c*.1100 (Photo: Sasha Grishin)

Plate 18.11 Monastery of Hosios Loukas, Greece, late tenth and early eleventh centuries. Exterior view from the east (Photo: Sasha Grishin)

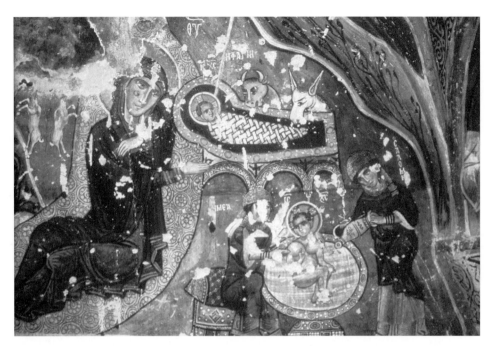

Plate 18.12   Nativity of Christ, fresco. Karanlik Kilise, Göreme Valley, Cappadocia, *c.*1060s (Photo: Sasha Grishin)

Plate 18.13   Threnos (Lamentation), fresco. Nerezi, Macedonia, 1164 (Photo: Sasha Grishin)

Plate 18.14 Crucifixion, fresco. *Katholikon* of the Monastery of the Virgin, Studenica, Serbia, 1209 (Photo: Sasha Grishin)

Plate 18.15 Anastasis, aspidal fresco. *Parekklesion*, Chora Monastery, Constantinople, *c.*1315–21 (Photo: Sasha Grishin)

Plate 19.1 Qalb Lozeh Church. View from the south-east (Photo: Conway Library, Courtauld Institute of Art)

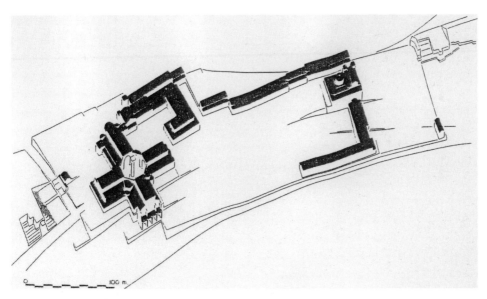

Plate 19.2 Qal'at Sim'an. Reconstruction of the pilgrimage shrine of St Symeon the Stylite (after G. Tchalenko, *Villages antiques de la Syrie du Nord*, Paris, 1953, vol. II, pl. LXXVIII)

Plate 19.3 Entry into Jerusalem. From a thirteenth-century Syriac lectionary. London, British Library, MS Add. 7170 fol. 115r (Photo: © British Library Board; all rights reserved)

Plate 19.4 Aght'amar. Church of the Holy Cross, west façade (Photo: A. F. Kersting)

Plate 19.5 Khatchk'ar of Aputayli. Stone cross, 1225. London, British Museum M&LA 1977, 5-5, 1 (Photo: © The Trustees of The British Museum)

Plate 19.6 Last Judgement. From a Gospel book illustrated by T'oros Roslin, 1262. The Walters Art Museum, Baltimore, MS no. W 539 fol. 109v (Photo: The Walters Art Museum, Baltimore)

Plate 19.7 Nativity. Wall-painting, sanctuary, southern semi-dome, Church of the Virgin, Dayr al-Suryan, Wadi Natrun, Egypt (Photo: L.-A. Hunt)

Plate 19.8 Panel of choir doors. Church of the Virgin, Dayr al-Suryan, Wadi Natrun,
Egypt (Photo: L.-A. Hunt)

Plate 19.9 Entry into Jerusalem. Carved wooden panel from the Church of al-Mu'allaqa, Old Cairo (Photo: © The Trustees of The British Museum)

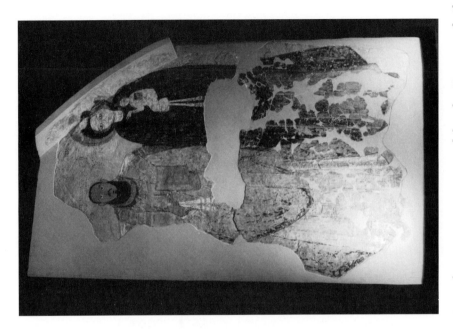

Plate 19.11 Bishop Marianos protected by the Virgin and Child. Wall-painting from Faras Cathedral. Warsaw. National Museum (Photo: L.-A. Hunt, by permission of the National Museum in Warsaw)

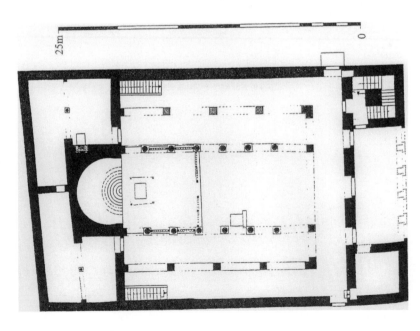

Plate 19.10 Cathedral, Qasr Ibrim. Plan (after P. M. Gartkiewicz, 'Remarks on the Cathedral at Qasr Ibrim', in J. M. Plumley (ed.), *Nubian Studies*, Warminster, Aris and Phillips, 1982, pp. 87–94, figure 4)

Plate 19.12 Section of stone frieze from the first Cathedral at Faras (Photo: © The Trustees of The British Museum)

Plate 19.13 Christ healing the blind. From a seventeenth-century Gospel book. London, British Library, MS Or. 510 fol. 51r (Photo: © British Library Board; all rights reserved)

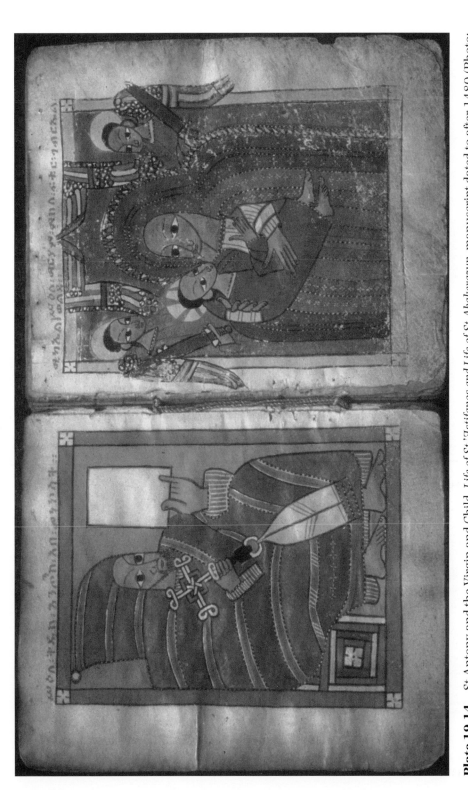

Plate 19.14 St Antony and the Virgin and Child. *Life of St 'Estifanos and Life of St Abakerazun*, manuscript dated to after 1480 (Photo: Spencer Collection, New York Public Library, Astor, Lenox and Tilden Foundations)

Plate 19.15 Processional Cross. Ethiopian, fifteenth century. The Walters Art Museum, Baltimore, no. 54.2894 (Photo: The Walters Art Museum, Baltimore)

second Bulgarian kingdom (1193–1393) the church at Boyana was built in the form of a cruciform, centrally planned building, which appears to bring together local and Byzantine architectural forms.

In the fourteenth century, prior to the Turkish invasion of the Balkans, in the *katholikon* of the Dečani monastery, decorated *c*.1335–50, we encounter one of the most elaborate and remarkable iconographic programmes from Serbia, containing a very complex fresco of the Nemanjić family tree. It demonstrates a sophisticated manner of working and points to the wonderful late flowering of the Morava school at Ravanica, *c*.1378, Kalenić *c*.1413–17 and Manasija (or Resava) *c*.1406–18, where the paintings have a visionary spiritual power. A considerable number of icons from the Balkan region also survive, including a curious Bulgarian ceramic icon of St Theodore with a Bulgarian inscription, possibly *c*.900, in Sofia, and a large number of icons in the collections of the Hilandar Monastery, in Ohrid and in Skopje.

In Romania, in the traditional territories of Wallachia, Moldavia and Transylvania, by the mid-fourteenth century there was sufficient economic prosperity and political stability for the construction and decoration of the major churches of Cozia and St Nicholas at Curtea-de-Arges, *c*.1362–6, whose frescoes may be compared with those of the Chora Monastery in Constantinople (plate 18.15). A golden age of Romanian architecture occurred in the fifteenth century during the reign of Stephen the Great, while one of the most original contributions to the Orthodox tradition was made by Moldavians in the sixteenth century, with a series of churches with externally frescoed walls. These include the St George church at Voronet, *c*.1488–96, with its impressive Last Judgement exterior wall painting, and those in St George in Suceava (1522), Humor (1535), Moldovita (1537) and Sucevita (*c*.1600) (Nandris 1970). The defeat of the Serbs at the Battle of Kosovo in 1389 by the Ottoman Turks and the final abolition of the Serbian state in 1459, and the Turkish occupation of Bulgaria from 1394 to 1878, severely restricted the development of Orthodox art in the Balkans. It was only after the liberation of Bulgaria in the Russo-Turkish wars in 1878 and the liberation of much of Serbia in the 1860s that the production of Orthodox art was once again revived, but now largely in neo-Baroque and neo-Renaissance styles.

Russia

Russia adopted the Byzantine conventions of art and architecture in the late tenth century, at the same time as its conversion to Christianity. The first early flowering of Christian art continued until 1237–40 and the Mongol invasion of Russia, when the Russian principalities became political dependencies of the Tartar khans of the Golden Horde. The three main centres for Russian art of the pre-Mongolian period were Kiev, Novgorod and in the north-east, Rostov and Vladimir-Suzdal. In the eleventh century, under Prince Yaroslav, Kiev's cathedral of St Sophia was built and decorated between 1037 and 1046. Architecturally it employed as its basic module an adaptation of the Byzantine cross-in-square design, but now greatly multiplied in scale, so that there were five apses and thirteen domes, while the mosaics and frescoes generally adhered to Byzantine conventions. The cathedral of St Sophia in Novgorod, *c*.1045–50, to some extent was a small-scale adaptation of the church in Kiev; however the bell-shaped cupolas, rather than the flatter Byzantine domes, were employed, although not quite the onion-shaped cupolas which were to appear shortly in northern Russian churches.

Russian frescoes of the twelfth century, such as those in the churches of St George in Staraya Ladoga, c.1167, and the Saviour Nereditsa in Novgorod, 1199, both severely damaged in the Nazi invasion, interpret a Byzantine iconography but with a majestic solemnity. The existence of low-relief sculpture on the exterior walls of some of these churches, including St Dmitry in Vladimir, c.1194–7, and St George in Yur'ev Pol'sky, c.1230–4, probably reflects a Byzantine imperial tradition that is also found in other buildings with imperial pretensions. From the mid-twelfth century, tower-like churches with onion-shaped cupolas built on very high drums emerged as the dominant architectural form and became very popular in the thirteenth century, as in the church of Paraskeva Pyatnitsa in Chernihiv of the early thirteenth century.

The icon *Our Lady of Vladimir* was brought from Constantinople to Kiev in 1131 and about twenty years later was transferred to Vladimir and then on to Moscow, where it became the country's palladium. Unlike the more austere Hodegetria image, *Our Lady of Vladimir* belongs to the 'Eleousa' or 'tenderness' iconographic type, where the human side of the deity is stressed. The note of compassion, of the God who suffers for humankind, became a strong feature in Russian medieval art. The mystical aestheticism of Byzantine art was certainly given prominence in Russian writings at the time, and in the Russian Primary Chronicle, compiled in the eleventh and twelfth centuries, it is suggested that Prince Vladimir only accepted Byzantine Christianity after the Russian envoys reported on their experience of the liturgy in Hagia Sophia in Constantinople:

> we knew not whether we were in heaven, or earth: for on earth there is no such vision or beauty, and we know not how to describe it; we know only that there God dwells among men.

During the period of the Mongol invasion, the princes of north-eastern Russia in Novgorod and Pskov maintained their independence and through trade accumulated considerable wealth, so that the archbishop of Novgorod in 1338 could commission a Byzantine master to paint churches in the city. The flowering of Palaiologan art found vivid reflection in the frescoes in the churches of Kovalevo (1378), and Volotova (c.1380s), both severely damaged by the Nazis. Theophanes the Greek, an artist who had painted in Constantinople and the Crimea, settled in Novgorod for some thirty years, where he painted the church of the Transfiguration, 1378; he then travelled to Moscow, where he painted the Cathedral of the Annunciation, dying in Moscow at sometime between 1405 and 1415. Theophanes' style is possibly associated with mystical Hesychasm and is characterized by its pale colours and extensive areas of white highlights; it had a profound impact on Russian icon-painting. Also at about this time the multi-tiered Russian icon screen – the iconostasis – developed (Cheremeteff 1990), and from Moscow appears to have spread to Mount Athos and throughout the Balkans.

Icons on wood, rather than wall paintings, in Russia assumed a greater significance than in Byzantium, possibly in part reflecting the immense timber resources of the country and its indigenous traditions of working in wood. Generally the pre-Mongolian icons were immense in scale with a dark and restrained palette. During the Tartar occupation, the thirteenth- and fourteenth-century icons of Novgorod were distinguished by their rich sonorous palette and graceful linear articulation. Many of the saints including St George, SS Florus and Laurus, the Prophet Elijah, St Nicholas and St Paraskeva Pyatnitsa were possibly connected with pagan agrarian cults or with the practical concerns of merchants and travellers (Lazarev 1983), and were painted in brilliant ritualistic colours without disrupting the traditional conventions of Byzantine iconography.

The Russian's first major victory over the Tartars at the battle of Kulikovo in 1380 and the rise of centralized state of Moscow led to the extensive building campaigns in the city and attracted many of the best artists in the country. St Andrey Rublev (c.1370–1430) is Russia's most esteemed icon-painter. Building on the heritage of his teacher St Daniil Cherny, with whom he decorated the Uspensky Cathedral in Vladimir, and later collaborating with Theophanes the Greek on the Cathedral of the Annunciation in Moscow, he developed a personal and deeply moving style in icon-painting, one characterized by its tenderness and humanism. In icons like his Old Testament Trinity, c.1411, and the Zvenigorod Deesis, c.1409, Rublev created some of the most profoundly moving images in the Orthodox tradition of art, which led one scholar to note that 'the Russian icon is the highest expression in art of godlike humility' (Ouspensky and Lossky 1982: 45). In the second half of the fifteenth century Moscow icon-painting was dominated by Dionysius and his workshop, which produced tender and moving images with graceful flowing lines and rich colour saturation. Generally, in the sixteenth century, Russian icons demonstrate a growing interest in historical subjects with realistic descriptive detail eroding the iconographic traditions. The last major period in Russian icon-painting is associated with the Stroganov workshops working on the outskirts of Siberia, when much of the country was gripped by political turmoil. They generally produced small, exquisitely refined, icons for their merchant patrons. This was before the onslaught of the secularization of the sacred iconography and the introduction of the completely inappropriate style of western illusionism which destroyed the spiritual effectiveness of the icon.

With the centralized state in Moscow, particularly under Tsar Ivan III (r. 1462–1505), several major cathedrals were built in the Moscow Kremlin, including the Uspensky (Dormition) Cathedral, 1475–9, designed by Aristotele Fioravanti, but based on the Uspensky Cathedral in Vladimir; the Archangel Michael Cathedral, 1505–8, by Aleviz Novy; and the Cathedral of the Annunciation, 1484–9 and the Church of the Deposition, 1484–5, both built by masons from Pskov. These served as models for numerous other Russian churches. There also existed several regional styles of architecture, such as churches with fantastic pyramidal roofs, like the Uspensky Cathedral at the Kirillo-Belozersky monastery of 1497, or the hip-roofed tower churches, like the Church of the Ascension at Kolomenskoye of 1532. Many of these styles of architecture were sacrificed in the eighteenth century when Tsar Peter the Great (r. 1682–1725) relocated the capital to St Petersburg and commenced a wholesale westernization of

Russian art, culture and religious life. Neoclassical, Baroque and, later Art Nouveau styles dominated much of eighteenth- and nineteenth-century Russian art and architecture.

Late Orthodox Traditions in Art and Architecture

The fifteenth-century Ottoman Turkish occupation of much of the traditional territory of the Byzantine Empire, as well as Greece and most of eastern Europe, did severely limit the scale and quality of production of religious art. On Mount Athos, art production continued in what is commonly referred to as the post-Byzantine period, although much of it was strongly influenced by Russian developments. Russia both funded and protected many Orthodox communities. On Crete icon-painting continued, but frequently under a strong Venetian influence, creating a hybrid mix of Byzantine and western traditions. Some of the prominent artists in Crete, including Michael Damaskenos, and Victor, Zanfurnari and Theodore Poulakis, signed their icons, while Domenikos Theotokopoulos, on leaving Crete and painting in Italy and then in Spain became known as El Greco. In Russia itself a westernized Baroque style gained popularity which had little to do with the spiritual forms of the Byzantine heritage. With the threat of a loss in continuity of tradition, in the sixteenth century model books and books with iconographic prescriptions became widespread.

In the twentieth century there have been many conscious attempts made to revive Byzantine art whether it be in Greece after its liberation after the 1821 War of Independence or in Bulgaria where in Sofia the huge Alexander Nevsky Cathedral was built, 1904–12 (consecrated 1924) by the Russian architect Aleksandr Pomerantsev; it is a domed basilica in what may be termed a neo-Russo-Byzantine style. Active icon-painting workshops have continued to function on Athos, Crete, Cyprus, Serbia, Macedonia and Greece and more recently have been re-established in Russia and are found throughout the Orthodox diaspora.

References and further reading

Belting, H., Mango, C. and Mouriki, D. (1978) *The Mosaics and Frescoes of St Mary Pammakaristos*. Dumbarton Oaks Studies 15. Washington, DC: Dumbarton Oaks.

Brubaker, L. and Haldon, J. (2001) *Byzantium in the Iconoclast Era (ca. 680–850): The Sources. An Annotated Survey*. London: Ashgate.

Carr, A. W. (1987) *Byzantine Illumination, 1150–1250*. Chicago: University of Chicago Press.

Cheremeteff, M. (1990) The transformation of the Russian sanctuary barrier and the role of Theophanes the Greek. In A. Leong (ed.) *The Millennium: Christianity and Russia*. Crestwood, NY: St Vladimir's Seminary Press.

Cormack, R. (1997) *Painting the Soul: Icons, Death Masks, and Shrouds*. London: Reaktion Books.

Demus, O. (1948) *Byzantine Mosaic Decoration: Aspects of Monumental Art in Byzantium*. London: Routledge and Kegan Paul. Reprinted 1976.

Epstein, A. W. (1981) The Middle-Byzantine sanctuary barrier: templon or iconostasis? *Journal of the British Archaeological Association* 134: 1–20.

Forsyth, G. and Weitzmann, K. (1973) *The Monastery of St Catherine at Mount Sinai: Church and Fortress of Justinian.* Ann Arbor: University of Michigan Press.

Freely, J. and Çakmak, A. S. (2004) *Byzantine Monuments of Istanbul.* Cambridge: Cambridge University Press.

Gavrilović, Z. (2001) *Studies in Byzantine and Serbian Christian Art.* London: Pindar Press.

Grabar, A. (1968) *Christian Iconography: A Study of its Origins.* Princeton, NJ and Washington, DC: National Gallery of Art.

Lazarev, V. N. (1983) *Russian Icon Painting from its Origins to the Beginning of the 16th Century.* Moscow: Iskusstvo.

Lowden, J. (1997) *Early Christian and Byzantine Art.* London: Phaidon.

Mango, C. (1976) *Byzantine Architecture.* New York: Harry N. Abrams.

—— (2000) *Chora: The Scroll of Heaven.* Istanbul: Ertug and Kocabiyik.

Mathews, T. F. (1993) *The Clash of Gods: A Reinterpretation of Early Christian Art.* Princeton, NJ: Princeton University Press.

Nandris, G. (1970) *Christian Humanism in the Neo-Byzantine Mural Paintings of Eastern Europe.* Wiesbaden: Harrawssowitz.

Obolensky, D. (1971) *The Byzantine Commonwealth: Eastern Europe, 500–1453.* London: Weidenfeld and Nicolson.

Ouspensky, L. (1992) *Theology of the Icon,* 2 vols. Crestwood, NY: St Vladimir's Seminary Press.

Ouspensky, L. and Lossky, V. (1982) *The Meaning of Icons.* Crestwood, NY: St Vladimir's Seminary Press.

Parry, K. (1996) *Depicting the Word: Byzantine Iconophile Thought of the Eighth and Ninth Centuries.* Leiden: Brill.

Piatnitsky, Y. et al. (2000) *Sinai, Byzantium, Russia: Orthodox Art from the Sixth to the Twentieth Century.* London: Saint Catherine Foundation in association with the State Hermitage Museum, St Petersburg.

Rice, D. T. (1968) *Byzantine Painting: The Last Phase.* New York: Dial Press.

Skawran, K. M. (1982) *The Development of Middle Byzantine Fresco Painting in Greece.* Pretoria: University of South Africa.

Stylianou, A. and J. A. (1985) *The Painted Churches of Cyprus.* London: Trigraph for A. G. Leventis Foundation.

Underwood, P. (1966–75) *The Kariye Djami,* 4 vols. London: Routledge and Kegan Paul.

Vassilaki, M. (ed.) (2000) *Mother of God: Representations of the Virgin in Byzantine Art.* Skira: Milan.

CHAPTER 19

Eastern Christian Iconographic and Architectural Traditions

Oriental Orthodox

Lucy-Anne Hunt

Introduction

This survey is concerned with the architecture and visual arts of the five Miaphysite churches: the Syrian, Armenian, Coptic, Nubian and Ethiopian. What they have theologically in common is that in 451 they all separated from the Council of Chalcedon, which prescribed the official definition of the nature of Christ adopted by the Byzantine Church. However, the oriental churches maintained links with the Byzantine church as well as with each other throughout the Middle Ages. But there was also divergence as each expressed of its own cultural and religious identity, an expression in which the visual played a major part.

The Syrian Orthodox Church

The Syrian churches are defined culturally as those sharing Syriac as the liturgical language. The Syrian Orthodox is the largest of these, interacting in the Middle Ages with the Melkite community and also with the Church of the East. The geographical area is centred on Syria, and also encompasses Iraq, Lebanon and Ṭur ʿAbdin in Eastern Turkey, as well as India, and in the earlier period central Asia and China, and the more recent diaspora communities in the USA and Australia.

Antioch, one of the great cities of the classical world alongside Rome and Alexandria, thrived in the early Christian period. Among its magnificent churches was that built by the Emperor Constantine in the fourth century on an octagonal plan. Edessa (present day Urfa), on the other hand, was the Aramaic-Syriac, as opposed to Graeco-Roman, cultural centre. It was here that King Abgar (r. 4BCE–7CE and 13–50) was converted to Christianity, giving rise to the famous story of the portrait of Christ sent to Edessa, the *mandylion*. Edessa became a major literary and theological centre, after the ceding of Nisibis in Mesopotamia as part of a peace treaty with Persia. This was when St Ephrem made his home in Edessa. Edessa was also famed as the burial site of St Thomas, in the so-called Ancient Church, rebuilt in the fourth century. This is not to say that links were cut with the Melkite Church. On the contrary, the cathedral, dedicated to St Sophia and consecrated in 345–6, was rebuilt as a Melkite place of worship in the 540 s by the Emperor Justinian. It vied with that emperor's great Church of Holy Wisdom in Constantinople in being a square, domed structure, with mosaics ornamenting its interior. But Edessene Christianity extended beyond the urban setting and was also famed for the numerous monasteries of the Holy Mountain near Edessa.

Architecture and sculpture

Better preserved than monuments in the great cities of Antioch and Edessa are rural monuments in Syria, especially those of the limestone massif of the north. In the fourth to sixth centuries this was a well populated area, at the peak of its prosperity in the second half of the sixth century, just before it was abandoned in the early seventh century because of Islamic incursion. The now 'dead cities' had been, under the Byzantine Empire, thriving towns, villages and communities of farmers. Their estates and smallholdings depended on the production and export of grain and wine, and of olive oil in particular. Their architecture in stone is a case study in the organization, settlement patterns and buildings of a self-sufficient society, as it emerged out of the Greco-Roman world, adopted Christianity and adapted its physical environment to its economic, physical and spiritual needs.

Although there were close links between Syrian and Byzantine architecture it would be a mistake to deny the former's independent features. These include the almost exclusive use of stone, in preference to the brick and mortar of Byzantine architecture. Design elements are different too, the emphasis being on the exterior of the building, with its sculpted bands and lintels, as opposed to the interior of the church, as in Byzantium. There were no galleries, and relics were kept in separate chapels rather than under the altar as in the West. The Eucharist was kept in a niche in the sanctuary wall, and several churches had ablution fountains. A particularly characteristic piece of liturgical furniture found in some Syrian churches was the bema. Sited in the centre of the nave, this low, semicircular, enclosed, platform had a door on the east side and a pulpit structure on the west side, where biblical lessons were read, sermons given and psalms sung.

Settlements in towns and villages arose organically, but with a number of common architectural elements. Churches were built – with separate structures functioning as martyr's chapels and baptisteries – alongside houses, communal and administrative buildings, funerary monuments and baths. Monasteries, originally comprising a group of hut cells around a chapel, developed into a standard arrangement of the conventual church, communal buildings, areas of habitation and tombs; examples are at Deir Turmanin, Kafr Deriān and Deir Sim'an. In the case of pilgrimage shrines an additional lodge or upper room was sometimes located over the entrance to the holy place or tomb of the saint, for monks or visitors to commune with the saint. The ecclesiastical and the secular rubbed shoulders; bazaars and inns were particularly well preserved between

Antioch and Aleppo, in, for example, Dar Qita, which was restored in 436. In some places, for example at Serğilla (473) and Babisqa, these secular establishments also included baths.

The first churches were house churches, the earliest example being that of Qirqbize, dating from the beginning of the fourth century. Rectangular in shape, it is orientated from east to west, with separate entrances for men and for women on the south side. Basilicas became the prevalent architectural form in the mid-fourth century. By the end of that century the basilica was prescribed as rectangular, on an east–west axis, twice as long as broad, with a nave and aisles supported on two rows of columns supporting arches, on the top of which were walls rising from the nave with windows at the top. The apse was vaulted and flanked by two side chambers, that to the north the *diaconicon* or sacristy, that to the south the martyr's chapel. At the end of the fourth century other features appear, including an external baptistery, lodging house, and tower.

One of the main structural elements of Syrian churches that developed in this area was that of the piers supporting arches, a feature which first appears in the basilica at Qalb Lozeh, and which divides its nave and two side aisles. Other characteristic features of this church were the flat wooden roof of the nave, with a double-pitched roof outside and a tiled sloping roof over each of the side naves, the tripartite narthex, the sculpted decoration around the doorways, and the protruding apse at the east end with engaged columns (Figure 19.1).

External architectural decoration was, indeed, a special feature of Syrian ecclesiastical architecture. Over time this decoration became increasingly elaborate, comprising moulding running around lintels, articulating the length of the structure's façade, windows, lintels, and doors, as well as carved capitals. Consistency between various churches and groups of churches suggests that the same teams of masons and stonecutters were employed. While these are anonymous, the names of some architects are known. Fragmentary painted plaster has been found in some churches, indicating that they were once painted; examples are the central nave at Qalb Lozeh, the south branch of the cruciform church at Qal'at Sim'an, and along the exterior wall surface of the church of Taqle. Mosaics would also have been employed, probably made by workers coming from the towns. A prominent example of the early use of mosaic work by Miaphysites is in the Church of Mar Gabriel near Qartmin in the Ṭ'ur ʿAbdin. Commissioned by the Emperor Anastasius in 512 the sanctuary vault shows vines issuing from amphorae placed in the four corners, on a gold ground, with crosses in the centre, east and west. The lunette on the south side depicts an altar with eucharistic vessels, under a ciborium lit by hanging lamps. Cypress trees on either side symbolize paradise. Here the triumph over death was expressed through a metaphorical representation of the liturgy.

The most famous site in Northern Syria, lying about 60 km north of Antioch, is that of St Symeon Stylites at Qal'at Sim'an. This site commemorates the stylite saint, Symeon the Elder, who lived on a column, attracting people from far and wide to come and benefit from his wisdom. At his death in 459 the body of St Symeon was taken to Antioch where it was, according to the chronicler John Malalas, eventually housed in a purpose-built church. But in 476 work commenced at the pilgrimage centre around his column to accommodate the crowds who continued to visit it. The column was encased within a structure topped with an octagonal drum, most probably open to the sky. Extending from it, placed symmetrically, are four basilicas, faced with porticoes (Figure 19.2). Although no liturgical descriptions of Qal'at Sim'an exist, it is certain that the eastern basilica was used for the eucharistic liturgy, thereby functioning as a sanctuary, while the faithful occupied the other three arms of the church. The octagon therefore occupied the same position – although not of course function – as the bema in other Syrian churches. Ornamental sculpted bands and sculpted mouldings are characteristic of churches of the area. It remained an important shrine until its almost total destruction by the Hamdanid emir of Aleppo in 985.

Visual arts

Preserved silver church vessels include patens and chalices, as well as spoons and liturgical fans (*flabella*), with which deacons kept flies away from the Eucharistic offerings. Several of these came to light in spectacular finds in the twentieth century and are now in museums across the world, especially in Europe and the USA. Some of these finds indicate that silver liturgical vessels were brought to Syria from Constantinople, where they were copied by silversmiths locally. Most are datable by their stamps to between the mid-sixth and early seventh centuries and it has been suggested that several of them may have been made for churches in Resafa, the centre of the cult of St Sergius and home to several other churches, including a famous cathedral. An example of a silver communion paten, or silver plate, is now in the Archaeological Museum in Istanbul; it is from the Stuma treasure, but the church to which it was dedicated is unknown. Its imagery depicts the Communion of the Apostles, with Christ shown twice as he performs the Eucharist, once giving bread on the viewer's right to the first of the six waiting Apostles and on the left dispensing the wine to the rest. Above the altar where the scene takes place is a dome from which a lamp is hung, directly above the Host. This paten was donated by a silversmith named Sergius, who had acquired the paten from Constantinople but probably completed the decoration himself, basing his designs on another paten in the same church's collection, the decoration of which had been completed in Constantinople prior to its donation by an official named Megalos.

Pilgrimage tokens, like small coins made of terracotta, celebrate St Symeon the Elder. These show the figure on a column with flying angels bearing crowns on each side and figures below, probably petitioners to the saint. Such objects, cheap to produce and to buy, some engraved in Syriac, gave blessing and protection to the pilgrim. Similar imagery was repeated on objects of value, such as the votive plaque in silver gilt dating to the sixth century in the Louvre in Paris. This plaque shows the saint on his column, a shell above him, and, entwined around the column, a large snake, bearded – as is the saint – and either personifying evil or, conversely, representing the healing god Asclepius. It is inscribed in Greek as a thanks-offering to the saint, testimony to the deference paid to a Syrian saint in Byzantine-held Syria. It has been suggested that it could have been displayed on the wall or *templon* of a church in a village near Ma'arret en-Noman, where it was found.

Churches were painted, as we have seen, and more became known of wall-painting in Syria and Lebanon during the last quarter of the twentieth century. A painting of the Annunciation, dating probably to between the early sixth and early eighth centuries, has been discovered in a secular building. It is on a pillar in the Kastron of al-Andarin (Androna), which was founded in 558–9. An important wall-painting is preserved in the monastery church of Mar Musa Habashi, near Nebek, a foundation of the fifth century, and work is still being undertaken, in the early twenty-first century, to uncover it. So far two layers of painting have been identified, one of after 1058 and the other of 1192. The earlier layer includes a dramatic scene of the Ascension of Elijah, a scene which also appears in the eleventh century in the Church of St Elijah at Ma'arret Saidnaya. The late twelfth century layer displays an extensive programme. In the bema, the lower part of the apse, stands the Virgin, her arms outstretched, holding a medallion of the Christ child, the so-called Blachernitissa image, flanked by church fathers. In the main semi-dome of the apse above is the image of the Deesis (Christ supplicated by the Virgin and St John the Baptist) with Christ in Majesty. These are paralleled by apse painting in Lebanese churches, including those at the church of Mar Tadros in Bahdeidat, and the churches of Mar Mitri and Saqqiyat el-Hait.

The portrait of the young Christ Emmanuel in the church at Mar Musa beams down from the top of the triumphal arch leading to the central sanctuary, above a window and below the roof gable. On either side of the window are Mary and Gabriel, depicting the Annunciation. These scenes are shown against a blue ground with inscriptions in both Syriac and Greek. Below the Annunciation, at the base of the window, is the older Christ Pantocrator, flanked by St Peter and St Paul and four Evangelists. In the upper register of the nave on both north and south are equestrian saints, including St George, Bacchus(?), St Sergius and St Theodore. Equestrian saints are commonly found in wall-painting in this period, other examples being at the nearby Melkite Church of Mar Sarkis at Qara and the chapel of the Monastery of Mar Yaqub, which is also at Qara, in the Qalamoun mountains, and was inhabited by Melkites until the mid-thirteenth century. In the spandrels of the nave arches are the writing Evangelists, with female saints and martyrs decorating the arch soffits. At the east end of the north aisle is the restored Baptism of Christ, and on the north wall is the scene of David and the Lion. The west wall depicts the Last Judgement. At the top are Peter and Paul. Below them is the *Hetoimasia*, the Prepared Throne, with Apostles and Evangelists. Below the *Hetoimasia* are Adam and Eve, with the three patriarchs and Mary on the viewer's left and heretical bishops on the viewer's right. Finally, the rest of the scene is taken up with the saved, on the viewer's left, and the damned on the right.

The image painted by King Abgar's messenger to Christ in Jerusalem was replicated in the form of an icon painted on wood prior to the eighth century, when the image was transferred to a cloth or *mandylion*. It is in this form that it was taken to Constantinople by order of the Emperor Romanos I in 944, and was depicted in an actual icon of the tenth century which is at the Monastery of St Catherine, Mount Sinai. This icon depicts King Abgar receiving the *mandylion*, with saints, including St Ephrem and St Basil, with monastic saints and the Apostle St Thaddeus. Wall-painting in Syria and present-day Lebanon can be studied in conjunction with painted icons preserved at the Monastery of St Catherine on Mount Sinai. Belonging to the contested domain of 'Crusader' art, these include panels given by Christian Arab and Latin donors, an example being a small panel of a woman supplicating the equestrian saint Sergius. He carries a red cross banner and his arms suggest he was fighting with the Mongol army as part of the East Christian support in driving the Mamlūks out of Syria. Another, an icon of the Virgin and Child of the Hodegetria type at the Greek Orthodox Monastery of Kaftun, located between Tripoli and Batrun, which has the Baptism of Christ on the reverse, has also been compared to icon painting at Sinai. Its inscriptions in Greek, Arabic and Syriac, as well as its similarity to wall-painting in the Qadisha valley, suggest its Melkite use.

The art of the book is well represented in Syrian church culture. An early, famous, manuscript is the Rabbula Gospels, now in the Biblioteca Laurentiana in Florence; it was copied by the monk Rabbula at the Monastery of St John at Beth Zagba on the Euphrates in 586.The manuscript opens with an elaborate set of canon tables, the list of concordance between the four Gospels. The Syriac reference to the appropriate Gospel is written between columns which support elaborately decorated arches and then canopies above. At the top stand birds with foliage and sometimes vases. At the top on either side are Old Testament figures, with New Testament figures and scenes in the margins below. Full-page illustrations of the Virgin and Child, the Crucifixion, Ascension, Christ Enthroned, the Election of St Matthew as an Apostle, and Pentecost are clustered at the beginning of the book.

Scribes were commissioned to produce manuscripts for monasteries and individuals throughout the areas of the Middle East where Syriac was spoken or, at a later date, retained its use as a liturgical language. This is known from scribal signatures and the colophon, or concluding statement at the end of a manuscript, as well as notes written in several manuscripts at various times. Manuscripts were also moved between one monastery and another, either to act as a model for a copy, or for safe-keeping, or to initiate or replenish the stock of manuscripts. An example of the latter instance is the removal of manuscripts from Iraq to Dayr al-Suryan, the Monastery of the Syrians, in the Scetis desert in Egypt. This was undertaken by the Abbot Moses in the tenth century as part of his refurbishment of the monastery, a renovation which included the adding of 'Abbasid, Iraqi-style, stuccoes in the sanctuary of the monastery church of the Virgin. Several of these manuscripts are now in the British Library in London and are undergoing restoration. Another is the collection and production of manuscripts by the great Syrian patriarch and chronicler of the twelfth century, Michael the Syrian (patriarch 1166–99), at his Monastery of Mar Barsauma near Malatya (Melitene).

A number of particularly fine illustrated lectionaries are preserved from the flourishing period of the later twelfth to thirteenth centuries known as the 'Syrian Renaissance'. This is the period of the crusades, when Eastern Christian culture intersects with that of the incoming westerners. St Mark's in Jerusalem, which was patronized by Queen Melisende of Jerusalem in the twelfth century, is an example of a monastery in which manuscripts were produced, as is attested by preserved unillustrated ones. One example of a lectionary, that from Deir ez-Zapharan and now in the Library of the Church of the Forty Martyrs in Mardin, was made by Dioscorus Theodorus, later Bishop of Hisn Zaid (now Kharput) in the mid-thirteenth century. Bound between thick wooden covers, it has miniatures whose iconography can be traced to Syriac hymns, homilies and exegesis. Its scene of the Communion of the Apostles is similar to that of the Stuma paten already mentioned. The illustrations in lectionaries such as these contain elements of everyday life and of direct contemporary relevance. Turbaned figures and highly decorative architecture occur in the Entry into Jerusalem scene in the thirteenth-century Syriac lectionary in London (B.L. Add 7170, Figure 19.3), features which also appear in contemporary secular Arabic manuscripts.

Another contemporary element is the appearance of Constantine and his mother Helena, the finder of the True Cross in Jerusalem, with Mongol facial features. The clearest example is the image in another lectionary made at the Monastery of Mar Mattaï near Mosul in 1260, which shows Constantine and his mother Helena holding the True Cross between them. Their Mongol features associate them with the contemporary Mongol Ilkhan Hülagü and his Christian wife Doghuz Khatun. This reflects the faith and trust in the alliance which Eastern Christians made with the Mongol forces at the time, when battling to stave off the Mamlūk Islamic armies and with the hope of regaining the Holy Land. The Christian–Mongol alliance is further celebrated by the contemporary portrait of Hülagü's Christian general Kitbugha as one of the three Magi, again with Mongol features, in a Nativity/Adoration scene on an iconostasis beam at the Greek Orthodox Monastery of St Catherine at Mount Sinai. This was arguably painted by a Syrian Melkite artist. Kitbugha was a member of the Church of the East, as was Khatun, and both were regarded as descendants of the Magi.

The Armenian Church

Positioned as it is between Turkey and Iran, Armenia was converted by Christians travelling to the Persian Empire by way of Edessa. Armenia is, strictly speaking, the first Christian state, Christianity being proclaimed there around 314, whereas Constantine merely promulgated an Edict of Toleration in 313. Tradition says the Apostles Bartholomew and Thaddeus preached in Armenia. But it was Gregory the Illuminator, who converted King Trdat, and the early female martyrs, Gayane and Hrip'sime, who became the great national saints of Armenia. Many churches were subsequently dedicated to these saints. The social structure was founded on the great feudal families who patronized churches and monasteries, with the catholicos, the spiritual head of the church, at Dvin. Secular structures are also preserved, including defensive building. In the later twelfth century, with the migration to Cilicia on the south coast of Turkey, fortresses began to be built. They were at their height between the twelfth to fourteenth century, and include those at Sis and Lambron.

Architecture and sculpture

The inventiveness of Armenian architecture is apparent in its use of stone cutting, mostly in tufa. Building traditions were derived from the pre-Christian era, as in the kingdom of Urartu, known through excavations. More recently the site of Garni, near modern Erevan, with its Greco-Roman temple and other monuments of the first or second century CE, also provided precedents for monumental building in stone. The late sixth to early seventh centuries CE saw the first phase of Christian architecture. An example of an early basilica is that of the ruined church known as Dsiranavor of Ashtarak, dated to 548–57 near Erevan, and probably founded by Catholicos Nerses II

(548–57). It had three aisles – functioning as the nave and two side aisles – and four bays, as well as the apse, which was approached through a horseshoe-shaped arch, with two flanking side rooms, all contained within the rectangular outer walls. The surviving arch-springing bears witness to the fact that the nave and side aisles were vaulted. Stone was used for the vaulting, in place of the wood used for the flat roofing in Syria, and the brick used in Byzantium. Entry was gained to the church from its south façade. The carefully cut tufa stone slabs, put into place without mortar, were strengthened and consolidated with the use of a concrete-like core. Resistance to earthquakes was maintained by the balancing of the size of slabs, with larger slabs generally being reserved for cornering. Decorative effect was achieved by using various coloured stone as well as by sculptured friezes around windows and doors. The stone facing gives buildings a sheer, compact, aesthetic, which often belies the complexity of the interior.

Another inventive feature is the development of the dome. By the fifth century Armenian architects were applying themselves to the task of building a dome over a rectangular space. The church at Ptghni in the sixth century shows how this was achieved: with the use of massive piers, linked by arches on which the cupola was raised using pendentives, one of which is still preserved. Elsewhere, such as at the cathedral at Mren in the first half of the seventh century, the solution was to place the octagonal drum, ribbed internally and with four windows, over the central part of the nave with the weight spreading through the arches to four barrel vaults.

Much architectural experimentation took place during the sixth and seventh centuries, during which churches were built according to myriad plans. The Church of St Hrip'sime at Vagharshapat, built in 618 on the site of the original *martyrium* dedicated to her by Catholicos Komitas, is a good example of a centrally planned church with domes. Its plan shows that internally it is formed as a quatrefoil, with three-quarter circle niches at the four corners where the apses intersect. These in turn link with four rectangular rooms at the outer edges so as to form a rectangle. But the main walls of the building do not appear straightforwardly rectangular on the exterior. Instead, the walls are interrupted by two niches on each side marking the four interior apses. The church is completed by the cylindrical dome which is supported by squinches and strengthened with ribs and decorated with circles. This church was influential in Armenia and early imitations of it are found in Georgia.

A related church is that of the cathedral of Zvart'nots, built by Catholicos Nerses III between 641 and 653 and dedicated to the Angels of Heaven. While only the lower courses of the walls are preserved today, the church can be reconstructed. It was a quatrefoil in plan, contained within a circular ambulatory. It can be envisaged as having a solid, eastern, main apse and an ambo in the central space. A rectangular chancel was appended to the circle on the east side. The cupola was supported by pendentives on arches linking four massive piers between the arms of the quatrefoils. Its sculptural remains points to an originally highly decorated form. The find of fragments of mosaic cubes inside the building shows that it was decorated with mosaic work. This church in its turn provided the prototype for other buildings in Armenia, including the Church of St Gregory at Ani built by Gagik I in the eleventh century, and elsewhere in the Caucasus, in both Armenia and Georgia.

Later Armenian architecture develops the themes of the experimental period of the sixth to seventh centuries. However, one feature that appeared later was the porch (*gavit*), which was often attached to the longitudinal side of a church. Appearing particularly in monasteries during the twelfth to fourteenth centuries, the *gavit* was used as a meeting hall and the burial site of abbots and feudal lords who had made large gifts to the monastery. An example is the Church of the Redeemer at the Monastery of Sanahin on to which the square structure of the *gavit* was added in 1181, comprising four columns joined by semicircular arches supporting a dome. It is linked to the main church through a door on the east side, although it is itself entered through the north side. Another was built at the same monastery in 1211 in front of the Church of the Virgin. Another architectural development was the addition of the free-standing bell tower in the thirteenth century. An example is the three-storied bell tower at the Monastery of Haghbat, built in 1245.

Several of these and other churches were decorated with sculpture, its position dictated by the architecture; it often framed windows or portals, or rested on capitals, or formed friezes, or was put in particular places on exterior walls. Sculpture also appears in funerary and commemorative contexts. A tradition of stone carving had already existed in the pagan monuments in pre-Christian Armenia and the extensive architectural use of stone lent itself to carving. The designs used in Armenian sculpture range widely from figurative capitals to ornamental motifs including vines, palmettes, rosettes and interwoven circles. Architectural examples include those at the sixth century church at Ptgni where, preserved on the south façade, there are panels of Christ, with the Apostles and donors. At the top of the arch over the window is a medallion containing Christ, supported by flying angels, with busts of Apostles on either side. Beyond, at the arch return on either side, figures are carved. On the west side is a horseman named by inscription as Manual, lord of the Amatuni who shoots at a lioness. Opposite, on the east side, is a hunting scene showing a man approaching a lion with a spear. These reflect the royal hunting iconography of the former Sasanian Empire and are common in mortuary chapels. The lion motif is continued on the west side of the façade, just below the arch where with the scene of Daniel in the lion's den, that familiar image of early Christian art, was inset. The hunting image is returned to at the church of the White Virgin (Spitakovar) built in 1321 near Areni on the estate of the powerful Proshian family. Here Amir Hasan, the son of the founder, is shown on horseback turning behind him to shoot at a doe in panels removed from the north façade of the church and now in the Historical Museum at Erevan. The emir is shown again, this time under the gable of the façade standing next to his father, Eatchi Proshian, the founder of the church, who appears seated. But here the garments he wears are characteristic of Islamic art and he has Mongol facial features.

A particularly well preserved example of the lively use of architectural sculpture is that preserved at the Church of the Holy Cross on the island of Aght'amar, in the southern part of Lake Van. A portrait of the donor, King Gagik Ardsruni, Prince of Vaspurakan, appears on the west façade of the church carrying a model of his church which he dedicates to Christ (Figure 19.4). Built by the architect Manuel between 915 and 921, alongside a palace, gardens and orchards, its plan is similar to that of the Church of St Hrip'sime already mentioned, but it has only two rectangular chapels at the east end. Under the conical roof of the dome and of the hemicycles and niches are friezes with animals, with human heads interspersed. On each of the façades under the gables is a standing Evangelist. On the upper part of the walls are vine-scrolls containing humans and animals. Below are animals and birds with, below them, rows of figurative scenes completed at the base with a palmette scroll. On the east façade saints and prophets are carved. On the north and south façades are Old Testament scenes including David and Goliath, with Saul added to the scene, with figures of Christ and the Virgin and Child enthroned. The windows of the church are also articulated with sculpture.

Typical of Armenian art are the stone crosses, or *khatchk'ars*, dating to between the ninth and eighteenth centuries, whose purpose is to commemorate the person whose name is often inscribed on the stone in the form of a prayer for the salvation of their soul. The *khatchk'ar* represents the Tree of Life, a meaning that is literally depicted in the sprouting foliage and fruit of the crosses. An example of a *khatchk'ar* is that of Aputayli (Figure 19.5) dating to 1225 from the Noraduz cemetery at Sewan; it was donated to the British Museum by His Holness Vazgen I, Catholicos of All Armenians in 1978. The inscription on the left edge seeks God's mercy for Aputayli. The front face of the rectangular slab has a leaved-cross with two smaller crosses below. The crosses are framed with a trefoil above from which bunches of grapes project on either side, and is banded with interlace panels. A band of interlocking circles with palmettes above complete the decoration at the top. Later *khatchk'ars* reflect the stylistic features of their times. That carved in 1308 by Momik, the architect and sculptor of the church at Areni, is lace-like in its delicacy, showing at the top the trio of the Deesis group, with Christ in the centre flanked by the intercessionary figures of the Virgin on his right and St John on the left, with a large cross below, above an ornamented circle and ornament in quatrefoils down both sides. A final point to be made is that the stepped cross which is found on some *khatchk'ars* is the same as that tooled on Armenian, as well as Syriac, book bindings.

Also commemorative are the stelae or stone slabs which were set up in memory of abbots and members of the feudal families. They are found in necropolises or near to churches. Some, obelisk in shape, are raised on a cubic base. They are often carved with figurative scenes in panels on two or three of their sides. At Odzun a pair of these seventh-century standing stones are set under arches on a platform reached by seven steps. Among the figures shown are the Virgin and Child at the top of the north stele and the Apostles, in pairs, on the west face of the southern stele. Other scenes include the Hebrews in the fiery furnace. There are taller stele, now mostly incomplete, which are cubic, flaring slightly at the top, and usually decorated on all four faces. Their square bases are decorated with figures or crosses. The stele at Haridj, for example, shows Christ blessing and the Virgin and Child on different faces, and Daniel in the lion's den at the base.

Visual arts

While fragments of mosaic work have been found in churches and excavations in Armenia, one of the best examples is that excavated near Damascus Gate in Jerusalem in the late nineteenth century. Although the most central imagery, that of a vine-scroll issuing from an amphora with peacocks on either side, and birds and animals with the scrolls, is common to sixth-century Judaeo-Christian mosaics in Palestine, the inscription marks out the mosaic as Armenian, reading as it does: 'To the memory and the salvation of all Armenians, whose names are known only to God'.

Armenian churches were decorated with wall-paintings, which have mostly only been preserved in a fragmentary state. The church at Aght'amar contains remains of a Genesis cycle in the drum of the dome, derived from early Christian models, and a New Testament cycle in the main body of the church, with Apostle figures remaining in the lower part of the apse.

Illustrated manuscripts have always been a treasured part of Armenian life and faith. Several kinds of religious books were illustrated, especially Gospel books, but also Bibles, lectionaries, prayer books, books of saints' lives. Secular books, including the Romance of Alexander and historical texts, can be added to the list. Dedicatory inscriptions and colophons, as well as additional notes give valuable information about the circumstances of the commissioning, production and subsequent history and ownership of Armenian manuscripts. Today, as a result of the wide Armenian diaspora, manuscripts are held in collections all over the world, including Erevan (the Matenadaran Library), Jerusalem (Armenian Patriarchate), Venice (Library of the Mekhitarist Fathers), the Walters Art Gallery in Baltimore, Topkapi Saray Library in Istanbul, Chester Beatty Library in Dublin, the Calouste Gulbenkian Collection in Lisbon, the British Library, and the John Rylands Library in Manchester, as well as other collections.

The development of the Armenian language after the invention of the Armenian alphabet around 406 saw the translation into Armenian of the Bible, from Greek and Syriac books brought from Constantinople and the other major cities of the Christian East. Some books epitomize the rich overlaying of culture. The sixth-century ivory book covers of the Armenian Ejmiadsin Gospels (Erevan, Matenadaran 2374) are in fact Byzantine works of art, having scenes of Christ in Majesty and the Virgin and Child, with crosses in wreaths borne by angels above. The sixth- or seventh-century full-page illustrations of the book itself were added at the end of the manuscript, which is itself dated to 989. They depict the Announcement to Zacharia, the Annunciation, the Adoration of the Magi and the Baptism of Christ. An early eleventh-century Gospel manuscript also in Ereven (Matenadaran 10780), the so-called Vehap'ar Gospels, follows the frequent layout of canon tables and prefatory miniatures, in this case the Hospitality of Abraham and a donor portrait, and thereafter sixty-four illustrations as a 'running narrative' set. The illustrations link the manuscript with those made in Melitene in the early eleventh century, and have been shown to have affiliations with Syriac manuscript illumination. Particularly interesting is the miniature with the Hospitality of Abraham, with its depiction of the godhead as the Trinity of three individuals in one. These are the three angels who sit at Abraham's table attended by Abraham and his wife Sarah, according to Genesis 18: 1–15, imagery that is found in early Byzantine art from the sixth century, although infrequently. It would be wrong, however, to underestimate the inventiveness of Armenian writers and artists in adapting iconography or to invent new themes for new purposes.

An example of a uniquely Armenian text is the *Book of Lamentations* written in 1102 by Gregory, a monk of the Monastery of Narek, at Lake Van. It comprises ninety-five spiritual, elegiac, poems in which Gregory converses with God. The earliest dated copy of this text, on vellum, is in the Matenadaran Library in Erevan; it was made by a named scribe (Grigor Mlichetsi) in 1173 for Archbishop Nerses of Lambron, undoubtedly in Skevra, the archbishop's seat. The manuscript also contains a biography of St Gregory by the archbishop. At the front of it are four portraits of Gregory of Narek. The last of these shows Gregory prostrate before Christ, who is seated under a canopy, holding the book and with his hand held out in reception and blessing. A tree in flower on the left completes the scene.

In the scriptoria of the kingdom of Cilicia, ruled by the Rubenid and Het'umid princely families during the late twelfth to fourteenth centuries, manuscript illumination reached its creative apogee. Centred on the former Byzantine domain south of the Taurus, on the Mediterranean coast, it opened up artists to contacts and influences from the Italian city-states as well as the areas established by crusaders. A period of sustained development can be seen, under the patronage of the ruling families. A richer colour range than that employed by Byzantine miniaturists was possible, owing to the greater use of the more durable mineral pigments, as opposed to organic pigments. As was the case in Greater Armenia, Gospel books were illustrated more often than any other category.

The most famous Armenian artist is T'oros Roslin, the master of the patriarchal scriptorium in Hromkla in the third quarter of the thirteenth century (the patriarchal see had been transferred here in 1151). Seven manuscripts illustrated, and sometimes transcribed, by him between 1256 and 1268 have been preserved. While he continued some of the conventions established by his predecessors his imagination and inventiveness are evident in his use of a wider range of narrative iconography, stimulated in part by his knowledge of western art. His painting style shows fluidity in depicting figures and draperies. One of his masterpieces is the Gospel book in the Walters Art Gallery in Baltmore (W. 539) of 1262, made of vellum. The Last Judgement on fol. 109v (Figure 19.6) illustrates how T'oros Roslin enlivens the theme while retaining a monumental composition. Christ is seated in the centre at the top of the scene, his hands outstretched to the Virgin and St John; this is the Deesis image, indicated earlier. On either side angels hail the scene with trumpets while others bear the skies in the form of furled scrolls, according to the text of Isaiah 34: 4. The Apostles are seated in the row below, on either side of the cross, with the Foolish Virgins in the left margin, literally excluded from paradise, which is beyond the closed door to the left. The two lowest rows divide the saved on the viewer's left from the damned on the right, with Adam and Eve in the central pivotal position, above a cherubim.

The greater recognition of the artist in Cilicia is apparent in the fourteenth century. A Gospel book, also of vellum, in the Chester Beatty library in Dublin (Nr. 614) was written in 1342 at the Monastery of Drazark in Cilicia for the priest Tiratur. It has (fol. 13v) a portrait of Christ with the donor on his left side and scribe on his right, depicted as an elderly man. Another major Armenian book, this time an early fourteenth-century one, is the Glazor Gospel book, now in the Library of UCLA (Armenian MS no. 1). It is dedicated to the abbot of Glazor in the province of Siwnik, a key figure in the defence of Orthodox (Miaphysite) Armenian culture against the inroads of Roman Catholicism in particular. It was produced by two scribes and five artists, working first in one of the provincial centres of Orbelian influence and then at Glazor, the monastery of the Proshian family, where the manuscript was completed. It has been argued that it is through the contemporary exegetical work at the monastery, through its defence of the faith and the preservation of Armenian traditions and liturgy, that the iconography of the manuscript's scenes can be interpreted. For example, the miniature of the Crucifixion shows two streams issuing from Christ's side, of blood and of water. This is interpreted as the refutation of, in this case, the Greek insistence of mixing water with the eucharistic wine.

Manuscripts produced in Greater Armenia and, particularly Cilicia, remained a benchmark for Armenians. Later, a fertile period in Armenian cultural history was made possible by the wealth of Armenian merchants living in New Julfa, a suburb of Isfahan in the seventeenth century, who had been moved there by Shah Abbas at the beginning of the century. There are several examples of earlier manuscripts being acquired and restored and in turn providing the inspiration for seventeenth-century illuminators. One example is the portrait of St John in a Gospel book produced in 1628, which is derived from the Glazor Gospel book just discussed. Constantinople and the Crimea were other centres that continued the traditions of the past at this time. One example is the restoration in the Crimea in 1621 of the covers of the Gospels of Catholicos Kostandin I Bardzraberdtsi (Erevan, Matenadaran, In. Nr. 7690). This book, written in Hromkla in 1249, was bound in silver gilt covers some time after 1255. The front cover depicts the Deesis, the back the four Evangelists.

Armenian metalworkers also produced liturgical objects such as censers and pyxes. Reliquaries were also produced, such as that of the Holy Cross of Khotakerats' of 1300, now in the Museum of the Catholicate at Ejmiadsin, which was made in Siunik' of silver gilt and inlaid with precious stones. When closed, the reliquary shows Christ Pantocrator at the top, his scroll inscribed with the words 'I am the Light of the World', and it has St Gregory the Illuminator (who also appears on a reliquary of 1293 from the Monastery of Skevra) and St John the Baptist on the doors. The Virgin and St John the Evangelist on the frames on either side recall their positions at the Crucifixion. The praying figure of the donor, Prince Eatchi of the Proshian famly is flanked by St Peter and St Paul, all three in bust-form. The doors open to reveal a jewelled cross surrounded with palmette scrolls and two seated harts below, symbolizing the longing of the human soul for God, according to Psalm 41: 1–20. The archangels Michael and Gabriel complete the programme on the inner sides of the door leaves.

Luxury goods were made in textiles, wood, and ceramic. The eleventh-century Gospel of King Gagik of Kars (Jerusalem, Armenian Patriarchate no. 2556) includes a royal portrait, added to the manuscript, in which the king is shown seated with his wife and daughter. The royal family wear rich garments, woven with medallions and decorated roundels, and they sit on sumptuous floor coverings. Examples of preserved Armenian textiles range from the silk bindings of manuscripts to the rich silk embroidery of eighteenth-century altar curtains, mitres, and altar frontals. There was particular interest in the late twentieth century in the manufacture of carpets by Armenians – carpets that were mentioned by Arab historians in the seventh and eighth centuries. In them a rich repertoire of real and imaginary animals, including dragons, eagles and serpents, alongside ornamental motifs, was created.

Another area of production is woodwork, especially that of church doors, lecterns, and even capitals, such as those from Sevan. Work in wood between the eleventh and thirteenth centuries is best represented by the carved relief of the Descent from the Cross, given by Gregory Magistros to the Monastery of Havuts T'ar in 1031, which emphasizes Christ's triumph over death. Christ is being crucified on the jewelled cross of Golgotha, his arm[s] leaning on the figure of Joseph of Arimathea while Nicodemus removes the nails.

Finally, ceramic goods have been found in excavations at Ani and Dvin. Examples of the use of ceramic objects in a religious context are found in the extensive collection of Kütahya work objects in the patriarchal collection of St James in Jerusalem, brought by pilgrims from Turkish Armenia. These include tiles, a blue and white ewer and bowl, pilgrim flasks and the collection of decorated ceramic hanging eggs which are suspended from lamp chains in the church.

The Coptic Church

Architectural and iconographic traditions in the Coptic Church developed as a result of several stimuli, internal and external, past and contemporary. The pharaonic past remained a potent force in the Coptic psyche. The Coptic language itself, retained as a liturgical if not a spoken language, was a continuation of the pharaonic language. In the fourth century, churches were built into pharaonic temples, such as Luxor and Deir el Bahari. Throughout the medieval period links were retained with the other Eastern Christian Churches and with Byzantium in Asia Minor, especially through trade.

Architecture, sculpture and painting

In Upper (northern) Egypt the development of early Christian architecture has been seen as predominantly influenced by association with the Mediterranean and Byzantine worlds through the coastal region, while monasticism has been seen as the stimulus for indigenous developments in the towns, cities and monasteries in central and Lower Egypt, although this division cannot be too strictly applied. As elsewhere in the eastern Mediterranean, the basilica was the core architectural form, with variations. Thus the fourth-century Church of Antinopolis (Antinoë) and the fourth- or fifth-century Church of Pbow had a narrow central nave flanked by side aisles, all of which was encircled by a form of narrow ambulatory that gave on to a small internal apse flanked by side chapels. Others, like the church at Hermopolis (Al-Ashmunein) of the fifth century, had a wide central nave with two side aisles which opened out into a transept with rounded ends to the arms on the north and south sides, beyond which the apse projected to the east. This latter plan was also used in Byzantine architecture, as was the triconch sanctuary at the eastern end of churches in middle Egypt of the fifth to seven centuries. These include the White and Red Monasteries (Dayr al-Abiad and Dayr al-Ahmar) at Sohag. A fully central plan appears in the sixth century in the east basilica of the sanctuary of St Menas, as also in the *martyrium* at the same site, which has a quatrefoil plan.

The basilica remained the standard form, with a widened central nave and side aisles and internal apse flanked by side rooms. Between the fifth and seventh centuries this is the form employed in the construction of the Monastery of Saqqara and in the churches of Old Cairo in the seventh century itself. The Old Cairo churches with those of the monasteries of the Wadi Natrun (in the Scetis desert) provide examples of that most characteristic feature of Coptic architecture, the *khurus*. This is the lateral room that was introduced between the central sanctuary (*haikal*) and the nave, effectively dividing the clergy from the laity. It was common in churches being built from the mid-seventh century onwards, and was also added to certain earlier churches. With the introduction of the vaulted roof, as opposed to the traditional wooden roof, between the tenth and twelfth centuries came the use of a barrel vault over the central nave and the *khurus* in Lower Egypt, and the appearance of cupolae (domes) over the nave in Upper Egypt.

The complex of buildings at Dayr Abu Mena grew up as a pilgrimage site around the shrine of St Menas, a local saint, martyr and miracle-worker who died at the end of the fourth century. Both archaeological work and the study of literary references have contributed to an understanding of the site, which in the early twenty-first century was listed by UNESCO as a world heritage site in danger. Originally the body of the saint was transferred to a crypt under a cruciform church, but the pressure of vistor numbers led to the building campaign of the early fifth century under imperial patronage. By the end of the fifth century, at the time of Emperor Zeno, the shrine had further developed, having acquired a large basilica (about 55 m long) with wide transepts on the east side of the complex and a projecting apse, divided from the crypt and shrine of St Menas to the west by a tetraconch building between. There was a separate baptistery. With the apse used primarily for burials, the bishop's throne and flanking raised seats for the clergy (*synthronon*) occupied the area to the west behind the high altar at the transept crossing. With the generous use of marble together with the extensive monastic buildings, baths and accommodation for vistors, and cemeteries, it is easy to see how Abu Mena rivalled the complex of St Symeon Stylites in Syria. As with that pilgrimage site, pilgrims could take away symbolic tokens. In the case of Abu Mena these were pilgrim bottles, which are usually known as ampullae. These small, rounded, terracotta flasks with handles were made at Abu Mena and were also available at other sites connected with the saint's life. They contained holy oil blessed at the site, and water from the spring at Abu Mena. They are moulded with the scene of St Menas standing frontally in the *orans* pose, with his arms stretched to the sides with palms facing forward, between two camels which kneel with their heads bowed to the saint. This image, of St Menas standing between camels, appeared on a marble panel at the beginning of the fifth century, when the crypt was enlarged. To the west of the tomb chamber was a small underground chapel decorated with mosaic.

The Greco-Roman period in Egypt saw the development of Alexandria as the major centre, whose Hellenized legacy was felt into the Middle Ages. The fifth-century city is only known from documents, as only fragments remain of ancient and early Christian and medieval Alexandria. Here in the former catacombs of Karmuz, funerary chapels with painted apses displayed imagery symbolic of the resurrection. Similar imagery can be seen in other funerary monuments and in churches. An example is the miracle of the loaves and fishes, which makes reference to the Christian symbolism of resurrection through the Eucharist. Of the mausolea in the Bagawit necropolis in the Kharga oasis in the (Libyan) Western Desert, two are particularly significant for their similar displays of the imagery of salvation. The fourth-century programme of the so-called Chapel of the Exodus includes the scene of Moses leading the Israelites out of Egypt to the Promised Land. The fifth-century 'Chapel of Peace'(containing the figure of Eirene (Peace) among the personifications around its dome) has paintings of Daniel in the lion's den and of the Sacrifice of Isaac.

At the rock-cut Church of Deir Abu Hennis near Antinoë friezes of the life of Christ are preserved. Dating to the late sixth century is a frieze with New Testament scenes including the Massacre of the Innocents, taking place by order of King Herod, and the Flight into Egypt, to which was added, in the eighth century, a cycle of the life of Zacharias. Carvings in bone and ivory have been found which reflect religious, as well as luxury use. These include liturgical combs with New Testament scenes, one of which, from Antinoë, depicts the raising of Lazarus and the miracle of the healing of the blind man and, on the reverse, an equestrian saint within a wreath supported by two angels (now in the Coptic Museum in Cairo).

Particularly important are the remains from the Monasteries of Bawit and Saqqara, in Middle Egypt, dating to between the sixth and eighth centuries. The Monastery of Bawit, on the west bank of the Nile about 320 km south of Cairo, was excavated in the early years of the twentieth century. Its carved sculpture and paintings are scattered in various collections. Although the most important sites were designated the north and south churches by the excavators, several finds are now believed to have come from private houses and taken subsequently to the monastery. Several capitals and friezes from Bawit are in the Coptic Museum in Old Cairo. The niches of the oratories were painted with imagery which combines the Virgin as the Mother of God with the Child in the lower register with an apocalyptic vision above. One, for example, which dates to the sixth to seventh century, shows the Virgin and Child below, with twelve Apostles and two local saints, and Christ in Majesty enthroned above in a *mandorla*, on a chariot with wheels. Four wings issue from the side of the *mandorla* incorporating the four apocalyptic beasts, and there is an angel on either side. This is the imagery of the theophany of Christ, illustrating the Old Testament apocalyptic texts of Ezekiel, Isaiah and Daniel, as well as that of John. Painting and sculpture is also preserved from the Monastery of St Jeremiah at Saqqara, the necropolis of ancient Memphis. Particularly significant is its sculpture of different periods, much of it from between the fifth and early sixth centuries, which includes the so-called 'wind-blown' capitals of Constantinopolitan sixth-century style. Painting and sculpture can also be seen at the churches of the Red and White Monasteries at Sohag (Dayr al-Ahmar and Dayr al-Abiad).

Other monastic sites in Egypt continue the tradition of wall-painting. In the Wadi Natrun there are vibrant images in the Church of the Virgin at Dayr al-Suryan, the Syrian monastery. At the east end, in the trefoil sanctuary, early thirteenth-century paintings of the Annunciation and Nativity (Figure 19.7) occupy the southern semi-dome, with the Dormition in the northern semi-dome. The western semi-dome in the church depicted an Ascension scene of the same date. These have bilingual inscriptions in Syriac and Greek indicating a multicultural community of monks in the early thirteenth century. Work at the end of the twentieth and beginning of the twenty-first

centuries in the church consisted of both the uncovering and restoration of other paintings of various dates. Below the scene of the Ascension in the western semi-dome is
that of the Annunciation to the Virgin, which includes Old Testament prophets and, in
the centre, a lighted censer with burning incense, a visual celebration paralleling the
liturgical hymns of the Virgin. Other paintings in the same church include the Nursing
Virgin and Child on the half column to the right of the main entrance to the
sanctuary.

The Church of the Virgin at Dayr al-Baramus displays recently discovered New
Testament paintings on the south wall of *c*.1200. In the eastern sanctuary are eucha-
ristic scenes showing the Sacrifice of Isaac and Abraham with the Old Testament priest
Mechisedek. In the apse the Virgin and Child between two angels occupies the lower
register with Christ enthroned above. There are paintings of saints in the southern
sanctuary. Little is known of the artists of these paintings. However, at St Antony's
Monastery near the Red Sea a painter named Theodore undertook work in 1232–3.
The programme at St Antony's includes that in a smaller chapel, dedicated to the Four
Living Creatures, with the enthroned Christ in Majesty and the apocalyptic beasts
between the Virgin and St John. Equestrian saints and monks join the similar apocalyptic imagery found at the monastery churches at Deir el-Fakouri and Deir el-Shuhada
at Esna. Three equestrian saints appear, with the archangel Gabriel, on the north wall
of the monastery church of the Archangel Gabriel at Naqlun in the Fayyum, built after
the ninth century and containing paintings preserved from the eleventh century. These
also include the fragmentary Christ in Majesty in the conch of the apse with Apostles
below, and niche paintings of the Virgin and Child, St Mark the Evangelist, and St
Athanasius. The Virgin and Child with St Michael are depicted on the southern part of
the west wall of what is now the narthex

Painting on wood in Egypt is known from the burial portraits from the Fayyum
which disappeared from use at the end of the fourth century. Painted icons for Christian
use were found on site of the south church of the Monastery of Bawit. A panel of Christ
with his arm around St Menas in a gesture of protection, found at Bawit, is now in the
Louvre. Contrary to the previously accepted view, which was that icons were abandoned in Egypt between the seventh and the eighteenth centuries, they probably flourished. Several icons are today preserved in collections in Egypt, such as those in the
Coptic Museum the Church of Dayr Abu Sayfayn in Old Cairo; some of those in the
great icon collection from St Catherine's monastery on Mount Sinai can be attributed
to Egypt.

Woodwork has been well preserved in the Egyptian climate. This comprises lintels,
door frames and screens as well as icons. Friezes and panels for architectural use reproduced a variety of imagery. A particularly Egyptian example is the appearance of Nilotic
scenes, with ducks, crocodiles, fish and hippopotamuses, imagery which was interpreted by sixth-century Christian writers as representing the waters of the Nile and the
Creation. The two pairs of doors, of the *khurus* (choir) and those of the sanctuary of
the Church of the Virgin at Dayr al-Suryan in the Wadi Natrun are a good example of
wooden doors giving access to a sacred space in a church context. They are dated to
the early tenth century and are of great intricacy. The *khurus* doors, of ebony inlaid
with ivory, are dated 926–7, from the time of Abbot Moses of Nisibis. They show, in

the upper register, St Peter on the upper left opposite St Mark on the upper right. These are the founders of the patriarchates of Antioch and Alexandria. Between them are the central panels, left, of the Virgin, and on the right, of Christ. Christ is designated Emmanuel, a Miaphysite trait, of which an example is illustrated here, as Figure 19.8. Below are five rows of intricate aniconic panels with geometric and cross designs. The sanctuary screen, dated 913–14, repeats the imagery of the Virgin and Christ Emmanuel, and St Mark. Here the Antioch patriarchate is instead represented by St Ignatius, accompanied by the Egyptian Dioscorus and the Syrian Severus. Aniconic panels again appear below. Later surviving panels from church doors include those from the baptistery of the Church of al-Mu'allaqa in Old Cairo, datable to c.1300 and now in the British Museum in London. These include feast scenes, such as that of the Entry into Jerusalem (Figure 19.9).

Textiles

One of the areas of Coptic culture that has attracted attention in the late twentieth and early twenty-first centuries is that of textiles. Many thousands of fragments and partial garments from cemeteries are scattered throughout collections worldwide, often with insufficient information about their find-spots. Many of these were from excavations initiated in the nineteenth and early twentieth centuries in the search for papyri, predominantly in Middle and Lower Egypt, including those in the desert sands of Akmîm and Antinopolis. Modern study is refining the description of items with the aim of standardizing cataloguing. There is attention to weaving techniques, and textile production as well as the use of colour and conservation methods. Aspects of life, material culture and death of late Roman and east Christian communities are revealed through the textiles. There had been a gradual change from ancient Egyptian mummification practices. Characteristic of the change is the use of the wax portraits, commonly known as Fayyum portraits from the area in which many were found, in the early second to third centuries CE. By the Christian period people were buried in their own clothes. Commonly worn were tunics woven from sleeve to sleeve in one piece and sewn together at the sides, and tucked in at the side to fit the individual. Some church fathers disapproved of the fine clothes used in burying the dead.

Where there is information about the contents of a burial, the objects and materials retrieved are very personal to the individual. Sometimes the headgear, beads and jewellery and the outer wrapping, which was occasionally a hanging, has been retained. The fabrics were made of wool and linen. Decoration took the form of tapestry and embroidered medallions, neck borders, shoulder bands and shoulder or knee patches. This decoration, which was consistent with the late Roman decorative repertoire, used figures as well as animal, plant, fruit, flower and geometric motifs. Alongside this was the use of Christian imagery from the Old and New Testament. An example of the former is a roundel in the Städtischen Museum Simeonstift in Trier in Germany that has scenes from the life of Jacob. This is one of two in this particular collection and several are preserved elsewhere, including Athens, Berlin, London, Moscow, Paris and Prague. The bands which ring the scenes demonstrate the richness of Coptic textile ornament, while the colours, red for the base, with red, greens, yellow ochre and black, are an example of the vivid use of colour in Coptic textiles. Carbon 14 dating of a piece in a private collection has dated this group of textiles to between the eighth and tenth centuries.

New Testament scenes include the Annunciation, the Nativity, which is depicted on a linen fragment from Akmim dated to the fifth to sixth centuries in the Victoria and Albert Museum in London, and miracle scenes, including the raising of Lazarus. The Alpha and Omega appear on textiles, as does the symbol of the fish. Some of this imagery can be related to that preserved in Coptic sculpture. Other images are of praying saints, military saints, as well as animals and plants. A large hanging of the Virgin and Child flanked by angels, from the sixth century (now in the Cleveland Museum of Art), has the function of an icon, and is similar to wall-painting as found at Bawit.

Illustrated manuscripts

In common with the other Eastern Christian churches the Coptic Church had a flour-ishing tradition of illustrated manuscripts, many produced in monastery scriptoria. Several manuscripts survived in the Egyptian climate, including the well-known Nag Hammadi Gnostic codices, written on papyrus, whose preservation also extends to their bindings. Others too are of singular importance. The Glazier codex, named after William S. Glazier who acquired it in 1962, is in the Pierpont Morgan Library in New York (G. 67); it is a vellum codex of c.400, its text being part of the Acts of the Apostles written in an archaic Coptic dialect of Middle Egyptian proper. It survives with its original binding of wooden boards and has a tooled leather spine secured by wrapping bands with ornamental bone pieces. At the end of the book is a finispiece depicting a cross, which was common practice in early Christian books. But this is the particularly Egyp-tian ankh cross, which is shaped as a *tau* connected to a circle above it. A representative symbol of life, the upper part is derived from an Egyptian hieroglyph with this meaning. The cross is filled with interlace patterning, with a bird in centre of the circle, while others are perched at ends of the cross arms and peacocks are on either side below. The peacocks, like the bird at the centre of the circle, are pecking at branches. This repre-sents the Resurrection and the eternal life that its offers.

Monastic communities relied on their scriptoria for their spiritual, liturgical and other religious needs. Examples of monastic libraries are those in the Wadi Natrun (Scetis) monasteries between Alexandria and Cairo, the Monastery of St Shenoute, the White Monastery near present-day Sohag and the Monastery of St Michael at Hamouli in the Fayyum in Middle Egypt. Among the illustrated manuscripts are some with full-page illustrations. Frontispieces in ninth-to-tenth-century manuscripts sometimes have 'icons' of frontally-facing holy figures. An example is the frontispiece of a ninth-century manuscript containing the works of Shenoute from the White Monastery which shows the nursing Virgin flanked by angels, framed with an interlace band (now in New York, Pierpont Morgan Library, M. 612). This emphasizes the Incarnation and the humanity of Christ and is comparable to wall-paintings from the Monasteries of Bawit and Saqqara. Below the feet of the Virgin the scribe, or artist, Isaac has signed his name. The equestrian St Theodore, as defender of the faith, striking an enemy as the devil shown with a human head and the body of a serpent, appears in the frontispiece of an early tenth-century manuscript with hagiographical texts (in New York, Pierpont Morgan Library, M. 613). Manuscripts of this period are often decorated with marginal vegetal, animal and bird motifs. Similar motifs also appear calligraphically to form capital letters. Punctuation and paragraph marks are also used.

Manuscripts of the twelfth-to-fourteenth centuries reflect contact with Byzantine and other Eastern Christian manuscript traditions, including the evangelist portraits and other illustrations in New Testament books. An example is the Gospel book with an extensive cycle of scenes (in Paris, Bibliotèque Nationale, Copte 13), which was made in Damietta in northern Egypt between 1178 and 1180. Others balance Byzantine with secular Arab concerns. An example is the New Testament now divided between Cairo and Paris (Institut Cathlique Copte-Aabe 1/Cairo Coptic Museum Bibl. 94), produced in Cairo in 1249–50, which is written in Bohairic Coptic and Arabic. While its figurative imagery relates to Byzantine and other Eastern Christian book illumination, its ornamentation and aniconic imagery is more in keeping with Arabic books, including Qur'an manuscripts, and this trend continues through the Mamlūk and Ottoman periods. A manuscript copy was made as late as 1733, which is now in the British Library in London (BL. Or. 1316), the line of descent from the Cairene New Testament mediated by way of engravings in Tempesta's printed Arabic Gospels in Rome of 1590.

The Nubian Church

Geographically Nubia is defined as the area between the First Cataract of the Nile at Aswan to beyond the Third Cataract. This comprised the three medieval kingdoms of Nobadia in the north, Makouria and Alwa to the south. Nobadia was taken over by Makouria, the latter's capital being Old Dongola, between the mid-seventh and the early eighth centuries. The extensive archaeological work at Old Dongola suggests its cultural hegemony, but as more work is done to the south this assumption may change. Nubia was officially evangelized from Byzantium in the sixth century, through the intervention of the Emperor Justinian and his Miaphysite wife Theodora, and initially pagan and Kushite burial customs coexisted with the Christian. Remaining independent from Muslim rule, the Nubian kingdoms retained their Christian identity until their decline in the thirteenth to the fifteenth centuries. This independence was based on the twin authorities of the royal courts, with the administration they generated, and the church hierarchy. The latter, under the jurisdiction of the patriarchate of Alexandria, comprised thirteen recorded sees, of which the bishoprics of Kurte, Qasr Ibrim, Faras, Sais, and Old Dongola, as well as that probably at Soba East, the capital of Alwa, were the most important. It is not surprising, therefore, that Nubia retained artistic and cultural, including architectural and iconographical, links with Byzantium and Egypt, as well as the Holy Land, with the use of Greek, Coptic and Old Nubian inscriptions and texts, although the distinctively Nubian characteristics should not be underestimated.

The building of the Aswan high dam prompted rescue archaeological work by national and international missions sponsored by UNESCO which led to major discoveries in northern Nubia in the early 1960s. This was followed by archaeological exploration by missions in central and southern Nubia, as well as ongoing work at the site of Qasr Ibrim in the southernmost part of Egypt known as Lower Nubia. Archaeological work is continuing to publish finds from excavations already undertaken, explore unknown sites, as well as to refine the chronology and relationship between the architectural and artistic production of the three kingdoms.

Architecture

Early churches ran on an east–west axis, with a narthex at the west end, probably used for penitents, which was discontinued after the seventh century. They had flat wooden roofs, replaced in later architecture with vaulted brick roof, often with a central cupola. The baptistery is invariably located in the south-east room in churches where there are three chambers at the east end. In larger churches it usually occupies the room to the south of the sanctuary. Alternative locations for a baptistery are an external structure or another internal chamber. The depth of fonts in early churches suggests that they allowed for the total immersion of adults.

A main feature of Nubian church architecture is its block-like character, the rectangular shape belying the internal arrangement of space. The classic Nubian plan is divided into nine sections. At the east end are sacristies flanking the main sanctuary; both the central area and the west end are also tripartite. Some of the earliest churches were accommodated within pharaonic temples, of which preserved examples date to between the sixth and eleventh centuries. Of purpose-built church architecture, the basilica was the most commonly used plan in the early period, invariably with three aisles. Cut stone was the most common material used, brick being rare in early churches except in the more southern areas (Upper Nubia). Generally speaking, the largest churches are the earliest ones, church architecture having been reduced in size proportionally to the decline of institutionalized Christianity by the fifteenth century. The largest church in Nobadia is the basilica at Qasr Ibrim, datable to the late seventh century. It and its relatives have been described as most likely to have served as the cathedrals of the region. Its plan (Figure 19.10), including the internal apse, is of a common early Christian type which would have been adopted via Egypt, although built of local materials, stone and brick. In the case of Qasr Ibrim, the building is dressed with reused stone blocks from the Kushite period. The nave is flanked by two side aisles, with the narthex to west. It has carved stone lintels, cornices, capitals and grilles.

During the 'classic' period of Nubian architecture from the eighth century to *c*.1200 an indigenous feature is the passageway linking the central apse chamber to the side chapels on either side. This was partly necessitated by the introduction of the curving seats in the main apse ('tribune' or *synthronon*), with the elevated bishop's seat at the top. This called for the extension of the main sanctuary (*haikal*) into the nave and the replacement of the altar to the west. A screen (*hijab*) cut off the nave from this extended sanctuary area (*presbyterium*). While some *synthronons* were of cut stone, most were of whitewashed mud brick. The narthex at the west end had been replaced by a tripartite set of rooms, the central one of which was the only one to give access to the nave, an arrangement that was used consistently up to the fifteenth century. This had already, in the early Nubian period, been a feature of churches within 20 km north and south of Faras, giving a 'cross-in-rectangle' type of plan with cupolae, more likely from Near Eastern, Byzantine, architecture than Coptic, with galleries, perhaps for the use of female worshippers. This structure, based on the central nave with pillars and a central cupola, evolving more generally from the eleventh century, saw the development of the central nave section of the church, with the main entry points through doors on the north and south sides. Architectural decoration is far less frequent in the interior of buildings than in the earlier ones.

Rescue archaeology since the Aswan dam rescue project uncovered several more churches in Makouria and Alwa which do not conform to the typology of Lower Nubia as established by W. Y. Adams. Indeed it has been noted that the reverse seems to occur in Makouria, where the early predominance of the centrally planned structure evolved into the use of the basilica supported on granite columns. The large sixth-century church known as Building X at Old Dongola was built of brick on a cross-in-rectangle plan, with a centrally planned naos. It was replaced in the early seventh century by the church, suggested to have been the cathedral, known as the Church of the Stone Pavement. After the destruction caused by Arab raids is the early seventh century this church was rebuilt as a domed basilica, drawing on Byzantine and Syrian inspiration. Among other major churches in Makouria is the Church of the Granite Columns at Old Dongola, probably of the later seventh century, rebuilt on the site of the Old Church. Here a local plan is employed, with a cruciform central section enclosed within a five-aisled basilica, its side aisles divided by grey granite columns, with a narthex to the west, and pasto-phoria (sacristies) at the east end linked with a corridor behind the apse. A cruciform baptismal font occupied a side chapel on the south side and there was a *synthronon* in the eastern apse, and an altar screen. Its plan, combining the five aisles with a cruciform central section, makes it a likely candidate as the model for the cathedral at Faras. Churches excavated at Alwa indicate that prior to the ninth century they were mostly basilical, with three or five aisles, made of red brick, and without *synthronons*.

From the thirteenth century churches were built of fired or mud brick, and simplified to a square hall shape on the four-pillar system, reducing the division between the clergy and the congregation. An example of the reduced, domed basilica is that in the small village church of 'Abd el-Qadir in Nobada, which was decorated with wall-paintings and was probably built in the mid-thirteenth century. With the size of the congregation drastically reduced, liturgy underwent changes and churches dispensed with many of the liturgical furnishings formerly used, including the *synthronon*. Although the cathedral churches of the early and classic periods in the major centres of Qasr Ibrim, Faras, as well as the churches in Old Dongola continued to be used, they suffered as a result of the Mamlūk invasions of the later thirteenth century.

Wall-painting and other arts

Churches were decorated with wall-paintings, but few have survived from the earliest churches. The earliest wall-paintings discovered are at Abu Oda, from the seventh century; they are followed by those at Wadi es-Sebua, Faras and 'Abd el-Qadir as well as the church at Abdallah Nirqi and Naqa el Oqba and elsewhere. The wall-paintings at Faras are the best known of those preserved from medieval Nubia. British excavations had been undertaken at the monastic site, on the west bank of the Nile between Egypt and the Republic of Sudan, by F. L. Griffiths in 1910–12. But it was the work by the Polish Centre of Mediterranean Archaeology during the first half of the 1960s that uncovered the cathedral and bishop's palace, revealing nearly two hundred wall-paintings on the walls of the cathedral and nearby bishops' tombs. These are now divided between the Sudan National Museum in Khartoum and the National Museum in Warsaw. The apse was crowned with the Christ in Majesty with the apocalyptic beings with, below, the Mother of God with the Apostles, and below that the painted equivalent of the already-mentioned eagle/dove frieze that had decorated the earlier church here. The scene of the Nativity was painted on the north side, and the head of Christ and four Evangelists were on the south wall. Equestrian saints, including George, were also depicted. One painting, dated to 1092, shows the three Hebrews in the fiery furnace, each named, protected by St Michael.

There are also other images of the Virgin and Child and several portraits of saints, royal personages, bishops and eparchs, the latter being those officials who ruled at Qasr Ibrim on behalf of the king and held control of defence and commercial relations with Egypt. The portrait of Bishop Marianos protected by the Virgin and Child, dateable to c.1005–39, is reproduced here (Figure 19.11). Although the name of this particular bishop is not included in the list of bishops from Faras, he can be identified through his stele which was found at Qasr Ibrim and which designates him as the Bishop of Pakhoras. He must have died during a visit to Qasr Ibrim. Characteristic of the portrait is the rich colouring and ornamentation of his episcopal garments. Four styles were identified at Faras by Kazimierz Michałowski: the violet style of the early eighth to mid-ninth century; the white between the mid-ninth to early tenth century; the red and yellow style attributed to the tenth century, and the multicoloured work of the late tenth to early twelfth century. A final phase is identifiable from the thirteenth century. These categorizations have been refined by subsequent work, including that at Kom H and at the Monastery of the Holy Trinity at Old Dongola.

Unlike ordinary mortals, who were simply buried wrapped in a shroud, ecclesiastics were buried in their robes with objects pertinent to their office. One example is Bishop Timotheus, who was buried in the north crypt of the cathedral at Faras in the late fourteenth century wearing ecclesiastical robes and with his cross staff and other objects (now in the British Museum) and scrolls bearing testimonial letters from the Patriarch of Alexandria in Coptic and Arabic (now in Cairo).

Early churches display extensive stone and wood carving, using floral motifs as well as some Christian symbols, including the cross and birds. An example is the section of sandstone frieze from the first cathedral at Faras, built in the early seventh century, and now in the British Museum (Figure 19.12), where a cross is depicted immediately above twenty-four birds, eagles or doves, with outstretched wings standing next to an altar between columns and looking towards the apse. Traces of a blue ground indicate that the frieze was originally painted. Altars in early Nubian churches were located within the central sanctuary, and were most likely of wood; of these only the sockets remain, showing that they would have been raised on four wooden legs. Some altars had marble tops, imported from the Aegean, similar to those in the monasteries of the Wadi Natrun in Egypt. Sculpture in the round is rarely found, although columns and column bases and capitals are common. During the sixth and most of the seventh century the sandstone capitals from Nobadia are Greco-Roman in inspiration while those of Makouria and Alwa, generally carved of hard stone, are in lower relief. Stone was commonly used for screens and window grilles, an example of the latter appearing in the Church of the Granite Columns in Old Dongola, ornamented with crosses and geometric patterns. Floor mosaics made of pebbles to form geometric shapes and crosses are known in a few churches in Old Dongola and Meinarti of the seventh to the turn of the eighth centuries. Woodwork was also used, not only for roof construction but also screens, including the *hijab*, the main sanctuary screen, as in Coptic churches. It was also used for lintels, altars, stairs and tribunes. It has been suggested that this wood was imported, as its use was reduced after the Arab conquests of the early seventh century.

Old Nubian, written in Coptic script, was the everyday language, and was also used for religious and liturgical texts, alongside Greek, in monasteries and churches. Papyri and parchment have been well preserved at the site of Qasr Ibrim. Pectoral crosses, terracotta figurines and ceramic 'icons' with relief representations of saints have also been found in excavations in Nubia.

Pottery from the north is exemplified by the 'Dongola ware' of the ninth to tenth centuries. Particularly characteristic of this ware are bowls with white or cream buff slip decorated with animals or Christian symbols. In the south, the 'Soba ware' from the kingdom of Alwa is known for its chalices, bowls and other vessels, the exterior and sometimes the interior of which are decorated with dots, rosettes and crosses as well as a variety of patterns, painted over a brown, red or cream slip. Some use animal motifs, such as lions, gazelles, frogs and birds, as well as the human face. Some of these motifs are copies of designs found in wall-paintings. Ibn el Aswani wrote of the prosperity of Alwa when he visited it in the late tenth century. Survey and excavation work at Soba since the 1980s, uncovering both churches and palatial structures, as well as the fine pottery, including chalices, bowls and other vessels, suggests its likely prosperity. Its continuing prosperity is attested by the fine imported Islamic glass, probably of the fourteenth century.

The Ethiopian Orthodox *Täwahǝdo* Church

Ethiopian Christianity, exceptionally, straddles the African and Semitic worlds. But Christianity in Ethiopia, adopted in the fourth century by the Aksumite king Ezana, also retained links with other Eastern Christian areas as well as with western Europe. Christianity purportedly came to Ethiopia with two brothers from Syria, with its first and subsequent bishops appointed by Coptic patriarchs from the Coptic church of Alexandria. The first bishop, Frumentius, one of the brothers, was a contemporary of St Antony; monasticism had developed in Ethiopia by the sixth century and, as in Egypt, became a hallmark of art and culture. The holy man remained an influential spiritual force, contributing to the spread of Christianity in the early centuries as well as acting as a powerful reminder of the traditional roots of Ethiopian religion at times of political and religious change, such as that experienced in the fourteenth century. Much is lost of Ethiopia's heritage, as a result of the destruction by the Falasha Queen Yodit in the tenth century, and in the sixteenth to seventeenth centuries, and during the invasions by the Muslim leader from eastern Ethiopia, Aḥmad ibn-Ibrahim al-Ghazi (Ahmäd Grañ in Ethiopian) in the 1530s. He was eventually defeated and killed in 1543 with the aid of the Portuguese, ushering in an era of Jesuit influence. Home of the western legend of the Christian ruler Prester John since the early fourteenth century, Ethiopia had long been sought as an ally by western and other eastern Christians as an ally against Islam.

Monuments and religious buildings

Kingship was crucially important to Ethiopian Christian society. Early cultural activity, until the tenth century, was based at Aksum in the north of the country. Aksum was a prosperous trading centre linking the Mediterranean with India, as its gold coinage attests. Early stone stelae (obelisks) survive from before 400, carved in storeys or registers, with blind windows. These are believed to mark the burial places of kings. The sacred Solomonic lineage, traced to the house of Solomon and David, remained unbroken, aside from the period of the Zag^{w}e dynasty (from the Lasta province) in the twelfth century CE to the time of the Emperor Haile Selassie, overthrown in 1974. According to Ethiopian tradition, the first king of Ethiopia, Mənəlik, was the son of Solomon and the Queen of Sheba (the Ethiopian Queen Makeda), who is believed to have travelled to Jerusalem to see his father and to have brought back the true Ark of the Covenant. It is still claimed to reside in the Cathedral of St Mary of Zion in Aksum.

This is the basis of the several Judaic features of Ethiopic Christianity, under which a symbolic replica of the Ark of the Covenant, known as the *tabot*, is in every church. This takes the form of a consecrated stone tablet in a wooden chest. These chests are carved with crosses and several are also inscribed with the name of the thirteenth-century Zag^{w}e ruler, Lalibäla. It is the tablet of stone, rather than the structure of the church in which it is housed, that is the focus of consecration. The tablet is laid out on the chest for the celebration of the Eucharist and is always covered in the presence of the laity. Other Judaic elements include a form of the observance of the Sabbath and circumcision. Jerusalem and the holy places of Christ's life in the Holy Land remain of crucial importance. Throughout history pilgrims have travelled to the Holy Land from Ethiopia and desired the building of Jerusalem in Ethiopia, particularly at the site of Lalibäla, named after the ruler. The names of the twelfth-century rock-cut churches of Lalibäla replicate after individual holy sites, including Golgotha, the Holy Sepulchre and the site of the Nativity. The river at Lalibäla is named Yrdanos after the River Jordan.

The Church and the court working together were the main stimuli for artistic production. Monasticism remained at the heart of Ethiopian Christianity. The great centres of early Ethiopian Christian culture and learning were founded in the north, notably those monasteries founded by the Nine Saints in Tigray which included the well-known monastery of Däbra Damo. The mid- to late thirteenth century saw monasteries being founded further south, such as the island monastery at Lake Hayq at Amhara (Däbrä Hayq 'Əstifanos). Däbrä Asbo at Shawa (later called Däbrä Libanos from the mid-fifteenth century) was established by St Täklä Haymanot of Shawa (d. 1313). Later the area of Lake Ṭana was developed as a monastic centre, mostly in the first half of the fourteenth century; the Monasteries of Däbrä Däga 'Əstifanos and Däbrä Gwegweben were established on its eastern shore. One of the great courtly centres in Ethiopian Christian history was developed at Gondar, which flourished between the mid-seventeenth and mid-eighteenth centuries. At this time the activities of Church and state were entwined, producing an unprecedented wealth of art, culture and scholarship. The rulers of Gondar built stone castles, built palaces and founded new churches and monasteries. They even rebuilt the cathedral of Aksum, which had been destroyed during the invasions of the 1530s, in the rectangular Gondar style.

Churches in Ethiopia were usually built of mud brick, with the emphasis on the sanctuary in which the *tabot* was displayed. The predominant plan, especially in the post-medieval period, was a tripartite plan, in which there was a central square sanctuary surrounded by two circles. The roof was thatched. Churches were decorated with paintings, especially over the altar. The paintings were frequently on linen, and included donor portraits and a record of the donation, and were attached to the walls. The richness of the churches of Shawa, for example, was described shortly before their destruction by the sixteenth-century Portuguese priest Francisco Alvares. Concerning earlier architecture, of which less is known, recent scholarship has emphasized the connection with and influence of early Christian architecture elsewhere, including the use of the basilica plan, of local materials and imported marble fragments in the building. The Cathedral of St Mary at Aksum, for example, was modelled on Jerusalemite architecture of the fourth century.

Manuscripts and religious objects

Many manuscripts that were produced in the monastic and court scriptoria have been destroyed; those that remain date largely from the fifteenth century onward. These include service books, Gospels, psalters, Apocalypses and devotional books with texts of the Miracles of the Virgin, written in the classical Ethiopian language of Ge'ez, a Semitic language. While the earliest preserved Ethiopian manuscript, the Abba Garima Gospels of the late twelfth to early thirteenth centuries, is not illustrated, other Gospel books are extensively decorated. Some of this decoration can be related to other Eastern Christian traditions. Characteristic of Ethiopian illumination is the *harag*, the system of interlacing bands which frame the page, coloured in reds, greens, yellows and grey-blues. These were particularly finely painted in manuscripts of the fourteenth and fifteenth centuries, especially at the Monastery of Gunda Gundi in Agame, the centre of the 'Əstifanosite movement in the fifteenth century. The designs were simplified thereafter, to undergo a revival in the late nineteenth and early twentieth centuries. The *harag* bears a similarity to Coptic and Syriac as well as Byzantine illumination.

Decorated Eusebian canon tables head Ethiopian Gospel books, especially those of the fourteenth and fifteenth centuries, in common with other Eastern Christian Gospel books. Those from the Monastery of Gunda Gundi can be differentiated by the use they make of a more architectural framing device. Ethiopian Gospel books also conform with Eastern Christian practice in including portraits of each Evangelist, as well as scenes from the life of Christ. One such example is a large Gospel book in the British Library (London B.L. Or. 510). The manuscript was written in the court at Gondar in 1664–5, in the official Gwelh script, probably for the Emperor Yohannes I and the Empress Sabla Wangel. Its illustrations are painted in the style known as the 'First Gondarene style', which uses clear, bright colours, especially yellow, orange-red and blue, on the figures' garments; the figures are animated by their gestures and eye contact with one another (see fol. 51r, the Healing of the Two Blind Men, illustrating Matt. 9: 27–31, in Figure 19.13). The arrangement of the figures and the neutral ground is also influenced by western woodcuts, specifically those of the Arabic Gospels, the *Evangelium arabicum*, printed in Rome in 1591 for Pope Gregory XIII.

By introducing the cult of the Mother of God into Ethiopia the Emperor Zär'a Ya'qob intended to create a focus of Ethiopian spirituality at a time of internal rupture (caused by the attempt to reduce practice of Sabbath worship), in 1441. The reading of the text of Miracles of Mary (*Taamra Maryam*), which had been translated into Ge'ez from Arabic under his father Emperor Dawit (r. 1382–1413), was introduced into the liturgy at this time. This stimulated the drive for images of the Virgin in both icon and manuscript painting. The most famous icon painter of the fifteenth century is Fere Seyon. His signature on an icon at Däga 'Əstifanos enables further panels to be attributed to him, including those in the collection of the Institute of Ethiopian Studies in Addis Ababa. The formula of the image of the Virgin and Child flanked by the archangels Michael and Gabriel is adapted in each case to accommodate accompanying scenes and saints. Elements of the iconography can be examined with reference to Zär'a Ya'qob's own theological writing on the Virgin.

Another shift is the introduction of western elements, including a sprig of flowers held by the Virgin in one of the Addis Ababa panels, a motif borrowed from Italian panel painting. Zär'a Ya'qob was determined to prevent the 'Əstifanosite movement from undermining the Church-state that he had fostered. Devotion to the Virgin, however, overrode spiritual and political differences, as the pictorial imagery shows. For example, St Antony with the Virgin and Child (Figure 19.14), is to be found in a manuscript dated after 1480 from Gunda Gundi, now in the New York Public Library (Spencer Collection 7) of the Lives of two saints of the movement, 'Əstifanos and Abakerazun. Later images were added to the repertoire. One such was the Virgin of Santa Maria Maggiore in Rome, introduced into Ethiopia by Portuguese Jesuits in the later seventeenth century, and thereafter frequently reproduced there.

Of the liturgical objects kept in Ethiopian churches, crosses are especially famed. Made of silver bronze or copper, some were, and still are, for processional use, and during ceremonies are held aloft on poles on to which coloured fabric is attached. An example of a processional cross is one now in the Walters Art Gallery in Baltimore (no. 54.2894, Figure 19.15), probably dating to the fifteenth century. Its four-lobed shape contains a repeating design of small crosses with serpents at the edges. The pierced work, enabling silhouetting against natural or candle light, was particularly effective and appropriate for processional use. The feature of the projecting semicircular arms at the base of the cross also occur on a processional cross given by the Emperor Zär'a Ya'qob to the monastery at Däbrä Nagwadgwad in Tagwela in central Ethiopia. The serpents represent wisdom and can be associated with the serpent made of brass by Moses. The cross is made of bronze that was cast according to the lost wax technique, whereby the image is first made in wax, then coated with clay to form a mould into which the molten metal is poured, replacing the wax. Other crosses were used as hand crosses for blessing by the clergy. Pilgrims and monks in particular wore crosses around the neck. Crosses display interlace designs not unlike those of Coptic woven leather crosses made in monasteries in Egypt to the present day. These designs are also repeated on the more widely-available wooden crosses.

Further reading

The Syrian Orthodox Church

Baer, E. (1998) *Ayyubid Metalwork with Christian Images*. Leiden: Brill.

Brock, S. P. (ed.) (2001) *The Hidden Pearl: The Syrian Orthodox Church and its Ancient Aramaic Heritage*, vols 1–2 [of 4], edited with the assistance of D. G. K. Taylor. Rome: Trans World Film Italia. See also: S. P. Brock (2002) Some Basic Annotation to *"The Hidden Pearl": The Syrian Orthodox Church and its Ancient Aramaic Heritage*, I-III (Rome, 2001), *Hugoye: Journal of Syriac Studies* 5, 1. http://syrcom.cua.edu/Hugoye/

Bell, G. L. (1982) *The Churches and Monasteries of the ṬurʿAbdin*, with introduction and notes by M. Mundell Mango. London: Pindar Press.

de la Croix, A.-M. and Zabbal, F. (2003) *Icônes arabes: art chrétien du Levant*. Exposition présentée à l'Institut du Monde Arabe du 6 mai au 17 août 2003. Paris: Éditions Grégoriennes.

Dodd, E. Cruikshank (2001) *The Frescoes of Mar Musa al-Habashi: A Study in Medieval Painting in Syria*. Toronto: Pontifical Institute of Medieval Studies.

—— (2004) *Medieval Painting in the Lebanon*. Wiesbaden: Reichert.

Hollerweger, H. (1999) *Tur Abdin: Lebendiges Kulturerbe – Living Cultural Heritage – Canli Kultur Mirasi*. Linz: Friends of Turabdin.

Hunt, L.-A. (1991) A woman's prayer to St Sergios in Latin Syria: interpreting a thirteenth-century icon at Mount Sinai. *Byzantine and Modern Greek Studies* 15: 96–145. Reprinted in *Byzantium, Eastern Christendom and Islam: Art at the Crossroads of the Medieval Mediterranean*, vol. 2. London: Pindar Press, 2000.

—— (2005) Orientalischer Christen: Kunst und Kultur zur Zeit der Kreuzfahrer. In A. Wieczorek, M. Fansa and H. Meller (eds.) *Saladin und die Kreuzfahrer*, Catalogue of an exhibition held 21 October 2005 to 5 November 2006 in the Landesmuseum für Vogeschichte, and other venues. Mainz am Rhein: von Zabern.

—— (2008) Eastern Christian Art and Culture in the Ayyubid and Early Mamluk Periods: cultural convergence between Jerusalem, Greater Syria and Egypt. In S. Auld and R. Hillenbrand (eds.) *Ayyubid Jerusalem: The Holy City in Context, 1187–1250*. London: Altajir World of Islam Festival Trust.

Immerzeel, M. (2004) Holy horsemen and crusader banners: equestrian saints in wall paintings in Lebanon and Syria. *Eastern Christian Art* 1: 29–60.

Leroy, J. (1964) *Les Manuscrits syriaques à peintures conserveés dans les bibliothèques d'Europe et d'Orient*. Paris: P. Geuthner.

Lossley, E. (2003) *The Architecture and Literature of the Bema in Fourth- to Sixth-Century Churches.* Patrimoine Syriaque. Kaslik: Parole d'Orient.

Mundell Mango, M. (1986) *Silver from Early Byzantium: The Kaper Koraon and Related Treasures.* Published in conjunction with the exhibition 'Silver Treasures from Early Byzantium', Walters Art Museum, Baltimore, 18 April to 17 August 1986, and on the occasion of the 17th International Byzantine Congress, Dumbarton Oaks/Georgetown University, 3–8 August 1986.

Palmer, A. (1990) *Monk and Mason on the Tigris Frontier: The Early History of Ṭur ʿAbdin.* Cambridge: Cambridge University Press.

Peña, I. (1997) *The Christian Art of Byzantine Syria.* London: Garnet Publishing.

Sader, W. (1997) *Painted Churches and Rock Cut Chapels of Lebanon.* Beirut: Dar Sader.

Schmidt, A. and Westphalen, S. (2005) *Christliche Wandmalerein in Syrien: Qara und das Kloster Mar Yakub.* Wiesbaden: Reichert.

Tchalenko, G. (1953) *Villages antiques de la Syrie du Nord: le massif du Bélus à l'époque romaine*, 3 vols. Paris: P. Geuthner.

The Armenian Church

Carswell, J. and Dowsett, C. J. F. (1972) *Kütahya Tiles and Pottery from the Armenian Cathedral of St James, Jerusalem*, 2 vols. Oxford: Clarendon Press.

Der Nersessian, S. (1978) *Armenian Art.* London: Thames and Hudson.

—— (1993) *Miniature Painting in the Armenian Kingdom of Cilicia from the Twelfth to the Fourteenth Century*, 2 vols. Washington, DC: Dumbarton Oaks.

Documents of Armenian Architecture/Documenti di architettura armena, 20 vols. (1968–89). Milan: Milan Polytechnic and the Armenian Academy of Sciences.

Gantzhorn, V. (1991) *The Christian Oriental Carpet.* Cologne: Taschen.

Kévorkian, R. H. (1996) *Arménie entre Orient et Occident, trois milles ans de civilisation.* Catalogue of the exhibition, Bibliothèque Nationale de France, 12 June to 20 October 1996. Paris: Bibliothèque Nationale de France.

Maranci, C. (2001) *Medieval Armenian Architecture: Constructions of Race and Nation.* Louvain: Peeters.

Mathews, T. F. and Sanjian, A. K. (1991) *Armenian Gospel Iconography: The Tradition of the Glajor Gospel.* Washington, DC: Dumbarton Oaks.

Mathews, T. F. and Wieck R. S. (eds.) (1994) *Treasures in Heaven: Armenian Illuminated Manuscripts.* Catalogue of the exhibition, Pierpont Morgan Library, New York, 4 May to 7 August 1994. New York: Pierpont Morgan Library.

Mathews, T. (1995) *Art and Architecture in Byzantium and Armenia: liturgical and exegetical approaches.* Aldershot: Ashgate.

Narkiss, B. (ed.) (1979) *Armenian Art Treasures of Jerusalem*, edited in collaboration with M. E. Stone and A. K. Sanjian. Jerusalem: Massada Press. Repr. Phaidon, London, 1989.

Nersessian, V. (2001) *Treasures from the Ark: 1700 Years of Armenian Christian Art.* London: British Library.

The Coptic Church

Badawy, A. (1978) *Coptic Archaeology: The Art of the Christian Egyptians from the Late Antique to the Middle Ages.* Cambridge, Mass.: MIT Press.

Bolman, E. (ed.) (2002) *Monastic Visions: Wall Paintings in the Monastery of St. Antony at the Red Sea.* New Haven, Conn. and London: Yale University Press.

Capuani, M. (2002) *Christian Egypt: Coptic Art and Monuments through Two Millennia.* Edited and introduced by G. Gabra, and with contributions from O. F. A. Meinardus, M.-H. Rutschowscaya. Cairo: American University in Cairo Press.

Clédat, J. (1999) *Le Monastère et la nécropole de Baouit.* Notes mises en oeuvre et editées par D. Bénazeth et M.-H. Rutschowscaya. Cairo: Institut français d'archéologie orientale.

Depuydt, L. (1993) *Catalogue of Coptic Manuscripts in the Pierpont Morgan Library.* Louvain: Peeters.

Effenberger, E. and von Falck, M. (1996) *Ägypten, Schätze aus dem Wüstensand: Kunst und Kultur der Christen am Nil.* Catalogue of the exhibition held at vom Gustav Lübcke Museum der Stadt Hamm, 16 June to 13 October 1996. Wiesbaden: Reichert.

Gabra, G. (1993, 1999) *Cairo: The Coptic Museum and Old Churches.* Cairo: Egyptian International Publishing Co.

—— (2002) *Coptic Monasteries: Egypt's Monastic Art and Architecture.* Cairo and New York: American University in Cairo.

Grossman, P. (1989) *Abu Mena* I: *Die Gruftkirche und die Gruft.* Mainz am Rhein: von Zabern.

—— (2002) *Christliche Architektur in Ägypten.* Leiden: Brill.

—— (2004) *Abu Mena* II: *Das Baptisterium.* Mainz am Rhein: von Zabern.

Grossmann, P., Godlewski, W. and Severin, H.-G. (1991) Architectural elements of churches. In A. S. Atiya (ed. in chief) *The Coptic Encyclopedia*, vol. 1 (pp. 194–221). New York: Macmillan.

Hunt, L.-A. (1998) *Byzantium, Eastern Christendom and Islam: Art at the Crossroads of the Medieval Mediterranean*, vol. 1. London: Pindar Press.

—— (2007) Artistic Interchange in Old Cairo in the Thirteenth to Early Fourteenth Century: The Role of Painted and Carved Icons. In C. Hourihane (ed), *Interactions: Artistic Interchange between the Eastern and Western Worlds in the Medieval Period.* Index of Christian Art, Department of Art & Archaeology Princeton University in association with Pennsylvania State University. Pennsylvania State University Press: University Park, PA.

Immerzeel, M., Langen, L. and van Moorsel, P. (1994) *Catalogue general du musée copte: The Icons.* Cairo: Supreme Council of Antiquities Press/Department of Early Christian Art, Leiden University.

Innéemee, K. C. et al. (1998) New discoveries in the Al-'Adra Church of Dayr Al-Suryan in the Wadi al-Natrun. *Mitteilungen zur christlichen Archäologie* 4: 79–103.

Innémee, K. C., Van Rompay, L. and Sobczynski, E. (1999) Deir al-Surian (Egypt): its wall-paintings, wall-texts, and manuscripts. *Hugoye: Journal of Syriac Studies* 2(2), online.

Innémee, K. C. and Van Rompay, L. (2002) Deir al-Surian (Egypt): new discoveries of 2001–2002. *Hugoye: Journal of Syriac Studies* 5(2), online.

Kendrick, A. F. (1920, 1921, 1922) *Catalogue of Textiles from Burying-Grounds in Egypt*, 1: *Greco-Roman Period*; 2: *Period of Transition and of Christian Emblems*; 3: *Coptic Period.* London: Victoria and Albert Museum.

Krause, M. et al. (ed.) (1998) *Ägypten in spätantik-christlicher Zeit: Einführung in die koptische Kultur.* Wiesbaden: Reichert.

Leroy, J. (1974) *Les Manuscripts coptes et coptes-arabes illustrés* Paris: P. Geuthner.

van Loon, G. J. M. (1999) *The Gate of Heaven: Wall Paintings with Old Testament Scenes in the Altar Room and the Ḥûrus of Coptic Churches.* Istanbul: Nederlands Historisch-Archaeologisch Instituut te Istanbul.

Nauerth, C. (1978) *Koptische Textilkunst im spätantiken Ägypten.* Trier: Spee-Verlag.

Rutschowscaya, M.-H. and Bénazeth, D. (eds.) (2000) *L'Art Copte en Égypte: 2000 ans de Christianisme.* Catalogue of the exhibition held at Institut du monde arabe, Paris, 15 May to 3 September 2000. Paris: Institut du monde arabe/Éditions Gallimard.

Severin, G. and H.-G. (1987) *Marmor vom heiligen Menas.* Frankfurt am Main: Liebieghaus.

Skalova, Z. and Gabra, G. (2003) *Icons in the Nile Valley.* Cairo: Egyptian International Publishing Company/Longman.

Thomas, T. K. (1990) *Textiles from Medieval Egypt 300–1300*, with a glossary by D. G. Harding. Pittsburgh, Pa.: Carnegie Museum of Natural History.

——— (2000) *Late Antique Egyptian Funerary Sculpture: Images from This World and the Next.* Princeton, NJ: Princeton University Press.

The Nubian Church

Adams, W. Y. (1965) Architectural evolution of the Nubian Church, 500–1400 AD. *Journal of the American Research Center in Egypt* 4: 87–139.

——— (1977) *Nubia: Corridor to Africa.* London: Allen Lane.

——— (1991) Nubian church art. In A. S. Atiya (ed. in chief) *The Coptic Encyclopedia*, vol. 6 (pp. 1811–12). New York: Macmillan.

Dinkler, E. (ed.) (1970) *Kunst und Geschichte Nubiens in Christlicher Zeit.* Recklinghausen: A. Bongers.

Gartkiewicz, P. M. (1982) An introduction to the history of Nubian church architecture. In S. Jakobielski (ed.) *Nubia Christiana*, vol. 1. Warsaw: Akademia theologii katolickiej.

——— (1990) *The Cathedral in Old Dongola and its Antecedents.* Warsaw: Paänstwowe Wylawn.

——— (1992) Remarks on the cathedral at Qasr Ibrim. In J. M. Plumley (ed.) *Nubian Studies: Proceedings of the Symposium for Nubian Studies, Selwyn College, 1978.* Warminster: Aris and Phillips.

Godlewski, W. (1994) Christian Nubia: after the Nubian Campaign. *Nubia Thirty Years Later*, Society for Nubian Studies Eighth International Conference, pre-publication of main papers, assembled by F. Geus, Lille, July 1994. http://www.arkamani.org/arkamani-library/christian/godlewski.htm, website of *Arkamani: Sudan Journal of Archaeology and Anthropology.*

Grossmann, P. (1991) Nubian architecture. In A. S. Atiya (ed. in chief) *The Coptic Encyclopedia*, vol. 6 (pp. 1807–11). New York: Macmillan.

Jakobielski, S. (1961) Nubian Christian architecture. *Zeitschrift für ägyptische Sprache und Altertumskunde* 108: 33–48.

Kjølbye-Biddle, B. (1994) The small early church in Nubia with reference to the church on the point at Qasr Ibrim. In K. Painter (ed.) *Churches Built in Ancient Times: Recent Studies in Early Christian Archaeology.* London: Society of Antiquaries of London.

Martens-Czarencka, M. (1982) *Les Éléments décoratifs sur les peintures de la cathédrale de Faras: Faras VII.* Warsaw: Éditions scientifiques de Pologne.

——— (1996) Wall paintings from the monastery on Kom H at Old Dongola. In S. Emmel, M. Krause, S. Richter and S. Schaten (eds) *Akten des 6. Internationalen Koptologenkongresses* (pp. 273–84). Münster, 21–6 July 1996.

Michałowski, K. (1966) *Faras: Centre artistique de la Nubie chrétienne.* Leiden: Nederlands Instituut voor het Nabije Ooster.

——— (1967) *Faras, Die Kathedrale aus dem Wüstensand.* Zurich and Cologne: Benziger.

——— (1974) *Faras: Wall Paintings in the Collection of the National Museum in Warsaw.* Warsaw: Wydawnictwo Artystyczno-Graficzne.

Taylor, J. H. (1991) *Egypt and Nubia.* London: British Museum Press.

Van Moorsel, P., Jacquet, J. and Schneider, H. (1975) *The Central Church of Abdallah Nirqi*. Leiden: Brill.

Welsby, D. A. (1992) Archaeology and history: their contribution to our understanding of medieval Nubia. In *Études Nubiennes, Actes du VIIe Congrès international d'études nubiennes*. Geneva: Bonnet.

—— (2002) *The Medieval Kingdoms of Nubia: Pagans, Christians and Muslims along the Middle Nile*. London: British Museum Press.

Welsby, D. A. and Anderson, J. R. (eds.) (2004) *Sudan: Ancient Treasures, an Exhibition of Recent Discoveries from the Sudan National Museum*. London: British Museum Press.

The Ethiopian Church

L'Arche éthiopienne: art chrétien d'Éthiopie (2000) Catalogue of the exhibition, Pavilion des Arts, Paris, 27 September 2000 to 7 January 2001 and the Fundació Caixo de Girona, Girona, 23 January to 31 March 2001 (Commissariat B. Riottot El-Habib, J. Mercier). Paris: Paris Musées; Girona: Fundació Caixa de Girona.

Chojnacki, S. (1983) *Major Themes in Ethiopian Painting: Indigenous Developments, the Influence of Foreign Models and their Adaptation from the 13th to the 19th Century*. Wiesbaden: F. Steiner.

Friedlander, M.-J. (2007) *Ethiopia's Hidden Treasures: A Guide to the Paintings of the Remote Churches of Ethiopia*. Addis Ababa.

Gerster, G. (1970) *Churches in Rock: Early Christian Art in Ethiopia*. London: Phaidon.

Grierson, R. (ed.) (1993) *African Zion: The Sacred Art of Ethiopia*. New Haven, Conn. and London: Yale University Press in association with InterCultura, Fort Worth, Walters Art Museum, Baltimore, Institute of Ethiopian Studies, Addis Ababa.

Heldman, M. E. (1992) Architectural symbolism, sacred geography and the Ethiopian Church. *Journal of Religion in Africa* 22: 222–41.

—— (1994) *The Marian Icons of the Painter Fré Seyon: A Study of Fifteenth-Century Ethiopian Art*. Wiesbaden: Harrassowitz.

Leroy, J. (1961) L'Évangeliaire éthiopien illustré du British Museum (Or. 510) et ses sources iconographiques. *Annales d'Éthiopie* 4: 155–80.

Mercier, J. (1997) *Art that Heals: The Image as Medicine in Ethiopia*. New York: Museum for African Art.

Proceedings of the First International Conference on the History of Ethiopian Art (1989) Conference sponsored by the Royal Asiatic Society, and held at the Warburg Institute, University of London, 21–2 October 1986. London: Pindar Press.

Ramos, M. J. and Boavida, I. (2004) *The Indigenous and the Foreign in Christian Ethiopian Art: On Portugese–Ethiopian contacts in the 16th–17th Centuries*. Papers from the Fifth International Conference on the History of Ethiopian Art, Arrábida 26–30 November 1999. Aldershot: Ashgate.

Simović, M. (2000–1) *Daughter of Zion: Orthodox Christian Art from Ethiopia*, published in conjunction with the exhibition by this name, spring 2000–1. Jerusalem: The Israel Museum.

CHAPTER 20

Eastern Christian Hagiographical Traditions

Eastern Orthodox

Dimitri Brady

The Holy Physicians

As there are literally many thousands of saints' lives in the various Eastern Orthodox Churches, I have chosen to concentrate on the Anargyroi or the Holy Physicians in this section and to follow it with a second section on the New Martyrs.

In Orthodox churches anywhere in the world one is certain to come across icons or wall-paintings depicting the Holy Physicians of Eastern Christian tradition. These saints are immediately distinguished by the medical chests and spatulas they display and by voluminous robes. Invariably, these are the 'Hagioi Anargyroi' or 'Unmercenary Physicians', sober-looking men of all ages, only rarely accompanied by women helpers. The Anargyroi are the widely venerated patrons of medical practitioners and the infirm alike and are reputed to have never accepted any recompense for their services and to remain efficacious intercessors to the present day.

The Anargyroi are commemorated individually or in groups alongside the Prophets, Apostles, Martyrs, Holy Priests and Monks recognized by the Church. Like these, the Anargyroi are singled out for a general office in the Greek and Slavic Menaia – indicating that they form a unique category for the Orthodox Churches. In the ecclesiastical calendars of the Byzantine tradition feasts related to one or another of these Anargyroi fall in every month. From their prominence it can be argued that this group of saints represents a model (one amongst several) for sanctity in the Christian East. The iconography associated with the Anargyroi is distinctive and ubiquitous. Church dedications are quite common. Names associated with this group remain a popular Orthodox choice worldwide.

This model of sanctity has been presented to the faithful for centuries, illustrated in art, readings and supported by many customs. Ultimately, this was inspired by the miracles of healing recorded in the New Testament. The passage in the Gospel of Matthew (10: 1, 5–8) that includes the instruction given by Christ to his disciples: 'Heal the sick, cleanse the lepers, raise the dead, cast out devils: freely you have received, freely give' is crucial. This text is always read in church on the feast-days of the Anar-gyroi and clearly inscribed on the scrolls decorating icons of this group. This and related passages endorse the link between Christian living and ministering to the sick, but also connect bodily ailments to those of the soul. The miraculous element, which features prominently in the Lives of the Anargyroi, also has scriptural precedents.

Church, state and individuals in Byzantium followed what was perceived to be the example set by the early Christians in founding charitable hospitals, sanatoria and institutions for those afflicted with mental ill-health. Such founders and benefactors included bishops like Basil the Great (d. 379), John Chrysostom (d. 407), Stratonikos of Harran (d. 502), Apollinarios of Alexandria (d. 568), John the Almsgiver (d. 616), Andrew of Crete (d. 740) and Theophylaktos of Nicomedia (d. 840). Others were abbots like Pachomios (d. 346), Theodosios the Koinobiarch (d. 529) and Sabas the Sanctified (d. 532). Notable amongst emperors were Justinian (d. 565), Alexios Komnenos (d. 1118) and John II Komnenos (d. 1143). The Emperor Isaak II Angelos (d. 1195) was remembered for having even transformed his palace into a hospital. Saints such as Andronikos and Athanasia of Antioch (fourth century) were lauded for leaving all their possessions to existing hospitals. Naturally, the donations of pious or socially minded individuals supplemented endowments but generally went unrecorded.

Throughout the Byzantine period hospitals and related institutions were generally attached to churches and monasteries. Even if these were not actually dedicated to Anargyroi saints they were commemorated by icons and special chapels. At the Meteora Monasteries of Thessaly and elsewhere this connection survived the fall of Constanti-nople in 1453. Above all, ministering to the sick and afflicted remained an important aspect of Christian witness in the Orthodox tradition. This needs to be emphasized as it is often overlooked by those western Christians who are primarily interested in desert spirituality and the Hesychast traditions of the Eastern Churches. It is also important to note that the Orthodox approach to this primarily social issue was mirrored in Islamic practice.

The Anargyroi are the saintly doctors and nurses of the Christian East whose lives, literary legends and associated folklore encapsulate a long-established Orthodox approach to health issues. They can be seen as the popular healers of previous centuries who used prayer alongside medicine and what we would now term alternative medi-cine or homeopathic techniques to help or cure people and animals alike. Church tradi-tion presents the Anargyroi as having worked in pairs or groups and maintains that besides performing cures they engaged in general charitable and evangelical work. In the surviving Lives this latter aspect is greatly enhanced by the generally miraculous nature of many of the healings attributed to the saints. The miraculous underlines the truths of the Christian faith. Popular devotion to the Anargyroi is reinforced by numer-ous stories, recorded and orally transmitted, of their potent intercession and direct intervention in the daily affairs of individuals and communities, historically and up to the present day. If anything, pious accounts show the Anargyroi to be more widely active and effective after their earthly demise than during their lives.

Above all it is stressed that this group of saints were totally unlike their contempo-rary colleagues in the medical profession. The Anargyroi are characterized as uphold-ing intransigent principles regarding recompense: they steadfastly refused to accept any form of payment or reward for their activity. Indeed, according to the Lives, this principle was so rigorously implemented that lifelong partners are shown as falling out when one suspected that the other was guilty of having accepted some gift, no matter how insignificant. The message is underlined by the implication that the early Anargyroi were persecuted and martyred by the Roman authorities, not only because they were subversives who promoted the Christian faith but also because they undermined the entire medical profession by never charging any fees. According to the Lives the therapies supervised by the Anargyroi and their miracles of healing discredited both the pagan physicians and their deities alike. We read that the temples of Asklepios and Isis were emptied as all in need flocked to the Christian Anargyroi. The temples remained empty because the Anargyroi continued to tirelessly heal the sick and ailing from beyond the grave. It follows that churches and tombs of these saints emerged as important centres for pilgrimage in the Byzantine era.

Some detective work might indicate that Greater Syria was the original homeland of the Anargyroi phenomenon, particularly the northern regions presently within Turkey. Tradition asserts that a number were martyred in Aigai (Ayas) or in the general vicinity of Antioch (Antakya). Significantly, Kyrros (Kilis), north of Antioch, was renamed Hagiopolis to draw attention to the claim that it held the tombs of the major Anargyroi, Kosmas and Damianos. Many Anargyroi are considered by the church to be martyrs. Some are titled great-martyrs, indicating that they suffered prolonged and particularly horrific tortures. As great-martyrs they are held to be major patrons of the Christian life. However, this is not the most important attribute of saints in the Anargyroi grouping, nor necessary for their inclusion. The epithet 'Anargyroi' came to be applied ever more widely in the Byzantine period to include not only Christian-minded doctors and nurses but also saintly people who organized or supervised charitable hospitals and hospices. Furthermore, all saints famed for miraculous cures were associated with this prestigious title, at least in the church offices and hymnody. It can be argued that some saints, like Therapon, probably came to be considered as Anargyroi owing to their names inviting a connection with healing (*therapia*, healing). This was an ongoing process as miracles of healing are attributed to the majority of saints, east and west. Nevertheless, the Anargyroi remain a clearly defined group amongst saints glorified by the Church.

The Kosmas and Damianos triangle

The main Anargyroi are surely the three pairs of 'Kosmas and Damianos' who are distinguished by being termed the Syrians, the Romans and the Arabs. An amount of confusion has always been engendered by them all bearing the same names. Unsurprisingly, scholars have argued that this triplication of pairs simply represents conflicting traditions about one pair – almost certainly the Syrians entombed in Kyrros/Hagiopolis. The Roman Catholics now appear to hold an approximation of this view and the Roman Martyrology commemorates just one pair, a conflation of the Syrians and the Arabs. The belief in an extra pair active in Rome is now thought to have arisen after relics were translated to the West at a relatively early date. However, the Orthodox Churches continue to commemorate all three pairs with gusto. It is argued that the

Romans and Arabs emulated their earlier Syrian counterparts and, out of respect, adopted their names.

The Syrians Kosmas and Damianos are still the focus of much popular devotion amongst Eastern Christians, but not to the point of entirely eclipsing the Romans or the Arabs. In parts of Macedonia the feast of the Roman Kosmas and Damianos is the occasion for gatherings in honour of all the healing saints. More widespread is the custom of commemorating all the Anargyroi (the Synaxis) on the feast-day of the Arabs Kosmas and Damianos. In Greece today this is marked by celebrations at a modern shrine in Ilioupolis on the outskirts of Athens.

In Greek folklore the Syrians Kosmas (often called Kosmianos) and Damianos, have arguably supplanted the ancient Greek deity Asklepios. In folk tales they are characterized as being the first Christian healers. A cave chapel at the Acropolis of Athens and a monastery at Ermioni in Argolis are among many examples of shrines dedicated to the saints on ruins of temples of Asklepios. Most are by springs or wells that have probably been considered sacred since ancient times. Pilgrims or those hoping for help or a specific cure traditionally slept overnight in churches of the saints, received guidance in their dreams, and customarily left votive offerings if convinced that they had indeed been healed. Incubation and related customs point to the likelihood that Kosmas and Damianos inherited certain aspects of pre-Christian cults, at least in Greek-speaking regions. Their enduring popularity is evident in the multiplicity of churches and chapels dedicated to the saints, the naming of towns, villages and neighbourhoods in their honour and the christening of infants invoking the protection of their names. Amongst the Greeks men called Anargyros/Argyris or women called Anargyro/Argyro/Iro generally observe their name-days on the feast-day of Kosmas and Damianos.

Dating from at least 1293, the Vassara Monastery in Lakonia remains an important centre of pilgrimage to the Anargyroi in Greece. Repeatedly damaged during Turkish punitive actions in the Ottoman centuries it is now adorned by works of the iconographer Photis Kontoglou.

The twelve and the twenty Anargyroi

From the early Byzantine period Panteleimon was also given the title Anargyros owing to the obvious parallels between his Life and the Kosmas and Damianos group. He was credited with healing and reviving a number of people, many of whom accompanied him to martyrdom. Kyros and John were also promoted as equal in stature to Kosmas and Damianos. It is evident from the stories of their posthumous miracles that this was done specifically to counter and eclipse the cult of the goddess Isis. From the sixth century onwards Sampson Xenodochos was also titled Anargyros and it is likely that by this time the notion of a group of heavenly physicians was quite well established. Indeed, Sampson emerged as the patron of the medical profession in Constantinople and presumably was viewed as presiding over a group of their saintly counterparts. The major Anargyroi correspond to the cultural units that made up the Byzantine world. They can be mapped out as Panteleimon in Nicomedia/Asia Minor, Kosmas and Damianos in Greater Syria, John and Kyros in Egypt and Sampson Xenodochos in Constantinople/Europe.

In the printed Greek texts there is evidence of at least two related traditions. In these we can find mention of a grouping of twelve Anargyroi saints and of another group of twenty that includes the former also. The twelve are: Aniketos, Diomedes, Damianos the Syrian, Hermolaos, John, Kosmas the Syrian, Kyros, Mokios, Panteleimon, Sampson, Thallelaios and Tryphon. The twenty number the above and also: Anthimos, Damianos the Arab, Damianos the Roman, Eutropios, Julian, Kosmas the Arab, Kosmas the Roman and Leontios. Sometimes Julian is left out to bring in Orestes or the widely venerated Photios/Photinos, the companion of Aniketos. In either form greater weight is given to the Byzantine heartlands of Asia Minor and Syria as opposed to outlying regions. The Russian Orthodox would at least add Agapit of the Kiev Caves to such lists and the Greek Catholics have ensured that Fabiola (d. 399) is closely associated with the Anargyroi. At least seven of the saints mentioned in this context are also styled great-martyrs and share the fame and veneration of both popular groups. It is not clear in which period Panteleimon, equally revered in the West as Pantoleon, overtook and replaced Sampson as the patron of the entire medical profession. Luke the Evangelist is generally included amongst the Anargyroi, as in Church tradition he is reputed to have been a physician.

Clearly, existing lists of Anargyroi in the printed Greek texts are governed as much by the conventions of numbering groups (twelve or twenty rather than thirteen or twenty-one) as by the perceived similarities between various surviving lives and legends of the Orthodox hagiographical tradition. The saints depicted in the ever popular group icons of the Anargyroi (the synaxis or gathering) clearly vary according to the commission or the icon-painter's preferences.

Women Anargyroi?

Disappointingly, there is no echo in Orthodox iconography of women Anargyroi nor is the title unequivocally given to any women saints. Nevertheless, Euboule, the mother of Panteleimon, and Theodote, the mother of the Syrian Kosmas and Damianos, are represented as assistants to their sons and are far from unknown amongst Orthodox Christians. Traditions relating to Anysia of Thessalonica (d. 298) indicate that she worked as a nurse, but emphasize her missionary endeavours and martyrdom. Women healers are not remarkable because women saints were generally presented as nursing the sick and performing miracle cures. It might be assumed that the established Church overlooked women active in the field of medicine. However, the Menaia specifically commemorate Sophia the Physician (Iatraina) and it is likely that she is one of the missing women Anargyroi. Presumably, careful study of the manuscripts would unearth information about Christian women healers and other forgotten Anargyroi.

National and regional Anargyroi

Every individual Orthodox Church preserves the memory of saints, like Agapit of the Kiev Caves, whose lives parallel those of the universally acclaimed Anargyroi. Most notable amongst these is Kolouthos (Akolouthos in the Greek Menaia) commemorated by the Copts on 19 May. He was a third-century physician martyred in the Thebaid and greatly revered in Egypt to the present day. Whether genuine Anargyroi, working for absolutely no recompense, or simply philanthropic doctors there are many other saints whose lives and legends contribute to and illuminate this particular model of Christian living and sanctity.

Marginal Anargyroi

On the other hand, many saints who were never reputed to be doctors, nurses or folk healers by profession have been given the title Anargyroi because they have been associated with faith healing or miraculous cures. Indeed, all the recognized Orthodox saints are portrayed not only as prayerful intercessors but as healers; quite simply they are like Christ and their prayers ought to be potentially curative. A few examples should suffice: Paraskevi the Roman is thought to cure eye diseases, Antipas of Pergamum to cure dental and related problems, Charalampos to ward off epidemics and Patapios to banish cancer. Other saints, like George 'the physician of the sick' or Artemios are thought to assist believers with a variety of medical conditions.

The Holy Fools or Saloi, particularly Andrew the Scythian, were traditionally considered the patrons of those suffering from mental ill-health. This latter group forms a distinct category and a recognized model of sanctity quite at variance to the strand represented by the Anargyroi. The feigned madness and eccentricities of the Holy Fools appears remote to the sober, self-effacing Anargyroi.

Some saints, like Modestos of Jerusalem, Phloros and Lavros, are primarily considered to be the patrons of animals with a particular interest in healing livestock. Above all Our Lady, the Theotokos, is seen as coming to the aid of humanity and all creation in all situations, including sickness. The feast of the Life-Giving Spring and icons of Our Lady as 'Iatrissa' or 'Megaloyiatrissa' (physician or great physician) clearly connect the Theotokos with specifically medical cures. Interestingly, the regional 'Myrtidiotissa' (myrtle tree) and 'Kassiopia' (of Kassiope) commemorations of the Theotokos are both associated with restoration of sight to the blind.

The Anargyroi in the church calendars

Even a brief survey of the Menaia and Heortologia currently in use would provide us with a list of over forty commemorations associated with the Anargyroi saints and other holy physicians. This clearly demonstrates the significance of the Anargyroi in the cycle of the Orthodox Church year and, by implication, the relevance of this group to the faithful and the centrality of this model of sanctity in traditional teaching. Of course, not all the feasts listed are widely celebrated today but those relating to the 'Twelve and Twenty' certainly do not pass unnoticed. This list could legitimately include saints such as Zotikos and Stephen of Armatiou, who apparently supervised rather than worked as doctors in hospitals. Basil the Great and Patriarch Photios have

been included in such compilations, presumably on the basis of having founded or supported medical institutions.

The feast of the Life-Giving Spring commemorates the Theotokos as heavenly inter-
cessor and healer but the offices of this movable celebration (the first Friday after Easter)
most clearly encapsulate Eastern Christian thought relating to ministering to the sick
and healing. As noted, in the posthumous miracles attributed to the Theotokos there
is a clear focus on healing. Therefore, the implicit suggestion is that in freely 'receiving
and giving' the Theotokos intervenes in the lives of the faithful as one of the heavenly
Anargyroi.

Significance of the Anargyroi

The Eastern Orthodox Menaia still in use list over forty major and minor feasts associated with the Anargyroi group and at least four relating to the Theotokos as healer.
Orthodox Christians in every country continue to dedicate churches and chapels in
honour of the Anargyroi, commission their icons and name children after leading
saints in this group. The Anargyroi remain central as a group to Orthodox ideas of
sanctity and the teaching related to the Christian life in general. This is of great significance to the wider community as this is a model of sanctity entirely rooted in lay life
and witness. Of course, medical practitioners in every society occupy a prestigious position but the Anargyroi are not all what we would term medical doctors. For instance,
Tryphon of Lampsakos and Argyris the New Martyr are depicted as folk healers rather
than medical doctors. Only a few of the Anargyroi are recorded as being bishops, priests
or even monastics. They therefore form one of the major lay groups of saints and maintain a high profile in the church calendars, which are otherwise dominated by holy
bishops, priests and monks or nuns.

It can be argued that the cult of the Anargyroi is a uniquely Eastern Christian phenomenon. Of course, relics of the Anargyroi are still enshrined in Catholic and Orthodox churches across Europe and the Near East. Many of the Anargyroi are individually
commemorated in western calendars and as far back as 530 Pope Felix IV erected a
church to honour a collection of relics, including those of Anargyroi, in Rome. John de
Beaumont brought relics of the Anargyroi from Syrian Edessa (Sanli-Urfa) to Paris in
the twelfth century. In the period of the crusades some of the Eastern Anargyroi became
better known to western Christians – primarily through renewed contact with Eastern
Christians and the removal of relics, icons etc. – but only as individual saints. The cult
of a defined group of saints did not follow either the relics or returning crusaders to
western Europe.

A closer examination of the various printed Menaia, Heortologia and calendars
would undoubtedly reveal other related feasts. Manuscripts almost certainly contain
further references to feasts no longer observed and, possibly, Lives of other Anargyroi
figures that could compliment and enhance our view of this group of saints. However,
it is unclear whether uncovering extra materials would increase the standing of the
Anargyroi in the life of the Eastern Churches. Here the significance of the Anargyroi is

underlined, above all, by their invocation during the Divine Liturgy. In the Byzantine rite it is customary to remember the Anargyroi during the Proskomide. In this context, at least the following are invoked by name: Kosmas and Damianos the Syrians, Kyros and John of Egypt, Panteleimon, Hermolaos and Diomedes of Nicaea and Sampson Xenodochos of Constantinople. Considering the centrality of the Divine Liturgy to Eastern Christian spirituality this can be taken as the ultimate proof of the recognized importance of the Anargyroi group in an Orthodox context. The lay status of the Anargyroi would further indicate that they illustrate an ideal of the Christian life that was viewed as more accessible to ordinary people.

The legacy of the Anargyroi

The Anargyroi are not simply a phenomenon of the early Christian era or the Byzantine centuries. A cursory look at the Orthodox calendars demonstrates that an active witness, represented in this instance by the Anargyroi, has always complemented the contemplative tradition in the Orthodox East.

In the twentieth century Elizabeth Feodorovna, guided by the Pskov elder Gabriel of Eleazar (d. 1915), established a hospital in her Moscow convent of Saints Mary and Martha. The very dedication of the new convent was intended to draw attention to the links between the active and contemplative traditions of the Church. Elizabeth, a German Grand Duchess and niece of Queen Victoria, was martyred by the Bolsheviks in 1918 and canonized in 1981. In Paris, Mother Maria Skobtsova emphasized ministering to the sick, refugees, homeless and persecuted. She ended her life in 1945 at the Ravensbruck concentration camp where she took the place of a Jewish woman condemned to the Nazi gas chambers.

In the closing years of the twentieth century the Ecumenical Patriarchate canonized Anthimos Vayianos (1869–1960), a priest who worked tirelessly amongst the lepers, infirm and poor refugees of Chios Island, Greece. Like Elizabeth Feodorovna, he founded hospitals and organized a monastic community (dedicated to Our Lady of Help) to work amongst the needy. Archbishop Luke of Simferopol and Crimea (1877–1961) is a clear example of a modern 'unmercenary physician'. He was both an outstanding surgeon and Orthodox Christian minister and elder who can be viewed as operating entirely within the tradition of the Anargyroi saints while ministering in the context of the strictly atheist Soviet Union.

In Greece, the Cretan monk Chrysanthos Katsouloyiannakis worked exclusively amongst the lepers of the notorious Spinalonga colony. Chrysanthos ended his life as a revered hermit and elder in 1972, thus uniting in himself two traditions that are often thought to be disparate in the wider Christian context. More controversially, the Athenian surgeon Dimitrios Lekkas (1947–79) became the focus of popular veneration and pilgrimage shortly after his death from cancer. The Church has been uncomfortable with the emergence of an unrecognized cult but the spontaneity of this movement indicates the abiding popularity of Anargyroi figures in the contemporary, secular world.

The Anargyroi in the Orthodox calendar

Below are notes on the main feasts of saints associated with the Anargyroi group as they appear sequentially in the Eastern Orthodox calendars. Variant commemorations indicate western practice. These notes do not attempt to distinguish between historical and legendary materials in traditional sources. It must be assumed that stories regarding early Christian figures in particular are greatly embellished.

> *4 September*: Hermione and Eutychia, the daughters of Philip the Deacon. Church tradition attributes to these sisters the foundation of charitable hospitals, first in Caesarea Mazaca and later in Ephesus (the Pandocheion). It is believed that they were martyred with others in the reign of Hadrian. (d. first century?)

> *11 October*: Zenais and Philonilla of Tarsus in Cilicia Pedias. Legendary figures who were held to have worked first in their home town and later, when expelled, in neighbouring Demetrias of Kataonia. Cypriot tradition maintains that they ended their lives in Paphos rather than on the Asia Minor mainland. Other accounts would have it that they were related to the Apostle Paul and that they travelled as far afield as Spain. (d. first century?)

> *13 October/13 April in the West*: Karpos the Bishop of Thyateira and Papylos the deacon. Originally from Pergamum they were martyred in Sardis, the ancient Lydian capital, with Agathodoros, a slave, and Agathonike, the sister of Papylos. An early *martyrium* dedicated to the saints survives under the church of St Menas in Kyparissia in Istanbul. (d. 251)

> *17 October/27 September in the West*: Kosmas, Damianos, Leontios, Anthimos, Eutropios/Euprepios the Arabs. A team of doctors reputed to have travelled throughout the East and to have been martyred at Aigai (Ayas) in Cilicia. (d. 313)

> *17 October or 28 October*: On this day, with the Arab physicians, the Greek Orthodox commemorate the Synaxis or Council of all the Anargyroi saints. Supposedly, this is originally an Athonite custom.

> *18 October*: Luke the Evangelist. According to Church tradition he was martyred in Thebes of Greece, where a tomb of the saint is still venerated. The reputed relics of the saint were removed first to Constantinople, then to Rogous in Epirus and finally to the West. The Eastern Orthodox attribute a number (between three and seventy) of icons, the first ever painted, to this Evangelist. (d. 80)

> *30 October*: Zenobios the bishop and Zenobia, his sister. They were natives of Aigai (Ayas) in Cilicia and were martyred in that city. (d. 285)

> *1 November*: Kosmas and Damianos of Phereman near Kyrrhos (later titled Hagiopolis, now Kilis) in Syria. Their mother, Theodote, helped them in their

missionary and charitable works and is commemorated separately (2 January). These brothers died natural deaths and their tombs became an important centre for pilgrimage in Syria. By the fifth century two important churches had been dedicated to the saints in Constantinople (in Zeugma and Kosmidion). It was the cult of these Anargyroi brothers that spread across the Christian East and they are still the main focus of Orthodox veneration. (d. third century)

10 November/9 November in the West: Orestes of Tyana (later titled Christopolis) in Cappadocia. He was martyred at Batos, close to Nigde. (d. third century)

26 November: Stylianos of Paphlagonia, the wonder-worker, sometimes identified with Alypios the Kionite (d. 640). He is famous for his miracles amongst ailing children and always depicted on icons cradling an infant. The Greek Orthodox now revere this saint as the patron of all infants. (d. fifth century?)

3 December: Angelis of Chios, a new martyr put to death by the Ottoman Turks for reverting to Christianity. (d. 1813)

31 December: Zotikos the Orphanotrophos. A Roman priest, he worked amongst the many homeless children of the Byzantine capital and with those suffering from incurable diseases. He founded an institution to house and care for orphans (hence his title) and another for lepers. Both included hospitals. Zotikos was martyred by the Arians. (d. 350)

1 January: Basil the Great, Bishop of Caesarea Mazaca in Cappadocia. A famous theologian, he was also the founder of Annesoi and the Basileias. The former was a monastic centre in Pontus but the latter was an urban charitable complex that included hospitals. He firmly established the link between the monastic life and social work. The saint's good works are celebrated in Greek folklore and by numerous carols sung at the New Year – over which he is seen to preside; he can be considered an Orthodox counterpart to the western 'Father Christmas'. As one of the Three Hierarchs (commemorated together on 30 January) Basil is also the patron of education in the Christian East. (d. 379)

31 January: Kyros (Abu Kir) of Alexandria and John of Edessa. The latter was a soldier who came to Egypt to assist Kyros in his work amongst the sick and marginalized. The two friends are represented as having been quite hostile to the medical profession of their day. They were martyred with their assistants, Athanasia, Eudoxia, Theodote and Theoktiste at Canopus of Egypt Augustamnica in the reign of Diocletian. In Constantinople there was an important church dedicated to this group at Sphorakiou. (d. 262)

1 February: Tryphon of Lampsakos in Hellespontine Phrygia. He was an uneducated farmhand who healed people and animals alike by using traditional country methods and prayer. He was martyred in Nicaea of Bithynia and came to be revered across the East as the protector of crops and rural life in general. He is also specifically invoked to ward off all kinds of vermin. A number of churches were dedicated to this saint in Constantinople. (d. 250)

6 February: Julian of Emesa in Coele Syria. He was martyred with Sylvan the bishop and Mokios the reader. (d. 284)

11 February/3 February in the West: Blasios the bishop. He was martyred near Sebastea Megalopolis (Sivas) in the Armenian Marches. From an early date the cult of this saint (known as Blaise in Britain) spread across the Mediterranean world and beyond. Blasios was invoked against infections of the throat and in Constantinople his *martyrium*, at Meltiadou, was a centre of pilgrimage. He is particularly venerated in Croatia, as his reputed relics were transferred to Dubrovnik in the medieval period. (d. 316)

27 February and 6 March: Stephen of Armatiou. He founded a complex of charitable institutions called the Gerokomeion. This housed and ministered to the old and ailing of Constantinople and was organized around a church dedicated to the Theotokos (commemorated separately). (d. 503)

9 March/25 February in the West: Kaisarios of Arianzos in Cappadocia. He was a medical doctor from a sainted family of theologians, most notably including his sister Gorgonia and their brother Gregory Nazianzene. (d. 396)

15 March: Nikandros of Egypt. He ministered to the needs of the many imprisoned and persecuted Christians of the Thebaid, Upper Egypt, eventually being martyred with a number of companions. (d. third century)

26 April: Kalandrion of Aroda, an ascetic physician of Paphos in Cyprus. He is numbered amongst the 'Three Hundred Palestinian Fathers' who sought refuge in Cyprus from the Saracens. (d. seventh century?)

6 May: Kosmas and Damianos of Phereman, the Syrian Anargyroi. On this date is commemorated the foundation of a church dedicated to the saints in Psamathia (Samatya) of Constantinople (around 890). The great monastery of Kosmidion, also dedicated to the brothers, was rebuilt after being sacked by the Avars on 5 June 623. Other churches and a convent (restored in the thirteenth century) were erected in their honour in the Byzantine capital.

11 May: Mokios the Roman, a priest of Amphipolis on the Strymon who was martyred in Byzantium. Emperor Constantine officially refounded the city as New Rome on his feast-day and Mokios was declared patron saint of the now Christian capital. The saint was buried in the old temple of Herakles, where his relics were later joined by those of Sampson Xenodochos. Originally the Emperor Constantine was commemorated with Mokios on this date. (d. 295)

13 May: Pausikakos the Physician, Bishop of Synnada in Phrygia Salutaria. He was originally from Myrleia-Apamea of Bithynia and achieved fame after healing the Byzantine Emperor Maurice. (d. sixth century)

14 May: Therapon the Lydian, Bishop of Cyprus. There is no mention of this saint having been a doctor but he is regularly titled Anargyros. According to the legendary Life he was exiled by the Byzantine iconoclasts and travelled as a pilgrim across the East. Reaching Cyprus he was elected bishop and was later martyred by Muslim raiders while celebrating the liturgy – making him an early new martyr. His relics were eventually moved to Constantinople and there a church dedicated to the saint was built by a holy well. (d. 632?)

20 May: Thallelaios the Phoenician. Based at Anazarbos (Anavarza) he worked across Osrhoene and Syria. He was martyred with Asterios, Alexander and others at Aigai (Ayas) in Cilicia. (d. 284)

22 May: Sophia the Egyptian physician and martyr. (d. third century)

1 June: Agapit of Ukraine. He was a monk doctor of the Great Caves Lavra near Kiev. Russian Orthodox pilgrims brought his cult to Mount Athos and the Holy Land. (d. 1095)

11 June: Luke, Archbishop of Simferopol and Crimea. He was a modern unmercenery physician who combined Christian ministry and mission with medical care and teaching in the face of anti-Christian persecution in the USSR. (d. 1961)

20 June: Luke the Evangelist. This feast commemorates the translation of the reputed relics of the saint from Greek Thebes to Constantinople in the reign of Constantine. Here they were placed in the Church of the Holy Apostles on the Mese (a site now occupied by the beautiful Fatih Cami). As an 'equal to the Apostles' Constantine and his mother Helena were also buried in this church, as were later Byzantine rulers. According to Church tradition another saint, Artemios, was entrusted with this mission before being martyred by Julian the Apostate around 363. Commemorated on 20 October, Artemios is virtually ranked with the Anargyroi and considered the healer of many illnesses, not least ailments particular to men.

27 June: Sampson the Xenodochos. Originally from Rome, he moved to Constantinople, was ordained priest and founded a charitable complex that included a large hospital. This Xenon received the support of the Byzantine Emperor Justinian. Sampson was buried in the shrine of another doctor, Mokios, and came to be considered the patron of the entire medical profession (whose guild would march to his tomb on the feast-day). During the Latin occupation the Xenon was taken over by the Knights Templar. (d. sixth century)

28 June: Paul of Corinth. (d. seventh century)

28 June: Kyros and John. This feast is in memory of the transferral of reputed relics to Menouthis during the patriarchate of Cyril (fifth century). It is claimed that when this occurred the local temple of the goddess Isis sank into the sands. From then on the saints were considered patrons of the Egyptian delta region but eventually the relics were again removed and taken to Rome.

1 July: Kosmas and Damianos of Rome. These brothers are believed to have healed people and animals, to have been denounced by colleagues who were jealous of their success and annoyed that they charged no fees, and subsequently to have been martyred in Italy. (d. 284?)

9 July: Orestes of Tyana in Cappadocia. This date probably commemorates the transferral of relics or the foundation of some major church to honour the saint, perhaps in Constantinople.

9 July: The Theotokos of the Zoodochos Pege (life-giving spring). On this date is commemorated the foundation of this church in 559 by the Byzantine Emperor Justinian. Associated with numerous feast-days, this title firmly characterizes the Theotokos as a heavenly healer and sets a precedent for later accounts that attribute miracles of healing to Mary. Rebuilt many times the church and monastery still exist outside the medieval walls of Istanbul and are called Balikli or 'Fishy Place' in Turkish.

25 July/22 April in the West: Alexander the Phrygian, martyr of Lugdunum in Gaul (France).

26 July/27 July in the West: Hermolaos the priest of Nicomedia in Bithynia. Associated with Panteleimon, he is commemorated with his fellow martyrs Hermippos and Hermokrates, also priests. (d. 306)

27 July: Panteleimon/Pantaleon of Nicomedia in Bithynia. His mother and assistant, Euboule, is remembered on 30 March and he is commemorated with numerous companions. Panteleimon is the best-loved saintly doctor of the East and was greatly revered in Italy also. Churches and monasteries were dedicated to the saint in Constantinople; one at Narsou claimed to treasure his head. His oldest shrine outside Nicomedia (Izmit-Kocaeli) was devastated by the Turks in the eighteenth century but survived as a major centre of pilgrimage up to 1922. The Russian monastery on Mount Athos, founded in the twelfth century, is dedicated to Panteleimon. In Greece today, a church at Aharne on the outskirts of Athens provides a focus for veneration of the saint. (d. 305)

12 August: Aniketos and Photios/Photinos, martyrs of Nicomedia in Bithynia. In Constantinople there was a church dedicated to these saints, allegedly an uncle and nephew, at Strategion. They were obviously popular on the island of Crete where local tradition maintains that a medieval saint, Kyr John, had a church built in their honour in the eleventh century, near Kissamos. (d. 305)

16 August: Diomedes the martyr of Nicaea (Iznik) in Bithynia. Originally from Tarsus of Cilicia, he was executed in the persecutions of Diocletian. A church of this saint by the walls of Constantinople served as a *metochion* for the Jerusalem Patriarchate. This was restored by Emperor Basil the Macedonian (or Bulgar-slayer) and it would appear that he regarded Diomedes as his personal patron and the protector of the Byzantines. (d. 288)

The Significance of the Orthodox New Martyrs

In the Greek Orthodox context the term 'new martyrs' refers to Orthodox Christians martyred in the period after the fall of Constantinople, that is, from 1453 onwards. In most Greek sources this term is applied exclusively to the martyrs of the Ottoman centuries or *Tourkokratia* and is not generally a title given after the 1920s. Indeed, it is apparent that new martyrs are popularly held to have not only witnessed to their faith in the Ottoman era but also to have been killed by Ottoman Turks, rather than in some other persecution of the Orthodox Church.

However, an examination of the Byzantine synaxaries reveals that this term was first used for the iconophile martyrs of an earlier era. In this context the title was conferred to underline the extent and brutality of the persecutions unleashed by the iconoclast authorities, Church and state. Even in the period of the controversy over icons a link was made between widespread persecution of the iconophiles and their tenacious resistance to imperial edicts, with the pagan persecutions of the first Christian centuries.

This linking not only legitimized and honoured resistance but also implied that iconoclast and pagan emperors posed an equivalent threat to the very survival of the Christian *oikoumene*. In these terms, it can be argued that the Orthodox Church both already possessed the language to refer to Christian witness within the expanding Ottoman Empire *and* was prepared to immediately redeploy a proven and potent concept. By redefining the term, Orthodox writers were proclaiming that although Orthodox Church institutions accepted the Pax Ottomana, individual Christians who witnessed to their faith to the point of death were heroic. New martyrs were depicted as the contemporary equals of the revered great-martyrs of the persecution under Diocletian and other pagan emperors. Furthermore, it was implied that the Ottoman authorities shared the opprobrium of the despised iconoclasts and hated pagans, and that Ottoman hegemony would prove to be equally transient. It can be argued, therefore, that the use of this term was quite as subversive as irredentist folk songs, popular sayings or the prophetic tracts that circulated in Greek throughout the Ottoman period. Localized veneration of revolutionary leaders like Dionysios Skylosophos of Larissa (d. 1600) clearly establishes this connection.

In the surviving accounts the new martyrs were only rarely represented as being victims of a simple miscarriage of Ottoman justice. Rather they emerged as extraordinary individuals who developed the courage and conviction to witness to their faith during ongoing, widespread and ordinary levels of harassment or persecution. The passion of John the Tailor (d. 1526) illustrates this point.

The Lives of the new martyrs and traditions relating to their passion present a grim account of Ottoman rule and of the situation of the Orthodox Christian population. However, it must be noted that they are neither unremittingly anti-Muslim nor consistently disparaging of the Ottoman order. Ultimately, they are concerned with moments of crisis and a complete breakdown in inter-communal relations. As the texts address fellow Orthodox Christians they are neither overtly polemical nor commentaries on the status of the non-Muslim groups. For a more balanced view of inter-faith relations we must turn to accounts of saints such as Ignatios Agallianos of Methymne (d. 1566), Eugenios Yiannoulis (d. 1682), John the Russian of Prokopion (d. 1730) or other Christians whose contribution to the wider community was normally respected or even encouraged.

Although the new martyrs were drawn from every walk of life they were extraordinary in so far as they were uncompromising in matters of faith. In this sense they were clearly a force of renewal within Christian communities that had been ground down by centuries of compromise, complacency and apostasy. Indeed, as new converts to Christianity are included amongst the new martyrs this group can be held to represent symbolically a reversal for the rising tide of Islam. This is the case even in the pre-Ottoman period as we discover that the Georgians venerated Neophytos-Omar the Arab (d. 590), a martyred convert from Islam. The cults of former Muslims, including George of the Copts (d. 959), Hoja Amir (d. 1614), Ahmet Kalfa (d. 1682), John-Hasan (d. 1814), Constantine the Hagarene (d. 1819) and Boris the Pomak (d. 1913), surely served to reassure the Christians that conversion was a two-way process.

Regardless of the historical accuracy of local traditions, or individual accounts, or the validity of the bleak vision of the *dhimmi* presented, it is significant that the cult of the new martyrs was promoted primarily by the Orthodox laity. Even monastic or ecclesiastical writers, collectors of information and disseminators of the tracts viewed the new martyrs as a sign of renewal in the life of the Church. Interestingly, within the Ottoman Empire new martyrs were adopted as the patrons of guilds and communities, not least George of Chiopolis (d. 1807) by Kydonia/Ayvalik and Demetrios (d. 1657) of Philadelphia/Alasehir in Asia Minor. This in itself indicates that the Ottomans were normally tolerant, even of new martyr patrons.

The very term 'new martyr' underlined both their importance to the Orthodox and that the Church was thought to be in danger of extinction. The subversive nature of this message was reflected by the reluctance of the Ecumenical Patriarchate openly to acknowledge or canonize these figures, in some cases even up to the present day. In almost every case popular veneration of new martyrs always preceded official church recognition. Lay veneration for certain new martyrs, for instance Panteleimon Dousa (d. 1848), is still officially discouraged. Likewise, it made sense that the term was only applied to martyrs of the Ottoman centuries and became redundant after the collapse of the Ottoman Empire and the exchange of populations between Greece, Turkey and neighbours (in the 1920s).

Even within the Greek Orthodox context an earlier move in this direction can be detected. This is clearly indicated in the accounts of Eustathios of Harran (d. 741), the

Forty-two Martyrs of Amorion, executed in Baghdad (*c.* 845), or Theodore Gavras of Atran (d. 1028), martyred by the Seljuks in Erzerum. It is sensible to assume that the patriarchates of Alexandria, Antioch and Jerusalem alongside the Churches of Armenia, Georgia and the East first developed the rhetoric of the new martyr model in an earlier context; whenever they first experienced Muslim incursions or rule and associated persecutions. Examples include the traditions associated with Bashnūfa of Egypt (d. 1092), the Tbilisi martyrs (thirteenth century) and Ruwais of Egypt (d. 1404). Popular veneration of Emperor Constantine XII Palaeologus and Christians killed in the conquest of Constantinople in 1453 was probably spontaneous and due to long-standing precedents.

Nevertheless, even for the Armenian, Syrian and Assyrian Christians 'new martyrs' remains a term largely applied to the victims of Ottoman Turkish persecution in the run-up to and during the First World War. It can be postulated that the term denotes resistance and is intrinsically linked with historical moments when the continued existence of the Church or the Christian community was threatened. It is reserved for those whose witness parallels that of the Christian heroes of the first era of martyrs, particularly the persecutions of Diocletian.

The term ethno-martyrs can be viewed as a variation on the same theme. However, the differentiation might be taken to imply that their witness is mainly of local significance. Although some, like Ecumenical Patriarchs Cyril VI and Gregory V (d. 1821), are revered by Orthodox Christians of several traditions, the very title suggests that they were martyrs for the national cause as much as for the wider Christian commonwealth. This subgroup represent a shift in focus to local churches that, from the 1820s to the 1920s, increasingly represented national aspirations. The term was revived to explain and legitimize the involvement of Orthodox Christians in the cause of the Resistance during the Second World War. Essentially this is a group linked to the politics of national liberation and self-determination. Thomas Paschides (d. 1890), Ilia Chavchavadze (d. 1907), Maxim Sandovich (d. 1914), Chrysostom Kalaphatis of Smyrna (d. 1922), Plato Jovanović of Banja Luka (d. 1941) and Hariton Lukić of Kosovo (d. 1999) are amongst Christian figures who were martyred for their national affiliation as much as for their religious convictions. Gorazd Pavlik (d. 1942) was executed for his involvement with the resistance movement in Czechoslovakia and Maria Skobtsova (d. 1945) for her stand against Nazi anti-Semitism.

Outside the Ottoman context the new martyrs are mainly a product of the turbulent twentieth century. The century opened ominously for the Orthodox Church with the martyrdom of Mitrophan Chi and many others in China during the Boxer Uprising (1900). Most notably the recognized new martyrs of the Soviet Union clearly outnumber their predecessors of the Ottoman era. They include Orthodox Christians who were killed during the 1917 Revolution, Stalinist and other purges. Vladimir Bogoiavlenskij (d. 1917), Veniamin Kazanskij (d. 1922), Pavel Florensky (d. 1937), Seraphim Chichagov (d. 1937), Basil Preobrazhenskij (d. 1945) and other outstanding figures in this group are commonly overshadowed by Elisabeth Feodorovna (d. 1918), Tsar Nicolas II and the Russian imperial family. The 800,000 Serbian and Montenegrin new martyrs largely represent the Orthodox Christian response to ethnic cleansing in Yugoslavia during the Second World War. These latter two groups represent the Orthodox Church in conflict with both extremes of the political spectrum: Communist and Fascist regimes. Again, the use of the term emphasizes the heroism of individual Orthodox Christians alongside the injustices of an era and the gravity of the threat to the continued existence of Orthodox Christian communities and their way of life.

It must be noted that in the conflicts of the twentieth century the new martyrs are necessarily political figures and therefore by definition controversial. Even the new martyrs who witnessed to their faith within the collapsing Ottoman Empire in the early decades of the twentieth century represent victims of modern political conflicts. Genocide, ethnic cleansing and ideological purges were not entirely inventions of the twentieth century but they were refined as political tools from the eve of the First World War onwards. In this sense, the phenomenon of the new martyrs has arguably transcended the Eastern Christian context in the modern period. It is documented that in the prisons and concentration camps of assorted totalitarian regimes, now canonized Orthodox Christian new martyrs rubbed shoulders with Roman Catholic, Protestant, Jewish, Muslim and other martyrs. All are indisputably martyrs to injustice, racism and sectarianism. Increasingly, the term is now used for witnesses to a variety of faiths of the last hundred years or the modern period generally.

Faithful to their pedigree, the Orthodox new martyrs include individuals from most walks of life alongside large groups that are often commemorated anonymously. Like the martyrs of Christian antiquity, they are a mix of clergy and laity, men, women and children, loyal Christians, 'reverting' apostates and new converts. Necessarily extraordinary individuals, in that they witnessed to their faith to the point of death, the new martyrs theologically represent the transfiguration of ordinary people, concerns and even entire communities. The new martyrs indicate the tenacity of the Orthodox Christian vision in the face of inter-faith rivalry or inter-communal conflict and the onslaught of a succession of nationalist or secular ideologies. The promotion of the cult of the new martyrs within Orthodox Churches, whether clandestinely or publicly, has proved to be a profound gesture of resistance, hope for, and confidence in the future. The new martyrs have illustrated most aspects of Orthodox spirituality across many centuries and in changing circumstances. Above all, they have symbolized the dignity of the Church in adverse circumstances and the inevitability of Christian renewal.

The above assertion flies in the face of comments of generations of outside observers who perceived the Orthodox Churches as being most moribund in the very years that produced the greatest numbers of new martyrs. In contrast to the witness of contemporary ascetic or contemplative figures the witness of the new martyrs clearly had an immediate and inspirational impact. Undoubtedly, the continued existence of saintly elders, male and female, remained an issue of prestige to devout Orthodox Christians. However, the passion of new martyrs surely served as an outward declaration of the faithfulness of the entire community. Clearly, this has been a particularly potent message in times when the Church has been under attack or in retreat. It stands to reason, therefore, that the new martyrs are not simply a historical phenomenon. We must assume that the example of many new martyrs will continue to inspire Christians and others, and that unfolding political and related upheavals will add to their number, at least in the foreseeable future.

The political dimension to the cult of the new martyrs has generally been over-looked. The importance within the group of dynamic women, including Philothei of Athens (d. 1589), Kassandra Ypsilanti of Trebizond (d. 1677), Elisabeth Feodorovna (d. 1918) and Maria Skobtsova (d. 1945) deserves closer study. The centrality to move-ments of 'national reawakening' of new martyrs like Theodore Sladich (d. 1788) or Kosmas Aitolos (d. 1779) needs to be reassessed in a wider, pan-Orthodox context. Furthermore, the existence of new martyrs who challenged the marriage of Church and state itself, including Kosmas Phlamiatos (d. 1852) in Greece, Ilia Chavchavadze (d. 1907) in Georgia and dissidents like Catherine Rouka (d. 1927), merits analysis. Regarding dissent, the mainstream Orthodox Churches need to consider whether Old Believer and Old Calendar new martyrs are indeed peripheral to the wider group. It is important to disentangle the politics of inter-communal conflict in accounts of martyr-doms, not least because this remains an issue in many countries. The case of St Sidhum Bishai (d. 1844) in Egypt remains relevant as the Copts have continued to experience sporadic pogroms. Above all, it is necessary to define the Christian vision that unites most Orthodox new martyrs and discover how this enabled people such as Anthimos the Georgian (d. 1716) to transcend their culture and origins to achieve pan-Orthodox significance. The very cult of the new martyrs attests to the persistence of unique fea-tures of Eastern Christian civilization. Veneration of John of Trebizond (d. 1492), George of Sofia (d. 1515), Zlata/Chryse of Moglena (d. 1795) or George of Ioannina (d. 1838) and other new martyrs has both withstood the test of time and remained trans-national, thus reaffirming an underlying unity amongst Eastern Christians.

Further reading

The Anargyroi

Antonopoulos, N. (1999) *Loukas Simpheroupoleos* (Luke of Simferopol). Athens: Akritas.

Asmatike Akolouthia (1988) *Ton en Kypro Agion, Moni Stavrovouniou* (Offices to the Saints of Cyprus, Monastery of Stavrovouni). Nicosia: Leucosia.

Baring-Gould, S. (1882) *The Lives of the Saints*. London: J. Hodges.

Butler, A. (1937) *The Lives of the Saints*. London: Burns, Oates and Washbourne.

Constantelos, D. (1984) *Byzantine Philanthropy and Social Welfare*. Athens: Phos.

Cowie, L. W. and Selwyn Gummer, J. (1974) *The Christian Calendar*. London: Weidenfeld and Nicolson.

Garneli, D. (1988) *Neophanes Dimitrios Lekkas*. Athens.

Gedeon, M. (1899) *Byzantinon Heortologion* (Byzantine Heortologion). Constantinople.

Koehler, L. (1988) *Saint Elizabeth the New Martyr*. New York: Orthodox Palestine Society.

Kontaxopoulos, K. (1990) *Agioi Iatroi tes Orthodoxias* (Holy Physicians of Orthodoxy). Athens: Kardias Publications.

Menaia (1977) Athens: Ekdoseis Apostolikis Diakonias.

Militsi, Y. (1997) *The Holy Twenty Anargyroi*. Trikala: Myripnoa Anthi.

Moustaki, V. (1973) *Vioi Agion* (Lives of the Saints). Athens: Astir.

Platanitou, K. (1989) *Eortologion tis Orthodoxou Ekklisias* (Heortologion of the Greek Orthodox Church). Athens: Ekdoseis Apostolikis Diakonias.

Psilakis, N. (1986) *The Monasteries of Crete*. Athens: Gramme.

Reymond, E. A. E. and Barns, J. W. B. (1973) *Four Martyrdoms from the Pierpoint Coptic Codices*. Oxford: Clarendon Press.

Seraphim Byzantios, Bishop of Argyropolis (1863) *Thesavros Hagion* (Thesaurus/Treasury of Saints). Constantinople.

Theoklitos, D. (1987) *Agios Anthimos tis Chiou* (Saint Anthimos of Chios). Athens: Astir.

Timotheos, A. (1990) *Patericon of the Kiev Caves Lavra, Ekdoseis Hieras Mones Parakletou*. Attiki: Oropos.

Tsolakidi, H. (2000) *Agiologio tis Orthodoxias* (Orthodox Hagiology). Athens.

Vasilopoulos, H. (1987) *Vioi ton Agion* (Lives of the Saints). Athens: Orthodoxos Typos.

Velimirović, N., Bishop of Zitsa (1985) *The Prologue of Ohrid*, vols I–IV. Birmingham: Lazarica Press.

The New Martyrs

Antonopoulos, N. (1999) *Archiepiskopos Loukas* (Archbishop Luke of Simferopol). Athens: Akritas.

Cavarnos, C. (1992) *The Significance of the New Martyrs*. Etna, Calif.: Centre for Traditionalist Orthodox Studies.

Stefan Decani (2005) Monk Hariton, the New Martyr of Kosovo. *The Orthodox Word* 241 (Platina, Calif.).

Dionysiou, G. (1989) *Martyres tes Katoches* (Martyrs of the Second World War). Athens: Tinos.

Hackel, S. (1981) *Pearl of Great Price: The Life of Mother Maria Skobtsova*. Crestwood, NY: St Vladimir's Seminary Press.

Ikonomou, F. (1991) *Hagiologion Panton ton en Epeirou Hagion* (Lives of the Saints of Epirus). Athens.

Mager, H. (1998) *Elizabeth, Grand Duchess of Russia*. New York: Carroll and Graf.

Meinardus, O. F. A. (1999) *Two Thousand Years of Coptic Christianity*. Cairo: American University in Cairo Press.

Mikrayiannanitis, G. (1978) *Eurytanikon Leimonarion* (Offices to the Saints of Eurytania). Athens.

Millar, L. (1991) *Grand Duchess Elizabeth of Russia, New Martyr*. Redding, Calif.: Nikodemos Press.

Papadopoulos, L. J. and Lizardos, G. (1985) *New Martyrs of the Turkish Yoke*. Seattle: St Nektarios Press.

Paris, E. (1990) *Convert or Die: Catholic Persecution in Yugoslavia during World War Two*. Chino, Calif.: Chick Press.

Polsky, M. (1979) *The New Martyrs of Russia*. Munich: St Job of Pochaev Press.

Praktika Theologikou Synedriou (1988) (Papers presented to the Theological Conference), Thessaloniki.

Solonos, N. (1994) *Neoi Martyres tes Rosikes Ekklesias* (New Martyrs of the Russian Church). Athens.

Vaporis, M. N. (2000) *Witnesses for Christ*. Crestwood, NY: St Vladimir's Seminary Press.

CHAPTER 21

Eastern Christian Hagiographical Traditions

Oriental Orthodox: Syriac Hagiography

Eva Synek

The Golden Age of Syriac Hagiography

The Golden Age of Syriac hagiography was late antiquity, so this period will be empha-sized in this survey. Some *vitae* of that period, which are of Syrian origin, won interna-tional popularity for their heroes: for example, the story of St Alexis of Edessa (Mar Resha), the 'Man of God' (the core of the Life from the fifth century); and the *vita* of St Pelagia, a converted courtesan (pseudonym of the fifth-century 'deacon Jacob'). The last-mentioned life became even the model for a particular type of Byzantine *vita*, prais-ing 'transvestite' saints, usually women living a disguised life as a monk. Besides these, the legend of the two famous physician saints, Cosmas and Damian, is first testified by Syriac manuscripts of the fifth or sixth century.

On the other hand, the hagiographic production of other churches was added to the genuine Syriac heritage. Such a mutual process has to be taken into consideration whenever we try to single out particular features of 'Syrian' sainthood. The translation of original Greek versions of *vitae*, such as the Life of St Antony the Great, as well as early collections of sayings (*apophthegmata*) from the Egyptian monastic milieu, and collections of short lives, such as Palladius' *Lausiac History*, were major contributions to the hagiographic sources transmitted to the Syriac-speaking world. One of the most famous examples for Syriac sources of this kind is Anan Isho's seventh-century collec-tion *The Paradise of the Holy Fathers*. At the same time, style and motifs from 'foreign' hagiography influenced the native Syriac literary tradition and the shaping of indige-nous *vitae*. It became a common practice, for example, to claim that a Syrian saint had links with Egyptian monasticism.

The development of hagiography in the multicultural world of late antique Syria has been described as 'a fluid interchange of cultures and experiences' (Ashbrook Harvey, 1980: 67). From the very beginning, Syriac hagiography borrowed a great deal from Greek hagiography. Particularly the hagiography of the anti-Chalcedonian faction also interacted intensively with Coptic hagiography. However, Syriac hagiography did not only take from others, there was 'an even exchange of goods', as the Syriac tradition was 'trading with ample wealth of its own' (Ashbrook Harvey, 1980: 67).

Particularization from the Seventh Century Onwards

From the seventh century onwards Syriac hagiographic works continued to be produced. However, compared with the older *vitae*, most of the texts written in honour of medieval indigenous Syrian saints had no more than a local or temporal influence, often a very restricted one. Thus, we have clearly to distinguish between the meaning of such a text in its original historical and ecclesiastical context, and its modern meaning, which may be quite different for Syrian Christians themselves who, in most cases, will never have heard of it, and for scholars who might be extremely interested in a single surviving manuscript. The Life of Theodotos of Amida (d. 698), a wandering charismatic, is a good example of this type of text. It is an untypical *vita*, as it obviously goes back to the dictation of an eyewitness who lacked literary skill, so that he had to rely on a scribe in order to put down the memory of 'his' saint. The authenticity of the report, its closeness to the historical saint, as well as its provenance from a low social environment, makes it extremely interesting reading for modern scholars, and not only for those interested in social history. However, as pointed out by Andrew Palmer (1987), we should not think that Theodotos' cult was ever widespread. There are almost no copies of his Life nor does he appear in any liturgical commemorations. Even at ṬurʿAbdin, where this late imitator of Jesus and his movement of wandering charismatics spent the latter part of his unsettled life, and where he was buried, there are few traces today.

Tendencies towards Acculturation

Particularization of medieval Syriac hagiography was combined with a gradual process of 'Byzantinization' of the West Syrian heritage. The so-called 'Melkite' communities which followed the Chalcedonian Creed in particular show signs of alienation from indigenous traditions. As already mentioned, Greek influence loomed large from the very beginning. During the fifth and sixth centuries, some writings show cultural syncretism at its best. But in the wake of the Christological controversies, the Hellenic influence on the West Syrian Orient took on a new quality, owing to a mixture of religious and political events that undermined the independence and confidence of Syrian theological writers. Gradually the feasts of Greek saints became even more popular with Melkite Christians than most of their indigenous celebrations.

The even greater impact of 'foreign' traditions can be traced in some of those particular churches that were integrated into the Catholic community. In modern times, Latinization followed upon medieval Byzantinization. In the period between the Council of Trent in 1545–1563 and the Second Vatican Council in 1962–1965, the Maronites, Chaldeans, and Syrian Catholics suffered considerable pressure on their indigenous traditions. In some respects, 'acculturation' is a more appropriate term to use than 'influence' or 'reception'. The Indian daughter-church of the Syrian Orthodox Church is a particular case: for those Indian Christians who were unhappy with Latinization and therefore sought shelter under the hegemony of the Syrian Orthodox Church, this union meant not only a significant change of liturgical traditions, but also the traditional lists of controversial saints and heretics were changed.

However, in no case was there a total loss of the old Syrian heritage. Nor was the development strictly one-sided. Byzantine Menaia list many oriental saints. The churches that united with Rome brought their own liturgical and spiritual heritage into the Catholic community. Thus hitherto existing saints of the various denominations who had not yet found their way into the Roman calendar entered the Catholic Church 'through the back door', as it were. The evidence suggests some degree of reciprocity between the different communities and Rome. Moreover, there were various formal beatifications and canonizations of Syrian Christians after their communities had united with Rome. The Catholic Church as such was involved, for example, when the pope canonized St Sharbel (1977) and St Rafqa (2001), and beatified Blessed Hardini (1998), all members of the Lebanese Maronite Order who had lived in the nineteenth century.

The Creation of New Saints

This leads us to the question of the creation of new saints. From the tenth century onwards, in the Latin context, the universal veneration of new saints had to be confirmed by papal processes. In modern times, this procedure was also expanded to the Oriental Catholic Churches. Also, some Orthodox Churches developed more formalized procedures for approving new saints, although none adopted in full the specific Roman procedure. In the twentieth century both Indian jurisdictions of the Syrian Orthodox Church recognized Mar Gregorios Geevarghese (d. 1902) as their indigenous saint. A new Syrian Orthodox saint generally accepted by his Church is Patriarch Elias III, who was canonized in 1982, fifty years after his death in India.

The traditional way of granting a holy man or woman afterlife (in the veneration of Christian believers) was the establishment of a cult and the composition of a *vita*. If a name also made its way into a martyrologion or heterologion there was a good chance that it would receive favourable and long-lasting reception. The earliest known source of this kind, the so-called *Breviarium* or *Martyrologium Syriacum*, is the Syriac translation of a Greek collection from Nicomedia which can be dated precisely to 362. The Syriac text was composed in Edessa in 411. The earlier a name entered such a collection the greater the chance of its wider dissemination. As far as later collections are concerned, they often never won more than local and limited significance.

Normally, a new cult had to be approved at least by the local bishop or an abbot. In some cases it appears that the bishop or abbot himself was instrumental in initiating a cult. In other cases, popular veneration could force the hierarchy to react. Sometimes an emerging cult can be traced back as far as a saint's own lifetime or to his or her death, but in such cases historical accuracy and initial hagiographic styling cannot be easily separated. In other cases, it is even more difficult to reconstruct the point when a cult of veneration began. Thus, quite a number of saints whose lives and deaths are set in the early Christian period are legendary figures. Their *vitae* and passions might have been woven around historical names, and there may even have been some oral traditions before hagiographic writings formed the image of an ancient hero. The construction of sanctuaries might be linked to some local knowledge about burials. But in several cases such traces are very faint and the scholarly community has not reached a çonsensus on their evaluation. Some cults did not start until someone affirmed that he or she had experienced supernatural phenomena, such as miracles or visions, which led to the 'discovery' of relics of a person who had long been dead.

It was in any case a good step to produce a *vita* or passion in order to promote a cult and to keep a saint's memory alive for the future. As far as most of the new medieval saints were concerned, local cults and the restricted circulation of their *vitae* were the only medium. In the East Syrian liturgical tradition in particular a comparatively small number of saints, most of them from the early Christian period, are honoured by individual liturgical commemoration and commonly celebrated feasts. But also in the other Syrian Churches, the number of saints who are generally commemorated is quite restricted today. Thus, those traditions which are easily accessible from modern church calendars cover only a very small field. To have a full picture of Syrian cults and hagiographic writings, it would be necessary to include a broad historical overview including various local traditions from the past and the present. This remains a challenge for future scholarship.

Special Features of Syriac Hagiography

Ascetic orientation

The strong ascetic orientation of Syrian Christianity may be its most widely known feature. No wonder that asceticism had also a significant impact on Syriac hagiography. From the very beginning, until the most recent beatifications and canonizations of nineteenth-century Maronites, almost all saints who were not venerated as martyrs have an ascetic element in some way or another. The *vitae* praise monks and nuns, church officials and hierarchs with an ascetic background, but also a considerable number of lay ascetics, men and women who lived a life of continence and prayer without taking any formal vows. Although not unique to Syrian Christianity this latter feature is quite prominent. As Ashbrook Harvey and Brock put it: 'What binds the stories' of Syrian martyrs and ascetics 'is the fact that holy lives and holy deaths are about the same thing. What is at stake is not the idea that asceticism might be an alternative form of martyrdom or vice versa, but that martyrdom and asceticism are two forms of the same event: humanity's encounter with the divine' (Ashbrook Harvey and Brock, 1998: 19).

There are famous hierarchs and learned theologians as well as heroes of charity, among the Syrian ascetics. Moreover, a considerable number are known for asceticism in rather extreme forms. In his *History of the Monks of Syria*, Theodoret of Cyrrhus (d. 466) describes such ascetics of his time, for example, wandering ascetics who continued the charismatic tradition of the New Testament, and 'grazers', who lived more or less naked in the wilderness, enacting the life of Adam and Eve in Eden. The prototype of the stylites, St Symeon (d. 459), who, according to Theodoret, was famous all over the Roman Empire during his lifetime, spent most of his life on top of a pillar. Of course, almost all hagiographic testimonies – even those which are close to a saint's life, such as Theodoret's stories, and rely more or less on eyewitnesses – attribute to their heroes other aims than those of modern biographers and historical researchers. Nevertheless, the historical kernel of the story of a famous ascetic should not be underestimated, if only for the reason that it describes an ascetic practice which hardly fits in with modern western ideas of holiness. Some of the more striking forms of asceticism may have irritated the church authorities at the time, as we can see from canons outlawing itinerant ascetics. At times there were also profound tensions between the ascetics and the hierarchy, particularly in the Church of the East. But in general one must be aware that what is described in the lives of these saints was attractive to contemporaries; it echoed their perception of a holy man or woman. Thus, St Symeon on top of his pillar is said to have attracted 'Arabs, Persians, Armenians, Iberians, Himyarites, Spaniards, Britons, Gauls and Italians'. As Theodoret puts it, people of all nations and classes came seeking his advice and intercession with God.

Literalization of symbols and bodily representation of biblical models

The phenomenon of stylites has to be interpreted in the larger framework of Syrian spirituality. It seems that the general tendency in early Christianity to literalize symbols, and to represent biblical models bodily, is prevalent in the Syrian tradition. Symeon and his successors standing on a pillar, that is to say, standing midway between heaven and earth, symbolically fulfilled the call to imitate Christ in a radical sense. Standing with their arms outstretched in prayer, they were living images of the crucified. Thus also St Alexis, the prototype of a Mesopotamian 'holy man', is not only to be seen in a functional way but has to be interpreted in terms of the *imitatio Christi*. The story of this young man from a wealthy family who leaves everything behind to take up the life of a beggar at the church door, can be read as the literal translation of Jesus' *kenosis* as found in Phil. 2: 7. So Alexis' Life has also to end with an empty grave, a motive which seems to belong to the original core of the legend. Likewise, those who went naked, surviving on a vegetarian diet, living among wild animals, exposing themselves to all kinds of weather, 'and leading an uninterrupted life of prayer and devotion to the divine as indeed Adam and Eve had done. They acted out with their bodies the spiritual truth of their faith' (Ashbrook Harvey and Brock 1998: 9) that Christ, the second Adam, made it possible to live as it were in paradise before the Fall. Most of those features of Syriac hagiography, which might be bewildering for many modern western Christians, can simply be understood as the consequence of the embodiment of Christian belief in practical behaviour.

These are obviously rooted in biblical models: first of all in Jesus himself and his chosen disciples, but also Old Testament prophets such as Elijah and Elisha, and John the Baptist, Paul and his female counterpart St Thecla, who became particularly prominent in Syrian Christianity, thanks to the widespread and quasi-canonical reception of the apocryphal *Acts of Paul and Thecla*. Less prominent figures from the New Testament, such as Tabitha, who served the early Christian community with works of charity, according to Acts 9: 36, could also be models. It is the common teaching of Syriac hagiographic sources that it is through the believer's life and death that his or her faith becomes manifest. For Euphemia, a saintly widow from Amida, whom John of Ephesus in the sixth century portrayed as a second Tabitha, that meant not only prayer and fasting but also begging for the poor and working hard to earn her own sustenance.

Martyrdom as a continuing challenge

Another important point in this and other stories collected in John of Ephesus' *Lives of the Eastern Saints* is full commitment to the truth. From the perspective of John, who wrote during the Christological controversies of the sixth century, this meant resistance to the Chalcedonian Creed, which the imperial authorities tried to impose upon all Christians. Owing to political and geographical circumstances, becoming a confessor or martyr was a true challenge for the Syrian faithful. They had to stand up for their beliefs against their fellow Christians and the persecuting power of the Christian empire. This might explain why the Maccabean mother (St Shmuni according to Syriac tradition) and her children, who figure as prototypes for the later Christian martyrs, together with St Stephen and St Thecla, became more prominent in the Syrian churches than elsewhere. Not only have the adherents of the Church of the East always been a minority, under either Zoroastrianism or Islam, but they have had to manage various conflicts with neighbours and rulers of other beliefs. The martyrs of Najran in southern Arabia were massacred under Jewish rulers in the sixth century. Even in the Roman Empire Christians stood against Christians soon after the consolidation of Christianity as the state religion.

From the seventh century onwards West Syrian Christians had to live under Islamic rule, which might have seemed at times the more favourable proposition for those dissenting from the Emperor's Creed. However, the toll of Syrian Christians killed in late antiquity was relatively low. A much greater number died during the Mongol invasions of the thirteenth and fourteenth centuries, and during the nineteenth and twentieth centuries. At that time many ethnic Syrian Christians were driven out of their traditional settlements in Eastern Turkey or lost their lives in local conflicts with Kurds and Turks. The Maronite community was particularly afflicted during a massacre committed by the Druze in 1860. Considering the political context, it is hardly surprising that the celebration of new martyrs, such as Anthony, a martyr from the times of the caliph Hārūn ar-Rašīd (786–809), according to Melkite *Synaxaria*, was retained rather than the celebration of early Christian figures, particularly in the Church of the East. However, general liturgical commemoration of unnamed saints and the continuing copying and rewriting of the lives of ancient heroes provoked less suspicion, but served the same purpose.

Shared Saints

Biblical saints

The first and foremost category of 'shared saints' goes back to the biblical writings and
related literature. Not only the canonical texts but also apocryphal works, such as the
Acts of St Thomas, contributed highly to the development of hagiography in general and
to Syriac hagiography in particular. Biblical and quasi-biblical figures have been direct
models for Syrian Christians of all times, as well as for hagiographers for their interpretation of holy men and women. They interchange these figures (such as St Thecla) with
later saints as models for the future. So already Jacob of Sarug in the fifth or sixth
century, a saint himself according to the Syrian Orthodox and Maronite traditions,
linked St Shmuni and her children with the Edessan martyr Habib and his mother.
Significantly, most of the biblical figures who are more famous in Syrian Christianity
are models of the ascetic life and martyrdom. This is obvious from feasts and calendars,
hymns and prayers, but is also reflected in all kinds of hagiographical writings such as
lives, passions and homilies dedicated to post-biblical saints.

Besides the Maccabean mother and her children, the prophet Elias is most prominent
from the Old Testament. From the New Testament John the Baptist, St Stephen, the
innocent children of Bethlehem and some Apostles, such as Peter, Paul and Thomas,
who is said to have taken the Gospel as far as India, are still celebrated today. From the
Apocrypha, Addai and his disciple Mari, the Apostles of Edessa, as well as Edessa's first
Christian king, Abgar, have to be added. The tradition of the 'first bishop' of Jerusalem
is also alive among Syrians; Peter, Addai and Mari, James, the brother of the Lord are
traditionally assigned an old anaphora (eucharistic formula), which is still in use.
Among the women, Paul's female companion, the 'apostle-like protomartyr' and model
of female ascetics, Thecla, was more important in former times, when her 'Acts' enjoyed
quasi canonical status. The traditional place connected with her was Merymelik, and
today there is a prosperous cultic centre at Ma'alula near Damascus. The sanctuary is
guarded by Orthodox Syrian nuns but visited by the faithful of all denominations, thus
figuring as a good example for the ecumenical significance of Syrian saints and their
cults. Finally we should not forget Mary, the Mother of Christ, who enjoys particular
veneration in all Syrian Churches. She has various fixed feast days in all Syrian Churches
including the Church of the East, although it does not generally use the title 'Theotokos'
(Godbearer), which the Council of Ephesus in 431 confirmed, against the teaching of
Nestorius.

Martyrs

As with their biblical forerunners, many martyrs from early Christian times are not
only shared saints but 'universal' saints as well, such as the Forty Martyrs of Sebaste,
St George and St Theodore, St Barbara and St Juliana, St Cosmas and St Damian, St
Julitta and her son St Kyriakos. But at the same time one might claim that some of

them, such as St Ignatius of Antioch are 'Syrian' in a more narrow sense. Also the 'ecclesiastical career' of Sergius and Bacchus, soldiers who died in Syria under the Emperor Maximian, is strongly linked to late antique Syria. In the sixth century they were so popular that not only the Empress Theodora, wife of the Chalcedonian Emperor Justinian, but also the Persian King Chosroes II, husband of the Church of the Christian Queen Shirin (a member of the Church of the East), sent gifts to their cultic centre at Resafa-Sergiopolis in Syria. Today the Catholic (Melkite) community of Ma'alula claims that their church dedicated to St Sergius has been in liturgical use without interruption since the fourth century. Some saints are from historically proven (or traditionally claimed) local Syrian origin. Ancient martyrs who can be called Syrian in the sense of their ethnicity or language competence are the Edessan martyrs Shmona, Guria and Habib.

The Syriac acts of the Persian martyrs are also of particular interest from a historical point of view. The historical core of their Lives goes back to the early fourth century, but many of the martyrs' stories are remote in place and time. This phenomenon can be observed in the development of the Edessan cycle, which has been expanded to include legendary material from the fifth century onwards. Only then were the stories of the so-called Doctrina Addai, and the acts of Sharbil, Babai and Barsamya added, perhaps in an attempt to improve the image of early Edessan Christianity. We should not forget that stories and legends can be confused and confounded, particularly when saints bearing the same name are misidentified, for example, Julian Anazarbos with Julian of Emesa and Julian of Antino. As far as ancient calendars are concerned it is often difficult to distinguish between such homonymous saints.

Ascetic figures, hierarchs and theologians from the first Christian centuries

The third group that figures prominently in the calendars of all Syrian Churches are early hierarchs and theologians. Some of them are indigenous Syrians such as St Ephrem, 'the harp of the Spirit', whose hymns greatly enriched the Syrian liturgy. Most of them have an ascetic slant, as already indicated. St Jacob, who was Bishop of Nisibis during the early fourth century, is famous as an ascetic as well as a teacher. The same is true for most of the Greek fathers, among whom may be mentioned Athanasius, the Cappadocian Fathers, and John Chrysostom, a native of Antioch and later Bishop of Constantinople, who entered the calendars of the Syrian Churches, even when there was no extended hagiographic tradition in Syriac.

Naturally not all famous ascetics became hierarchs. Antony the Great, for example, whose Syriac Life had a great impact on the formation of Syrian monasticism, or Symeon Stylites, the forefather of a considerable number of later Syrian stylites. A particular case is Mor Awgen. According to his legend, he was an Egyptian monk who became one of the fathers of Mesopotamian monasticism under the Persian King Shapur II in the fourth century. Although today he figures prominently in the East Syrian as well is in the West Syrian tradition it is not certain that there is any historical truth to his life story.

Shared traditions from later times

This brings us to the fact that the store of shared saints and hagiographic sources was enlarged when Syrian Christianity began to separate in the fifth century. To some extent the saints' lives crossed doctrinal borders, as did canon law and ascetic writings, sometimes, but not always, with a false attribution to an author whose doctrinal background was not under suspicion. Isaac of Nineveh, a famous seventh-century East Syrian writer of ascetic literature, proves that doctrinal quarrels did not necessarily dominate all spheres of ecclesiastical life. Isaac's writings have been honoured among all Christians, so that he has become a common saint of the East and West Syrians as well as the Byzantine and Latin traditions. When a saint such as Mor Awgen is said to have lived before the outbreak of the Christological differences, cross-border reception of hagiographic literature is even more likely. Febronia, who is praised as a 'super-saint' in her *vita* (a learned nun and teacher who gave her life in the Diocletian persecution) is a good example. Not only is it unknown if Febronia's *vita*, which is dated to the sixth or seventh century, is of East or West Syrian origin, but her cult which seems to have started in sixth-century Nisibis, had reached Constantinople by the seventh century. From there St Febronia continued her career to southern Italy and to France as well as to the Slavic world.

On the other hand, the reception of Byzantine hagiography was not restricted to the Melkite communities. It is apparent that Rabban Sliba, the Syrian Orthodox author of a local medieval martyrologion, used Melkite books for his collection, though in a selective manner. So St Nicholas and various martyrs typically celebrated by the Melkites entered the Syrian Orthodox and the Maronite calendars. There are examples of Maronite calendars which even commemorate various patriarchs of Constantinople along with 'typical' Syrian Orthodox saints.

Denominational Specification

Particular prominence in one church

Today the promotion of saints who are shared by different Syrian Churches reflects ecumenical concerns and the increasing desire for political cooperation of ethnic Syrians, as well as the efforts of some churches that have suffered considerable acculturation in the past, to rediscover their own roots. The recent liturgical reforms of the Maronite Church have included a revision of the calendar with the result that only a few feasts of Latin origin, which had become particularly popular among the Maronite faithful, remain.

Nevertheless denominational specification cannot be denied. First, there is the fact that some ancient saints are more prominent in one church than in another, and are therefore less well known and celebrated, or even totally neglected. So the martyr Mar Papa, the early fourth-century organizer of the Church of the East, is a particularly East

Syrian saint. Or Mar Maron and his disciple Jacob, ascetics already praised by Theodoret of Cyrrhus, can be called typically Maronite saints. It is of course from Mar Maron that the Maronites take their name.

In a sense, all those later saints of individual churches, who were not involved in doctrinal controversies, might also be counted in this category. The point is that the most popular ascetic figures, martyrs and hierarchs from medieval and modern times, are 'local saints' of a church, and may even be quite 'local' within that church, as explained above. It is not that they are confessional saints, so to speak. Conversely, some of them are even remembered for their conciliatory spirit, for example, the great medieval theologian and canonist of the Syrian Orthodox Church, Grīgōr bar 'Ebrāyā, better known as Barhebraeus (1226–86). Such saints do not create ecumenical problems. Of interest is also the above mentioned Empress Theodora who is celebrated by the Syrian Orthodox for having supported the non-Chalcedonians during the rule of Justinian. In the year 2000 a Patriarchal encyclical has secured her place in the calendar of the Oriental Orthodox Churches.

Holy 'heretics' and 'schismatic' saints

In contrast to the border-crossing saints introduced above there are saints who remained confessional. They are connected with the Christological quarrels of late antiquity. John of Ephesus has already been mentioned. His collection of 'Eastern saints' lives leads us straight to the question of ecclesiastical plurality within Syrian Christianity and its impact on hagiographical composition. Hagiography was certainly used as a weapon during the rising theological conflicts as it served confessional interests. Thus Jacob Baradeus (c.500–78), the organizer of the Syrian Orthodox Church, is an example of one of those saints who are commemorated in its diptychs.

In some particular cases the saint of one church is the theological *enfant terrible*, or even the formally condemned heretic of the other. Archbishop Mesrob Krikorian provided a list of such 'holy heretics' and 'schismatic saints'. For example, Patriarch Mar Severus of Antioch and Bishop Philoxenos of Mabbug, as well as the Alexandrian Patriarchs Dioscorus and Timothy Aelurus are venerated by the Oriental Orthodox Churches, but anathematized by the Eastern Orthodox and the Latin Churches. On the other hand, Pope Leo the Great and the Patriarchs Flavian, Anatolius and Gennadius are all anathematized by the Oriental Orthodox Churches, but count as saints in the Chalcedonian Churches. The problem has been discussed, but the issue has not yet been resolved in the ecumenical approach of modern times, and is particularly topical between the Syrian Orthodox Church and the Church of the East. There Diodore of Tarsus, Theodore of Mopsuestia, Narsai (Narses of Edessa) and occasionally Nestorius are celebrated as saints. But as far as other inter-church relations are concerned in the world of Eastern Christianity the general doctrinal approach helps to play down the problem of the status of saints from different traditions. There is a tendency instead to stress the shared hagiographical patrimony, as pointed out already.

New Catholic saints

From an ecumenical point of view those newly canonized or beatified persons of the Catholic Syrian Churches whose lives were directly connected with church-unions in some way have to be distinguished from other new saints. The nineteenth-century Malabar priest Kuriakose Elias Chavara (d. 1871, beatified 1986), a descendant of an old Indian Christian family, is not only known as the founder of a new monastic congregation, but also for his particular commitment to the Holy See. It was definitely the pope's side that he took when conflicts arose in his Church, because people were longing for an indigenous hierarchy and a better protection of Indian (Syrian) Christian traditions against Latinization. Such a person can hardly figure as a bridge-builder between the churches, while respect and veneration across boarders is more likely for Catholic saints without controversial backgrounds.

References and further reading

Alfeyev, H. (2000) *The Spiritual World of Isaac the Syrian.* Kalamazoo, Mich.: Cistercian Publications.

Ashbrook Harvey. S. (1980) Syriac Hagiography: An Emporium of Cultural Influences. In J. H. Eaton (ed) *Horizons in Semitic Studies.* Birmingham: University of Birmingham.

Ashbrook Harvey, S. (1990) *Asceticism and Society: John of Ephesus and the Lives of the Eastern Saints.* Berkeley: University of California Press.

—— (1996) Sacred bonding: mothers and daughters in early Syriac hagiography. *Journal of Early Christian Studies* 4: 27–56.

Ashbrook Harvey, S. and Brock, S. P. (1998, revised edition) *Holy Women of the Syrian Orient.* Berkeley: University of California Press.

Brock, S. P. (1997) *A Brief Outline of Syriac Literature.* Moran Etho 9. Kottayam: St Ephrem Ecumenical Research Institute.

Chaillot, C. (1998) *The Syrian Orthodox Church of Antioch and All the East: A Brief Introduction to its Life and Spirituality.* Geneva: Inter-Orthodox Dialogue.

Doran, R. (1992) *The Lives of Symeon Stylites.* Kalamazoo, Mich.: Cistercian Publications.

Key Fowden, E. (1999) *The Barbarian Plain: Saint Sergius between Rome and Iran.* Berkeley: University of California Press.

Krikorian, M. K. (1990) The Theological Significance of the Results of the Five Vienna Consultations. In *Pro Oriente – Vienna Dialogue. Communiques and Joint Documents.* Booklet 1. Horn: Austria.

Palmer, A. (1987) Saints' lives with a difference. Elijah on John of Tella (d. 538) and Joseph on Theodotos of Amida (d. 698). *Orientalia Christiana Analecta* 229: 203–16.

Parry, K. (2005) Vegetarianism in late antiquity and Byzantium: the transmission of a regimen. In W. Mayer and S. Trzcionka (eds.) *Feast, Fast or Famine: Food and Drink in Byzantium.* Brisbane: Australian Association for Byzantine Studies.

Price, R. M. (1985) *The History of the Monks of Syria.* Kalamazoo, Mich.: Cistercian Publications.

Takeda, F. F. (1998) The Syriac version of the Life of Antony: a meeting point of Egyptian monasticism with Syriac native asceticism. *Orientalia Christiana Analecta* 256: 185–94.

Witakowski, W. (1994) Mart(y) Shmuni, the mother of the Maccabean martyrs, in Syriac tradition. *Orientalia Christiana Analecta* 247: 153–68.

CHAPTER 22

Eastern Christian Hagiographical Traditions

Oriental Orthodox: Coptic Hagiography

Youhanna Nessim Youssef

The Coptic Calendar

Of all the survivals from pharaonic Egypt, the calendar is the most striking. Each of the twelve months of the Coptic calendar still carries the name of one of the deities or feasts of ancient Egypt. The year was divided into three seasons of equal length, each comprising four months. Possibly as early as the Ramesside period, each month came to be named after an important festival that was celebrated during that period of time. The twelve months and the origins of their names are as follows:

1 Tut (11/12 September to 9/10 October). The first month of the Coptic year was dedicated to Thoth, god of wisdom and science, inventor of writing.
2 Babah (10/11 October to 9/10 November). In the second month came the celebration of the 'beautiful feast of Opet', whose name Paopi signifies 'that of Opet'.
3 Hatur (10/11 November to 9/10 December). This month commemorated Hathor, a very ancient goddess.
4 Kiyahk (10/11 December to 8/9 January). This month derives its name from a ritual vase that was probably used for measuring incense.
5 Tubah (9/10 January to 7/8 February). The festival of the Great Sacrifice, occurs in this month.
6 Amshir (8/9 February to 9 March). This is the month of the 'large fire' because it is the coldest time of year.
7 Baramhat (10 March to 8 April). This month was originally consecrated to a festival; but after the death of Amenhotep, first king of the eighteenth dynasty, he became the object of a particular cult, which was observed in this month.
8 Baramudah (9 April to 8 May). This month was dedicated to Ermonthis, goddess of the harvest.

9   Bashans (9 May to 7 June). This month took its name from the ancient festival of Khonsou, a lunar god.

10   Ba'unah (8 June to 7 July). The Festival of the Valley was a local Theban
festival.

11   Abib (8 July to 6 August). This month was consecrated to Ipy, goddess of
fecundity, who assumed the form of a hippopotamus.

12   Misra (7 August to 5 September). In the last month of the year the birth of
the sun god Ra was celebrated.

Finally, Nasi, the epagomenal, or intercalary days, called the 'delayed days' or the
'little month', are five extra days that follow the month of Misra (six during a leap
year).

Coptic Hagiography

Coptic Egypt was influenced by Greek Christian culture hence many of its hagiographical texts were written first in that language and translated later into Coptic. It is important to consult the classical hagiographical tools, such as the *Bibliotheca Hagiographica
Orientalis*, *Subsidia Hagiographica*, and the *Bibliotheca Sanctorum*. There are several ways
to approach the study of hagiography; we have chosen to start with the liturgical
approach or how the Coptic Church presents its saints through the Coptic liturgical
books.

There is no formal procedure for canonization in the Coptic Church. The saints are
commemorated through several rites, such as the rite of Glorifications, or by using
special hymns such as the *psalies*, the doxologies, and the *turuhat*. A short account of
a saint's life is included in the Synaxarion, and the Antiphonarion (Arabic: *Difnar*),
which contains a collection of hymns for the whole year. The hymn of the Antiphonarion is sung in the service of the Psalmodia which follows the office of Compline.
For the liturgical celebration, the Coptic Church possesses the Synaxarion of the
saints which asks for their intercession and their prayers. Another *synaxis* is also
recited before the Mass during the midnight prayer

Categories of Saints and Martyrs

The commemorated saints of the Coptic Church can be put into several categories. First
of all there is the Virgin Mary. She is celebrated on the feast of her birth, the feast of her
entrance into the temple, the feast of her rest during the flight into Egypt, the feast of
the Assumption of her body, and the consecration of the Church in the city of Philippi.
In addition, the whole month of Kiyahk, preceding the feast of the Nativity of Christ on
the 28th or 29th day of the month, is consecrated to the praise of the Virgin Mary, and
to comparing her image with various symbols in the Old Testament.

After Mary there are the angels and heavenly creatures. The Archangel Michael
(celebrated on 12 Hatur and 12 Ba'unah) is the most popular heavenly creature among

the Copts. He inherited several attributes from the ancient Egyptian religion, such as a special cake which was presented in ancient times to Osiris. According to Coptic tradition it was Michael the Archangel who announced Christ's resurrection to the women at the tomb. Michael is also the angel of the Last Judgement, holding a balance in his hand like the Egyptian god Anubis. Several churches and monasteries are named after him. The Archangel Gabriel (22 Kiyahk) is the angel of the Annunciation, hence his commemoration is included in the fasting at Advent, during the month of Kiyahk, and at the Feast of the Annunciation. In Coptic iconography he is always represented with the Virgin in the Annunciation, or with the Archangel Michael, holding a sword. The Archangel Raphael (celebrated on 3 Nasi) has been assimilated in the Coptic mind with the story of Tobit, and he is always presented as a guardian angel. The Archangel Suriel is, according to Coptic tradition, the trumpeter of the Apocalypse. There is also the feast of the four bodiless creatures (8 Hatur), as mentioned in Ezekiel 1: 4–11, and depicted in Christian iconography as the tetramorph, symbolizing the four Evangelists. A few churches are dedicated to them, among which is the ancient church of the Monastery of Saint Antony in the Egyptian desert.

The twenty-four elders of the Apocalypse (24 Hatur) represent a type of the priest on earth, their doxology being used to welcome new priests and bishops. John the Baptist (2 and 26 Tut, 2 and 30 Ba'unah, 30 Misra), known as the precursor or fore-runner of Christ, has a very special place in the Coptic *synaxis*. The Church asks for his intercession, as it does with the Virgin, the angels and the heavenly creatures, while with the other saints it only asks for their prayers. Also included among the commemorated saints are the prophets of the Old Testament, and the Evangelists and Apostles of the New Testament.

Few martyrs are known before the persecution by the Emperor Diocletian (r. 284–305). Those that are found in the Coptic calendar are non-Egyptians, such as Ignatius of Antioch, who died under the Emperor Trajan (r. 98–117), and the Seven Sleepers of Ephesus, who died under the Emperor Decius (r. 249–51). There is a legend about the martyr Eudoemon, who was from Erment in Upper Egypt. An angel is said to have informed him of the presence of Jesus, Joseph and the Virgin Mary at Ashmunein, while they were fleeing from Herod. He went there and worshipped the infant Jesus. After his return to his village, he refused to worship the pagan gods and as a result suffered martyrdom. The tradition of his martyrdom occurs only in the Synaxarion of Upper Egypt.

Among the martyrs of Egypt deriving from the great persecution under Diocletian there is an important category of clergy and bishops. There is historical evidence from the beginning of the fourth century for the martyrdom of Phileas Bishop of Thmui, Sarapamon Bishop of Nikiou (celebrated on 28 Hatur), Pisoura of Masil, Macrobius of Nikiou, Psate Bishop of Psoi, Gallinicus, and Ammonius. Sarapamon of Nikiu, whose name derives from Egyptian words meaning 'Son of Re who belongs to Amon', was a native of Jerusalem; upon the death of his parents he wanted to become a Christian. After an angelic vision, he went to Bishop John of Jerusalem and this bishop directed him to the Patriarch of Alexandria, Theonas, who baptised him. Sarapamon then became a monk. Peter, the successor of Theonas, called Sarapamon to assist him in the administration of the patriarchate, and then ordained him Bishop of Nikiu. After he had performed many miracles, the governor of Alexandria sent him to Upper Egypt, where he was beheaded.

There were martyrs from noble families such as Ptoleme of Dendarah (11 Kiyahk) and Kaou (28 Tubah). Kaou was a native of Bimay in the Fayyum. When the governor received orders from Diocletian to persecute the Christians, an angel appeared to Kaou and told him to go to the governor and confess his belief in Christ. On his way to the governor Kaou is said to have performed many miracles. After refusing to make a sacrifice required of him, Kaou was tortured and cast into prison. The governor then sent him to Upper Egypt where he confessed Christ and was beheaded.

Among the soldier martyrs there is Apa Dios (25 Tubah), Abakradjon (25 Abib) and Menas, a popular saint of the early Church. Another group of soldier martyrs is known as the martyrs of Antioch; they were supposedly members of a legendary noble family called Basilides. There are several genealogies mentioned in accounts of their martyrdoms, but they are largely unreliable because of inconsistencies. This collection of martyrdoms includes those of Basilides, Claudius, Apater and Iraaie, Macarius, Eusebius, sometimes Theodore, Victor, Besamon, Apoli and Justus.

Another cycle of martyrdom stories is attributed to a legendary individual called Julius of Akfahs. The research on this cycle reveals that most of the martyrdoms were written between the sixth or seventh century and the eleventh century. From a study of the events, administrative titles, geography, and personal names it is possible to subdivide the corpus into homogenous groups. The first group consists of martyrs related to Middle Egypt, such as Epima, Shenoufe, Heraclides, Didymus, Pansnew and Chamoul. It is evident that the compiler knew the geography of the district very well, and each story begins and ends the same way. The second group consists of stories about Ari and Anoub, which were written in Lower Egypt. Julius of Akfahs is presented in few lines and no useful geographical data are given that would help in dating. The third group consists of the story of Paese and Thecla. Written in a different style, it tells of a brother and a sister, and the text we have seems to be a combination of at least two narratives. Macarius of Antioch and Nahrawa represent the fourth group. This is characterized by exaggeration; the judge in the story is the emperor himself, and the events take place in Antioch, the capital. The eleventh-century story of the martyrdoms of John and Simon is also ascribed to Julius of Akfahs. There are also several texts in Arabic attributed to him, but it is hard to determine their real authorship.

There is a group of non-Egyptian martyrs that includes, for example, Isidore (19 Bashans), and Philotheus (16 Tubah). In the story, Philotheus was a native of Antioch whose parents worshipped a calf. At the age of 10 he rebelled against this worship and refused to prostrate himself before the calf, and became convinced that the sun was God. But a voice came from heaven and declared 'I am only a servant'. Then an angel visited him and taught him the truth. One year after this his parents arranged a feast and asked their sons to offer incense to the calf. The youth refused to take part in the feast. Diocletian is informed of these events, and sends for Philotheus, who after being questioned and tortured by the emperor, is finally executed.

A category of new martyrs belongs to the period following the Arab conquest of Egypt in the seventh century, and includes John of Phanidjoit, Salib (3 Kiyahk), and George al-Mozahim (19 Ba'unah). The accounts of these martyrdoms are quite graphic in their descriptions of atrocious tortures and physical sufferings as well as of amazing miracles. The general story line centres on the saints renouncing their Muslim faith, which they held either because they had been brought up as Muslims or because they had converted to Islam. Sometimes they are killed in an outbreak of mob violence or as a result of Muslim rulers looking for scapegoats. On the whole the geographical and historical data in these descriptions of martyrdoms are accurate and reliable.

It is known that Egypt was the cradle of the Christian monasticism, and monastic saints have a special place in the Coptic tradition. The first among these is Antony the Great, the founder of Christian monasticism, but there are also other important monks such as Macarius, Paul the Hermit, John Kama and Symeon the Stylite. The saintly monks can be grouped according to geographical location, so that we may speak of monks from Lower Egypt, such as Scetis, Nitria, and Kellia; monks from Middle Egypt, such as the disciples of Antony and those of the Fayyumic regions; and monks from Upper Egypt, such as Pachomius and Shenute. In this category we should include the foreigners who became monks in Egypt. If they are grouped according to the ascetic rule or lifestyle they followed, we find hermits, semi-hermits (cross-bearers), coenobitic monks and stylites. Categorized chronologically, they may be found in the fourth century, the fifth century, and so on.

The accounts of the eastern fathers of the Church, in contrast to those of some of the martyrs, are fairly accurate, historically, and authentic. Some of them are figures known only locally, while others, such as Basil the Great, are known throughout the Christian world. In this category are those fathers who played an important role in the Miaphysite movement, for example Dioscorus of Alexandria and Severus of Antioch, and in the establishment of a separate Church in Egypt. More information about Coptic saints and martyrs can be found in the publications in the reading list at the end of this chapter.

Nineteenth- and Twentieth-Century Martyrs and Saints

During the nineteenth and twentieth centuries several riots by Muslims have produced new martyrs for the Coptic Church. Among those of the nineteenth century is Sidhum Bishai (1804–44). He served as clerk at the port of Damietta when a Muslim-instigated revolt broke out and he was accused of insulting Islam. He was killed and his body now reposes in the Church of the Holy Virgin in Damietta.

Under the leadership of President Sadat Islamist fundamentalist movements were encouraged in Egypt. These groups began a systematic persecution of Christians, especially in Upper Egypt. The persecutions resulted in the deaths of many who became martyrs, some of them known by name while others remain anonymous. Islamic fundamentalism began to gain ground in Egypt in the late 1960s and was aggravated when Sadat became president in 1970. The new president was a pious Muslim and his name had been linked with the Muslim Brotherhood, whose founder and head, Hasan al-Banna, he had met as early as 1940. Sadat was appointed Secretary General of the Islamic Congress in 1954–5, and he represented President Nasser at the first Islamic summit in Rabbat in 1969. Under Sadat's regime Islamic extremism spread rapidly. He suspected that the vigorous and opinionated spiritual leader of the Copts, Pope Shenouda III, was willing to take advantage of the seeming weakness of the pre-October 1973 government to press for the fulfilment of Coptic demands. Sadat did not take any action after the Khanqa incidents in 1972 when a Coptic church was burned.

In 1977, under pressure from Islamic militants, the Egyptian government announced its intention of reinstating capital punishment for those Christians who converted to Islam and then reneged on their new faith and returned to Christianity. The Coptic Church protested with a five-day fasting period. In 1978 and 1979 Muslim fundamentalist violence against Coptic Christians escalated, and Sadat was unwilling or unable to suppress it. During these years a priest, Marcus Aziz, was killed in the city of Samalut in the province of Minya. In the same city, Father Gabriel abd al Mutagaly, and a woman and a child were killed. In Qalubyia province, in Mansha Delo, two Coptic men were killed for being Christian. The government took the part of the Islamists and promulgated the idea that shariah law should be the basis for legislation in Egypt.

In June 1981, six months before the assassination of President Sadat, in the Cairene suburb of Zawiya al-Hamra, Muslim fundamentalists tried to build a mosque on a parcel of land belonging to a Copt. The landowner was surrounded and threatened by a crowd of Muslims, and he opened fire in self-defence. The police did not intervene and at the end of the three-day on-and-off battle, there were many victims.

A relatively calm period followed the assassination of Sadat in 1981 and the election of President Mubarak. However, Muslim fundamentalists started receiving funds associated with oil revenues and some of this money helped to finance extremist activities against the Copts. As a result Islamist groups started to control several regions. In Assiut province, in the city of Abu Tig, Father Ruweiss Fakher, parish priest of the Church of Dweina in Abu Tig was killed in 1988, having resisted pressure to close his church.

There was much aggression against Christians under a new interior minister, Abdel Halim Musa, who was known for his Islamist sympathies. In April 1990 seven Copts died in an attack against a Coptic church in Alexandria. In September 1991, at Embaba in Cairo, several Copts were murdered and their homes destroyed. In May 1992, at Dayrout in Assiut province, twelve Coptic students were murdered along with their teacher while they were in class. The government was unable to control the situation. Again in 1993 many violent incidents took place in the provinces of Assiut and Sohag, for which various Islamic radical and militant groups were responsible. In January 2000 at El-Kosheh in Sohag province twenty-one Copts were murdered and many shops were destroyed as a result of random armed raids on the community.

Several modern monastics are venerated by the Coptic people as saints, among whom is 'Abd al-Masih al-Makari (1892–1963). He was a monk at the Monastery of Saint Macarius, but lived at times in other monasteries. He served as a parish priest in the village of al-Manahra and used sometimes to act strangely, to hide his holiness. He is venerated as a wonderworker and is buried in the Church of al-Manahra. Abraham

Bishop of Fayyum (1829–1914) was the abbot of the Monastery of al-Muharraq in Upper Egypt. After being accused of mismanagement he was tracked down to the Monastery of Baramus. There he met the abbot who was to become Patriarch Cyril V, and who would ordain him Bishop of Fayyum. Abraham is known for his charity to the poor, and as a wonderworker. He is buried in Dair al-'Azab, Fayyum. Mikha'il al-Buhayri (1847–1923), a monk in the Monastery of al-Muharraq and a disciple of Anba Abraham, Bishop of Fayyum, practised sanctity by observing total silence.

Patriarch Cyril VI (1959–71) was first a monk at the Monastery of Baramus, before he became a hermit in the hills near Cairo. During the Second World War he was forced to leave his cell, which was in a windmill, and to live in Cairo. He built a church and named it after his patron saint, Menas. After his enthronement he built the Monastery of Saint Menas and the Cathedral of Cairo, and during his patriarchate some relics of Saint Mark were returned to Egypt. In the latter part of his period of office apparitions of the Virgin Mary began to be seen in the church of Zeitun, a suburb of Cairo. He is venerated as a wonderworker, and his shrine at the Monastery of Saint Menas, along with the cells he occupied at the Monastery of Baramus and at the windmill, attract many pilgrims.

Newly Discovered Saints

The remains of several saints and martyrs of the Coptic Church have been newly discovered. While the ambo of the Church of Abū Sarjah in Cairo was being restored, some bones were brought to light on 25 April 1991. There were identified as the relics of Saint Bashnūfa, who was mentioned in the *History of the Patriarchs*, and the story of whose martyrdom was composed in 1164. This martyr, according to the *History of the Patriarchs*, was

> A monk (who) was martyred at their hands (of the mob). His name was Shanūfah (or Bashnūfa) from the monastery of Abba Macarius. They seized him and gave him the choice of converting to Islam, but he refused to do so and they killed him, and they intended to burn his body, but the Christians took it, and they buried it in the Church of Abū Sargah in Cairo on the 24th day of the month Bashans of the year eight hundred and eight of the Martyrs = 1092 A.D.

Polish archaeologists working at the site of the Monastery of St Gabriel, Naqlun Fayyum, in 1990 discovered thirteen complete bodies of men, women and children, bearing traces of torture. They were considered to be martyrs, but the circumstance of their deaths is unknown. The remains of Simeon the Tanner were discovered in the Church of the Virgin Babylon al-Darag in August 1991.

Finally, it needs to be said that Coptic hagiography is not a closed book. We can see that almost every year new names are added to the list of saints, martyrs, and miracle workers. The situation for the Coptic Church in Egypt is still one in which there is enormous pressure from militants who wish to establish an Islamic state and to deny the provision for Christians to practise their faith.

Further reading

Kamil, J. (2002) *Christianity in the Land of the Pharaohs: The Coptic Orthodox Church*. London: Routledge.

Cannuyer, C. (2001) *Coptic Egypt: The Christians of the Nile*. London: Thames and Hudson.

Evetts, B. (ed.) (1910) *History of the Patriarchs of the Coptic Church of Alexandria*. Patrologia Orientalis 1. Paris: Firmin-Didot.

Gabra, G. (ed.) (2005) *Christianity and Monasticism in the Fayoum Oasis: Essays from the 2004 International Symposium of the Saint Mark Foundation and the Saint Shenouda the Archimandrite Coptic Society in Honor of Martin Krause*. A Saint Mark Foundation Publication. Cairo and New York: American University in Cairo.

Lacy O'Leary, D. (1937) *The Saints of Egypt*. London. Repr. Amsterdam, 1974.

Meinardus, O. F. A. (2002a) *Coptic Saints and Pilgrimages*. Cairo: American University in Cairo.

—— (2002b) *Two Thousand Years of Coptic Christianity*. Cairo: American University in Cairo.

Youssef, Y. N. (1992) De nouveau, la christianisation des dates des fêtes de l'ancienne religion égyptienne. *Bulletin de la Société d'Archéologie Copte* 31: 109–11.

—— (1993) Recherches sur Jules d'Akfahs. Thèse de Doctorat soutenue a l'Université de Montpellier III.

—— (1997) Une relecture des Théotokies Coptes. *Bulletin de la Société d'Archéologie Copte* 36: 157–70.

—— (1998) Book Review, R.-G. Coquin. *Bulletin de la Société d'Archéologie Copte* 37: 149–55.

CHAPTER 23

Eastern Christian Hagiographical Traditions

Oriental Orthodox: Armenian Hagiography

Vrej Nerses Nersessian

The fundamental work on Armenian hagiography began with the Mkhit'arist scholar Fr. Mkrtitch Avgerian (1762–1854) (pseud. Aucher), who, between 1810 and 1815, published the 12 volumes of his famous work *Liakatar vark' ew vkayabanut'iwn srbots, vork' kan i Hin tonatsutsi ekeghetswoy Hayastaneayts* (The Complete Lives of the Saints Found in the Old Calendar of the Armenian Church). Of particular importance is the twelfth volume, entitled *Mnatsordk' Varuts srbots artak'oy tonatsutsin meroy, yishatake-lots i Yaysmawwurs kam i Charentirs Hayots orpes ew Yunats ew Latinatswots* (The Remaining Lives of Saints not Found in Our Calendar, Commemorated in the Synax-aries and Lectionaries of the Greeks and the Latins). Anthologies of works by other authors include *Sop'erk' Haykakank'* (Armenian Hagiography) in 22 volumes, pub-lished in Venice between 1853 and 1861, and *Vark' ew Vkayabanut'iwnk' srbots hatentir k'aghealk' i char entrats* (Selection of Lives and Martyrdoms of Saints Abridged from Selected Homilies) published in 2 volumes in Venice in 1874. The 'Lives' of modern Armenian martyrs from the period 1155–1843 were collected by H. Acharyan and H. Manandyan under the title *Hayots nor vkaner* (New Armenian Martyrs) and published in Ejmiadsin in 1903.

The Armenian Synaxary, which contains the lives or acts of saints to be read in church on the day of their commemorations, is called *Yaysmawurk*, literally 'On this day'; it is arranged according to the Armenian year, whose opening day, since the variable year has been changed to a fixed one, corresponds to 11 August. The Synaxary has several redactions:

(1) Ter Israel's (d. 1249) redaction (Matenadaran MSS 1339, 2695, 4512, among others) has the Armenian translation of the Greek Menologion done in 991 by Yovsep' as its base text, to which he adds the Armenian commemorations. However, he does not begin the year in September nor does he follow the practice laid down by Grigor II Vkayaser regarding Navasard (August), but follows the Latin tradition starting on 1 January, with the feast day of St Basil of Caesarea.

(2)   Kirakosvardapet Areweltsi's (d. 1272) redaction (Matenadaran MSS 7433, 7529, 7530, among others), begins the liturgical year according to the Armenian calendar on 1 Navasard (i.e., 11 August, the feast day of St John the Baptist), ending in the following August. In the first edition, which he completed in 1253, he added 122 new Acts, while in the second, which he completed in Sis in 1269, he increased the number of Acts by 170. He employed the Armenian calendar, and in order to make it more interesting, he also provided dating according to the Latin and Syriac-Hebrew calendar.

(3)   Grigor VII Anawarzetsi's (d. 1307) redaction (1293–1307), although preserving the general outline of Ter Israel's edition, departed from the Armenian tradition both theologically and structurally. He introduced a number of Catholic rituals, began the year on 1 September, and placed the Annunciation, Birth of Christ and Epiphany, and Presentation in the Temple according to the Greek and Latin calendar, on 25 March, 25 December, 6 January, and 2 February respectively. The Armenian Church did not accept the Menologion composed by Grigor Anawarzetsi, which was deliberately designed to please the Latinizing party in their pursuit of Armenian-Catholic unity, and this is why so few manuscripts have survived (Matenadaran MSS 7529 dated 1326, and 4873 dated 1427).

(4)   Grigorvardapet Khlatetsi Dserents (d. 1425) composed his redaction in 1401, and this is the most voluminous and popular. Over two hundred manuscripts have survived and it was the first to be published, in Constantinople in 1706 (reprinted 1708, 1730, 1834). Its popularity is based on the fact that he introduced into the classical text the acts of popular, folkloric figures such as Himar Vanetsi (the Idiot of Van), T'amar Mokatsi, Eghisabet the martyr, Melik'set' and Karapet Vanetsi and 'many new saints, martyred in our times'.

The Armenian Church does not have a formal ritual for granting sainthood. The last saint accepted into the Armenian Synaxary was the scholar and philosopher Grigor Tat'evatsi (1346–1409) whose feast day falls on the Saturday before the fourth Sunday in Lent. The accounts of Christian martyrdoms are divided into three types: *Acta* (accounts of trials and condemnation written for the purpose of spiritual edification), *Passiones* or *Martyria* (descriptions of the martyr's life and death by contemporary eyewitnesses), and Martyr's Legends (legendary stories and narratives of later times).

An Armenian Synaxary (Or. 6555) in the British Library's collection defines the purpose and contents of the *Yaysmawurk'* in these terms: 'Here, then, are completed the glorious Feasts of all saintly champions, ascetics of old, and all Dominical Feasts . . . which the priest teaches by reading and recounting to all the lives and martyrdoms of the lovers of Christ and of them that fulfilled his commands.'

Literature dealing with the lives of saints was among the earliest translations into Armenian. Between 454 and 464, Abraham Khostovanogh translated into Armenian Marutha of Maiperkatensis' *Book of Martyrs*, containing accounts of those who suffered for the Christian faith under the Sassanian kings Shapur II, Yazdegerd I and Vahram V. The first lives to appear in Armenian were those of the Apostles Thaddeus, Bartholomew, St Gregory the Illuminator, Princess Sandukht and Princess Shushanik, St Hrip'sime and St Gayane, incorporated into the historical writings of Movses Khorenatsi, P'awstos Buzand and Agat'angeghos.

The most important achievement of this genre was the works of Koriwn and Eghishe vardapet. Koriwn, as witness, wrote a biography of St Mesrop Mashtots entitled *Vark' Mashtotsi* (*The Life of Mashtots*), in which he remarks 'We related this not for the glory of the saints of God who already have been honoured for their most luminous faith and life, but as an inspiring example to their spiritual sons and to all who, through them, will be taught from generation to generation.' Eghishe vardapet, who also wrote a witness account of the 451 battle of Avarayr, in his *History of Vardan and the Armenian War* calls his work simply a *Yishatakaran* (Memorial). The struggle of Vardanank' was, in the view of Eghishe, a struggle for the preservation of the glory and liberty of the Church. The troops going into battle prayed: 'May our death be equal to the death of the righteous and the shedding of our blood to that of the sainted martyrs; and may God be pleased with our voluntary sacrifice and deliver not his Church unto the hands of the heathens.' They also vowed: 'We are ready to suffer persecution, death, and all sorts of violence and afflictions for our Lord Jesus Christ, through whom we were reborn . . . Since we recognize . . . the Apostolic Catholic Church our Mother.'

The most indefatigable translator of *Lives of the Saints* was Grigor II Vkayaser (1066–1105), nicknamed 'Martyrophile', who is described as 'a wise and virtuous man'. The historian Kirakos Ghandzaketsi says of him: 'This wonderful patriarch translated from Greek and Syriac numerous hagiographical works and encomia.' The poet Nerses Shnorhali, in his *Vipasanut'iwn* (an epic poem) writes of him:

> He appeared to us as a second Mesrop,
> Translated numerous books from Greek and Syriac [originals],
> And works on the lives of the saints.

The complete contribution of Grigor Vkayaser was first published under the title *Girk' vor kotchi Harants Vark'* in New Julfa in 1641, and was reprinted in Constantinople in 1720 and in Venice in 1855.

In the Armenian Church calendar 112 days are put aside for 'the celebration', which can fall on Mondays, Tuesdays, Thursdays and Saturdays, since Wednesdays and Fridays are deemed fast days and Sunday is reserved for the Lord's Resurrection. All in all, there are 400 saints divided into three groups: (a) biblical; (b) saints of the Universal Church up to the Council of Chalcedon in 451, and (c) Armenian saints. The Armenian Church does not possess a procedure in canon law as does the Roman Church for the sanctification of saints. Generally, it has been through the piety of the faithful and through their acceptance of the exemplary spiritual strength of an individual that believers themselves recognize and honour them. Then the proper ecclesiastical authorities, after being likewise convinced of their spiritual strength and exemplary behaviour, canonize them through inclusion in the Directorium. Although the majority of the Acts in the Armenian Synaxary are also found in the Latin and the Greek, the versions differ considerably. Of the acts described in all the synaxaries, the most interesting are those belonging to the lives of St Martin, Bishop of Tours; St Benedict; St Thomas Becket; and saints who lived after Chalcedon and who were Chalcedonians, such as Pope Agapetus (d. 536) and Pope Gregory the Great (d. 604); we also find St. Augustine included. By continuing to commemorate these early and non-Armenian saints, the

Armenian Church lays emphasis on the fact that in its mission to its people, as the mother and fortress of the faith of the Holy Gospels, it is and shall remain 'apostolic' and 'universal'.

Further reading

Adontz, N. (1924) Note sur les Synaxaires Armeniens, *Revue de l'Orient Chretien* IV.3: 211–18.

Bayan, G. (1910–30) *Le Synaxaire Armenien de Ter Israel. Patrologia Orientalia* 349; 187; 297; 5; 5; 5 and 443.

Eghishe vardapet (1982) *History of Vardan and the Armenian War*, trans. R. W. Thomson. Cambridge, Mass.: Harvard University Press.

Gushakian, T'orgom, Patriarch (1981) *Surbk' ew Tonk' Hayastaneayts Ekeghetswoy*, 3rd edn. Lebanon: Antilias Catholicate. English trans. by Fr. Haigazoun Melkonian, *Saints and Feasts of the Armenian Church*, New York: St Vartan Press, 1988.

Koriwn (1964) *The Life of Mashtots*, trans. Bedros Norehad. New York: AGBU.

Ter Petrosyan, L. (1976) *Abraham Khostovanoghi 'Vkayk' Arewelitse'* (The 'Martyrs of the East' by Abraham Khostovanogh). Erevan: Armenian Academy of Sciences.

CHAPTER 24

Sociology and Eastern Orthodoxy

Peter McMylor and Maria Vorozhishcheva

Introduction

As the reader will have noted, this essay is not entitled 'a sociology of' or 'an anthropology of' Eastern Orthodoxy, denoting an object of study caught within the frame of an academic field of enquiry. We believe such an act of academic closure is premature, for a range of complex social, historical and cultural reasons, some of which are explored below. Socio-political and cultural analysis is based upon a number of unspoken, often long-standing and rarely explicated assumptions, and this affects the way we view all cultures, especially alien ones. In the case of Eastern Orthodoxy these influences are manifold: they are clearly present in the way other Christian Churches or religious groupings understand it, and also shape the manner in which mainly secular western commentators understand the Church and the societies in which it plays an important role. So it is the doubtful relationship between Eastern Orthodoxy and largely western social scientific thought that we explore. It can be argued that there is a remarkable historical amnesia and a woeful lack of comparative analysis in many contemporary accounts of the role of the Orthodox churches in the contemporary era. It is not that history is missing in many of these accounts; indeed, it could be argued that a profoundly misplaced historicism is at work, which profoundly distorts our understanding of Churches per se and leads frequently to a kind of theological reductionism in which supposed aspects of church theology are seen to lead inexorably to certain social outcomes.

One point must be made clear: despite the considerable significance of Eastern Orthodox Christianity both in terms of sheer numbers and historical significance there is in reality very little in the way of a sociology of it. It has not been a focus of scholarly attention by either the classical founders of sociology in the nineteenth century or amongst contemporary academic sociologists in western universities, whose work dominates the academic journals of the discipline and to a large measure defines its subject matter. If we just take one example from the British context, the standard textbooks used on most courses focusing on the sociology of religion in British universities are two works written by the well-known British scholar Malcolm Hamilton: *The Sociology of Religion: Theoretical and Comparative Perspectives* (1995) and *Sociology and the World's Religions* (1998). Neither of these texts contains any discussion of Eastern Orthodox Christianity; you could read both these books without ever realizing, if you did not know already, that there existed any such tradition within Christianity. This should not be seen as an idiosyncratic failure on the part of Hamilton, far from it. In the *Blackwell Companion to the Sociology of Religion*, edited by R. Fenn (2001) the reader will find that Eastern Orthodox Churches are mentioned twice and only in passing, in just one essay in the volume by J. A. Beckford, compared with, say, Taoism which is referred to on some ten occasions.

This should not be seen as any criticism of particular authors. Both Hamilton and Fenn are widely and correctly recognized as distinguished in this field but it is, rather, symptomatic of a much wider phenomenon which reveals much about the nature of sociology, and western understandings of the 'East' and the positioning of Orthodoxy, culturally and geographically within what might be termed the 'western gaze'. A central point we wish to argue here is that to gain a sense of the social dimensions and locatedness of Eastern Orthodoxy one needs to pay careful attention to the mode by which Eastern Orthodoxy is made either present or absent within the dominant conceptions of secular western thought, a key element of which is the social sciences. Sociological understanding of Eastern Orthodoxy, then, is also an exercise in an understanding of the relationship of the discipline as a self-conscious form of modernity to the tradition of Eastern Orthodoxy. For example it is surely very revealing that the monumental 'International Encyclopaedia of the Social and Behavioural Sciences' (2002), an electronic resource intended to be comprehensive and exhaustive in its coverage, has only one reference to Eastern Orthodox Christianity and that is under the category 'Globalization: political aspects'.

Sociology of Religion as an Intellectual Practice

To grasp the way Eastern Orthodoxy is understood as it is, it is necessary to look very briefly at the nature of sociology as a discipline, particularly the role played by the sociology of religion within it. True to its Enlightenment origins within the wider discipline of sociology itself, the sociology of religion seems to promise rational understanding of that which the Enlightenment and its heirs deemed the 'irrational'. However, this background in practice produced a set of difficulties about the relationship between sociology and religion. In the first instance this Enlightenment heritage meant sociology had, at least originally, an element – which now may be latent – that made it hostile to the claims of religion. The key founding figures of nineteenth-century sociology – Weber, Marx and Durkheim – were at best sceptical secularist in spirit. Even in more recent years a sociologist of religion and holder of the Chair in Sociology at Cambridge University can say, 'I was converted to Christianity under the auspices of the Methodist Church. My subsequent interest in the sociology of religion has been an attempt to understand that event and to escape from it' (Turner 1983: vii). The theologian John

Milbank has written an important and necessary book, *Theology and Social Theory* (1991) which uncovers much of the strongly competitive relationship of social thought with Christian theology. Milbank argues that the secular was not just the 'natural' awakening of understanding that occurred when the forces of secularization had stripped away from society the apparently unnecessary 'religious' element. Instead he argues that the secular had to be imagined into existence via secular philosophies and practices, against the trend of religious understandings. There would seem to be a good deal of plausibility in the view that much social thought is a kind of secular theology – perhaps especially clear in Marxism – in which elements from religion are borrowed for secular purposes (see MacIntyre 1968).

For Milbank, then, much social theory that underpins traditional sociology smuggles in a rather doubtful metaphysics that is, ironically, parasitic on religious thought. But this does not mean that Milbank argues for a rejection of the ongoing significance of social practices and contexts for the shaping of religious understandings and behaviour. Milbank and most contemporary sociologists would agree that atheist or agnostic beliefs and movements are also shaped by social contexts and practices. Intellectual modesty, with no legislative claims about the truth and falsity of beliefs smuggled in, is the best position for the social scientific account of the field of religion. Indeed, sophisticated sociologists of religion are now generally careful to avoid reductive accounts of religion and do not seek to explain away the phenomenon, but sometimes have even been prone to be protective of the religious groups studied, especially if those groups have a controversial public image. However, when dealing with the complex realities of large-scale religious organizations, their international connections and their local, national, even regional variations, the sociology of religion cannot claim to have made great advances over and above the work of the classic nineteenth-century founders. This is even more the case when we add the intractable issues raised by comparative sociology of religion, for here the sociology of religion remains, as Malcolm Hamilton has noted (1998), very much the product of the great German sociologist Max Weber's pioneering work.

Even when we look to Weber's work (1964) we are not given a great deal of guidance in regard to Eastern Orthodoxy. We might note, with the distinguished Weberian scholar W. Schluchter, that in comparison with Islam or Occidental Christianity Weber's 'view of Oriental Christianity and the development of the Eastern Churches is more difficult to grasp' (cited in Arnason 2000: 66 n. 3). Johann Arnason adds, 'This would seem to be a cautious understatement' (ibid.). The lack of treatment of Orthodoxy in Weber's work is not susceptible to a simple empirical remedy, because of some general problems in the nature of his approach to the sociology of Christianity. Despite Weber's undoubted erudition and the vast intellectual significance of his work it does have a general bias against traditional Orthodox liturgical Christianity and towards a highly 'rationalized' version of Christianity as embodied, as he believed, in its Protestant forms. Weber was really interested in finding the roots in the Judaic and Christian faiths of modern rationalized processes in society and economy. In his work, aspects of ancient Judaism are important but most vital is early modern Protestantism; this plays the starring role because of its relatively unusual combination of 'this-worldliness' and 'asceticism' which, he suggests, encourages attitudes supportive of early industrial capitalism (see Schluchter 1981). However, this emphasis can be seen to lead him to misunderstand and neglect other centrally important Christian traditions and doctrines. As the great twentieth-century sociologist of religion, Werner Stark, has pointed out Weber shared with the founder of positivist sociology, Auguste Comte, the quite erroneous and unhistorical belief that monotheism is a rather late development in the history of the great world religions; for Weber, even Christian Trinitarian theology was, Stark suggests, one of the 'early and crude forms of theology, phantasmogoric and not rational in character' (Stark 1968: 203).

It follows of course that if Trinitarian beliefs emerge after Judaism, as they do in Christianity, then this is 'to him a regrettable throwback to outmoded primitive ideas' (ibid.). Weber seems to have had no inkling that such Trinitarian thought could be understood as a development and an intellectual achievement, which provided for believers some understanding of the inner purposes of the deity and clues to the sacral meanings of creation achieved. As Stark puts it:

> it was seen that in the Godhead there is a principle of love, the Son, as well as a principle of power, the Father, and that love means a yearning for completion of the One by the many, a going out and making of a world which would tend back towards Him who had given it being – the Father and the Son and the Holy Spirit, three persons, yet one God. (1968: 203)

It is remarkable that Weber failed to appreciate such ideas, which – aside from their theological significance – were to resonate so deeply in philosophical thought, especially in Germany in the nineteenth century in relation to ideas of immanence and transcendence, which Weber certainly was informed about.

Weber's biases against Catholic and by implication of course Eastern Orthodox versions of Christianity, and for an apparently rationalizing Protestantism, bring into even sharper focus his failure of understanding in regard to ritual and devotional worship. He states in the text we know in English as *The Sociology of Religion*, 'In practice the Roman Catholic cult of masses and saints actually comes fairly close to polytheism' (cited in Stark 1968: 203), when clearly he should know that the cult of saints (to be found in both the Eastern and Western Church) is clearly a post-monotheistic development that is given clear theological recognition in the idea of the Communion of Saints. To cap this Stark points out that Weber has no real grasp of the nature of sacramental practice, even seeing in the Christian Eucharist some kind of manipulative magic (1968: 204). It is difficult not to see that for all Weber's astonishing scholarship he was unable to escape in his sociology of Christianity the prejudices of late nineteenth-century Protestant and post-Protestant culture. As we note below, such prejudice still limits our understanding of Eastern Christianity – and not just Eastern Christianity. However, it is also the case that, given Weber's enormous significance for comparative and civilizational based sociological analysis, his failure to provide a full and comprehensive understanding of Christianity has stood in the way of comparative civilizational analysis. This area of his work has not led to a genuinely balanced account of the nature of culture in Europe, including eastern Europe.

In practice many western writers and analysts, including able social historians, still start from a set of modern, frequently Protestant, prejudices about what Christianity is and by extension what Eastern Orthodoxy is and perhaps what it ought to be, if purged of backward superstitious mindsets and practices.

A good example of the latter position can be found in the work of one of the most eminent of British historians of Russia and in particular the Russian peasantry, Orlando Figes. In Figes's monumental history of the Russian Revolution, *A People's Tragedy* (1996), his understanding of Russian peasants is fascinating not least for what it reveals about the author's own assumptions of what Christian religious belief and practice mean. To begin with, Figes tells us that 'the religiosity of the Russian peasant has been one of the most enduring myths . . . in the history of Russia' but that 'in reality the Russian peasant had never more than a semi-detached relation with the Orthodox religion. Only a thin coat of Christianity had been painted over the ancient pagan folk-culture' (p. 66). However, having made this confident assertion he goes on to say:

> to be sure, the Russian peasant displayed a great deal of external devotion. He crossed himself continually, pronounced the Lord's name in every sentence, regularly went to church, always observed the Lenten fast, never worked on religious holidays, and was even known to from time to time to go on pilgrimage to holy shrines. (1996: 66)

He even concedes that most peasants thought of themselves as Orthodox and admits that if you had gone into a Russian village in 1900 and asked the inhabitants who they were they would have told you that they were Orthodox. However it seems that the widespread religious practices and clear self-definition are not adequate for our historian, for he seems to believe that he knows what true Christianity is and that these peasants are falling short of the mark. What is this mark that the Russian peasant failed to meet? It seems it was because 'the peasant's religion was far from the bookish Christianity of the clergy' and that the peasant 'mixed pagan cults and superstition' with Orthodox belief and he makes the surprising claim that 'being illiterate the average peasant knew very little of the Gospels' and that they would not know the Lord's Prayer – surely a most unlikely situation given their regular attendance at liturgies where it was regularly repeated.

Basically the model and standard that Figes is using to define real Christianity is a western post-Reformation Protestant one in which Christianity is defined in highly individualized textual and propositional terms. Now, crucially for the Eastern Orthodox tradition and indeed for the western Roman Catholic one, liturgical worship, the participation in the sacraments, Lenten devotion and discipline, religious holidays and feasts were not simply 'external devotion' implicitly to be contrasted with some other and perhaps higher form, but rather the essence of the Christian life. The liturgical year, with its rich and complex pattern of celebration and enactment of the Christian story, was deeply entwined with the whole life of the village community. If the world of the peasant and the natural world surrounding it seemed to be one in which spirits and the supernatural were ever-present then they were, and perhaps are still, closer to the world view of the early Christians than the modern literate and doctrinally well-taught modern western Christian, who spends at least six days out of seven in the bureaucratic and disenchanted world of modernity so distant from the liturgically ordered world of the nineteenth-century Russian village. Nor should we postulate very great distinctions between educated priests and ignorant or illiterate peasants. Figes himself, without realizing it, indicates crucial connections when he points to 'the icon' being 'the focus of the peasant's faith' (1996: 67), central after all to all Orthodox believers and not simply the poorly educated, and this includes the belief in their capacity for miraculous influence.

East as Orientalist

After Edward Said's path-breaking work on the western scholarly constructions of Arab and Islamic culture the concept of Orientalism has been significant in the human sciences. It is well defined as follows:

> Orientalism as a discourse divides the globe unambiguously into Occident and Orient; the latter is essentially strange, exotic and mysterious, but also sensual, irrational and potentially dangerous . . . The task of orientalism was to reduce the bewildering complexity of Oriental societies and Oriental culture to some manageable comprehensible level. (Turner 1983: 31)

It is not difficult to see this intellectual process at work in regard to the culture of Eastern Orthodoxy.

Western intellectuals and scholars have long had a problem in identifying or typifying the eastern lands and cultures of the Orthodox world. The problem has of course almost always been pressing because it was so frequently connected with constructing an identity for the societies of the West. A particular issue was Russia: a significant power and a significant regional space but was it 'Europe' or something else – i.e., alien? The history of the successive 'locations' of Russia since the Renaissance is, as Perry Anderson has noted (1976), a revealing and significant subject. Machiavelli regarded Russia as basically the 'Scythia' of classical times, 'a land that is cold and poor, where there are too many men for the soil to support' so beyond the bounds of Europe, while Jean Bodin saw Russia as within Europe but also unique: the only example of a despotic monarchy, so quite apart from the general European pattern. Later Montesquieu, impressed by Peter the Great's westernizing efforts, saw Russia as part of Europe (see Anderson 1976: 491 n. 14). However, in the nineteenth century Marx and Engels once more banished Russia to Asia and viewed it as a land of despotism. But the problem of exclusion or inclusion was not limited to Russia; it begins with the issue of Byzantium.

The key dynamic behind much commentary has involved not only a desire to demarcate West and East but in more recent centuries to mark the progressiveness of the West compared with the backward, reactionary, and even threatening East. The prejudice and feeling was presented most vividly and influentially by Gibbon, when he put it thus:

The subjects of the Byzantine Empire, who assume and dishonour the names of both Greeks and Romans, present a dead uniformity of abject vices, which are neither softened by the weakness of humanity nor animated by the vigour of memorable crimes. From these considerations I should have abandoned without regret the Greek slaves and their servile historians, had I not reflected that the fate of the Byzantine monarchy is passively connected with the most splendid and important revolutions which have changed the state of the world. (1995: 24)

This quotation from Gibbon, even when stripped of its hyperbole and hectoring moral tone, still contains crucial clues for understanding the structure of explanation in much western commentary. As Johann Arnason points out in his innovative essay on the historical sociology of Byzantium and its continuing contemporary significance:

the key term [Gibbon uses] is 'passively connected'. Gibbon is acknowledging and at the same time minimizing the most obvious objection to his narrative of decline and fall: the Roman Empire did survive in the East when its defences crumbled in the West. The answer is that the surviving fragment had no created history and had no significant experience of its own, although it can be used – as a purely negative counter-example – to highlight the upheavals outside its borders. This verdict on the Byzantine millennium is, in other words, inseparable from the genealogy of the West that is implicit in Gibbon's story-line, and it has obvious implications for the whole relationship between Western and Eastern Europe. (Arnason 2000)

We might well reasonably quibble about the obviousness of the consequences of this kind of analysis for we can suggest that they are far-reaching, complex and all too frequently taken for granted. But Aranason goes on to note that more than two centuries after Gibbon was writing (the first volume of *Decline and Fall* was published in 1775), Michael Mann, in his substantial work of historical sociology (1986), reproduces the same vision of an inert survivor that was 'later swept aside, except in its heartland around Constantinople, by a religion of greater mobilizing power, Islam' and also that Byzantium lay outside the medieval civilization of Christendom (Mann 1986, cited in Arnason 2000: 45). What is clearly involved here is judgements about the values of differing cultures, some progressive and powerful, some backward and weak. Gibbon's work can be taken as the beginning of a whole project of historical explanation the real subject of which is the uniqueness of the West; it often implicitly involves negative comparative judgements of other civilizations, which are somehow seen as falling short of an ideal. In essence what seems most crucial for this narrative (inevitably compressing a complex argument) is locating a common origin for East and West in late antiquity in the politically innovatory rule of Constantine the Great, and in his adoption of Christianity and the role the new religion played in the political system. In this view the adoption by Constantine of monotheistic Christianity and its fusion with a universal empire is literally epoch-making. It seems to have produced an exceptionally powerful and long-lasting model of authority, which can be taken to explain 'the continuity of "autocracy, absolutism, centralization, divine sanction" ... throughout successive phases of history' (Arnason 2000: 40).

This is really an argument for great continuity in the East but a very different pattern for the West. On this view, as Arnason notes, 'for Western Europe, its trajectory is marked by cumulative ruptures of the Constantinian union of sacred and mundane power. The story begins with the collapse of imperial structures in the West, in contrast to the survival of their eastern counterpart' (2000: 41). Again, Arnason emphasizes that in many standard interpretations 'the Constantinian turn' is seen 'as a historical watershed of such dimensions that only the concatenation of and accumulation of transformative factors in Western Europe – never matched on the eastern side – could undo its effects' (p. 46). Within this apparent breach events gradually enlarge to eventually produce two radically different trajectories with radically different social political and religious outcomes. The story normally highlights the 'two swords' theory of spiritual and earthly government, formally adopted by Pope Gelasius I. The Church granted the former and the empire the latter in the process of western development, whilst in the East a pattern of so-called 'caesaropapism' is assumed to have more fully emerged.

Caesaropapism is normally understood as a system of rule in which the head of state is also head of the Church and the supreme judge in religious matters; Byzantium and Russia are generally cited as examples (quite why is not really clear when England from the Henrican Reformation to the present day seems a rather splendid example). It is, however, very doubtful that the Byzantine case could qualify as caesaropapist. Although the patriarch of the imperial capital owed his position to the political power of the emperor, Byzantine Orthodoxy knew no instance of ultimate doctrinal authority except the church councils (see Arnason 2000: 62); we can add that nor does any form of Eastern Orthodox Christianity. We might also note that in the opinion of a leading historical sociologist, and contributor to civilizational analysis, S. N. Eisenstadt, Byzantium and its daughter religious cultures must firstly be understood within the wider compass of Christian civilization rather than as a distinct civilizational centre itself. This is a point of absolutely vital significance when we come to consider the various theorists of the so-called clash of civilizations. Eisenstadt suggested that the key aspect of the culture was strong differentiation between Church and state and amongst different elite groups such as the bureaucratic, military and clerical, rather than any monolithic qualities (Eisenstadt 1995).

Much of the above could seem only the concern of scholars and specialists but in practice these views have an urgent saliency, owing to the renewed interest in civilizational sociology. Within the realm of policy analysis and public political discourse what might be called a more popular and politically influential version of civilizational social science analysis exists, in which we find the older visions of Europe and Christianity as fundamentally divided once more gaining currency. Why should this be happening?

The very short answer, which is perhaps as predictable as it is true, is that the end of the Cold War and the collapse of Communism as both ideological competitor and perceived threat to the western capitalist world changed the relations between states across the planet. In a brief wave of 'bourgeois triumphalism' the ghost of Hegel was summoned to the aid of the US State Department in the shape of the famous 'End of History' thesis by its former employee Francis Fukyama. This postulated, not that there would be no more conflict or change (as some really quite extraordinarily badly informed commentary in the British press would have had it), but rather that liberal democracy in its various forms would mark the horizon within which future change and conflict would occur, with the non-western societies gradually adopting its forms, albeit with lots of ups and downs on the way.

However, the euphoria that broke out in western policy circles with the end of the Soviet control of Eastern Europe in 1989 and the collapse of the Soviet Union itself in 1991 soon began to fade and more sober opinions emerged that were perhaps more far-sighted. Even if the analysis was wrong at least it could point to some global realities that western commentators would ignore at their peril. Indeed one might say that in the mid-1990s a relatively pessimistic but more realistic analysis reappeared that had been occluded in the feverish atmosphere of the late eighties. Looking back to the dominant elite policy discussions in the early and mid-eighties one discovers concern about western and especially American decline in the face of the rise of the powers of Asia, Japan and especially China; all this is persuasively argued in the substantial work of Paul Kennedy, especially his 1987 book *The Rise and Fall of the Great Powers*. Such matters were temporarily forgotten at the time of Japan's severe economic problems, which coincided to some degree with the collapse of Communism and with a revival in strength of the US economy. Such fundamental and long-standing structural issues could not go away and with the Cold War fading into memory the new context required some reversion to long-term thinking but with a distinctive shift in the form of the analysis.

The result was the most influential book of western foreign policy analysis of the 1990s, Samuel P. Huntington's *The Clash of Civilizations and the Remaking of World Order* (1996). Huntington argues his position through an exposition of five wide-ranging and interrelated propositions:

(1)   For the first time in history world politics and international relations now operate in a multi-polar and multi-civilizational environment. Social and economic modernization is now understood as something distinct from westernization and is now producing neither a universal civilization in any meaningful sense nor the westernization of non-western societies. It should be immediately noted that this distinction between westernization and modernization should be welcomed as an important development. It overcomes some of the Eurocentric biases of much traditional sociology and is being explored in the comparative sociology of that cautious scholar S. N. Eisenstadt under the rubric of multiple modernities (see Eisenstadt 2003).

(2)   The balance of power is understood to be moving, with the West undergoing a decline in influence. On the other hand, Asian civilizations are seen to be expanding their economic, military and political strength. Islam, it is noted, is undergoing a massive demographic expansion with notable destabilizing effects for many Muslim countries and their neighbours. In general non-western civilizations are also reaffirming the value of their own cultures and beliefs. Huntington noted the confrontation in 1993 at the Vienna Human Rights Conference between the West, led by the then US Secretary of State Warren Christopher, who denounced 'cultural relativism', and an apparent coalition of Islamic and Confucian states who rejected 'western universalism'.

(3)   A civilizational-based world order is understood to be emerging in which societies that share cultural affinities cooperate with each other and efforts to shift a society from one civilization to another are largely unsuccessful. In addition we start to see behaviour that suggests that countries group themselves around the lead or core state of their civilization. Huntington points amongst other things to the emergence of patterns of regionalism in multi-country-based economic associations that frequently have a distinct cultural pattern as well as an economic one. For example, the European Union has gone furthest in economic integration in part, it is suggested, because of cultural commonalities.

(4)   The West's universalist pretensions increasingly brings it into conflict with other civilizations, most notably and most seriously with Islam and China. It is also noted that at the local regional level there emerge what could be called fault-line wars between members of different civilizational groupings, largely up till now between Muslim and non-Muslim. These conflicts generate what Huntington terms 'kin-country rallying', which produces the threat of broader escalation, but so far this has been contained by core civilizational states seeking to halt such wars.

(5)   The survival of the West depends on Americans reaffirming their western identity and westerners accepting their civilization as unique and not universal, and uniting to renew and preserve it against the challenges that are emerging from non-western societies. Avoidance of a global war of civilizations depends on world leaders accepting and cooperating in order to maintain the multi-civilizational character of global world politics. (Points 1 to 5 are derived, with some alteration, from Huntingon 1996: 20–1.)

The multi-civilizational model of the contemporary world order consists, then, in adumbrating and assessing the significance of the key world civilizations and their interrelations. For Huntington, the key contemporary world civilizations are: (1) Sinic, essentially the Chinese civilization with a common culture of China proper as well as the Chinese communities of south-east Asia; (2) Japanese, an offspring of Chinese but now quite distinct; (3) Hindu, largely based in the Indian subcontinent but with a substantial diaspora; (4) Islamic, with several sub-civilizations including Arab, Turkic, Persian and Malay; (5) western, with three major components: Europe, North America and Latin America. However, controversially, Huntington counts Latin America (6) as a distinct civilizational entity because of its different historical experience, the key aspect of which is the lack of impact of the Reformation and its uniformly – until recently – Catholic religious formation, which was also partially influenced by the surviving indigenous religions and culture. Because, Huntington notes, both Europe and North America have mixed Catholic and Protestant religious formations it is implicitly and revealingly the case that it is Latin America's lack of Protestantism, or rather the unfettered influence of Catholicism, that makes it ineligible for full membership of the West. This is a curious and perhaps revealing view given the overwhelming influence of Catholicism in southern Europe, and one perhaps indicating the lingering of the Weberian prejudice against Catholic and also Orthodox Christianity, that we noted above.

Finally, and most importantly for our purposes, the seventh contemporary world civilization is Orthodox, now centred on Russia and seen as separate from western

Christendom as a consequence. In Huntington's words, it is 'of Byzantine parentage, [a] distinct religion' (here a question mark surely jumps before us as it surely doubtful that Eastern Orthodoxy is a more distinct form of Christianity than say Protestantism is from Catholicism), and has '200 years of Tatar rule, bureaucratic despotism, and limited exposure to the Renaissance, Reformation, Enlightenment, and other central Western experiences' (Huntington 1996: 45–6). He does not specify what these other experiences might be but it is clear that, as in the case of Latin America, the absence of the Protestant Reformation influence is for him a prominent issue.

Huntington is in fact very blunt about the clear significance of an Orthodox civilization. He says, for example, that 'Greece is not part of Western Civilization' (1996: 162). He does however note – how could he not – that Greece has been an important source of western civilization and has been closely entwined with the West in the conflict with the Ottoman Empire. Nonetheless Huntington is insistent that Greece 'is also an anomaly, the Orthodox outsider in Western organizations. It has never been an easy member of either the EU or NATO and has had difficulty adapting itself to the principles and mores of both' (ibid.). He goes on to point out that from the mid-1960s to the mid-1970s it was ruled by a military junta, which prevented it joining the EU (but it did not, as he fails to point out, prevent it from joining NATO) until its democratic turn. We might note in passing that both the non-Orthodox countries of Spain and Portugal were in a similar position and indeed for a much longer period than Greece.

Huntington's key prediction for Greece is that it will become part of a greater Orthodox bloc of countries centred on Russia. He suggests that events after the collapse of Communism in the region point in this direction. So he argues:

> with respect to the conflicts in the former Yugoslavia, Greece separated itself from the policies pursued by the principal Western powers, actively supporting the Serbs . . . With the end of the Soviet Union and the Communist threat, Greece has mutual interests with Russia in opposition to their common enemy Turkey. It has permitted Russia to establish a significant presence in Greek Cyprus and as a result of 'their Eastern Orthodox religion', the Greek Cypriots have welcomed both Russians and Serbs to the Island. (1996: 163)

Huntington suggests that although Greece will remain a formal member of the EU and of NATO the links will become more tenuous and that eventually Greece will be a post-Cold War ally of Russia. Ultimately he seems to be suggesting this will happen because of the shared culture, in this case the shared religious culture of Eastern Orthodoxy, which will propel Greece towards its natural civilizational home. This is a profoundly unsatisfactory mode of analysis, as we will explain below, but before turning to criticism we must complete Huntington's account of Orthodox civilization.

As must now be clear, at the heart of his account of Orthodoxy and its civilizational role is Russia. For him, 'the successor to the tsarist and communist empires is the civilizational bloc paralleling in many respects that of the West in Europe. At the core is Russia, the equivalent of France and Germany' (1996: 163), with close links to Belarus, Ukraine, Moldova and Armenia. When Huntington wrote his book he expected the expansion of NATO tacitly to accept the boundaries of western Christendom and the Orthodox civilizational sphere by excluding 'Serbia, Bulgaria, Romania, Moldova, Belarus and Ukraine, as long as Ukraine remained united' (p. 162). However, in practice, NATO has included Romania and Bulgaria – admittedly much to Russia's annoy-ance. He has been no more accurate about the EU's expansion now that it has moved to include such Orthodox countries as Bulgaria and Romania, and the inclusion of Turkey would certainly run counter to his model. For Huntington, then, 'overall Russia is creating a bloc with an Orthodox heartland under its leadership and a surrounding buffer of relatively weak Islamic states which it will in varying degrees dominate and from which it will attempt to exclude the influence of other powers' (p. 164).

So in essence this brand of social scientific thought suggests that Eastern Orthodoxy constitutes one civilizational group in competition and conflict with various others, including the Islamic and the western groups. We have indicated already that we think that this is not a plausible way of looking at the situation and we suggest that it pro-duces a quite unhelpful framework for understanding the significance of Eastern Orthodoxy in the world today. To understand why this is we must first look at some general problems with this approach and then some particular empirical issues. In the first instance one has to ask questions about the core assumptions of approaches like Huntington's concerning the explanatory power of the concept of 'civilization'. The concept is applied as if it possessed capacities of agency in the social and historical field. In other words, can it really make sense to talk about civilizations that clash?

Civilizations are notoriously difficult entities to get into complete focus; indeed the geographical diversity and the sheer historical longevity of such entities inevitably leads to generalization, with the danger of producing oversimplified descriptions. So most social scientists are likely tacitly or overtly to use some kind of ideal-type form of strategy as a means of producing a manageable model to work with – a strategy pio-neered, of course, by Max Weber. In many respects this practice is perfectly justifiable when discussing, perhaps for comparative purposes, say doctrinal beliefs about God or gods, or forms of political power and authority. However, the practice can be become problematic when the social scientist begins to reify the model, allowing it to fully stand in for the complexity of the reality of the civilization under discussion. The practice becomes especially problematic when, as G. Melleuish notes in respect of Huntington, it tries to 'treat civilizations as if they were unified political and cultural entities, that is, states capable of behaving as historical actors in a unified and forceful fashion' (Melleuish 2000: 112). The implication of this is that in some sense they are, in Melleuish's term, 'deep structures' fairly resistant to change and influence from outside themselves and with fairly clear and distinct borders. Indeed, as Melleuish notes:

> The model of clashing civilizations only really works if we make specific states the carriers of particular civilizations, and so combine political and military power with the more peaceful pursuits of civilization. Other states then should line up behind the major carrier and support them because of their shared civilization. (p. 115)

Now clearly this is what Huntington wants to argue is happening now, but Melleuish is correct to see this as a highly anachronistic model of long term social change, for it takes a twentieth-century 'ideal' of an ethnically and culturally homo-geneous nation-state, projecting it back on to a past that was composed of much more heterogeneous civilizations (Melleuish 2000: 115). Bearing this in mind, can

Huntington come back and claim that in practice, this is what is happening now in the context of modern nation-states with cultural consciousness? Are we to believe that an Eastern Orthodox civilizational grouping is emerging or re-emerging, in conflict with something called the West and no doubt with an entity called Islam?

The answer to this last question must surely be 'No' – principally because civilizations are not states and they are not even in a full sense cultures, since any particular national culture, say Greek or Russian, is the product of too many forces and influences to be simply defined as Orthodox, except in the most simple of shorthand. To do more is a form of cultural reductionism. Civilizations are complex background contexts and inheritances, always heterogeneous and capable of developing in a wide variety of directions. In practice they frequently provide a seedbed or resource for a variety of different cultures. Nonetheless, can Huntington point to evidence to support his claims? In particular, do recent wars and conflicts point towards his clash theory having some limited validity now? Huntington and another American author, Robert Kaplan (1993), certainly believe that the conflict in the Balkans in the 1990s confirm their view that the new post-Cold-War conflicts are civilizational, and even religiously driven. They believe they are pointing towards new patterns of global alignment, as in Huntington's prediction of the direction of Greece will move, that is, towards an alliance with Orthodox Russia.

In essence it is hard not to see such analysis as superficial in giving a determining role to the religious dimensions of civilizations that even the most ambitious archbishop or cardinal would shrink from. Naturally religion and culture generally play an important role in virtually all human civilizations, most notably as forms of symbolic resources that are available for a wide variety of purposes. In reality it is much more productive and plausible to view the conflicts in post-Yugoslavian Balkans not at all as some supposed atavistic civilizational hatreds or wars of religion but as rooted in the forms and processes of modernity and modernization itself. This is most notably true in regard to the role of nationalism and that of the uneven patterns of social and economic development in the area. Victor Roudometof has argued persuasively that the problems and conflicts that have occurred in the former Yugoslavia and in Macedonia and Albania and in the less well-known case of Bulgaria (even to a certain extent in Greece) are rooted in 'the political, economic and cultural reorganization of south-eastern Europe according to the model of the homogeneous nation-state over the past two centuries' (Roudometof 1999: 241). In the nineteenth century, inspired by European Romanticism and especially the new nationalist movements in Germany and Italy, the emerging nationalist intelligentsia shaped 'the Greek, Serb and Bulgarian versions of the "nation" through such devices as historical narrative, religious symbolism, reinterpretation of folklore and the writing of nationalist literature and poetry' (pp. 239–40). Crucially, Roudometof sees this process of nation building and the nationalist modernizing intellectuals as rooted in the long-term 'secularization of South-eastern Europe beginning with the Grecophone Balkan Enlightenment of the late eighteenth century' (ibid.). However, given that the bulk of the Balkan population was religious these nationalist intellectuals' first step 'was to manipulate religious institutions so as to transform . . . [them] . . . into national ones' (ibid.). This was done by creating – for the first time in the area – separate national churches: for Greece in 1832, Serbia in 1832 and the Bulgarian Exarchate in 1870. In effect this turned the meaning of religious affiliation into a 'national' one and ominously provided 'the means through which the traditional ties of the Orthodox Balkan people could be severed and new national ties constructed' (ibid.). Also, as M. Bakic-Hayden notes, given that the nationalist movements 'were generally anti-clerical, the place of religion in the newly emerging nations was defined, as in the West, in subordination to the secular power of the state' (Bakic-Hayden 2002: 69).

So it was modernity that brought the Orthodox Churches to submit to the state. In the Russian case, Peter the Great actually followed the example of the English Anglican Church when he nationalized the Russian Church. Indeed the Church was worried about the implications of the new nationalism in the Eastern Mediterranean arena. At an important Synod in August 1872, the Ecumenical Patriarch of Constantinople, the Patriarchs of Alexandria, Antioch and Jerusalem, and the Archbishop of Cyprus all condemned nationalism and racism as phyletism: 'We renounce, censure and condemn racism, that is racial discrimination, ethnic feuds, hatreds and dissensions within the Church of Christ' (Bakic-Hayden 2002: 69).

It is clear that complex difficulties and conflicts in the Balkans must be seen not as ancient and civilizational but rather part of a familiar problematic of ethnic nationalism and war that have bedevilled the politics of much of Europe and its neighbours in the twentieth century, from Turkish treatment of the Armenians to German Nazi policies. Nor would it be right to accept at face value the claims that Greece's behaviour inside the EU and its relative political instability stem from some fundamental non-western or Orthodox civilizational matrix. Rather, once again the way Greece and the Balkans area were inserted into the modern social and economic order is the key. Nicos Moulzelis has insightfully compared the socio-economic experience of the Balkans with Latin America as semi-peripheral to industrial capitalism. The effect of western industrialization on 'semi-peripheral' societies in the nineteenth century was a substantial degree of commercialization, but not – until a much later period – of industrialization. But it did cause an 'early' non-industrial urbanization and an expanded state, a bureaucracy and an educational system, all combined with a very influential agrarian population. (Mouzelis 1986). It is social structural factors such as these which point to differing socio-politico logics and political outcomes rather than the workings out in Latin America of Catholicism or Orthodoxy in the Balkans. It should go without saying, but perhaps it does not for some commentators, that the experience and inheritance of Soviet Communism on the whole economic and social order of Russia should be the starting point for social explanations of its present nature and international posture towards other societies.

Cultural Reductionism

The re-emergence of cultural and civilizational analysis in sociology has led to claims being made about the supposed internal consequences of Orthodoxy in Russia and other former Communist societies. The same kinds of mechanisms at work in the Huntington school are also deployed here. This means that religious traditions, in this case Orthodoxy, has characteristics imputed to it from a particular reading of theological texts and then presumed to have fairly direct cultural and societal consequences, especially in the economic and political sphere, and not only on believers but, it seems, on the majority of the population. For example, A. Pollis (1993) claims that Eastern Orthodoxy is incompatible with modern western conceptions of individual rights. In the economic sphere a range of commentators, both academics and journalists, have made claims about Eastern Orthodoxy and comparisons between it and Catholicism in relation to market-based business activity, citing the former's supposed hostility to it or lack of aptitude (Dinello 1998; Kaplan 2000; Nedelchev 2002).

The basic problem of all these arguments and studies is their cultural reductionism in which whole societies are typified and apparently explained by reference to their being Orthodox or Catholic. So, for example, Nedelchev (2002) wants to argue that Catholicism promotes a cultural environment conducive to a market transition and Orthodoxy does not. He seeks to establish this via a comparison of two 'Catholic' countries, Poland and Hungary, and two 'Orthodox' countries, Bulgaria and Rumania. By doing so he subsumes the complex and deeply differentiated histories under these global categories of apparently religious differences. Or take the following assertion presented by Kaplan (2000): 'Since 1989, the economies of the Catholic and Protestant countries of Poland, Hungary, Slovenia and the Czech Republic have all grown faster, or at least have been less stagnant, than those of Orthodox Romania, Bulgaria and Macedonia, and largely Muslim Albania.' M. Bakic-Hayden provides some sensible commentary on this statement when she writes:

> What is being qualified here: [the] economy as Catholic? Protestant, or Orthodox? Or, Catholicism and Protestantism as faster growing or less stagnant than Orthodoxy? In what way, one wonders, can these religious designations be helpful in understanding the logic of investment in post-communist Eastern Europe? Why, indeed, has Hungary had more investment than Romania? Can politics perhaps explain more than religion in this case? (2002: 73)

The answer must of course be: Yes, politics, and social structure and wider economic and international relations are necessary elements of a more complete explanation. (Once more Mouzelis's book makes for some interesting starting points and comparisons.) One of the interesting findings in Nedelchev's research is that (opinion) polling between Catholic and Orthodox countries indicates that 'Catholics demonstrate greater preference for incentive driven distribution of income and a more positive view of wealth than the Orthodox' and in general 'are closer to the profile of modern personality than the characteristics of the Orthodox' (Nedelchev 2002: 1). This is especially interesting given classical status in the discipline of sociology of Max Weber's *The Protestant Ethic and the Spirit of Capitalism*, which sought to establish the traditionalism of Catholicism in regard to wealth. This should at least give us pause for thought and suggest the possibility of quite dramatic cultural change or that there might indeed be something wrong in thinking about the relationship between religion and society in this kind of way.

Religion is nothing if it is not about meanings and the communication of those meanings over time. Eastern Orthodoxy is a Church or group of churches that exists

Huntington's civilizational map of Europe. Redrawn from Huntington (1993).

within the broad and deep civilizational framework of Christianity. It has within it varied currents, it is not indefinably fluid but neither is it entirely rigid and predetermined, it has never been entirely uninfluenced by, or uninfluential upon, the Christian Churches of the West, Catholic and Protestant, or in regard to its sister Churches in the East, the so-called Oriental Churches. It makes no sense to define the history of Orthodoxy or western churches as A. Pollis does, as existing from the 'fourteenth century [with] a nearly impermeable iron curtain [having descended between Orthodoxy and Catholicism. The former emphasized liturgy and conformity to rites and rituals' (1993: 341). To support this claim she quotes George Florovsky, who says 'Christianity is a liturgical religion and the Church is first of all a worshipping community' (1993: 341 n. 3). It is virtually impossible to imagine any Roman Catholic theologian dissenting from this view of what the Church and its life is. However, historical detail is less important than the methodological point concerning the mode by which religion exists in a modern complex society. It is perhaps best to draw on the understanding of the French sociologist of religon Daniele Hervieu-Leger, who speaks of religion as 'a chain of memory' (Hervieu-Leger 2000). It consists of the tradition as a kind of collective memory for the religious community, with the chain being as it were the way the memory acts via individuals (certainly not just theologians), making them members of a community of past, present and future members. The members of the Christian Churches both East and West are the bearers of their tradition in both institutional and non-institutional ways. Those who believe that Orthodoxy 'remains frozen in the past' and 'unable to say anything about the nature of persons and their possible rights' (Pollis 1993: 353) should ponder both the hermeneutical richness of the Orthodox Christian tradition and the history of the Christian Churches in general. Critics who see no possible chance of change and development should ponder the history of the Roman Catholic Church in the twentieth century in particular.

The chain of memory is not broken in the Orthodox Churches in spite of the great difficulties and hardships it has had to endure in the twentieth century. In a world that is now more open to critical thought about secularity and modernity the spiritual traditions of Eastern Orthodoxy will have space to help shape the minds and hearts of new generations.

References

Anderson, P. (1976) *Lineages of the Absolutist State*. London: New Left Books.
Arnason, J. (2000) Approaching Byzantium: identity, predicament and afterlife. *Thesis Eleven* 62: 39–69.
Bakic-Hayden, M. (2002) What's so Byzantine about the Balkans? In D. I. Bjelic and O. Savic (eds.) *Balkan as Metaphor: Between Globalization and Fragmentation*. Cambridge, Mass.: MIT Press.
Dinello, N. (1998) Russian religious rejections of money and 'Homo Economicus': the self-identifications of the 'pioneers of a money economy' in post-Soviet Russia. *Sociology of Religion* 59(1): 45–64.
Eisenstadt, S. N. (1995) *Power, Trust and Meaning*. Chicago: Chicago University Press.
—— (2003) *Comparative Civilizations and Multiple Modernities*. Leiden and Boston: Brill.

Fenn, R. (ed.) (2001) *The Blackwell Companion to the Sociology of Religion.* Oxford: Blackwell.

Figes, O. (1996) *A People's Tragedy: The Russian Revolution 1891–1924.* London: Jonathan Cape.

Gibbon, E. (1995) *The Decline and Fall of the Roman Empire,* vol. III. Harmondsworth: Penguin Books.

Hamilton, M. (1995) *The Sociology of Religion: Theoretical and Comparative Perspectives.* London: Routledge.

—— (1998) *Sociology and the World's Religions.* London: Macmillan.

Hervieu-Leger, D. (2000) *Religion as a Chain of Memory.* Cambridge: Polity Press.

Huntington, S. (1993) The clash of civilizations. *Foreign Affairs* 72(3): 22–49.

—— (1996) *The Clash of Civilizations and the Remaking of World Order.* New York: Simon and Schuster.

Kaplan, R. (1993) *Balkan Ghosts: A Journey through History.* New York: St Martin's Press.

—— (2000) Yugoslavia's fate, and Europe's. *New York Times,* opinion and editorial sect., 6 October.

Kennedy, P. (1987) *The Rise and Fall of the Great Powers.* New York: Random House.

MacIntyre, A. (1968) *Marxism and Christianity.* New York: Schocken Books.

Mann, M. (1986) *Sources of Social Power,* vol.1. Cambridge: Cambridge University Press.

Melleuish, G. (2000) The clash of civilizations: a model of historical development? *Thesis Eleven* 62: 109–20.

Milbank, J. (1991) *Theology and Social Theory.* Oxford: Oxford University Press.

Mouzelis, N. (1986) *Politics in the Semi-Periphery: Early Parliamentarianism and Late Industrialization in the Balkans and Latin America.* London: Macmillan.

Nedelchev, E. T. (2002) Catholicism and Eastern Orthodoxy: cultural influences on the transition in Central and Eastern Europe. PhD dissertation, University of Delaware, Accession number 200214927.

Pollis, A. (1993) Eastern Orthodoxy and human rights. *Human Rights Quarterly* 15: 339–56.

Roudometof, V. (1999) Nationalism, globalization, Eastern Orthodoxy: 'unthinking' the 'clash of civilizations' in south-eastern Europe. *European Journal of Social Theory* 2(2): 233–47.

Schluchter, W. (1981) *The Rise of Western Rationalism.* Berkeley: University of California Press.

Stark, W. (1968) The place of Catholicism in Max Weber's *Sociology of Religion. Sociological Analysis* 29 (winter): 202–10.

Turner, B. (1983) *Religion and Social Thought.* London: Heinemann.

Weber, M. (1964) *The Sociology of Religion.* Boston: Beacon Press.

Index